OCP

Oracle® Certified Professional
Java® SE 8 Programmer II
Study Guide

OCP

Oracle® Certified Professional Java® SE 8 Programmer II
Study Guide

Jeanne Boyarsky

Scott Selikoff

A Wiley Brand

Senior Acquisitions Editor: Kenyon Brown
Development Editor: Gary Schwartz
Technical Editors: Ernest Friedman-Hill and Matt Dalen
Production Editor: Dassi Zeidel
Copy Editor: Linda Recktenwald
Editorial Manager: Mary Beth Wakefield
Production Manager: Kathleen Wisor
Associate Publisher: Jim Minatel
Supervising Producer: Rich Graves
Book Designers: Judy Fung and Bill Gibson
Proofreader: Josh Chase, Word One New York
Indexer: Ted Laux
Project Coordinator, Cover: Brent Savage
Cover Designer: Wiley
Cover Image: ©Getty Images Inc./Jeremy Woodhouse

Copyright © 2016 by John Wiley & Sons, Inc., Indianapolis, Indiana

Published simultaneously in Canada

ISBN: 978-1-119-06790-0
ISBN: 978-1-119-06788-7 (ebk.)
ISBN: 978-1-119-06789-4 (ebk.)

Manufactured in the United States of America

For general information on our other products and services or to obtain technical support, please contact our Customer Care Department within the U.S. at (877) 762-2974, outside the U.S. at (317) 572-3993 or fax (317) 572-4002.

Wiley publishes in a variety of print and electronic formats and by print-on-demand. Some material included with standard print versions of this book may not be included in e-books or in print-on-demand. If this book refers to media such as a CD or DVD that is not included in the version you purchased, you may download this material at http://booksupport.wiley.com. For more information about Wiley products, visit www.wiley.com.

Library of Congress Control Number: 2015951679

V10015698 120619

To the programmers on FIRST robotics team FRC 694 StuyPulse
— Jeanne

To my newborn daughters Olivia and Sophia, I love you both more and more every day.
— Scott

Acknowledgments

Jeanne and Scott would like to thank numerous individuals for their contribution to this book. Thank you, Gary Schwartz, for guiding us through the process and making the book better in so many ways. Thank you, Ernest Friedman-Hill, for being our Technical Editor as we wrote this book. Ernest pointed out many subtle errors in addition to the big ones. And thank you, Matt Dalen, for being our Technical Proofreader and finding the errors that managed to sneak by even Ernest. This book also wouldn't be possible without many people at Wiley, including Kenyon Brown, Dassi Zeidel, Mary Beth Wakefield, and so many others.

Jeanne would personally like to thank Chris Kreussling and Elena Felder for their feedback on early drafts of the trickier material. Elena even helped figure out a good way to explain upper bounds. Roel De Nijs reviewed the Java 8 date/time material for words that native English speakers take for granted, and he responded to lots of posts in the CodeRanch.com OCA forum on our first book. To all of the people at work and at CodeRanch.com who were so excited for me about writing this book, you made it even more exciting when we published our first book. Jeanne would like to thank the members of FIRST robotics FRC team 694 for their support. It was an awesome feeling seeing high school students pore over the book while waiting for dinner the night the hard copy arrived. Go StuyPulse! See if you can find JoeBot in this book. Finally, Jeanne would like to thank Scott for being a great co-author again.

Scott could not have reached this point without the help of a small army of people, led by his perpetually understanding wife Patti, the most wonderful mother their twin daughters could ask for. Professor Johannes Gehrke of Cornell University always believed in him and knew he would excel in his career. Jeanne's patience and striving for excellence was invaluable in creating this second book. A big thanks to fellow new father Matt Dalen, who has been a wonderful friend, sounding board, and technical reviewer over the last year. Joel McNary introduced Scott to CodeRanch.com and encouraged him to post regularly—a step that changed his life. Finally, Scott would like to thank his mother and retired teacher Barbara Selikoff, for teaching him the value of education, and his father Mark Selikoff, for instilling in him the benefits of working hard.

Finally, both Jeanne and Scott would like to give a big thank-you to the readers of our OCA 8 book. Hearing from all of you who enjoyed the book and passed the exam was great. We'd also like to thank those who pointed out errors and made suggestions for improvements in our OCA book. As of July 2015, the top three were Mushfiq Mammadov, Elena Felder, and Cédric Georges. Thank you for your attention to detail! We also would like to thank Mathias Bader, Maaike Zijderveld, Vincent Botteman, Edward Rance, Gabriel Jesus, Ilya Danilov, Marc ter Braak, Dominik Bauer, Saad Benbouzid, Evgeny Kapinos, Helen Colson, Alex Lord, and Kevin Abel.

About the Authors

Jeanne Boyarsky has worked as a Java developer for more than 13 years at a bank in New York City, where she develops, mentors, and conducts training. Besides being a senior moderator at CodeRanch.com in her free time, she leads the team that works on the forum's code base. Jeanne also mentors the programming division of a FIRST robotics team, where she works with students just getting started with Java.

Jeanne got her Bachelor of Arts degree in 2002 in Computer Science and her Master's in Computer Information Technology in 2005. She enjoyed getting her Master's degree in an online program while working full time. This was before online education was cool! Jeanne is also a Distinguished Toastmaster and a Scrum Master. You can find out more about Jeanne at http://www.coderanch.com/how-to/java/BioJeanneBoyarsky.

Scott Selikoff is a professional software consultant, author, and owner of Selikoff Solutions, LLC, which provides software development solutions to businesses in the tri-state New York City area. Skilled in a plethora of software languages and platforms, Scott specializes in database-driven systems, web-based applications, and service-oriented architectures.

A native of Toms River, New Jersey, Scott achieved his Bachelor of Arts from Cornell University in Mathematics and Computer Science in 2002, after three years of study. In 2003, he received his Master of Engineering in Computer Science, also from Cornell University.

As someone with a deep love of education, Scott has always enjoyed teaching others new concepts. He's given lectures at Cornell University and Rutgers University, as well as conferences including The Server Side Java Symposium. Scott lives in New Jersey with his loving wife, amazing twin baby girls, and two very playful dogs. You can find out more about Scott at http://www.linkedin.com/in/selikoff.

Jeanne and Scott are both moderators on the CodeRanch.com forums, and they can be reached there for questions and comments. They also co-author a technical blog called Down Home Country Coding at http://www.selikoff.net.

Contents at a Glance

Contents

Introduction

Java recently celebrated its 20th birthday, since it was "born" in 1995. As with anything 20 years old, there is a good amount of history and variation between different versions of Java. Over the years, the certification exams have changed to cover different topics. The names of the exams have even changed. This book covers the Java 8 OCP exam along with the upgrade exams to Java 8.

If you read about the exam on the web, you may see information about the older names for the exam. The name changes are shown in Figure I.1. Here's what happened. Back when Sun Microsystems owned Java, they used to have two exams. The SCJA (Sun Certified Java Associate) was meant for new programmers and the SCJP (Sun Certified Java Programmer) was meant for those who wanted broader knowledge. When Oracle bought Sun Microsystems, they renamed all of the exams from Sun to Oracle, giving us the OCJA (Oracle Certified Java Associate) and OCJP (Oracle Certified Java Programmer).

FIGURE I.1   Names for the exam

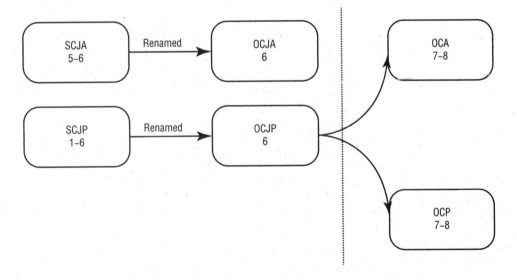

Then Oracle made two strategic decisions with Java 7. They decided to stop updating the OCJA exam. They also decided to cover more in the programmer space, and they split it into two exams. Now you first take the OCAJP (Oracle Certified Associate Java Programmer), also known as Java Programmer I or OCA. Then you take the OCPJP (Oracle Certified Professional Java Programmer), also known as Java Programmer II or OCP, and that's what this book is about. Most people refer to the current exams as OCA 8 and OCP 8.

Oracle also has upgrade exams in case you took an older version of the SCJP or OCPJP and you want to upgrade. While most people refer to them as the Java 8 upgrade exam, there are really two exams, and you choose the correct one based on the certification you currently hold. Table I.1 describes the exams that this book covers, while Figure I.2 helps you decide what exam to take next, assuming that you have passed a prior Java certification exam. Our book is designed to help you prepare for any of these three exams, all of which result in you being OCP 8 certified.

TABLE I.1   Exams this book covers

Exam Code	Name	Who Should Take
1Z0–809	Java Programmer II	Holders of the OCA **8** certification
1Z0–810	Upgrade Java SE 7 to Java SE 8 OCP Programmer	Holders of the OCPJP **7** certification
1Z0–813	Upgrade to Java SE 8 OCP (Java SE 6 and all prior versions)	Holders of any of the following certifications: • SCJP/OCJP 6 • SCJP/OCJP 5 • SCJP 1.4 • Any older SCJP certs

FIGURE I.2   Exam prerequisites

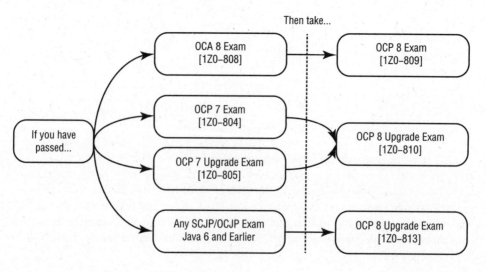

We try to keep the history to a minimum in this book. There are some places on the exam where you need to know both an old way and a new way of doing things. When that happens, we will be sure to tell you what version of Java introduced which way. We will also let you know about topics that are not on the exam anymore, in case you see questions on them in the older free online mock exams.

The OCP Exam

All you need to do to become an Oracle Certified Professional for Java 8 is to pass an exam! That's it.

Oracle has a tendency to fiddle with the length of the exam and the passing score once it comes out. Since it's pretty much guaranteed that whatever we tell you here will become obsolete, we will instead give you a feel for the range. The OCP exam has varied between 60 and 90 questions since it was first introduced. The score to pass the exam has varied between 60 percent and 80 percent. The time allowed to take the exam has varied from two hours to two-and-a-half hours.

Oracle has a tendency to tweak the exam objectives over time as well. They do make minor additions and deletions from what is covered on the exam. For example, serialization has been added and removed from the objectives many times over the life of the OCP. As of this writing, it is on the exam.

While there will likely be minor changes to the scope of the exam, they certainly aren't a secret. We've created a book page on our blog: http://www.selikoff.net/ocp. If there are any changes to the topics on the exam after this book is published, we will note them there.

That book page also contains a link to the official exam page, so you can check the length and passing score that Oracle has chosen for the moment. Finally, all known errata and links to discussion can be found at http://www.coderanch.com.

Scheduling the Exam

Pearson VUE administers the exam, and it can be taken at any Pearson VUE testing center. To find a testing center or to register for the exam, go to http://pearsonvue.com. Choose IT and then Oracle. If you haven't been to the test center before, we recommend visiting in advance. Some testing centers are nice and professionally run. Others stick you in a closet with lots of people talking around you. You don't want to be taking the test with someone complaining about his or her broken laptop nearby!

At this time, you can reschedule the exam without penalty until up to 24 hours in advance. This means that you can register for a convenient time slot well in advance knowing that you can delay taking the exam if you aren't ready by that time. Rescheduling is easy and can be done completely on the Pearson VUE website. This may change, so check the rules before paying.

The Day of the Exam

When you go to take the exam, remember to bring two forms of ID, including one that is government issued. See Pearson's list of what is an acceptable ID at http://www.pearsonvue.com/policies/1S.pdf. Try not to bring too much extra with you, because it will not be allowed into the exam room. While you will be allowed to check your belongings, it is better to leave extra items at home or in your car.

You will not be allowed to bring paper, your phone, and so on into the exam room with you. Some centers are stricter than others. At one center, tissues were even taken away from us! Most centers allow you to keep your ID and money. They watch you taking the exam, though, so don't even think about writing notes on money. Some centers place these articles in a locker and give you the key, whereas others just throw them in an administrator's desk drawer. Suffice it to say, if you have something that you really don't want to lose, we recommend that you leave it at home.

The exam center will give you writing materials to use during the exam. These are to be used as scratch paper during the exam to figure out answers and to keep track of your thought process. The exam center will dispose of them at the end. Notice how we said "writing materials" rather than "pen and paper." Actually getting pen and paper is rare. Most centers provide a small erasable board and a dry erase marker. Before going into the exam room, we recommend testing that the marker writes and erases.

As we alluded to earlier, some exam centers are more professionally run than others, so we recommend visiting your local exam center before scheduling the exam if you have never been there before. Some exam centers also have problems keeping the temperature at a comfortable level. Regardless of whether it is winter or summer, when you take the exam, we strongly recommend that you dress in layers, such as a long-sleeve shirt or sweatshirt over a short-sleeve shirt. This way, you can add/remove layers of clothing to adjust for your own comfort.

Some exam centers are located in quiet suburban areas while others are near busy city streets with noisy traffic. Furthermore, you might get lucky and be the only person in your exam room the day you show up, or you might be unlucky and have 10 other people in the room coming and going at different times. If you are someone who gets easily distracted by noise and other people moving around, we recommend that you bring a pair of earplugs for the exam. Some exam centers will even offer you a pair of sterile earplugs if you ask. Double-check with your test administrator before using your own, so that they don't think you're trying to cheat!

While many exam centers permit bathroom breaks during the exam with permission, very few allow you to bring drinks inside. Since these exams are at least two hours long, make sure that you are well hydrated before you arrive. Just be aware that if you do need to use the facilities, your exam clock will not be paused.

Finally, if you have any issues like it being unbearably hot, cold, or noisy in your exam room, you should contact Oracle after you finish taking the exam to let them know the quality of the particular testing center was poor. Some exam centers have shown improvement after receiving such reports.

Finding Out Your Score

In the past, you would find out whether you passed or not right after finishing the exam. Now you have to wait nervously until you can check your score online.

If you go to the Pearson VUE website, it will just show a status of "Taken" rather than your result. Oracle uses a separate system for scores. You'll need to go to http://certview.oracle.com to find out whether you passed and your score. It doesn't update immediately upon taking the test, but we haven't heard of it taking more than an hour. In addition to your score, you'll also see objectives for which you got a question wrong and instructions on how to get a hardcopy certificate.

At some point, you'll get an electronic certificate, and some more time after that, you'll receive a printed certificate. Sound vague? It is. The times reported to receive certificates vary widely.

Exam Questions

The OCP exam consists of multiple-choice questions. There are typically four to six possible answers for each question. If a question has more than one correct answer, the question specifically states exactly how many correct answers there are. This book does not do that. We say "choose all that apply" if there might be more than one correct answer to make the questions harder. This means that the questions in this book are generally harder than those on the exam. The idea is to give you more practice so that you can spot the correct answer more easily on the real exam.

You can right-click questions to cross out answers. This lets you mark answers as incorrect as you go so that you have less to think about as you read. It also helps you remember what you've eliminated when you go back to questions.

The exam uses two different formats for identifying line numbers. We use both approaches in this book to get you prepared. The first approach is a comment at the end of a line such as this:

```
list.stream()
    .map(s-> s.length())    // k1
    .forEach(System.out::println);
```

One or more answer choices will refer to k1. With this approach, imports will be provided for any class definitions. For code snippets, you can assume that all necessary surrounding code is implied. The other approach is placing line numbers at the beginning of each line, like so:

```
4:     list.stream()
5:         .map(s-> s.length())
6:         .forEach(System.out::println);
```

With this approach, the line numbers often begin with numbers higher than 1. This is to indicate that you are looking at a code snippet rather than a complete class.

If you read about older versions of the exam online, you might see references to drag-and-drop questions. These questions had you do a puzzle on how to complete a piece of code. There was also a bug in the exam software that caused your answers to be lost if you reviewed them. Luckily, these are no longer on the exam.

Getting Started

We recommend reading Appendix B, "Study Tips," before diving into the technical material in this book. Knowing how to approach studying will help you make better use of your study time.

Next, make sure that you have downloaded version 8 of the JDK. If you learned Java some time ago, you might have version 7 or even earlier. Many of the examples won't even compile in Java 7.

Also, please check our book page to make sure that Oracle hasn't changed the objectives. For example, if Oracle changed their mind on whether to include serialization yet again, you'd want to know that before studying. We will post any updates that you should know about at http://www.selikoff.net/ocp.

Getting Help

Both of the authors are moderators at CodeRanch.com, a very large and active programming forum that is very friendly toward Java beginners. It has a forum just for this exam called "SCJP/OCPJP." It also has a forum called "Java in General" for non-exam-specific questions. As you read the book, feel free to ask your questions in either of those forums. It could be that you are having trouble compiling a class or that you are just plain confused about something. You'll get an answer from a knowledgeable Java programmer. It might even be one of us.

Who Should Buy This Book

If you want to become Oracle Certified Java Programmer, this book is definitely for you. If you want to acquire a solid foundation in Java, and your goal is to prepare for the exam, this book is also for you. You'll find clear explanations of the concepts you need to grasp and plenty of help to achieve the high level of professional competency you need in order to succeed in your chosen field.

This book is intended to be understandable to anyone who knows basic Java. Since the exam has a prerequisite of the Associate exam, we assume that you have a good handle on that much Java. We don't assume that you know the Java 8–specific parts of the Associate exam, since some readers are taking the upgrade exam and are new to Java 8.

This book is for anyone from high school students to those beginning their programming journey to experienced professionals who need a review for the certification.

How This Book Is Organized

This book consists of 10 chapters plus supplementary information: a glossary, this introduction, four appendices, and the assessment test after this introduction. You might have noticed that there are more than 10 exam objectives. We split up what you need to know to make it easy to learn and remember. Each chapter begins with a list of the objectives that are covered in that chapter.

Java 8 lambdas and functional programming streams are prevalent throughout the exam and appear in questions on many topics. You have to know this topic as well as you knew loops on the OCA exam. We've made sure to use them in many chapters so that you will be ready. For example, Chapter 2 reviews functional interfaces and Chapter 3 introduces method references. Chapter 4 covers the Streams API in detail. Later chapters use "the new approach" to writing code often so that you keep using it and become fluent.

The chapters are organized as follows:

Chapter 1: Advanced Class Design   This chapter covers inheritance, including abstract classes and the final keyword. It also discusses inner classes and enums.

Chapter 2: Design Patterns and Principles   This chapter teaches you best practices for designing and writing applications that lead to code that is easier to understand and more maintainable.

Chapter 3: Generics and Collections   This chapter goes beyond ArrayList and shows Sets, Maps, and Queues. It also shows new methods in Java 8 on these classes.

Chapter 4: Functional Programming   This chapter explains lambdas and stream pipelines in detail. It also covers the built-in functional interfaces and the Optional class.

Chapter 5: Dates, Strings, and Localization   This chapter shows the improved date and time classes in Java 8. It also covers more advanced String concepts that you need to know and how to make your application work in multiple languages.

Chapter 6: Exceptions and Assertions   This chapter shows more advanced syntax for exceptions than what appears on the OCA. It also covers how to use assertions to verify the state of your program.

Chapter 7: Concurrency   This chapter introduces the concept of thread management, and it teaches you how to write multi-threaded programs using the Concurrency API.

Chapter 8: IO   This chapter introduces you to managing files and directories using the java.io API. It also instructs you on how to read and write file data using I/O streams.

Chapter 9: NIO.2   This chapter shows you how to manage files and directories using the newer NIO.2 API. It includes techniques for reading and writing file attributes, as well as traversing and searching for files using lambdas and streams.

Chapter 10: JDBC   This chapter provides the basics of working with databases in Java including different types of ResultSets.

Appendix A: Answers to Review Questions   This appendix lists the answers to the Review Questions along with explanations.

Appendix B: Study Tips   This appendix covers how to approach studying for the exam.

Appendix C: Upgrading from Java 6 or Earlier   This appendix covers topics that are on the upgrade exam for those holding a Java 6 or earlier programmer certification. These topics are not on the main OCP 8 exam, nor are they on the upgrade exam for holders of the OCP 7 certification.

At the end of each chapter, you'll find a few elements that you can use to prepare for the exam:

Summary   This section reviews the most important topics that were covered in the chapter, and it serves as a good review.

Exam Essentials   This section summarizes the main points that were covered in the chapter. You should be able to convey the information requested.

Review Questions   Each chapter concludes with at least 20 Review Questions. You should answer these questions and check your answers against the ones provided after the questions. If you can't answer at least 80 percent of these questions correctly, go back and review the chapter, or at least review those sections that seem to be giving you difficulty.

The Review Questions, Assessment Test, and other testing elements included in this book are *not* derived from the real exam questions, so don't memorize the answers to these questions and assume that doing so will enable you to pass the exam. You should learn the underlying topic, as described in the text of the book. This will let you answer the questions provided with this book *and* pass the exam. Learning the underlying topic is also the approach that will serve you best in the workplace—the ultimate goal of a certification.

To get the most out of this book, you should read each chapter from start to finish before going to the end-of-chapter elements. They are most useful for checking and reinforcing your understanding. Even if you're already familiar with a topic, you should at least skim the chapter. There are a number of subtleties to Java that you may not encounter even when working with Java for years.

Interactive Online Learning Environment and Test Bank

The interactive online learning environment that accompanies *OCP Oracle Certified Professional SE 8 Programmer II: Exam 1Z0-809* provides a test bank with study tools to help you prepare for the certification exam, and it increases your chances of passing it the first time! The test bank includes the following:

Sample Tests   All of the questions in this book are provided, including the Assessment Test, which you'll find at the end of this introduction, and the Chapter Tests, which include the Review Questions at the end of each chapter. In addition, there are three Practice Exams—180 questions in total! Use these questions to test your knowledge of the study guide material. The online test bank runs on multiple devices.

Flashcards   Over 250 questions are provided in digital flashcard format (a question followed by a single correct answer). You can use the flashcards to reinforce your learning and provide last-minute test prep before the exam.

Other Study Tools   Several bonus study tools are included:

> **Glossary**   A glossary of key terms from this book and their definitions is available as a fully searchable PDF.

> **Nashorn Materials**   Early drafts of the exam objectives had Nashorn on the exam for using JavaScript with Java. Since it isn't on the exam anymore, this topic isn't in the printed book. The appendix is available in the bonus contents in case you want to learn about this topic, independent of the exam.

 Go to http://sybextestbanks.wiley.com to register and gain access to this interactive online learning environment and test bank with study tools.

Conventions Used in This Book

This book uses certain typographic styles in order to help you quickly identify important information and to avoid confusion over the meaning of words such as on-screen prompts. In particular, look for the following styles:

- *Italicized text* indicates key terms that are described at length for the first time in a chapter. (Italics are also used for emphasis.)
- A `monospaced` font indicates code or command-line text.
- *`Italicized monospaced text`* indicates a variable.

In addition to these text conventions, which can apply to individual words or entire paragraphs, a few conventions highlight segments of text:

A note indicates information that's useful or interesting. It is often something to which you should pay special attention for the exam.

> **Sidebars**
>
> A sidebar is like a note but longer. The information in a sidebar is useful, but it doesn't fit into the main flow of the text.

 Real World Scenario

Real World Scenario

A real world scenario is a type of sidebar that describes a task or an example that's particularly grounded in the real world. This is something that is useful in the real world but is not going to show up on the exam.

OCP Exam Objectives

This book has been written to cover every objective on the OCP 8 exam along with both upgrade exams.

OCP 8 (1Z0–809)

The following table provides a breakdown of this book's exam coverage for the OCP 8 (1Z0–809) exam, showing you the chapter where each objective or sub-objective is covered:

Exam Objective	Chapter
Java Class Design	
Implement encapsulation	2
Implement inheritance including visibility modifiers and composition	1,2
Implement polymorphism	2

Exam Objective	Chapter
Override hashCode, equals, and toString methods from Object class	1
Create and use singleton classes and immutable classes	2
Develop code that uses static keyword on initialize blocks, variables, methods, and classes	1
Advanced Java Class Design	
Develop code that uses abstract classes and methods	1
Develop code that uses final keyword	1
Create inner classes including static inner class, local class, nested class, and anonymous inner class	1
Use enumerated types including methods and constructors in an enum type	1
Develop code that declares, implements and/or extends interfaces and use the @Override annotation.	1,2
Create and use Lambda expressions	2,3
Generics and Collections	
Create and use a generic class	3
Create and use ArrayList, TreeSet, TreeMap, and ArrayDeque objects	3
Use java.util.Comparator and java.lang.Comparable interfaces	3
Collections Streams and Filters	4
Iterate using forEach methods of Streams and List	3,4
Describe Stream interface and Stream pipeline	4
Filter a collection by using lambda expressions	3
Use method references with Streams	3,4
Lambda Built-in Functional Interfaces	
Use the built-in interfaces included in the java.util.function package such as Predicate, Consumer, Function, and Supplier	2,4

Exam Objective	Chapter
Develop code that uses primitive versions of functional interfaces	4
Develop code that uses binary versions of functional interfaces	4
Develop code that uses the UnaryOperator interface	4
Java Stream API	
Develop code to extract data from an object using peek() and map() methods including primitive versions of the map() method	4
Search for data by using search methods of the Stream classes including findFirst, findAny, anyMatch, allMatch, noneMatch	4
Develop code that uses the Optional class	4
Develop code that uses Stream data methods and calculation methods	4
Sort a collection using Stream API	4
Save results to a collection using the collect method and group/partition data using the Collectors class	4
Use of merge() and flatMap() methods of the Stream API	3,4
Exceptions and Assertions	
Use try-catch and throw statements	6
Use catch, multi-catch, and finally clauses	6
Use Autoclose resources with a try-with-resources statement	6
Create custom exceptions and AutoCloseable resources	6
Test invariants by using assertions	6
Use Java SE 8 Date/Time API	
Create and manage date-based and time-based events including a combination of date and time into a single object using LocalDate, LocalTime, LocalDateTime, Instant, Period, and Duration	5
Work with dates and times across time zones and manage changes resulting from daylight savings including Format date and times values	5

Exam Objective	Chapter
Submit queries and read results from the database (including creating statements, returning result sets, iterating through the results, and properly closing result sets, statements, and connections)	10
Localization	
Read and set the locale by using the Locale object	5
Create and read a Properties file	5
Build a resource bundle for each locale and load a resource bundle in an application	5

Upgrade from Java 7 (1Z0–810)

This table shows the chapter where each objective or sub-objective is covered for the upgrade exam from Java 7 to Java 8 OCP (1Z0–810):

Exam Objective	Chapter
Lambda Expressions	
Describe and develop code that uses Java inner classes, including nested class, static class, local class, and anonymous classes	1
Describe and write functional interfaces	2
Describe a lambda expression; refactor the code that uses an anonymous inner class to use a lambda expression; describe type inference and target typing	4
Using Built-in Lambda Types	
Describe the interfaces of the java.util.function package	4
Develop code that uses the Function interface	4
Develop code that uses the Consumer interface	4
Develop code that uses the Supplier interface	4
Develop code that uses the UnaryOperator interface	4
Develop code that uses the Predicate interface	4

Exam Objective	Chapter
Develop code that uses the primitive and binary variations of the base interfaces of the java.util.function package	4
Develop code that uses a method reference, including refactoring a lambda expression to a method reference	3,4
Filtering Collections with Lambdas	
Develop code that iterates a collection by using the forEach() method and method chaining	3
Describe the Stream interface and pipelines	4
Filter a collection by using lambda expressions	3
Identify the lambda operations that are lazy	4
Collection Operations with Lambda	
Develop code to extract data from an object by using the map() method	3
Search for data by using methods such as findFirst(), findAny(), anyMatch(), allMatch(), and noneMatch()	4
Describe the unique characteristics of the Optional class	4
Perform calculations by using Java Stream methods, such as count(), max(), min(), average(), and sum()	4
Sort a collection by using lambda expressions	4
Develop code that uses the Stream.collect() method and Collectors class methods, such as averagingDouble(), groupingBy(), joining(), and partitioningBy()	4
Parallel Streams	
Develop code that uses parallel streams	7
Implement decomposition and reduction in streams	4,7
Lambda Cookbook	
Develop code that uses Java SE 8 collection improvements, including Collection.removeIf(), List.replaceAll(), Map.computeIfAbsent(), and Map.computeIfPresent() methods	3

Exam Objective	Chapter
Develop code that uses Java SE 8 I/O improvements, including Files.find(), Files. walk(), and lines() methods	9
Use the merge() and flatMap() methods	3,4
Develop code that creates a stream by using the Arrays.stream() and IntStream. range() methods	
Method Enhancements	
Add static methods to interfaces	2
Define and use a default method of an interface and describe the inheritance rules for the default method	2
Use Java SE 8 Date/Time API	
Create and manage date- and time-based events, including a combination of date and time in a single object, by using LocalDate, LocalTime, LocalDateTime, Instant, Period, and Duration	5
Work with dates and times across time zones and manage changes resulting from daylight savings, including Format date and times values	5
Define, create, and manage date- and time-based events using Instant, Period, Duration, and TemporalUnit	5

Upgrade from Java 6 or lower (1Z0–813)

If you are studying for the 1Z0–813 exam, you *must* read Appendix C. It covers topics that are on your exam but not the other exams covered by the book.

This table shows the chapter where each objective or sub-objective is covered for the upgrade exam from a Java 6 or lower certification to Java 8 OCP (1Z0–813).

Exam Objective	Chapter
Language Enhancements	
Develop code that uses String objects in the switch statement, binary literals, and numeric literals, including underscores in literals	Appendix C
Develop code that uses try-with-resources statements, including using classes that implement the AutoCloseable interface	6

Exam Objective	Chapter
Develop code that handles multiple Exception types in a single catch block	6
Use static and default methods of an interface including inheritance rules for a default method	2
Concurrency	
Use collections from the java.util.concurrent package with a focus on the advantages over and differences from the traditional java.util collections	7
Use Lock, ReadWriteLock, and ReentrantLock classes in the java.util. concurrent.locks and java.util.concurrent.atomic packages to support lock-free thread-safe programming on single variables	Appendix C
Use Executor, ExecutorService, Executors, Callable, and Future to execute tasks using thread pools	7
Use the parallel Fork/Join Framework	7
Localization	
Describe the advantages of localizing an application and developing code that defines, reads, and sets the locale with a Locale object	5
Build a resource bundle for a locale and call a resource bundle from an application	5
Create and manage date- and time-based events by using LocalDate, LocalTime, LocalDateTime, Instant, Period, and Duration, including a combination of date and time in a single object	5
Format dates, numbers, and currency values for localization with the NumberFormat and DateFormat classes, including number and date format patterns	5, Appendix C
Work with dates and times across time zones and manage changes resulting from daylight savings	5
Java File I/O (NIO.2)	
Operate on file and directory paths by using the Path class	9
Check, delete, copy, or move a file or directory by using the Files class	9
Recursively access a directory tree by using the DirectoryStream and FileVisitor interfaces	Appendix C

Exam Objective	Chapter
Find a file by using the PathMatcher interface, and use Java SE 8 I/O improvements, including Files.find(), Files.walk(), and lines() methods	9
Observe the changes in a directory by using the WatchService interface	Appendix C
Lambda	
Define and write functional interfaces and describe the interfaces of the java.util.function package	3,4
Describe a lambda expression; refactor the code that uses an anonymous inner class to use a lambda expression; describe type inference and target typing	3,4
Develop code that uses the built-in interfaces included in the java.util. function package, such as Function, Consumer, Supplier, UnaryOperator, Predicate, and Optional APIs, including the primitive and binary variations of the interfaces	4
Develop code that uses a method reference, including refactoring a lambda expression to a method reference	3
Java Collections	
Develop code that uses diamond with generic declarations	Appendix C
Develop code that iterates a collection, filters a collection, and sorts a collection by using lambda expressions	3
Search for data by using methods, such as findFirst(), findAny(), any-Match(), allMatch(), and noneMatch()	4
Perform calculations on Java Streams by using count, max, min, average, and sum methods and save results to a collection by using the collect method and Collector class, including the averagingDouble, groupingBy, joining, partitioningBy methods	4
Develop code that uses Java SE 8 collection improvements, including the Collection.removeIf(), List.replaceAll(), Map.computeIfAbsent(), and Map.computeIfPresent() methods	3
Develop code that uses the merge(), flatMap(), and map() methods on Java Streams	4

Exam Objective	Chapter
Java Streams	
Describe the Stream interface and pipelines; create a stream by using the Arrays.stream() and IntStream.range() methods; identify the lambda operations that are lazy	4
Develop code that uses parallel streams, including decomposition operation and reduction operation in streams	7

Assessment Test

1. What is the result of executing the following application? (Choose all that apply.)

```java
import java.util.concurrent.*;
import java.util.stream.*;
public class BabyPandaBathManager {
    public static void await(CyclicBarrier cb) {
        try {
            cb.await();
        } catch (InterruptedException | BrokenBarrierException e) {
            // Handle exception
        }
    }
    public static void main(String[] args) {
        final CyclicBarrier cb = new CyclicBarrier(3,()-> System.out.
        println("Clean!"));// u1
        ExecutorService service = Executors.newScheduledThreadPool(2);
        IntStream.iterate(1, i-> 1) // u2
            .limit(12)
            .forEach(i-> service.submit( // u3
                    ()-> await(cb))); // u4
        service.shutdown();
    }
}
```

  A. It outputs Clean! at least once.

  B. It outputs Clean! four times.

  C. The code will not compile because of line u1.

  D. The code will not compile because of line u2.

  E. The code will not compile because of line u3.

  F. The code will not compile because of line u4.

  G. It compiles but throws an exception at runtime.

  H. It compiles but waits forever at runtime.

2. What is the result of the following program?

```java
1:    public abstract class Message {
2:        public String recipient;
3:        public abstract final void sendMessage();
4:        public static void main(String[] args) {
```

```
5:            Message m = new TextMessage();
6:            m.recipient = "1234567890";
7:            m.sendMessage();
8:        }
9:        static class TextMessage extends Message {
10:            public final void sendMessage() {
11:                System.out.println("Text message to " + recipient);
12:        } } }
```

A. Text message to null.

B. Text message to 1234567890.

C. A compiler error occurs on line 1.

D. A compiler error occurs on line 3.

E. A compiler error occurs on line 7.

F. A compiler error occurs on another line.

3. What is the result of executing the following code? (Choose all that apply.)

```
1: import java.io.*;
2: public class Tail {}
3: public class Bird implements Serializable {
4:      private String name;
5:      private transient int age;
6:      private Tail tail;
7:
8:      public String getName() { return name; }
9:      public Tail getTail() { return tail; }
10:     public void setName(String name) { this.name = name; }
11:     public void setTail(Tail tail) { this.tail = tail; }
12:     public int getAge() { return age; }
13:     public void setAge(int age) { this.age = age; }
14:
15:     public void main(String[] args) {
16:         try(InputStream is = new ObjectInputStream(
17:             new BufferedInputStream(new FileInputStream("birds.dat")))) {
18:             Bird bird = is.readObject();
19:         }
20:     }
21: }
```

A. It compiles and runs without issue.

B. The code will not compile because of line 3.

C. The code will not compile because of line 5.

D. The code will not compile because of lines 16–17.

E. The code will not compile because of line 18.

F. It compiles but throws an exception at runtime.

4. What is the result of the following class?

```
1:   public class Box<T> {
2:       T value;
3:
4:       public Box(T value) {
5:           this.value = value;
6:       }
7:       public T getValue() {
8:           return value;
9:       }
10:      public static void main(String[] args) {
11:          Box<String> one = new Box<String>("a string");
12:          Box<Integer> two = new Box<>(123);
13:          System.out.print(one.getValue());
14:          System.out.print(two.getValue());
15:      } }
```

A. Compiler error on line 1.

B. Compiler error on line 2.

C. Compiler error on line 11.

D. Compiler error on line 12.

E. a string123

F. An exception is thrown.

5. What is the result of executing the following code snippet?

```
List<Integer> source = new ArrayList<>(Arrays.asList(1,2,3,4));
List<Integer> fish = new CopyOnWriteArrayList<>(source);
List<Integer> mammals = Collections.synchronizedList(source);
Set<Integer> birds = new ConcurrentSkipListSet<>();
birds.addAll(source);

synchronized(new Integer(10)) {
    for(Integer f: fish) fish.add(4); // c1
```

```
    for(Integer m: mammals) mammals.add(4); // c2
    for(Integer b: birds) birds.add(5); // c3
    System.out.println(fish.size()+" "+mammals.size()+" "+birds.size());
}
```

A. It outputs 4 8 5.

B. It outputs 8 4 5.

C. It outputs 8 8 8.

D. The code does not compile.

E. It compiles but throws an exception at runtime on line c1.

F. It compiles but throws an exception at runtime on line c2.

G. It compiles but throws an exception at runtime on line c3.

H. It compiles but enters an infinite loop at runtime.

6. What changes would need to be made to make the following immutable object pattern correct? (Choose all that apply.)

```
import java.util.List;
public class Duck {
    private String name;
    private List<Duck> ducklings;
    public Duck(String name, List<Duck> ducklings) {
        this.name = name;
        this.ducklings = new ArrayList<Duck>(ducklings);
    }
    public String getName() { return name; }
    public List<Duck> getDucklings() { return ducklings; }
    public String hasDucklings(Predicate<Duck> p) {
        return p.test(this) ? "Quack Quack": "";
    }
}
```

A. None, the immutable object pattern is properly implemented.

B. Mark name and ducklings final.

C. Mark the Duck class final.

D. Have Duck implement the Immutable interface.

E. Remove the hasDucklings() method since any lambda expressions passed to it could modify the Duck object.

F. Replace the getDucklings() with a method (or methods) that do not give the caller direct access to the List<Duck> ducklings.

G. Change the type of List<Duck> to be List<Object>.

7. Assuming the current directory /bats/day and all of the files and directories referenced here exist and are available within the file system, what is the result of executing the following code?

```
Path path1 = Paths.get("/bats/night","../").resolve(Paths.get(
"./sleep.txt")).normalize();
Path path2 = new File("../sleep.txt").toPath().toRealPath();

System.out.print(Files.isSameFile(path1,path2));
System.out.print(" "+path1.equals(path2));
```

A. true true

B. false false

C. true false

D. false true

E. The code does not compile.

F. The code compiles but throws an exception at runtime.

8. What statements are true about the following code? (Choose all that apply.)

```
public class Tail {}
public class Animal {
    public String name;
}
public class Canine extends Animal {
    public Tail tail;
}
public class Wolf extends Canine {}
```

A. Wolf has-a name.

B. Wolf has-a Tail.

C. Wolf is-a Tail.

D. Wolf is-a Animal.

E. Canine is-a Wolf.

F. Animal has-a Tail.

9. Which of the following can fill in the blank? (Choose all that apply.)

```
public void stmt(Connection conn, int a) throws SQLException {
    Statement stmt = conn.createStatement(a, _____);
}
```

A. ResultSet.CONCUR_READ_ONLY

B. ResultSet.CONCUR_INSERTABLE

C. ResultSet.CONCUR_UPDATABLE

D. ResultSet.TYPE_FORWARD_ONLY

E. ResultSet.TYPE_SCROLL_INSENSITIVE

F. ResultSet.TYPE_SCROLL_SENSITIVE

10. Which of the following statements is true when the code is run with `java AssertDemo`?

```
1:    public class AssertDemo {
2:       public static void main(String [] args) {
3:          Integer x = 10;
4:          x++;
5:          assert x == null && x >= 0;
6:          System.out.println(x);
7:       }
8:    }
```

A. Line 3 generates a compiler error.

B. Line 4 generates a compiler error.

C. Line 5 generates a compiler error.

D. Line 5 throws an AssertionError at runtime.

E. The output is 10.

F. The output is 11.

11. Which of the following are true? (Choose all that apply.)

```
private static void magic(Stream<Integer> s) {
   Optional o = s.filter(x -> x < 5).limit(3).max((x, y) -> x-y);
   System.out.println(o.get());
}
```

A. magic(Stream.empty()); runs infinitely.

B. magic(Stream.empty()); throws an exception.

C. magic(Stream.iterate(1, x ->> x++)); runs infinitely.

D. magic(Stream.iterate(1, x ->> x++)); throws an exception.

E. magic(Stream.of(5, 10)); runs infinitely.

F. magic(Stream.of(5, 10)); throws an exception.

G. The method does not compile.

12. Suppose that we have the following property files and code. Which bundle is used on lines 7 and 8, respectively?

```
Dolphins.properties
name=The Dolphin
```

```
age=0

Dolphins_fr.properties
name=Dolly

Dolphins_fr_CA.properties
name=Dolly
age=4
```

```
5:      Locale fr = new Locale("fr");
6:      ResourceBundle b = ResourceBundle.getBundle("Dolphins", fr);
7:      b.getString("name");
8:      b.getString("age");
```

A. Dolphins.properties and Dolphins.properties

B. Dolphins.properties and Dolphins_fr.properties

C. Dolphins_fr.properties and Dolphins_fr.properties

D. Dolphins_fr.properties and Dolphins.properties

E. Dolphins_fr.properties and Dolphins_fr_CA.properties

F. Dolphins_fr_CA.properties and Dolphins_fr.properties

13. What is the result of executing the following code? (Choose all that apply.)

```
String line;
Console c = System.console();
if ((line = c.readLine()) != null)
    System.out.println(line);
```

A. The code runs without error but prints nothing.

B. The code prints what was entered by the user.

C. An ArrayIndexOutOfBoundsException might be thrown.

D. A NullPointerException might be thrown.

E. An IOException might be thrown.

F. The code does not compile.

14. How many compilation issues are in the following code?

```
1:      public class Compiles {
2:          class RainException extends Exception {}
3:
4:          public static void main(String[] args) {
5:              try(Scanner s = new Scanner("rain"); String line = "";) {
```

```
6:              if (s.nextLine().equals("rain"))
7:                  throw new RainException();
8:          } finally {
9:              s.close();
10:      } } }
```

A. 0

B. 1

C. 2

D. 3

E. 4

F. 5

15. What is the result of the following code?

```
1:    public class VisitPark {
2:        enum AnimalsInPark {
3:            SQUIRREL, CHIPMUNK, SPARROW;
4:        }
5:        public static void main(String[] args) {
6:            AnimalsInPark[] animals = AnimalsInPark.values();
7:            System.out.println(animals[1]);
8:        } }
```

A. CHIPMUNK

B. SQUIRREL

C. The code compiles, but the output is indeterminate.

D. A compiler error occurs on line 2.

E. A compiler error occurs on line 6.

F. A compiler error occurs on line 7.

16. Which of the answer choices is printed out by the following code?

```
String d = Duration.ofDays(1).toString();
String p = Period.ofDays(1).toString();

boolean b1 = d == p;
boolean b2 = d.equals(p);
System.out.println(b1 + " " + b2);
```

A. false false

B. false true

   C.   true false

   D.   true true

   E.   The code does not compile.

   F.   A runtime exception is thrown.

17. Assuming that the directory /gorilla exists within the file system with the numerous files including signed-words.txt, what is the result of executing the following code? (Choose all that apply.)

```
Path path = Paths.get("/gorilla/signed-words.txt");

Files.find(path.getParent(),10.0,   // k1
    (Path p) -> p.toString().endsWith(".txt") && Files.isDirectory(p)) // k2
    .collect(Collectors.toList())
    .forEach(System.out::println);

Files.readAllLines(path) // k3
    .flatMap(p -> Stream.of(p.split(" "))) // k4
    .map(s -> s.toLowerCase()) // k5
    .forEach(System.out::println);
```

   A.   The code compiles but does not produce any output at runtime.

   B.   It does not compile because of line k1.

   C.   It does not compile because of line k2.

   D.   It does not compile because of line k3.

   E.   It does not compile because of line k4.

   F.   The code prints all of the .txt files in the directory tree.

   G.   The code prints all of the words in the signed-words.txt file, each on a different line.

18. Which of the following statements can fill in the blank to make the code compile successfully? (Choose all that apply.)

```
Set<? extends RuntimeException> set = _____
```

   A.   new HashSet<? extends RuntimeException>();

   B.   new HashSet<Exception>();

   C.   new TreeSet<RuntimeException>();

   D.   new TreeSet<NullPointerException>();

   E.   None of the above

19. Which of the following position a `ResultSet` cursor to a location immediately before the first row? (Choose all that apply.)

A. `rs.absolute(-1)`

B. `rs.absolute(0)`

C. `rs.absolute(1)`

D. `rs.beforeFirst()`

E. `rs.first()`

F. `rs.next()`

20. Assume that today is June 1, 2016. What is the result of the following?

```
Stream<LocalDate> s = Stream.of(LocalDate.now());
UnaryOperator<LocalDate> u = l -> l;
s.filter(l -> l != null).map(u).peek(System.out::println);
```

A. `2016-05-01`

B. B. `2016-06-01`

C. There is no output.

D. The output is something other than `2016-05-01` or `2016-06-01`.

E. The code does not compile.

F. An exception is thrown.

Answers to Assessment Test

1. H. The code compiles without issue, so C, D, E, and F are incorrect. The key to understanding this code is to notice that our thread pool size is only 2, but our CyclicBarrier limit is 3. Even though 12 tasks are all successfully submitted to the thread executor service by way of the stream forEach() method, the first two tasks will use up both available threads and wait indefinitely. Since a third await() is never executed, the barrier is never broken and the program hangs, making H the only correct answer. Nothing is ever outputted nor is any exception thrown, so A, B, and G are incorrect. See Chapter 7 for more information.

2. D. The code does not compile because a method is not allowed to be both abstract and final. If final were removed, the answer would be B. An abstract class may contain an abstract method. A static nested class may extend other classes. For more information, see Chapter 1.

3. D, E. The code does not compile due to a number of issues, so A and F are incorrect. First off, the readObject() method is not available to the InputStream class, and since the ObjectInputStream has been upcast to InputStream, the code will not compile due to line 18, so E is correct. Line 18 will also not compile because the return type of readObject() is of type Object and must be cast explicitly to Bird in order to be assigned to the Bird reference. Furthermore, constructors and methods on lines 16, 17, and 18 throw checked IOExceptions that must be caught, so D is also correct. Note that line 18 also throws ClassNotFoundException. Lines 3 and 5 compile without issue, so B and C are incorrect. It should be noted that even if the compilation problems were resolved, the code would still throw an exception at runtime since the Bird class includes a Tail reference as a member, and the Tail class does not implement Serializable. For more information, see Chapter 8.

4. E. This class is a proper use of generics. Box uses a generic type named T. On line 11, the generic type is String. On line 12 the generic type is Integer. Line 12 also uses the diamond operator. See Chapter 3 for more information.

5. F. The code compiles without issue, so D is incorrect. The code throws a ConcurrentModificationException at runtime on line c2, because mammals is a synchronized list and not a concurrent one. Therefore, it is not safe to be used inside an iterator, and F is the correct answer. Note that if line c2 were removed, the rest of the code would run without throwing an exception, outputting 8 4 5. See Chapter 7 for more information.

6. B, C, F. A is incorrect, since there are definitely some problems with the immutable objects implementation. B is correct, because all instance variables should be marked final and private for the class to be considered immutable. C is correct, because it prevents the methods from being overridden. D is incorrect, since there is no such thing as the Immutable interface defined in the Java API. E is also incorrect, because any passed lambda expression would have access to only the public methods of the class. F is correct, because the mutable object ducklings should not be exposed directly, since this allows the user to modify it. G is incorrect, because this has nothing to do with immutability. For more information, see Chapter 2.

7. A. The code compiles and runs without issue, so E and F are incorrect. For this question, it helps if you resolve each path to a simplified form component before answering it. The path1 variable simplifies to /bats/sleep.txt after the Path operations have been applied. The path2 variable using the current directory of /bats/day is assigned a path value of /bats/sleep.txt. Since the file Path objects represent the same path within the file system, they will return true for both equals() and isSameFile(), so A is the correct answer and B, C, and D are incorrect. For more information, see Chapter 9.

8. A, B, D. A is correct because name is public and therefore inherited by the Wolf class. B is correct because Wolf is-a Canine and Canine has-a Tail; therefore, since tail is public, it is inherited and Wolf has-a Tail. C is incorrect, because Wolf is not inherited from Tail. D is correct, because Wolf is-a Canine and Canine is-a Animal; therefore, Wolf is-a Animal. E is incorrect, because the relationship is reversed. F is incorrect, since Animal does not have a Tail attribute. For more information, see Chapter 2.

9. A, C. The first parameter is the ResultSet type. The second parameter is the ResultSet concurrency mode. Choices D, E, and F are incorrect because they represent the first parameter. Choice B is incorrect because it is not a constant in JDBC. Choices A and C are correct. For more information, see Chapter 10.

10. F. The code compiles due to autoboxing. The command line does not enable assertions, so D cannot happen. Line 6 executes and prints out 11, so the answer is F. For more information, see Chapter 6.

11. B, F. Calling get() on an empty Optional causes an exception to be thrown, making options B and F correct. Option C is incorrect because the infinite stream is made finite by the intermediate limit() operation. Options A and E are incorrect because the source streams are not infinite. Therefore, the call to max() sees only three elements and terminates. For more information, see Chapter 4.

12. D. Java will use Dolphins_fr.properties as the matching resource bundle on line 6 because it is an exact match on the language. Line 7 finds a matching key in this file. Line 8 does not find a match in that file, and therefore it has to look higher up in the hierarchy. For more information, see Chapter 5.

13. B, D. Option B is correct because this is the right way to read data from the Console. Option D is also correct. If there is no console available, a NullPointerException is thrown. The read method does not throw an IOException. For more information, see Chapter 8.

14. D. Line 5 is incorrect because String does not implement AutoCloseable. Not all objects can be declared in a try-with-resources try clause. Line 7 is incorrect because RainException is a checked exception and is not declared or handled. Line 9 is incorrect because s is declared in the try clause and is therefore out of scope for the finally block.

15. A. The code compiles. An enum may be an inner class. The values() method returns an array with the enum values in the order in which they were declared in the code. Since Java uses 0-based indexes, the answer is A. For more information, see Chapter 1.

16. A. d is the String P1D and p is the String PT24H. They are neither the same object nor the same value. Remember that Duration uses hours/minutes/seconds and Period uses years/months/days for measures. For more information, see Chapter 5.

17. B, C, E. Numerous lines would have to be corrected for the code to compile, so A, F, and G are incorrect. First off, the second parameter to Files.find() is the depth limit and must be an int, so line k1 would have to be changed to make the code compile, and B is correct. Next, the Files.find() method uses a BiPredictate<Path,BasicFileAttribute>, not a Predicate<Path>, for its lambda expression, so line k2 would also need to be changed to allow the code to compile, and C is also correct. Finally, Files.readAllLines() returns a List<String>, not a stream, so the following line, k4, which applies flatMap(), would also prevent the code from compiling, and E is correct. D is incorrect, since line k3 by itself does not cause any compilation issues. For more information, see Chapter 9.

18. C, D. Set defines an upper bound of type RuntimeException. This means that classes may specify RuntimeException or any subclass of RuntimeException as the type parameter. Choice A is incorrect because the wildcard cannot occur on the right side of the assignment. See Chapter 3 for more information.

19. B, D. On a scrollable ResultSet, the absolute() method positions the cursor. -1 means the last row. 1 means the first row. 0 means before the first row. Therefore, choice B is correct. There is also a method beforeFirst() that is equivalent, making choice D correct as well. For more information, see Chapter 10.

20. C. There is no terminal operation. Since the intermediate operations use lazy evaluation, they wait for a terminal operation to run. Since there is no terminal operation, peek() never runs. For more information, see Chapter 4.

Chapter

1

Advanced Class Design

THE OCP EXAM TOPICS COVERED IN THIS CHAPTER INCLUDE THE FOLLOWING:

✓ **Java Class Design**

- Implement inheritance including visibility modifiers and composition

- Implement polymorphism

- Override hashCode, equals, and toString methods from Object class

- Develop code that uses the static keyword on initialize blocks, variables, methods, and classes

✓ **Advanced Java Class Design**

- Develop code that uses abstract classes and methods

- Develop code that uses final keyword

- Create inner classes including static inner class, local class, nested class, and anonymous inner class

- Use enumerated types including methods, and constructors in an enum type

- Develop code that declares, implements, and/or extends interface and use the @Override annotation

Congratulations! If you are reading this, you've probably passed the Java Programmer I OCA (Oracle Certified Associate) exam, and you are now ready to start your journey through the Java Programmer II OCP (Oracle Certified Professional) exam. Or perhaps you came here from an older version of the certification and are now upgrading.

The OCP builds upon the OCA. You are expected to know the material on the OCA when taking the OCP. Some objectives on the OCP are the same as those on the OCA, such as those concerning access modifiers, overloading, overriding, abstract classes, static, and final. Most are implied. For example, the OCP objectives don't mention if statements and loops. Clearly, you still need to know these. We will also point out differences in Java 8 to help those of you coming in from an older version of Java.

If you didn't score well on the OCA exam, or if it has been a while since you took it, we recommend reviewing the book you used to study for it. The OCP questions are a lot tougher. You really need to know the fundamentals well. If you've misplaced your review materials, feel free to check out our OCA book, *OCA: Oracle Certified Associate Java SE 8 Programmer I Study Guide* (Sybex, 2014).

This chapter includes a brief review of overlapping topics and then moves on to new material. You'll see how to use instanceof, implement equals/hashCode/toString, create enumerations, and create nested classes.

Reviewing OCA Concepts

In this section, we review the OCA objectives that are explicitly listed as being on the OCP. Since this is review, we will ask you questions followed by a brief reminder of the key points. These questions are harder than the ones on the OCA because they require you to reflect on a lot of what you learned at the same time.

Access Modifiers

First up on the review are the access modifiers public, protected, and private and default access. Imagine the following method exists. For now, just remember the instance variables it tries to access:

```java
public static void main(String[] args) {
    BigCat cat = new BigCat();
    System.out.println(cat.name);
```

```
System.out.println(cat.hasFur);
System.out.println(cat.hasPaws);
System.out.println(cat.id);
```

Now, suppose each of these classes has this `main` method that instantiates a `BigCat` and tries to print out all four variables. Which variables will be allowed in each case?

```
package cat;
public class BigCat {
    public String name = "cat";
    protected boolean hasFur = true;
    boolean hasPaws = true;
    private int id;
}

package cat.species;
public class Lynx extends BigCat { }

package cat;
public class CatAdmirer { }

package mouse;
public class Mouse { }
```

Think about it for a minute—no really. Pause and try to answer. Ready now? While this code compiles for `BigCat`, it doesn't in all of the classes.

The line with `cat.name` compiles in all four classes because any code can access `public` members. The line with `cat.id` compiles only in `BigCat` because only code in the same class can access `private` members. The line with `cat.hasPaws` compiles only in `BigCat` and `CatAdmirer` because only code in the same package can access code with default access.

Finally, the line with `cat.hasFur` also compiles only in `BigCat` and `CatAdmirer`. `protected` allows subclasses and code in the same package to access members. Lynx is a tricky one. Since the code is being accessed via the variable rather than by inheritance, it does not benefit from `protected`. However, if the code in main was `Lynx cat = new Lynx();`, Lynx would be able to access `cat.hasFur` using `protected` access because it would be seen as a subclass.

Remember that there was a `default` keyword introduced in Java 8 for interfaces. That keyword is not an access modifier.

To review the rules for access modifiers at a glance, see Table 1.1.

TABLE 1.1 Access modifiers

Can access	If that member is private?	If that member has default (package private) access?	If that member is protected?	If that member is public?
Member in the same class	yes	yes	yes	yes
Member in another class in the same package	no	yes	yes	yes
Member in a superclass in a different package	no	no	yes	yes
Method/field in a class (that is not a superclass) in a different package	no	no	no	yes

Overloading and Overriding

Next we review the differences between overloading and overriding. Which method(s) in BobcatKitten overload or override the one in Bobcat?

```
1:    public class Bobcat {
2:        public void findDen() { }
3:    }
```

```
1:    public class BobcatKitten extends Bobcat {
2:        public void findDen() { }
3:        public void findDen(boolean b) { }
4:        public int findden() throws Exception { return 0; }
5:    }
```

The one on line 2 is an override because it has the same method signature. The one on line 3 is an overloaded method because it has the same method name but a different parameter list. The one on line 4 is not an override or overload because it has a different method name. Remember that Java is case sensitive.

To review, overloading and overriding happen only when the method name is the same. Further, *overriding* occurs only when the method signature is the same. The *method signature* is the method name and the parameter list. For *overloading*, the method parameters must vary by type and/or number.

When multiple overloaded methods are present, Java looks for the closest match first. It tries to find the following:

- Exact match by type
- Matching a superclass type
- Converting to a larger primitive type
- Converting to an autoboxed type
- Varargs

For overriding, the overridden method has a few rules:

- The access modifier must be the same or more accessible.
- The return type must be the same or a more restrictive type, also known as *covariant return types*.
- If any checked exceptions are thrown, only the same exceptions or subclasses of those exceptions are allowed to be thrown.

The methods must not be static. (If they are, the method is hidden and not overridden.)

Abstract Classes

Now we move on to reviewing abstract classes and methods. What are three ways that you can fill in the blank to make this code compile? Try to think of ways that use the clean() method rather than just putting a comment there.

```
abstract class Cat {

   --------------------
}
class Lion extends Cat {
   void clean() {}
}
```

Did you get three? One of them is a little tricky. The tricky one is that you could leave it blank. An abstract class is not required to have any methods in it, let alone any abstract ones. A second answer is the one that you probably thought of right away:

```
abstract void clean();
```

This one is the actual abstract method. It has the abstract keyword and a semicolon instead of a method body. A third answer is a default implementation:

```
void clean () {}
```

An abstract class may contain any number of methods including zero. The methods can be abstract or concrete. Abstract methods may not appear in a class that is not abstract. The first concrete subclass of an abstract class is required to implement all abstract methods that were not implemented by a superclass.

Notice that we said three ways. There are plenty of other ways. For example, you could have the clean() method throw a RuntimeException.

Static and Final

Next on the review list are the static and final modifiers. To which lines in the following code could you independently add static and/or final without introducing a compiler error?

```
1:    abstract class Cat {
2:        String name = "The Cat";
3:        void clean() { }
4:    }
5:    class Lion extends Cat {
6:        void clean() { }
7:    }
```

Both static and final can be added to line 2. This allows the variable to be accessed as Cat.name and prevents it from being changed. static cannot be added to line 3 or 6 independently because the subclass overrides it. It could be added to both, but then you wouldn't be inheriting the method. The final keyword cannot be added to line 3 because the subclass method would no longer be able to override it. final can be added to line 6 since there are no subclasses of Lion.

To review, final prevents a variable from changing or a method from being overridden. static makes a variable shared at the class level and uses the class name to refer to a method.

static and final are allowed to be added on the class level too. You will see static classes in the section on nested classes at the end of this chapter, so don't worry if you didn't pick up on those. Using final on a class means that it cannot be subclassed. As with methods, a class cannot be both abstract and final. In the Java core classes, String is final.

Imports

Oracle no longer lists packages and imports in the objectives for the OCP 8 exam. They do include visibility modifiers, which means that you still need to understand packages and imports. So let's review. How many different ways can you think of to write imports that will make this code compile?

```
public class ListHelper {
    public List <String> copyAndSortList(List <String> original) {
```

```
    List <String> list = new ArrayList <String>(original);
    sort(list);
    return list;
}
}
```

The key is to note that this question really has two parts. One thing to figure out is how to get sort(list) to compile. Since sort() is a static method on Collections, you definitely need a static import. Either of these will do it:

```
import static java.util.Collections.sort;
import static java.util.Collections.*;
```

The other part of the question is to note that List and ArrayList are both referenced. These are regular classes and need regular imports. One option is to use a wildcard:

```
import java.util.*;
```

The other option is to list them out:

```
import java.util.List;
import java.util.ArrayList;
```

There are other imports you can add, but they have redundancy or are unnecessary. For example, you could import java.lang.*. However, this package is always imported whether you specify it or not.

Using *instanceof*

Now we move on to the new topics. On the OCA, you learned about many operators including < and ==. Now it is time to learn another: instanceof.

In a instanceof B, the expression returns true if the reference to which a points is an instance of class B, a subclass of B (directly or indirectly), or a class that implements the B interface (directly or indirectly).

Let's see how this works. You have three classes with which to work:

```
class HeavyAnimal { }
class Hippo extends HeavyAnimal { }
class Elephant extends HeavyAnimal { }
```

You see that Hippo is a subclass of HeavyAnimal but not Elephant. Remember that the exam starts with line numbers other than 1 when showing a code snippet. This is to tell you that you can assume the correct code comes before what you see. You can assume any missing code is correct and all imports are present.

```
12:    HeavyAnimal hippo = new Hippo();
13:    boolean b1 = hippo instanceof Hippo;         // true
14:    boolean b2 = hippo instanceof HeavyAnimal;   // true
15:    boolean b3 = hippo instanceof Elephant;      // false
```

On line 13, you see that hippo is an instance of itself. We'd certainly hope so! Line 14 returns true because hippo is an instance of its superclass. Line 15 returns false because hippo is not an Elephant. The variable reference is HeavyAnimal, so there could be an Elephant in there. At runtime, Java knows that the variable is in fact pointing to a Hippo.

All Java classes inherit from Object, which means that x instanceof Object is usually true, except for one case where it is false. If the literal null or a variable reference pointing to null is used to check instanceof, the result is false. null is not an Object. For example:

```
26:    HeavyAnimal hippo = new Hippo();
27:    boolean b4 = hippo instanceof Object;     // true
28:    Hippo nullHippo = null;
29:    boolean b5 = nullHippo instanceof Object;  // false
```

Line 27 returns true because Hippo extends from Object indirectly as do all classes. Line 29 returns false because the nullHippo variable reference points to null and null is not a Hippo. This next one is interesting:

```
30:    Hippo anotherHippo = new Hippo();
31:    boolean b5 = anotherHippo instanceof Elephant; // DOES NOT COMPILE
```

Line 31 is a tricky one. The compiler knows that there is no possible way for a Hippo variable reference to be an Elephant, since Hippo doesn't extend Elephant directly or indirectly.

The compilation check only applies when instanceof is called on a class. When checking whether an object is an instanceof an interface, Java waits until runtime to do the check. The reason is that a subclass could implement that interface and the compiler wouldn't know it. There is no way for Hippo to be a subclass of Elephant.

For example, suppose that you have an interface Mother and Hippo does not implement it:

```
public interface Mother {}
class Hippo extends HeavyAnimal { }
```

This code compiles:

```
42:    HeavyAnimal hippo = new Hippo();
43:    boolean b6 = hippo instanceof Mother;
```

It so happens that Hippo does not implement Mother. The compiler allows the statement because there could later be a class such as this:

```
class MotherHippo extends Hippo implements Mother { }
```

The compiler knows an interface could be added, so the instanceof statement could be true for some subclasses, whereas there is no possible way to turn a Hippo into an Elephant.

The instanceof operator is commonly used to determine if an instance is a subclass of a particular object before applying an explicit cast. For example, consider a method that takes as input an Animal reference and performs an operation based on that animal's type:

```java
public void feedAnimal(Animal animal) {
    if(animal instanceof Cow) {
        ((Cow)animal).addHay();
    } else if(animal instanceof Bird) {
        ((Bird)animal).addSeed();
    } else if(animal instanceof Lion) {
        ((Lion)animal).addMeat();
    } else {
        throw new RuntimeException("Unsupported animal");
    } }
```

In this example, you needed to know if the animal was an instance of each subclass before applying the cast and calling the appropriate method. For example, a Bird or Lion probably will not have an addHay() method, a Cow or Lion probably will not have an addSeed() method, and so on. The else throwing an exception is common. It allows the code to fail when an unexpected Animal is passed in. This is a good thing. It tells the programmer to fix the code rather than quietly letting the new animal go hungry.

This is not a good way to write code. instanceof and the practice of casting with if statements is extremely rare outside of the exam. It is mostly used when writing a library that will be used by many others. On the exam, you need to understand how instanceof works though.

Understanding Virtual Method Invocation

You just saw a poor way of feeding some animals. A better way would be to make each Animal know how to feed itself. Granted this won't work in the real world, but there could be a sign in each animal habitat or the like.

```java
abstract class Animal {
    public abstract void feed(); }
}
class Cow extends Animal {
    public void feed() { addHay(); }
    private void addHay() { }
}
```

```
class Bird extends Animal {
   public void feed() { addSeed(); }
   private void addSeed() { }
}
class Lion extends Animal {
   public void feed() { addMeat(); }
   private void addMeat() { }
}
```

The Animal class is abstract, and it requires that any concrete Animal subclass have a feed() method. The three subclasses that we defined have a one-line feed() method that delegates to the class-specific method. A Bird still gets seed, a Cow still gets hay, and so forth. Now the method to feed the animals is really easy. We just call feed() and the proper subclass's version is run.

This approach has a huge advantage. The feedAnimal() method doesn't need to change when we add a new Animal subclass. We could have methods to feed the animals all over the code. Maybe the animals get fed at different times on different days. No matter. feed() still gets called to do the work.

```
public void feedAnimal(Animal animal) {
   animal.feed();
}
```

We've just relied on *virtual method invocation*. We actually saw virtual methods on the OCA. They are just regular non-static methods. Java looks for an overridden method rather than necessarily using the one in the class that the compiler says we have. The only thing new about virtual methods on the OCP is that Oracle now *calls* them virtual methods in the objectives. You can simply think of them as methods.

In the above example, we have an Animal instance, but Java didn't call feed on the Animal class. Instead Java looked at the actual type of animal at runtime and called feed on that.

Notice how this technique is called virtual *method* invocation. Instance variables don't work this way. In this example, the Animal class refers to name. It uses the one in the super-class and not the subclass.

```
abstract class Animal {
   String name = "???";
   public void printName() {
      System.out.println(name);
   }
}
class Lion extends Animal {
   String name = "Leo";
}
```

```
public class PlayWithAnimal {
   public static void main(String... args) {
      Animal animal = new Lion();
      animal.printName();
   }
}
```

This outputs ???. The name declared in Lion would only be used if name was referred to from Lion (or a subclass of Lion.) But no matter how you call printName(), it will use the Animal's name, not the Lion's name.

Aside from the formal sounding name, there isn't anything new here. Let's try one more example to make sure that the exam can't trick you. What does the following print?

```
abstract class Animal {
   public void careFor() {
      play();
   }
   public void play() {
      System.out.println("pet animal");
   } }
class Lion extends Animal {
   public void play() {
      System.out.println("toss in meat");
   } }
public class PlayWithAnimal {
   public static void main(String... args) {
      Animal animal = new Lion();
      animal.careFor();
   } }
```

The correct answer is toss in meat. The main method creates a new Lion and calls careFor. Since only the Animal superclass has a careFor method, it executes. That method calls play. Java looks for overridden methods, and it sees that Lion implements play. Even though the call is from the Animal class, Java still looks at subclasses, which is good because you don't want to pet a Lion!

Annotating Overridden Methods

You already know how to override a method. Java provides a way to indicate explicitly in the code that a method is being overridden. In Java, when you see code that begins with an @ symbol, it is an annotation. An *annotation* is extra information about the program, and it is a type of *metadata*. It can be used by the compiler or even at runtime.

The @Override annotation is used to express that you, the programmer, intend for this method to override one in a superclass or implement one from an interface. You don't traditionally think of implementing an interface as overriding, but it actually is an override. It so happens that the method being overridden is an abstract one.

The following example shows this annotation in use:

```
1:   class Bobcat {
2:     public void findDen() { }
3:   }
4:   class BobcatMother extends Bobcat {
5:     @Override
6:     public void findDen() { }
7:   }
```

Line 5 tells the compiler that the method on line 6 is intended to override another method. Java ignores whitespace, which means that lines 5 and 6 could be merged into one:

```
6:   @Override public void findDen(boolean b) { }
```

This is helpful because the compiler now has enough information to tell you when you've messed up. Imagine if you wrote

```
1:   class Bobcat {
2:     public void findDen() { }
3:   }
4:   class BobcatMother extends Bobcat {
5:     @Override
6:     public void findDen(boolean b) { } // DOES NOT COMPILE
7:   }
```

Line 5 still tells Java the method that line 6 is intended to override another method. However, the method on line 6 overloads the method rather than overriding it. Java recognizes that this is a broken promise and gives it a compiler error.

It is useful to have the compiler tell you that you are not actually overriding when you think that you are. The problem could be a typo. Or it could be that the superclass or interface changed without your knowledge. Either way, it is useful information to know so that you can fix the code. It is a great idea to get in the habit of using @Override in order to avoid accidentally overloading a method.

@Override is allowed only when referencing a method. Just as there is no such thing as overriding a field, the annotation cannot be used on a field either.

Much of the time, you will not see @Override used on the exam when a method is being overridden. The exam is testing whether you can recognize an overridden method. However, when you see @Override show up on the exam, you must check carefully that the method is doing one of three things:

- Implementing a method from an interface
- Overriding a superclass method of a class shown in the example
- Overriding a method declared in Object, such as hashCode, equals, or toString

To be fair, the third one is a special case of the second. It is less obvious. Since the methods aren't declared on the page in front of you, we mention it specifically. Pay attention to the signatures of these three methods in the next sections so that you know the method signatures well and can spot where they are overridden.

Coding *equals, hashCode,* and *toString*

All classes in Java inherit from java.lang.Object, either directly or indirectly, which means that all classes inherit any methods defined in Object. Three of these methods are common for subclasses to override with a custom implementation. First, we will look at toString(). Then we will talk about equals() and hashCode(). Finally, we will discuss how equals() and hashCode() relate.

toString

When studying for the OCA, we learned that Java automatically calls the toString() method if you try to print out an object. We also learned that some classes supply a human-readable implementation of toString() and others do not. When running the following example, we see one of each:

```
public static void main(String[] args) {
    System.out.println(new ArrayList());      // []
    System.out.println(new String[0]);        // [Ljava.lang.String;@65cc892e
}
```

ArrayList provided an implementation of toString() that listed the contents of the ArrayList, in this case, an empty ArrayList. (If you want to be technical about it, a superclass of ArrayList implemented toString() and ArrayList inherited that one instead of the one in Object, whereas the array used the default implementation from Object.) You don't need to know that for the exam, though.

Clearly, providing nice human-readable output is going to make things easier for developers working with your code. They can simply print out your object and understand what it represents. Luckily, it is easy to override toString() and provide your own implementation.

Let's start with a nice, simple example:

```
public class Hippo {
    private String name;
    private double weight;
```

```java
public Hippo(String name, double weight) {
    this.name = name;
    this.weight = weight;
}
@Override
public String toString() {
    return name;
}
public static void main(String[] args) {
    Hippo h1 = new Hippo("Harry", 3100);
    System.out.println(h1);      // Harry
} }
```

Now when we run this code, it prints Harry. Granted that we have only one Hippo, so it isn't hard to keep track of this! But when the zoo later gets a whole family of hippos, it will be easier to remember who is who.

When you implement the toString() method, you can provide as much or as little information as you would like. In this example, we use all of the instance variables in the object:

```java
public String toString() {
    return "Name: " + name + ", Weight: " + weight;
}
```

 Real World Scenario

The Easy Way to Write toString() Methods

Once you've written a toString() method, it starts to get boring to write more—especially if you want to include a lot of instance variables. Luckily, there is an open source library that takes care of it for you. Apache Commons Lang (http://commons.apache.org/proper/commons-lang/) provides some methods that you might wish were in core Java.

This is all you have to write to have Apache Commons return all of the instance variables in a String:

```java
public String toString() {
    return ToStringBuilder.reflectionToString(this);
}
```

Calling our Hippo test class with this toString() method outputs something like toString.Hippo@12da89a7[name=Harry,weight=3100.0]. You might be wondering what this reflection thing is that is mentioned in the method name. *Reflection* is a technique used in Java to look at information about the class at runtime. This lets the ToString-Builder class determine what are all of the instance variables and to construct a String with each.

When testing your code, there is a benefit to not having information in toString() that isn't useful to your caller (12da89a7). Apache Commons accounts for this as well. You can write

```
@Override public String toString() {
  return ToStringBuilder.reflectionToString(this,
    ToStringStyle.SHORT_PREFIX_STYLE);
}
```

This time our Hippo test class outputs Hippo[name=Harry,weight=3100.0]. There are a few other styles that support letting you choose to omit the class names or the instance variable names.

equals

Remember that Java uses == to compare primitives and for checking if two variables refer to the same object. Checking if two objects are equivalent uses the equals() method, or at least it does if the developer implementing the method overrides equals(). In this example, you can see that only one of the two classes provides a custom implementation of equals():

```
String s1 = new String("lion");
String s2 = new String("lion");
System.out.println(s1.equals(s2));              // true
StringBuilder sb1 = new StringBuilder("lion");
StringBuilder sb2 = new StringBuilder("lion");
System.out.println(sb1.equals(sb2));            // false
```

String does have an equals() method. It checks that the values are the same. StringBuilder uses the implementation of equals() provided by Object, which simply checks if the two objects being referred to are the same.

There is more to writing your own equals() method than there was to writing toString(). Suppose the zoo gives every lion a unique identification number. The following Lion class implements equals() to say that any two Lion objects with the same ID are the same Lion:

```
1:    public class Lion {
2:        private int idNumber;
```

```
3:      private int age;
4:      private String name;
5:      public Lion(int idNumber, int age, String name) {
6:          this.idNumber = idNumber;
7:          this.age = age;
8:          this.name = name;
9:      }
10:     @Override public boolean equals(Object obj) {
11:         if ( !(obj instanceof Lion)) return false;
12:         Lion otherLion = (Lion) obj;
13:         return this.idNumber == otherLion.idNumber;
14:     }
15: }
```

First, pay attention to the method signature on line 10. It takes an Object as the method parameter rather than a Lion. Line 11 checks whether a cast would be allowed. You get to use the new instanceof operator that you just learned! There is no way that a Lion is going to be equal to a String. The method needs to return false when this occurs. If you get to line 12, a cast is OK. Then line 13 checks whether the two objects have the same identification number.

The this. syntax is not required. Line 12 could have been return idNumber == otherLion.idNumber. Many programmers explicitly code this. to be explicit about the object being referenced.

The Contract for equals() Methods

Since equals() is such a key method, Java provides a number of rules in the contract for the method. The exam expects you to recognize correct and incorrect equals() methods, but it will not ask you to name which property is broken. That said, it is helpful to have seen it at least once.

The equals() method implements an equivalence relation on non-null object references:

- *It is reflexive*: For any non-null reference value x, x.equals(x) should return true.

- *It is symmetric*: For any non-null reference values x and y, x.equals(y) should return true if and only if y.equals(x) returns true.

- *It is transitive*: For any non-null reference values x, y, and z, if x.equals(y) returns true and y.equals(z) returns true, then x.equals(z) should return true.

- *It is consistent*: For any non-null reference values x and y, multiple invocations of x.equals(y) consistently return true or consistently return false, provided no information used in equals comparisons on the objects is modified.

- For any non-null reference value x, x.equals(null) should return false.

Much of this is common sense. The definition of equality doesn't change at random, and the same objects can't be equal "sometimes." The most interesting rule is the last one. It should be obvious that an object and `null` aren't equal. The key is that `equals()` needs to return `false` when this occurs rather than throw a `NullPointerException`.

For practice, can you see what is wrong with this equals() method?

```
public boolean equals(Lion obj) {
   if (obj == null) return false;
   return this.idNumber == obj.idNumber;
}
```

There is actually nothing wrong with this method. It is a perfectly good method. However, it does not override `equals()` from `Object`. It overloads that method, which is probably not what was intended.

 Real World Scenario

The Easy Way to Write `equals()` Methods

Like `toString()`, you can use Apache Commons Lang to do a lot of the work for you. If you want all of the instance variables to be checked, your `equals()` method can be one line:

```
public boolean equals(Object obj) {
   return EqualsBuilder.reflectionEquals(this, obj);
}
```

This is nice. However, for `equals()`, it is common to look at just one or two instance variables rather than all of them.

```
public boolean equals(Object obj) {
   if ( !(obj instanceof LionEqualsBuilder)) return false;
   Lion other = (Lion) obj;
   return new EqualsBuilder().appendSuper(super.equals(obj))
      .append(idNumber, other.idNumber)
      .append(name, other.name)
      .isEquals();
}
```

Not quite as elegant, right? You have to remember to handle the `null` and `instanceof` guard conditions first. It is still better than having to code the whole thing by hand, though. Comparing the `idNumber` is easy because you can call `==`. Comparing the name means checking that either both names are `null` or the names are the same. If either name is `null`, you need to return `false`. This logic is a bit messy if you write it out by hand.

hashCode

Whenever you override `equals()`, you are also expected to override `hashCode()`. The hash code is used when storing the object as a key in a map. You will see this in Chapter 3, "Generics and Collections."

A *hash code* is a number that puts instances of a class into a finite number of categories. Imagine that I gave you a deck of cards, and I told you that I was going to ask you for specific cards and I want to get the right card back quickly. You have as long as you want to prepare, but I'm in a big hurry when I start asking for cards. You might make 13 piles of cards: All of the aces in one pile, all the twos in another pile, and so forth. That way, when I ask for the five of hearts, you can just pull the right card out of the four cards in the pile with fives. It is certainly faster than going through the whole deck of 52 cards! You could even make 52 piles if you had enough space on the table.

The following is the code that goes with our little story. Cards are equal if they have the same rank and suit. They go in the same pile (hash code) if they have the same rank.

```java
public class Card {
    private String rank;
    private String suit;
    public Card(String r, String s) {
        if (r == null || s == null)
            throw new IllegalArgumentException();
        rank = r;
        suit = s;
    }
    public boolean equals(Object obj) {
        if ( !(obj instanceof Card)) return false;
        Card c = (Card) obj;
        return rank.equals(c.rank) && suit.equals(c.suit);
    }
    public int hashCode() {
        return rank.hashCode();
    }
}
```

In the constructor, you make sure that neither instance variable is null. This check allows equals() to be simpler because you don't have to worry about null there. The hashCode() method is quite simple. It asks the *rank* for its hash code and uses that.

That's all well and good. But what do you do if you have a primitive and need the hash code? The hash code is just a number. On the exam, you can just use a primitive number as is or divide to get a smaller int. Remember that all of the instance variables don't need to be used in a hashCode() method. It is common not to include boolean and char variables in the hash code.

The official JavaDoc contract for hashCode() is harder to read than it needs to be. The three points in the contract boil down to these:

- Within the same program, the result of hashCode() must not change. This means that you shouldn't include variables that change in figuring out the hash code. In our hippo example, including the name is fine. Including the weight is not because hippos change weight regularly.

- If equals() returns true when called with two objects, calling hashCode() on each of those objects must return the same result. This means hashCode() can use a subset of the variables that equals() uses. You saw this in the card example. We used only one of the variables to determine the hash code.

- If equals() returns false when called with two objects, calling hashCode() on each of those objects does not have to return a different result. This means hashCode() results do not need to be unique when called on unequal objects.

Going back to our Lion, which has three instance variables and only used idNumber in the equals() method, which of these do you think are legal hashCode() methods?

```
16:    public int hashCode() { return idNumber; }
17:    public int hashCode() { return 6; }
18:    public long hashcode() { return idNumber; }
19:    public int hashCode() { return idNumber * 7 + age; }
```

Line 16 is what you would expect the hashCode() method to be. Line 17 is also legal. It isn't particularly efficient. It is like putting the deck of cards in one giant pile. But it is legal. Line 18 is not an override of hashCode(). It uses a lowercase c, which makes it a different method. If it were an override, it wouldn't compile because the return type is wrong. Line 19 is not legal because it uses more variables than equals().

 Real World Scenario

The Easy Way to Write hashCode() Methods

You probably thought that this was going to be about the Apache Commons Lang class for hash code. There is one, but it isn't the easiest way to write hash code.

It is easier to code your own. Just pick the key fields that identify your object (and don't change during the program) and combine them:

```
public int hashCode() {
    return keyField + 7 * otherKeyField.hashCode();
}
```

It is common to multiply by a prime number when combining multiple fields in the hash code. This makes the hash code more unique, which helps when distributing objects into buckets.

Working with *Enums*

In programming, it is common to have a type that can only have a finite set of values. An *enumeration* is like a fixed set of constants. In Java, an *enum* is a class that represents an enumeration. It is much better than a bunch of constants because it provides type-safe checking. With numeric constants, you can pass an invalid value and not find out until runtime. With enums, it is impossible to create an invalid enum type without introducing a compiler error.

Enumerations show up whenever you have a set of items whose types are known at compile time. Common examples are the days of the week, months of the year, the planets in the solar system, or the cards in a deck. Well, maybe not the planets in a solar system, given that Pluto had its planetary status revoked.

To create an enum, use the enum keyword instead of the class keyword. Then list all of the valid types for that enum.

```
public enum Season {
    WINTER, SPRING, SUMMER, FALL
}
```

Since an enum is like a set of constants, use the uppercase letter convention that you used for constants.

Behind the scenes, an enum is a type of class that mainly contains static members. It also includes some helper methods like name() that you will see shortly. Using an enum is easy:

```
Season s = Season.SUMMER;
System.out.println(Season.SUMMER);           // SUMMER
System.out.println(s == Season.SUMMER);      // true
```

As you can see, enums print the name of the enum when toString() is called. They are also comparable using == because they are like static final constants.

An enum provides a method to get an array of all of the values. You can use this like any normal array, including in a loop:

```
for(Season season: Season.values()) {
    System.out.println(season.name() + " " + season.ordinal());
}
```

The output shows that each enum value has a corresponding int value in the order in which they are declared. The int value will remain the same during your program, but the program is easier to read if you stick to the human-readable enum value.

```
WINTER 0
SPRING 1
SUMMER 2
FALL 3
```

You can't compare an int and enum value directly anyway. Remember that an enum is a type and *not* an int.

```
if ( Season.SUMMER == 2) {} // DOES NOT COMPILE
```

You can also create an enum from a String. This is helpful when working with older code. The String passed in must match exactly, though.

```
Season s1 = Season.valueOf("SUMMER");     // SUMMER
Season s2 = Season.valueOf("summer");     // exception
```

The first statement works and assigns the proper enum value to s1. The second statement encounters a problem. There is no enum value with the lowercase name "summer." Java throws up its hands in defeat and throws an IllegalArgumentException.

```
Exception in thread "main" java.lang.IllegalArgumentException: No enum constant
enums.Season.summer
```

Another thing that you can't do is extend an enum.

```
public enum ExtendedSeason extends Season { } // DOES NOT COMPILE
```

The values in an enum are all that are allowed. You cannot add more at runtime by extending the enum.

Now that we've covered the basics, we look at using enums in switch statements and how to add extra functionality to enums.

Using *Enums* in *Switch* Statements

Enums may be used in switch statements. Pay attention to the case value in this code:

```
Season summer = Season.SUMMER;
switch (summer) {
```

```
    case WINTER:
       System.out.println("Get out the sled!");
       break;
    case SUMMER:
       System.out.println("Time for the pool!");
       break;
    default:
       System.out.println("Is it summer yet?");
}
```

The code prints "Time for the pool!" since it matches SUMMER. Notice that we just typed the value of the enum rather than writing Season.WINTER. The reason is that Java already knows that the only possible matches can be enum values. Java treats the enum type as implied. In fact, if you were to type case Season.WINTER, it would not compile. Keep in mind that an enum type is not an int. The following code does not compile:

```
switch (summer) {
    case 0:       // DOES NOT COMPILE
       System.out.println("Get out the sled!");
       break;
}
```

You can't compare an int with an enum. Pay special attention when working with enums that they are used only as enums.

Adding Constructors, Fields, and Methods

Enums can have more in them than just values. It is common to give state to each one. Our zoo wants to keep track of traffic patterns for which seasons get the most visitors.

```
1:    public enum Season {
2:       WINTER("Low"), SPRING("Medium"), SUMMER("High"), FALL("Medium");
3:       private String expectedVisitors;
4:       private Season(String expectedVisitors) {
5:          this.expectedVisitors = expectedVisitors;
6:       }
7:       public void printExpectedVisitors() {
8:          System.out.println(expectedVisitors);
9:       } ]
```

There are a few things to notice here. On line 2, we have a semicolon. This is required if there is anything in the enum besides the values.

Lines 3–9 are regular Java code. We have an instance variable, a constructor, and a method. The constructor is `private` because it can only be called from within the enum. The code will not compile with a `public` constructor.

Calling this new method is easy:

```
Season.SUMMER.printExpectedVisitors();
```

Notice how we don't appear to call the constructor. We just say that we want the enum value. The first time that we ask for any of the enum values, Java constructs all of the enum values. After that, Java just returns the already-constructed enum values. Given that explanation, you can see why this code calls the constructor only once:

```
public enum OnlyOne {
    ONCE(true);
    private OnlyOne(boolean b) {
        System.out.println("constructing");
    }
    public static void main(String[] args) {
        OnlyOne firstCall = OnlyOne.ONCE;     // prints constructing
        OnlyOne secondCall = OnlyOne.ONCE;    // doesn't print anything
    } }
```

This technique of a constructor and state allows you to combine logic with the benefit of a list of values. Sometimes, you want to do more. For example, our zoo has different seasonal hours. It is cold and gets dark early in the winter. We could keep track of the hours through instance variables, or we can let each enum value manage hours itself:

```
public enum Season {
    WINTER {
        public void printHours() { System.out.println("9am-3pm"); }
    }, SPRING {
        public void printHours() { System.out.println("9am-5pm"); }
    }, SUMMER {
        public void printHours() { System.out.println("9am-7pm"); }
    }, FALL {
        public void printHours() { System.out.println("9am-5pm"); }
    };
    public abstract void printHours();
}
```

What's going on here? It looks like we created an abstract class and a bunch of tiny sub-classes. In a way we did. The enum itself has an abstract method. This means that each and every enum value is required to implement this method. If we forget one, we get a compiler error.

If we don't want each and every enum value to have a method, we can create a default implementation and override it only for the special cases:

```java
public enum Season3 {
    WINTER {
        public void printHours() { System.out.println("short hours"); }
    }, SUMMER {
        public void printHours() { System.out.println("long hours"); }
    }, SPRING, FALL;
    public void printHours() { System.out.println("default hours"); }
}
```

This one looks better. We only code the special cases and let the others use the enum-provided implementation. Notice how we still have the semicolon after FALL. This is needed when we have anything other than just the values. In this case, we have a default method implementation.

Just because an enum can have lots of methods, doesn't mean that it should. Try to keep your enums simple. If your enum is more than a page or two, it is way too long. Most enums are just a handful of lines. The main reason they get long is that when you start with a one- or two-line method and then declare it for each of your dozen enum types, it grows long. When they get too long or too complex, it makes the enum hard to read.

Creating Nested Classes

A *nested class* is a class that is defined within another class. A nested class that is not static is called an *inner class*. There are four of types of nested classes:

- A member inner class is a class defined at the same level as instance variables. It is not static. Often, this is just referred to as an inner class without explicitly saying the type.

- A local inner class is defined within a method.

- An anonymous inner class is a special case of a local inner class that does not have a name.

- A static nested class is a static class that is defined at the same level as static variables.

There are a few benefits of using inner classes. They can encapsulate helper classes by restricting them to the containing class. They can make it easy to create a class that will be used in only one place. They can make the code easier to read. They can also make the code harder to read when used improperly. Unfortunately, the exam tests these edge cases where programmers wouldn't actually use a nested class. This section covers all four types of nested classes.

Member Inner Classes

A *member inner class* is defined at the member level of a class (the same level as the methods, instance variables, and constructors). Member inner classes have the following properties:

- Can be declared public, private, or protected or use default access
- Can extend any class and implement interfaces
- Can be abstract or final
- Cannot declare static fields or methods
- Can access members of the outer class including private members

The last property is actually pretty cool. It means that the inner class can access the outer class without doing anything special. Ready for a complicated way to print "Hi" three times?

```
1:    public class Outer {
2:        private String greeting = "Hi";
3:
4:        protected class Inner {
5:            public int repeat = 3;
6:            public void go() {
7:            for (int i = 0; i < repeat; i++)
8:                System.out.println(greeting);
9:        }
10:    }
11:
12:    public void callInner() {
13:        Inner inner = new Inner();
14:        inner.go();
15:    }
16:    public static void main(String[] args) {
17:        Outer outer = new Outer();
18:        outer.callInner();
19: } }
```

A member inner class declaration looks just like a stand-alone class declaration except that it happens to be located inside another class—oh, and that it can use the instance variables declared in the outer class. Line 8 shows that the inner class just refers to greeting as if it were available. This works because it is in fact available. Even though the variable is private, it is within that same class.

Since a member inner class is not static, it has to be used with an instance of the outer class. Line 13 shows that an instance of the outer class can instantiate Inner normally. This works because callInner() is an instance method on Outer. Both Inner and callInner() are members of Outer. Since they are peers, they just write the name.

There is another way to instantiate Inner that looks odd at first. OK, well maybe not just at first. This syntax isn't used often enough to get used to it:

```
20:   public static void main(String[] args) {
21:       Outer outer = new Outer();
22:       Inner inner = outer.new Inner();   // create the inner class
23:       inner.go();
24: }
```

Let's take a closer look at line 22. We need an instance of Outer in order to create Inner. We can't just call new Inner() because Java won't know with which instance of Outer it is associated. Java solves this by calling new as if it were a method on the *outer* variable.

.class Files for Inner Classes

Compiling the Outer.java class with which we have been working creates two class files. Outer.class you should be expecting. For the inner class, the compiler creates Outer$Inner.class. You don't need to know this syntax for the exam. We mention it so that you aren't surprised to see files with $ appearing in your directories. You do need to understand that multiple class files are created.

Inner classes can have the same variable names as outer classes. There is a special way of calling this to say which class you want to access. You also aren't limited to just one inner class. Please never do this in code you write. Here is how to nest multiple classes and access a variable with the same name in each:

```
1:    public class A {
2:        private int x = 10;
3:        class B {
4:          private int x = 20;
5:          class C {
6:            private int x = 30;
7:            public void allTheX() {
8:                System.out.println(x);           // 30
9:                System.out.println(this.x);      // 30
10:               System.out.println(B.this.x);    // 20
11:               System.out.println(A.this.x);    // 10
```

```
12:      } } }
13:      public static void main(String[] args) {
14:          A a = new A();
15:          A.B b = a.new B();
16:          A.B.C c = b.new C();
17:          c.allTheX();
18:   }}
```

Yes, this code makes us cringe too. It has two nested classes. Line 14 instantiates the outermost one. Line 15 uses the awkward syntax to instantiate a B. Notice the type is A.B. We could have written B as the type because that is available at the member level of B. Java knows where to look for it. On line 16, we instantiate a C. This time, the A.B.C type is necessary to specify. C is too deep for Java to know where to look. Then line 17 calls a method on c.

Lines 8 and 9 are the type of code that we are used to seeing. They refer to the instance variable on the current class—the one declared on line 6 to be precise. Line 10 uses this in a special way. We still want an instance variable. But this time we want the one on the B class, which is the variable on line 4. Line 11 does the same thing for class A, getting the variable from line 2.

Private Interfaces

This following code looks weird but is legal:

```
public class CaseOfThePrivateInterface {
    private interface Secret {
      public void shh();
    }
    class DontTell implements Secret {
      public void shh() { }
    } }
```

The rule that all methods in an interface are public still applies. A class that implements the interface must define that method as public.

The interface itself does not have to be public, though. Just like any inner class, an inner interface can be private. This means that the interface can only be referred to within the current outer class.

Local Inner Classes

A *local inner class* is a nested class defined within a method. Like local variables, a local inner class declaration does not exist until the method is invoked, and it goes out of scope when the method returns. This means that you can create instances only from within the method. Those instances can still be returned from the method. This is just how local variables work. Local inner classes have the following properties:

- They do not have an access specifier.
- They cannot be declared static and cannot declare static fields or methods.
- They have access to all fields and methods of the enclosing class.
- They do not have access to local variables of a method unless those variables are final or effectively final. More on this shortly.

Ready for an example? Here's a complicated way to multiply two numbers:

```
1:    public class Outer {
2:        private int length = 5;
3:        public void calculate() {
4:            final int width = 20;
5:            class Inner {
6:                public void multiply() {
7:                    System.out.println(length * width);
8:                }
9:            }
10:           Inner inner = new Inner();
11:           inner.multiply();
12:       }
13:       public static void main(String[] args) {
14:           Outer outer = new Outer();
15:           outer.calculate();
16:       }
17: }
```

Lines 5 through 9 are the local inner class. That class's scope ends on line 12 where the method ends. Line 7 refers to an instance variable and a final local variable, so both variable references are allowed from within the local inner class.

Earlier, we made the statement that local variable references are allowed if they are final or effectively final. Let's talk about that now. The compiler is generating a class file from your inner class. A separate class has no way to refer to local variables. If the local variable is final, Java can handle it by passing it to the constructor of the inner class or by storing it in the class file. If it weren't effectively final, these tricks wouldn't work because the value could change after the copy was made. Up until Java 7, the programmer actually had to type the final keyword. In Java 8, the "effectively final" concept was introduced. If the code could still compile with the keyword final inserted before the local variable, the variable is effectively final.

NOTE   Remember that the "effectively final" concept was introduced in Java 8. If you are looking at older mock exam questions online, some of the answers about local variables and inner classes might be different.

Which of the variables do you think are effectively final in this code?

```
34:    public void isItFinal() {
35:        int one = 20;
36:        int two = one;
37:        two++;
38:        int three;
39:        if ( one == 4) three = 3;
40:        else three = 4;
41:        int four = 4;
42:        class Inner { }
43:        four = 5;
44: }
```

one is effectively final. It is only set in the line in which it is declared. two is not effectively final. The value is changed on line 37 after it is declared. three is effectively final because it is assigned only once. This assignment may happen in either branch of the if statement, but it can happen in only one of them. four is not effectively final. Even though the assignment happens after the inner class, it is not allowed.

Anonymous Inner Classes

An *anonymous inner class* is a local inner class that does not have a name. It is declared and instantiated all in one statement using the new keyword. Anonymous inner classes are required to extend an existing class or implement an existing interface. They are useful when you have a short implementation that will not be used anywhere else. Here's an example:

```
1:    public class AnonInner {
2:        abstract class SaleTodayOnly {
3:            abstract int dollarsOff();
4:        }
5:        public int admission(int basePrice) {
6:            SaleTodayOnly sale = new SaleTodayOnly() {
7:                int dollarsOff() { return 3; }
8:            };
9:            return basePrice - sale.dollarsOff();
10: } }
```

Lines 2 through 4 define an abstract class. Lines 6 through 8 define the inner class. Notice how this inner class does not have a name. The code says to instantiate a new SaleTodayOnly object. But wait. SaleTodayOnly is abstract. This is OK because we provide the class body right there—anonymously.

Pay special attention to the semicolon on line 8. We are declaring a local variable on these lines. Local variable declarations are required to end with semicolons, just like other Java statements—even if they are long and happen to contain an anonymous inner class.

Now we convert this same example to implement an `interface` instead of extending an abstract class:

```
1:    public class AnonInner {
2:       interface SaleTodayOnly {
3:          int dollarsOff();
4:       }
5:       public int admission(int basePrice) {
6:          SaleTodayOnly sale = new SaleTodayOnly() {
7:             public int dollarsOff() { return 3; }
8:          };
9:          return basePrice - sale.dollarsOff();
10:   } }
```

The most interesting thing here is how little has changed. Lines 2 through 4 declare an `interface` instead of an abstract class. Line 7 is `public` instead of using default access since interfaces require `public` methods. And that is it. The anonymous inner class is the same whether you implement an `interface` or extend a class! Java figures out which one you want automatically.

But what if we want to implement both an `interface` and extend a class? You can't with an anonymous inner class, unless the class to extend is `java.lang.Object`. `Object` is a special class, so it doesn't count in the rule. Remember that an anonymous inner class is just an unnamed local inner class. You can write a local inner class and give it a name if you have this problem. Then you can extend a class and implement as many `interfaces` as you like. If your code is this complex, a local inner class probably isn't the most readable option anyway.

There is one more thing that you can do with anonymous inner classes. You can define them right where they are needed, even if that is an argument to another method:

```
1:    public class AnonInner {
2:       interface SaleTodayOnly {
3:          int dollarsOff();
4:       }
5:       public int pay() {
6:          return admission(5, new SaleTodayOnly() {
7:             public int dollarsOff() { return 3;      }
8:          });
9:       }
10:      public int admission(int basePrice, SaleTodayOnly sale) {
```

```
11:            return basePrice - sale.dollarsOff();
12:    }}
```

Lines 6 through 8 are the anonymous inner class. We don't even store it in a local variable. Instead, we pass it directly to the method that needs it. Reading this style of code does take some getting used to. But it is a concise way to create a class that you will use only once.

Before you get too attached to anonymous inner classes, know that you'll see a shorter way of coding them in Chapter 4, "Functional Programming."

 Real World Scenario

Inner Classes as Event Handlers

Writing graphical user interface code isn't on the exam. Nonetheless, it is a very common use of inner classes, so we'll give you a taste of it here:

```
JButton button = new JButton("red");
button.addActionListener(new ActionListener() {

    public void actionPerformed(ActionEvent e) {
        // handle the button click
    }
});
```

This technique gives the event handler access to the instance variables in the class with which it goes. It works well for simple event handling.

You should be aware that inner classes go against some fundamental concepts, such as reuse of classes and high cohesion (discussed in the next chapter). Therefore, make sure that inner classes make sense before you use them in your code.

Static Nested Classes

The final type of nested class is not an inner class. A *static nested class* is a static class defined at the member level. It can be instantiated without an object of the enclosing class, so it can't access the instance variables without an explicit object of the enclosing class. For example, new OuterClass().var allows access to the instance variable var.

In other words, it is like a regular class except for the following:

- The nesting creates a namespace because the enclosing class name must be used to refer to it.

- It can be made `private` or use one of the other access modifiers to encapsulate it.

- The enclosing class can refer to the fields and methods of the `static` nested class.

```
1:    public class Enclosing {
2:       static class Nested {
3:          private int price = 6;
4:       }
5:       public static void main(String[] args) {
6:          Nested nested = new Nested();
7:          System.out.println(nested.price);
8:    } }
```

Line 6 instantiates the nested class. Since the class is `static`, you do not need an instance of Enclosing in order to use it. You are allowed to access `private` instance variables, which is shown on line 7.

Importing a `static` Nested Class

Importing a `static` nested class is interesting. You can import it using a regular import:

```
package bird;
public class Toucan {
    public static class Beak {}
}
package watcher;
import bird.Toucan.Beak;    // regular import ok
public class BirdWatcher {
    Beak beak;
}
```

And since it is `static`, alternatively you can use a `static` import:

```
import static bird.Toucan.Beak;
```

Either one will compile. Surprising, isn't it? Java treats the `static` nested class as if it were a namespace.

To review the four types of nested classes, make sure that you know the information in Table 1.2.

TABLE 1.2   Types of nested classes

	Member inner class	Local inner class	Anonymous inner class	static nested class
Access modifiers allowed	public, protected, private, or default access	None. Already local to method.	None. Already local to statement.	public, protected, private, or default access
Can extend any class and any number of interfaces	Yes	Yes	No—must have exactly one superclass or one interface	Yes
Can be abstract	Yes	Yes	N/A—because no class definition	Yes
Can be final	Yes	Yes	N/A—because no class definition	Yes
Can access instance members of enclosing class	Yes	Yes	Yes	No (not directly; requires an instance of the enclosing class)
Can access local variables of enclosing class	No	Yes—if final or effectively final	Yes—if final or effectively final	No
Can declare static methods	No	No	No	Yes

Summary

The instanceof keyword compares an object to a class or interface type. It also looks at subclasses and subinterfaces. x instanceof Object returns true unless x is null. If the compiler can determine that there is no way for instanceof to return true, it will generate a compiler error. Virtual method invocation means that Java will look at subclasses when finding the right method to call. This is true, even from within a method in the superclass.

The methods toString(), equals(), and hashCode() are implemented in Objects that classes can override to change their behavior. toString() is used to provide a human-readable representation of the object. equals() is used to specify which instance variables should be considered for equality. equals() is required to return false when the object passed in is null or is of the wrong type. hashCode() is used to provide a grouping in some collections. hashCode() is required to return the same number when called with objects that are equals().

The enum keyword is short for enumerated values or a list of values. Enums can be used in switch statements. They are not int values and cannot be compared to int values. In a switch, the enum value is placed in the case. Enums are allowed to have instance variables, constructors, and methods. Enums can also have value-specific methods. The enum itself declares that method as well. It can be abstract, in which case all enum values must provide an implementation. Alternatively, it can be concrete, in which case enum values can choose whether they want to override the default implementation.

There are four types of nested classes. Member inner classes require an instance of the outer class to use. They can access private members of that outer class. Local inner classes are classes defined within a method. They can also access private members of the outer class. Local inner classes can also access final or effectively final local variables. Anonymous inner classes are a special type of local inner class that does not have a name. Anonymous inner classes are required to extend exactly one class by name or implement exactly one interface. Static nested classes can exist without an instance of the outer class.

This chapter also contained a review of access modifiers, overloading, overriding, abstract classes, static, final, and imports. It also introduced the optional @Override annotation for overridden methods or methods implemented from an interface.

Exam Essentials

Be able to identify the output of code using instanceof.   instanceof checks if the left operand is the same class or interface (or a subclass) as the right operand. If the left operand is null, the result is false. If the two operands are not in the same class hierarchy, the code will not compile.

Recognize correct and incorrect implementations of equals(), hashCode(), and toString().   public boolean equals(Object obj) returns false when called with null or a class of the wrong type. public int hashCode() returns a number calculated with all or some of the instance variables used in equals(). public String toString() returns any String.

Be able to create enum classes.   enums have a list of values. If that is all that is in the enum, the semicolon after the values is optional. Enums can have instance variables, constructors, and methods. The constructors are required to be private or package private. Methods are allowed to be on the enum top level or in the individual enum values. If the enum declares an abstract method, each enum value must implement it.

Identify and use nested classes.   A member inner class is instantiated with code such as `outer.new Inner();`. Local inner classes are scoped to the end of the current block of code and not allowed to have `static` members. Anonymous inner classes are limited to extending a class or implementing one `interface`. A semicolon must end the statement creating an anonymous inner class. Static nested classes cannot access the enclosing class instance variables.

Know how to use imports and static imports.   Classes can be imported by class name or wildcard. Wildcards do not look at subdirectories. In the event of a conflict, class name imports take precedence. Static imports import static members. They are written as `import static`, not static import. Make sure that they are importing static methods or variables rather than class names.

Understand the rules for method overriding and overloading.   The Java compiler allows methods to be overridden in subclasses if certain rules are followed: a method must have the same signature, be at least as accessible as the parent method, must not declare any new or broader exceptions, and must use covariant return types. Methods are overloaded if they have the same method name but a different argument list. An overridden method may use the optional `@Override` annotation.

Review Questions

1. What is the result of the following code?

```
1:    public class Employee {
2:        public int employeeId;
3:        public String firstName, lastName;
4:        public int yearStarted;
5:        @Override public int hashCode() {
6:            return employeeId;
7:        }
8:        public boolean equals(Employee e) {
9:            return this.employeeId == e.employeeId;
10:       }
11:       public static void main(String[] args) {
12:           Employee one = new Employee();
13:           one.employeeId = 101;
14:           Employee two = new Employee();
15:           two.employeeId = 101;
16:           if (one.equals(two)) System.out.println("Success");
17:           else System.out.println("Failure");
18:    } }
```

   A. Success

   B. Failure

   C. The hashCode() method fails to compile.

   D. The equals() method fails to compile.

   E. Another line of code fails to compile.

   F. A runtime exception is thrown.

2. What is the result of compiling the following class?

```
public class Book {
   private int ISBN;
   private String title, author;
   private int pageCount;
   public int hashCode() {
      return ISBN;
   }
   @Override public boolean equals(Object obj) {
     if ( !(obj instanceof Book)) {
```

```
        return false;
    }
    Book other = (Book) obj;
     return this.ISBN == other.ISBN;
    }
// imagine getters and setters are here
}
```

A. The code compiles.

B. The code does not compile because hashCode() is incorrect.

C. The code does not compile because equals() does not override the parent method correctly.

D. The code does not compile because equals() tries to refer to a private field.

E. The code does not compile because the ClassCastException is not handled or declared.

F. The code does not compile for another reason.

3. What is the result of the following code?

```
String s1 = "Canada";
String s2 = new String(s1);
if(s1 == s2) System.out.println("s1 == s2");
if(s1.equals(s2)) System.out.println("s1.equals(s2)");
```

A. There is no output.

B. s1 == s2

C. s1.equals(s2)

D. Both B and C.

E. The code does not compile.

F. The code throws a runtime exception.

4. What is true about the following code? You may assume city and mascot are never null.

```
public class BaseballTeam {
    private String city, mascot;
    private int numberOfPlayers;
    public boolean equals(Object obj) {
        if ( !(obj instanceof BaseballTeam))
          return false;
        BaseballTeam other = (BaseballTeam) obj;
        return (city.equals(other.city) && mascot.equals(other.mascot));
    }
```

```
    public int hashCode() {
        return numberOfPlayers;
    }
// imagine getters and setters are here
}
```

    A. The class does not compile.

    B. The class compiles but has an improper equals() method.

    C. The class compiles but has an improper hashCode() method.

    D. The class compiles and has proper equals() and hashCode() methods.

5. Which of the following statements are true, assuming a and b are String objects? (Choose all that apply.)

    A. If a.equals(b) is true, a.hashCode() == b.hashCode() is always true.

    B. If a.equals(b) is true, a.hashCode() == b.hashCode() is sometimes but not always true.

    C. If a.equals(b) is false, a.hashCode() == b.hashCode() can never be true.

    D. If a.equals(b) is false, a.hashCode() == b.hashCode() can sometimes be true.

6. What is the result of the following code?

```
public class FlavorsEnum {
    enum Flavors {
        VANILLA, CHOCOLATE, STRAWBERRY
    }
    public static void main(String[] args) {
        System.out.println(Flavors.CHOCOLATE.ordinal());
    }
}
```

    A. 0

    B. 1

    C. 9

    D. CHOCOLATE

    E. The code does not compile due to a missing semicolon.

    F. The code does not compile for a different reason.

7. What is the result of the following code? (Choose all that apply.)

```
public class IceCream {
    enum Flavors {
        VANILLA, CHOCOLATE, STRAWBERRY
    }
    public static void main(String[] args) {
```

```
Flavors f = Flavors.STRAWBERRY;
switch (f) {
    case 0: System.out.println("vanilla");
    case 1: System.out.println("chocolate");
    case 2: System.out.println("strawberry");
        break;
    default: System.out.println("missing flavor");
} } }
```

A. vanilla

B. chocolate

C. strawberry

D. missing flavor

E. The code does not compile.

F. An exception is thrown.

8. What is the result of the following code?

```
1:     public class Outer {
2:         private int x = 5;
3:         protected class Inner {
4:             public static int x = 10;
5:             public void go() { System.out.println(x); }
6:         }
7:         public static void main(String[] args) {
8:             Outer out = new Outer();
9:             Outer.Inner in = out.new Inner();
10:            in.go();
11:  } }
```

A. The output is 5.

B. The output is 10.

C. Line 4 generates a compiler error.

D. Line 8 generates a compiler error.

E. Line 9 generates a compiler error.

F. An exception is thrown.

9. What is the result of the following code?

```
1:     public class Outer {
2:     private int x = 24;
3:     public int getX() {
4:         String message = "x is ";
```

```
5:          class Inner {
6:              private int x = Outer.this.x;
7:              public void printX() {
8:                  System.out.println(message + x);
9:              }
10:         }
11:         Inner in = new Inner();
12:         in.printX();
13:         return x;
14:     }
15:     public static void main(String[] args) {
16:         new Outer().getX();
17:     } }
```

A.   x is 0.

B.   x is 24.

C.   Line 6 generates a compiler error.

D.   Line 8 generates a compiler error.

E.   Line 11 generates a compiler error.

F.   An exception is thrown.

10. The following code appears in a file named Book.java. What is the result of compiling the source file?

```
1:    public class Book {
2:        private int pageNumber;
3:        private class BookReader {
4:            public int getPage() {
5:                return pageNumber;
6:    } } }
```

A.   The code compiles successfully, and one bytecode file is generated: Book.class.

B.   The code compiles successfully, and two bytecode files are generated: Book.class and BookReader.class.

C.   The code compiles successfully, and two bytecode files are generated: Book.class and Book$BookReader.class.

D.   A compiler error occurs on line 3.

E.   A compiler error occurs on line 5.

11. Which of the following statements can be inserted to make FootballGame compile?

```
package my.sports;
public class Football {
```

```
    public static final int TEAM_SIZE = 11;
}
package my.apps;
// INSERT CODE HERE
public class FootballGame {
    public int getTeamSize() { return TEAM_SIZE; }
}
```

A. import my.sports.Football;

B. import static my.sports.*;

C. import static my.sports.Football;

D. import static my.sports.Football.*;

E. static import my.sports.*;

F. static import my.sports.Football;

G. static import my.sports.Football.*;

12. What is the result of the following code?

```
public class Browsers {
    static class Browser {
        public void go() {
            System.out.println("Inside Browser");
        }
    }
    static class Firefox extends Browser {
        public void go() {
            System.out.println("Inside Firefox");
        }
    }
    static class IE extends Browser {
        @Override public void go() {
            System.out.println("Inside IE");
        }
    }
    public static void main(String[] args) {
        Browser b = new Firefox();
        IE e = (IE) b;
        e.go();
    }
}
```

    A. Inside Browser

    B. Inside Firefox

    C. Inside IE

    D. The code does not compile.

    E. A runtime exception is thrown.

13. Which is a true statement about the following code?

```java
public class IsItFurry {
    static interface Mammal { }
    static class Furry implements Mammal { }
    static class Chipmunk extends Furry { }
    public static void main(String[] args) {
        Chipmunk c = new Chipmunk();
        Mammal m = c;
        Furry f = c;
        int result = 0;
        if (c instanceof Mammal) result += 1;
        if (c instanceof Furry) result += 2;
        if (null instanceof Chipmunk) result += 4;
        System.out.println(result);
} }
```

    A. The output is 0.

    B. The output is 3.

    C. The output is 7.

    D. `c instanceof Mammal` does not compile.

    E. `c instanceof Furry` does not compile.

    F. `null instanceof Chipmunk` does not compile.

14. Which is a true statement about the following code? (Choose all that apply.)

```java
import java.util. *;
public class IsItFurry {
    static class Chipmunk { }
    public static void main(String[] args) {
        Chipmunk c = new Chipmunk();
        ArrayList <Chipmunk> l = new ArrayList<>();
        Runnable r = new Thread();
        int result = 0;
        if (c instanceof Chipmunk) result += 1;
```

```
        if (l instanceof Chipmunk) result += 2;
        if (r instanceof Chipmunk) result += 4;
        System.out.println(result);
   } }
```

A. The code compiles, and the output is 0.

B. The code compiles, and the output is 3.

C. The code compiles, and the output is 7.

D. c instanceof Chipmunk does not compile.

E. l instanceof Chipmunk does not compile.

F. r instanceof Chipmunk does not compile.

15. Which of the following statements are true about the equals() method? (Choose all that apply.)

A. If equals(null) is called, the method should throw an exception.

B. If equals(null) is called, the method should return false.

C. If equals(null) is called, the method should return true.

D. If equals() is passed the wrong type, the method should throw an exception.

E. If equals() is passed the wrong type, the method should return false.

F. If equals() is passed the wrong type, the method should return true.

16. Which of the following can be inserted in main?

```
public class Outer {
    class Inner { }

    public static void main(String[] args) {
        // INSERT CODE HERE
    } }
```

A. Inner in = new Inner();

B. Inner in = Outer.new Inner();

C. Outer.Inner in = new Outer.Inner();

D. Outer.Inner in = new Outer().Inner();

E. Outer.Inner in = new Outer().new Inner();

F. Outer.Inner in = Outer.new Inner();

17. What is the result of the following code? (Choose all that apply.)

```
1:    public enum AnimalClasses {
2:        MAMMAL(true), FISH(Boolean.FALSE), BIRD(false),
```

```
3:      REPTILE(false), AMPHIBIAN(false), INVERTEBRATE(false)
4:          boolean hasHair;
5:          public AnimalClasses(boolean hasHair) {
6:              this.hasHair = hasHair;
7:          }
8:          public boolean hasHair() {
9:              return hasHair;
10:         }
11:         public void giveWig() {
12:             hasHair = true;
13:         } }
```

A. Compiler error on line 2.

B. Compiler error on line 3.

C. Compiler error on line 5.

D. Compiler error on line 8.

E. Compiler error on line 12.

F. Compiler error on another line.

G. The code compiles successfully.

18. What is the result of the following code? (Choose all that apply.)

```
public class Swimmer {
   enum AnimalClasses {
      MAMMAL, FISH {
         public boolean hasFins() { return true; }},
      BIRD, REPTILE, AMPHIBIAN, INVERTEBRATE;
      public abstract boolean hasFins();
   }
   public static void main(String[] args) {
      System.out.println(AnimalClasses.FISH);
      System.out.println(AnimalClasses.FISH.ordinal());
      System.out.println(AnimalClasses.FISH.hasFins());
      System.out.println(AnimalClasses.BIRD.hasFins());
   }
}
```

A. fish

B. FISH

C. 0

D. 1

E. false

F. true

G. The code does not compile.

19. Which of the following can be inserted to override the superclass method? (Choose all that apply.)

```
public class LearnToWalk {
   public void toddle() {}
   class BabyRhino extends LearnToWalk {
      // INSERT CODE HERE
   }
}
```

A. `public void toddle() {}`

B. `public void Toddle() {}`

C. `public final void toddle() {}`

D. `public static void toddle() {}`

E. `public void toddle() throws Exception {}`

F. `public void toddle(boolean fall) {}`

20. What is the result of the following code?

```
public class FourLegged {
   String walk = "walk,";
   static class BabyRhino extends FourLegged {
      String walk = "toddle,";
   }
   public static void main(String[] args) {
      FourLegged f = new BabyRhino();
      BabyRhino b = new BabyRhino();
      System.out.println(f.walk);
      System.out.println(b.walk);
   } }
```

A. toddle,toddle,

B. toddle,walk,

C. walk,toddle,

D. walk,walk,

E. The code does not compile.

F. A runtime exception is thrown.

21. Which of the following could be inserted to fill in the blank? (Choose all that apply.)

```
public interface Otter {
    default void play() { }
}
class RiverOtter implements Otter {

    -----------------------------
}
```

A. @Override public boolean equals(Object o) { return false; }
B. @Override public boolean equals(Otter o) { return false; }
C. @Override public int hashCode() { return 42; }
D. @Override public long hashCode() { return 42; }
E. @Override public void play() { }
F. @Override void play() { }

Chapter

2

Design Patterns and Principles

THE OCP EXAM TOPICS COVERED IN THIS CHAPTER INCLUDE THE FOLLOWING:

✓ **Advanced Java Class Design**

- Develop code that declares, implements, and/or extends interfaces and use the @Override annotation
- Create and use Lambda expressions

✓ **Lambda Built-in Functional Interfaces**

- Use the built-in interfaces included in the java.util.function package such as Predicate, Consumer, Function, and Supplier

✓ **Java Class Design**

- Implement encapsulation
- Implement inheritance including visibility modifiers and composition
- Implement polymorphism
- Create and use singleton classes and immutable classes

What does it mean to write good code? How do you measure code and differentiate good code from bad code? Although your previous study may have focused on learning how to develop Java code that compiles and executes properly at runtime, this chapter assumes that you already know how to do that. The primary goal of this chapter is to teach you best practices for designing Java classes and writing applications that lead to code that is easier to understand, more maintainable, and that you and other developers can leverage in future projects.

Adhering to the design principles and design patterns enables you to create complex class models that smoothly interact with other developers' applications. The better your software application is designed, the better it may adapt to changes in requirements, allowing it to scale naturally over the course of the project lifespan. Many of the Java libraries that you rely on to build your own applications may have started as simple projects that someone built to solve a commonly reoccurring problem.

To put it another way, this chapter is about teaching you powerful techniques for writing software so that you can build complex applications while avoiding the mistakes and pitfalls that previous developers have encountered.

Designing an Interface

While studying for the OCA, you learned about Java interfaces, including how to declare, extend, and implement them. We touched on some of these topics in Chapter 1, "Advanced Class Design," when we presented the @Override annotation. In this chapter, we will review interfaces in more detail, although we recommend returning to your OCA study material for a more detailed explanation if you are unfamiliar with these rules.

As you may recall, an interface is an abstract data type, similar to a class that defines a list of public abstract methods that any class implementing the interface must provide. An interface may also include constant public static final variables, default methods, and static methods. The following is an example of an interface and a class that implements it:

```
public interface Fly {
   public int getWingSpan() throws Exception;
   public static final int MAX_SPEED = 100;

   public default void land() {
      System.out.println("Animal is landing");
   }
```

```java
    public static double calculateSpeed(float distance, double time) {
        return distance/time;
    }
}

public class Eagle implements Fly {
    public int getWingSpan() {
        return 15;
    }
    public void land() {
        System.out.println("Eagle is diving fast");
    }
}
```

In this example, the first method of the interface, getWingSpan(), declares an exception in the interface. Due to the rules of method overriding, this does not require the exception to be declared in the overridden method in the Eagle class. The second declaration, MAX_SPEED, is a constant static variable available anywhere within our application. The next method, land(), is a default method that has been optionally overridden in the Eagle class. Finally, the method calculateSpeed() is a static member and, like MAX_SPEED, it is available without an instance of the interface.

An interface may extend another interface, and in doing so it inherits all of the abstract methods. The following is an example of an interface that extends another interface:

```java
public interface Walk {
    boolean isQuadruped();
    abstract double getMaxSpeed();
}

public interface Run extends Walk {
    public abstract boolean canHuntWhileRunning();
    abstract double getMaxSpeed();
}

public class Lion implements Run {
    public boolean isQuadruped() {
        return true;
    }

    public boolean canHuntWhileRunning() {
        return true;
    }
```

```
   public double getMaxSpeed() {
      return 100;
   }
}
```

In this example, the interface Run extends Walk and inherits all of the abstract methods of the parent interface. Notice that modifiers used in the methods isQuadruped(), getMaxSpeed(), and canHuntWhileRunning() are different between the class and interface definitions, such as public and abstract. The compiler automatically adds public to all interface methods and abstract to all non-static and non-default methods, if the developer does not provide them. By contrast, the class implementing the interface must provide the proper modifiers. For example, the code would not compile if getMaxSpeed() was not marked public in the Lion class.

Since the Lion class implements Run, and Run extends Walk, the Lion class must provide concrete implementations of all inherited abstract methods. As shown in this example with getMaxSpeed(), interface method definitions may be duplicated in a child interface without issue.

Remember that an interface cannot extend a class, nor can a class extend an interface. For these reasons, none of the following definitions using our previous Walk interface and Lion class will compile:

```
public interface Sleep extends Lion {}        // DOES NOT COMPILE

public class Tiger extends Walk {}            // DOES NOT COMPILE
```

In the first definition, the interface Sleep cannot extend Lion, since Lion is a class. Likewise, the class Tiger cannot extend the interface Walk.

Interfaces also serve to provide limited support for multiple inheritance within the Java language, as a class may implement multiple interfaces, such as in the following example:

```
public interface Swim {
}

public interface Hop {
}

public class Frog implements Swim, Hop {
}
```

In this example, the Frog class implements both the Swim and Hop interfaces. An instance of Frog may be passed to any method that accepts Swim, Hop, Frog, or java.lang.Object as an input parameter. As shown in this example, you can also construct interfaces that have neither methods nor class members, traditionally referred to as marker interfaces. In Chapter 8, "IO," you will see that the java.io.Serializable interface, which contains no methods, is an example of a marker interface.

There are numerous rules associated with implementing interfaces that you should know quite well at this point. For example, interfaces cannot extend classes, nor can classes extend interfaces. Interfaces may also not be marked final or instantiated directly. There are additional rules for default methods, such as Java failing to compile if a class or interface inherits two default methods with the same signature and doesn't provide its own implementation.

If you are a bit out of practice with interfaces, we recommend returning to your OCA study material for a full explanation of rules regarding interfaces and method overriding.

Purpose of an Interface

An interface provides a way for one individual to develop code that uses another individual's code, without having access to the other individual's underlying implementation. Interfaces can facilitate rapid application development by enabling development teams to create applications in parallel, rather than being directly dependent on each other.

For example, two teams can work together to develop a one-page standard interface at the start of a project. One team then develops code that *uses* the interfaces while the other team develops code that *implements* the interface. The development teams can then combine their implementations toward the end of the project, and as long as both teams developed with the same interface, they will be compatible. Of course, testing will still be required to make sure that the class implementing the interface behaves as expected.

 Real World Scenario

Mock Objects

You might wonder how a developer using the interface can build their code without access to a class that implements the interface. The developer using the interface can create a temporary *mock object*, sometimes referred to as dummy code, which simulates the real object that implements the interface with a simple implementation. The mock object does not need to be very complex, with one line per abstract method, for example, as it only serves as a placeholder for the real implementation. This allows the developer using the interface to compile, run, and test their code.

For example, imagine that you were working on a racing application with the code that calculates the winners handled by a different team. Both your team and the other team agreed on a RaceManager interface, as shown in the following code, with your team using the interface and the other team implementing it:

```
public class Animal {}
public class Tortoise extends Animal {}
public class Hare extends Animal {}
public interface RaceManager {
    public Animal getWinner(List<Animal> animals);
}
```

The good news is that your team has finished its part of the project first. The bad news is that the other team has nothing for you to test with. While waiting for the other team to finish, you can create a mock version of the RaceManager class, as shown in the following sample code:

```
public class DummyRaceManager implements RaceManager {
    public Animal getWinner(List<Animal> animals) {
        return animals==null || animals.size()==0 ? null: animals.get(0);
    }
}
```

The code isn't particularly intelligent; after all it just returns the first item in the list, but it is useful for testing purposes because it allows your team to execute your code while the other team finishes their implementation. You could also write a version that always returns Tortoise or Hare. The goal is just to give you something temporary that you can work with and that allows your code to compile, regardless of whether it works exactly as expected. After all, the full implementation of getWinner() could be hundreds of lines long and based on very complex business rules.

Introducing Functional Programming

Java defines a *functional interface* as an interface that contains a single abstract method. Functional interfaces are used as the basis for lambda expressions in functional programming. A *lambda expression* is a block of code that gets passed around, like an anonymous method.

Since lambda expressions and functional programming are a cornerstone of Java 8, we will review the basics from the OCA exam in this chapter. In Chapter 3, "Generics and Collections," we will apply lambda expressions to Collections classes. When we get to Chapter 4, "Functional Programming," we will expand our definition of functional programming to include numerous functional interface classes, as well as show you how to use them with streams. As you read through the rest of the book, you'll see how support for lambdas and streams has been added to numerous APIs in Java 8.

Defining a Functional Interface

Let's take a look at an example of a functional interface and a class that implements it:

```
@FunctionalInterface
public interface Sprint {
    public void sprint(Animal animal);
}

public class Tiger implements Sprint {
    public void sprint(Animal animal) {
        System.out.println("Animal is sprinting fast! "+animal.toString());
    }
}
```

In this example, the Sprint class is a functional interface, because it contains exactly one abstract method, and the Tiger class is a valid class that implements the interface.

Applying the *@FunctionalInterface* Annotation

While it is a good practice to mark a functional interface with the @FunctionalInterface annotation for clarity, it is not required with functional programming. The Java compiler implicitly assumes that any interface that contains exactly one abstract method is a functional interface. Conversely, if a class marked with the @FunctionalInterface annotation contains more than one abstract method, or no abstract methods at all, then the compiler will detect this error and not compile.

One problem with not always marking your functional interfaces with this annotation is that another developer may treat any interface you create that has only one method as a functional interface. If you later modify the interface to have other abstract methods, suddenly their code will break since it will no longer be a functional interface.

Therefore, it is recommend that you explicitly mark the interface with the @FunctionalInterface annotation so that other developers know which interfaces they can safely apply lambdas to without the possibility that they may stop being functional interfaces down the road.

The exam writers aren't likely to use this annotation, as they expect you to be able to determine whether an interface is a functional interface on your own.

Consider the following three interfaces. Assuming Sprint is our previously defined functional interface, which ones would also be functional interfaces?

```
public interface Run extends Sprint {}

public interface SprintFaster extends Sprint {
   public void sprint(Animal animal);
}

public interface Skip extends Sprint {
   public default int getHopCount(Kangaroo kangaroo) {return 10;}
   public static void skip(int speed) {}
}
```

The answer? All three are valid functional interfaces! The first interface, Run, defines no new methods, but since it extends Sprint, which defines a single abstract method, it is also a functional interface. The second interface, SprintFaster, extends Sprint and defines an abstract method, but this is an override of the parent sprint() method; therefore, the resulting interface has only one abstract method, and it is considered a functional interface. The third interface, Skip, extends Sprint and defines a static method and a default method, each with an implementation. Since neither of these methods is abstract, the resulting interface has only one abstract method and is a functional interface.

Now that you've seen some variations of valid functional interfaces, let's look at some invalid ones using our previous Sprint functional interface definition:

```
public interface Walk {}

public interface Dance extends Sprint {
   public void dance(Animal animal);
}

public interface Crawl {
   public void crawl();
   public int getCount();
}
```

Although all three of these interfaces will compile, none of them are considered functional interfaces. The Walk interface neither extends any functional interface classes nor defines any methods, so it is not a functional interface. The Dance method extends Sprint, which already includes a single abstract method, bringing the total to two abstract methods; therefore, Dance is not a functional interface. Finally, the Crawl method defines two abstract methods; therefore it cannot be a functional interface.

In these examples, applying the @FunctionalInterface annotation to any of these interfaces would result in a compiler error, as would attempting to use them implicitly as functional interfaces in a lambda expression.

Implementing Functional Interfaces with Lambdas

Now that we have defined a functional interface, we'll show you how to implement them using lambda expressions. As we said earlier, a lambda expression is a block of code that gets passed around, like an anonymous method. Let's start with a simple CheckTrait functional interface, which has a single method test(), which takes as input an instance of an Animal class. The definitions of the class and functional interface are as follows:

```java
public class Animal {
    private String species;
    private boolean canHop;
    private boolean canSwim;
    public Animal(String speciesName, boolean hopper, boolean swimmer) {
        species = speciesName;
        canHop = hopper;
        canSwim = swimmer;
    }
    public boolean canHop() { return canHop; }
    public boolean canSwim() { return canSwim; }
    public String toString() { return species; }
}

public interface CheckTrait {
    public boolean test(Animal a);
}
```

Now that we've defined a structure, let's do something with it. The following simple program uses a lambda expression to determine if some sample animals match the specified criteria:

```java
public class FindMatchingAnimals {
    private static void print(Animal animal, CheckTrait trait) {
        if(trait.test(animal))
            System.out.println(animal);
    }

    public static void main(String[] args) {
        print(new Animal("fish", false, true), a -> a.canHop());
        print(new Animal("kangaroo", true, false), a -> a.canHop());
    }
}
```

For illustrative purposes, the lambda expression chosen for this program is quite simple:

```java
a -> a.canHop();
```

This expression means that Java should call a method with an `Animal` parameter that returns a `boolean` value that's the result of `a.canHop()`. We know all this because we wrote the code. But how does Java know?

Java relies on context when figuring out what lambda expressions mean. We are passing this lambda as the second parameter of the `print()` method. That method expects a `CheckTrait` as the second parameter. Since we are passing a lambda instead, Java treats `CheckTrait` as a functional interface and tries to map it to the single abstract method:

```
boolean test(Animal a);
```

Since this interface's method takes an `Animal`, it means the lambda parameter has to be an `Animal`. And since that interface's method returns a `boolean`, we know that the lambda returns a `boolean`.

Recall that lambda expressions rely on the notion of deferred execution. *Deferred execution* means that code is specified now but runs later. In this case, *later* is when the `print()` method calls it. Even though the execution is deferred, the compiler will still validate that the code syntax is properly formed.

Understanding Lambda Syntax

The syntax of lambda expressions is tricky because many parts are optional. These two lines are equivalent and do the exact same thing:

```
a -> a.canHop()
```

```
(Animal a) -> { return a.canHop(); }
```

Let's look at what is going on here. The left side of the arrow operator `->` indicates the input parameters for the lambda expression. It can be consumed by a functional interface whose abstract method has the same number of parameters and compatible data types. The right side is referred to as the body of the lambda expression. It can be consumed by a functional interface whose abstract method returns a compatible data type.

Since the syntax of these two expressions is a bit different, let's look at them more closely. The first example, shown in Figure 2.1, has three parts:

- We specify a single parameter with the name a.

- The arrow operator → separates the parameter from the body.

- The body calls a single method and returns the result of that method.

FIGURE 2.1   Lambda syntax omitting optional parts

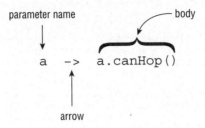

The second example also has three parts, as shown in Figure 2.2; it's just more verbose:

- We specify a single parameter with the name a and state that the type is Animal, wrapping the input parameters in parentheses ().
- The arrow operator -> separates the parameter from the body.
- The body has one or more lines of code, including braces {}, a semicolon ;, and a return statement.

FIGURE 2.2   Lambda syntax, including optional parts

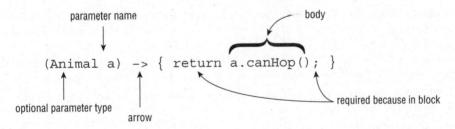

Let's review some of the differences between these two figures. The first difference that you may notice is that Figure 2.2 uses parentheses (), while Figure 2.1 does not. The parentheses () can be omitted in a lambda expression if there is exactly one input parameter and the type is not explicitly stated in the expression. This means that expressions that have zero or more than one input parameter will still require parentheses. For example, the following are all valid lambda expressions, assuming that there are valid functional interfaces that can consume them:

```
() -> new Duck()
d -> {return d.quack();}
(Duck d) -> d.quack()
(Animal a, Duck d) -> d.quack()
```

The first lambda expression could be used by a functional interface containing a method that takes no arguments and returns a Duck object. The second and third lambda expressions can both be used by a functional interface that takes a Duck as input and returns whatever the return type of quack() is. The last lambda expression can be used by a functional interface that takes as input Animal and Duck objects and returns whatever the return type of quack() is.

Spotting Invalid Lambdas

Can you figure out why each of the following lambda expressions is invalid and will not compile when used as an argument to a method?

```
Duck d -> d.quack()               // DOES NOT COMPILE
a,d -> d.quack()                  // DOES NOT COMPILE
Animal a, Duck d -> d.quack()     // DOES NOT COMPILE
```

They each require parentheses ()! As we said, parentheses can be omitted only if there is exactly one parameter and the data type is not specified.

Next, you see that Figure 2.2 has a pair of statement braces {} around the body of the lambda expression. This allows you to write multiple lines of code in the body of the lambda expression, as you might do when working with an if statement or while loop. What's tricky here is that when you add braces {}, you must explicitly terminate each statement in the body with a semicolon;.

In Figure 2.1, we were able to omit the braces {}, semi-colon;, and return statement, because this is a special shortcut that Java allows for single-line lambda bodies. This special shortcut doesn't work when you have two or more statements. At least this is consistent with using {} to create blocks of code elsewhere in Java. When using {} in the body of the lambda expression, you must use the return statement if the functional interface method that lambda implements returns a value. Alternatively, a return statement is optional when the return type of the method is void.

Let's look at some more examples:

```
() -> true                              // 0 parameters
a -> {return a.startsWith("test");}     // 1 parameter
(String a) -> a.startsWith("test")      // 1 parameter
(int x) -> {}                           // 1 parameter
(int y) -> {return;}                    // 1 parameter
```

The first example takes no arguments and always returns true. The second and third examples both take a single String value, using different syntax to accomplish the same thing. Notice that in the first two examples we mixed and matched syntax between Figure 2.1 and Figure 2.2 by having the first example use parentheses () but no braces {} and reversing this in the second example. The last two examples are equivalent because they take an integer value and do not return anything.

Now let's look at some lambda expressions that take more than one parameter:

```
(a, b) -> a.startsWith("test")            // 2 parameters
(String a, String b) -> a.startsWith("test")    // 2 parameters
```

These examples both take two parameters and ignore one of them, since there is no rule that says the lambda expression must use all of the input parameters.

Let's review some additional lambda expressions to see how your grasp of lambda syntax is progressing. Do you see what's wrong with each of these lambda expressions?

```
a, b -> a.startsWith("test")            // DOES NOT COMPILE
c -> return 10;                         // DOES NOT COMPILE
a -> { return a.startsWith("test") }    // DOES NOT COMPILE
```

The first lambda needs parentheses () around the parameter list. Remember that the parentheses are optional only when there is one parameter and it doesn't have a type declared. The second line uses the return keyword without using braces {}. The last line is missing the semicolon after the return statement. The following rewritten lambda expressions are each valid:

```
(a, b) -> a.startsWith("test")
c -> { return 10; }
a -> { return a.startsWith("test"); }
```

As mentioned, the data types for the input parameters of a lambda expression are optional. When one parameter has a data type listed, though, all parameters must provide a data type. The following lambda expressions are each invalid for this reason:

```
(int y, z) -> {int x=1; return y+10; }      // DOES NOT COMPILE
(String s, z) -> { return s.length()+z; }   // DOES NOT COMPILE
(a, Animal b, c) -> a.getName()             // DOES NOT COMPILE
```

If we add or remove all of the data types, then these lambda expressions do compile. For example, the following rewritten lambda expressions are each valid:

```
(y, z) -> {int x=1; return y+10; }
(String s, int z) -> { return s.length()+z; }
(a, b, c) -> a.getName()
```

There is one more issue you might see with lambdas. We've been defining an argument list in our lambda expressions. Since Java doesn't allow us to re-declare a local variable, the following is an issue:

```
(a, b) -> { int a = 0; return 5;}       // DOES NOT COMPILE
```

We tried to re-declare a, which is not allowed. By contrast, the following line is permitted because it uses a different variable name:

```
(a, b) -> { int c = 0; return 5;}
```

Applying the Predicate Interface

In our earlier example, we created a simple functional interface to test an Animal trait:

```
public interface CheckTrait {
    public boolean test(Animal a);
}
```

You can imagine that we'd have to create lots of interfaces like this to use lambdas. We want to test animals, plants, String values, and just about anything else that we come across.

Luckily, Java recognizes that this is a common problem and provides such an interface for us. It's in the package java.util.function, and the gist of it is as follows:

```
public interface Predicate<T> {
    public boolean test(T t);
}
```

That looks a lot like our method. The only difference is that it uses type T instead of Animal. As you may remember from your OCA studies, this is the syntax for an interface that uses a generic type. If you're a bit out of practice with generics, don't worry. We'll be reviewing generics in more detail in Chapter 3.

The result of using Predicate is that we no longer need our own functional interface. The following is a rewrite of our program to use the Predicate class:

```
import java.util.function.Predicate;

public class FindMatchingAnimals {
    private static void print(Animal animal, Predicate<Animal> trait) {
        if(trait.test(animal))
            System.out.println(animal);
    }

    public static void main(String[] args) {
        print(new Animal("fish", false, true), a -> a.canHop());
        print(new Animal("kangaroo", true, false), a -> a.canHop());
    }
}
```

This is very similar to our original program, except that we wrote it with one less interface. As you will see in Chapter 3 when we work with collections, as well as throughout the book, Java 8 integrates the Predicate interface into a variety of methods and APIs. In Chapter 4, we will be presenting lambda expressions based on interfaces that take other inputs and return other data types besides boolean.

Implementing Polymorphism

Polymorphism is the ability of a single interface to support multiple underlying forms. In Java, this allows multiple types of objects to be passed to a single method or class. Let's take a look at an example of this for illustrative purposes:

```java
public interface LivesInOcean { public void makeSound(); }

public class Dolphin implements LivesInOcean {
    public void makeSound() { System.out.println("whistle"); }
}

public class Whale implements LivesInOcean {
    public void makeSound() { System.out.println("sing"); }
}

public class Oceanographer {
    public void checkSound(LivesInOcean animal) {
        animal.makeSound();
    }
    public void main(String[] args) {
        Oceanographer o = new Oceanographer();
        o.checkSound(new Dolphin());
        o.checkSound(new Whale());
    }
}
```

This code compiles and executes without issue and yields the following output:

```
whistle
sing
```

In this sample code, our `Oceanographer` class includes a method named `checkSound()` that is capable of accepting any object whose class implements the `LivesInOcean` interface. We can also create new objects, such as `Fish` or `Lobster`, that also implement the `LivesInOcean` interface and that would be compatible with our `Oceanographer` class.

Polymorphism also allows one object to take on many different forms. As you may remember from studying for the OCA exam, a Java object may be accessed using a reference with the same type as the object, a reference that is a superclass of the object, or a reference that defines an interface that the object implements, either directly or through a superclass. Furthermore, a cast is not required if the object is being reassigned to a supertype or interface of the object.

The following example illustrates this polymorphic property:

```java
public class Primate {
   public boolean hasHair() {
      return true;
   }
}


public interface HasTail {
   public boolean isTailStriped();
}


public class Lemur extends Primate implements HasTail {
   public int age = 10;

   public boolean isTailStriped() {
      return false;
   }

   public static void main(String[] args) {
      Lemur lemur = new Lemur();
      System.out.println(lemur.age);

      HasTail hasTail = lemur;
      System.out.println(hasTail.isTailStriped());

      Primate primate = lemur;
      System.out.println(primate.hasHair());
   }
}
```

This code compiles and executes without issue and yields the following output:

```
10
false
true
```

The most important thing to note about this example is that only one object, Lemur, is created and referenced. The ability of the Lemur object to be passed as an instance of an interface it implements, HasTail, as well as an instance of one of its superclasses, Primate, is the nature of polymorphism.

If you use a variable to refer to an object, then only the methods or variables that are part of the variable's reference type can be called without an explicit cast. For example, the following snippets of code will not compile:

```
HasTail hasTail = lemur;
System.out.println(hasTail.age);              // DOES NOT COMPILE

Primate primate = lemur;
System.out.println(primate.isTailStriped());  // DOES NOT COMPILE
```

In this example, the reference hasTail has direct access only to methods defined with the HasTail interface; therefore, it doesn't know that the variable age is part of the object. Likewise, the reference primate has access only to methods defined in the Primate class, and it doesn't have direct access to the isTailStriped() method.

Distinguishing between an Object and a Reference

In Java, all objects are accessed by reference, so as a developer you never have direct access to the memory of the object itself. Conceptually, though, you should consider the object as the entity that exists in memory, allocated by the Java runtime environment. Regardless of the type of the reference that you have for the object in memory, the object itself doesn't change. For example, since all objects inherit java.lang.Object, they can all be reassigned to java.lang.Object, as shown in the following example:

```
Lemur lemur = new Lemur();

Object lemurAsObject = lemur;
```

Even though the Lemur object has been assigned a reference with a different type, the object itself has not changed and still exists as a Lemur object in memory. What has changed, then, is our ability to access methods within the Lemur class with the lemurAsObject reference. Without an explicit cast back to Lemur, as you'll see in the next section, we no longer have access to the Lemur properties of the object.

We can summarize this principle with the following two rules:

1. The type of the object determines which properties exist within the object in memory.

2. The type of the reference to the object determines which methods and variables are accessible to the Java program.

It therefore follows that successfully changing a reference of an object to a new reference type may give you access to new properties of the object, but those properties existed before the reference change occurred.

We illustrate this property using the previous example again, as shown in Figure 2.3. As you can see in the figure, the same object exists in memory regardless of which reference is pointing to it. Depending on the type of the reference, we may have access only to certain methods. For example, the hasTail reference has access to the method isTailStriped(), but it doesn't have access to the variable age defined in the Lemur class. As you'll learn in the next section, it is possible to reclaim access to the variable age by explicitly casting the hasTail reference to a Lemur reference.

FIGURE 2.3   Object vs. reference

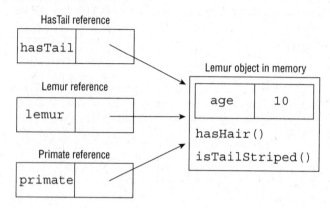

Casting Object References

In the previous example, we created a single instance of a Lemur object and accessed it via superclass and interface references. Once we changed the reference type, though, we lost access to more specific methods defined in the subclass that still exists within the object. We can reclaim those references by casting the object back to the specific subclass it came from:

```
Primate primate = lemur;

Lemur lemur2 = primate; // DOES NOT COMPILE

Lemur lemur3 = (Lemur)primate;
System.out.println(lemur3.age);
```

In this example, we first try to convert the primate reference back to a lemur reference, lemur2, without an explicit cast. The result is that the code will not compile. In the second example, though, we explicitly cast the object to a subclass of the object Primate, and we gain access to all the methods available to the Lemur class.

Here are some basic rules to keep in mind when casting variables:

1. Casting an object from a subclass to a superclass doesn't require an explicit cast.

2. Casting an object from a superclass to a subclass requires an explicit cast.

3. The compiler will not allow casts to unrelated types.

4. Even when the code compiles without issue, an exception may be thrown at runtime if the object being cast is not actually an instance of that class.

The third rule is important; the exam may try to trick you with a cast that the compiler doesn't allow. For example, we were able to cast a Primate reference to a Lemur reference as Lemur is a subclass of Primate and therefore related.

Consider this example:

```
public class Bird {}

public class Fish {
   public static void main(String[] args) {
      Fish fish = new Fish();
      Bird bird = (Fish)bird;   // DOES NOT COMPILE
   }
}
```

In this example, the classes Fish and Bird are not related through any class hierarchy; therefore, the code will not compile.

Casting is not without its limitations. Even though two classes share a related hierarchy, that doesn't mean an instance of one can automatically be cast to another. Here's an example:

```
public class Rodent {
}

public class Capybara extends Rodent {
   public static void main(String[] args) {
      Rodent rodent = new Rodent();
      Capybara capybara = (Capybara)rodent;   // Throws ClassCastException at
                                              // runtime
   }
}
```

This code creates an instance of Rodent and then tries to cast it to a subclass of Rodent, Capybara. Although this code will compile without issue, it will throw a ClassCastException at runtime since the object being referenced is not an instance of the Capybara class. As you may recall from Chapter 1, you can use the instanceof operator prior to casting the object to avoid throwing ClassCastException at runtime:

```
if(rodent instanceof Capybara) {
   Capybara capybara = (Capybara)rodent;
}
```

When faced with a question on the exam that involves casting and polymorphism, be sure to remember what the instance of the object actually is. Then focus on whether the compiler will allow the object to be referenced with or without explicit casts.

Understanding Design Principles

A *design principle* is an established idea or best practice that facilitates the software design process. In this section, we will discuss design principles for creating Java classes and why those principles lead to better and more manageable code bases. In general, following good design principles leads to

- More logical code
- Code that is easier to understand
- Classes that are easier to reuse in other relationships and applications
- Code that is easier to maintain and that adapts more readily to changes in the application requirements

Throughout this section, we will refer to the decision of how to structure class relationships as the underlying data model. In software development, a *data model* is the representation of our objects and their properties within our application and how they relate to items in the real world. For example, we compose numerous data models of zoo animals throughout this book, containing only the attributes with which we are concerned in our sample programs.

Encapsulating Data

One fundamental principle of object-oriented design is the concept of encapsulating data. In software development, *encapsulation* is the idea of combining fields and methods in a class such that the methods operate on the data, as opposed to the users of the class accessing the fields directly. In Java, it is commonly implemented with private instance members that have public methods to retrieve or modify the data, commonly referred to as getters and setters, respectively.

For the sake of brevity, we sometimes present classes with publically accessible instance variables in this book. The exam writers do this as well. Although instance variables are allowed to be public, the practice is strongly discouraged in professional software development.

The underlying idea of encapsulation is that no actor other than the class itself should have direct access to its data. The class is said to encapsulate the data it contains and prevent anyone from directly accessing it.

With encapsulation, a class is able to maintain certain invariants about its internal data. An *invariant* is a property or truth that is maintained even after the data is modified. For example, imagine that we are designing a new Animal class, and we have the following design requirements:

- Each animal has a non-null, non-empty species field
- Each animal has an age field that is greater than or equal to zero

The goal of designing our `Animal` class would be to make sure that we never arrive at an instance of `Animal` that violates one of these properties. By using `private` instance members along with getter and setter methods that validate the input data, we can ensure that these invariants remain true. In Chapter 6, "Exceptions and Assertions," we will describe how to test these class invariants using assertions.

An illustrative example may shed some light on this concept. We first define our `Animal` class without encapsulation:

```
public class Animal {
    public String species;
    public int age;
}
```

As the `Animal` class is defined, it's easy to create an instance of `Animal` that violates both of our invariants:

```
Animal animal = new Animal();
animal.age = -100;
```

In this example, the first invariant is violated as soon as the object is created, with `species` defaulting to `null`. The user then sets the `age` field to `-100`, since this field is publically accessible, resulting in the second invariant being violated. This object may now be passed around to methods, with users unaware that both invariants have been violated.

How can we fix this problem using encapsulation? First we need to make instance variables `private`. This way, the class is the only one that can modify the data directly. Then we need to define constructors, getters, and setters that enforce these invariants. Here is an implementation that enforces the invariants using encapsulation:

```
public class Animal {
    private String species;
    private int age;

    public Animal(String species) {
        this.setSpecies(species);
    }

    public String getSpecies() {
        return species;
    }

    public void setSpecies(String species) {
        if(species == null || species.trim().length()==0) {
            throw new IllegalArgumentException("Species is required");
        }
```

```
        this.species = species;
    }

    public int getAge() {
        return age;
    }

    public void setAge(int age) {
        if(age<0) {
            throw new IllegalArgumentException("Age cannot be a negative number");
        }
        this.age = age;
    }
}
```

As you can see in this example, species and age are both marked private, with public methods getSpecies() and getAge() to read the data. Next, our setSpecies() and setAge() methods now validate the input and throw an exception if one of our invariants is violated. Finally, a non-default constructor has been added that requires a species value and uses the setter method to validate the input.

The advantage of this new implementation of the Animal class is that it uses encapsulation to enforce the design principles of the class. Anytime an instance of an Animal object is passed to a method, it can be used without requiring that its invariants be validated.

 Real World Scenario

Blocking Direct Access to Private Class Variables

When you come across a getter or setter in practice, it is often generated and offers near-direct access to its private variables, such as in the following example:

```
private String name;

public String getName() {
    return name;
}

public void setName(String name) {
    this.name = name;
}
```

At first, this may look like poor encapsulation. After all, the name field can be changed without enforcing any rules. In actuality, this is still worlds better than allowing direct access to the `private` variable name. The advantage comes from the fact that the writers of the class can update the getter or setter method to have more complex rules without causing the users of the class to have to recompile their code. Suppose that we have a requirement to treat empty strings or those containing only whitespace characters as `null` values. Then `setName()` could be rewritten as this:

```
public void setName(String name) {
    this.name = (name == null || name.trim().length()==0) ? null: name;
}
```

Since the method signature `setName()` did not change, the callers of this method would not have to modify and recompile their code.

What if the writer of the class had first allowed `public` access to the name field and later switched the field to be `private` and added a `public` getter and setter? This would result in all users of the class being forced to recompile their code, since the manner in which the name field is accessed has changed. Therefore, it is considered a good design practice always to encapsulate all variables in a class, even if there are no established data rules, as a way to protect the data when such rules may be added in the future.

Creating JavaBeans

Encapsulation is so prevalent in Java that there is a standard for creating classes that store data, called JavaBeans. A *JavaBean* is a design principle for encapsulating data in an object in Java. Table 2.1 lists the rules for naming JavaBeans.

TABLE 2.1   JavaBean naming conventions

Rule	Example
Properties are `private`.	`private int age;`

Getter for non-boolean properties begins with get.	`public int getAge() {`
	`    return age;`
	`}`

TABLE 2.1   JavaBean naming conventions *(continued)*

Rule	Example
Getters for boolean properties may begin with is or get.	```java\npublic boolean isBird() {\n return bird;\n}\npublic boolean getBird() {\n return bird;\n}\n```
Setter methods begin with set.	```java\npublic void setAge(int age) {\n this.age = age;\n}\n```
The method name must have a prefix of set/get/is followed by the first letter of the property in uppercase and followed by the rest of the property name.	```java\npublic void setNumChildren\n (int numChildren) {\n this.numChildren = numChildren;\n}\n```

Although boolean values use is to start their getter method, the same does not apply to instances of the wrapper Boolean class, which use get.

Let's take a look at some examples. Let's say that we have the following two private variables defined in our class:

```java
private boolean playing;
private Boolean dancing;
```

Which of the following could be correctly included in a JavaBean?

```java
public boolean isPlaying() { return playing; }
public boolean getPlaying() { return playing; }
public Boolean isDancing() { return dancing; }
```

The first line is correct because it defines a proper getter for a boolean variable. The second example is also correct, since boolean may use is or get. The third line is incorrect, because a Boolean wrapper should start with get, since it is an object. What about these examples?

```java
public String name;
public String name() { return name; }
public void updateName(String n) { name = n; }
public void setname(String n) { name = n; }
```

None of these lines follow correct JavaBean practices! The first line makes `name` `public`, whereas it should be `private`. The second line does not define a proper getter and should be `getName()`. The last two lines are both incorrect setters, since the first does not start with `set` and the second does not have the first letter of the attribute `name` in uppercase.

Applying the Is-a Relationship

In Chapter 1, you were introduced to the `instanceof` operator and shown how it could be used to determine when an object is an instance of a particular class, superclass, or interface. In object-oriented design, we describe the property of an object being an instance of a data type as having an *is-a relationship*. The is-a relationship is also known as the inheritance test.

The fundamental result of the is-a principle is that if A is-a B, then any instance of A can be treated like an instance of B. This holds true for a child that is a subclass of any parent, be it a direct subclass or a distant child. As we discussed with polymorphism, objects can take many different forms.

When constructing an inheritance-based data model, it is important to apply the is-a relationship regularly, so that you are designing classes that conceptually make sense. For example, imagine that we have a class `Cat` that extends a class `Pet`, as shown in Figure 2.4.

FIGURE 2.4   Good design—A `Cat` is-a `Pet`, because `Cat` extends `Pet`.

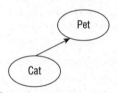

The parent class, `Pet`, has commonly used fields such as name and age. As a developer, you might also design a class `Tiger`, and since tigers also have an age and a name, you might be inclined to reuse the parent `Pet` class for the purposes of saving time and lines of code, as shown in Figure 2.5.

FIGURE 2.5   Poor design—A `Tiger` is-a `Pet`, because `Tiger` extends `Pet`.

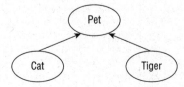

Unfortunately, Pet also has a cuddle() method, with the result being that you are encouraging people to cuddle tigers! By reusing the parent Pet class, you are conceptually stating that a Tiger is-a Pet, even though a Tiger is not a Pet. Although this example is functionally correct and does save time and lines of code, the result of failing to apply the is-a relationship is that you have created a relationship that violates the data model.

Let's try to fix the problem by placing Pet and Tiger underneath a Feline parent class and see if that solves the problem, as shown in Figure 2.6.

FIGURE 2.6   Still poor design—All Pets are now Felines.

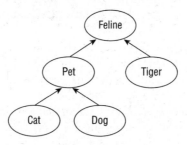

Our class structure now works and is consistent, but as shown in Figure 2.6, if we add a child Dog to Pet, we encounter a problem with the is-a test. A Dog is-a Pet, and a Pet is-a Feline, but the model implies that a Dog is-a Feline, which obviously is not true.

As you saw in this example, the is-a relationship test helps us avoid creating object models that contain contradictions. One solution in this example is to not combine Tiger and Pet in the same model, preferring to write duplicate code rather than create inconsistent data. Another solution might be to use the multi-inheritance properties of interfaces and declare Pet an interface rather than a parent class, as shown in Figure 2.7.

FIGURE 2.7   Good design—Pet is now an interface.

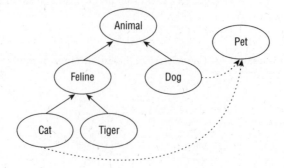

You see in this example that the object model is now correct using the is-a test. For example, `Cat` is-a `Animal`, `Tiger` is-a `Feline`, `Dog` is-a `Animal`, and so forth. `Pet` is now separate from the class inheritance model, but by using interfaces, we preserve the relationship that `Cat` is-a `Pet` and `Dog` is-a `Pet`.

Applying the Has-a Relationship

In object-oriented design, we often want to test whether an object contains a particular property or value. We refer to the *has-a relationship* as the property of an object having a named data object or primitive as a member. The has-a relationship is also known as the object composition test, described in the next section.

Let's take a look at an example with `Bird` and `Beak` classes, as shown in Figure 2.8.

FIGURE 2.8   `Bird` has-a `Beak`.

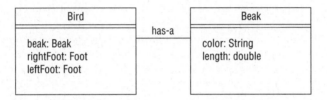

In this example, `Bird` and `Beak` are both classes with different attributes and values. While they obviously fail the is-a test, since a `Bird` is not a `Beak`, nor is a `Beak` a `Bird`, they do pass the has-a test, as a `Bird` has-a `Beak`.

Inheritance goes one step further by allowing us to say that any child of `Bird` must also have a `Beak`. More generally, if a parent has-a object as a `protected` or `public` member, then any child of the parent must also have that object as a member. Note that this does not hold true for `private` members defined in parent classes, because `private` members are not inherited in Java.

Uncovering Problems with the Data Model Using Is-a and Has-a

Sometimes relationships appear to pass the is-a test but fail when combined with the has-a test via inheritance. For example, take a look at the following code:

```
public class Tail {}
public class Primate {
    protected Tail tail;
}
```

```
public class Monkey extends Primate { // Monkey has-a Tail since it is-a Primate
}
public class Chimpanzee extends Primate { // Chimpanzee has-a Tail since it is-a Primate
}
```

In this example, a `Monkey` is-a `Primate` and a `Chimpanzee` is-a `Primate`. The model also states that a `Primate` has-a `Tail`, and through inheritance a `Monkey` has-a `Tail` and a `Chimpanzee` has-a `Tail`. Unfortunately, chimpanzees do not have tails in the real world, so the underlying data model is incorrect.

We saw that the model appeared to be correct when examined individually, but by using inheritance, we uncovered a flaw in the data model. The result is that we should remove the `Tail` property from the `Primate` class, since not all primates have tails.

Composing Objects

In object-oriented design, we refer to *object composition* as the property of constructing a class using references to other classes in order to reuse the functionality of the other classes. In particular, the class contains the other classes in the has-a sense and may delegate methods to the other classes.

Object composition should be thought of as an alternate to inheritance and is often used to simulate polymorphic behavior that cannot be achieved via single inheritance. For example, imagine that we have the following two classes:

```
public class Flippers {
   public void flap() {
      System.out.println("The flippers flap back and forth");
   }
}
```

```
public class WebbedFeet {
   public void kick() {
      System.out.println("The webbed feet kick to and fro");
   }
}
```

Trying to relate these objects using inheritance does not make sense, as `WebbedFeet` are not the same as `Flippers`. Instead, we can compose a new class that contains both of these objects and delegates its methods to them, such as in the following code:

```
public class Penguin {
   private final Flippers flippers;
   private final WebbedFeet webbedFeet;
```

```
   public Penguin() {
      this.flippers = new Flippers();
      this.webbedFeet = new WebbedFeet();
   }

   public void flap() {
      this.flippers.flap();
   }
   public void kick() {
      this.webbedFeet.kick();
   }
}
```

As you can see, this new class Penguin is composed of instances of Flippers and WebbedFeet. Furthermore, the heavy lifting of flap() and kick() is delegated to the other classes, with the methods in the Penguin class being only one line long. Note that implementations of these methods in the delegate classes are also only one line long, although they could conceivably be much more complex.

One of the advantages of object composition over inheritance is that it tends to promote greater code reuse. By using object composition, you gain access to other classes and methods that would be difficult to obtain via Java's single-inheritance model.

In our previous example, the Flippers class can be reused in classes completely unrelated to a Penguin or a Bird, such as in a Dolphin or Turtle class. Alternatively, if the Flippers class had been inherited from the Penguin class, then using it in other unrelated classes would be difficult without breaking the class model or having the other class contain an instance of a Penguin. For example, it would be silly to say a Dolphin is inherited from a Penguin or has an instance of a Penguin class, just because a Dolphin has Flippers, and Flippers inherits from the Penguin class.

Object composition may seem more attractive than inheritance because of its reusable nature, but bear in mind that one of the strengths of Java is its powerful inheritance model. Object composition still requires you to explicitly expose the underlying methods and values manually, whereas inheritance includes protected and public members automatically. Also, using method overloading to determine dynamically which method to select at runtime is an extremely powerful tool for building intelligent classes. In other words, both object composition and inheritance have their proper place in developing good code, and in many cases it may be difficult to decide which path to choose.

Working with Design Patterns

A *design pattern* is an established general solution to a commonly occurring software development problem. The purpose of a design pattern is to leverage the wealth of knowledge of developers who have come before you in order to solve old problems that you may encounter easily. It also gives developers a common vocabulary in which they can discuss common problems and solutions. For example, if you say that you wrote getters/setters or implemented the singleton pattern, most developers will understand the structure of your code without having to get into the low-level details.

In this chapter, we are primarily focused on *creational patterns*, a type of software design pattern that manages the creation of objects within an application. Obviously, you already know how to create objects in Java with the new keyword, as shown in the following code:

```
Animal animal = new Camel();
```

The problem with object creation, though, lies in how you create and manage objects in more complex systems. In this example, we were required to know exactly which type of Animal object, in this case Camel, we wanted to create at compile time. But what if this is not known until runtime? Furthermore, what if we wanted to create a single Animal object in memory that is shared by all classes within our application? We will investigate these kinds of design creation problems and their associated patterns in this section.

One thing to keep in mind as you read this section is that under the covers, the new keyword is still used to create objects in memory. The creational patterns simply apply a level of indirection to object creation by creating the object in some other class, rather than creating the object directly in your application. *Level of indirection* is a general term for solving a software design problem by conceptually separating the task into multiple levels.

For the OCP 8 exam, you are required to know only the first two of the four design patterns that we present in this section: the singleton pattern and the immutable object pattern. Because of this, we will test you only on the first two patterns in any review questions in this book. That said, we suggest that you become familiar with all four of these patterns as they are used throughout the Java API, as well as in later chapters of this book.

Applying the Singleton Pattern

The first creational pattern we will discuss is the singleton pattern.

Problem   How do we create an object in memory only once in an application and have it shared by multiple classes?

Motivation   There are times when we want only one instance of a particular type of object in memory. For example, we might want to manage the amount of hay available for food to the zoo animals across all classes that use it. We could pass the same shared HayManager object to every class and method that uses it, although this would create a lot of extra pointers and could be difficult to manage if the object is used throughout the application. By creating a singleton HayManager object, we centralize the data and remove the need to pass it around the application.

Solution   The *singleton pattern* is a creational pattern focused on creating only one instance of an object in memory within an application, sharable by all classes and threads within the application. The globally available object created by the singleton pattern is referred to as a *singleton*. Singletons may also improve performance by loading reusable data that would otherwise be time consuming to store and reload each time it is needed.

We present a simple implementation of our HayManager class as a singleton and discuss its various properties:

```java
public class HayStorage {

   private int quantity = 0;
   private HayStorage() {}

   private static final HayStorage instance = new HayStorage();

   public static HayStorage getInstance() {
      return instance;
   }
   public synchronized void addHay(int amount) {
      quantity += amount;
   }
   public synchronized boolean removeHay (int amount) {
      if(quantity < amount) return false;
      quantity -= amount;
      return true;
   }
   public synchronized int getHayQuantity() {
      return quantity;
   }
}
```

As shown in the preceding code, singletons in Java are created as `private static` variables within the class, often with the name `instance`. They are accessed via a single `public static` method, often named `getInstance()`, which returns the reference to the singleton object. Finally, all constructors in a singleton class are marked `private`, which ensures that no other class is capable of instantiating another version of the class.

By marking the constructors `private`, we have implicitly marked the class `final`. Recall that every class requires at least one constructor, with the default no-argument constructor being added if none are provided. Furthermore, the first line of any constructor is a call to a parent constructor with the `super()` command. If all of the constructors are declared `private` in the singleton class, then it is impossible to create a subclass with a valid constructor; therefore, the singleton class is effectively `final`.

You might have noticed that we added the modifier synchronized to addHay(), removeHay(), and getHayQuantity(). We will discuss these concepts in more detail in Chapter 7, "Concurrency." For now, however, you just need to know that they prevent two processes from running the same method at the exact same time.

Returning to our HayStorage example, a process that wants to use this singleton first calls getInstance() and then calls the appropriate public method:

```
public class LlamaTrainer {
    public boolean feedLlamas(int numberOfLlamas) {
        int amountNeeded = 5 * numberOfLlamas;
        HayStorage hayStorage = HayStorage.getInstance();
        if(hayStorage.getHayQuantity() < amountNeeded) {
            hayStorage.addHay(amountNeeded + 10);
        }
        boolean fed = hayStorage.removeHay(amountNeeded);
        if(fed) System.out.println("Llamas have been fed");
        return fed;
    }
}
```

One thing to keep in mind is that there might be multiple llama trainers at the zoo but only one food storage location. Within our data model, this would amount to many LlamaTrainer instances but only a single instance of HayStorage. We also checked the return type of removeHay(), as it is possible that someone else could have taken the food that we just restocked before we had a chance to use it.

In our first HayStorage example, we instantiated the singleton object directly in the definition of the instance reference. We can also instantiate a singleton in two other ways. The following example creates a singleton using a static initialization block when the class is loaded. For simplicity, we skip defining the data methods on these classes and present only the creation and instance retrieval logic:

```
// Instantiation using a static block
public class StaffRegister {
    private static final StaffRegister instance;
    static {
        instance = new StaffRegister();
        // Perform additional steps
    }
    private StaffRegister() {
    }
    public static StaffRegister getInstance() {
```

```
      return instance;
   }

   // Data access methods
   ...

}
```

Both the `StaffRegister` class and our previous `HayStorage` class instantiate the singleton at the time the class is loaded. Unlike the `HayStorage` class, though, the `StaffRegister` class instantiates the singleton as part of a `static` initialization block. Conceptually, these two implementations are equivalent, since both create the singleton when the class is loaded, although the `static` initialization block allows additional steps to be taken to set up the singleton after it has been created. It also allows us to handle cases in which the `StaffRegister` constructor throws an exception. Since the singleton is created when the class is loaded, we are able to mark the reference `final`, which guarantees only one instance will be created within our application.

Singletons are used in situations where we need access to a single set of data throughout an application. For example, application configuration data and reusable data caches are commonly implemented using singletons. Singletons may also be used to coordinate access to shared resources, such as coordinating write access to a file.

Applying Lazy Instantiation to Singletons

Another technique is to delay creation of the singleton until the first time the `getInstance()` method is called:

```
// Lazy instantiation
public class VisitorTicketTracker {
   private static VisitorTicketTracker instance;
   private VisitorTicketTracker() {
   }
   public static VisitorTicketTracker getInstance() {
      if(instance == null) {
         instance = new VisitorTicketTracker();   // NOT THREAD-SAFE!
      }
      return instance;
   }

   // Data access methods
   ...

}
```

The `VisitorTicketTracker`, like our singleton classes, declares only `private` constructors, creates a singleton instance, and returns the singleton with a `getInstance()`

method. The `VisitorTicketTracker` class, though, does not create the singleton object when the class is loaded but rather the first time it is requested by a client. Creating a reusable object the first time it is requested is a software design pattern known as *lazy instantiation*. It used often in conjunction with the singleton pattern.

Lazy instantiation reduces memory usage and improves performance when an application starts up. In fact, without lazy instantiation, most operating systems and applications that you run would take significantly longer to load and consume a great deal more memory, perhaps more memory than is even available on your computer. The downside of lazy instantiation is that users may see a noticeable delay the first time a particular type of resource is needed.

For example, you may have seen lazy instantiation in applications that you use to write software and not even noticed it. One such freely available software development tool, Eclipse, often demonstrates a slight delay the first time you open a Java file in an editor window after starting the program. This delay disappears, though, when you open additional Java files. This is an example of lazy instantiation, since Eclipse is only loading the libraries to parse and present Java files the first time a Java file is open.

 Real World Scenario

Singletons in Server Environments

For the purposes of the exam, singletons are always unique. When you get to writing applications that run across multiple computers, the `static` singleton solution starts to require special consideration, as each computer would have its own JVM.

In those situations, you might still use the singleton pattern, although it might be implemented with a database or queue server rather than as a `static` object. However, the discussion of which to employ is beyond the scope of the exam.

Creating Unique Singletons

To truly implement the singleton pattern, we must ensure that only one instance of the singleton is ever created. Marking the constructor `private` is a good first step as it prevents the singleton from being created by other classes, but we also need to ensure that the object is only created once within the singleton class itself. We guaranteed this in the `HayStorage` and `StaffRegister` classes by using the `final` modifier on the `static` reference.

Unfortunately, because we used lazy instantiation in the `VisitorTicketTracker` class, the compiler won't let us assign the `final` modifier to the `static` reference. The implementation of `VisitorTicketTracker`, as shown, is not considered thread-safe in that two threads could call `getInstance()` at the same time, resulting in two objects being created. After both threads finish executing, only one object will be set and used by other threads going forward, but the object that the two initial threads received may not be the same.

Thread safety is the property of an object that guarantees safe execution by multiple threads at the same time. We will discuss thread safety in Chapter 7, but for now we present a simple solution that is compatible with lazy instantiation using the synchronized modifier:

```java
public static synchronized VisitorTicketTracker getInstance() {
    if(instance == null) {
        instance = new VisitorTicketTracker();
    }
    return instance;
}
```

The getInstance() method is now synchronized, which means only one thread will be allowed in the method at a time, ensuring that only one object is created.

 Real World Scenario

Singletons with Double-Checked Locking

The synchronized implementation of getInstance(), while correctly preventing multiple singleton objects from being created, has the problem that every single call to this method will require synchronization. In practice, this can be costly and can impact performance. Synchronization is only needed the first time that the object is created.

The solution is to use double-checked locking, a design pattern in which we first test if synchronization is needed before actually acquiring any locks. The following is an example rewrite of this method using double-checked locking:

```java
private static volatile VisitorTicketTracker instance;
public static VisitorTicketTracker getInstance() {
    if(instance == null) {
        synchronized(VisitorTicketTracker.class) {
            if(instance == null) {
                instance = new VisitorTicketTracker();
            }
        }
    }
    return instance;
}
```

As you may have noticed, we added the volatile modifier to our singleton object. This keyword prevents a subtle case where the compiler tries to optimize the code such that that the object is accessed before it is finished being constructed. For the exam, you are not required to know how volatile works or about any compiler optimizations.

This solution is better than our previous version, as it performs the synchronization step only when the singleton does not exist. If our singleton is accessed thousands of times over many hours or days, this means that only the first few calls would require synchronization, and the rest would not.

Creating Immutable Objects

The next creational pattern we will discuss is the immutable objects pattern.

Problem   How do we create read-only objects that can be shared and used by multiple classes?

Motivation   Sometimes we want to create simple objects that can be shared across multiple classes, but for security reasons we don't want their value to be modified. We could copy the object before sending it to another method, but this creates a large overhead that duplicates the object every time it is passed. Furthermore, if we have multiple threads accessing the same object, we could run into concurrency issues, as you will see in Chapter 7.

Solution   The *immutable object pattern* is a creational pattern based on the idea of creating objects whose state does not change after they are created and can be easily shared across multiple classes. Immutable objects go hand and hand with encapsulation, except that no setter methods exist that modify the object. Since the state of an immutable object never changes, they are inherently thread-safe.

 You've actually been working with immutable objects throughout your OCA studies. You may remember that the String class was called *immutable*. In this section, we'll show you how to define your own immutable classes.

Applying an Immutable Strategy

Although there are a variety of techniques for writing an immutable class, you should be familiar with a common strategy for making a class immutable for the exam:

1. Use a constructor to set all properties of the object.
2. Mark all of the instance variables private and final.
3. Don't define any setter methods.
4. Don't allow referenced mutable objects to be modified or accessed directly.
5. Prevent methods from being overridden.

The first rule defines how we create the immutable object, by passing the information to the constructor, so that all of the data is set upon creation. The second and third rules are straightforward, as they stem from proper encapsulation. If the instance variables are private and final, and there are no setter methods, then there is no direct way to change the property of an object. All references and primitive values contained in the object are set at creation and cannot be modified.

The fourth rule requires a little more explanation. Let's say that you have an immutable Animal object, which contains a reference to a List of the animal's favorite foods, as shown in the following example:

```
import java.util.*

public final class Animal {
    private final List<String> favoriteFoods;

    public Animal(List<String> favoriteFoods) {
        if(favoriteFoods == null) {
            throw new RuntimeException("favoriteFoods is required");
        }
        this.favoriteFoods = new ArrayList<String>(favoriteFoods);
    }

    public List<String> getFavoriteFoods() { // MAKES CLASS MUTABLE!
        return favoriteFoods;
    }
}
```

In order to ensure that the favoriteFoods List is not null, we validate it in the constructor and throw an exception if it is not provided. The problem in this example is that the user has direct access to the List defined in our instance of Animal. Even though they can't change the List object to which it points, they can modify the items in the List, for example, deleting all of the items by calling getFavoriteFoods().clear(). They could also replace, remove, or even sort the List.

The solution, then, is never to return that List reference to the user. More generally stated, you should never share references to a mutable object contained within an immutable object. If the user does need access to the data in the List, either create wrapper methods to iterate over the data or create a one-time copy of the data that is returned to the user and never stored as part of the object. In fact, the Collections API includes the Collections.unmodifiableList() method, which does exactly this. The key here is that none of the methods that you create should modify the mutable object.

Returning to our five rules, the last rule is important because it prevents someone from creating a subclass of your class in which a previously immutable value now appears mutable. For example, they could override a method that modifies a different variable in the subclass, essentially hiding the private variable defined in the parent class. The simplest solution is to mark the class or methods with the final modifier, although this does limit the usage of the class. Another option is to make the constructor private and apply the factory pattern, which we will discuss later in this chapter.

Here is an example of an immutable Animal class:

```java
import java.util.*

public final class Animal {
    private final String species;
    private final int age;
    private final List<String> favoriteFoods;

    public Animal(String species, int age, List<String> favoriteFoods) {
        this.species = species;
        this.age = age;
        if(favoriteFoods == null) {
            throw new RuntimeException("favoriteFoods is required");
        }
        this.favoriteFoods = new ArrayList<String>(favoriteFoods);
    }

    public String getSpecies() {
        return species;
    }

    public int getAge() {
        return age;
    }

    public int getFavoriteFoodsCount() {
        return favoriteFoods.size();
    }

    public String getFavoriteFood(int index) {
        return favoriteFoods.get(index);
    }
}
```

Does this sample follow all five rules? Well, all fields are marked private and final, and the constructor sets them upon object creation. Next, there are no setter methods and the class itself is marked final, so the methods cannot be overridden by a subclass. The class does contain a mutable object, List, but no references to the object are publically available. We provide two methods for retrieving the total number of favorite foods as well as a method to retrieve a food based on an index value. Note that String is given to be immutable, so we don't have to worry about any of the String objects being modified. Therefore, all five rules are preserved and instances of this class are immutable.

Handling Mutable Objects in the Constructors of Immutable Objects

You may notice that we created a new `ArrayList` in the `Animal` constructor. This is absolutely important to prevent the class that initially creates the object from maintaining a reference to the mutable `List` used by `Animal`. Consider if we had just done the following in the constructor:

```
this.favoriteFoods = favoriteFoods;
```

With this change, the caller that creates the object is using the same reference as the immutable object, which means that it has the ability to change the `List`! It is important when creating immutable objects that any mutable input arguments are copied to the instance instead of being used directly.

"Modifying" an Immutable Object

How do we modify immutable objects if they are inherently unmodifiable? The answer is, we can't! Alternatively, we can create new immutable objects that contain all of the same information as the original object plus whatever we wanted to change. This happens every time we combine two strings:

```
String firstName = "Grace";
String fullName = firstName + " Hopper";
```

In this example, the `firstName` is immutable and is not modified when added to the `fullName`, which is also an immutable object. We can also do the same thing with our `Animal` class. Imagine that we want to increase the age of an `Animal` by one. The following creates two `Animal` instances, the second using a copy of the data from the first instance:

```
// Create a new Animal instance
Animal lion = new Animal("lion", 5, Arrays.asList("meat","more meat"));

// Create a new Animal instance using data from the first instance
List<String> favoriteFoods = new ArrayList<String>();
for(int i=0; i<lion.getFavoriteFoodsCount(); i++) {
    favoriteFoods.add(lion.getFavoriteFood(i));
}
Animal updatedLion = new Animal(lion.getSpecies(), lion.getAge()+1,
    favoriteFoods);
```

Since we did not have direct access to the `favoriteFoods` mutable `List`, we had to copy it using the methods available in the immutable class. We could also simplify this by defining a method in `Animal` that returns a copy of the `favoriteFood List`, provided that the caller understands that modifying this copied `List` does not change the original `Animal` object in any way.

> As we stated earlier, you are not currently required to know how to implement the builder design pattern and the factory design pattern, although we recommend that at least you be familiar with them, as it will help you to understand techniques used in later parts of the book.

Using the Builder Pattern

The third creational pattern we will discuss is the builder pattern.

Problem   How do we create an object that requires numerous values to be set at the time the object is instantiated?

Motivation   As our data objects grow in size, the constructor may grow to contain many attributes. For example, in our most recent immutable `Animal` class example, we had three input parameters: `species`, `age`, and `favoriteFoods`. If we want to add five new attributes to the object, we'd have to add five new values in the constructor. Every time we add a parameter, the constructor grows! Users who reference our object would also be required to update their constructor calls each time that the object was modified, resulting in a class that would be difficult to use and maintain. Alternatively, we could add a new constructor each time we add a parameter, but having too many constructors can be quite difficult to manage in practice.

One solution is to use setter methods instead of the constructor to configure the object, but this doesn't work for immutable objects since they can't be modified after creation. For mutable objects, it could also lead to class invariants being temporarily broken. For example, the attributes of the class may be dependent on each other, and setting them one at a time may expose a state where the object is not properly configured.

 Real World Scenario

Introducing Anti-Patterns

The problem of a constructor growing too large actually has a name, referred to as the telescoping constructor anti-pattern. An *anti-pattern* is a common solution to a reoccurring problem that tends to lead to unmanageable or difficult-to-use code. Anti-patterns often appear in complex systems as time goes on, when developers implement a series of successive changes without considering the long-term effects of their actions.

For example, with the telescoping constructor anti-pattern, the class may start off with only two parameters in the constructor. Another developer may come in and added another parameter, thinking "It's only one more!" A third developer may update the class and add a fourth parameter, and so on, until the class has 50 or 60 parameters in the constructor and is in desperate need of rewriting, also called *refactoring*.

The reason why this is an anti-pattern is that each time the class is modified, the developer is only doing minor damage to the class. However, it eventually grows out of control. If the class is used in a number of important places throughout the system, refactoring it may become difficult—in some cases nearly impossible. Design patterns are often written to help prevent anti-patterns from forming.

Solution   The *builder pattern* is a creational pattern in which parameters are passed to a builder object, often through method chaining, and an object is generated with a final build call. It is often used with immutable objects, since immutable objects do not have setter methods and must be created with all of their parameters set, although it can be used with mutable objects as well.

The following is an AnimalBuilder class, which uses our immutable Animal class:

```java
import java.util.*;

public class AnimalBuilder {
    private String species;
    private int age;
    private List<String> favoriteFoods;

    public AnimalBuilder setAge(int age) {
        this.age = age;
        return this;
    }

    public AnimalBuilder setSpecies(String species) {
        this.species = species;
        return this;
    }

    public AnimalBuilder setFavoriteFoods(List<String> favoriteFoods) {
        this.favoriteFoods = favoriteFoods;
        return this;
    }

    public Animal build() {
```

```
      return new Animal(species,age,favoriteFoods);
   }
}
```

At first glance, this code might look a lot like the immutable Animal class, so much so that it seems like we redefined it exactly. But there are some important differences. First, this class is mutable, whereas the Animal class is immutable. We can modify this class as we build it, and the result of the build method will be an immutable object. In some ways, using the builder pattern is analogous to taking a mutable object and making it read-only.

The next thing that you might notice is that all of the setter methods return an instance of the builder object this. Builder methods are commonly chained together, often callable in any order. For example, the following two code snippets are both valid uses of this builder:

```
AnimalBuilder duckBuilder = new AnimalBuilder();
duckBuilder
    .setAge(4)
    .setFavoriteFoods(Arrays.asList("grass","fish")).setSpecies("duck");
Animal duck = duckBuilder.build();

Animal flamingo = new AnimalBuilder()
    .setFavoriteFoods(Arrays.asList("algae","insects"))
    .setSpecies("flamingo").build();
```

Notice that in the second Animal example, we never even save an instance to our builder object! Oftentimes, builder objects are used once and then discarded. Finally, we create our target object build method, usually named build(), allowing it to interact with the Animal's constructor directly.

You might also notice that we never explicitly set the age in the second example. In this scenario, age may not be required, although we could certainly write our build() method to throw an exception if certain required fields are not set. Alternatively, the build() method may also set default values for anything the user failed to specify on the builder object.

The primary advantage of the builder pattern is that, over time, this approach leads to far more maintainable code. If a new optional field is added to the Animal class, then our code that creates objects using the AnimalBuilder class will not need to be changed. In practice, a builder object often supports dozens of parameters, only a handful of which may be set by users of the builder at a given time.

Builder Pattern and Tightly Coupled Code

As stated, the AnimalBuilder class looks a lot like our target Animal class. Furthermore, it requires direct knowledge of how to use the Animal constructor, mentioned earlier, which could grow to 50 or 60 parameters over time. In this manner, the builder class and target class are considered tightly coupled. *Tight coupling* is the practice of developing coupled classes that are highly dependent, such that a minor change in one class may greatly impact the other class. Alternatively, *loose coupling* is the practice of developing coupled classes with minimum dependencies on one another.

Although loose coupling is preferred in practice, tight coupling is required here so that callers of the `AnimalBuilder` class never have to use the `Animal` class constructor directly, 60 parameters and all.

In practice, a builder class is often packaged alongside its target class, either as a `static` inner class within the target class or within the same Java package. One advantage of packing them together is that if one is changed, then the other can be quickly updated. Another advantage is that writers of the target class can then choose to make the constructor a `private` or default package, forcing the user to rely on the builder object to obtain instances of the target class. For example, if the `Animal` class did not have a `public` constructor, programs calling it from other packages would be required to use the `AnimalBuilder` class to create instances of `Animal`.

Creating Objects with the Factory Pattern

The final creational pattern we will discuss is the factory pattern.

Problem   How do we write code that creates objects in which the precise type of the object may not be known until runtime?

Motivation   As you saw with the builder pattern, object creation can be quite complex. We'd like some way of encapsulating object creation to deal with the complexity of object creation, including selecting which subclass to use, as well as loosely coupling the underlying creation implementation.

Solution   The *factory pattern*, sometimes referred to as the factory method pattern, is a creational pattern based on the idea of using a factory class to produce instances of objects based on a set of input parameters. It is similar to the builder pattern, although it is focused on supporting class polymorphism.

Factory patterns are often, although not always, implemented using `static` methods that return objects and do not require a pointer to an instance of the factory class. It is also a good coding practice to postfix the class name with the word `Factory`, such as in `AnimalFactory`, `ZooFactory`, and so forth.

Let's try an example of the factory pattern involving zoo animals and food. Imagine a zookeeper who needs to feed a variety of animals in the zoo different types of foods. Some animals eat specialized food, while others share the same type food. Furthermore, a quantity value is associated with each distribution of food to an animal. We illustrate this example with the following class definitions:

```java
public abstract class Food {
    private int quantity;
    public Food(int quantity) {
```

```
        this.quantity = quantity;
    }
    public int getQuantity() {
        return quantity;
    }
    public abstract void consumed();
}

public class Hay extends Food {
    public Hay(int quantity) {
        super(quantity);
    }
    public void consumed() {
        System.out.println("Hay eaten: "+getQuantity());
    }
}

public class Pellets extends Food {
    public Pellets(int quantity) {
        super(quantity);
    }
    public void consumed() {
        System.out.println("Pellets eaten: "+getQuantity());
    }
}

public class Fish extends Food {
    public Fish(int quantity) {
        super(quantity);
    }
    public void consumed() {
        System.out.println("Fish eaten: "+getQuantity());
    }
}
```

Now, let's define a FoodFactory using the factory pattern that returns a food type based on some set of inputs, as shown in the following code and in Figure 2.9. For simplicity, we will use a java.lang.String representing the animal name as input, although you could certainly expand the data model using a class type or set of input parameters.

FIGURE 2.9   FoodFactory data model

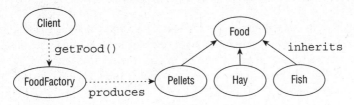

```
public class FoodFactory {
    public static Food getFood(String animalName) {
        switch(animalName) {
            case "zebra": return new Hay(100);
            case "rabbit": return new Pellets(5);
            case "goat": return new Pellets(30);
            case "polar bear": return new Fish(10);
        }

        // Good practice to throw an exception if no matching subclass could be found
        throw new UnsupportedOperationException("Unsupported animal: "+animalName);
    }
}
public class ZooKeeper {
    public static void main(String[] args) {
        final Food food = FoodFactory.getFood("polar bear");
        food.consumed();
    }
}
```

Depending on the value of animalName, we return different types of food for use in our factory. The factory pattern gives us a number of features. First of all, different animals can share the same food, such as goat and rabbit both eating pellets but with varying quantities. Next, notice in our ZooKeeper method that we don't care about the particular type of food that we get, as long as it implements the Food interface. This loose coupling of ZooKeeper and Food allows us to change the rules in the FoodFactory at a later date without requiring any code changes to our ZooKeeper class. Of course, the developer could cast the object to a particular subclass of Food after it is returned from the FoodFactory, although that practice is generally discouraged when using a factory pattern as it creates a tightly coupled solution.

Factory Pattern and Default Class Constructors

You may notice that in this example all of the Food class and subclass constructors are marked public. We obviously could not mark the constructors private, as this would prevent the FoodFactory class from creating any instances of Food classes. We could also not mark them protected, since the FoodFactory class is not a subclass of any of the Food classes, nor should it be.

The only problem with marking them public is that any class could bypass our factory pattern and create instances of the Food classes directly. If we wanted to tighten our access control, we could have declared these constructors with default or package-level access in which there is no modifier.

The advantage of using default access is that it forces any class outside the package into using the FoodFactory class to create an instance of a Food object, thereby preventing it from instantiating a Food object directly. The only limitation is that our FoodFactory and all of our Food classes must be set in the same Java package. If a Food class exists in a different package than FoodFactory, and we want to use FoodFactory to create an instance of it, then it must provide a public method.

As an alternative to using a factory pattern, a developer could implement a set of Animal classes and define a getFood() method in each class that returns a Food object. The limitation in this solution is that it tightly couples what an animal is and what food an animal eats. For example, if a particular food were no longer available, all of the many classes that use that particular food would need to be changed. By using a factory pattern, we create loosely coupled code that is more resistant to changes in animal feeding behaviors.

Design Patterns: Elements of Reusable Object-Oriented Software

If you have enjoyed this chapter on software design patterns, we recommend that you read the book _Design Patterns_ (Addison-Wesley Professional, 1994), whose authors Erich Gamma, Richard Helm, Ralph Johnson, and John Vlissides are often referred to humorously as the "Gang of Four."

Design Patterns is considered one of the most influential software engineering books ever written, and it established the foundation of many of the design patterns that we use today. Although we have reviewed everything you need to know to answer questions about design patterns on the OCP exam, the value of the knowledge offered in _Design Patterns_ on building better and more powerful software applications cannot be overstated.

Summary

One of the primary goals of this chapter was to teach you how to write better code. We demonstrated techniques for designing class structures that scale naturally over time, integrate well with other applications, and are easy for other developers to read and understand.

We started off with a brief review of interfaces from your OCA studies showing how to declare, implement, and extend them. We then moved on to functional programming and reviewed the various syntax options available for defining functional interfaces and writing lambda expressions. Given the prevalence of lambda expressions throughout Java 8, you absolutely need to practice writing and using lambda expressions before taking the exam. We concluded the discussion with a review of the generics-based Predicate interface and showed how it can be used in place of your own functional interface. We will return to lambdas and streams in Chapter 3 and Chapter 4 in much greater detail.

This chapter introduced the concept of polymorphism, which is central to the Java language, and showed how objects can be accessed in a variety of forms. Make sure that you understand when casts are needed for accessing objects, and be able to spot the difference between compile-time and runtime cast problems.

In the design principles section, we taught you how to encapsulate your classes in Java properly, allowing you to enforce class invariants in your data model. We then described the is-a and has-a principles and showed how you can apply them to your data model. Finally, we introduced the technique of creating class structures using object composition that rely on the has-a principle as an alternative to inheritance.

We completed this chapter by explaining what a design pattern is and presenting you with four well-known design patterns. Design patterns provide you with a way to solve a problem that you encounter using solutions that other developers have already built and generalized. The singleton pattern is excellent for managing a single shared instance of an object within an application. The immutable object pattern is useful for creating read-only objects that cannot be modified by other classes. The builder pattern solves the problem of how to create complex objects cleanly, and it is often used in conjunction with the immutable object pattern. Finally, the factory pattern is useful for creating various objects without exposing the underlying constructors and complex rules for selecting a particular object subtype.

Exam Essentials

Be able to write code that declares, implements, and/or extends interfaces. An interface is like an abstract class that defines a set of `public` abstract methods, which classes implementing the interface must provide. A class may implement multiple interfaces as well as extend classes that implement interfaces, allowing for limited multiple inheritance in Java. Interfaces may extend other interfaces, although they may not extend a class and vice versa. Interfaces may also contain `public static final` constant values, `public static` methods, and `public default` methods.

Know how to create and recognize a functional interface.   A functional interface is one that has exactly one abstract method. It is the primary manner in which lambda expressions are passed between methods. Java includes a `Predicate` interface for testing a generic type and returning a `boolean` expression.

Be able to write valid lambda expressions.   A lambda expression is like an anonymous method that can be passed to a method, relying on deferred execution to process the expression at a later time. It has various syntax options, both long and short. Lambda expressions are used throughout Java 8 and in numerous questions on the exam.

Understand polymorphism.   An object in Java may take on a variety of forms, in part depending on the reference used to access the object. The type of the object determines which properties exist within the object in memory, whereas the type of the reference to the object determines which methods and variables are accessible to the Java program. An instance can be automatically cast to a superclass or interface reference without an explicit cast. Alternatively, an explicit cast is required if the reference is being narrowed to a subclass of the object. The Java compiler doesn't permit casting to unrelated types. Finally, you should be able to distinguish between compile-time casting errors and those that will not occur until runtime, throwing a `ClassCastException`.

Understand the importance of design principles and design patterns.   A design principle is an established idea or best practice that facilitates the software design process. A design pattern is an established general solution to a commonly occurring software development problem.

Know how to implement encapsulation.   Encapsulation is based on the idea of combining fields and methods in a class such that the methods operate on the data, as opposed to users of the class accessing the fields directly. It can be used to prevent users from creating object states that violate class invariants. In Java, it is often implemented with JavaBeans, using the `private` access modifier on instance variables and `public` getter and setter methods.

Be able to apply the is-a and has-a tests.   The is-a test is used to test whether an object is of a particular type, and it is used for both classes and interfaces. The has-a test is used to determine whether an object contains a reference to another object as an instance property.

Be able to apply object composition and distinguish it from inheritance.   Object composition is the idea of creating a class by connecting other classes as members using the has-a principle. Inheritance is the idea of creating a class that inherits all of its reusable methods and objects from a parent class. Both are used to create complex data models, each with its own advantages and disadvantages.

Be able to apply creational patterns including the singleton pattern and the immutable object pattern.   The singleton and immutable object patterns are both types of creational patterns, which are design patterns that facilitate the creation of objects with an application. The singleton pattern solves the problem of how to create a single instance of an object in memory that multiple classes can share by centralizing the object-creation mechanisms. The immutable object pattern is used to create read-only objects that cannot be modified by other classes. Although immutable objects cannot be modified, they can be copied to new immutable objects with the updated information.

Review Questions

1. Which of the following statements about design principles and design patterns are true? (Choose all that apply.)

    A. A design principle is focused on solving a specific commonly occurring problem.

    B. Design principles and design patterns are the same thing.

    C. Design principles are often applied throughout an application, whereas design patterns are applied to solve specific problems.

    D. Design patterns can only be applied to static classes.

    E. Design principles and design patterns tend to produce code that is easier to maintain and easier for other developers to read.

2. What is the result of the following code?

```
1: public interface CanClimb {
2:     public abstract void climb();
3: }
4: public interface CanClimbTrees extends CanClimb {}
5: public abstract class Chipmunk implements CanClimbTrees {
6:     public abstract void chew();
7: }
8: public class EasternChipmunk extends Chipmunk {
9:     public void chew() { System.out.println("Eastern Chipmunk is Chewing"); }
10: }
```

    A. It compiles and runs without issue.

    B. The code will not compile because of line 2.

    C. The code will not compile because of line 4.

    D. The code will not compile because of line 5.

    E. The code will not compile because of line 8.

    F. It compiles but throws an exception at runtime.

3. Which of the following are valid functional interfaces? (Choose all that apply.)

```
public interface Climb {
    public int climb();
}
public abstract class Swim {
    public abstract Object swim(double speed, int duration);
}
public interface ArcticMountainClimb extends MountainClimb {
    public default int getSpeed();
```

```
    }
        public interface MountainClimb extends Climb {}
```

A. Climb

B. Swim

C. ArcticMountainClimb

D. MountainClimb

E. None of these are valid functional interfaces.

4. Which of the following are valid lambda expressions? (Choose all that apply.)

   A. () -> ""

   B. x,y -> x+y

   C. (Coyote y) -> return 0;

   D. (Camel c) -> {return;}

   E. Wolf w -> 39

   F. () ->

   G. (Animal z, m) -> a

5. What are some of the properties of using the singleton pattern? (Choose all that apply.)

   A. Singleton object can be replaced with encapsulated setter method.

   B. Requires constructor of singleton class to be private.

   C. Singleton object must be named instance.

   D. Singleton object may be private or protected.

   E. Ensures that there is only one instance of an object in memory.

   F. Requires a public static method to retrieve the instance of the singleton.

6. What is the result of the following class?

```
import java.util.function.*;
public class Panda {
    int age;
    public static void main(String[] args) {
        Panda p1 = new Panda();
        p1.age = 1;
        check(p1, p -> p.age < 5);  // h1
    }
    private static void check(Panda panda, Predicate<Panda> pred) { // h2
        String result = pred.test(panda) ? "match": "not match";  // h3
        System.out.print(result);
} }
```

A. match

B. not match

C. Compiler error on line h1.

D. Compiler error on line h2.

E. Compile error on line h3.

F. A runtime exception is thrown.

7. What changes need to be made to make the following immutable object pattern correct? (Choose all that apply.)

```java
import java.util.List;
public class Seal {
    String name;
    private final List<Seal> friends;
    public Seal(String name, List<Seal> friends) {
        this.name = name;
        this.friends = friends;
    }
    public String getName() { return name; }
    public List<Seal> getFriends() { return friends; }
}
```

A. None; the immutable object pattern is properly implemented.

B. Have Seal implement the Immutable interface.

C. Mark name final and private.

D. Add setters for name and List<Seal> friends.

E. Replace the getFriends() method with methods that do not give the caller direct access to the List<Seal> friends.

F. Change the type of List<Seal> to List<Object>.

G. Make a copy of the List<Seal> friends in the constructor.

H. Mark the Seal class final.

8. Which of the following are true of interfaces? (Choose all that apply.)

A. They can extend other classes.

B. They cannot be extended.

C. They enable classes to have multiple inheritance.

D. They can only contain abstract methods.

E. They can be declared final.

F. All members of an interface are public.

9. What changes need to be made to make the following singleton pattern correct? (Choose all that apply.)

```
public class CheetahManager {
    public static CheetahManager cheetahManager;
    private CheetahManager() {}
    public static CheetahManager getCheetahManager() {
        if(cheetahManager == null) {
            cheetahManager = new CheetahManager();
        }
        return cheetahManager;
    }
}
```

   A. None; the singleton pattern is properly implemented.
   B. Rename cheetahManager to instance.
   C. Rename getCheetahManager() to getInstance().
   D. Change the access modifier of cheetahManager from public to private.
   E. Mark cheetahManager final.
   F. Add synchronized to getCheetahManager().

10. What is the result of the following code?

```
1: public interface CanWalk {
2:     default void walk() { System.out.println("Walking"); }
3: }
4: public interface CanRun {
5:     public default void walk() { System.out.println("Walking"); }
6:     public abstract void run();
7: }
8: public interface CanSprint extends CanWalk, CanRun {
9:     void sprint();
10: }
```

   A. The code compiles without issue.
   B. The code will not compile because of line 5.
   C. The code will not compile because of line 6.
   D. The code will not compile because of line 8.
   E. The code will not compile because of line 9.

11. Which lambda can replace the MySecret class to return the same value? (Choose all that apply.)

```
public interface Secret {
    String magic(double d);
}

public class MySecret implements Secret {
    public String magic(double d) {
        return "Poof";
    }
}
```

A. caller((e) -> "Poof");
B. caller((e) -> {"Poof"});
C. caller((e) -> { String e = ""; "Poof" });
D. caller((e) -> { String e = ""; return "Poof"; });
E. caller((e) -> { String e = ""; return "Poof" });
F. caller((e) -> { String f = ""; return "Poof"; });

12. What is the result of the following code?

```
public interface Climb {
    boolean isTooHigh(int height, int limit);
}
public class Climber {
    public static void main(String[] args) {
        check((h, l) -> h.toString(), 5);  // x1
    }
    private static void check(Climb climb, int height) {
        if (climb.isTooHigh(height, 10))  // x2
            System.out.println("too high");
        else System.out.println("ok");
    } }
```

A. ok
B. too high
C. Compiler error on line x1.
D. Compiler error on line x2.
E. Compiler error on a different line.
F. A runtime exception is thrown.

13. Which of the following are properties of classes that define immutable objects? (Choose all that apply.)

    A. They don't define any getter methods.

    B. All of the instance variables marked `private` and `final`.

    C. They don't define any setter methods.

    D. They mark all instance variables `static`.

    E. They prevent methods from being overridden.

    F. All getter methods are marked `synchronized`.

14. Which of the following statements can be inserted in the blank line so that the code will compile successfully? (Choose all that apply.)

```
public interface CanHop {}
public class Frog implements CanHop {
    public static void main(String[] args) {
        _____ frog = new TurtleFrog();
    }
}
public class BrazilianHornedFrog extends Frog {}
public class TurtleFrog extends Frog {}
```

    A. `Frog`

    B. `TurtleFrog`

    C. `BrazilianHornedFrog`

    D. `CanHop`

    E. `Object`

    F. `Long`

15. Which of the following statements about polymorphism are true? (Choose all that apply.)

    A. A reference to an object may be cast to a subclass of the object without an explicit cast.

    B. If a method takes a class that is the superclass of three different object references, then any of those objects may be passed as a parameter to the method.

    C. A reference to an object may be cast to a superclass of the object without an explicit cast.

    D. All cast exceptions can be detected at compile time.

    E. By defining a `public` instance method in the superclass, you guarantee that the specific method will be called in the parent class at runtime.

16. Choose the correct statement about the following code:

```
1: public interface Herbivore {
2:    int amount = 10;
3:    public static void eatGrass();
```

```
4:     public int chew() {
5:         return 13;
6:     }
7: }
```

A. It compiles and runs without issue.

B. The code will not compile because of line 2.

C. The code will not compile because of line 3.

D. The code will not compile because of line 4.

E. The code will not compile because of lines 2 and 3.

F. The code will not compile because of lines 3 and 4.

17. Which of the following are properties of classes that are properly encapsulated as a JavaBean? (Choose all that apply.)

A. All instance variables are marked `final`.

B. `boolean` instance variables are accessed with `is` or get.

C. All instance variables are marked `private`.

D. They implement the `JavaBean` interface.

E. Variables are created using lazy instantiation.

F. The first letter of the any getter/setter, after the get, set, or is prefix, must be uppercase.

18. Which of the following statements about inheritance and object composition are correct? (Choose all that apply.)

A. Inheritance supports access to `protected` variables.

B. Object composition tends to promote greater code reuse than inheritance.

C. Inheritance relies on the has-a principle.

D. Object composition supports method overriding at runtime.

E. Object composition requires a class variable to be declared `public` or accessible from a `public` method to be used by a class in a different package.

F. Object composition is always preferred to inheritance.

19. Which three scenarios would best benefit from using a singleton pattern? (Choose all three.)

A. Create read-only objects that are thread-safe.

B. Manage a reusable cache of objects.

C. Ensure that all objects are lazily instantiated.

D. Manage write access to a log file.

E. Provide central access to application configuration data.

F. Allow multiple instances of a `static` object to be managed in memory.

20. Choose the correct statement about the following code:

```
1: public interface CanFly {
2:    void fly();
3: }
4: interface HasWings {
5:        public abstract Object getWingSpan();
6: }
7: abstract class Falcon implements CanFly, HasWings {
8: }
```

A. It compiles without issue.

B. The code will not compile because of line 2.

C. The code will not compile because of line 4.

D. The code will not compile because of line 5.

E. The code will not compile because of lines 2 and 5.

F. The code will not compile because the class Falcon doesn't implement the interface methods.

Chapter 3

Generics and Collections

THE OCP EXAM TOPICS COVERED IN THIS CHAPTER INCLUDE THE FOLLOWING:

✓ **Generics and Collections**

- Create and use a generic class
- Create and use ArrayList, TreeSet, TreeMap and ArrayDeque objects
- Use java.util.Comparator and java.lang.Comparable interfaces
- Iterate using forEach methods on Streams and List
- Use method references with Streams

✓ **Advanced Java Class Design**

- Create and use lambda expressions

✓ **Generics and Collections**

- Filter a collection using lambda expressions

✓ **Java Stream API**

- Use of merge() and flatMap() methods of the Stream API

You learned about `ArrayList` on the OCA. This chapter covers the rest of the Java Collections Framework that you need to know for the exam. This includes other lists, sets, queues, and maps. The thread-safe collection types will be discussed in Chapter 7, "Concurrency."

We will also discuss how to create your own classes and methods that use generics so that the same class can be used with many types. You'll learn how to customize searching and sorting using `Comparable` and `Comparator`. We will end with some methods that use functional interfaces, such as `forEach()` and `merge()`.

In the next chapter, we will cover the Stream API. Note that the exam objectives are sloppy and sometimes use "stream" to include "stream" and "lambda." The `merge()` method is on `Map` and not really a stream API.

Reviewing OCA Collections

The *Java Collections Framework* includes classes that implement `List`, `Map`, `Queue`, and `Set`. On the OCA, you saw one such class. The class `ArrayList` implements the interface `List`. You will learn about more of these later in this chapter. You also saw arrays on the OCA, such as `int[]`. An array is not part of the Collections Framework. Since sorting and searching are similar between lists and arrays, both are covered on the exam. Furthermore, since the OCP is cumulative, you are still expected to know how to work with arrays from the OCA.

In the following sections, we will review arrays, `ArrayLists`, wrapper classes, autoboxing, the diamond operator, searching, and sorting.

Array and *ArrayList*

An *ArrayList* is an object that contains other objects. An `ArrayList` cannot contain primitives. An array is a built-in data structure that contains other objects or primitives. The following code reviews how to use an array and `ArrayList`:

```
List<String> list = new ArrayList<>();          // empty list
list.add("Fluffy");                             // [Fluffy]
list.add("Webby");                              // [Fluffy, Webby]

String[] array = new String[list.size()];       // empty array
```

```
array[0] = list.get(1);                    // [Webby]
array[1] = list.get(0);                    // [Webby, Fluffy]
for (int i = 0; i < array.length; i++)
   System.out.print(array[i] + "-");
```

The output is Webby-Fluffy-. This code reminds us that Java counts starting with 0 for indexes. It also reminds us that we access elements in ArrayLists with get(), and we check the number of elements with size(). By contrast, we access elements in arrays using brackets and check the number of elements with the length variable.

Now, let's review the link created when converting between an array and ArrayList.

```
4:    String[] array = { "gerbil", "mouse" };        // [gerbil, mouse]
5:    List<String> list = Arrays.asList(array);       // returns fixed size list
6:    list.set(1, "test");                            // [gerbil, test]
7:    array[0] = "new";                               // [new, test]
8:    String[] array2 = (String[]) list.toArray();    // [new, test]
9:    list.remove(1);                                 // throws UnsupportedOperationException
```

Line 5 converts an array to a List. It happens to be an implementation of List that is not an ArrayList. Remember that a List is like a resizable array. It makes sense to convert an array to a List. It doesn't make sense to convert an array to a Set. You still can do so, however, although it takes an extra step. You'd have to convert the array to a List and then the List to a Set. Lines 6 and 7 show that you can change the elements in either the array or the List. Changes are reflected in both, since they are backed by the same data.

Implementations of List are allowed to add their own behavior. The implementation used when calling asList() has the added feature of not being resizable but honoring all of the other methods in the interface. Line 8 converts the List back to an array. Finally, line 9 shows that list is not resizable because it is backed by the underlying array.

Searching and Sorting

Our last topic to review is searching and sorting. Do you remember why this works the way it does?

```
11:    int[] numbers = {6,9,1,8};
12:    Arrays.sort(numbers);                                            // [1,6,8,9]
13:    System.out.println(Arrays.binarySearch(numbers, 6)); // 1
14:    System.out.println(Arrays.binarySearch(numbers, 3)); // -2
```

Line 12 sorts the array because binary search assumes the input is sorted. Line 13 prints the index at which a match is found. Line 14 prints one less than the negated index of where the requested value would need to be inserted. The number 3 would need to be inserted at index 1 (after the number 1 but before the number 6). Negating that gives us -1 and subtracting 1 gives us -2.

Let's try that again with a List:

```
15:   List<Integer> list = Arrays.asList(9,7,5,3);
16:   Collections.sort(list);   // [3, 5, 7, 9]
17:   System.out.println(Collections.binarySearch(list, 3)); // 0
18:   System.out.println(Collections.binarySearch(list, 2)); // -1
```

Similarly, we needed to sort first. Line 17 prints the index of a match. For line 18, we would need to insert 2 at index 0, since it is smaller than any of the numbers in the list. Negating 0 is still 0 and subtracting 1 gives us -1.

> We call sort() and binarySearch() on Collections rather than Collection. In the past, Collection could not have concrete methods because it is an interface. Some were added in Java 8. We will explore these in Chapter 4, "Functional Programming." Keep this change in mind if you practice with any older mock exams.

You will see searching and sorting again later in this chapter, after you learn about the Comparable interface.

Wrapper Classes and Autoboxing

As a brief review, each primitive has a corresponding wrapper class, as shown in Table 3.1. *Autoboxing* automatically converts a primitive to the corresponding wrapper classes when needed if the generic type is specified in the declaration. Unsurprisingly, *unboxing* automatically converts a wrapper class back to a primitive.

TABLE 3.1   Wrapper classes

Primitive type	Wrapper class	Example of initializing
boolean	Boolean	new Boolean(true)
byte	Byte	new Byte((byte) 1)
short	Short	new Short((short) 1)
int	Integer	new Integer(1)

Primitive type	Wrapper class	Example of initializing
long	Long	new Long(1)
float	Float	new Float(1.0)
double	Double	new Double(1.0)
char	Character	new Character('c')

Let's try an example, which also points out the only trick in this space. What do you think this code does?

```
3:    List<Integer> numbers = new ArrayList<Integer>();
4:    numbers.add(1);
5:    numbers.add(new Integer(3));
6:    numbers.add(new Integer(5));
7:    numbers.remove(1);
8:    numbers.remove(new Integer(5));
9:    System.out.println(numbers);
```

The answer is it leaves just [1]. Let's walk through why that is. On lines 4 through 6, we add three Integer objects to numbers. The one on line 4 relies on autoboxing to do so, but it gets added just fine. At this point, numbers contains [1, 3, 5].

Line 7 contains the trick. The remove() method is overloaded. One signature takes an int as the index of the element to remove. The other takes an Object that should be removed. On line 7, Java sees a matching signature for int, so it doesn't need to autobox the call to the method. Now numbers contains [1, 5]. Line 8 calls the other remove() method, and it removes the matching object, which leaves us with just [1].

Java also converts the wrapper classes to primitives via unboxing:

```
int num = numbers.get(0);
```

The Diamond Operator

Java has come a long way. Before Java 5 came out, you had to write code like the following and hope that programmers remembered that you wanted only String objects in there:

```
List names = new ArrayList();
```

This required a bit of mind reading. You had no way of knowing names were expected to contain String objects rather than StringBuilder or something else. In Java 5, you could actually document this assumption in code through a new feature called *generics*! The compiler even helps enforce this assumption for you:

```
List<String> names = new ArrayList<String>();
```

When Java 7 came out, its developers made it even better. The previous statement required you to type six extra characters (`String`). Java 7 lets you shorten it a bit:

```
List<String> names = new ArrayList<>();
```

The shortened form uses the diamond operator. It is called that because <> looks like a diamond if you tilt your head to the side.

You may laugh a bit about saving six characters. The diamond operator becomes more helpful if you have more complex code. By the end of the chapter, you'll know how to write code like this:

```
HashMap<String, HashMap<String, String>> map1 =
    new HashMap<String, HashMap<String, String>>();

HashMap<String, HashMap<String, String>> map2 = new HashMap<>();
```

Both of these statements contain a nested map. The second line is a lot easier to read because it doesn't contain the redundant type information. In case you are wondering, this nested map arrangement might be useful if you have a number of data caches that you want to query by key.

The diamond operator isn't limited to one-line declarations. In this example, you can see it used with an instance variable and a local variable:

```
import java.util.*;
class Doggies {
    List<String> names;
    Doggies() {
        names = new ArrayList<>();        // matches instance variable declaration
    }
    public void copyNames() {
        ArrayList<String> copyOfNames;
        copyOfNames = new ArrayList<>(); // matches local variable declaration
    } }
```

In the case of the constructor, use your judgment as to whether the diamond operator makes the code easier to read. It is a good bit away from the declaration at that point. For the exam, you just have to know that this is legal.

Working with Generics

Why do we need generics? Well, remember when we said that we had to hope the caller didn't put something in the list that we didn't expect? The following does just that:

```
14:    static void printNames(List list) {
15:        for (int i = 0; i < list.size(); i++) {
16:            String name = (String) list.get(i);    // class cast exception here
17:            System.out.println(name);
18:        }
19:    }
20:    public static void main(String[] args) {
21:        List names = new ArrayList();
22:        names.add(new StringBuilder("Webby"));
23:        printNames(names);
24:    }
```

This code throws a ClassCastException. Line 22 adds a StringBuilder to list. This is legal because a non-generic list can contain anything. However, line 16 is written to expect a specific class to be in there. It casts to a String, reflecting this assumption. Since the assumption is incorrect, the code throws a ClassCastException that java.lang .StringBuilder cannot be cast to java.lang.String.

Generics fix this by allowing you to write and use parameterized types. You specify that you want an ArrayList of String objects. Now the compiler has enough information to prevent you from causing this problem in the first place:

```
List<String> names = new ArrayList<String>();
names.add(new StringBuilder("Webby"));           // DOES NOT COMPILE
```

Getting a compiler error is good. You'll know right away that something is wrong rather than hoping to discover it later.

Generic Classes

You can introduce generics into your own classes. The syntax for introducing a generic is to declare a *formal type parameter* in angle brackets. For example, the following class named Crate has a generic type variable declared after the name of the class:

```
public class Crate<T> {
    private T contents;
    public T emptyCrate() {
        return contents;
    }

    public void packCrate(T contents) {
        this.contents = contents;
    }
}
```

The generic type T is available anywhere within the Crate class. When you instantiate the class, you tell the compiler what T should be for that particular instance.

Naming Conventions for Generics

A type parameter can be named anything you want. The convention is to use single uppercase letters to make it obvious that they aren't real class names. The following are common letters to use:

- E for an element
- K for a map key
- V for a map value
- N for a number
- T for a generic data type
- S, U, V, and so forth for multiple generic types

For example, suppose an Elephant class exists, and we are moving our elephant to a new and larger enclosure in our zoo. (The San Diego Zoo did this in 2009. It was interesting seeing the large metal crate.)

```
Elephant elephant = new Elephant();
Crate<Elephant> crateForElephant = new Crate<>();
crateForElephant.packCrate(elephant);
Elephant inNewHome = crateForElephant.emptyCrate();
```

To be fair, we didn't pack the crate so much as the elephant walked into it. However, you can see that the Crate class is able to deal with an Elephant without knowing anything about it.

This probably doesn't seem particularly impressive yet. We could have just typed in Elephant instead of T when coding Crate. What if we wanted to create a Crate for another animal?

```
Crate<Zebra> crateForZebra = new Crate<>();
```

Now we couldn't have simply hard-coded Elephant in the Crate class, since a Zebra is not an Elephant. However, we could have created an Animal superclass or interface and used that in Crate.

Generic classes become useful when the classes used as the type parameter can have absolutely nothing to do with each other. For example, we need to ship our 120-pound robot to another city:

```
Robot joeBot = new Robot();
Crate<Robot> robotCrate = new Crate<>();
robotCrate.packCrate(joeBot);

// ship to St. Louis
Robot atDestination = robotCrate.emptyCrate();
```

Now it is starting to get interesting. The Crate class works with any type of class. Before generics, we would have needed Crate to use the Object class for its instance variable, which would have put the burden on the caller of needing to cast the object it receives on emptying the crate.

In addition to Crate not needing to know about the objects that go into it, those objects don't need to know about Crate either. We aren't requiring the objects to implement an interface named Crateable or the like. A class can be put in the Crate without any changes at all.

Don't worry if you can't think of a use for generic classes of your own. Unless you are writing a library for others to reuse, generics hardly show up in the class definitions you write. They do show up frequently in the code you call, such as the Java Collections Framework.

Generic classes aren't limited to having a single type parameter. This class shows two generic parameters:

```
public class SizeLimitedCrate<T, U> {
   private T contents;
   private U sizeLimit;
   public SizeLimitedCrate(T contents, U sizeLimit) {
      this.contents = contents;
      this.sizeLimit = sizeLimit;
} }
```

T represents the type that we are putting in the crate. U represents the unit that we are using to measure the maximum size for the crate. To use this generic class, we can write the following:

```
Elephant elephant = new Elephant();
Integer numPounds = 15_000;
SizeLimitedCrate<Elephant, Integer> c1 = new SizeLimitedCrate<>(elephant,
numPounds);
```

Here we specify that the type is Elephant and the unit is Integer. We also throw in a reminder that numeric literals have been able to contain underscores since Java 7.

Type Erasure

Specifying a generic type allows the compiler to enforce proper use of the generic type. For example, specifying the generic type of Crate as Robot is like replacing the T in the Crate class with Robot. However, this is just for compile time.

Behind the scenes, the compiler replaces all references to T in Crate with Object. In other words, after the code compiles, your generics are actually just Object types. The Crate class looks like the following:

```
public class Crate {
    private Object contents;
    public Object emptyCrate() {
        return contents;
    }
    public void packCrate(Object contents) {
        this.contents = contents;
    }
}
```

This means there is only one class file. There aren't different copies for different parameterized types. (Some other languages work that way.)

This process of removing the generics syntax from your code is referred to as *type erasure*. Type erasure allows your code to be compatible with older versions of Java that do not contain generics.

The compiler adds the relevant casts for your code to work with this type of erased class. For example, you type

```
Robot r = crate.emptyCrate();
```

and the compiler turns it into

```
Robot r = (Robot) crate.emptyCrate();
```

Generic Interfaces

Just like a class, an interface can declare a formal type parameter. For example, the following Shippable interface uses a generic type as the argument to its ship() method:

```
public interface Shippable<T> {
    void ship(T t);
}
```

There are three ways a class can approach implementing this interface. The first is to specify the generic type in the class. The following concrete class says that it deals only with robots. This lets it declare the ship() method with a Robot parameter:

```
class ShippableRobotCrate implements Shippable<Robot> {
    public void ship(Robot t) { }
}
```

The next way is to create a generic class. The following concrete class allows the caller to specify the type of the generic:

```
class ShippableAbstractCrate<U> implements Shippable<U> {
   public void ship(U t) { }
}
```

In this example, the type parameter could have been named anything, including T. We used U in the example so that it isn't confusing as to what T refers to. The exam won't mind trying to confuse you by using the same type parameter name.

The final way is to not use generics at all. This is the old way of writing code. It generates a compiler warning about Shippable being a *raw type*, but it does compile. Here the ship() method has an Object parameter since the generic type is not defined:

```
class ShippableCrate implements Shippable {
   public void ship(Object t) { }
}
```

 Real World Scenario

What You Can't Do with Generic Types

There are some limitations on what you can do with a generic type. These aren't on the exam, but it will helpful to refer back to this scenario when you are writing practice programs and run into one of these.

Most of the limitations are due to type erasure. Oracle refers to types whose information is fully available at runtime as *reifiable*. Reifiable types can do anything that Java allows. Non-reifiable types have some limitations.

Here are the things that you can't do with generics. (And by "can't," we mean without resorting to contortions like passing in a class object.)

- *Call the constructor.* new T() is not allowed because at runtime it would be new Object().

- *Create an array of that static type.* This one is the most annoying, but it makes sense because you'd be creating an array of Objects.

- *Call* instanceof. This is not allowed because at runtime List<Integer> and List<String> look the same to Java thanks to type erasure.

- *Use a primitive type as a generic type parameter.* This isn't a big deal because you can use the wrapper class instead. If you want a type of int, just use Integer.

- *Create a static variable as a generic type parameter.* This is not allowed because the type is linked to the instance of the class.

Generic Methods

Up until this point, you've seen formal type parameters declared on the class or interface level. It is also possible to declare them on the method level. This is often useful for `static` methods since they aren't part of an instance that can declare the type. However, it is also allowed on non-static methods as well.

In this example, the method uses a generic parameter:

```
public static <T> Crate<T> ship(T t) {
   System.out.println("Preparing " + t);
   return new Crate<T>();
}
```

The method parameter is the generic type T. The return type is a Crate<T>. Before the return type, we declare the formal type parameter of <T>.

Unless a method is obtaining the generic formal type parameter from the class/interface, it is specified immediately before the return type of the method. This can lead to some interesting-looking code!

```
3:    public static <T> void sink(T t) { }
4:    public static <T> T identity(T t) { return t; }
5:    public static T noGood(T t) { return t; }   // DOES NOT COMPILE
```

Line 3 shows the formal parameter type immediately before the return type of void. Line 4 shows the return type being the formal parameter type. It looks weird, but it is correct. Line 5 omits the formal parameter type, and therefore it does not compile.

 Real World Scenario

Optional Syntax for Invoking a Generic Method

You can call a generic method normally, and the compiler will figure out which one you want. Alternatively, you can specify the type explicitly to make it obvious what the type is:

```
Box.<String>ship("package");
Box.<String[]>ship(args);
```

As to whether this makes things clearer, it is up to you. You should at least be aware that this syntax exists.

Interacting with Legacy Code

Legacy code is older code. It is usually code that is in a different style than you would write if you were writing the code today. In this section, we are referring to code that was written to target Java 1.4 or lower, and therefore it does not use generics. Collections written without generics are also known as *raw collections*.

Remember that using generics gives us compile time safety. At least it does when all of the code involved uses generics. When some code uses generics and other code does not, it is easy to get lulled into a false sense of security. Let's look at an example:

```
class Dragon {}
class Unicorn { }
public class LegacyDragons {
   public static void main(String[] args) {
      List unicorns = new ArrayList();
      unicorns.add(new Unicorn());
      printDragons(unicorns);
   }
   private static void printDragons(List<Dragon> dragons) {
      for (Dragon dragon: dragons) {    // ClassCastException
         System.out.println(dragon);
   } } }
```

In this example, we get a ClassCastException on a line that is working with a generic list. At first, this seems odd. This is the problem that generics are supposed to solve. The difference is that all of the code doesn't use generics here. The main() method calls print-Dragons() with a raw type. Due to type erasure, Java doesn't know this is a problem until runtime, when it attempts to cast a Unicorn to a Dragon. The cast is tricky because it doesn't appear in the code. With generic types, Java writes the casts for us.

Although Java doesn't know that there is a problem, it does know there *might* be a problem. Java knows that raw types are asking for trouble, and it presents a *compiler warning* for this case. A compiler warning is different from a compiler error in that all of the code still compiles with a compiler error. The compiler warning is Java informing you that you should take a closer look at something.

 Real World Scenario

Compiler Warnings

On the exam, you have to identify when a compiler warning will occur. You will not be expected to know how to run the commands to list the compiler warnings or read the output. In the real world, you will need that skill. When compiling the LegacyDragon class, the compiler warnings look something like this:

```
$ javac *.java
Note: Some input files use unchecked or unsafe operations.
Note: Recompile with -Xlint:unchecked for details.
```

Java is basically telling you that it knows you are using old code and asking if you want to know more. If you pass that flag, you get something like the following. (The exact messages will depend on your compiler. For example, on some compilers, you'll get a fourth warning where the unicorns object is declared.)

```
$ javac -Xlint:unchecked *.java
LegacyDragons.java:9: warning: [unchecked] unchecked call to add(E) as a member
of the raw type List
    unicorns.add(new Unicorn());
              ^
  where E is a type-variable:
    E extends Object declared in interface List
LegacyDragons.java:11: warning: [unchecked] unchecked method invocation: method
printDragons in class LegacyDragons is applied to given types
    printDragons(unicorns);
              ^
  required: List<Dragon>
  found: List
LegacyDragons.java:11: warning: [unchecked] unchecked conversion
    printDragons(unicorns);
              ^
  required: List<Dragon>
  found:    List
3 warnings
```

The messages look a little scary, but all Java is trying to tell you is that you should really be using generics.

It shouldn't be a surprise that you can get a ClassCastException in the other direction either, for example:

```
1:    public class LegacyUnicorns {
2:        public static void main(String[] args) {
3:            java.util.List<Unicorn> unicorns = new java.util.ArrayList<>();
4:            addUnicorn(unicorns);
5:            Unicorn unicorn = unicorns.get(0);    // ClassCastException
6:        }
7:        private static void addUnicorn(List unicorn) {
8:            unicorn.add(new Dragon());
9:    } }
```

The main() method correctly uses generics. The problem is that it calls a legacy method that claims to add a Unicorn to the list. But this method does not actually work as advertised and adds a Dragon on line 8 instead. Then when line 5 tries to put that Dragon in a Unicorn reference, a ClassCastException occurs. Of course, this code has compiler warnings in it as well.

This problem is fairly straightforward. If the legacy code doesn't use the right types, the generics code will still fail at runtime. Autoboxing has a different problem:

```
1:    public class LegacyAutoboxing {
2:        public static void main(String[] args) {
3:            java.util.List numbers = new java.util.ArrayList();
4:            numbers.add(5);
5:            int result = numbers.get(0);    // DOES NOT COMPILE
6:        }
7:    }
```

The good news is that unboxing fails with a compiler error rather than a runtime error. On line 3, we create a raw list. On line 4, we try to add an int to the list. This works because Java automatically autoboxes to an Integer. On line 5, we have a problem. Since we aren't using generics, Java doesn't know that the list contains an Integer. It just knows that we have an Object. And an Object can't be unboxed into an int.

To review, the lesson is to be careful when you see code that doesn't use generics. Pay special attention to looking for compiler warnings, ClassCastExceptions, and compiler errors.

Bounds

By now, you might have noticed that generics don't seem particularly useful since they are treated as Objects and therefore don't have many methods available. Bounded wildcards solve this by restricting what types can be used in that wildcard position.

A *bounded parameter type* is a generic type that specifies a bound for the generic. Be warned that this is the hardest section in the chapter, so don't feel bad if you have to read it more than once.

A *wildcard generic type* is an unknown generic type represented with a question mark (?). You can use generic wildcards in three ways, as shown in Table 3.2. This section looks at each of these three wildcard types.

TABLE 3.2   Types of bounds

Type of bound	Syntax	Example
Unbounded wildcard	?	List<?> l =new ArrayList<String>();
Wildcard with an upper bound	? extends type	List<? extends Exception> l =new ArrayList<RuntimeException>();
Wildcard with a lower bound	? super type	List<? super Exception> l =new ArrayList<Object>();

Unbounded Wildcards

An unbounded wildcard represents any data type. You use ? when you want to specify that any type is OK with you. Let's suppose that we want to write a method that looks through a list of any type:

```
public static void printList(List<Object> list) {
    for (Object x: list) System.out.println(x);
}
public static void main(String[] args) {
    List<String> keywords = new ArrayList<>();
    keywords.add("java");
    printList(keywords);    // DOES NOT COMPILE
}
```

Wait. What's wrong? A String is a subclass of an Object. This is true. However, List<String> cannot be assigned to List<Object>. We know; it doesn't sound logical. Java is trying to protect us from ourselves with this one. Imagine if we could write code like this:

```
4:    List<Integer> numbers = new ArrayList<>();
5:    numbers.add(new Integer(42));
6:    List<Object> objects = numbers;   // DOES NOT COMPILE
7:    objects.add("forty two");
8:    System.out.println(numbers.get(1));
```

On line 4, the compiler promises us that only Integer objects will appear in numbers. If line 6 were to have compiled, line 7 would break that promise by putting a String in there since numbers and objects are references to the same object. Good thing that the compiler prevents this.

Storing the Wrong Objects—Arrays vs. ArrayLists

We can't write List<Object> l = new ArrayList<String>(); because Java is trying to protect us from a runtime exception. You might think this would mean that we can't write Object[] o = new String[0];. That isn't the case. This code does compile:

```
Integer[] numbers = { new Integer(42)};
Object[] objects = numbers;
objects[0] = "forty two";               // throws ArrayStoreException
```

Although the code does compile, it throws an exception at runtime. With arrays, Java knows the type that is allowed in the array. Just because we've assigned an Integer[] to an Object[] doesn't change the fact that Java knows it is really an Integer[].

Due to type erasure, we have no such protection for an ArrayList. At runtime, the ArrayList doesn't know what is allowed in it. Therefore, Java uses the compiler to prevent this situation from coming up in the first place. OK, so why doesn't Java *add* this knowledge to ArrayList? The reason is backward compatibility; that is, Java is big on not breaking existing code.

Going back to printing a list, we cannot assign a List<String> to a List<Object>. That's fine; we don't really need a List<Object>. What we really need is a List of "whatever." That's what List<?> is. The following code does what we expect:

```
public static void printList(List<?> list) {
    for (Object x: list)  System.out.println(x);
}
public static void main(String[] args) {
    List<String> keywords = new ArrayList<>();
    keywords.add("java");
    printList(keywords);
}
```

printList() takes any type of list as a parameter. keywords is of type List<String>. We have a match! List<String> is a list of anything. "Anything" just happens to be a String here.

Upper-Bounded Wildcards

Let's try to write a method that adds up the total of a list of numbers. We've established that a generic type can't just use a subclass:

```
ArrayList<Number> list = new ArrayList<Integer>(); // DOES NOT COMPILE
```

Instead, we need to use a wildcard:

```
List<? extends Number> list = new ArrayList<Integer>();
```

The upper-bounded wildcard says that any class that extends Number or Number itself can be used as the formal parameter type:

```
public static long total(List<? extends Number> list) {
    long count = 0;
    for (Number number: list)
        count += number.longValue();
    return count;
}
```

Remember how we kept saying that type erasure makes Java think that a generic type is an Object? That is still happening here. Java converts the previous code to something equivalent to the following:

```java
public static long total(List list) {
   long count = 0;
   for (Object obj: list) {
      Number number = (Number) obj;
      count += number.longValue();
   }
   return count;
}
```

Something interesting happens when we work with upper bounds or unbounded wildcards. The list becomes logically immutable. Immutable means that the object cannot be modified, as you saw in Chapter 2, "Design Patterns and Principles." Technically, you can remove elements from the list, but the exam won't ask about this.

```java
2:     static class Sparrow extends Bird { }
3:     static class Bird { }
4:
5:     public static void main(String[] args) {
6:        List<? extends Bird> birds = new ArrayList<Bird>();
7:        birds.add(new Sparrow());        // DOES NOT COMPILE
8:        birds.add(new Bird());           // DOES NOT COMPILE
9: }
```

The problem stems from the fact that Java doesn't know what type List<? extends Bird> really is. It could be List<Bird> or List<Sparrow> or some other generic type that hasn't even been written yet. Line 7 doesn't compile because we can't add a Sparrow to List<Bird>, and line 8 doesn't compile because we can't add a Bird to List<Sparrow>. From Java's point of view, both scenarios are equally possible so neither is allowed.

Now let's try an example with an interface. We have an interface and two classes that implement it:

```java
interface Flyer { void fly(); }
class HangGlider implements Flyer { public void fly() {} }
class Goose implements Flyer { public void fly() {} }
```

We also have two methods that use it. One just lists the interface and the other uses an upper bound:

```java
private void anyFlyer(List<Flyer> flyer) {}
private void groupOfFlyers(List<? extends Flyer> flyer) {}
```

Note that we used the keyword extends rather than implements. Upper bounds are like anonymous classes in that they use extends regardless of whether we are working with a class or an interface.

You already learned that a variable of type List<Flyer> can be passed to either method. A variable of type List<Goose> can be passed only to the one with the upper bound. This shows one of the benefits of generics. Random flyers don't fly together. We want our groupOfFlyers() method to be called only with the same type. Geese fly together but don't fly with hang gliders.

Lower-Bounded Wildcards

Let's try to write a method that adds a string "quack" to two lists:

```
List<String> strings = new ArrayList<String>();
strings.add("tweet");
List<Object> objects = new ArrayList<Object>(strings);
addSound(strings);
addSound(objects);
```

The problem is that we want to pass a List<String> and a List<Object> to the same method. First, make sure that you understand why the first three examples in Table 3.3 do *not* solve this problem.

TABLE 3.3   Why we need a lower bound

Code	Method compiles	Can pass a List<String>	Can pass a List<Object>
public static void addSound(List<?> list) {list.add("quack");}	No (unbounded generics are immutable)	Yes	Yes
public static void addSound(List<? extends Object> list) {list.add("quack");}	No (upper-bounded generics are immutable)	Yes	Yes
public static void addSound(List<Object> list) {list.add("quack");}	Yes	No (with generics, must pass exact match)	Yes
public static void addSound(List<? super String> list) {list.add("quack");}	Yes	Yes	Yes

To solve this problem, we need to use a lower bound:

```
public static void addSound(List<? super String> list) {     // lower bound
    list.add("quack");
}
```

With a lower bound, we are telling Java that the list will be a list of String objects or a list of some objects that are a superclass of String. Either way, it is safe to add a String to that list.

Just like generic classes, you probably won't use this in your code unless you are writing code for others to reuse. Even then it would be rare. But it's on the exam, so now is the time to learn it!

Understand Generic Supertypes

When you have subclasses and superclasses, lower bounds can get tricky:

```
3:    List<? super IOException> exceptions = new ArrayList<Exception>();
4:    exceptions.add(new Exception());   // DOES NOT COMPILE
5:    exceptions.add(new IOException());
6:    exceptions.add(new FileNotFoundException());
```

Line 3 references a List that could be List<IOException> or List<Exception> or List<Object>. Line 4 does not compile because we could have a List<IOException> and an Exception object wouldn't fit in there.

Line 4 is fine. IOException can be added to any of those types. Line 5 is also fine. FileNotFoundException can also be added to any of those three types. This is tricky because FileNotFoundException is a subclass of IOException and the keyword says super. What happens is that Java says "Well, FileNotFoundException also happens to be an IOException, so everything is fine."

Putting It All Together

At this point, you know everything that you need to know to ace the exam questions on generics. It is possible to put these concepts together to write some *really* confusing code, which the exam likes to do.

This section is going to be difficult to read. It contains the hardest questions that you could possibly be asked about generics. The exam questions will probably be easier to read than these. We want you to encounter the really tough ones here so that you are ready for the exam. In other words, don't panic. Take it slow, and reread the code a few times. You'll get it.

Let's try an example. First, we declare three classes that the example will use:

```
class A {}
class B extends A { }
class C extends B { }
```

Ready? Can you figure out why these do or don't compile? Also, try to figure out what they do.

```
6:    List<?> list1 = new ArrayList<A>();
7:    List<? extends A> list2 = new ArrayList<A>();
8:    List<? super A> list3 = new ArrayList<A>();
9:    List<? extends B> list4 = new ArrayList<A>();    // DOES NOT COMPILE
10:   List<? super B> list5 = new ArrayList<A>();
11:   List<?> list6 = new ArrayList<? extends A>();  // DOES NOT COMPILE
```

Line 6 creates an ArrayList that can hold instances of class A. It is stored in a variable with an unbounded wildcard. Any generic type can be referenced from an unbounded wildcard, making this OK.

Line 7 tries to store a list in a variable declaration with an upper-bounded wildcard. This is OK. You can have ArrayList<A>, ArrayList<B>, or ArrayList<C> stored in that reference. Line 8 is also OK. This time, you have a lower-bounded wildcard. The lowest type you can reference is A. Since that is what you have, it compiles.

Line 9 has an upper-bounded wildcard that allows ArrayList<B> or ArrayList<C> to be referenced. Since you have ArrayList<A> that is trying to be referenced, the code does not compile. Line 10 has a lower-bounded wildcard, which allows a reference to ArrayList<A>, ArrayList<B>, or ArrayList<Object>.

Finally, line 11 allows a reference to any generic type since it is an unbounded wildcard. The problem is that you need to know what that type will be when instantiating the ArrayList. It wouldn't be useful anyway, because you can't add any elements to that ArrayList.

Now on to the methods. Same question: try to figure out why they don't compile and what they do. We will present the methods one at a time because there is more to think about.

```
<T> T method1(List<? extends T> list) {
    return list.get(0);
}
```

method1() is a perfectly normal use of generics. It uses a method-specific type parameter, T. It takes a parameter of List<T>, or some subclass of T, and it returns a single object of that T type. For example, you could call it with a List<String> parameter and have it return a String. Or you could call it with a List<Number> parameter and have it return a Number. Or...well, you get the idea.

Given that, you should be able to see what is wrong with this one:

```
<T> <? extends T> method2(List<? extends T> list) {  // DOES NOT COMPILE
    return list.get(0);
}
```

method2() does not compile because the return type isn't actually a type. You are writing the method. You know what type it is supposed to return. You don't get to specify this as a wildcard.

Now be careful—this one is extra tricky:

```
<B extends A> B method3(List<B> list) {
    return new B();   // DOES NOT COMPILE
}
```

method3() does not compile. <B extends A> says that you want to use B as a type parameter just for this method and that it needs to extend the A class. Coincidentally, B is also the name of a class. It isn't a coincidence. It's an evil trick. Within the scope of the method, B can represent classes A, B, or C, because all extend the A class. Since B no longer refers to the B class in the method, you can't instantiate it.

After that, it would be nice to get something straightforward:

```
void method4(List<? super B> list) {
}
```

method4() is a normal use of generics. You can pass the types List<B>, List<A>, or List<Object>.

Finally, here is our last question for you:

```
<X> void method5(List<X super B> list) {   // DOES NOT COMPILE
}
```

method5() does not compile because it tries to mix a method-specific type parameter with a wildcard. A wildcard must have a ? in it.

We are happy to tell you that the rest of the chapter is far easier. We are also happy to tell you that only the basics of generics are used in the rest of the chapter. Well, at least until you get to the review questions. This means that you can keep reading the rest of this chapter and come back to reread the generics section tomorrow when you have a fresh mind.

Using Lists, Sets, Maps, and Queues

A *collection* is a group of objects contained in a single object. The *Java Collections Framework* is a set of classes in java.util for storing collections. There are four main interfaces in the Java Collections Framework:

- List: A *list* is an ordered collection of elements that allows duplicate entries. Elements in a list can be accessed by an int index.

- Set: A *set* is a collection that does not allow duplicate entries.

- Queue: A *queue* is a collection that orders its elements in a specific order for processing. A typical queue processes its elements in a first-in, first-out order, but other orderings are possible.

- Map: A *map* is a collection that maps keys to values, with no duplicate keys allowed. The elements in a map are key/value pairs.

Figure 3.1 shows the Collection interface and its core subinterfaces. Notice that Map doesn't implement the Collection interface. It is considered part of the Java Collections Framework, even though it isn't technically a Collection. It is a collection (note the lowercase), though, in that it contains a group of objects. The reason why maps are treated differently is that they need different methods due to being key/value pairs.

We will first discuss the methods Collection provides to all implementing classes. Then we will cover the different types of collections, including when to use each one and the concrete subclasses. Then we will compare the different types.

FIGURE 3.1   The Collection interface is the root of all collections except maps.

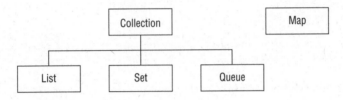

Common Collections Methods

The Collection interface contains useful methods for working with lists, sets, and queues. We will also cover maps. In the following sections, we will discuss the most common ones. We will cover stream in the next chapter and a couple others added in Java 8 at the end of this chapter.

You might have noticed that this book covers more Collections than the exam objectives. The Java 7 version of the exam covered more implementations. Since they behave in similar ways, we cover them as well to ensure that you are prepared in case an old question sneaks onto the exam and also as a warning not to use some of them!

add()

The add() method inserts a new element into the Collection and returns whether it was successful. The method signature is

```
boolean add(E element)
```

Remember that the Collections Framework uses generics. You will see E appear frequently. It means the generic type that was used to create the collection. For some collection types, add() always returns true. For other types, there is logic as to whether the add was successful. The following shows how to use this method:

```
3:    List<String> list = new ArrayList<>();
4:    System.out.println(list.add("Sparrow"));    // true
```

```
5:    System.out.println(list.add("Sparrow"));    // true
6:
7:    Set<String> set = new HashSet<>();
8:    System.out.println(set.add("Sparrow"));     // true
9:    System.out.println(set.add("Sparrow"));     // false
```

A List allows duplicates, making the return value true each time. A Set does not allow duplicates. On line 9, we tried to add a duplicate so that Java returns false from the add() method.

remove()

The remove() method removes a single matching value in the Collection and returns whether it was successful. The method signature is

```
boolean remove(Object object)
```

This time, the boolean return value tells us whether a match was removed. The following shows how to use this method:

```
3:    List<String> birds = new ArrayList<>();
4:    birds.add("hawk");                                    // [hawk]
5:    birds.add("hawk");                                    // [hawk, hawk]
6:    System.out.println(birds.remove("cardinal"));  // prints false
7:    System.out.println(birds.remove("hawk"));       // prints true
8:    System.out.println(birds);                            // [hawk]
```

Line 6 tries to remove an element that is not in birds. It returns false because no such element is found. Line 7 tries to remove an element that is in birds, so it returns true. Notice that it removes only one match.

Since calling remove() with an int uses the index, an index that doesn't exist will throw an exception. For example, birds.remove(100); throws an IndexOutOfBoundsException. Remember that there are overloaded remove() methods. One takes the element to remove. The other takes the index of the element to remove. The latter is being called here.

isEmpty() and size()

The isEmpty() and size() methods look at how many elements are in the Collection. The method signatures are

```
boolean isEmpty()
int size()
```

The following shows how to use these methods:

```
System.out.println(birds.isEmpty()); // true
System.out.println(birds.size());    // 0
```

```
birds.add("hawk");                        // [hawk]
birds.add("hawk");                        // [hawk, hawk]
System.out.println(birds.isEmpty()); // false
System.out.println(birds.size());    // 2
```

At the beginning, birds has a size of 0 and is empty. It has a capacity that is greater than 0. After we add elements, the size becomes positive and it is no longer empty.

clear()

The clear() method provides an easy way to discard all elements of the Collection. The method signature is

```
void clear()
```

The following shows how to use this method:

```
List<String> birds = new ArrayList<>();
birds.add("hawk");                         // [hawk]
birds.add("hawk");                         // [hawk, hawk]
System.out.println(birds.isEmpty());  // false
System.out.println(birds.size());     // 2
birds.clear();                             // []
System.out.println(birds.isEmpty());  // true
System.out.println(birds.size());     // 0
```

After calling clear(), birds is back to being an empty ArrayList of size 0.

contains()

The contains() method checks if a certain value is in the Collection. The method signature is

```
boolean contains(Object object)
```

The following shows how to use this method:

```
List<String> birds = new ArrayList<>();
birds.add("hawk");                                  // [hawk]
System.out.println(birds.contains("hawk"));  // true
System.out.println(birds.contains("robin")); // false
```

This method calls equals() on each element of the ArrayList to see if there are any matches.

Using the *List* Interface

You use a list when you want an ordered collection that can contain duplicate entries. Items can be retrieved and inserted at specific positions in the list based on an int index much like an array. Lists are commonly used because there are many situations in programming where you need to keep track of a list of objects.

For example, you might make a list of what you want to see at the zoo: First, see the lions because they go to sleep early. Second, see the pandas because there is a long line later in the day. And so forth.

Figure 3.2 shows how you can envision a List. Each element of the List has an index, and the indexes begin with zero.

FIGURE 3.2   Example of a List

Sometimes, you don't actually care about the order of elements in a list. List is like the "go to" data type. When we make a shopping list before going to the store, the order of the list happens to be the order in which we thought of the items. We probably aren't attached to that particular order, but it isn't hurting anything.

While the classes implementing the List interface have many methods, you need to know only the most common ones. Conveniently, these are the same for all of the implementations that might show up on the exam.

The main thing that all List implementations have in common is that they are ordered and allow duplicates. Beyond that, they each offer different functionality. We will look at the implementations that you need to know and the available methods.

> **NOTE**   Pay special attention to which names are classes and which are interfaces. The exam may ask you which is the best class or which is the best interface for a scenario.

Comparing *List* Implementations

An ArrayList is like a resizable array. When elements are added, the ArrayList automatically grows. When you aren't sure which collection to use, use an ArrayList. This class is so common that it was tested on the OCA too.

The main benefit of an ArrayList is that you can look up any element in constant time. Adding or removing an element is slower than accessing an element. This makes an ArrayList a good choice when you are reading more often than (or the same amount as) writing to the ArrayList.

🌐 Real World Scenario

Big O Notation

In computer programming, we use big O notation to talk about the performance of algorithms. It's pretty clear that it is better for code to take 1 second than 10 seconds to do the same thing. This is called an *order of magnitude* difference.

Big O notation lets you compare the order of magnitude of performance rather than the exact performance. It also assumes the worst-case response time. If you write an algorithm that could take a while or be instantaneous, big O uses the longer one. It uses an *n* to reflect the number of elements or size of the data you are talking about. The following lists the most common big O notation values that you will see and what they mean:

- *O(1)*—constant time: It doesn't matter how large the collection is, the answer will always take the same time to return. Returning the string literal "Panda" from a method will take constant time, as will returning the last element of an array.

- *O(log n)*—logarithmic time: A logarithm is a mathematical function that grows much more slowly than the data size. You don't need to know this for the exam, but log(8) gives you 3 in base 2 and log(1024) gives you 10 in base 2. The point is that logarithmic time is better than linear time. Binary search runs in logarithmic time because it doesn't look at the majority of the elements for large collections.

- *O(n)*—linear time: The performance will grow linearly with respect to the size of the collection. Looping through a list and returning the number of elements matching "Panda" will take linear time.

- *O(n²)*—n squared time: Code that has nested loops where each loop goes through the data takes n squared time. An example would be putting every pair of pandas together to see if they'll share an exhibit.

A LinkedList is special because it implements both List and Queue. It has all of the methods of a List. It also has additional methods to facilitate adding or removing from the beginning and/or end of the list.

The main benefits of a LinkedList are that you can access, add, and remove from the beginning and end of the list in constant time. The tradeoff is that dealing with an arbitrary index takes linear time. This makes a LinkedList a good choice when you'll be using it as Queue.

There are also two old implementations. Way back when, Vector was the only choice if you wanted a list. In Java 1.2, ArrayList essentially replaced it. Vector does the same thing as ArrayList except more slowly. The benefit to that decrease in speed is that it is thread-safe, but as you'll see in Chapter 8, there is a better way to do that now. This means that the real reason that you need to know about Vector is that really old code might refer to it.

A Stack is a data structure where you add and remove elements from the top of the stack. Think about a stack of paper as an example. Like Vector, Stack hasn't been used for new code in ages. In fact, Stack extends Vector. If you need a stack, use an ArrayDeque instead. More on this when we get to the Queue section.

Working with *List* Methods

The methods in the List interface are for working with indexes. In addition to the inherited Collection methods, the method signatures that you need to know are in Table 3.4.

TABLE 3.4 List methods

Method	Description
void add(E element)	Adds element to end
void add(int index, E element)	Adds element at index and moves the rest toward the end
E get(int index)	Returns element at index
int indexOf(Object o)	Returns first matching index or -1 if not found
int lastIndexOf(Object o)	Returns last matching index or -1 if not found
void remove(int index)	Removes element at index and moves the rest toward the front
E set(int index, E e)	Replaces element at index and returns original

The following statements demonstrate these basic methods for adding and removing items from a list:

```
4:    List<String> list = new ArrayList<>();
5:    list.add("SD");             // [SD]
6:    list.add(0, "NY");          // [NY,SD]
7:    list.set(1, "FL");          // [NY,FL]
8:    list.remove("NY");          // [FL]
9:    list.remove(0);             // []
```

On line 4, list starts out empty. Line 5 adds an element to the end of the list. Line 6 adds an element at index 0 that bumps the original index 0 to index 1. Notice how the ArrayList is now automatically one larger. Line 7 replaces the element at index 1 with a new value. Line 8 removes the element matching "NY". Finally, line 9 removes the element at index 0 and list is empty again.

Let's look at one more example that queries the list:

```
5:    list.add("OH");             // [OH]
6:    list.add("CO");             // [OH,CO]
```

```
7:    list.add("NJ");                    // [OH,CO,NJ]
8:    String state = list.get(0);        // OH
9:    int index = list.indexOf("NJ");    // 2
```

Lines 5 through 7 add elements to list in order. Line 8 requests the element at index 2. Line 9 searches the list until it hits an element with "NJ". The elements do not need to be in order for this to work because indexOf() looks through the whole list until it finds a match.

The output would be the same if you tried these examples with LinkedList, Vector, or Stack. Although the code would be less efficient, it wouldn't be noticeable until you have very large lists.

Looping through a List

Back on the OCA, you learned how to loop through a list using an enhanced for loop:

```
for (String string: list) {
    System.out.println(string);
}
```

You'll see another longer way to do this in code written before Java 5:

```
Iterator iter = list.iterator();
while(iter.hasNext()) {
    String string = (String) iter.next();
    System.out.println(string);
}
```

The old way requires casting because it predates generics. It also requires checking if the Iterator has any more elements followed by requesting the next element. There's also a hybrid way where you still use Iterator with generics. You get rid of the cast but still have to handle the looping logic yourself.

```
Iterator<String> iter = list.iterator();
while(iter.hasNext()) {
    String string = iter.next();
    System.out.println(string);
}
```

Pay attention to the difference between these methods. hasNext() checks if there is a next value. In other words, it tells you whether next() will execute without throwing an exception. next() actually moves the Iterator to the next element.

Using the *Set* Interface

You use a set when you don't want to allow duplicate entries. For example, you might want to keep track of the unique animals that you want to see at the zoo. You aren't concerned with the order in which you see these animals, but there isn't time to see them more than once. You just want to make sure that you see the ones that are important to you and remove them from the set of outstanding animals to see after you see them.

Figure 3.3 shows how you can envision a Set. The main thing that all Set implementations have in common is that they do not allow duplicates. Beyond that, they each offer different functionality. We will look at each implementation that you need to know for the exam and how to write code using Set.

FIGURE 3.3   Example of a Set

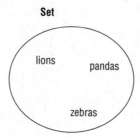

Comparing *Set* Implementations

A HashSet stores its elements in a hash table. This means that it uses the hashCode() method of the objects to retrieve them more efficiently. If you forgot how hashCode() works, please review Chapter 1, "Advanced Class Design."

The main benefit is that adding elements and checking if an element is in the set both have constant time. The tradeoff is that you lose the order in which you inserted the elements. Most of the time, you aren't concerned with this in a set anyway, making HashSet the most common set.

A TreeSet stores its elements in a sorted tree structure. The main benefit is that the set is always in sorted order. The tradeoff is that adding and checking if an element is present are both O(log n). TreeSet implements a special interface called NavigableSet, which lets you slice up the collection as you will see in the next sidebar, "The *NavigableSet* Interface".

Figure 3.4 shows how you can envision HashSet and TreeSet being stored. HashSet is more complicated in reality because it has empty rows as well, but this is fine for the purpose of the exam.

FIGURE 3.4   Examples of a HashSet and TreeSet

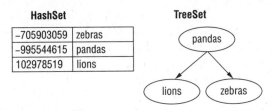

Working with *Set* Methods

The Set interface doesn't add any extra methods that you need to know for the exam. You just have to know how sets behave with respect to the traditional Collection methods. You also have to know the differences between the types of sets. Let's start with HashSet:

```
3:    Set<Integer> set = new HashSet<>();
4:    boolean b1 = set.add(66);                                   // true
5:    boolean b2 = set.add(10);                                   // true
6:    boolean b3 = set.add(66);                                   // false
7:    boolean b4 = set.add(8);                                    // true
8:    for (Integer integer: set) System.out.print(integer + ","); // 66,8,10,
```

The add() methods should be straightforward. They return true unless the Integer is already in the set. Line 6 returns false, because we already have 66 in the set and a set must preserve uniqueness. Line 8 prints the elements of the set in an arbitrary order. In this case, it happens not to be sorted order, or the order in which we added the elements.

Remember that the equals() method is used to determine equality. The hashCode() method is used to know which bucket to look in so that Java doesn't have to look through the whole set to find out if an object is there. The best case is that hash codes are unique, and Java has to call equals() on only one object. The worst case is that all implementations return the same hashCode(), and Java has to call equals() on every element of the set anyway.

Now let's look at the same example with TreeSet:

```
3:    Set<Integer> set = new HashSet<>();
4:    boolean b1 = set.add(66);                                   // true
5:    boolean b2 = set.add(10);                                   // true
6:    boolean b3 = set.add(66);                                   // false
7:    boolean b4 = set.add(8);                                    // true
8:    for (Integer integer: set) System.out.print(integer + ","); // 8,10,66
```

This time, the elements are printed out in their natural sorted order. Numbers implement the Comparable interface in Java, which is used for sorting. Later in the chapter, you will learn how to create your own Comparable objects.

The *NavigableSet* Interface

TreeSet implements the NavigableSet interface. This interface provides some interesting methods. Their method signatures are as follows:

Method	Description
E lower(E e)	Returns greatest element that is < e, or null if no such element
E floor(E e)	Returns greatest element that is <= e, or null if no such element
E ceiling(E e)	Returns smallest element that is >= e, or null if no such element
E higher(E e)	Returns smallest element that is > e, or null if no such element

These methods were added to the exam with Java 6, so you might come across them. Let's look at an example of these methods:

```
36:    NavigableSet<Integer> set = new TreeSet<>();
37:    for (int i = 1; i <= 20; i++) set.add(i);
38:    System.out.println(set.lower(10));    // 9
39:    System.out.println(set.floor(10));    // 10
40:    System.out.println(set.ceiling(20));  // 20
41:    System.out.println(set.higher(20));   // null
```

The TreeSet contains 20 Integer objects whose values are 1 to 20. In this example, line 38 must return the highest element that is less than 10. Line 39 must return the highest element that is no higher than 10. See the difference? One includes the target element and the other does not.

Line 40 must return the lowest element greater than or equal to 20. Line 41 must return the lowest element greater than 20. There is no such element that meets these criteria, making the result null.

These methods sound similar. Just remember that lower and higher elements do not include the target element. This also makes sense in English. If something needs to be lower than a coffee table, it must completely fit under the coffee table.

Using the *Queue* Interface

You use a queue when elements are added and removed in a specific order. Queues are typically used for sorting elements prior to processing them. For example, when you want to buy a ticket and someone is waiting in line, you get in line behind that person. And if you are British, you get in the queue behind that person, making this really easy to remember!

Unless stated otherwise, a queue is assumed to be *FIFO* (first-in, first-out). Some queue implementations change this to use a different order. You can envision a FIFO queue as shown in Figure 3.5. The other common format is *LIFO* (last-in, first-out.)

FIGURE 3.5   Example of a Queue

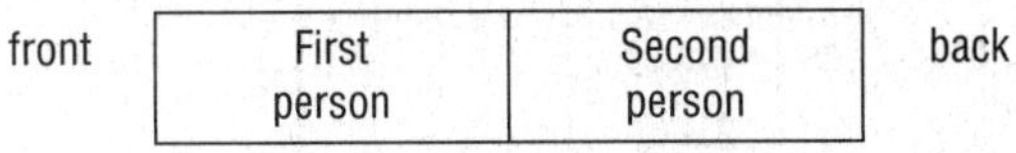

front	First person	Second person	back

All queues have specific requirements for adding and removing the next element. Beyond that, they each offer different functionality. We will look at the implementations that you need to know and the available methods.

Comparing *Queue* Implementations

You saw LinkedList earlier in the List section. In addition to being a list, it is a double-ended queue. A double-ended queue is different from a regular queue in that you can insert and remove elements from both the front and back of the queue. Think, "Mr. President, come right to the front. You are the only one who gets this special treatment. Everyone else will have to start at the back of the line."

The main benefit of a LinkedList is that it implements both the List and Queue interfaces. The tradeoff is that it isn't as efficient as a "pure" queue.

An ArrayDeque is a "pure" double-ended queue. It was introduced in Java 6, and it stores its elements in a resizable array. The main benefit of an ArrayDeque is that it is more efficient than a LinkedList. *Deque* is supposed to be pronounced "deck," but many people, including the authors, say it wrong as "d-queue."

Working with *Queue* Methods

The ArrayDeque contains many methods. Luckily, there are only seven methods that you need to know in addition to the inherited Collection ones. These methods are shown in Table 3.5.

TABLE 3.5   ArrayDeque

Method	Description	For queue	For stack
boolean add(E e)	Adds an element to the back of the queue and returns true or throws an exception	Yes	No
E element()	Returns next element or throws an exception if empty queue	Yes	No
boolean offer(E e)	Adds an element to the back of the queue and returns whether successful	Yes	No

TABLE 3.5   ArrayDeque *(continued)*

Method	Description	For queue	For stack
E remove()	Removes and returns next element or throws an exception if empty queue	Yes	No
void push(E e)	Adds an element to the front of the queue	Yes	Yes
E poll()	Removes and returns next element or returns null if empty queue	Yes	No
E peek()	Returns next element or returns null if empty queue	Yes	Yes
E pop()	Removes and returns next element or throws an exception if empty queue	No	Yes

Except for push, all are in the Queue interface as well. push is what makes it a double-ended queue.

As you can see, there are basically two sets of methods. One set throws an exception when something goes wrong. The other uses a different return value when something goes wrong. The offer/poll/peek methods are more common. This is the standard language people use when working with queues.

Let's look at an example that uses some of these methods:

```
12:    Queue<Integer> queue = new ArrayDeque<>();
13:    System.out.println(queue.offer(10));    // true
14:    System.out.println(queue.offer(4));     // true
15:    System.out.println(queue.peek());       // 10
16:    System.out.println(queue.poll());       // 10
17:    System.out.println(queue.poll());       // 4
18:    System.out.println(queue.peek());       // null
```

Figure 3.6 shows what the queue looks like at each step of the code. Lines 13 and 14 successfully add an element to the end of the queue. Some queues are limited in size, which would cause offering an element to the queue to fail. You won't encounter a scenario like that on the exam. Line 15 looks at the first element in the queue, but it does not remove it. Lines 16 and 17 actually remove the elements from the queue, which results in an empty queue. Line 18 tries to look at the first element of a queue, which results in null.

We've said that ArrayDeque is a double-ended queue. What if we want to insert an element at the other end, just as we could with a Stack? No problem. We just call the push() method. It works just like offer() except at the other end of the queue. When talking about LIFO (stack), people say push/poll/peek. When talking about FIFO (single-ended queue), people say offer/poll/peek.

FIGURE 3.6   Working with a queue

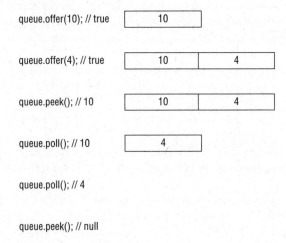

Now let's rewrite that example using the stack functionality:

```
12:    ArrayDeque<Integer> stack = new ArrayDeque<>();
13:    stack.push(10);
14:    stack.push(4);
15:    System.out.println(stack.peek());    // 4
16:    System.out.println(stack.poll());    // 4
17:    System.out.println(stack.poll());    // 10
18:    System.out.println(stack.peek());    // null
```

Figure 3.7 shows what the queue looks like at each step of the code. Lines 13 and 14 successfully put an element on the front/top of the stack. The remaining code looks at the front as well.

FIGURE 3.7   Working with a stack

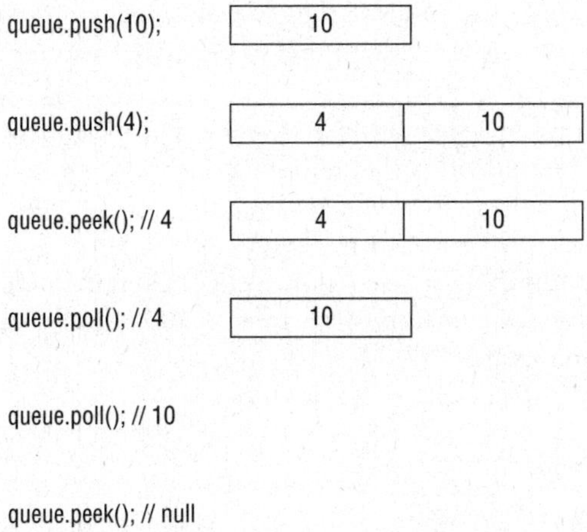

queue.push(10); | 10 |

queue.push(4); | 4 | 10 |

queue.peek(); // 4 | 4 | 10 |

queue.poll(); // 4 | 10 |

queue.poll(); // 10

queue.peek(); // null

The difference between whether an ArrayDeque is being used as a stack or a queue is really important. To review, a queue is like a line of people. You get on in the back and off in the front. A stack is like a stack of plates. You put the plate on the top and take it off the top. Since the stack is implemented using ArrayDeque, we refer to "top" and "front" interchangeably.

A LinkedList works the exact same way as ArrayDeque, so we will skip showing the code for that one.

Map

You use a map when you want to identify values by a key. For example, when you use the contact list in your phone, you look up "George" rather than looking through each phone number in turn.

You can envision a Map as shown in Figure 3.8. You don't need to know the names of the specific interfaces that the different maps implement, but you do need to know that TreeMap is sorted and navigable.

FIGURE 3.8 Example of a Map

George	555-555-5555
Mary	777-777-7777

The main thing that all four classes have in common is that they all have keys and values. Beyond that, they each offer different functionality. We will look at the implementations that you need to know and the available methods.

Comparing *Map* Implementations

A HashMap stores the keys in a hash table. This means that it uses the hashCode() method of the keys to retrieve their values more efficiently.

The main benefit is that adding elements and retrieving the element by key both have constant time. The tradeoff is that you lose the order in which you inserted the elements. Most of the time, you aren't concerned with this in a map anyway. If you were, you could use LinkedHashMap.

A TreeMap stores the keys in a sorted tree structure. The main benefit is that the keys are always in sorted order. The tradeoff is that adding and checking if a key is present are both O(log n).

A Hashtable is like Vector in that it is really old and thread-safe and that you won't be expected to use it. It contains a lowercase *t* as a mistake from the olden days. All you have to do is be able to pick it out in a lineup. In the form of old school analogies, ArrayList is to Vector as HashMap is to Hashtable.

Working with *Map* Methods

Given that Map doesn't extend Collection, there are more methods specified on the Map interface. Since there are both keys and values, we need generic type parameters for both. The class uses K for key and V for value. Most of the method signatures that you need to know for the exam are shown in Table 3.6.

TABLE 3.6   Map methods

Method	Description
void clear()	Removes all keys and values from the map.
boolean isEmpty()	Returns whether the map is empty.
int size()	Returns the number of entries (key/value pairs) in the map.
V get(Object key)	Returns the value mapped by key or null if none is mapped.
V put(K key, V value)	Adds or replaces key/value pair. Returns previous value or null.
V remove(Object key)	Removes and returns value mapped to key. Returns null if none.
boolean containsKey(Object key)	Returns whether key is in map.
boolean containsValue(Object)	Returns value is in map.
Set<K> keySet()	Returns set of all keys.
Collection<V> values()	Returns Collection of all values.

As usual, let's compare running the same code with two Map types. First up is HashMap:

```
Map<String, String> map = new HashMap<>();
map.put("koala", "bamboo");
map.put("lion", "meat");
map.put("giraffe", "leaf");
String food = map.get("koala");  // bamboo
for (String key: map.keySet())
    System.out.print(key + ","); // koala,giraffe,lion,
```

Java uses the hashCode() of the key to determine the order. The order here happens to not be sorted order, or the order in which we typed the values. Now let's look at TreeMap:

```
Map<String, String> map = new TreeMap<>();
map.put("koala", "bamboo");
map.put("lion", "meat");
map.put("giraffe", "leaf");
String food = map.get("koala");  // bamboo
for (String key: map.keySet())
   System.out.print(key + ","); // giraffe,koala,lion,
```

TreeMap sorts the keys as we would expect. If we were to have called values() instead of keySet(), the order of the values would correspond to the order of the keys.

With our same map, we can try some boolean checks:

```
System.out.println(map.contains("lion"));       // DOES NOT COMPILE
System.out.println(map.containsKey("lion"));    // true
System.out.println(map.containsValue("lion"));  // false
System.out.println(map.size());                 // 3
```

The first line is a little tricky. contains() is a method on the Collection interface but not the Map interface. The next two lines show that keys and values are checked separately. Finally, we see that there are three key/value pairs in our map.

Comparing Collection Types

Let's start off with a brief review of the characteristics of the different types. Make sure that you can fill in Table 3.7 and Table 3.8 from memory.

TABLE 3.7 Java Collections Framework types

Type	Can contain duplicate elements?	Elements ordered?	Has keys and values?	Must add/remove in specific order?
List	Yes	Yes (by index)	No	No
Map	Yes (for values)	No	Yes	No
Queue	Yes	Yes (retrieved in defined order)	No	Yes
Set	No	No	No	No

TABLE 3.8   Collection attributes

Type	Java Collections Framework interface	Sorted?	Calls hashCode?	Calls compareTo?
ArrayList	List	No	No	No
ArrayDeque	Queue	No	No	No
HashMap	Map	No	Yes	No
HashSet	Set	No	Yes	No
Hashtable	Map	No	Yes	No
LinkedList	List, Queue	No	No	No
Stack	List	No	No	No
TreeMap	Map	Yes	No	Yes
TreeSet	Set	Yes	No	Yes
Vector	List	No	No	No

Next, the exam expects you to know which data structures allow nulls. Most do allow nulls, so we discuss only the exceptions. A few are even logical!

The data structures that involve sorting do not allow nulls. This makes sense. We can't compare a null and a String. They are completely different things. We wouldn't say that 5 is less than "Puppy." It doesn't make any more sense to say that null is less than "Puppy" either. This means that TreeSet cannot contain null elements. It also means that TreeMap cannot contain null keys. Null values are OK.

Next comes ArrayDeque. You can't put null in an ArrayDeque because methods like poll() use null as a special return value to indicate that the collection is empty. Since null has that meaning, Java forbids putting a null in there. That would just be confusing.

Finally, Hashtable doesn't allow null keys or values. There isn't really a good reason for this one. It's just because it is old and written that way. On the bright side, you aren't likely to get asked about this one since it is so old.

In handy list form, all data structures allow nulls except these:

TreeMap—no null keys

Hashtable—no null keys or values

TreeSet—no null elements

ArrayDeque—no null elements

Finally, the exam expects you to be able to choose the right collection type given a description of a problem. Table 3.9 walks you through that type of situation to give you practice. Pay attention to the Reason column. It gives you clues to look for when faced with this type of question on the exam.

TABLE 3.9   Choosing the right collection type

Which class do you choose when you want _____	Answer (single best type)	Reason
to pick the top zoo map off a stack of maps	ArrayDeque	The description is of a last-in, first-out data structure, so you need a stack, which is a type of Queue. (Stack would also match this description, but it shouldn't be used for new code.)
to sell tickets to people in the order in which they appear in line and tell them their position in line	LinkedList	The description is of a first-in, first-out data structure, so you need a queue. You also needed indexes, and LinkedList is the only class to match both requirements.
to write down the first names of all of the elephants so that you can tell them to your friend's three-year-old every time she asks. (The elephants do not have unique first names.)	ArrayList	Since there are duplicates, you need a list rather than a set. You will be accessing the list more often than updating it, since three-year-olds ask the same question over and over, making an ArrayList better than a LinkedList. Vector and Stack aren't used in new code.
to list the unique animals that you want to see at the zoo today	HashSet	The keyword in the description is *unique*. When you see "unique," think "set." Since there were no requirements to have a sorted order or to remember the insertion order, you use the most efficient set.
to list the unique animals that you want to see at the zoo today in alphabetical order	TreeSet	Since it says "unique," you need a set. This time, you need to sort, so you cannot use a HashSet.
to look up animals based on a unique identifier	HashMap	Looking up by key should make you think of a map. Since you have no ordering or sorting requirements, you should use the most basic map.

We recommend first identifying which type of collection the question is asking about. First, figure out whether you are looking for a list, map, queue, or set. This lets you eliminate a number of answers. Then you can figure out which of the remaining choices is the best answer.

Comparator vs. *Comparable*

We discussed "order" for the TreeSet and TreeMap classes. For numbers, order is obvious—it is numerical order. For String objects, order is defined according to the Unicode character mapping. As far as the exam is concerned, that means numbers sort before letters and uppercase letters sort before lowercase letters.

 Remember that numbers sort before letters and uppercase letters sort before lowercase letters.

You can also sort objects that you create. Java provides an interface called Comparable. If your class implements Comparable, it can be used in these data structures that require comparison. There is also a class called Comparator, which is used to specify that you want to use a different order than the object itself provides.

Comparable and Comparator are similar enough to be tricky. The exam likes to see if it can trick you into mixing up the two. Don't be confused! In this section, we will discuss Comparable first. Then, as we go through Comparator, we will point out all of the differences.

Comparable

The Comparable interface has only one method. In fact, this is the entire interface:

```java
public interface Comparable<T> {
    public int compareTo(T o);
}
```

See the use of generics in there? This lets you avoid the cast when implementing compareTo(). Any object can be Comparable. For example, we have a bunch of ducks and want to sort them by name:

```java
import java.util.*;
public class Duck implements Comparable<Duck> {
    private String name;
    public Duck(String name) {
        this.name = name;
```

```
      }
      public String toString() {          // use readable output
         return name;
      }
      public int compareTo(Duck d) {
         return name.compareTo(d.name);    // call String's compareTo
      }
      public static void main(String[] args) {
         List<Duck> ducks = new ArrayList<>();
         ducks.add(new Duck("Quack"));
         ducks.add(new Duck("Puddles"));
         Collections.sort(ducks);          // sort by name
         System.out.println(ducks);        // [Puddles, Quack]
   } }
```

The Duck class implements the Comparable interface. Without implementing that interface, all we have is a method named compareTo(), but it wouldn't be a Comparable object.

The Duck class overrides the toString() method from Object, so we can see useful output when printing out ducks. Without this override, the output would be something like [Duck@70dea4e, Duck@5c647e05]—hardly useful in seeing which duck's name comes first.

Finally, the Duck class implements compareTo(). Since Duck is comparing objects of type String and the String class already has a compareTo() method, it can just delegate.

We still need to know what the compareTo() method returns so that we can write our own. There are three rules to know:

- The number zero is returned when the current object is equal to the argument to compareTo().

- A number less than zero is returned when the current object is smaller than the argument to compareTo().

- A number greater than zero is returned when the current object is larger than the argument to compareTo().

Let's look at an implementation of compareTo() that compares numbers instead of String objects:

```
1:    public class Animal implements java.util.Comparable<Animal> {
2:       private int id;
3:       public int compareTo(Animal a) {
4:          return id - a.id;
5:       }
6:       public static void main(String[] args) {
7:          Animal a1 = new Animal();
8:          Animal a2 = new Animal();
```

```
9:            a1.id = 5;
10:           a2.id = 7;
11:           System.out.println(a1.compareTo(a2));    // -2
12:           System.out.println(a1.compareTo(a1));    // 0
13:           System.out.println(a2.compareTo(a1));    // 2
14:    } }
```

Lines 7 and 8 create two Animal objects. Lines 9 and 10 set their id values. This is not a good way to set instance variables. It would be better to use a constructor or setter method. Since the exam shows nontraditional code to make sure that you understand the rules, we throw in some as well.

Lines 3 through 5 implement the compareTo() method. Since an int is a primitive, we can't call a method on it. We could create the Integer wrapper class and call compareTo() on that. It's not necessary, though, since it is so easy to implement compareTo() correctly on our own.

Lines 11 through 13 confirm that we've implemented compareTo() correctly. Line 11 compares a smaller id to a larger one, and therefore it prints a negative number. Line 12 compares animals with the same id, and therefore it prints 0. Line 13 compares a larger id to a smaller one, and therefore it returns a positive number.

> Remember that id - a.id sorts in ascending order and a.id - id sorts in descending order.

When dealing with legacy code, the compareTo() method requires a cast since it is passed an Object:

```
public class LegacyDuck implements java.util.Comparable {
   private String name;
   public int compareTo(Object obj) {
      LegacyDuck d = (LegacyDuck) obj;    // cast because no generics
      return name.compareTo(d.name);
   }
}
```

Since we don't specify a generic type for Comparable, Java assumes that we want an Object, which means that we have to cast to LegacyDuck before accessing instance variables on it.

You might have noticed by now that we have been writing java.util.Comparable. That's because it is in the java.util package. Most of the time, you won't see the package name on the exam. You can tell that the imports have been omitted because the code will have line numbers that do not begin with line 1.

***compareTo() and equals()* Consistency**

If you write a class that implements Comparable, you introduce new business logic for determining equality. The compareTo() method returns 0 if two objects are equal, while your equals() method returns true if two objects are equal. A *natural ordering* that uses compareTo() is said to be *consistent with equals* if, and only if, x.equals(y) is true whenever x.compareTo(y) equals 0. You are strongly encouraged to make your Comparable classes consistent with equals because not all collection classes behave predictably if the compareTo() and equals() methods are not consistent.

For example, the following Product class defines a compareTo() method that is not consistent with equals:

```java
public class Product implements Comparable<Product> {
    int id;
    String name;
    public boolean equals(Object obj) {
        if(!(obj instanceof Product)) {
            return false;
        }
        Product other = (Product) obj;
        return this.id == other.id;
    }
    public int compareTo(Product obj) {
        return this.name.compareTo(obj.name);
    }
} }
```

You might be sorting Product objects by name, but names are not unique. Therefore, the return value of compareTo() might not be 0 when comparing two equal Product objects, so this compareTo() method is not consistent with equals. One way to fix that is to use a Comparator to define the sort elsewhere.

Now that you know how to implement Comparable objects, you get to look at Comparators and focus on the differences.

Comparator

Sometimes you want to sort an object that did not implement Comparable, or you want to sort objects in different ways at different times.

Suppose that we add weight to our Duck class. We now have the following:

```java
public class Duck implements Comparable<Duck> {
    private String name;
```

```
   private int weight;
   public Duck(String name, int weight) {
      this.name = name;
      this.weight = weight;
   }
   public String getName() {  return name; }
   public int getWeight() {  return weight; }
   public String toString() { return name; }
   public int compareTo(Duck d) {
      return name.compareTo(d.name);
   }
}
```

The Duck class itself can define compareTo() in only one way. In this case, name was chosen. If we want to sort by something else, we have to define that sort order outside the compareTo() method:

```
public static void main(String[] args) {
   Comparator<Duck> byWeight = new Comparator<Duck>() {
      public int compare(Duck d1, Duck d2) {
         return d1.getWeight()-d2.getWeight();
      }
   };
   List<Duck> ducks = new ArrayList<>();
   ducks.add(new Duck("Quack", 7));
   ducks.add(new Duck("Puddles", 10));
   Collections.sort(ducks);
   System.out.println(ducks);           // [Puddles, Quack]
   Collections.sort(ducks, byWeight);
   System.out.println(ducks);           // [Quack, Puddles]
}
```

First, we defined an inner class with the comparator. Then we sorted without the comparator and with the comparator to see the difference in output.

Comparator is a functional interface since there is only one abstract method to implement. This means that we can rewrite the comparator in the previous example as any of the following:

```
Comparator<Duck> byWeight = (d1, d2) -> d1.getWeight()-d2.getWeight();
Comparator<Duck> byWeight = (Duck d1, Duck d2) -> d1.getWeight()-d2.getWeight();
Comparator<Duck> byWeight = (d1, d2) -> { return d1.getWeight()-d2.getWeight(); };
Comparator<Duck> byWeight = (Duck d1, Duck d2) -> {return d1.getWeight()-
d2.getWeight(); };
```

All of these examples show taking two parameters and returning an int—just as Comparator specifies. Remember that the type is optional. Java will infer it by what is needed in that spot in the code. This is cool. You can rewrite five lines of code using a funky syntax into one line in a different funky syntax! It is really cool because you get used to the lambda syntax, whereas the anonymous inner class always feels kludgy. We will use a mix of lambdas and anonymous inner classes in this book since you should expect to see both approaches on the exam.

Is *Comparable* a Functional Interface?

We said that Comparator is a functional interface because it has a single abstract method. Comparable is also a functional interface since it also has a single abstract method. However, using a lambda for Comparable would be silly. The point of Comparable is to implement it inside the object being compared.

There are a good number of differences between Comparable and Comparator. We've listed them for you in Table 3.10.

TABLE 3.10   Comparison of Comparable and Comparator

Difference	Comparable	Comparator
Package name	java.lang	java.util
Interface must be implemented by class comparing?	Yes	No
Method name in interface	compareTo	compare
Number of parameters	1	2
Common to declare using a lambda	No	Yes

Memorize this table—really. The exam will try to trick you by mixing up the two and seeing if you can catch it. Do you see why this one doesn't compile?

```
Comparator<Duck> byWeight = new Comparator<Duck>() { //DOES NOT COMPILE
   public int compareTo(Duck d1, Duck d2) {
      return d1.getWeight()-d2.getWeight();
   }
};
```

The method name is wrong. A Comparator must implement a method named compare(). Pay special attention to method names and the number of parameters when you see Comparator and Comparable in questions.

 Real World Scenario

An Easier Way of Comparing Multiple Fields

When writing a Comparator that compares multiple instance variables, the code gets a little messy. Suppose that we have a Squirrel class and assume that the species name will never be null. We could write a constructor to enforce that if we wanted to:

```
public class Squirrel {
    private int weight;
    private String species;
      public Squirrel(String theSpecies) {
          if (theSpecies == null) throw new IllegalArgumentException();
          species = theSpecies;
      }
    public int getWeight() { return weight; }
    public void setWeight(int weight) { this.weight = weight; }
    public String getSpecies() { return species; }
}
```

We want to write a Comparator to sort by species name. If two squirrels are from the species, we want to sort the one that weighs the least first. We could do this with code that looks like this:

```
public class MultiFieldComparator implements Comparator<Squirrel> {
    public int compare(Squirrel s1, Squirrel s2) {
        int result = s1.getSpecies().compareTo(s2.getSpecies());
        if (result != 0) return result;
        return s1.getWeight()-s2.getWeight();
}}
```

This works. It checks one field. If they don't match, we are finished sorting. If they do match, it looks at the next field. This isn't that easy to read, though. It is also easy to get wrong. Changing != to == breaks the sort completely.

Java 8 makes this much easier. With the introduction of static and default methods on interfaces, there are now some new helper methods on Comparator. The code can now be written as this:

```
public class ChainingComparator implements Comparator<Squirrel> {
   public int compare(Squirrel s1, Squirrel s2) {
      Comparator<Squirrel> c = Comparator.comparing(s -> s.getSpecies());
      c = c.thenComparingInt(s -> s.getWeight());
      return c.compare(s1, s2);
}}
```

The lambda means to get the species value out of the squirrel and pass it to the method. You will see lots of functional programming code in the next chapter.

We grant you that it is the same number of lines. The second one is easier to read, though. It describes what we are doing nicely. First we sort by species, and then we sort by weight. We could have used method chaining to write this all on one line.

You've probably noticed by now that we have ignored nulls in checking equality and comparing objects. This works fine for the exam. In the real world, though, things aren't so neat. You will have to decide how to handle nulls or prevent them from being in your object. It is common to decide that nulls sort before any other values.

Searching and Sorting

You already know the basics of searching and sorting. You now know a little more about Comparable and Comparator.

The sort method uses the compareTo() method to sort. It expects the objects to be sorted to be Comparable.

```
1:   import java.util.*;
2:   public class SortRabbits {
3:   static class Rabbit{ int id; }
4:   public static void main(String[] args) {
5:      List<Rabbit> rabbits = new ArrayList<>();
6:      rabbits.add(new Rabbit());
7:      Collections.sort(rabbits);      // DOES NOT COMPILE
8: } }
```

Java knows that the Rabbit class is not Comparable. It knows sorting will fail, so it doesn't even let the code compile. You can fix this by passing a Comparator to sort(). Remember that a Comparator is useful when you want to specify sort order without using a compareTo() method:

```
import java.util.*;
public class SortRabbits {
    static class Rabbit{ int id; }
    public static void main(String[] args) {
        List<Rabbit> rabbits = new ArrayList<>();
        rabbits.add(new Rabbit());
        Comparator<Rabbit> c = (r1, r2) -> r1.id - r2.id;
        Collections.sort(rabbits, c);
} }
```

sort() and binarySearch() allow you to pass in a Comparator object when you don't want to use the natural order. There is a trick in this space. What do you think the following outputs?

```
3:    List<String> names = Arrays.asList("Fluffy", "Hoppy");
4:    Comparator<String> c = Comparator.reverseOrder();
5:    int index = Collections.binarySearch(names, "Hoppy", c);
6:    System.out.println(index);
```

The correct answer is -1. Before you panic, you don't need to know that the answer is -1. You do need to know that the answer is not defined. Line 3 creates a list, [Fluffy, Hoppy]. This list happens to be sorted in ascending order. Line 4 creates a Comparator that reverses the natural order. Line 5 requests a binary search in descending order. Since the list is in ascending order, we don't meet the precondition for doing a search.

Earlier in the chapter, we talked about collections that require classes to implement Comparable. Unlike sorting, they don't check that you have actually implemented Comparable at compile time.

Going back to our Rabbit that does not implement Comparable, we try to add it to a TreeSet:

```
2:    public class UseTreeSet {
3:    static class Rabbit{ int id; }
4:     public static void main(String[] args) {
5:        Set<Duck> ducks = new TreeSet<>();
6:        ducks.add(new Duck("Puddles"));
7:        Set<Rabbit> rabbit = new TreeSet<>();
8:        rabbit.add(new Rabbit());        // throws an exception
9:  } }
```

Line 6 is fine. Duck does implement Comparable. TreeSet is able to sort it into the proper position in the set. Line 8 is a problem. When TreeSet tries to sort it, Java discovers the fact that Rabbit does not implement Comparable. Java throws an exception that looks like this:

```
Exception in thread "main" java.lang.ClassCastException: comparing.Rabbit cannot
be cast to java.lang.Comparable
```

It seems weird for this exception to be thrown when the first object is added to the set. After all, there is nothing to compare yet. Java works this way for consistency.

Just like searching and sorting, you can tell collections that require sorting that you wish to use a specific Comparator, for example:

```java
Set<Rabbit> rabbit = new TreeSet<>(new Comparator<Rabbit>() {
    public int compare(Rabbit r1, Rabbit r2) {
        return r1.id = r2.id;
    }
});
rabbit.add(new Rabbit());
```

Now Java knows that you want to sort by id and all is well. Comparators are helpful objects. They let you separate sort order from the object to be sorted.

Additions in Java 8

Aside from using lambdas for the Comparator implementation, nothing in this chapter has been unique to Java 8. This section is where that changes. Most of the changes in Java 8 revolve around streams, which we will cover in the next chapter. In this chapter, we will also introduce method references to show how to make code more compact. Method references and lambdas are core Java structures now, which means that you should expect to see them in questions about other topics too. We will show you how to use the new removeIf(), forEach(), merge(), computeIfPresent(), and computeIfAbsent() methods.

Using Method References

Method references are a way to make the code shorter by reducing some of the code that can be inferred and simply mentioning the name of the method. Like lambdas, it takes time to get used to the new syntax.

Suppose that we have a Duck class with name and weight attributes along with this helper class:

```java
public class DuckHelper {
    public static int compareByWeight(Duck d1, Duck d2) {
        return d1.getWeight()-d2.getWeight();
    }
    public static int compareByName(Duck d1, Duck d2) {
        return d1.getName().compareTo(d2.getName());
    }
}
```

Now think about how we would write a `Comparator` for it if we wanted to sort by weight. Using lambdas, we'd have the following:

```
Comparator<Duck> byWeight = (d1, d2) -> DuckHelper.compareByWeight(d1, d2);
```

Not bad. There's a bit of redundancy, though. The lambda takes two parameters and does nothing but pass those parameters to another method. Java 8 lets us remove that redundancy and simply write this:

```
Comparator<Duck> byWeight = DuckHelper::compareByWeight;
```

The `::` operator tells Java to pass the parameters automatically into `compareByWeight`.

 NOTE `DuckHelper::compareByWeight` returns a functional interface and not an int. Remember that `::` is like lambdas, and it is typically used for deferred execution.

There are four formats for method references:

- Static methods
- Instance methods on a particular instance
- Instance methods on an instance to be determined at runtime
- Constructors

In this chapter, we will be using three functional interfaces in our examples. We will use more in the next chapter. Remember from Chapter 2 that `Predicate` is a functional interface that takes a single parameter of any type and returns a `boolean`. Another functional interface is `Consumer`, which takes a single parameter of any type and has a `void` return type. Finally, `Supplier` doesn't take any parameters and returns any type.

Let's look at some examples from the Java API. In each set, we show the lambda equivalent. Remember that none of these method references are actually called in the code that follows. They are simply available to be called in the future. Let's start with a static method:

```
14:    Consumer<List<Integer>> methodRef1 = Collections::sort;
15:    Consumer<List<Integer>> lambda1 = l -> Collections.sort(l);
```

On line 14, we call a method with one parameter, and Java knows that it should create a lambda with one parameter and pass it to the method.

Wait a minute. We know that the sort method is overloaded. How does Java know that we want to call the version that omits the comparator? With both lambdas and method references, Java is inferring information from the context. In this case, we said that we were declaring a `Consumer`, which takes only one parameter. Java looks for a method that matches that description.

Next up is calling an instance method on a specific instance:

```
16:    String str = "abc";
17:    Predicate<String> methodRef2 = str::startsWith;
18:    Predicate<String> lambda2 = s -> str.startsWith(s);
```

Line 17 shows that we want to call `string.startsWith()` and pass a single parameter to be supplied at runtime. This would be a nice way of filtering the data in a list. Next, we call an instance method without knowing the instance in advance:

```
19:    Predicate<String> methodRef3 = String::isEmpty;
20:    Predicate<String> lambda3 = s -> s.isEmpty();
```

Line 19 says the method that we want to call is declared in `String`. It looks like a static method, but it isn't. Instead, Java knows that `isEmpty` is an instance method that does not take any parameters. Java uses the parameter supplied at runtime as the instance on which the method is called. Finally, we have a constructor reference:

```
21:    Supplier<ArrayList> methodRef4 = ArrayList::new;
22:    Supplier<ArrayList> lambda4 = () -> new ArrayList();
```

A *constructor reference* is a special type of method reference that uses new instead of a method, and it creates a new object. It expands like the method references you have seen so far. You'll see method references again in the next chapter when we cover more types of functional interfaces.

Removing Conditionally

Java 8 introduces a new method called `removeIf`. Before this, we had the ability to remove a specified object from a collection or a specified index from a list. Now we can specify what should be deleted using a block of code.

The method signature looks like this:

```
boolean removeIf(Predicate<? super E> filter)
```

It uses a `Predicate`, which is a lambda that takes one parameter and returns a `boolean`. Since lambdas use deferred execution, this allows specifying logic to run when that point in the code is reached. Let's take a look at an example:

```
4:    List<String> list = new ArrayList<>();
5:    list.add("Magician");
6:    list.add("Assistant");
7:    System.out.println(list);  // [Magician, Assistant]
8:    list.removeIf(s -> s.startsWith("A"));
9:    System.out.println(list);  // [Magician]
```

Line 8 shows how to remove all of the strings that begin with the letter A. This allows us to make the `Assistant` disappear.

How would you replace line 8 with a method reference? Trick question—you can't. Since `startsWith` takes a parameter that isn't s, it needs to be specified "the long way."

There isn't much to `removeIf` as long as long as you remember how `Predicate` works. If this isn't familiar, go back and review Chapter 2. We will be using lambdas a lot in the next chapter, and you need to have this down cold. The most important thing to remember about `removeIf` is that it is one of two methods that are on a collection and it takes a lambda parameter.

Updating All Elements

Another new method introduced on `Lists` is `replaceAll`. Java 8 lets you pass a lambda expression and have it applied to each element in the list. The result replaces the current value of that element.

The method signature looks like:

```
void replaceAll(UnaryOperator<E> o)
```

It uses a `UnaryOperator`, which takes one parameter and returns a value of the same type. Let's take a look at an example:

```
List<Integer> list = Arrays.asList(1, 2, 3);
list.replaceAll(x -> x*2);
System.out.println(list); // [2, 4, 6]
```

The lambda uses deferred execution to increase the value of each element in the list.

Looping through a Collection

Looping though a `Collection` is very common. For example, we often want to print out the values one per line. There are a few ways to do this. We could use an iterator, the enhanced for loop, or a number of other approaches—or we could use a Java 8 lambda.

Cats like to explore, so let's join two of them as we learn a shorter way to loop through a `Collection`. We start with the traditional way:

```
List<String> cats = Arrays.asList("Annie", "Ripley");
for(String cat: cats)
  System.out.println(cat);
```

This works. We can do the same thing with lambdas in one line:

```
cats.forEach(c -> System.out.println(c));
```

This time, we've used a `Consumer`, which takes a single parameter and doesn't return anything. You won't see this approach used too often because it is common to use a method reference instead:

```
cats.forEach(System.out::println);
```

The cats have now discovered a more efficient way of printing their names. Now they have more time to play (as do we)! In the next chapter, you will learn about using the `stream()` method to do much more powerful things with lambdas.

Using New Java 8 *Map* APIs

Java 8 added a number of new methods on the `Map` interface. Only `merge()` is listed in the OCP objectives. Two others, `computeIfPresent()` and `computeIfAbsent()`, are added in the upgrade exam objectives. We recommend checking http://www.selikoff.net/ocp to make sure that this is still the case before you take the exam.

Sometimes you need to update the value for a specific key in the map. There are a few ways that you can do this. The first is to replace the existing value unconditionally:

```
Map<String, String> favorites = new HashMap<>();
favorites.put("Jenny", "Bus Tour");

favorites.put("Jenny", "Tram");
System.out.println(favorites); // {Jenny=Tram}
```

There's another method, called putIfAbsent(), that you can call if you want to set a value in the map, but this method skips it if the value is already set to a non-null value:

```
Map<String, String> favorites = new HashMap<>();
favorites.put("Jenny", "Bus Tour");
favorites.put("Tom", null);

favorites.putIfAbsent("Jenny", "Tram");
favorites.putIfAbsent("Sam", "Tram");
favorites.putIfAbsent("Tom", "Tram");
System.out.println(favorites); // {Tom=Tram, Jenny=Bus Tour, Sam=Tram}
```

As you can see, Jenny's value is not updated because one was already present. Sam wasn't there at all, so he was added. Tom was present as a key but had a null value. Therefore, he was added as well. These two methods handle simple replacements. Sometimes, you need more logic to determine which value should be used. The following sections show three approaches.

merge

The merge() method allows adding logic to the problem of what to choose. Suppose that our guests are indecisive and can't pick a favorite. They agree that the ride that has the longest name must be the most fun. We can write code to express this by passing a mapping function to the merge() method:

```
11:    BiFunction<String, String, String> mapper = (v1, v2)
12:        -> v1.length() > v2.length() ? v1: v2;
13:
14:    Map<String, String> favorites = new HashMap<>();
15:    favorites.put("Jenny", "Bus Tour");
16:    favorites.put("Tom", "Tram");
17:
18:    String jenny = favorites.merge("Jenny", "Skyride", mapper);
19:    String tom = favorites.merge("Tom", "Skyride", mapper);
20:
21:    System.out.println(favorites); // {Tom=Skyride, Jenny=Bus Tour}
22:    System.out.println(jenny);      // Bus Tour
23:    System.out.println(tom);        // Skyride
```

Line 11 uses a functional interface called a BiFunction. In this case, it takes two parameters of the same type and returns a value of that type. Our implementation returns the one with the longest name. Line 18 calls this mapping function, and it sees that "Bus Tour" is longer than "Skyride," so it leaves the value as "Bus Tour." Line 19 calls this mapping function again. This time "Tram" is not longer than "Skyride," so the map is updated. Line 21 prints out the new map contents. Lines 22 and 23 show that the result gets returned from merge().

The merge() method also has logic for what happens if nulls or missing keys are involved. In this case, it doesn't call the BiFunction at all, and it simply uses the new value:

```
BiFunction<String, String, String> mapper = (v1, v2) -> v1.length() >
v2.length() ? v1 : v2;

Map<String, String> favorites = new HashMap<>();
favorites.put("Sam", null);

favorites.merge("Tom", "Skyride", mapper);
favorites.merge("Sam", "Skyride", mapper);

System.out.println(favorites); // {Tom=Skyride, Sam=Skyride}
```

Notice that the mapping function isn't called. If it were, we'd have a NullPointerException. The mapping function is used only when there are two actual values to decide between.

The final thing to know about merge() is what happens when the mapping function is called and returns null. The key is removed from the map when this happens:

```
BiFunction<String, String, String> mapper = (v1, v2) -> null;

Map<String, String> favorites = new HashMap<>();
favorites.put("Jenny", "Bus Tour");
favorites.put("Tom", "Bus Tour");

favorites.merge("Jenny", "Skyride", mapper);
favorites.merge("Sam", "Skyride", mapper);

System.out.println(favorites); // {Tom=Bus Tour, Sam=Skyride}
```

Tom was left alone since there was no merge() call for that key. Sam was added since that key was not in the original list. Jenny was removed because the mapping function returned null. You'll see merge again in the next chapter.

computeIfPresent and computeIfAbsent

These two methods are on the upgrade exam but not on the OCP exam. In a nutshell, computeIfPresent() calls the BiFunction if the requested key is found.

```
Map<String, Integer> counts = new HashMap<>();
counts.put("Jenny", 1);

BiFunction<String, Integer, Integer> mapper = (k, v) -> v + 1;
Integer jenny = counts.computeIfPresent("Jenny", mapper);
Integer sam = counts.computeIfPresent("Sam", mapper);
System.out.println(counts); // {Jenny=2}
System.out.println(jenny); // 2
System.out.println(sam); // null
```

The function interface is a BiFunction again. However, this time the key and value are passed rather than two values. Just like with merge(), the return value is the result of what changed in the map or null if that doesn't apply.

For computeIfAbsent(), the functional interface runs only when the key isn't present or is null:

```
Map<String, Integer> counts = new HashMap<>();
counts.put("Jenny", 15);
counts.put("Tom", null);

Function<String, Integer> mapper = (k) -> 1;
Integer jenny = counts.computeIfAbsent("Jenny", mapper); // 15
Integer sam = counts.computeIfAbsent("Sam", mapper); // 1
Integer tom = counts.computeIfAbsent("Tom", mapper); // 1
System.out.println(counts); // {Tom=1, Jenny=15, Sam=1}
```

Since there is no value already in the map, a Function is used instead of a BiFunction. Only the key is passed as input. As you can see, Jenny isn't changed because that key is already in the map. Tom is updated because null is treated like not being there.

If the mapping function is called and returns null, the key is removed from the map for computeIfPresent(). For computeIfAbsent(), the key is never added to the map in the first place, for example:

```
Map<String, Integer> counts = new HashMap<>();
counts.put("Jenny", 1);

counts.computeIfPresent("Jenny", (k, v) -> null);
counts.computeIfAbsent("Sam", k -> null);
System.out.println(counts); // {}
```

After running this code, the map is empty. The call to computeIfPresent() removes the key from the map. The call to computeIfAbsent() doesn't add a key.

Table 3.11 and Table 3.12 show all of these scenarios as a reference.

TABLE 3.11   The basics of the merge and compute methods

Scenario	merge	computeIfAbsent	computeIfPresent
Key already in map	Result of function	No action	Result of function
Key not already in map	Add new value to map	Result of function	No action
Functional Interface used	BiFunction (Takes existing value and new value. Returns new value.)	BiFunction (Takes key and existing value. Returns new value.)	Function (Takes key and returns new value.)

TABLE 3.12   Merge and compute methods when nulls are involved

Key has	Mapping functions returns	merge	computeIfAbsent	computeIfPresent
null value in map	null	Remove key from map.	Do not change map.	Do not change map.
null value in map	Not null	Set key to mapping function result.	Add key to map with mapping function result as value.	Do not change map.
Non-null value in map	null	Remove key from map.	Do not change map.	Remove key from map.
Non-null value in map	Not null	Set key to mapping function result.	Do not change map.	Set key to mapping function result.
Key not in map	null	Add key to map.	Do not change map.	Do not change map.
Key not in map	Not null	Add key to map.	Add key to map with mapping function result as value.	Do not change map.

Summary

Generics are type parameters for code. To create a class with a generic parameter, add <T> after the class name. You can use any name you want for the type parameter. Single upper-case letters are common choices.

The diamond operator (<>) is used to tell Java that the generic type matches the declaration without specifying it again. The diamond operator can be used for local variables or instance variables as well as one-line declarations.

Generics allow you to specify wildcards. <?> is an unbounded wildcard that means any type. <? extends Object> is an upper bound that means any type that is Object or extends it. <? extends MyInterface> means any type that implements MyInterface. <? super Number> is a lower bound that means any type that is Number or a superclass. A compiler error results from code that attempts to add or remove an item in a list with an unbounded or upper-bounded wildcard.

When working with code that doesn't use generics (also known as legacy code or raw types), Java gives a compiler warning. A compiler warning is different than a compiler error in that the compiler still produces a class file. If you ignore the compiler warning, the code might throw a ClassCastException at runtime. Unboxing gives a compiler error when generics are not used.

Each primitive class has a corresponding wrapper class. For example, long's wrapper class is Long. Java can automatically convert between primitive and wrapper classes when needed. This is called autoboxing and unboxing. Java will only use autoboxing if it doesn't find a matching method signature with the primitive. For example, remove(int n) will be called rather than remove(Object o) when called with an int.

The Java Collections Framework includes four main types of data structures: lists, sets, queues, and maps. The Collection interface is the parent interface of List, Set, and Queue. The Map interface does not extend Collection. You need to recognize the following:

- List—An ordered collection of elements that allows duplicate entries
  - ArrayList—Standard resizable list.
  - LinkedList—Can easily add/remove from beginning or end.
  - Vector—Older thread-safe version of ArrayList.
  - Stack—Older last-in, first-out class.
- Set—Does not allow duplicates
  - HashSet—Uses hashcode() to find unordered elements.
  - TreeSet—Sorted and navigable. Does not allow null values.
- Queue—Orders elements for processing
  - LinkedList—Can easily add/remove from beginning or end.
  - ArrayDeque—First-in, first-out or last-in, first-out. Does not allow null values.
- Map—Maps unique keys to values
  - HashMap—Uses hashcode() to find keys.
  - TreeMap—Sorted map. Does not allow null keys.
  - Hashtable—Older version of hashmap. Does not allow null keys or values.

The Comparable interface declares the compareTo() method. This method returns a negative number if the object is smaller than its argument, zero if the two objects are equal, and a positive number otherwise. compareTo() is declared on the object that is being compared, and it takes one parameter. The Comparator interface defines the compare() method. A negative number is returned if the first argument is smaller, zero if they are equal, and a positive number otherwise. compare() can be declared in any code, and it takes two parameters. Comparator is often implemented using a lambda.

The Arrays and Collections classes have methods for sort() and binarySearch(). Both take an optional Comparator parameter. It is necessary to use the same sort order for both sorting and searching, so the result is not undefined. Collection has a few methods that take lambdas, including removeIf(), forEach(), and merge().

A method reference is a compact syntax for writing lambdas that refer to methods. There are four types: static methods, instance methods referring to a specific instance, instance methods with the instance supplied at runtime, and constructor references.

Exam Essentials

Pick the correct type of collection from a description.   A List allows duplicates and orders the elements. A Set does not allow duplicates. A Queue orders its elements to allow retrievals from one or both ends. A Map maps keys to values. Be familiar with the differences of implementations of these interfaces.

Identify valid and invalid uses of generics.   <T> represents a type parameter. Any name can be used, but a single uppercase letter is the convention. <?> is an unbounded wildcard. <? extends X> is an upper-bounded wildcard and applies to both classes and interfaces. <? super X> is a lower-bounded wildcard.

Recognize the difference between compiler warnings and errors when dealing with legacy code.   A compiler warning occurs when using non-generic types, and a ClassCastException might occur at runtime. A compiler error occurs when trying to unbox from a legacy collection.

Differentiate between Comparable and Comparator.   Classes that implement Comparable are said to have a natural ordering and implement the compareTo() method. A class is allowed to have only one natural ordering. A Comparator takes two objects in the compare() method. Different Comparators can have different sort orders. A Comparator is often implemented using a lambda such as (a, b) -> a.num - b.num.

Understand the behavior and usage of the sort and binary search methods.   The Collections and Arrays classes provide overloaded sort() and binarySearch() methods. They take an optional Comparator parameter. The list or array must be sorted before it is searched using the same definition of order for both.

Map method references to the "long form" lambda.   Be able to convert method references into regular lambda expressions and vice versa. For example, System.out::print and x -> System.out.print(x) are equivalent.

Review Questions

1. Suppose that you have a collection of products for sale in a database and you need to display those products. The products are not unique. Which of the following collections classes in the `java.util` package best suit your needs for this scenario?

   A. Arrays

   B. ArrayList

   C. HashMap

   D. HashSet

   E. LinkedList

2. Suppose that you need to work with a collection of elements that need to be sorted in their natural order, and each element has a unique string associated with its value. Which of the following collections classes in the `java.util` package best suit your needs for this scenario?

   A. ArrayList

   B. HashMap

   C. HashSet

   D. TreeMap

   E. TreeSet

   F. Vector

3. What is the result of the following statements?

   ```
   3:    List list = new ArrayList();
   4:    list.add("one");
   5:    list.add("two");
   6:    list.add(7);
   7:    for (String s: list)
   8:    System.out.print(s);
   ```

   A. onetwo

   B. onetwo7

   C. onetwo followed by an exception

   D. Compiler error on line 6

   E. Compiler error on line 7

4. What is the result of the following statements?

   ```
   3:    ArrayDeque<String> greetings = new ArrayDeque<String>();
   4:    greetings.push("hello");
   5:    greetings.push("hi");
   6:    greetings.push("ola");
   ```

```
7:      greetings.pop();
8:      greetings.peek();
9:      while (greetings.peek() != null)
10:         System.out.print(greetings.pop());
```

A. hello

B. hellohi

C. hellohiola

D. hi

E. hihello

F. The code does not compile.

G. An exception is thrown.

5. Which of these statements compile? (Choose all that apply.)

A. `HashSet<Number> hs = new HashSet<Integer>();`

B. `HashSet<? super ClassCastException> set = new HashSet<Exception>();`

C. `List<String> list = new Vector<String>();`

D. `List<Object> values = new HashSet<Object>();`

E. `List<Object> objects = new ArrayList<? extends Object>();`

F. `Map<String, ? extends Number> hm = new HashMap<String, Integer>();`

6. What is the result of the following code?

```
1:      public class Hello<T> {
2:          T t;
3:          public Hello(T t) { this.t = t; }
4:          public String toString() { return t.toString(); }
5:          public static void main(String[] args) {
6:              System.out.print(new Hello<String>("hi"));
7:              System.out.print(new Hello("there"));
8:          } }
```

A. hi

B. hi followed by a runtime exception

C. hithere

D. Compiler error on line 4

E. Compiler error on line 6

F. Compiler error on line 7

7. Which of the following statements are true? (Select two.)

```
3:      Set<Number> numbers = new HashSet<>();
4:      numbers.add(new Integer(86));
```

```
5:      numbers.add(75);
6:      numbers.add(new Integer(86));
7:      numbers.add(null);
8:      numbers.add(309L);
9:      Iterator iter = numbers.iterator();
10:     while (iter.hasNext())
11:         System.out.print(iter.next());
```

A. The code compiles successfully.

B. The output is 8675null309.

C. The output is 867586null309.

D. The output is indeterminate.

E. There is a compiler error on line 3.

F. There is a compiler error on line 9.

G. An exception is thrown.

8. What is the result of the following code?

```
TreeSet<String> tree = new TreeSet<String>();
tree.add("one");
tree.add("One");
tree.add("ONE");
System.out.println(tree.ceiling("On"));
```

A. On

B. one

C. One

D. ONE

E. The code does not compile.

F. An exception is thrown.

9. Which of the answer choices are valid given the following declaration?

```
Map<String, Double> map = new HashMap<>();
```

A. map.add("pi", 3.14159);

B. map.add("e", 2L);

C. map.add("log(1)", new Double(0.0));

D. map.add('x', new Double(123.4));

E. None of the above

10. What is the result of the following program?

```
import java.util.*;

public class MyComparator implements Comparator<String> {
```

```
   public int compare(String a, String b) {
      return b.toLowerCase().compareTo(a.toLowerCase());
   }

   public static void main(String[] args) {
      String[] values = { "123", "Abb", "aab" };
      Arrays.sort(values, new MyComparator());
      for (String s: values)
         System.out.print(s + " ");
         }
}
```

A. Abb aab 123

B. aab Abb 123

C. 123 Abb aab

D. 123 aab Abb

E. The code does not compile.

F. A runtime exception is thrown.

11. What is the result of the following code?

```
3:    Map<Integer, Integer> map = new HashMap<>(10);
4:    for (int i = 1; i <= 10; i++) {
5:       map.put(i, i * i);
6:    }
7:    System.out.println(map.get(4));
```

A. 16

B. 25

C. Compiler error on line 3.

D. Compiler error on line 5.

E. Compiler error on line 7.

F. A runtime exception is thrown.

12. Which of these statements can fill in the blank so that the Helper class compiles successfully? (Choose all that apply.)

```
3:    public class Helper {
4:       public static <U extends Exception> void printException(U u) {
5:          System.out.println(u.getMessage());
6:       }
7:       public static void main(String[] args) {
8:          _____
9:       } }
```

A. `Helper.printException(new FileNotFoundException("A"));`

B. `Helper.printException(new Exception("B"));`

C. `Helper.<Throwable>printException(new Exception("C"));`

D. `Helper.<NullPointerException>printException(new NullPointerException`
`("D"));`

E. `Helper.printException(new Throwable("E"));`

13. Which of these statements can fill in the blank so that the `Wildcard` class compiles successfully? (Choose all that apply.)

```
import java.util.*;

public class Wildcard {
    public void showSize(List<?> list) {
        System.out.println(list.size());
    }
    public static void main(String[] args) {
        Wildcard card = new Wildcard();

        _____

        card.showSize(list);
    } }
```

A. `ArrayDeque<?> list = new ArrayDeque<String>();`

B. `ArrayList<? super Date> list = new ArrayList<Date>();`

C. `List<?> list = new ArrayList<?>();`

D. `List<Exception> list = new LinkedList<java.io.IOException>();`

E. `Vector<? extends Number> list = new Vector<Integer>();`

F. None of the above

14. What is the result of the following program?

```
import java.util.*;
public class Sorted implements Comparable<Sorted>, Comparator<Sorted> {
    private int num;
    private String text;

    Sorted(int n, String t) {
        this.num = n;
        this.text = t;
    }
    public String toString() { return "" + num; }
    public int compareTo(Sorted s) { return text.compareTo(s.text); }
    public int compare(Sorted s1, Sorted s2) { return s1.num - s2.num; }
```

```
public static void main(String[] args) {
    Sorted s1 = new Sorted(88, "a");
    Sorted s2 = new Sorted(55, "b");
    TreeSet<Sorted> t1 = new TreeSet<>();
    t1.add(s1);    t1.add(s2);
    TreeSet<Sorted> t2 = new TreeSet<>(s1);
    t2.add(s1); t2.add(s2);
    System.out.println(t1 + " " + t2);
} }
```

A. [55. 88] [55, 88]

B. [55. 88] [88, 55]

C. [88. 55] [55, 88]

D. [88. 55] [88, 55]

E. The code does not compile.

F. A runtime exception is thrown.

15. What is the result of the following code?

```
Comparator<Integer> c = (o1, o2) -> o2-o1;
List<Integer> list = Arrays.asList(5, 4, 7, 1);
Collections.sort(list, c);
System.out.println(Collections.binarySearch(list, 1));
```

A. 0

B. 1

C. 2

D. The result is undefined.

E. The code does not compile.

F. A runtime exception is thrown.

16. Which of the following statements are true? (Choose all that apply.)

A. Comparable is in the java.util package.

B. Comparator is in the java.util package.

C. compare() is in the Comparable interface.

D. compare() is in the Comparator interface.

E. compare() takes one method parameter.

F. compare() takes two method parameters.

17. Which two options can fill in the blanks to make this code compile? (Choose all that apply.)

```
1:      public class Generic_____ {
2:          public static void main(String[] args) {
```

```
3:              Generic<String> g = new Generic_____();
4:              Generic<Object> g2 = new Generic();
5:      }
6:  }
```

A. On line 1, fill in with <>.

B. On line 1, fill in with <T>.

C. On line 1, fill in with <?>.

D. On line 3, fill in with <>.

E. On line 3, fill in with <T>.

F. On line 3, fill in with <?>.

18. Which of the following lines can be inserted to make the code compile? (Choose all that apply.)

```
class A {}
class B extends A {}
class C extends B {}

class D<C> {
    // INSERT CODE HERE
}
```

A. A a1 = new A();

B. A a2 = new B();

C. A a3 = new C();

D. C c1 = new A();

E. C c2 = new B();

F. C c1 = new C();

19. Which options are true of the following code? (Choose all that apply.)

```
3:      _____<Integer> q = new LinkedList<>();
4:      q.add(10);
5:      q.add(12);
6:      q.remove(1);
7:      System.out.print(q);
```

A. If we fill in the blank with List, the output is [10].

B. If we fill in the blank with List, the output is [10, 12].

C. If we fill in the blank with Queue, the output is [10].

D. If we fill in the blank with `Queue`, the output is `[10, 12]`.

E. The code does not compile in either scenario.

F. A runtime exception is thrown.

20. What is the result of the following code?

```
4: Map m = new HashMap();
5: m.put(123, "456");
6: m.put("abc", "def");
7: System.out.println(m.contains("123"));
```

A. false

B. true

C. Compiler error on line 4.

D. Compiler error on line 5.

E. Compiler error on line 7.

F. A runtime exception is thrown.

21. Fill in the blanks to make this code compile and print 123. (Choose all that apply.)

```
4:    List<String> list = Arrays.asList("1", "2", "3");
5:    Iterator iter = list.iterator();
6:    while(iter._____())
7:        System.out.print(iter._____());
```

A. On line 6, fill in the blank with `hasNext()`.

B. On line 6, fill in the blank with `isNext()`.

C. On line 6, fill in the blank with `next()`.

D. On line 7, fill in the blank with `getNext()`.

E. On line 7, fill in the blank with `hasNext()`.

F. On line 7, fill in the blank with `next()`.

22. What code change is needed to make the method compile?

```
public static T identity(T t) {
    return t;
}
```

A. Add `<T>` after the `public` keyword.

B. Add `<T>` after the `static` keyword.

C. Add `<T>` after T.

D. Add `<?>` after the `public` keyword.

E. Add `<?>` after the `static` keyword.

F. No change required. The code already compiles.

23. Which of the answer choices make sense to implement with a lambda? (Choose all that apply.)

A. Comparable interface

B. Comparator interface

C. remove method on a Collection

D. removeAll method on a Collection

E. removeIf method on a Collection

24. Which of the following compiles and print outs the entire set? (Choose all that apply.)

```
Set<String> s = new HashSet<>();
s.add("lion");
s.add("tiger");
s.add("bear");
s.forEach(_____);
```

A. () -> System.out.println(s)

B. s -> System.out.println(s)

C. (s) -> System.out.println(s)

D. System.out.println(s)

E. System::out::println

F. System.out::println

25. What is the result of the following?

```
Map<Integer, Integer> map = new HashMap<>();
map.put(1, 10);
map.put(2, 20);
map.put(3, null);

map.merge(1, 3, (a,b) -> a + b);
map.merge(3, 3, (a,b) -> a + b);

System.out.println(map);
```

A. {1=10, 2=20}

B. {1=10, 2=20, 3=null}

C. {1=10, 2=20, 3=3}

D. {1=13, 2=20}

E. {1=13, 2=20, 3=null}

F. {1=13, 2=20, 3=3}

G. The code does not compile.

H. An exception is thrown.

Chapter 4

Functional Programming

THE OCP EXAM TOPICS COVERED IN THIS CHAPTER INCLUDE THE FOLLOWING:

✓ **Generics and Collections**

- Collections Streams and Filters

- Iterate using forEach methods of Streams and List

- Describe Stream interface and Stream pipeline

- Use method references with Streams

✓ **Lambda Built-In Functional Interfaces**

- Use the built-in interfaces included in the java.util.function package such as Predicate, Consumer, Function, and Supplier

- Develop code that uses primitive versions of functional interfaces

- Develop code that uses binary versions of functional interfaces

- Develop code that uses the UnaryOperator interface

✓ **Java Stream API**

- Develop code to extract data from an object using peek() and map() methods including primitive versions of the map() method

- Search for data by using search methods of the Stream classes including findFirst, findAny, anyMatch, allMatch, and noneMatch

- Develop code that uses the Optional class

- Develop code that uses Stream data methods and calculation methods

- Sort a collection using Stream API

- Save results to a collection using the collect method and group/partition data using the Collectors class

- Use of merge() and flatMap() methods of the Stream API

By now, you should be comfortable with the lambda and method reference syntax. Both are used when implementing functional interfaces. If you aren't comfortable with this, go back and review Chapter 2, "Design Patterns and Principles," and Chapter 3, "Generics and Collections." You even used methods like forEach() and merge() in Chapter 3. In this chapter, we'll add actual functional programming to that, focusing on the Streams API. Note that the Streams API in this chapter is used for functional programming. By contrast, there are also java.io streams, which we will talk about in Chapter 8, "IO."

In this chapter, we will introduce many more functional interfaces and Optional classes. Then we will introduce the Stream pipeline and tie it all together. You might have noticed that this chapter covers a long list of objectives. That's because they are extremely detailed and many of them cover a tiny topic each. Don't worry if you find the list daunting. By the time you finish the chapter, you'll see that many of the objectives cover similar topics. You might even want to read this chapter twice before doing the review questions, so that you really get the hang of it.

Using Variables in Lambdas

In Chapter 1, "Advanced Class Design," we talked about the idea of "effectively final." This meant that if you could add the final modifier to a local variable, it was "effectively final." Lambdas use the same access rules as inner classes.

Lambda expressions can access static variables, instance variables, effectively final method parameters, and effectively final local variables. How many of those can you find in this example?

```
1:    interface Gorilla { String move(); }
2:    class GorillaFamily {
3:       String walk = "walk";
4:       void everyonePlay(boolean baby) {
5:          String approach = "amble";
6:          //approach = "run";
7:
8:          play(() -> walk);
9:          play(() -> baby ? "hitch a ride": "run");
10:         play(() -> approach);
11:      }
```

```
12:     void play(Gorilla g) {
13:         System.out.println(g.move());
14:     }
15:   }
```

Line 8 uses an instance variable in the lambda. Line 9 uses a method parameter. We know it is effectively final since there are no reassignments to that variable. Line 10 uses an effectively final local variable. If we uncomment line 6, there will be a reassignment and the variable will no longer be effectively final. This would cause a compiler error on line 10 when it tries to access a non–effectively final variable.

The normal rules for access control still apply. For example, a lambda can't access private variables in another class. Remember that lambdas can access a subset of variables that are accessible, but never more than that.

Working with Built-In Functional Interfaces

As you remember, a functional interface has exactly one abstract method. All of the functional interfaces in Table 4.1 were introduced in Java 8 and are provided in the java.util.function package. The convention here is to use the generic type T for type parameter. If a second type parameter is needed, the next letter, U, is used. If a distinct return type is needed, R for *return* is used for the generic type.

TABLE 4.1   Common functional interfaces

Functional Interfaces	# Parameters	Return Type	Single Abstract Method
Supplier<T>	0	T	get
Consumer<T>	1 (T)	void	accept
BiConsumer<T, U>	2 (T, U)	void	accept
Predicate<T>	1 (T)	boolean	test
BiPredicate<T, U>	2 (T, U)	boolean	test
Function<T, R>	1 (T)	R	apply
BiFunction<T, U, R>	2 (T, U)	R	apply
UnaryOperator<T>	1 (T)	T	apply
BinaryOperator<T>	2 (T, T)	T	apply

Many other functional interfaces are defined in the java.util.function package. They are for working with primitives, which you'll see later in the chapter.

You do need to memorize this table. We will give you lots of practice in this section to help make this memorable. Before you ask, most of the time we don't actually assign the implementation of the interface to a variable. The interface name is implied, and it gets passed directly to the method that needs it. We are introducing the names so that you can better understand and remember what is going on. Once we get to the streams part of the chapter, we will assume that you have this down and stop creating the intermediate variable.

As you saw in Chapter 2, you can name a functional interface anything you want. The only requirements are that it must be a valid interface name and contain a single abstract method. Table 4.1 is significant because these interfaces are often used in streams and other classes that come with Java, which is why you need to memorize them for the exam.

 As you'll learn in Chapter 7, there's an interface called Runnable. It is used for concurrency the majority of the time. However, it may show up on the exam when you are asked to recognize which functional interface to use. All you need to know is that Runnable doesn't take any parameters, return any data, or use generics.

Let's look at how to implement each of these interfaces. Since both lambdas and method references show up all over, we show an implementation using both where possible.

Implementing *Supplier*

A Supplier is used when you want to generate or supply values without taking any input. The Supplier interface is defined as

```java
@FunctionalInterface public class Supplier<T> {
    public T get();
}
```

On the OCA, you learned that you could create a date using a factory. If you've forgotten how, don't worry. We will be covering it again in Chapter 5, "Dates, Strings, and Localization," in this book. You can use a Supplier to call this factory:

```java
Supplier<LocalDate> s1 = LocalDate::now;
Supplier<LocalDate> s2 = () -> LocalDate.now();

LocalDate d1 = s1.get();
LocalDate d2 = s2.get();

System.out.println(d1);
System.out.println(d2);
```

This example prints a date such as 2015-06-20 twice. It's also a good opportunity to review static method references. The LocalDate::now method reference is used to create a Supplier to assign to an intermediate variable s1. A Supplier is often used when constructing new objects. For example, we can print two empty StringBuilders:

```
Supplier<StringBuilder> s1 = StringBuilder::new;
Supplier<StringBuilder> s2 = () -> new StringBuilder();

System.out.println(s1.get());
System.out.println(s2.get());
```

This time, we use a constructor reference to create the object. We've been using generics to declare what type of Supplier we are using. This can get a little long to read. Can you figure out what the following does? Just take it one step at a time.

```
Supplier<ArrayList<String>> s1 = ArrayList<String>::new;
ArrayList<String> a1 = s1.get();
System.out.println(a1);
```

We have a Supplier of a certain type. That type happens to be ArrayList<String>. Then calling get() creates a new instance of ArrayList<String>, which is the generic type of the Supplier—in other words, a generic that contains another generic. It's not hard to understand, so just look at the code carefully when this type of thing comes up.

Notice how we called get() on the functional interface. What would happen if we tried to print out s1 itself?

System.out.println(s1); prints something like this:

```
functionalinterface.BuiltIns$$Lambda$1/791452441@1fb3ebeb
```

That's the result of calling toString() on a lambda. Yuck. This actually does mean something. Our test class is named BuiltIns, and it is in a package that we created named functionalinterface. Then comes $$, which means that the class doesn't exist in a class file on the file system. It exists only in memory. You don't need to worry about the rest.

Implementing *Consumer* and *BiConsumer*

You use a Consumer when you want to do something with a parameter but not return anything. BiConsumer does the same thing except that it takes two parameters. Omitting the default methods, the interfaces are defined as follows:

```
@FunctionalInterface public class Consumer<T> {
    void accept(T t);
}
@FunctionalInterface public class BiConsumer<T, U> {
    void accept(T t, U u);
}
```

You'll notice this pattern. *Bi* means two. It comes from Latin, but you can remember it from English words like *binary* (0 or 1) or *bicycle* (two wheels). Always add another parameter when you see *Bi* show up.

You used a Consumer in Chapter 3 with forEach. Here's that example actually being assigned to the Consumer interface:

```
Consumer<String> c1 =  System.out::println;
Consumer<String> c2 = x -> System.out.println(x);


c1.accept("Annie");
c2.accept("Annie");
```

This example prints Annie twice. You might notice that the Consumer examples used the method reference System.out::println. That's OK. Java uses the context of the lambda to determine which overloaded println() method it should call.

BiConsumer is called with two parameters. They don't have to be the same type. For example, we can put a key and a value in a map using this interface:

```
Map<String, Integer> map = new HashMap<>();
BiConsumer<String, Integer> b1 =  map::put;
BiConsumer<String, Integer> b2 = (k, v) -> map.put(k, v);


b1.accept("chicken", 7);
b2.accept("chick", 1);


System.out.println(map);
```

The output is {chicken=7, chick=1}, which shows that both BiConsumer implementations did get called. This time we used an instance method reference since we want to call a method on the local variable map. It's also the first time that we passed two parameters to a method reference. The code to instantiate b1 is a good bit shorter than the code for b2. This is probably why the exam is so fond of method references.

As another example, we use the same type for both generic parameters:

```
Map<String, String> map = new HashMap<>();
BiConsumer<String, String> b1 =  map::put;
BiConsumer<String, String> b2 = (k, v) -> map.put(k, v);


b1.accept("chicken", "Cluck");
b2.accept("chick", "Tweep");


System.out.println(map);
```

The output is {chicken=Cluck, chick=Tweep}, which shows that a BiConsumer can use the same type for both the T and U generic parameters.

Implementing *Predicate* and *BiPredicate*

You've been using Predicate since the OCA, and you saw it again more recently with removeIf() in Chapter 3. Predicate is often used when filtering or matching. Both are very common operations. A BiPredicate is just like a Predicate except that it takes two parameters instead of one. Omitting any default or static methods, the interfaces are defined as follows:

```
@FunctionalInterface public class Predicate<T> {
   boolean test(T t);
}
@FunctionalInterface public class BiPredicate<T, U> {
   boolean test(T t, U u);
}
```

It should be old news by now that you can use a Predicate to test a condition:

```
Predicate<String> p1 =  String::isEmpty;
Predicate<String> p2 = x -> x.isEmpty();

System.out.println(p1.test(""));
System.out.println(p2.test(""));
```

This prints true twice. More interesting is a BiPredicate. This example also prints true twice:

```
BiPredicate<String, String> b1 =  String::startsWith;
BiPredicate<String, String> b2 = (string, prefix) -> string.startsWith(prefix);

System.out.println(b1.test("chicken", "chick"));
System.out.println(b2.test("chicken", "chick"));
```

The method reference combines two techniques that you've already seen. startsWith() is an instance method. This means that the first parameter in the lambda is used as the instance on which to call the method. The second parameter is passed to the startsWith() method itself. This is another example of how method references save a good bit of typing. The downside is that they are less explicit, and you really have to understand what is going on!

Real World Scenario

Default Methods on Functional Interfaces

By definition, all functional interfaces have a single abstract method. This doesn't mean that they have only one method, though. Several of the common functional interfaces provide a number of helpful default methods. You don't need to know these for the exam, but they are helpful when you start building your own implementations out in the real world.

Suppose that we have these two Predicates:

```
Predicate<String> egg = s -> s.contains("egg");
Predicate<String> brown = s -> s.contains("brown");
```

Now we want a Predicate for brown eggs and another for all other colors of eggs. We could write this by hand:

```
Predicate<String> brownEggs = s -> s.contains("egg") && s.contains("brown");
Predicate<String> otherEggs = s -> s.contains("egg") && ! s.contains("brown");
```

This works, but it's not great. It's a bit long to read, and it contains duplication. What if we decide the letter *e* should be capitalized in *eggs*? We'd have to change it in three variables: egg, brownEggs, and otherEggs.

A better way to deal with this situation is to use two of the default methods on Predicate:

```
Predicate<String> brownEggs = egg.and(brown);
Predicate<String> otherEggs = egg.and(brown.negate());
```

Neat! Now we are reusing the logic in the original Predicates to build two new ones. It's shorter and clearer what the relationship is between the Predicates. We can also change the spelling of *egg* in one place, and the other two objects will have new logic because they reference it.

Implementing *Function* and *BiFunction*

A Function is responsible for turning one parameter into a value of a potentially different type and returning it. Similarly, a BiFunction is responsible for turning two parameters into a value and returning it. Omitting any default or static methods, the interfaces are defined as the following:

```
@FunctionalInterface public class Function<T, R> {
    R apply(T t);
}
```

```
@FunctionalInterface public class BiFunction<T, U, R> {
    R apply(T t, U u);
}
```

For example, this function converts a `String` to the length of the `String`:

```
Function<String, Integer> f1 =  String::length;
Function<String, Integer> f2 = x -> x.length();

System.out.println(f1.apply("cluck"));  // 5
System.out.println(f2.apply("cluck"));  // 5
```

This function turns a `String` into an `Integer`. Well, technically it turns the `String` into an `int`, which is autoboxed into an `Integer`. The types don't have to be different. The following combines two `String` objects and produces another `String`:

```
BiFunction<String, String, String> b1 =  String::concat;
BiFunction<String, String, String> b2 = (string, toAdd) -> string.concat(toAdd);

System.out.println(b1.apply("baby ", "chick")); // baby chick
System.out.println(b2.apply("baby ", "chick")); // baby chick
```

The first two types in the `BiFunction` are the input types. The third is the result type. For the method reference, the first parameter is the instance that concat() is called on and the second is passed to concat().

Creating Your Own Functional Interfaces

Java provides a built-in interface for functions with one or two parameters. What if you need more? No problem. Suppose that you want to create a functional interface for the wheel speed of each wheel on a tricycle. You could create a functional interface such as this:

```
interface TriFunction<T,U,V,R> {
    R apply(T t, U u, V v);
}
```

There are four type parameters. The first three supply the types of the three wheel speeds. The fourth is the return type. Now suppose that you want to create a function to determine how fast your quad-copter is going given the power of the four motors. You could create a functional interface such as the following:

```
interface QuadFunction<T,U,V,W,R> {
    R apply(T t, U u, V v, W w);
}
```

There are five type parameters here. The first four supply the types of the four motors. Ideally these would be the same type, but you never know. The fifth is the return type.

Java's built-in interfaces are meant to facilitate the most common functional interfaces that you'll need. It is by no means an exhaustive list. Remember that you can add any functional interfaces you'd like, and Java matches them when you use lambdas or method references.

Implementing *UnaryOperator* and *BinaryOperator*

UnaryOperator and BinaryOperator are a special case of a function. They require all type parameters to be the same type. A UnaryOperator transforms its value into one of the same type. For example, incrementing by one is a unary operation. In fact, UnaryOperator extends Function. A BinaryOperator merges two values into one of the same type. Adding two numbers is a binary operation. Similarly, BinaryOperator extends BiFunction. Omitting any default or static methods, the interfaces are defined as follows:

```
@FunctionalInterface public class UnaryOperator<T>
    extends Function<T, T> { }
@FunctionalInterface public class BinaryOperator<T>
    extends BiFunction<T, T, T> { }
```

This means that method signatures look like this:

```
T apply(T t);
T apply(T t1, T t2);
```

If you look at the Javadoc, you'll notice that these methods are actually declared on the Function/BiFunction superclass. The generic declarations on the subclass are what force the type to be the same. For the unary example, notice how the return type is the same type as the parameter:

```
UnaryOperator<String> u1 =  String::toUpperCase;
UnaryOperator<String> u2 = x -> x.toUpperCase();

System.out.println(u1.apply("chirp"));
System.out.println(u2.apply("chirp"));
```

This prints CHIRP twice. We don't need to specify the return type in the generics because UnaryOperator requires it to be the same as the parameter. And now for the binary example:

```
BinaryOperator<String> b1 =  String::concat;
BinaryOperator<String> b2 = (string, toAdd) -> string.concat(toAdd);
```

```
System.out.println(b1.apply("baby ", "chick")); // baby chick
System.out.println(b2.apply("baby ", "chick")); // baby chick
```

Notice that this does the same thing as the BiFunction example. The code is more succinct, which shows the importance of using the correct functional interface. It's nice to have one generic type specified instead of three.

Checking Functional Interfaces

It's really important to know the number of parameters, types, return value, and method name for each of the functional interfaces. Now would be a good time to memorize Table 4.1 if you haven't done so already. Let's do some examples to practice.

What functional interface would you use in these three situations?

- Returns a String without taking any parameters
- Returns a Boolean and takes a String
- Returns an Integer and takes two Integers

Ready? Think about your answer is before continuing. Really. You have to know this cold. OK. The first one is a Supplier because it generates an object and takes zero parameters. The second one is a Function because it takes one parameter and returns another type. It's a little tricky. You might think it is a Predicate. Note that a Predicate returns a boolean primitive and not a Boolean object. Finally, the third one is either a BinaryOperator or BiFunction. Since BinaryOperator is a special case of BiFunction, either is a correct answer. BinaryOperator is the better answer of the two since it is more specific.

Let's try this exercise again but with code. It's harder with code. With code, the first thing you do is look at how many parameters the lambda takes and whether there is a return value. What functional interface would you use to fill in the blank for these?

```
6:    ____<List> ex1 = x -> "".equals(x.get(0));
7:    ____<Long> ex2 = (Long l) -> System.out.println(l);
8:    ____ <String, String> ex3 = (s1, s2) -> false;
```

Again, think about the answers before continuing. Ready? Line 6 passes one String parameter to the lambda and returns a boolean. This tells us that it is a Predicate or Function. Since the generic declaration has only one parameter, it is a Predicate.

Line 7 passes one Long parameter to the lambda and doesn't return anything. This tells us that it is a Consumer. Line 8 takes two parameters and returns a boolean. When you see a boolean returned, think Predicate unless the generics specify a Boolean return type. In this case, there are two parameters, so it is a BiPredicate.

Are you finding these easy? If not, review Table 4.1 again. We aren't kidding. You need to know the table really well. Now that you are fresh from studying the table, we are going to play "identify the error." These are meant to be tricky:

```
6:   Function<List<String>> ex1 = x -> x.get(0); // DOES NOT COMPILE
7:   UnaryOperator<Long> ex2 = (Long l) -> 3.14; // DOES NOT COMIPLE
8:   Predicate ex4 = String::isEmpty;  // DOES NOT COMPILE
```

Line 6 claims to be a Function. A Function needs to specify two generics—the input parameter type and the return value type. The return value type is missing from line 6, causing the code not to compile. Line 7 is a UnaryOperator, which returns the same type as it is passed in. The example returns a double rather than a Long, causing the code not to compile.

Line 8 is missing the generic for Predicate. This makes the parameter that was passed an Object rather than a String. The lambda expects a String because it calls a method that exists on String rather than Object. Therefore, it doesn't compile.

Returning an *Optional*

Suppose that you are taking an introductory Java class and receive scores of 90 and 100 on the first two exams. Now, we ask you what your average is. An average is calculated by adding the scores and dividing by the number of scores, so you have (90+100)/2. This gives 190/2, so you answer with 95. Great!

Now suppose that you are taking your second class on Java, and it is the first day of class. We ask you what your average is in this class that just started. You haven't taken any exams yet, so you don't have anything to average. It wouldn't be accurate to say that your average is zero. That sounds bad, and it isn't true. There simply isn't any data, so you don't have an average yet.

How do we express this "we don't know" or "not applicable" answer in Java? Starting with Java 8, we use the Optional type. An Optional is created using a factory. You can either request an empty Optional or pass a value for the Optional to wrap. Think of an Optional as a box that might have something in it or might instead be empty. Figure 4.1 shows both options.

FIGURE 4.1   Optional

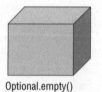

Optional.empty()

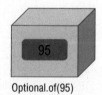

Optional.of(95)

Here's how to code our average method:

```
10:   public static Optional<Double> average(int… scores) {
11:       if (scores.length == 0) return Optional.empty();
```

```
12:      int sum = 0;
13:      for (int score: scores) sum += score;
14:      return Optional.of((double) sum / scores.length);
15:   }
```

Line 11 returns an empty Optional when we can't calculate an average. Lines 12 and 13 add up the scores. There is a functional programming way of doing this math, but we will get to that later in the chapter. In fact, the entire method could be written in one line, but that wouldn't teach you how Optional works! Line 14 creates an Optional to wrap the average.

Calling the method shows what is in our two boxes:

```
System.out.println(average(90, 100)); // Optional[95.0]
System.out.println(average());        // Optional.empty
```

You can see that one Optional contains a value and the other is empty. Normally, we want to check if a value is there and/or get it out of the box. Here's one way to do that:

```
20:   Optional<Double> opt = average(90, 100);
21:   if (opt.isPresent())
22:      System.out.println(opt.get()); // 95.0
```

Line 21 checks whether the Optional actually contains a value. Line 22 prints it out. What if we didn't do the check and the Optional was empty?

```
26:   Optional<Double> opt = average();
27:   System.out.println(opt.get());  // bad
```

We'd get an exception since there is no value inside the Optional:

```
java.util.NoSuchElementException: No value present
```

When creating an Optional, it is common to want to use empty when the value is null. You can do this with an if statement or ternary operator. We use the ternary operator to make sure that you remember how it works from the OCA:

```
Optional o = (value== null) ? Optional.empty(): Optional.of(value);
```

If value is null, o is assigned the empty Optional. Otherwise, we wrap the value. Since this is such a common pattern, Java provides a factory method to do the same thing:

```
Optional o = Optional.ofNullable(value);
```

That covers the static methods you need to know about Optional. Table 4.2 summarizes most of the instance methods on Optional that you need to know for the exam. There are a few others that involve chaining. We will cover those later in the chapter.

TABLE 4.2   Optional instance methods

Method	When Optional Is Empty	When Optional Contains a Value
get()	Throws an exception	Returns value
ifPresent(Consumer c)	Does nothing	Calls Consumer c with value
isPresent()	Returns false	Returns true
orElse(T other)	Returns other parameter	Returns value
orElseGet(Supplier s)	Returns result of calling Supplier	Returns value
orElseThrow(Supplier s)	Throws exception created by calling Supplier	Returns value

You've already seen get() and isPresent(). The other methods allow you to write code that uses an Optional in one line without having to use the ternary operator. This makes the code easier to read. Instead of using an if statement, which we used when checking the average earlier, we can specify a Consumer to be run when there is a value inside the Optional. When there isn't, the method simply skips running the Consumer:

```
Optional<Double> opt = average(90, 100);
opt.ifPresent(System.out::println);
```

Using ifPresent() better expresses our intent. We want something done if a value is present. The other methods allow you to specify what to do if a value isn't present. There are three choices:

```
30:    Optional<Double> opt = average();
31:    System.out.println(opt.orElse(Double.NaN));
32:    System.out.println(opt.orElseGet(() -> Math.random()));
33:    System.out.println(opt.orElseThrow(() -> new IllegalStateException()));
```

This prints something like the following:

```
NaN
0.49775932295380165
Exception in thread "main" java.lang.IllegalStateException
    at optional.Average.lambda$3(Average.java:56)
    at optional.Average$$Lambda$5/455659002.get(Unknown Source)
    at java.util.Optional.orElseThrow(Optional.java:290)
```

Line 31 shows that you can return a specific value or variable. In our case, we print the "not a number" value. Line 32 shows using a Supplier to generate a value at runtime to return instead. I'm glad our professors didn't give us a random average though! Line 33 shows using a different Supplier to create an exception that should be thrown. Remember that the stack trace looks weird because the lambdas are generated rather than named classes.

Notice that the two methods that take a Supplier have different names. Do you see why this code does not compile?

```
System.out.println(opt.orElseGet(
   () -> new IllegalStateException())); // DOES NOT COMPILE
```

opt is an Optional<Double>. This means the Supplier must return a Double. Since this supplier returns an exception, the type does not match.

The last example with Optional is really easy. What do you think this does?

```
Optional<Double> opt = average(90, 100);
System.out.println(opt.orElse(Double.NaN));
System.out.println(opt.orElseGet(() -> Math.random()));
System.out.println(opt.orElseThrow(() -> new IllegalStateException()));
```

It prints out 95 three times. Since the value does exist, there is no need to use the "or else" logic.

Is *Optional* the Same as *null*?

Before Java 8, programmers would return null instead of Optional. There were a few shortcomings with this approach. One was that there wasn't a clear way to express that null might be a special value. By contrast, returning an Optional is a clear statement in the API that there might not be a value in there.

Another advantage of Optional is that you can use a functional programming style with ifPresent() and the other methods rather than needing an if statement. Finally, you'll see toward the end of the chapter that you can chain Optional calls.

Using Streams

A *stream* in Java is a sequence of data. A *stream pipeline* is the operations that run on a stream to produce a result. Think of a stream pipeline as an assembly line in a factory. Suppose that we were running an assembly line to make signs for the animal exhibits at the zoo. We have a number of jobs. It is one person's job to take signs out of a box. It is a second person's job to paint the sign. It is a third person's job to stencil the name of the animal on the sign. It is a fourth person's job to put the completed sign in a box to be carried to the proper exhibit.

Notice that the second person can't do anything until one sign has been taken out of the box by the first person. Similarly, the third person can't do anything until one sign has been painted, and the fourth person can't do anything until it is stenciled.

The assembly line for making signs is finite. Once we process the contents of our box of signs, we are finished. *Finite* streams have a limit. Other assembly lines essentially run forever, like one for food production. Of course, they do stop at some point when the factory closes down, but pretend that doesn't happen. Or think of a sunrise/sunset cycle as *infinite*, since it doesn't end for an inordinately large period of time.

Another important feature of an assembly line is that each person touches each element to do their operation and then that piece of data is gone. It doesn't come back. The next person deals with it at that point. This is different than the lists and queues that you saw in the last chapter. With a list, you can access any element at any time. With a queue, you are limited in which elements you can access, but all of the elements are there. With streams, the data isn't generated up front—it is created when needed.

Many things can happen in the assembly line stations along the way. In programming, these are called *stream operations*. Just like with the assembly line, operations occur in a pipeline. Someone has to start and end the work, and there can be any number of stations in between. After all, a job with one person isn't an assembly line! There are three parts to a stream pipeline, as shown in Figure 4.2:

- *Source*: Where the stream comes from.

- *Intermediate operations*: Transforms the stream into another one. There can be as few or as many intermediate operations as you'd like. Since streams use lazy evaluation, the intermediate operations do not run until the terminal operation runs.

- *Terminal operation*: Actually produces a result. Since streams can be used only once, the stream is no longer valid after a terminal operation completes.

FIGURE 4.2   Stream pipeline

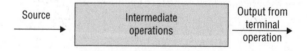

Notice that the intermediate operations are a black box. When viewing the assembly line from the outside, you care only about what comes in and goes out. What happens in between is an implementation detail.

You will need to know the differences between intermediate and terminal operations well. Make sure that you can fill in Table 4.3.

TABLE 4.3   Intermediate vs. terminal operations

Scenario	For Intermediate Operations?	For Terminal Operations?
Required part of a useful pipeline?	No	Yes
Can exist multiple times in a pipeline?	Yes	No
Return type is a stream type?	Yes	No
Executed upon method call?	No	Yes
Stream valid after call?	Yes	No

A factory typically has a foreman who oversees the work. Java serves as the foreman when working with stream pipelines. This is a really important role, especially when dealing with lazy evaluation and infinite streams. Think of declaring the stream as giving instructions to the foreman. As the foreman finds out what needs to be done, he sets up the stations and tells the workers what their duties will be. However, the workers do not start until the foreman tells them to begin. The foreman waits until he sees the terminal operation to actually kick off the work. He also watches the work and stops the line as soon as work is complete.

Let's look at a few examples of this. We aren't using code in these examples because it is really important to understand this stream pipeline concept before starting to write the code. Figure 4.3 shows a stream pipeline with one intermediate operation. Let's take a look at what happens from the point of the view of the foreman. First, he sees that the source is taking signs out of the box. The foreman sets up a worker at the table to unpack the box and says to await a signal to start. Then the foreman sees the intermediate operation to paint the sign. He sets up a worker with paint and says to await a signal to start. Finally, the foreman sees the terminal operation to put the signs into a pile. He sets up a worker to do this and yells out that all three workers should start.

FIGURE 4.3   Steps in running a stream pipeline

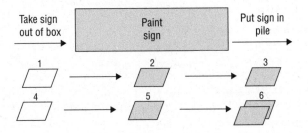

Suppose that there are two signs in the box. Step 1 is the first worker taking one sign out of the box and handing it to the second worker. Step 2 is the second worker painting it and handing it to the third worker. Step 3 is the third worker putting it in the pile. Steps 4–6 are this same process for the other sign. Then the foreman sees that there are no more signs left and shuts down the entire enterprise.

The foreman is smart. He can make decisions about how to best do the work based on what is needed. As an example, let's explore the stream pipeline in Figure 4.4.

FIGURE 4.4   A stream pipeline with a limit

The foreman still sees a source of taking signs out of the box and assigns a worker to do that on command. He still sees an intermediate operation to paint and sets up another worker with instructions to wait and then paint. Then he sees an intermediate step that we need only two signs. He sets up a worker to count the signs that go by and notify him when the worker has seen two. Finally, he sets up a worker for the terminal operation to put the signs in a pile.

This time, suppose that there are 10 signs in the box. We start out like last time. The first sign makes its way down the pipeline. The second sign also makes its way down the pipeline. When the worker in charge of counting sees the second sign, she tells the foreman. The foreman lets the terminal operation worker finish her task and then yells out "stop the line." It doesn't matter that that there are eight more signs in the box. We don't need them, so it would be unnecessary work to paint them. And we all want to avoid unnecessary work!

Similarly, the foreman would have stopped the line after the first sign if the terminal operation was to find the first sign that gets created.

In the following sections, we will cover the three parts of the pipeline. We will also discuss special types of streams for primitives and how to print a stream.

Creating Stream Sources

In Java, the Stream interface is in the java.util.stream package. There are a few ways to create a finite stream:

```
1: Stream<String> empty = Stream.empty();      // count = 0
2: Stream<Integer> singleElement = Stream.of(1);    // count = 1
3: Stream<Integer> fromArray = Stream.of(1, 2, 3);     // count = 2
```

Line 1 shows how to create an empty stream. Line 2 shows how to create a stream with a single element. Line 3 shows how to create a stream from an array. You've undoubtedly noticed that there isn't an array on line 3. The method signature uses varargs, which let you specify an array or individual elements. Since streams are new in Java 8, most code that's already written uses lists. Java provides a convenient way to convert from a list to a stream:

```
4: List<String> list = Arrays.asList("a", "b", "c");
5: Stream<String> fromList = list.stream();
6: Stream<String> fromListParallel = list.parallelStream();
```

Line 5 shows that it is a simple method call to create a stream from a list. Line 6 does the same, except that it creates a stream that is allowed to process elements in parallel. This is a great feature because you can write code that uses parallelism before even learning what a thread is. Using parallel streams is like setting up multiple tables of workers who are able to do the same task. Painting would be a lot faster if we could have five painters painting different signs at once. Just keep in mind that it isn't worth working in parallel for small streams. There is an overhead cost in coordinating the work among all of the workers operating in parallel. For small amounts of work, it is faster just to do it sequentially. You'll learn much more about running in parallel in Chapter 7, "Concurrency."

So far, this isn't particularly impressive. We could do all this with lists. We can't create an infinite list, though, which makes streams more powerful:

```
7: Stream<Double> randoms = Stream.generate(Math::random);
8: Stream<Integer> oddNumbers = Stream.iterate(1, n -> n + 2);
```

Line 7 generates a stream of random numbers. How many random numbers? However many you need. If you call randoms.forEach(System.out::println), the program will print random numbers until you kill it. Later in the chapter, you'll learn about operations like limit() to turn the infinite stream into a finite stream.

Line 8 gives you more control. iterate() takes a seed or starting value as the first parameter. This is the first element that will be part of the stream. The other parameter is a lambda expression that gets passed the previous value and generates the next value. As with the random numbers example, it will keep on producing odd numbers as long as you need them.

> If you try to call System.out.println(stream), you'll get something like java.util.stream.ReferencePipeline$3@4517d9a3. This is different than a Collection where you see the contents. You don't need to know this for the exam. We mention it so that you aren't caught by surprise when writing code for practice.

Using Common Terminal Operations

You can perform a terminal operation without any intermediate operations but not the other way around. This is why we will talk about terminal operations first. *Reductions* are a special type of terminal operation where all of the contents of the stream are combined into a single primitive or Object. For example, you might have an int or a Collection.

Table 4.4 summarizes this section. Feel free to use it as a guide to remember the most important points as we go through each one individually. We explain them from easiest to hardest rather than alphabetically.

TABLE 4.4   Terminal stream operations

Method	What Happens for Infinite Streams	Return Value	Reduction
allMatch() /anyMatch() /noneMatch()	Sometimes terminates	boolean	No
collect()	Does not terminate	Varies	Yes
count()	Does not terminate	long	Yes
findAny() /findFirst()	Terminates	Optional<T>	No
forEach()	Does not terminate	void	No
min()/max()	Does not terminate	Optional<T>	Yes
reduce()	Does not terminate	Varies	Yes

count()

The count() method determines the number of elements in a finite stream. For an infinite stream, it hangs. Why? Count from 1 to infinity and let us know when you are finished. Or rather don't do that because we'd rather you study for the exam than spend the rest of your life counting. count() is a reduction because it looks at each element in the stream and returns a single value. The method signature is this:

```
long count()
```

This example shows calling count() on a finite stream:

```
Stream<String> s = Stream.of("monkey", "gorilla", "bonobo");
System.out.println(s.count());     // 3
```

min() and max()

The min() and max() methods allow you to pass a custom comparator and find the smallest or largest value in a finite stream according to that sort order. Like count(), min() and max() hang on an infinite stream because they cannot be sure that a smaller or larger value isn't coming later in the stream. Both methods are reductions because they return a single value after looking at the entire stream. The method signatures are as follows:

```
Optional<T> min(<? super T> comparator)
Optional<T> max(<? super T> comparator)
```

This example finds the animal with the fewest letters in its name:

```
Stream<String> s = Stream.of("monkey", "ape", "bonobo");
Optional<String> min = s.min((s1, s2) -> s1.length()-s2.length());
min.ifPresent(System.out::println); // ape
```

Notice that the code returns an Optional rather than the value. This allows the method to specify that no minimum or maximum was found. We use the Optional method and a method reference to print out the minimum only if one is found. As an example of where there isn't a minimum, let's look at an empty stream:

```
Optional<?> minEmpty = Stream.empty().min((s1, s2) -> 0);
System.out.println(minEmpty.isPresent());    // false
```

Since the stream is empty, the comparator is never called and no value is present in the Optional.

findAny() and findFirst()

The findAny() and findFirst() methods return an element of the stream unless the stream is empty. If the stream is empty, they return an empty Optional. This is the first method you've seen that works with an infinite stream. Since Java generates only the amount of stream you need, the infinite stream needs to generate only one element. findAny() is useful when you are working with a parallel stream. It gives Java the flexibility to return to you the first element it comes by rather than the one that needs to be first in the stream based on the intermediate operations.

These methods are terminal operations but not reductions. The reason is that they sometimes return without processing all of the elements. This means that they return a value based on the stream but do not reduce the entire stream into one value.

The method signatures are these:

```
Optional<T> findAny()
Optional<T> findFirst()
```

This example finds an animal:

```
Stream<String> s = Stream.of("monkey", "gorilla", "bonobo");
Stream<String> infinite = Stream.generate(() -> "chimp");
s.findAny().ifPresent(System.out::println); // monkey
infinite.findAny().ifPresent(System.out::println); // chimp
```

Finding any one match is more useful than it sounds. Sometimes we just want to sample the results and get a representative element, but we don't need to waste the processing generating them all. After all, if we plan to work with only one element, why bother looking at more?

allMatch(), anyMatch() and noneMatch()

The `allMatch()`, `anyMatch()` and `noneMatch()` methods search a stream and return information about how the stream pertains to the predicate. These may or may not terminate for infinite streams. It depends on the data. Like the find methods, they are not reductions because they do not necessarily look at all of the elements.

The method signatures are as follows:

```
boolean anyMatch(Predicate <? super T> predicate)
boolean allMatch(Predicate <? super T> predicate)
boolean noneMatch(Predicate <? super T> predicate)
```

This example checks whether animal names begin with letters:

```
List<String> list = Arrays.asList("monkey", "2", "chimp");
Stream<String> infinite = Stream.generate(() -> "chimp");
Predicate<String> pred = x -> Character.isLetter(x.charAt(0));
System.out.println(list.stream().anyMatch(pred)); // true
System.out.println(list.stream().allMatch(pred)); // false
System.out.println(list.stream().noneMatch(pred)); // false
System.out.println(infinite.anyMatch(pred)); // true
```

This shows that we can reuse the same predicate, but we need a different stream each time. `anyMatch()` returns `true` because two of the three elements match. `allMatch()` returns `false` because one doesn't match. `noneMatch()` also returns `false` because one matches. On the infinite list, one match is found, so the call terminates. If we called `noneMatch()` or `allMatch()`, they would run until we killed the program.

> Remember that `allMatch()`, `anyMatch()`, and `noneMatch()` return a boolean. By contrast, the find methods return an `Optional` because they return an element of the stream.

forEach()

A looping construct is available. As expected, calling `forEach()` on an infinite stream does not terminate. Since there is no return value, it is not a reduction.

Before you use it, consider if another approach would be better. Developers who learned to write loops first tend to use them for everything. For example, a loop with an `if` statement should be a filter instead.

The method signature is the following:

```
void forEach(Consumer<? super T> action)
```

Notice that this is the only terminal operation with a return type of void. If you want something to happen, you have to make it happen in the loop. Here's one way to print the elements in the stream. There are other ways, which we cover later in the chapter.

```
Stream<String> s = Stream.of("Monkey", "Gorilla", "Bonobo");
s.forEach(System.out::print);    // MonkeyGorillaBonobo
```

 Remember that you can call forEach() directly on a Collection or on a Stream. Don't get confused on the exam when you see both approaches.

Notice that you can't use a traditional for loop on a stream:

```
Stream s = Stream.of(1);
for (Integer i: s) {} // DOES NOT COMPILE
```

While forEach() sounds like a loop, it is really a terminal operator for streams. Streams cannot use a traditional for loop to run because they don't implement the Iterable interface.

reduce()

The reduce() method combines a stream into a single object. As you can tell from the name, it is a reduction. The method signatures are these:

```
T reduce(T identity, BinaryOperator<T> accumulator)
Optional<T> reduce(BinaryOperator<T> accumulator)
<U> U reduce(U identity, BiFunction<U,? super T,U> accumulator,
BinaryOperator<U> combiner)
```

Let's take them one at a time. The most common way of doing a reduction is to start with an initial value and keep merging it with the next value. Think about how you would concatenate an array of Strings into a single String without functional programming. It might look something like this:

```
String[] array = new String[] { "w", "o", "l", "f" };
String result = "";
for (String s: array) result = result + s;
System.out.println(result);
```

The initial value of an empty String is the identity. The accumulator combines the current result with the current String. With lambdas, we can do the same thing with a stream and reduction:

```
Stream<String> stream = Stream.of("w", "o", "l", "f");
String word = stream.reduce("", (s, c) -> s + c);
System.out.println(word);    // wolf
```

Notice how we still have the empty String as the identity. We also still concatenate the Strings to get the next value. We can even rewrite this with a method reference:

```
Stream<String> stream = Stream.of("w", "o", "l", "f");
String word = stream.reduce("", String::concat);
System.out.println(word);    // wolf
```

Let's try another one. Can you write a reduction to multiply all of the Integer objects in a stream? Try it. Our solution is shown here:

```
Stream<Integer> stream = Stream.of(3, 5, 6);
System.out.println(stream.reduce(1, (a, b) -> a*b));
```

We set the identity to 1 and the accumulator to multiplication. In many cases, the identity isn't really necessary, so Java lets us omit it. When you don't specify an identity, an Optional is returned because there might not be any data. There are three choices for what is in the Optional:

- If the stream is empty, an empty Optional is returned.
- If the stream has one element, it is returned.
- If the stream has multiple elements, the accumulator is applied to combine them.

The following illustrates each of these scenarios:

```
BinaryOperator<Integer> op = (a, b) -> a * b;
Stream<Integer> empty = Stream.empty();
Stream<Integer> oneElement = Stream.of(3);
Stream<Integer> threeElements = Stream.of(3, 5, 6);

empty.reduce(op).ifPresent(System.out::print); // no output
oneElement.reduce(op).ifPresent(System.out::print); // 3
threeElements.reduce(op).ifPresent(System.out::print); // 90
```

Why are there two similar methods? Why not just always require the identity? Java could have done that. However, sometimes it is nice to differentiate the case where the stream is empty rather than the case where there is a value that happens to match the identity being returned from calculation. The signature returning an Optional lets us differentiate these cases. For example, we might return Optional.empty() when the stream is empty and Optional.of(3) when there is a value.

The third method signature is used when we are processing collections in parallel. It allows Java to create intermediate reductions and then combine them at the end. In our example, it looks similar. While we aren't actually using a parallel stream here, Java assumes that a stream might be parallel. This is helpful because it lets us switch to a parallel stream easily in the future:

```
BinaryOperator<Integer> op = (a, b) -> a * b;
Stream<Integer> stream = Stream.of(3, 5, 6);
System.out.println(stream.reduce(1, op, op)); // 90
```

collect()

The collect() method is a special type of reduction called a *mutable reduction*. It is more efficient than a regular reduction because we use the same mutable object while accumulating. Common mutable objects include `StringBuilder` and `ArrayList`. This is a really useful method, because it lets us get data out of streams and into another form. The method signatures are as follows:

```
<R> R collect(Supplier<R> supplier, BiConsumer<R, ? super T> accumulator,
BiConsumer<R, R> combiner)
<R,A> R collect(Collector<? super T, A,R> collector)
```

Let's start with the first signature, which is used when we want to code specifically how collecting should work. Our wolf example from reduce can be converted to use `collect()`:

```
Stream<String> stream = Stream.of("w", "o", "l", "f");
StringBuilder word = stream.collect(StringBuilder::new,
    StringBuilder::append, StringBuilder:append)
```

The first parameter is a `Supplier` that creates the object that will store the results as we collect data. Remember that a `Supplier` doesn't take any parameters and returns a value. In this case, it constructs a new `StringBuilder`.

The second parameter is a `BiConsumer`, which takes two parameters and doesn't return anything. It is responsible for adding one more element to the data collection. In this example, it appends the next `String` to the `StringBuilder`.

The final parameter is another `BiConsumer`. It is responsible for taking two data collections and merging them. This is useful when we are processing in parallel. Two smaller collections are formed and then merged into one. This would work with `StringBuilder` only if we didn't care about the order of the letters. In this case, the accumulator and combiner have similar logic.

Now let's look at an example where the logic is different in the accumulator and combiner:

```
Stream<String> stream = Stream.of("w", "o", "l", "f");
TreeSet<String> set = stream.collect(TreeSet::new, TreeSet::add,
TreeSet::addAll);
System.out.println(set); // [f, l, o, w]
```

The collector has three parts as before. The supplier creates an empty `TreeSet`. The accumulator adds a single `String` from the `Stream` to the `TreeSet`. The combiner adds all of the elements of one `TreeSet` to another in case the operations were done in parallel and need to be merged.

We started with the long signature because that's how you implement your own collector. It is important to know how to do this for the exam and to understand how collectors work. In practice, there are many common collectors that come up over and over. Rather than making developers keep reimplementing the same ones, Java provides an interface with common collectors. This approach also makes the code easier to read because it is more expressive. For example, we could rewrite the previous example as follows:

```
Stream<String> stream = Stream.of("w", "o", "l", "f");
TreeSet<String> set = stream.collect(Collectors.toCollection(TreeSet::new));
System.out.println(set); // [f, l, o, w]
```

If we didn't need the set to be sorted, we could make the code even shorter:

```
Stream<String> stream = Stream.of("w", "o", "l", "f");
Set<String> set = stream.collect(Collectors.toSet());
System.out.println(set); // [f, w, l, o]
```

You might get different output for this last one since toSet() makes no guarantees as to which implementation of Set you'll get. It is likely to be a HashSet, but you shouldn't expect or rely on that.

> The exam expects you to know about common predefined collectors in addition to being able to write your own by passing a supplier, accumulator, and combiner.

Later in this chapter, we will show many Collectors that are used for grouping data. It's a big topic, so it's best to master how streams work before adding too many Collectors into the mix.

Using Common Intermediate Operations

Unlike a terminal operation, intermediate operations deal with infinite streams simply by returning an infinite stream. Since elements are produced only as needed, this works fine. The assembly line worker doesn't need to worry about how many more elements are coming through and instead can focus on the current element.

filter()

The filter() method returns a Stream with elements that match a given expression. Here is the method signature:

```
Stream<T> filter(Predicate<? super T> predicate)
```

This operation is easy to remember and very powerful because we can pass any Predicate to it. For example, this filters all elements that begin with the letter *m*:

```
Stream<String> s = Stream.of("monkey", "gorilla", "bonobo");
s.filter(x -> x.startsWith("m")).forEach(System.out::print);    // monkey
```

distinct()

The distinct() method returns a stream with duplicate values removed. The duplicates do not need to be adjacent to be removed. As you might imagine, Java calls equals() to determine whether the objects are the same. The method signature is as follows:

```
Stream<T> distinct()
```

Here's an example:

```
Stream<String> s = Stream.of("duck", "duck", "duck", "goose");
s.distinct().forEach(System.out::print); // duckgoose
```

limit() and skip()

The limit() and skip() methods make a Stream smaller. They could make a finite stream smaller, or they could make a finite stream out of an infinite stream. The method signatures are shown here:

```
Stream<T> limit(int maxSize)
Stream<T> skip(int n)
```

The following code creates an infinite stream of numbers counting from 1. The skip() operation returns an infinite stream starting with the numbers counting from 6, since it skips the first five elements. The limit() call takes the first two of those. Now we have a finite stream with two elements:

```
Stream<Integer> s = Stream.iterate(1, n -> n + 1);
s.skip(5).limit(2).forEach(System.out::print);     // 67
```

map()

The map() method creates a one-to-one mapping from the elements in the stream to the elements of the next step in the stream. The method signature is as follows:

```
<R> Stream<R> map(Function<? super T, ? extends R> mapper)
```

This one looks more complicated than the others you have seen. It uses the lambda expression to figure out the type passed to that function and the one returned. The return type is the stream that gets returned.

The map() method on streams is for transforming data. Don't confuse it with the Map interface, which maps keys to values.

As an example, this code converts a list of String objects to a list of Integers representing their lengths:

```
Stream<String> s = Stream.of("monkey", "gorilla", "bonobo");
s.map(String::length).forEach(System.out::print);     // 676
```

Remember that String::length is shorthand for the lambda x -> x.length(), which clearly shows it is a function that turns a String into an Integer.

flatMap()

The flatMap() method takes each element in the stream and makes any elements it contains top-level elements in a single stream. This is helpful when you want to remove empty elements from a stream or you want to combine a stream of lists. We are showing you the method signature for consistency with the other methods, just so you don't think we are hiding anything. You aren't expected to be able to read this:

```
<R> Stream<R> flatMap(Function<? super T, ? extends Stream<? extends R>> mapper)
```

This gibberish basically says that it returns a Stream of the type that the function contains at a lower level. Don't worry about the signature. It's a headache.

What you should understand is the example. This gets all of the animals into the same level along with getting rid of the empty list:

```
List<String> zero = Arrays.asList();
List<String> one = Arrays.asList("Bonobo");
List<String> two = Arrays.asList("Mama Gorilla", "Baby Gorilla");
Stream<List<String>> animals = Stream.of(zero, one, two);

animals.flatMap(l -> l.stream()).forEach(System.out::println);
```

Here's the output:

```
Bonobo
Mama Gorilla
Baby Gorilla
```

As you can see, it removed the empty list completely and changed all elements of each list to be at the top level of the stream.

sorted()

The sorted() method returns a stream with the elements sorted. Just like sorting arrays, Java uses natural ordering unless we specify a comparator. The method signatures are these:

```
Stream<T> sorted()
Stream<T> sorted(Comparator<? super T> comparator)
```

Calling the first signature uses the default sort order:

```
Stream<String> s = Stream.of("brown-", "bear-");
s.sorted().forEach(System.out::print); // bear-brown-
```

Remember that we can pass a lambda expression as the comparator. For example, we can pass a Comparator implementation:

```
Stream<String> s = Stream.of("brown bear-", "grizzly-");
s.sorted(Comparator.reverseOrder())
    .forEach(System.out::print); // grizzly-brown bear-
```

Here we passed a Comparator to specify that we want to sort in the reverse of natural sort order. Ready for a tricky one? Do you see why this doesn't compile?

```
s.sorted(Comparator::reverseOrder); // DOES NOT COMPILE
```

Take a look at the method signatures again. Comparator is a functional interface. This means that we can use method references or lambdas to implement it. The Comparator interface implements one method that takes two String parameters and returns an int. However, Comparator::reverseOrder doesn't do that. It is a reference to a function that takes zero parameters and returns a Comparator. This is not compatible with the interface. This means that we have to use a method and not a method reference. We bring this up to remind you that you really do need to know method references well.

peek()

The peek() method is our final intermediate operation. It is useful for debugging because it allows us to perform a stream operation without actually changing the stream. The method signature is as follows:

```
Stream<T> peek(Consumer<? super T> action)
```

The most common use for peek() is to output the contents of the stream as it goes by. Suppose that we made a typo and counted bears beginning with the letter *g* instead of *b*. We are puzzled why the count is 1 instead of 2. We can add a peek() to find out why:

```
Stream<String> stream = Stream.of("black bear", "brown bear", "grizzly");
long count = stream.filter(s -> s.startsWith("g"))
    .peek(System.out::println).count();    // grizzly
System.out.println(count);    // 1
```

When working with a Queue, peek() looks only at the first element. In a stream, peek() looks at each element that goes through that part of the stream pipeline. It's like having a worker take notes on how a particular step of the process is doing.

Danger: Changing State with *peek()*

Remember that peek() is intended to perform an operation without changing the result. Here's a straightforward stream pipeline that doesn't use peek().

```
List<Integer> numbers = new ArrayList<>();
List<Character> letters = new ArrayList<>();
numbers.add(1);
letters.add('a');
Stream<List<?>> stream = Stream.of(numbers, letters);
stream.map(List::size).forEach(System.out::print); // 11
```

We can add a proper peek() operation:

```
StringBuilder builder = new StringBuilder();
Stream<List<?>> good = Stream.of(numbers, letters);
good.peek(l -> builder.append(l)).map(List::size).forEach(System.out::print); // 11
System.out.println(builder); // [1][a]
```

In this example, you can see that peek() updates a StringBuilder variable that doesn't affect the result of the stream pipeline. It still prints 11. Java doesn't prevent us from writing bad peek code:

```
Stream<List<?>> bad = Stream.of(numbers, letters);
bad.peek(l -> l.remove(0)).map(List::size).forEach(System.out::print);  // 00
```

This example is bad because peek() is modifying the data structure that is used in the stream, which causes the result of the stream pipeline to be different than if the peek wasn't present.

Putting Together the Pipeline

Streams allow you to use chaining and express what you want to accomplish rather than how to do so. Let's say that we wanted to get the first two names alphabetically that are four characters long. In Java 7, we'd have to write something like the following:

```
List<String> list = Arrays.asList("Toby", "Anna", "Leroy", "Alex");
List<String> filtered = new ArrayList<>();
for (String name: list) {
  if (name.length() == 4) filtered.add(name);
}
Collections.sort(filtered);
Iterator<String> iter = filtered.iterator();
```

```
if (iter.hasNext()) System.out.println(iter.next());
if (iter.hasNext()) System.out.println(iter.next());
```

This works. It takes some reading and thinking to figure out what is going on. The problem we are trying to solve gets lost in the implementation. It is also very focused on the how rather than on the what. In Java 8, the equivalent code is as follows:

```
List<String> list = Arrays.asList("Toby", "Anna", "Leroy", "Alex");
list.stream().filter(n -> n.length() == 4).sorted()
  .limit(2).forEach(System.out::println);
```

Before you say that it is harder to read, we can format it:

```
stream.filter(n -> n.length() == 4)
    .sorted()
    .limit(2)
    .forEach(System.out::println);
```

The difference is that we express what is going on. We care about String objects of length 4. Then we then want them sorted. Then we want to first two. Then we want to print them out. It maps better to the problem that we are trying to solve, and it is simpler because we don't have to deal with counters and such.

Once you start using streams in your code, you may find yourself using them in many places. Having shorter, briefer, and clearer code is definitely a good thing!

In this example, you see all three parts of the pipeline. Figure 4.5 shows how each intermediate operation in the pipeline feeds into the next.

FIGURE 4.5   Stream pipeline with multiple intermediate operations

Remember that the assembly line foreman is figuring out how to best implement the stream pipeline. He sets up all of the tables with instructions to wait before starting. He tells the limit() worker to inform him when two elements go by. He tells the sorted() worker that she should just collect all of the elements as they come in and sort them all at once. After sorting, she should start passing them to the limit() worker one at a time. The data flow looks like this:

1. stream() sends Toby to filter(). filter() sees that the length is good and sends Toby to sorted(). sorted() can't sort yet because it needs all of the data, so it holds Toby.

2. stream() sends Anna to filter(). filter() sees that the length is good and sends Anna to sorted(). sorted() can't sort yet because it needs all of the data, so it holds Anna.

3.   stream() sends Leroy to filter(). filter() sees that the length is not a match, and it takes Leroy out of the assembly line processing.

4.   stream() sends Alex to filter(). filter() sees that the length is good and sends Alex to sorted(). sorted() can't sort yet because it needs all of the data, so it holds Alex. It turns out sorted() does have all of the required data, but it doesn't know it yet.

5.   The foreman lets sorted() know that it is time to sort and the sort occurs.

6.   sorted() sends Alex to limit(). limit() remembers that it has seen one element and sends Alex to forEach(), printing Alex.

7.   sorted() sends Anna to limit(). limit() remembers that it has seen two elements and sends Anna to forEach(), printing Anna.

8.   limit() has now seen all of the elements that are needed and tells the foreman. The foreman stops the line, and no more processing occurs in the pipeline.

Make sense? Let's try two more examples to make sure that you understand this well. What do you think the following does?

```
Stream.generate(() -> "Elsa")
    .filter(n -> n.length() == 4)
    .sorted()
    .limit(2)
    .forEach(System.out::println);
```

It actually hangs until you kill the program or it throws an exception after running out of memory. The foreman has instructed sorted() to wait until everything to sort is present. That never happens because there is an infinite stream. What about this example?

```
Stream.generate(() -> "Elsa")
    .filter(n -> n.length() == 4)
    .limit(2)
    .sorted()
    .forEach(System.out::println);
```

This one prints Elsa twice. The filter lets elements through and limit() stops the earlier operations after two elements. Now sorted() can sort because we have a finite list. Finally, what do you think this does?

```
Stream.generate(() -> "Olaf Lazisson")
    .filter(n -> n.length() == 4)
    .limit(2)
    .sorted()
    .forEach(System.out::println);
```

This one hangs as well until we kill the program. The filter doesn't allow anything through, so limit() never sees two elements. This means that we have to keep waiting and hope that they show up.

 **Real World Scenario**

Peeking behind the Scenes

The peek() method is useful for seeing how a stream pipeline works behind the scenes. Remember that the methods run against each element one at a time until processing is done. Suppose that we have this code:

```
Stream<Integer> infinite = Stream.iterate(1, x -> x + 1);
infinite.limit(5)
        .filter(x -> x % 2 == 1)
        .forEach(System.out::print);   // 135
```

The source is an infinite stream of odd numbers. Only the first five elements are allowed through before the foreman instructs work to stop. The filter operation is limited to seeing if these five numbers from 1 to 5 are odd. Only three are, and those are the ones that get printed, giving 135.

Now what do you think this prints?

```
Stream<Integer> infinite = Stream.iterate(1, x -> x + 1);
infinite.limit(5)
        .peek(System.out::print)
        .filter(x -> x % 2 == 1)
        .forEach(System.out::print);
```

The correct answer is 11233455. As the first element passes through, 1 shows up in the peek() and print(). The second element makes it past the limit() and peek(), but it gets caught in the filter(). The third and fifth elements behave like the first element. The fourth behaves like the second.

Reversing the order of the intermediate operations changes the result:

```
Stream<Integer> infinite = Stream.iterate(1, x -> x + 1);
infinite.filter(x -> x % 2 == 1)
        .limit(5)
        .forEach(System.out::print); // 13579
```

The source is still an infinite stream of odd numbers. The first element still flows through the entire pipeline and limit() remembers that it allows one element through. The second element doesn't make it past filter(). The third element flows through the entire pipeline and limit() prevents its second element. This proceeds until the ninth element flows through and limit() has allowed its fifth element through.

Finally, what do you think this prints?

```
Stream<Integer> infinite = Stream.iterate(1, x -> x + 1);
infinite.filter(x -> x % 2 == 1)
        .peek(System.out::print)
        .limit(5)
        .forEach(System.out::print);
```

The answer is 1133557799. Since filter() is before peek(), we see only the odd numbers.

Printing a Stream

When code doesn't work as expected, it is traditional to add a println() or set a break-point to see the values of an object. With streams, this is trickier. Since intermediate operations don't run until needed, and Java is free to make them more efficient, new techniques are needed. Table 4.5 shows some options for printing out the contents of a stream. You'll find that you have less need to print out the values of a stream as you get more practice with stream pipelines. While learning, printing is *really* helpful!

TABLE 4.5 How to print a stream

Option	Works for Infinite Streams?	Destructive to Stream?
s.forEach(System.out::println);	No	Yes
System.out.println(s.collect(Collectors.toList()));	No	Yes
s.peek(System.out::println).count();	No	No
s.limit(5).forEach(System.out::println);	Yes	Yes

Notice that most of the approaches are destructive. This means that you cannot use the stream anymore after printing. This is fine when you are getting started and just want to see what the code does. It's a problem if you are trying to find out what a stream looks like as it passes through a certain part of the pipeline.

Also, notice that only one of the approaches works for an infinite stream. It limits the number of elements in the stream before printing. If you try the others with an infinite stream, they will run until you kill the program.

Working with Primitives

Up until now, we have been using wrapper classes when we needed primitives to go into streams. We did this with the Collections API so it would feel natural. With streams, there are also equivalents that work with the int, double, and long primitives. Let's take a look at why this is needed. Suppose that we want to calculate the sum of numbers in a finite stream:

```
Stream<Integer> stream = Stream.of(1, 2, 3);
System.out.println(stream.reduce(0, (s, n) -> s + n));
```

Not bad. It wasn't hard to write a reduction. We started the accumulator with zero. We then added each number to that running total as it came up in the stream. There is another way of doing that:

```
Stream<Integer> stream = Stream.of(1, 2, 3);
System.out.println(stream.mapToInt(x -> x).sum());
```

This time, we converted our Stream<Integer> to an IntStream and asked the IntStream to calculate the sum for us. The primitive streams know how to perform certain common operations automatically.

So far, this seems like a nice convenience but not terribly important. Now think about how you would compute an average. You need to divide the sum by the number of elements. The problem is that streams allow only one pass. Java recognizes that calculating an average is a common thing to do, and it provides a method to calculate the average on the stream classes for primitives:

```
IntStream intStream = IntStream.of(1, 2, 3);
OptionalDouble avg = intStream.average();
System.out.println(avg.getAsDouble());
```

Not only is it possible to calculate the average, but it is also easy to do so. Clearly primitive streams are important. We will look at creating and using such streams, including optionals and functional interfaces.

Creating Primitive Streams

Here are three types of primitive streams:

- IntStream: Used for the primitive types int, short, byte, and char
- LongStream: Used for the primitive type long
- DoubleStream: Used for the primitive types double and float

Why doesn't each primitive type have its own primitive stream? These three are the most common, so the API designers went with them.

Some of the methods for creating a primitive stream are equivalent to how we created the source for a regular Stream. You can create an empty stream with this:

```
DoubleStream empty = DoubleStream.empty();
```

Another way is to use the of() factory method from a single value or by using the varargs overload:

```
DoubleStream oneValue = DoubleStream.of(3.14);
DoubleStream varargs = DoubleStream.of(1.0, 1.1, 1.2);
oneValue.forEach(System.out::println);
System.out.println();
varargs.forEach(System.out::println);
```

This code outputs the following:

```
3.14

1.0
1.1
1.2
```

It works the same way for each type of primitive stream. You can also use the two methods for creating infinite streams, just like we did with Stream:

```
DoubleStream random = DoubleStream.generate(Math::random);
DoubleStream fractions = DoubleStream.iterate(.5, d -> d / 2);
random.limit(3).forEach(System.out::println);
System.out.println();
fractions.limit(3).forEach(System.out::println);
```

Since the streams are infinite, we added a limit intermediate operation so that the output doesn't print values forever. The first stream calls a static method on Math to get a random double. Since the numbers are random, your output will obviously be different. The second stream keeps creating smaller numbers, dividing the previous value by two each time. The output from when we ran this code was as follows:

```
0.07890654781186413
0.28564363465842346
0.6311403511266134
```

```
0.5
0.25
0.125
```

You don't need to know this for the exam, but the Random class provides a method to get primitives streams of random numbers directly. Fun fact! For example, ints() generates an infinite stream of int primitives.

When dealing with int or long primitives, it is common to count. Suppose that we wanted a stream with the numbers from 1 through 5. We could write this using what we've explained so far:

```
IntStream count = IntStream.iterate(1, n -> n+1).limit(5);
count.forEach(System.out::println);
```

This code does print out the numbers 1–5, one per line. However, it is a lot of code to do something so simple. Java provides a method that can generate a range of numbers:

```
IntStream range = IntStream.range(1, 6);
range.forEach(System.out::println);
```

This is better. The range() method indicates that we want the numbers 1–6, not including the number 6. However, it still could be clearer. We want the numbers 1–5. We should be able to type the number 5, and we can do so as follows:

```
IntStream rangeClosed = IntStream.rangeClosed(1, 5);
rangeClosed.forEach(System.out::println);
```

Even better. This time we expressed that we want a closed range, or an inclusive range. This method better matches how we express a range of numbers in plain English.

The final way to create a primitive stream is by mapping from another stream type. Table 4.6 shows that there is a method for mapping between any stream types.;

TABLE 4.6   Mapping methods between types of streams

Source Stream Class	To Create Stream	To Create DoubleStream	To Create IntStream	To Create LongStream
Stream	map	mapToDouble	mapToInt	mapToLong
DoubleStream	mapToObj	map	mapToInt	mapToLong
IntStream	mapToObj	mapToDouble	map	mapToLong
LongStream	mapToObj	mapToDouble	mapToInt	map

Obviously, they have to be compatible types for this to work. Java requires a mapping function to be provided as a parameter, for example:

```
Stream<String> objStream = Stream.of("penguin", "fish");

IntStream intStream = objStream.mapToInt(s -> s.length())
```

This function that takes an Object, which is a String in this case. The function returns an int. The function mappings are intuitive here. They take the source type and return the target type. In this example, the actual function type is ToIntFunction. Table 4.7 shows the mapping function names. As you can see, they do what you might expect.

TABLE 4.7   Function parameters when mapping between types of streams

Source Stream Class	To Create Stream	To Create DoubleStream	To Create IntStream	To Create LongStream
Stream	Function	ToDoubleFunction	ToIntFunction	ToLongFunction
DoubleStream	Double Function	DoubleUnary Operator	DoubleToInt Function	DoubleToLong Function
IntStream	IntFunction	IntToDouble Function	IntUnary Operator	IntToLong Function
LongStream	Long Function	LongToDouble Function	LongToInt Function	LongUnary Operator

You do have to memorize Table 4.6 and Table 4.7. It's not as hard as it might seem. There are patterns in the names if you remember a few rules. For Table 4.6, mapping to the same type you started with is just called map(). When returning an object stream, the method is mapToObj(). Beyond that, it's the name of the primitive type in the map method name.

For Table 4.7, you can start by thinking about the source and target types. When the target type is an object, you drop the To from the name. When the mapping is to the same type you started with, you use a unary operator instead of a function for the primitive streams.

You can also create a primitive stream from a Stream using flatMapToInt(), flatMapToDouble(), or flatMapToLong(). For example, IntStream ints = list.stream().flatMapToInt(x -> IntStream.of(x));

Using *Optional* with Primitive Streams

Earlier in the chapter, we wrote a method to calculate the average of an int[] and promised a better way later. Now that you know about primitive streams, you can calculate the average in one line:

```
IntStream stream = IntStream.rangeClosed(1,10);
OptionalDouble optional = stream.average();
```

The return type is not the Optional you have become accustomed to using. It is a new type called OptionalDouble. Why do we have a separate type, you might wonder? Why not just use Optional<Double>? The difference is that OptionalDouble is for a primitive and Optional<Double> is for the Double wrapper class. Working with the primitive optional class looks similar to working with the Optional class itself:

```
optional.ifPresent(System.out::println);
System.out.println(optional.getAsDouble());
System.out.println(optional.orElseGet(() -> Double.NaN));
```

The only noticeable difference is that we called getAsDouble() rather than get(). This makes it clear that we are working with a primitive. Also, orElseGet() takes a DoubleSupplier instead of a Supplier.

As with the primitive streams, there are three type-specific classes for primitives. Table 4.8 shows the minor differences among the three. You probably won't be surprised that you have to memorize it as well. This is really easy to remember since the only thing that changes is the primitive name. As you should remember from the terminal operations section, a number of stream methods return an optional such as min() or findAny(). These each return the corresponding optional type. The primitive stream implementations also add two new methods that you need to know. The sum() method does not return an optional. If you try to add up an empty stream, you simply get zero. The avg() method always returns an OptionalDouble, since an average can potentially have fractional data for any type.

TABLE 4.8   Optional types for primitives

	OptionalDouble	OptionalInt	OptionalLong
Getting as a primitive	getAsDouble()	getAsInt()	getAsLong()
orElseGet() parameter type	DoubleSupplier	IntSupplier	LongSupplier
Return type of max()	OptionalDouble	OptionalInt	OptionalLong
Return type of sum()	double	int	long
Return type of avg()	OptionalDouble	OptionalDouble	OptionalDouble

Let's try an example to make sure that you understand this:

```
5:     LongStream longs = LongStream.of(5, 10);
6:     long sum = longs.sum();
7:     System.out.println(sum); // 15
```

```
8:    DoubleStream doubles = DoubleStream.generate(() -> Math.PI);
9:    OptionalDouble min = doubles.min(); // runs infinitely
```

Line 5 creates a stream of long primitives with two elements. Line 6 shows that we don't use an optional to calculate a sum. Line 8 creates an infinite stream of double primitives. Line 9 is there to remind you that a question about code that runs infinitely can appear with primitive streams as well.

Summarizing Statistics

You've learned enough to be able to get the maximum value from a stream of int primitives. If the stream is empty, we want to throw an exception:

```
private static int max(IntStream ints) {
    OptionalInt optional = ints.max();
    return optional.orElseThrow(RuntimeException::new);
}
```

This should be old hat by now. We got an OptionalInt because we have an IntStream. If the optional contains a value, we return it. Otherwise, we throw a new RuntimeException.

Now we want to change the method to take an IntStream and return a range. The range is the minimum value subtracted from the maximum value. Uh-oh. Both min() and max() are terminal operations, which means that they use up the stream when they are run. We can't run two terminal operations against the same stream. Luckily, this is a common problem and the primitive streams solve it for us with summary statistics. *Statistic* is just a big word for a number that was calculated from data.

```
private static int range(IntStream ints) {
    IntSummaryStatistics stats = ints.summaryStatistics();
    if (stats.getCount() == 0) throw new RuntimeException();
    return stats.getMax()-stats.getMin();
}
```

Here we asked Java to perform many calculations about the stream. This includes the minimum, maximum, average, size, and the number of values in the stream. If the stream were empty, we'd have a count of zero. Otherwise, we can get the minimum and maximum out of the summary.

Learning the Functional Interfaces for Primitives

Remember when we told you to memorize Table 4.1, with the common functional interfaces, at the beginning of the chapter? Did you? If you didn't, go do it now. We are about to make it more involved. Just as there are special streams and optional classes for primitives, there are also special functional interfaces.

Luckily, most of them are for the double, int, and long types that you saw for streams and optionals. There is one exception, which is BooleanSupplier. We will cover that before introducing the ones for double, int, and long.

Functional Interfaces for *boolean*

BooleanSupplier is a separate type. It has one method to implement:

```
boolean getAsBoolean()
```

It works just as you've come to expect from functional interfaces, for example:

```
12:   BooleanSupplier b1 = () -> true;
13:   BooleanSupplier b2 = () -> Math.random() > .5;
14:   System.out.println(b1.getAsBoolean());
15:   System.out.println(b2.getAsBoolean());
```

Lines 12 and 13 each create a BooleanSupplier, which is the only functional interface for boolean. Line 14 prints true, since it is the result of b1. Line 15 prints out true or false, depending on the random value generated.

Functional Interfaces for *double, int,* and *long*

Most of the functional interfaces are for double, int, and long to match the streams and optionals that we've been using for primitives. Table 4.9 shows the equivalent of Table 4.1 for these primitives. You probably won't be surprised that you have to memorize it. Luckily, you've memorized Table 4.1 by now and can apply what you've learned to Table 4.9.

TABLE 4.9   Common functional interfaces for primitives

Functional Interfaces	# Parameters	Return Type	Single Abstract Method
DoubleSupplier	0	double	getAsDouble
IntSupplier		int	getAsInt
LongSupplier		long	getAsLong
DoubleConsumer	1 (double)	void	accept
IntConsumer	1 (int)		
LongConsumer	1 (long)		
DoublePredicate	1 (double)	boolean	test
IntPredicate	1 (int)		
LongPredicate	1 (long)		

TABLE 4.10   Common functional interfaces for primitives *(continued)*

Functional Interfaces	# Parameters	Return Type	Single Abstract Method
DoubleFunction<R> IntFunction<R> LongFunction<R>	1 (double) 1 (int) 1 (long)	R	apply
DoubleUnaryOperator IntUnaryOperator LongUnaryOperator	1 (double) 1 (int) 1 (long)	double int long	applyAsDouble applyAsInt applyAsLong
DoubleBinaryOperator IntBinaryOperator LongBinaryOperator	2 (double, double) 2 (int, int) 2 (long, long)	double int long	applyAsDouble applyAsInt applyAsLong

There are a few things to notice that are different between Table 4.1 and Table 4.9:

- Generics are gone from some of the interfaces, since the type name tells us what primitive type is involved. In other cases, such as IntFunction, only the return type generic is needed.

- The single abstract method is often, but not always, renamed to reflect the primitive type involved.

- BiConsumer, BiPredicate, and BiFunction are not in Table 4.9. The API designers stuck to the most common operations. For primitives, the functions with two different type parameters just aren't used often.

In addition to Table 4.1 equivalents, some interfaces are specific to primitives. Table 4.10 lists these.

TABLE 4.10   Primitive-specific functional interfaces

Functional Interfaces	# Parameters	Return Type	Single Abstract Method
ToDoubleFunction<T> ToIntFunction<T> ToLongFunction<T>	1 (T)	double int long	applyAsDouble applyAsInt applyAsLong
ToDoubleBiFunction<T, U> ToIntBiFunction<T, U> ToLongBiFunction<T, U>	2 (T, U)	double int long	applyAsDouble applyAsInt applyAsLong

Functional Interfaces	# Parameters	Return Type	Single Abstract Method
DoubleToIntFunction	1 (double)	int	applyAsInt
DoubleToLongFunction	1 (double)	long	applyAsLong
IntToDoubleFunction	1 (int)	double	applyAsDouble
IntToLongFunction	1 (int)	long	applyAsLong
LongToDoubleFunction	1 (long)	double	applyAsDouble
LongToIntFunction	1 (long)	int	applyAsInt
ObjDoubleConsumer<T>	2 (T, double)	void	accept
ObjIntConsumer<T>	2 (T, int)		
ObjLongConsumer<T>	2 (T, long)		

We've been using functional interfaces all chapter long, so you should have a good grasp of how to read the table by now. Let's do one example just to be sure. Which functional interface would you use to fill in the blank to make the following code compile?

```
double d = 1.0;
_____ f1 = x -> 1;
f1.applyAsInt(d);
```

When you see a question like this, look for clues. You can see that the functional interface in question takes a double parameter and returns an int. You can also see that it has a single abstract method named applyAsInt. The only functional interface meeting all three of those criteria is DoubleToIntFunction.

Working with Advanced Stream Pipeline Concepts

You've almost reached the end of learning about streams. We have only a few more topics left. You'll see the relationship between streams and the underlying data, chaining Optional and grouping collectors.

Linking Streams to the Underlying Data

What do you think this outputs?

```
25:    List<String> cats = new ArrayList<>();
26:    cats.add("Annie");
27:    cats.add("Ripley");
```

```
28:    Stream<String> stream = cats.stream();
29:    cats.add("KC");
30:    System.out.println(stream.count());
```

The correct answer is 3. Lines 25–27 create a List with two elements. Line 28 requests that a stream be created from that List. Remember that streams are lazily evaluated. This means that the stream isn't actually created on line 28. An object is created that knows where to look for the data when it is needed. On line 29, the List gets a new element. On line 30, the stream pipeline actually runs. The stream pipeline runs first, looking at the source and seeing three elements.

Chaining Optionals

By now, you are familiar with the benefits of chaining operations in a stream pipeline. A few of the intermediate operations for streams are available for Optional.

Suppose that you are given an Optional<Integer> and asked to print the value, but only if it is a three-digit number. Without functional programming, you could write the following:

```
private static void threeDigit(Optional<Integer> optional) {
    if (optional.isPresent()) {          // outer if
        Integer num = optional.get();
        String string = "" + num;
        if (string.length() == 3)        // inner if
            System.out.println(string);
} }
```

It works, but it contains nested if statements. That's extra complexity. Let's try this again with functional programming:

```
private static void threeDigit(Optional<Integer> optional) {
    optional.map(n -> "" + n)                // part 1
        .filter(s -> s.length() == 3)        // part 2
        .ifPresent(System.out::println);     // part 3
}
```

This is much shorter and more expressive. With lambdas, the exam is fond of carving up a single statement and identifying the pieces with a comment. We've done that here to show what happens with both the functional programming and non–functional programming approaches.

Suppose that we are given an empty Optional. The first approach returns false for the outer if. The second approach sees an empty Optional and has both map() and filter() pass it through. Then ifPresent() sees an empty Optional and doesn't call the Consumer parameter.

The next case is where we are given an Optional.of(4). The first approach returns false for the inner if. The second approach maps the number 4 to the String "4". The filter then returns an empty Optional since the filter doesn't match, and ifPresent() doesn't call the Consumer parameter.

The final case is where we are given an Optional.of(123). The first approach returns true for both if statements. The second approach maps the number 123 to the String "123". The filter than returns the same Optional, and ifPresent() now does call the Consumer parameter.

Now suppose that we wanted to get an Optional<Integer> representing the length of the String contained in another Optional. Easy enough:

```
Optional<Integer> result = optional.map(String::length);
```

What if we had a helper method that did the logic of calculating something for us and it had the signature static Optional<Integer> calculator(String s)? Using map doesn't work:

```
Optional<Integer> result = optional.map(ChainingOptionals::calculator); // DOES
NOT COMPILE
```

Real World Scenario

Checked Exceptions and Functional Interfaces

You might have noticed by now that the functional interfaces do not declare checked exceptions. This is normally OK. However, it is a problem when working with methods that declare checked exceptions. Suppose that we have a class with a method that throws a checked exception:

```
import java.io.*;
import java.util.*;

public class ExceptionCaseStudy {
    private static List<String> create() throws IOException {
        throw new IOException();
    }
}
```

Now we use it in a stream:

```
ExceptionCaseStudy.create().stream().count();
```

Nothing new here. The `create()` method throws a checked exception. The calling method handles or declares it. Now what about this one?

```
Supplier<List<String>> s = ExceptionCaseStudy::create; // DOES NOT COMPILE
```

The actual compiler error is

```
<code>unhandled exception type IOException
```

Say what now? The problem is that the lambda to which this method reference expands does declare an exception. The `Supplier` interface does not allow checked exceptions. There are two approaches to get around this problem. One is to catch the exception and turn it into an unchecked exception:

```
Supplier<List<String>> s = () -> {
    try {
        return ExceptionCaseStudy.create();
    } catch (IOException e) {
        throw new RuntimeException(e);
    }
};
```

This works. But the code is ugly. One of the benefits of functional programming is that the code is supposed to be easy to read and concise. Another alternative is to create a wrapper method with the try/catch:

```
private static List<String> createSafe() {
    try {
        return ExceptionCaseStudy.create();
    } catch (IOException e) {
        throw new RuntimeException(e);
    } }
```

Now we can use the safe wrapper in our `Supplier` without issue:

```
Supplier<List<String>> s2 = ExceptionCaseStudyHelper::createSafe;
```

The problem is that calculator returns `Optional<Integer>`. The `map()` method adds another Optional, giving us `Optional<Optional<Integer>>`. Well, that's no good. The solution is to call `flatMap()` instead:

```
Optional<Integer> result = optional.flatMap(ChainingOptionals::calculator);
```

This one works because flatMap removes the unnecessary layer. In other words, it flattens the result. Chaining calls to flatMap() is useful when you want to transform one Optional type to another.

Collecting Results

You're almost finished learning about streams. The last topic builds on what you've learned so far to group the results. Early in the chapter, you saw the collect() terminal operation. There are many predefined collectors, including those shown in Table 4.11. We will look at the different types of collectors in the following sections.

TABLE 4.11   Examples of grouping/partitioning collectors

Collector	Description	Return Value When Passed to collect
averagingDouble(ToDoubleFunction f) averagingInt(ToIntFunction f) averagingLong(ToLongFunction f)	Calculates the average for our three core primitive types	Double
counting()	Counts number of elements	Long
groupingBy(Function f) groupingBy(Function f, Collector dc) groupingBy(Function f, Supplier s, Collector dc)	Creates a map grouping by the specified function with the optional type and optional downstream collector	Map<K, List<T>>
joining() joining(CharSequence cs)	Creates a single String using cs as a delimiter between elements if one is specified	String
maxBy(Comparator c) minBy(Comparator c)	Finds the largest/smallest elements	Optional<T>
mapping(Function f, Collector dc)	Adds another level of collectors	Collector
partitioningBy(Predicate p) partitioningBy(Predicate p, Collector dc)	Creates a map grouping by the specified predicate with the optional further downstream collector	Map<Boolean, List<T>>

TABLE 4.11 Examples of grouping/partitioning collectors *(continued)*

Collector	Description	Return Value When Passed to collect
summarizingDouble(ToDoubleFunction f) summarizingInt(ToIntFunction f) summarizingLong(ToLongFunction f)	Calculates average, min, max, and so on	DoubleSummaryStatistics IntSummaryStatistics LongSummaryStatistics
summingDouble(ToDoubleFunction f) summingInt(ToIntFunction f) summingLong(ToLongFunction f)	Calculates the sum for our three core primitive types	Double Integer Long
toList() toSet()	Creates an arbitrary type of list or set	List Set
toCollection(Supplier s)	Creates a Collection of the specified type	Collection
toMap(Function k, Function v) toMap(Function k, Function v, BinaryOperator m) toMap(Function k, Function v, BinaryOperator m, Supplier s)	Creates a map using functions to map the keys, values, an optional merge function, and an optional type	Map

Collecting Using Basic Collectors

Luckily, many of these collectors work in the same way. Let's look at an example:

```
Stream<String> ohMy = Stream.of("lions", "tigers", "bears");
String result = ohMy.collect(Collectors.joining(", "));
System.out.println(result); // lions, tigers, bears
```

Notice how the predefined collectors are in the Collectors class rather than the Collector class. This is a common theme, which you saw with Collection vs. Collections. We pass the predefined joining() collector to the collect() method. All elements of the stream are then merged into a String with the specified delimiter between each element.

It is very important to pass the Collector to the collect method. It exists to help collect elements. A Collector doesn't do anything on its own.

Let's try another one. What is the average length of the three animal names?

```
Stream<String> ohMy = Stream.of("lions", "tigers", "bears");
Double result = ohMy.collect(Collectors.averagingInt(String::length));
System.out.println(result); // 5.333333333333333
```

The pattern is the same. We pass a collector to collect() and it performs the average for us. This time, we needed to pass a function to tell the collector what to average. We used a method reference, which returns an int upon execution. With primitive streams, the result of an average was always a double, regardless of what type is being averaged. For collectors, it is a Double since those need an Object.

Often, you'll find yourself interacting with code that was written prior to Java 8. This means that it will expect a Collection type rather than a Stream type. No problem. You can still express yourself using a Stream and then convert to a Collection at the end, for example:

```
Stream<String> ohMy = Stream.of("lions", "tigers", "bears");
TreeSet<String> result = ohMy.filter(s -> s.startsWith("t")
    .collect(Collectors.toCollection(TreeSet::new));
System.out.println(result); // [tigers]
```

This time we have all three parts of the stream pipeline. Stream.of() is the source for the stream. The intermediate operation is filter(). Finally, the terminal operation is collect(), which creates a TreeSet. If we didn't care which implement of Set we got, we could have written Collectors.toSet() instead.

At this point, you should be able to use all of the Collectors in Table 4.11 except groupingBy(), mapping(), partitioningBy(), and toMap().

Collecting into Maps

Collector code involving maps can get long. We will build it up slowly. Make sure that you understand each example before going on to the next one. Let's start out with a straightforward example to create a map from a stream:

```
Stream<String> ohMy = Stream.of("lions", "tigers", "bears");
Map<String, Integer> map = ohMy.collect(
    Collectors.toMap(s -> s, String::length));
System.out.println(map); // {lions=5, bears=5, tigers=6}
```

When creating a map, you need to specify two functions. The first function tells the collector how to create the key. In our example, we use the provided String as the key. The second function tells the collector how to create the value. In our example, we use the length of the String as the value.

Returning the same value passed into a lambda is a common operation, so Java provides a method for it. You can rewrite s -> s as Function.identity(). It is not shorter and may or may not be clearer, so use your judgment on whether to use it.

Now we want to do the reverse and map the length of the animal name to the name itself. Our first incorrect attempt is shown here:

```
Stream<String> ohMy = Stream.of("lions", "tigers", "bears");
Map<Integer, String> map = ohMy.collect(Collectors.toMap(String::length, k ->
k)); // BAD
```

Running this gives an exception similar to the following:

```
Exception in thread "main" java.lang.IllegalStateException: Duplicate key lions
    at java.util.stream.Collectors.lambda$throwingMerger$114(Collectors.java:133)
    at java.util.stream.Collectors$$Lambda$3/1044036744.apply(Unknown Source)
```

What's wrong? Two of the animal names are the same length. We didn't tell Java what to do. Should the collector choose the first one it encounters? The last one it encounters? Concatenate the two? Since the collector has no idea what to do, it "solves" the problem by throwing an exception and making it our problem. How thoughtful. Let's suppose that our requirement is to create a comma-separated String with the animal names. We could write this:

```
Stream<String> ohMy = Stream.of("lions", "tigers", "bears");
Map<Integer, String> map = ohMy.collect(Collectors.toMap(
    String::length, k -> k, (s1, s2) -> s1 + "," + s2));
System.out.println(map);  // {5=lions,bears, 6=tigers}
System.out.println(map.getClass());  // class. java.util.HashMap
```

It so happens that the Map returned is a HashMap. This behavior is not guaranteed. Suppose that we want to mandate that the code return a TreeMap instead. No problem. We would just add a constructor reference as a parameter:

```
Stream<String> ohMy = Stream.of("lions", "tigers", "bears");
TreeMap<Integer, String> map = ohMy.collect(Collectors.toMap(
    String::length, k -> k, (s1, s2) -> s1 + "," + s2, TreeMap::new));
System.out.println(map); // // {5=lions,bears, 6=tigers}
System.out.println(map.getClass());  // class. java.util.TreeMap
```

This time we got the type that we specified. With us so far? This code is long but not particularly complicated. We did promise you that the code would be long!

Collecting Using Grouping, Partitioning, and Mapping

Now suppose that we want to get groups of names by their length. We can do that by saying that we want to group by length:

```
Stream<String> ohMy = Stream.of("lions", "tigers", "bears");
Map<Integer, List<String>> map = ohMy.collect(
    Collectors.groupingBy(String::length));
System.out.println(map); // {5=[lions, bears], 6=[tigers]}
```

The groupingBy() collector tells collect() that it should group all of the elements of the stream into lists, organizing them by the function provided. This makes the keys in the map the function value and the values the function results.

Suppose that we don't want a List as the value in the map and prefer a Set instead. No problem. There's another method signature that lets us pass a *downstream collector*. This is a second collector that does something special with the values:

```
Stream<String> ohMy = Stream.of("lions", "tigers", "bears");
Map<Integer, Set<String>> map = ohMy.collect(
    Collectors.groupingBy(String::length, Collectors.toSet()));
System.out.println(map); // {5=[lions, bears], 6=[tigers]}
```

We can even change the type of Map returned through yet another parameter:

```
Stream<String> ohMy = Stream.of("lions", "tigers", "bears");
TreeMap<Integer, Set<String>> map = ohMy.collect(
    Collectors.groupingBy(String::length, TreeMap::new, Collectors.toSet()));
System.out.println(map); // {5=[lions, bears], 6=[tigers]}
```

This is very flexible. What if we want to change the type of Map returned but leave the type of values alone as a List? There isn't a method for this specifically because it is easy enough to write with the existing ones:

```
Stream<String> ohMy = Stream.of("lions", "tigers", "bears");
TreeMap<Integer, List<String>> map = ohMy.collect(
    Collectors.groupingBy(String::length, TreeMap::new, Collectors.toList()));
System.out.println(map);
```

Partitioning is a special case of grouping. With partitioning, there are only two possible groups—true and false. *Partitioning* is like splitting a list into two parts.

Suppose that we are making a sign to put outside each animal's exhibit. We have two sizes of signs. One can accommodate names with five or fewer characters. The other is needed for longer names. We can partition the list according to which sign we need:

```
Stream<String> ohMy = Stream.of("lions", "tigers", "bears");
Map<Boolean, List<String>> map = ohMy.collect(
    Collectors.partitioningBy(s -> s.length() <= 5));
System.out.println(map); // {false=[tigers], true=[lions, bears]}
```

Here we passed a Predicate with the logic for which group each animal name belongs in. Now suppose that we've figured out how to use a different font, and seven characters can now fit on the smaller sign. No worries. We just change the Predicate:

```
Stream<String> ohMy = Stream.of("lions", "tigers", "bears");
Map<Boolean, List<String>> map = ohMy.collect(
    Collectors.partitioningBy(s -> s.length() <= 7));
System.out.println(map); // {false=[], true=[lions, tigers, bears]}
```

Notice that there are still two keys in the map—one for each boolean value. It so happens that one of the values is an empty list, but it is still there. As with groupingBy(), we can change the type of List to something else:

Debugging Complicated Generics

When working with collect(), there are often many levels of generics, making compiler errors unreadable. Here are three useful techniques for dealing with this situation:

- Start over with a simple statement and keep adding to it. By making one tiny change at a time, you will know which code introduced the error.

- Extract parts of the statement into separate statements. For example, try writing Collectors.groupingBy(String::length, Collectors.counting());. If it compiles, you know that the problem lies elsewhere. If it doesn't compile, you have a much shorter statement to troubleshoot.

- Use generic wildcards for the return type of the final statement, for example, Map<?, ?>. If that change alone allows the code to compile, you'll know that the problem lies with the return type not being what you expect.

```
Stream<String> ohMy = Stream.of("lions", "tigers", "bears");
Map<Boolean, Set<String>> map = ohMy.collect(
   Collectors.partitioningBy(s -> s.length() <= 7, Collectors.toSet()));
System.out.println(map);// {false=[], true=[lions, tigers, bears]}
```

Unlike groupingBy(), we cannot change the type of Map that gets returned. However, there are only two keys in the map, so does it really matter which Map type we use?

Instead of using the downstream collector to specify the type, we can use any of the collectors that we've already shown. For example, we can group by the length of the animal name to see how many of each length we have:

```
Stream<String> ohMy = Stream.of("lions", "tigers", "bears");
Map<Integer, Long> map = ohMy.collect(Collectors.groupingBy(
   String::length, Collectors.counting()));
System.out.println(map); // {5=2, 6=1}
```

Finally, there is a mapping() collector that lets us go down a level and add another collector. Suppose that we wanted to get the first letter of the first animal alphabetically of each length. Why? Perhaps for random sampling. The examples on this part of the exam are fairly contrived as well. We'd write the following:

```
Stream<String> ohMy = Stream.of("lions", "tigers", "bears");
```

```
Map<Integer, Optional<Character>> map = ohMy.collect(
    Collectors.groupingBy(
        String::length,
        Collectors.mapping(s -> s.charAt(0),
            Collectors.minBy(Comparator.naturalOrder()))));
System.out.println(map); // {5=Optional[b], 6=Optional[t]}
```

We aren't going to tell you that this code is easy to read. We will tell you that it is the most complicated thing you should expect to see on the exam. Comparing it to the previous example, you can see that we replaced counting() with mapping(). It so happens that mapping() takes two parameters: the function for the value and how to group it further.

You might see collectors used with a static import to make the code shorter. This means that you might see something like this:

```
Stream<String> ohMy = Stream.of("lions", "tigers", "bears");
Map<Integer, Optional<Character>> map = ohMy.collect(
    groupingBy(
        String::length,
        mapping(s -> s.charAt(0),
            minBy(Comparator.naturalOrder()))));
System.out.println(map); // {5=Optional[b], 6=Optional[t]}
```

The code does the same thing as in the previous example. This means that it is important to recognize the collector names because you might not have the Collectors class name to call your attention to it.

There is one more collector called reducing(). You don't need to know it for the exam. It is a general reduction in case all of the previous collectors don't meet your needs.

Summary

Lambdas can reference static variables, instance variables, effectively final parameters, and effectively final local variables. A functional interface has a single abstract method. You must know the functional interfaces:

- Supplier<T>: Method get() returns T
- Consumer<T>: Method accept(T t) returns void
- BiConsumer<T>: Method accept(T t, U u) returns void
- Predicate<T>: Method test(T t) returns boolean
- BiPredicate<T>: Method test(T t, U u) returns boolean
- Function<T, R>: Method apply(T t) returns R
- BiFunction<T, U, R>: Method apply(T t, U u) returns R

- UnaryOperator<T>: Method apply(T t) returns T
- BinaryOperator<T>: Method apply(T t1, T t2) returns T

An Optional can be empty or store a value. You can check if it contains a value with ifPresent() and get() the value inside. There are also three methods that take functional interfaces as parameters: ifPresent(Consumer c), orElseGet(Supplier s), and orElseThrow(Supplier s). There are three optional types for primitives: DoubleSupplier, IntSupplier, and LongSupplier. These have the methods getDouble(), getInt(), and getLong(), respectively.

A stream pipeline has three parts. The source is required, and it creates the data in the stream. There can be zero or more intermediate operations, which aren't executed until the terminal operation runs. Examples of intermediate operations include filter(), flatMap(), and sorted(). Examples of terminal operations include allMatch(), count(), and forEach().

There are three primitive streams: DoubleStream, IntStream, and LongStream. In addition to the usual Stream methods, they have range() and rangeClosed(). The call range(1, 10) on IntStream and LongStream creates a stream of the primitives from 1 to 9. By contrast, rangeClosed(1, 10) creates a stream of the primitives from 1 to 10. The primitive streams have math operations including average(), max(), and sum(). They also have summaryStatistics() to get many statistics in one call. There are also functional interfaces specific to streams. Except for BooleanSupplier, they are all for double, int, and long primitives as well.

You can use a Collector to transform a stream into a traditional collection. You can even group fields to create a complex map in one line. Partitioning works the same way as grouping, except that the keys are always true and false. A partitioned map always has two keys even if the value is empty for the key.

You should review the tables in the chapter. You absolutely must memorize Table 4.1. You should memorize Table 4.6 and Table 4.7 but be able to spot incompatibilities, such as type differences, if you can't memorize these two. Finally, remember that streams are lazily evaluated. They take lambdas or method references as parameters, which occur later when the method is run.

Exam Essentials

Identify the correct functional interface given the number of parameters, return type, and method name—and vice versa.   The most common functional interfaces are Supplier, Consumer, Function, and Predicate. There are also binary versions and primitive versions of many of these methods.

Write code that uses Optional.   Creating an Optional uses Optional.empty() or Optional.of(). Retrieval frequently uses ifPresent() and get(). Alternatively, there are the functional ifPresent() and orElseGet() methods.

Recognize which operations cause a stream pipeline to execute.   Intermediate operations do not run until the terminal operation is encountered. If no terminal operation is in the pipeline, a Stream is returned but not executed. Examples of terminal operations include collect(), forEach(), min(), and reduce().

Determine which terminal operations are reductions.   Reductions use all elements of the stream in determining the result. The reductions that you need to know are collect(), count(), max(), min(), and reduce(). A mutable reduction collects into the same object as it goes. The collect() method is a mutable reduction.

Write code for common intermediate operations.   The filter() method returns a Stream filtering on a Predicate. The map() method returns a Stream transforming each element to another through a Function. The flatMap() method flattens nested lists into a single level and removes empty lists.

Compare primitive streams to Stream.   There are three primitive stream classes: DoubleStream, IntStream, and LongStream. There are also three primitive Optional classes: OptionalDouble, OptionalInt, and OptionalLong. There are a good number of functional interfaces for primitives. Aside from BooleanSupplier, they all involve the double, int, or long primitives.

Convert primitive stream types to other primitive stream types.   Normally when mapping, you just call the map() method. When changing the class used for the stream, a different method is needed. To convert to Stream, you use mapToObj(). To convert to DoubleStream, you use mapToDouble(). To convert to IntStream, you use mapToInt(). To convert to LongStream, you use mapToLong().

Translate coding using method references into lambdas and vice versa.   All code that uses method references can be rewritten as a lambda. For example, stream.forEach(System. out::println) does the same thing as stream.forEach(x -> System.out.println(x)). Not all code that uses lambdas can be rewritten to use a method reference.

Use peek() to inspect the stream.   The peek() method is an intermediate operation. It executes a lambda or method reference on the input and passes that same input through the pipeline to the next operator. It is useful for printing out what passes through a certain point in a stream.

Search a stream.   The findFirst() and findAny() methods return a single element from a stream in an Optional. The anyMatch(), allMatch(), and noneMatch() methods return a boolean. Be careful, because these three can hang if called on an infinite stream with some data. All of these methods are terminal operations.

Sort a stream.   The sorted() method is an intermediate operation that sorts a stream. There are two versions: the signature with zero parameters that sorts using the natural sort order, and the signature with one parameter that sorts using that Comparator as the sort order.

Review Questions

1. What is the output of the following?

```
Stream<String> stream = Stream.iterate("", (s) -> s + "1");
System.out.println(stream.limit(2).map(x -> x + "2"));
```

- **A.** 12112
- **B.** 212
- **C.** 212112
- **D.** java.util.stream.ReferencePipeline$3@4517d9a3
- **E.** The code does not compile.
- **F.** An exception is thrown.
- **G.** The code hangs.

2. What is the output of the following?

```
Predicate<? super String> predicate = s -> s.startsWith("g");
Stream<String> stream1 = Stream.generate(() -> "growl! ");
Stream<String> stream2 = Stream.generate(() -> "growl! ");
boolean b1 = stream1.anyMatch(predicate);
boolean b2 = stream2.allMatch(predicate);
System.out.println(b1 + " " + b2);
```

- **A.** true false
- **B.** true true
- **C.** java.util.stream.ReferencePipeline$3@4517d9a3
- **D.** The code does not compile.
- **E.** An exception is thrown.
- **F.** The code hangs.

3. What is the output of the following?

```
Predicate<? super String> predicate = s -> s.length() > 3;
Stream<String> stream = Stream.iterate("-", (s) -> s + s);
boolean b1 = stream.noneMatch(predicate);
boolean b2 = stream.anyMatch(predicate);
System.out.println(b1 + " " + b2);
```

- **A.** false true
- **B.** false false
- **C.** java.util.stream.ReferencePipeline$3@4517d9a3
- **D.** The code does not compile.

E. An exception is thrown.

F. The code hangs.

4. Which are true statements about terminal operations in a stream? (Choose all that apply.)

   A. At most one terminal operation can exist in a stream pipeline.

   B. Terminal operations are a required part of the stream pipeline in order to get a result.

   C. Terminal operations have `Stream` as the return type.

   D. The referenced `Stream` may be used after the calling a terminal operation.

   E. The peek() method is an example of a terminal operation.

5. Which terminal operations on the `Stream` class are reductions? (Choose all that apply.)

   A. `collect()`

   B. `count()`

   C. `findFirst()`

   D. `map()`

   E. `peek()`

   F. `sum()`

6. Which of the following can fill in the blank so that the code prints out `false`? (Choose all that apply.)

   ```
   Stream<String> s = Stream.generate(() -> "meow");
   boolean match = s._____(String::isEmpty);
   System.out.println(match);
   ```

   A. `allMatch`

   B. `anyMatch`

   C. `findAny`

   D. `findFirst`

   E. `noneMatch`

   F. None of the above

7. We have a method that returns a sorted list without changing the original. Which of the following can replace the method implementation to do the same with streams?

   ```
   private static List<String> sort(List<String> list) {
       List<String> copy = new ArrayList<>(list);
       Collections.sort(copy, (a, b) -> b.compareTo(a));
       return copy;
   }
   ```

   A. `return list.stream()`
       `.compare((a, b) -> b.compareTo(a))`
       `.collect(Collectors.toList());`

B. `return list.stream()`
    `.compare((a, b) -> b.compareTo(a))`
    `.sort();`

C. `return list.stream()`
    `.compareTo((a, b) -> b.compareTo(a))`
    `.collect(Collectors.toList());`

D. `return list.stream()`
    `.compareTo((a, b) -> b.compareTo(a))`
    `.sort();`

E. `return list.stream()`
    `.sorted((a, b) -> b.compareTo(a))`
    `.collect();`

F. `return list.stream()`
    `.sorted((a, b) -> b.compareTo(a))`
    `.collect(Collectors.toList());`

8. Which of the following are true given the declaration `IntStream is = IntStream.empty()`? (Choose all that apply.)

A. `is.average()` returns the type `int`.

B. `is.average()` returns the type `OptionalInt`.

C. `is.findAny()` returns the type `int`.

D. `is.findAny()` returns the type `OptionalInt`.

E. `is.sum()` returns the type `int`.

F. `is.sum()` returns the type `OptionalInt`.

9. Which of the following can we add after line 5 for the code to run without error and not produce any output? (Choose all that apply.)

```
4:    LongStream ls = LongStream.of(1, 2, 3);
5:    OptionalLong opt = ls.map(n -> n * 10).filter(n -> n < 5).findFirst();
```

A. `if (opt.isPresent()) System.out.println(opt.get());`

B. `if (opt.isPresent()) System.out.println(opt.getAsLong());`

C. `opt.ifPresent(System.out.println)`

D. `opt.ifPresent(System.out::println)`

E. None of these; the code does not compile.

F. None of these; line 5 throws an exception at runtime.

10. Select from the following statements and indicate the order in which they would appear to output 10 lines:

```
Stream.generate(() -> "1")
L:   .filter(x -> x.length() > 1)
M:   .forEach(System.out::println)
N:   .limit(10)
O:   .peek(System.out::println)
  ;
```

A. L, N

B. L, N, O

C. L, N, M

D. L, N, M, O

E. L, O, M

F. N, M

G. N, O

11. What changes need to be made for this code to print the string 12345? (Choose all that apply.)

```
Stream.iterate(1, x -> x++).limit(5).map(x -> x).collect(Collectors.
joining());
```

A. Change `Collectors.joining()` to `Collectors.joining("")`.

B. Change `map(x -> x)` to `map(x -> "" + x)`.

C. Change `x -> x++` to `x -> ++x`.

D. Add `forEach(System.out::print)` after the call to `collect()`.

E. Wrap the entire line in a `System.out.print` statement.

F. None of the above. The code already prints 12345.

12. Which functional interfaces complete the following code? (Choose all that apply.)

```
6:   _____ x = String::new;
7:   _____ y = (a, b) -> System.out.println();
8:   _____ z = a -> a + a;
```

A. `BiConsumer<String, String>`

B. `BiFunction<String, String>`

C. `BinaryConsumer<String, String>`

D. `BinaryFunction<String, String>`

E. `Consumer<String>`

F. `Supplier<String>`

G. `UnaryOperator<String>`

H. `UnaryOperator<String, String>`

13. Which of the following is true?

```
List<Integer> l1 = Arrays.asList(1, 2, 3);
List<Integer> l2 = Arrays.asList(4, 5, 6);
List<Integer> l3 = Arrays.asList();
Stream.of(l1, l2, l3).map(x -> x + 1)
    .flatMap(x -> x.stream()).forEach(System.out::print);
```

A. The code compiles and prints 123456.

B. The code compiles and prints 234567.

C. The code compiles but does not print anything.

D. The code compiles but prints stream references.

E. The code runs infinitely.

F. The code does not compile.

G. The code throws an exception

14. Which of the following is true?

```
4:    Stream<Integer> s = Stream.of(1);
5:    IntStream is = s.mapToInt(x -> x);
6:    DoubleStream ds = s.mapToDouble(x -> x);
7:    Stream<Integer> s2 = ds.mapToInt(x -> x);
8:    s2.forEach(System.out::print);
```

A. Line 4 does not compile.

B. Line 5 does not compile.

C. Line 6 does not compile.

D. Line 7 does not compile.

E. Line 8 does not compile.

F. The code throws an exception.

G. The code compiles and prints 1.

15. The partitioningBy() collector creates a Map<Boolean, List<String>> when passed to collect() by default. When specific parameters are passed to partitioningBy(), which return types can be created? (Choose all that apply.)

A. Map<boolean, List<String>>

B. Map<Boolean, Map<String>>

C. Map<Long, TreeSet<String>>

D. Map<Boolean, List<String>>

E. Map<Boolean, Set<String>>

F. None of the above

16. What is the output of the following?

```
Stream<String> s = Stream.empty();
Stream<String> s2 = Stream.empty();
Map<Boolean, List<String>> p = s.collect(
    Collectors.partitioningBy(b -> b.startsWith("c")));
Map<Boolean, List<String>> g = s2.collect(
    Collectors.groupingBy(b -> b.startsWith("c")));
System.out.println(p + " " + g);
```

A. {} {}

B. {} {false=[], true=[]}

C. {false=[], true=[]} {}

D. {false=[], true=[]} {false=[], true=[]}

E. The code does not compile.

F. An exception is thrown.

17. Which of the following is equivalent to this code?

```
UnaryOperator<Integer> u = x -> x * x;
```

A. BiFunction<Integer> f = x -> x*x;

B. BiFunction<Integer, Integer> f = x -> x*x;

C. BinaryOperator<Integer, Integer> f = x -> x*x;

D. Function<Integer> f = x -> x*x;

E. Function<Integer, Integer> f = x -> x*x;

F. None of the above

18. What is the result of the following?

```
DoubleStream s = DoubleStream.of(1.2, 2.4);
s.peek(System.out::println).filter(x -> x > 2).count();
```

A. 1

B. 2

C. 2.4

D. 1.2 and 2.4

E. There is no output.

F. The code does not compile.

G. An exception is thrown.

19. Which of the following return primitives? (Choose all that apply.)

   A. BooleanSupplier

   B. CharSupplier

   C. DoubleSupplier

   D. FloatSupplier

   E. IntSupplier

   F. StringSupplier

20. What is the simplest way of rewriting this code?

```
List<Integer> l = IntStream.range(1, 6)
    .mapToObj(i -> i).collect(Collectors.toList());
l.forEach(System.out::println);
```

   A. IntStream.range(1, 6);

   B.
```
IntStream.range(1, 6)
    .forEach(System.out::println);
```

   C.
```
IntStream.range(1, 6)
    .mapToObj(1 -> i)
    .forEach(System.out::println);
```

   D. None of the above is equivalent.

   E. The provided code does not compile.

Chapter

5

Dates, Strings, and Localization

THE OCP EXAM TOPICS COVERED IN THIS CHAPTER INCLUDE THE FOLLOWING:

✓ **Use Java SE 8 Date/Time API**

- Create and manage date-based and time-based events including a combination of date and time into a single object using LocalDate, LocalTime, LocalDateTime, Instant, Period and Duration

- Work with dates and times across time zones and manage changes resulting from daylight savings including Format date and time values

- Define and create and manage date-based and time-based events using Instant, Period, Duration and TemporalUnit

✓ **Localization**

- Read and set the local by using the Locale object

- Create and read a Properties file

- Build a resource bundle for each locale and load a resource bundle in an application

You learned about the basics of Java 8 dates for the OCA. In addition to reviewing these, we will cover more advanced date concepts including time zones, daylight savings time, and comparing values and instants. Be sure to read the whole section, because Oracle goes deeper into some topics that you've already learned.

You might notice that Strings are not listed in the exam objectives. Since they are such a fundamental concept that might pop up in other questions, we will do a brief review here as well.

After that, we will discuss how to make your application work in different languages with localization. We will end with how to read and write numbers, dates, and money using different international formats.

Working with Dates and Times

In Java 8, Oracle completely revamped how we work with dates and times. You can still write code the old way, but those classes aren't on the exam. We'll mention the old way in real-world scenarios, so that you can learn the new way more easily if you learned Java before version 8. Even if you are learning Java starting with version 8, this will help you when you need to read older code. Just know that the old way is not on the exam.

You need an import to work with the date and time classes. Most of them are in the java.time package. To use it, add this import to your program:

```
import java.time.*;          // import time classes
```

Day vs. Date

In American English, the word *date* is used to represent two different concepts. Sometimes, it is the month/day/year combination when something happened, such as January 1, 2000. Sometimes, it is the day of the month, such as today's date is the 6th.

That's right; the words *day* and *date* are often used as synonyms. Be alert to this on the exam, especially if you live someplace where people are more precise about this distinction.

In the following sections, we'll look at creating, manipulating, and formatting dates and times.

Creating Dates and Times

In the real world, we usually talk about dates and time zones as if the other person is located near us. For example, if you say to me "I'll call you at 11:00 on Tuesday morning," we assume that 11:00 means the same thing to both of us. But if I live in New York and you live in California, we need to be more specific. California is three hours earlier than New York because the states are in different time zones. You would instead say "I'll call you at 11:00 EST (eastern standard time) on Tuesday morning." Unlike on the OCA, you do have to know about time zones on the OCP.

When working with dates and times, the first thing to do is to decide how much information you need. The exam gives you four choices:

LocalDate   Contains just a date—no time and no time zone. A good example of LocalDate is your birthday this year. It is your birthday for a full day, regardless of what time it is.

LocalTime   Contains just a time—no date and no time zone. A good example of LocalTime is midnight. It is midnight at the same time every day.

LocalDateTime   Contains both a date and time but no time zone. A good example of LocalDateTime is "the stroke of midnight on New Year's Eve." Midnight on January 2 isn't nearly as special, making the date relatively unimportant, and clearly an hour after midnight isn't as special either.

ZonedDateTime   Contains a date, time, and time zone. A good example of ZonedDateTime is "a conference call at 9:00 a.m. EST." If you live in California, you'll have to get up really early since the call is at 6:00 a.m. local time!

Oracle recommends avoiding time zones unless you really need them. Try to act as if everyone is in the same time zone when you can.

As you may remember from the OCA, you obtain date and time instances using a static method:

```
System.out.println(LocalDate.now());
System.out.println(LocalTime.now());
System.out.println(LocalDateTime.now());
System.out.println(ZonedDateTime.now());
```

Each of the four classes has a static method called now(), which gives the current date and time. Your output is going to depend on the date/time when you run it and where you live. The authors live in the United States, making the output look like the following when run on May 25 at 9:13 a.m.:

```
2015-05-25
09:13:07.768
2015-05-25T09:13:07.768
2015-05-25T09:13:07.769-04:00[America/New_York]
```

The key is the type of information in the output. The first line contains only a date and no time. The second contains only a time and no date. The time displays hours, minutes, seconds, and fractional seconds. The third contains both a date and a time. Java uses T to separate the date and time when converting LocalDateTime to a String. Finally, the fourth adds the time zone offset and time zone. New York is four time zones away from Greenwich Mean Time (GMT).

Greenwich Mean Time is a time zone in Europe that is used as time zone zero when discussing offsets. You might have also heard of *Coordinated Universal Time*, which is a time zone standard. It is abbreviated as a UTC, as a compromise between the English and French names. (That's not a typo. UTC isn't actually the proper acronym in either language!) UTC uses the same time zone zero as GMT.

Let's make sure that you understand how UTC works. We include names of the time zones in the examples to make them easier to picture. The exam will give you the UTC offset. You are not expected to memorize any time zones.

First, let's try to figure out how far apart these moments are in time. Notice how India has a half-hour offset, not a full hour. To approach a problem like this, you subtract the time zone from the time. This gives you the GMT equivalent of the time:

```
2015-06-20T07:50+02:00[Europe/Paris]    // GMT 2015-06-20 5:50
2015-06-20T06:50+05:30[Asia/Kolkata]    // GMT 2015-06-20 1:20
```

After converting to GMT, you can see that the Paris time is four and a half hours behind the Kolkata time.

 The time zone offset can be listed in different ways: +02:00, GMT+2, and UTC+2 all mean the same thing. You might see any of them on the exam.

Let's try another one, this time with GMT. Remember that you need to add when subtracting a negative number.

```
2015-06-20T07:50 GMT-04:00   // GMT 2015-06-20 11:50
2015-06-20T04:50 GMT-07:00   // GMT 2015-06-20 11:50
```

For this example, both moments in time are the same. The eastern U.S. time zone is three hours ahead of the Pacific U.S. time zone.

If you have trouble remembering this, try to memorize one example where the time zones are a few zones apart and remember the direction. In the United States, most people know that the east coast is three hours ahead of the west coast. And most people know that Asia is ahead of Europe. Just don't cross time zone zero in the example that you choose to remember. The calculation works the same way, but it isn't as great a memory aid.

Speaking of which, how many hours apart are California in the Pacific U.S. time zone and India? Try to work this one out on your own. Really, get a pen and write it out. You need to be able to perform this math on the exam.

```
2015-06-20T07:50-07:00[US/Pacific]
2015-06-20T07:50+05:30[Asia/Kolkata]
```

The answer is 12 and a half hours. The first instance in time is GMT 14:50. The second is GMT 2:20. No wonder calls between California and India aren't convenient!

Wait—I Don't Live in the United States

The exam recognizes that exam takers live all over the world, and it will not ask you about the details of U.S. date and time formats.

In the United States, the month is written before the date. The exam won't ask you about the difference between 02/03/2015 and 03/02/2015. That would be mean and not internationally friendly, and it would be testing your knowledge of U.S. dates rather than your knowledge of Java. That said, our examples do use U.S. date and time formats, as will the questions on the exam. Just remember that the month comes before the date. Also Java tends to use a 24-hour clock even though the United States uses a 12-hour clock with a.m./p.m.

Now that you know how to create the current date and time, let's look at other specific dates and times. To begin, let's create just a date with no time. Both of these examples create the same date:

```
LocalDate date1 = LocalDate.of(2015, Month.JANUARY, 20);
LocalDate date2 = LocalDate.of(2015, 1, 20);
```

Both pass in the year, month, and date. Although it is good to use the Month constants (to make the code easier to read), you can pass the int number of the month directly. Just use the number of the month the same way you would if you were writing the date in real life.

The method signatures are as follows:

```
public static LocalDate of(int year, int month, int dayOfMonth)
public static LocalDate of(int year, Month month, int dayOfMonth)
```

Month is an enum. Remember that an enum is not an int and cannot be compared to one, for example:

```
12:   Month month = Month.JANUARY;
13:   boolean b1 = month == 1;          // DOES NOT COMPILE
14:   boolean b2 = month == Month.APRIL; // false
```

Line 13 doesn't compile because an enum is a different type than an int. Line 14 shows how to compare enum values properly.

Up to now, we've been continually telling you that Java counts starting with 0. Well, months are an exception. For months in the new date and time methods, Java counts starting from 1, just as we humans do.

When creating a time, you can choose how detailed you want to be. You can specify just the hour and minute, or you can include the number of seconds. You can even include nanoseconds if you want to be very precise. (A nanosecond is a billionth of a second, though you probably won't need to be that specific.)

```
LocalTime time1 = LocalTime.of(6, 15);              // hour and minute
LocalTime time2 = LocalTime.of(6, 15, 30);          // + seconds
LocalTime time3 = LocalTime.of(6, 15, 30, 200);     // + nanoseconds
```

These three times are all different but within a minute of each other. The method signatures are as follows:

```
public static LocalTime of(int hour, int minute)
public static LocalTime of(int hour, int minute, int second)
public static LocalTime of(int hour, int minute, int second, int nanos)
```

You can combine dates and times into one object:

```
LocalDateTime dateTime1 = LocalDateTime.of(2015, Month.JANUARY, 20, 6, 15, 30);
LocalDateTime dateTime2 = LocalDateTime.of(date1, time1);
```

The first line of code shows how you can specify all of the information about the LocalDateTime right in the same line. There are many method signatures allowing you to specify different things. Having that many numbers in a row gets to be hard to read, though. The second line of code shows how you can create LocalDate and LocalTime objects separately first and then combine them to create a LocalDateTime object.

Now there are a lot of method signatures since there are more combinations. The method signatures are as follows:

```
public static LocalDateTime of(int year, int month,
  int dayOfMonth, int hour, int minute)
public static LocalDateTime of(int year, int month,
  int dayOfMonth, int hour, int minute, int second)
public static LocalDateTime of(int year, int month,
  int dayOfMonth, int hour, int minute, int second, int nanos)
public static LocalDateTime of(int year, Month month,
  int dayOfMonth, int hour, int minute)
public static LocalDateTime of(int year, Month month,
  int dayOfMonth, int hour, int minute, int second)
public static LocalDateTime of(int year, Month month,
  int dayOfMonth, int hour, int minute, int second, int nanos)
public static LocalDateTime of(LocalDate date, LocalTime time)
```

In order to create a ZonedDateTime, we first need to get the desired time zone. We will use US/Eastern in our examples:

```
ZoneId zone = ZoneId.of("US/Eastern");
ZonedDateTime zoned1 = ZonedDateTime.of(2015, 1, 20,
    6, 15, 30, 200, zone);
ZonedDateTime zoned2 = ZonedDateTime.of(date1, time1, zone);
ZonedDateTime zoned3 = ZonedDateTime.of(dateTime1, zone);
```

We start by getting the time zone object. Then we use one of three approaches to create the ZonedDateTime. The first passes all of the fields individually. We don't recommend this approach—there are too many numbers, and it is hard to read. A better approach is to pass a LocalDate object and a LocalTime object, or a LocalDateTime object.

Although there are other ways of creating a ZonedDateTime, you only need to know three for the exam:

```
public static ZonedDateTime of(int year, int month,
    int dayOfMonth, int hour, int minute, int second, int nanos, ZoneId zone)
public static ZonedDateTime of(LocalDate date, LocalTime time, ZoneId zone)
public static ZonedDateTime of(LocalDateTime dateTime, ZoneId zone)
```

Notice that there isn't an option to pass in the Month enum. This seems like an oversight from the API creators and something that will be fixed in future versions of Java.

Finding a Time Zone

Finding out your time zone is easy. You can just print out ZoneId.systemDefault(). If you don't know what another time zone is, Java provides a method to list the supported ones. Using the functional programming techniques that you've learned, you can easily print out a sorted list of the ones that are potential candidates:

```
ZoneId.getAvailableZoneIds().stream()
    .filter(z -> z.contains("US") || z.contains("America"))
    .sorted().forEach(System.out::println);
```

This printed 177 lines when we ran it. We prefer the US/Eastern time zone to America/New_York since it is more general. There are so many time zones because there is a lot of duplication. When writing code, try to use whatever is clearest. In the United States, most people say "eastern" when talking about east coast time, so we like to use that in the code.

How do you know what to filter by? Try the country name or city name. Or you can print everything and look though that. Or you could use Google to find out the name of the target time zone.

Did you notice that we did not use a constructor in any of the examples? The date and time classes have private constructors to force you to use the factory's static methods. The exam creators may throw something like this at you:

```
LocalDate d = new LocalDate(); // DOES NOT COMPILE
```

Don't fall for this. You are not allowed to construct a date or time object directly. Another trick is what happens when you pass invalid numbers to of(), for example:

```
LocalDate.of(2015, Month.JANUARY, 32)     // throws DateTimeException
```

You don't need to know the exact exception that's thrown, but it's a clear one:

```
java.time.DateTimeException: Invalid value for DayOfMonth
  (valid values 1–28/31): 32
```

 Real World Scenario

Creating Dates in Java 7 and Earlier

You can see some of the problems with the old way in Table 5.1 There wasn't a way to specify just a date without the time. The Date class represented both the date and time whether you wanted it to or not. Trying to create a specific date required more code than it should have. Month indexes were 0 based instead of 1 based, which was confusing.

There's a really old way to create a date. In Java 1.1, you create a specific Date with this: Date jan = new Date(2015, Calendar.JANUARY, 1);. You could use the Calendar class beginning with Java 1.2. Date exists mainly for backward compatibility and in order that Calendar can work with code—making the new way the third way. The new way, as shown in Table 5.1, is much better, so it looks like this is a case of the third time is the charm!

TABLE 5.1   Old vs. new way of creating dates

	Old Way	New Way (Java 8 and Later)
Importing	import java.util.*;	import java.time.*;
Creating an object with the current date	Date d = new Date();	LocalDate d = LocalDate.now();
Creating an object with the current date and time	Date d = new Date();	LocalDateTime dt = LocalDateTime.now();

TABLE 5.1 Old vs. new way of creating dates *(continued)*

	Old Way	New Way (Java 8 and Later)

Creating an object representing January 1, 2015	`Calendar c = Calendar.getInstance(); c.set(2015, Calendar.JANUARY, 1); Date jan = c.getTime();`
	
	or
	
	`Calendar c = new GregorianCalendar(2015, Calendar.JANUARY, 1); Date jan = c.getTime();`
		`LocalDate jan = LocalDate.of(2015, Month.JANUARY, 1);`

Creating January 1, 2015 without the constant	`Calendar c = Calendar.getInstance(); c.set(2015, 0, 1); Date jan = c.getTime();`	`LocalDate jan = LocalDate.of(2015, 1, 1)`

Manipulating Dates and Times

Adding to a date is easy. The date and time classes are immutable. As you learned in Chapter 2, "Design Patterns and Principles," this means that we need to remember to assign the results of these methods to a reference variable so that they are not lost.

```
12: LocalDate date = LocalDate.of(2014, Month.JANUARY, 20);
13: System.out.println(date);          // 2014-01-20
14: date = date.plusDays(2);
15: System.out.println(date);          // 2014-01-22
16: date = date.plusWeeks(1);
17: System.out.println(date);          // 2014-01-29
18: date = date.plusMonths(1);
19: System.out.println(date);          // 2014-02-28
20: date = date.plusYears(5);
21: System.out.println(date);          // 2019-02-28
```

This code is nice because it does just what it looks like. We start out with January 20, 2014. On line 14, we add two days to it and reassign it to our reference variable. On line 16, we add a week. This method allows us to write clearer code than plusDays(7). Now date is January 29, 2014. On line 18, we add a month. This would bring us to February 29, 2014. However, 2014 is not a leap year. (2012 and 2016 are leap years.) Java is smart enough to realize that February 29, 2014, does not exist, and it gives us February 28, 2014, instead. Finally, line 20 adds five years.

 February 29 exists only in a leap year. Leap years are years that are a multiple of 4 or 400 but not other multiples of 100. For example, 2000 and 2016 are leap years, but 2100 is not.

There are also nice, easy methods to go backward in time. This time, let's work with LocalDateTime:

```
22: LocalDate date = LocalDate.of(2020, Month.JANUARY, 20);
23: LocalTime time = LocalTime.of(5, 15);
24: LocalDateTime dateTime = LocalDateTime.of(date, time);
25: System.out.println(dateTime);          // 2020-01-20T05:15
26: dateTime = dateTime.minusDays(1);
27: System.out.println(dateTime);          // 2020-01-19T05:15
28: dateTime = dateTime.minusHours(10);
29: System.out.println(dateTime);          // 2020-01-18T19:15
30: dateTime = dateTime.minusSeconds(30);
31: System.out.println(dateTime);          // 2020-01-18T19:14:30
```

Line 25 prints the original date of January 20, 2020, at 5:15 a.m. Line 26 subtracts a full day, bringing us to January 19, 2020, at 5:15 a.m. Line 28 subtracts 10 hours, showing that the date will change if the hours cause it to adjust, and it brings us to January 18, 2020, at 19:15 (7:15 p.m.). Finally, line 30 subtracts 30 seconds. You can see that all of a sudden the display value starts showing seconds. Java is smart enough to hide the seconds and nanoseconds when we aren't using them.

It is common for date and time methods to be chained. For example, without the print statements, the previous example could be rewritten as follows:

```
LocalDate date = LocalDate.of(2020, Month.JANUARY, 20);
LocalTime time = LocalTime.of(5, 15);
LocalDateTime dateTime = LocalDateTime.of(date, time)
    .minusDays(1).minusHours(10).minusSeconds(30);
```

When you have a lot of manipulations to make, this chaining comes in handy. There are two ways that the exam creators can try to trick you. What do you think this prints?

```
LocalDate date = LocalDate.of(2020, Month.JANUARY, 20);
date.plusDays(10);
System.out.println(date);
```

It prints January 20, 2020. Adding 10 days was useless because the program ignored the result. Whenever you see immutable types, pay attention to make sure that the return value of a method call isn't ignored. The exam also may test to see if you remember what each of the date and time objects includes. Do you see what is wrong here?

```
LocalDate date = LocalDate.of(2020, Month.JANUARY, 20);
date = date.plusMinutes(1);    // DOES NOT COMPILE
```

LocalDate does not contain time. This means that you cannot add minutes to it. This can be tricky in a chained sequence of addition/subtraction operations, so make sure that you know which methods in Table 5.2 can be called on which types.

TABLE 5.2   Methods in LocalDate, LocalTime, LocalDateTime, and ZonedDateTime

	Can Call on LocalDate?	Can Call on LocalTime?	Can Call on LocalDateTime or ZonedDateTime?
plusYears/ minusYears	Yes	No	Yes
plusMonths/ minusMonths	Yes	No	Yes
plusWeeks/ minusWeeks	Yes	No	Yes
plusDays/ minusDays	Yes	No	Yes
plusHours/ minusHours	No	Yes	Yes
plusMinutes/ minusMinutes	No	Yes	Yes
plusSeconds/ minusSeconds	No	Yes	Yes
plusNanos/ minusNanos	No	Yes	Yes

Manipulating Dates in Java 7 and Earlier

As you look at all the code in Table 5.3 to do time calculations in the old way, you can see why Java needed to revamp the date and time APIs! The old way took a lot of code to do something simple.

TABLE 5.3   Old vs. new way of creating dates

	Old Way	New Way (Java 8 and Later)
| Adding a day | ```java
public Date addDay(Date
date) {
  Calendar cal =
Calendar.getInstance();
  cal.setTime(date);
  cal.add(Calendar.DATE,
1);
  return cal.getTime();
}
``` | ```java
public LocalDate
addDay(LocalDate date)
{
  return
date.plusDays(1);
}
``` |
| Subtracting a day | ```java
public Date
subtractDay(Date date) {
  Calendar cal =
Calendar.getInstance();
  cal.setTime(date);
  cal.add(Calendar.DATE,
-1);
  return cal.getTime();
}
``` | ```java
public LocalDate
subtractDay(LocalDate
date) {
  return
date.minusDays(1);
}
``` |

Working with Periods

Now you know enough to do something fun with dates! Our zoo performs animal enrichment activities to give the animals something fun to do. The head zookeeper has decided to switch the toys every month. This system will continue for three months to see how it works out.

```java
public static void main(String[] args) {
  LocalDate start = LocalDate.of(2015, Month.JANUARY, 1);
  LocalDate end = LocalDate.of(2015, Month.MARCH, 30);
  performAnimalEnrichment(start, end);
}
private static void performAnimalEnrichment(LocalDate start, LocalDate end) {
  LocalDate upTo = start;
  while (upTo.isBefore(end)) {          // check if still before end
   System.out.println("give new toy: " + upTo);
   upTo = upTo.plusMonths(1);          // add a month
  } }
```

This code works fine. It adds a month to the date until it hits the end date. The problem is that this method can't be reused. Our zookeeper wants to try different schedules to see which works best.

Converting to a *long*

LocalDate and LocalDateTime have a method to convert themselves into long equivalents in relation to January 1, 1970. This special date is called the epoch. What's special about 1970? That's what Unix started using for date standards, so Java reused it. And don't worry—you don't have to memorize the names for the exam.

- LocalDate has toEpochDay(), which is the number of days since January 1, 1970.

- LocalDateTime and ZonedDateTime have toEpochSecond(), which is the number of seconds since January 1, 1970.

- LocalTime does not have an epoch method. Since it represents a time that can occur on any date, it doesn't make sense to compare it to 1970. Although the exam pretends that time zones don't exist, you may be wondering if this special January 1, 1970, is in a specific time zone. The answer is yes. This special time refers to when it was January 1, 1970, in GMT (Greenwich mean time). Greenwich is in England, and GMT does not participate in daylight savings time. This makes it a good reference point.

Luckily, Java has a Period class that we can pass in. This code does the same thing as the previous example:

```
public static void main(String[] args) {
  LocalDate start = LocalDate.of(2015, Month.JANUARY, 1);
  LocalDate end = LocalDate.of(2015, Month.MARCH, 30);
  Period period = Period.ofMonths(1);              // create a period
  performAnimalEnrichment(start, end, period);
}
private static void performAnimalEnrichment(LocalDate start, LocalDate end,
  Period period) {                    // uses the generic period
  LocalDate upTo = start;
  while (upTo.isBefore(end)) {
    System.out.println("give new toy: " + upTo);
    upTo = upTo.plus(period);      // adds the period
  }
```

The method can add an arbitrary period of time that gets passed in. This allows us to reuse the same method for different periods of time as our zookeeper changes her mind.

There are five ways to create a `Period` class:

```
Period annually = Period.ofYears(1);              // every 1 year
Period quarterly = Period.ofMonths(3);            // every 3 months
Period everyThreeWeeks = Period.ofWeeks(3);       // every 3 weeks
Period everyOtherDay = Period.ofDays(2);          // every 2 days
Period everyYearAndAWeek = Period.of(1, 0, 7);    // every year and 7 days
```

There's one catch. You cannot chain methods when creating a `Period`. The following code looks like it is equivalent to the everyYearAndAWeek example, but it's not. Only the last method is used because the `Period` of___ methods are `static` methods.

```
Period wrong = Period.ofYears(1).ofWeeks(1);      // every week
```

This tricky code is really like writing the following:

```
Period wrong = Period.ofYears(1);
wrong = Period.ofWeeks(1);
```

This is clearly not what you intended! That's why the `of()` method allows you to pass in the number of years, months, and days. They are all included in the same period. You will get a compiler warning about this. Compiler warnings tell you that something is wrong or suspicious without failing compilation.

The `of()` method takes only years, months, and days. The ability to use another factory method to pass weeks is merely a convenience. As you might imagine, the actual period is stored in terms of years, months, and days. When you print out the value, Oracle displays any non-zero parts using the format shown in Figure 5.1.

FIGURE 5.1   Period format

```
System.out.printIn(Period.of)1,2,3));
```

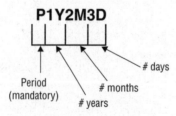

As you can see, the `P` always starts out the `String` to show it is a period measure. Then come the number of years, number of months, and number of days. If any of these are zero, they are omitted.

Can you figure out what this outputs?

```
System.out.println(Period.ofMonths(3));
```

The output is P3M. Remember that Java omits any measures that are zero. Let's try another:

```
System.out.println(Period.of(0, 20, 47));
```

The output is P20M47D. There are no years, so that part is skipped. It's OK to have more days than are in a month. Also it is OK to have more months than are in a year. Java uses the measures provided for each.

Now let's try a tricky one:

```
System.out.println(Period.ofWeeks(3));
```

This one outputs P21D. Remember that week is not one of the units a Period stores. Therefore, a week is converted to 7 days. Since we have 3 weeks, that's 21 days.

The last thing to know about Period is what objects it can be used with. Let's look at some code:

```
3: LocalDate date = LocalDate.of(2015, 1, 20);
4: LocalTime time = LocalTime.of(6, 15);
5: LocalDateTime dateTime = LocalDateTime.of(date, time);
6: Period period = Period.ofMonths(1);
7: System.out.println(date.plus(period));        // 2015-02-20
8: System.out.println(dateTime.plus(period));     // 2015-02-20T06:15
9: System.out.println(time.plus(period));     // UnsupportedTemporalTypeException
```

Lines 7 and 8 work as expected. They add a month to January 20, 2015, giving us February 20, 2015. The first has only the date, and the second has both the date and time.

Line 9 attempts to add a month to an object that has only a time. This won't work. Java throws an exception and complains that we attempted to use an Unsupported unit: Months.

As you can see, you'll have to pay attention to the type of date and time objects every place you see them.

Working with Durations

You've probably noticed by now that a Period is a day or more of time. There is also Duration, which is intended for smaller units of time. For Duration, you can specify the number of days, hours, minutes, seconds, or nanoseconds. And yes, you could pass 365 days to make a year, but you really shouldn't—that's what Period is for.

Conveniently, Duration roughly works the same way as Period, except it is used with objects that have time. Remember that a Period is output beginning with a P. Duration is output beginning with PT, which you can think of as a period of time. A Duration is stored in hours, minutes, and seconds. The number of seconds includes fractional seconds.

We can create a Duration using a number of different granularities:

```
Duration daily = Duration.ofDays(1);                    // PT24H
Duration hourly = Duration.ofHours(1);                  // PT1H
Duration everyMinute = Duration.ofMinutes(1);           // PT1M
Duration everyTenSeconds = Duration.ofSeconds(10);      // PT10S
Duration everyMilli = Duration.ofMillis(1);             // PT0.001S
Duration everyNano = Duration.ofNanos(1);               // PT0.000000001S
```

This is similar to Period. We pass a number to the proper method. We also try to make the code readable. We could say Duration.ofSeconds(3600) to mean one hour. That's just confusing. Although the exam prides itself on being confusing, it isn't testing your mathematical ability in converting between units of dates.

Duration doesn't have a constructor that takes multiple units like Period does. If you want something to happen every hour and a half, you would specify 90 minutes.

Duration includes another more generic factory method. It takes a number and a TemporalUnit. The idea is, say, something like "5 seconds." However, TemporalUnit is an interface. At the moment, there is only one implementation named ChronoUnit.

The previous example could be rewritten as this:

```
Duration daily = Duration.of(1, ChronoUnit.DAYS);
Duration hourly = Duration.of(1, ChronoUnit.HOURS);
Duration everyMinute = Duration.of(1, ChronoUnit.MINUTES);
Duration everyTenSeconds = Duration.of(10, ChronoUnit.SECONDS);
Duration everyMilli = Duration.of(1, ChronoUnit.MILLIS);
Duration everyNano = Duration.of(1, ChronoUnit.NANOS);
```

ChronoUnit also includes some convenient units such as ChronoUnit.HALF_DAYS to represent 12 hours.

ChronoUnit for Differences

ChronoUnit is a great way to determine how far apart two Temporal values are. Temporal includes LocalDate, LocalTime, and so on.

```
LocalTime one = LocalTime.of(5, 15);
LocalTime two = LocalTime.of(6, 30);
LocalDate date = LocalDate.of(2016, 1, 20);

System.out.println(ChronoUnit.HOURS.between(one, two));   // 1
System.out.println(ChronoUnit.MINUTES.between(one, two)); // 75
System.out.println(ChronoUnit.MINUTES.between(one, date)); // DateTimeException
```

> The first print statement shows that between truncates rather than rounds. The second shows how easy it is to count in different units. Just change the `ChronoUnit` type. The last reminds us that Java will throw an exception if we mix up what can be done on date vs. time objects.

Using a `Duration` works the same way as using a `Period`, for example:

```
7:   LocalDate date = LocalDate.of(2015, 1, 20);
8:   LocalTime time = LocalTime.of(6, 15);
9:   LocalDateTime dateTime = LocalDateTime.of(date, time);
10:  Duration duration = Duration.ofHours(6);
11:  System.out.println(dateTime.plus(duration)); // 2015-01-20T12:15
12:  System.out.println(time.plus(duration));     // 12:15
13:  System.out.println(date.plus(duration));     // UnsupportedTemporalException
```

Line 11 shows that we can add hours to a `LocalDateTime`, since it contains a time. Line 12 also works, since all we have is a time. Line 13 fails because we cannot add hours to an object that does not contain a time.

Let's try that again, but add 23 hours this time.

```
7:   LocalDate date = LocalDate.of(2015, 1, 20);
8:   LocalTime time = LocalTime.of(6, 15);
9:   LocalDateTime dateTime = LocalDateTime.of(date, time);
10:  Duration duration = Duration.ofHours(23);
11:  System.out.println(dateTime.plus(duration)); // 2015-01-21T05:15
12:  System.out.println(time.plus(duration));     // 05:15
13:  System.out.println(date.plus(duration));     // UnsupportedTemporalException
```

This time we see that Java moves forward past the end of the day. Line 11 goes to the next day since we pass midnight. Line 12 doesn't have a day, so the time just wraps around—just like on a real clock.

Remember that `Period` and `Duration` are not equivalent. This example shows a `Period` and `Duration` of the same length:

```
LocalDate date = LocalDate.of(2015, 5, 25);
Period period = Period.ofDays(1);
Duration days = Duration.ofDays(1);

System.out.println(date.plus(period)); // 2015-05-26
System.out.println(date.plus(days)); // Unsupported unit: Seconds
```

Since we are working with a `LocalDate`, we are required to use `Period`. `Duration` has time units in it, even if we don't see them and they are meant only for objects with time. Make sure that you can fill in Table 5.4 to identify which objects can use `Period` and `Duration`.

TABLE 5.4   Where to use Duration and Period

	Can Use with Period?	Can Use with Duration?
LocalDate	Yes	No
LocalDateTime	Yes	Yes
LocalTime	No	Yes
ZonedDateTime	Yes	Yes

Working with Instants

The Instant class represents a specific moment in time in the GMT time zone. Suppose that you want to run a timer:

```
Instant now = Instant.now();
// do something time consuming
Instant later = Instant.now();

Duration duration = Duration.between(now, later);
System.out.println(duration.toMillis());
```

In our case, the "something time consuming" was just over a second, and the program printed out 1025.

If you have a ZonedDateTime, you can turn it into an Instant:

```
LocalDate date = LocalDate.of(2015, 5, 25);
LocalTime time = LocalTime.of(11, 55, 00);
ZoneId zone = ZoneId.of("US/Eastern");
ZonedDateTime zonedDateTime = ZonedDateTime.of(date, time, zone);
Instant instant = zonedDateTime.toInstant(); // 2015-05-25T15:55:00Z
System.out.println(zonedDateTime); // 2015-05-25T11:55-04:00[US/Eastern]
System.out.println(instant); // 2015-05-25T15:55:00Z
```

The last two lines represent the same moment in time. The ZonedDateTime includes a time zone. The Instant gets rid of the time zone and turns it into an Instant of time in GMT.

You cannot convert a LocalDateTime to an Instant. Remember that an Instant is a point in time. A LocalDateTime does not contain a time zone, and it is therefore not universally recognized around the world as the same moment in time.

If you have the number of seconds since 1970, you can also create an Instant that way:

```
Instant instant = Instant.ofEpochSecond(epochSeconds);
System.out.println(instant);        // 2015-05-25T15:55:00Z
```

Using that `Instant`, you can do math. `Instant` allows you to add any unit day or smaller, for example:

```
Instant nextDay = instant.plus(1, ChronoUnit.DAYS);
System.out.println(nextDay); // 2015-05-26T15:55:00Z
Instant nextHour = instant.plus(1, ChronoUnit.HOURS);
System.out.println(nextHour); // 2015-05-25T16:55:00Z
Instant nextWeek = instant.plus(1, ChronoUnit.WEEKS); // exception
```

It's weird that an `Instant` displays a year and month while preventing you from doing math with those fields. Unfortunately, you need to memorize this fact.

Accounting for Daylight Savings Time

Some countries observe *daylight savings time*. This is where the clocks are adjusted by an hour twice a year to make better use of the sunlight. Not all countries participate, and those that do use different weekends for the change.

In the United States, we move the clocks an hour ahead in March and move them an hour back in November. The exam will let you know if a date/time mentioned falls on a weekend when the clocks are scheduled to be changed. If it is not mentioned in a question, you can assume that is a normal weekend. We officially change our clocks at 2 a.m., which falls very early Sunday morning.

Figure 5.2 shows what happens with the clocks. On a normal day, time proceeds linearly from 1:00 a.m. to 2:00 a.m. to 3:00 a.m. to 4:00 a.m. and so on. When we change our clocks in March, time springs forward from 1:59 a.m. to 3:00 a.m. Technically it is 1:59 a.m. and 59 seconds plus milliseconds; in other words, the moment immediately before 2:00 a.m. Luckily, the exam doesn't get that granular, and we can think of it as simply 1:59 a.m.

FIGURE 5.2 How daylight savings time works

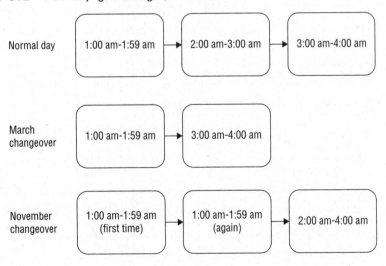

When we change our clocks in November, time falls back and we experience the hour from 2:00 a.m. to 2:59 a.m. Children learn this as spring forward in the spring and fall back in the fall.

Another way to look at it is that there is one day in March that is 23 hours long and one day in November that is 25 hours long. In programming, we call this an edge case. Oracle has decided that it is important enough to be on the exam. This means that you have to learn about it, even if you live in a country that doesn't participate in daylight savings time.

For example, on March 13, 2016, we move our clocks forward an hour and jump from 2:00 a.m. to 3:00 a.m. This means that there is no 2:30 a.m. that day. If we wanted to know the time an hour later than 1:30, it would be 3:30.

```
LocalDate date = LocalDate.of(2016, Month.MARCH, 13);
LocalTime time = LocalTime.of(1, 30);
ZoneId zone = ZoneId.of("US/Eastern");
ZonedDateTime dateTime = ZonedDateTime.of(date, time, zone);

System.out.println(dateTime); // 2016-03-13T01:30-05:00[US/Eastern]

dateTime = dateTime.plusHours(1);

System.out.println(dateTime); // 2016-03-13T03:30-04:00[US/Eastern]
```

Notice that two things change in this example. The time jumps from 1:30 to 3:30. The UTC offset also changes. Remember when we calculated GMT time by subtracting the time zone from the time? You can see that we went from 6:30 GMT (1:30 minus -5:00) to 7:30 GMT (3:30 minus -4:00). This shows that the time really did change by one hour from GMT's point of view.

Similarly in November, an hour after the initial 1:30 is also 1:30 because at 2:00 a.m. we repeat the hour. This time, try to calculate the GMT time yourself for all three times to confirm that we really do move back only one hour at a time.

```
LocalDate date = LocalDate.of(2016, Month.NOVEMBER, 6);
LocalTime time = LocalTime.of(1, 30);
ZoneId zone = ZoneId.of("US/Eastern");
ZonedDateTime dateTime = ZonedDateTime.of(date, time, zone);

System.out.println(dateTime); // 2016-11-06T01:30-04:00[US/Eastern]

dateTime = dateTime.plusHours(1);

System.out.println(dateTime); // 2016-11-06T01:30-05:00[US/Eastern]

dateTime = dateTime.plusHours(1);

System.out.println(dateTime); // 2016-11-06T02:30-05:00[US/Eastern]
```

Did you get it? We went from 5:30 GMT to 6:30 GMT to 7:30 GMT.

Finally, trying to create a time that doesn't exist just rolls forward:

```
LocalDate date = LocalDate.of(2016, Month.MARCH, 13);
LocalTime time = LocalTime.of(2, 30);
ZoneId zone = ZoneId.of("US/Eastern");
ZonedDateTime dateTime = ZonedDateTime.of(date, time, zone);
System.out.println(dateTime);   // 2016-03-13T03:30-04:00[US/Eastern]
```

Java is smart enough to know that there is no 2:30 a.m. that night and switches over to the appropriate GMT offset.

Yes, it is annoying that Oracle expects you to know this even if you aren't in the United States—or for that matter in a part of the United States that doesn't follow daylight savings time. The exam creators are in the United States, and they decided that everyone needs to know how United States time zones work.

Reviewing the *String* class

You might notice that the String class is not listed in the objectives for the OCP. However, it is used in most of the questions for output. We don't want you to get a question on another topic wrong because you forgot how concatenation works! As you know, a *string* is a sequence of characters.

Since there are so many String objects in a program, the String class is final and String objects are immutable. The value cannot change on an immutable object, as discussed in Chapter 2. This allows Java to optimize by storing string literals in the *string pool*. This also means that you can compare string literals with ==. However, it is still a good idea to compare with equals(), because String objects created via a constructor or a method call will not always match when using comparison with ==. Here's an example:

```
4:     String s1 = "bunny";
5:     String s2 = "bunny";
6:     String s3 = new String("bunny");
7:     System.out.println(s1 == s2);        // true
8:     System.out.println(s1 == s3);        // false
9:     System.out.println(s1.equals(s3));   // true
```

Line 7 prints true because the s1 and s2 references point to the same literal in the string pool. Line 8 prints false because line 6 intentionally creates a new object in memory by calling the constructor. Line 9 returns true because the values are the same, even though the location in memory is not.

Since String is such a fundamental class, Java allows using the + operator to combine them, which is called *concatenation*. *Concatenation* is a big word, but it just means creating a new String with the values from both original strings. Remember that Java processes these operators from left to right. Also remember that a String concatenated with anything else is a String. Do you see what makes these two examples different?

```
10:    String s4 = "1" + 2 + 3;
11:    String s5 = 1 + 2 + "3";
12:    System.out.println(s4);  // 123
13:    System.out.println(s5);  // 33
```

Line 12 prints out 123 because it sees a String first and then keeps concatenating, making new strings. Line 13 sees two numbers to add first, and it does that using integer arithmetic. It isn't until the end of the line that it sees a String and can concatenate.

Finally, here is an example that uses common String methods:

```
14:    String s = "abcde ";
15:    System.out.println(s.trim().length());                // 5
16:    System.out.println(s.charAt(4));                      // e
17:    System.out.println(s.indexOf('e'));                   // 4
18:    System.out.println(s.indexOf("de"));                  // 3
19:    System.out.println(s.substring(2, 4).toUpperCase());  // CD
20:    System.out.println(s.replace('a', '1'));              // 1bcde
21:    System.out.println(s.contains("DE"));                 // false
22:    System.out.println(s.startsWith("a"));                // true
```

Line 15 shows that trim() removes any whitespace characters from the beginning and end of a String. Line 16 reminds us that Java starts counting indexes with 0 instead of 1. Lines 17 and 18 show that we can find the zero-based index of a character or a String. Line 19 creates a smaller String from index 2 to right before index 4. It then uses method chaining to convert that String to capital letters. Line 20 does a character replacement. Lines 21 and 22 do a simple String search.

Since String is immutable, it is inefficient for when you are updating the value in a loop. StringBuilder is better for that scenario. A StringBuilder is *mutable*, which means that it can change value and increase in capacity. If multiple threads are updating the same object, you should use StringBuffer rather than StringBuilder.

As a review of StringBuilder code, see if you remember why each of these lines outputs what it does:

```
3:     StringBuilder b = new StringBuilder();
4:     b.append(12345).append('-');
5:     System.out.println(b.length());     // 6
6:     System.out.println(b.indexOf("-")); // 5
7:     System.out.println(b.charAt(2));    // 3
8:
9:     StringBuilder b2 = b.reverse();
10:    System.out.println(b.toString());   // -54321
11:    System.out.println(b == b2);        // true
```

Line 3 creates an empty StringBuilder. Line 4 uses method chaining to make multiple method calls and appends two different types to the StringBuilder. On line 5, there are six characters in b. Five are the numbers from the int and the sixth is the dash. On line 6, the last index is 5 because Java starts counting indexes with 0. Similarly, on line 7, the second index is the third character, which is 3. On line 9, we reverse the StringBuilder and return a reference to the same object. Line 10 prints this reversed value, and line 11 confirms that it is the same object.

And now for some more:

```
12:    StringBuilder s = new StringBuilder("abcde");
13:    s.insert(1, '-').delete(3, 4);
14:    System.out.println(s);                    //a-bde
15:    System.out.println(s.substring(2, 4)); // bd
```

Line 13 uses chaining. We insert at the index that is right before the second character, b, making the string a-bc. Then we delete from the third index until right before the fourth index, which happens to be only one character, c. On line 15, we get the characters starting with index 2 and ending right before index 4. This is the two characters, bd.

Table 5.5 reviews the differences between String, StringBuilder, and StringBuffer. If this is still fuzzy, please get out your study materials from the OCA before proceeding.

TABLE 5.5   Comparing String, StringBuilder, and StringBuffer

Characteristic	String	StringBuilder	StringBuffer
Immutable?	Yes	No	No
Pooled?	Yes	No	No
Thread-safe?	Yes	No	Yes
Can change size?	No	Yes	Yes

Adding Internationalization and Localization

Many applications need to work for different countries and with different languages. For example, consider the sentence "The zoo is holding a special event on 4/1/15 to look at animal behaviors." When is the event? In the United States, it is on April 1. However a British reader would interpret this as January 4. A British reader might also wonder why we didn't write "behaviours." If we are making a website or program that will run in multiple countries, we want to use the correct language and formatting.

Internationalization is the process of designing your program so it can be adapted. This involves placing strings in a property file and using classes like DateFormat so that the right format is used based on user preferences. You do not actually need to support more than one language or country to internationalize the program. Internationalization just means that you can.

Localization means actually supporting multiple locales. Oracle defines a locale as "a specific geographical, political, or cultural region." You can think of a locale as being like a language and country pairing. Localization includes translating strings to different languages. It also includes outputting dates and numbers in the correct format for that locale. You can go through the localization process many times in the same application as you add more languages and countries.

Since *internationalization* and *localization* are such long words, they are often abbreviated as *i18n* and *l10n*. The number refers to the number of characters between the first and last characters, in other words, the number of characters that are replaced with a number.

In this section, we will look at how to define a locale, work with resources bundles, and format dates and numbers.

Picking a Locale

While Oracle defines a locale as "a specific geographical, political, or cultural region," you'll only see languages and countries on the exam. Oracle certainly isn't going to delve into political regions that are not countries. That's too controversial for an exam!

The Locale class is in the java.util package. The first useful Locale to find is the user's current locale. Try running the following code on your computer:

```
Locale locale = Locale.getDefault();
System.out.println(locale);
```

When we run it, it prints en_US. It might be different for you. This default output tells us that our computers are using English and are sitting in the United States.

Notice the format. First comes the lowercase language code. Then comes an underscore followed by the uppercase country code. The underscore and country code are optional. It is valid for a Locale to be only a language. Figure 5.3 shows the two formats for Locale objects that you are expected to remember.

FIGURE 5.3   Locale string formats

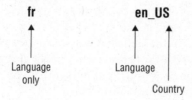

As practice, make sure that you understand why each of these Locales is invalid:

```
US       // can have a language without a country, but not the reverse
enUS     // missing underscore
US_en    // the country and language are reversed
EN       // language must be lowercase
```

The corrected versions are en and en_US.

 You do not need to memorize language or country codes. The exam will let you know about any that are being used. You do need to recognize valid and invalid formats. Pay attention to uppercase/lowercase and the underscore.

You can also use a Locale other than the default. There are three main ways of creating a Locale. First, the Locale class provides constants for some of the most commonly used locales:

```
System.out.println(Locale.GERMAN);  // de
System.out.println(Locale.GERMANY); // de_DE
```

Notice that the first one is the German language and the second is Germany the country— similar, but not the same. The other two main ways of creating a Locale are to use the constructors. You can pass just a language or both a language and country:

```
System.out.println(new Locale("fr"));          // fr
System.out.println(new Locale("hi", "IN"));    // hi_IN
```

The first is the language French and the second is Hindi in India. Again, you don't need to memorize the codes. There is another constructor that lets you be even more specific about the locale. That variant is not on the exam.

Java will let you create a Locale with an invalid language or country. However, it will not match the Locale that you want to use and your program will not behave as expected.

There's another way to create a Locale that is more flexible. The builder design pattern lets you set all of the properties that you care about and then build it at the end. This means that you can specify the properties in any order. The following two Locales both represent en_US.

```
Locale l1 = new Locale.Builder()
    .setLanguage("en")
    .setRegion("US")
    .build();
Locale l2 = new Locale.Builder()
    .setRegion("US")
    .setLanguage("en")
    .build();
```

As you saw in Chapter 2, the advantage of the builder pattern is that you can easily use different combinations of setter methods. `Locale.Builder` supports a number of other setter methods that you don't need to know for the exam.

How Not to Use `Locale.Builder`

The locale builder converts to uppercase or lowercase for you as needed, which means this is legal:

```
Locale l2 = new Locale.Builder()  // bad but legal
    .setRegion("us")
    .setLanguage("EN")
    .build();
```

Please don't write code that looks like this example. Your teammates will expect US to be in uppercase and en to be in lowercase. Switching it is just confusing.

`Locale.Builder` also lets you do other bad things like create a blank `Locale`. Please don't.

When testing a program, you might need to use a `Locale` other than the default for your computer. You can set a new default right in Java:

```
System.out.println(Locale.getDefault()); // en_US
Locale locale = new Locale("fr");
Locale.setDefault(locale);                // change the default
System.out.println(Locale.getDefault()); // fr
```

Try it, and don't worry—the `Locale` changes only for that one Java program. It does not change any settings on your computer. It does not even change future programs. If you run the previous code multiple times, the output will stay the same.

The exam uses `setDefault` a lot because it can't make assumptions about where you are located. In practice, `setDefault` is used extremely rarely.

Using a Resource Bundle

A *resource bundle* contains the local specific objects to be used by a program. It is like a map with keys and values. The resource bundle can be in a property file or in a Java class. A *property file* is a file in a specific format with key/value pairs.

Up until now, we've kept all of the strings from our program in the classes that use them. Localization requires externalizing them to elsewhere. This is typically a property file, but it could be a resource bundle class.

Our zoo program has been very successful. We are now getting requests to use it at three more zoos! We already have support for United States–based zoos. We now need to add Zoo de La Palmyre in France, the Greater Vancouver Zoo in English-speaking Canada, and Zoo de Granby in French-speaking Canada.

We immediately realized that we are going to need to internationalize our program. Resource bundles will be quite helpful. They will let us easily translate our application to multiple locales or even support multiple locales at once. It will also be easy to add more locales later if we get zoos in even more countries interested. We thought about which locales we need to support, and we came up with four:

```
Locale us = new Locale("en", "US");
Locale france = new Locale("fr", "FR");
Locale englishCanada = new Locale("en", "CA");
Locale frenchCanada = new Locale("fr", "CA");
```

In the next sections, we will create a resource bundle using a property file and a Java class. We will also look at how Java determines which resource bundle to use.

Creating a Property File Resource Bundle

Luckily, Java doesn't require us to create four different resource bundles. If we don't have a country-specific resource bundle, Java will use a language-specific one. It's a bit more involved than this, which we cover later in the chapter.

For now, we need English and French property file resource bundles. First, create two property files:

Zoo_en.properties
```
hello=Hello
open=The zoo is open.
```

Zoo_fr.properties
```
hello=Bonjour
open=Le zoo est ouvert
```

Notice that the filenames are the name of our resource bundle followed by an underscore followed by the target locale. We can write our very first program that uses a resource bundle to print this information:

```
1:    import java.util.*;
2:    public class ZooOpen {
3:
4:        public static void main(String[] args) {
5:            Locale us = new Locale("en", "US");
6:            Locale france = new Locale("fr", "FR");
7:
```

```
 8:            printProperties(us);
 9:            System.out.println();
10:            printProperties(france);
11:      }
12:
13:      public static void printProperties(Locale locale) {
14:          ResourceBundle rb = ResourceBundle.getBundle("Zoo", locale);
15:          System.out.println(rb.getString("hello"));
16:          System.out.println(rb.getString("open"));
17:      }
18:  }
```

Lines 5 and 6 create the locales that we want to test. The method on lines 13–17 does the actual work. Line 14 calls a factory method on ResourceBundle to get the right resource bundle. Lines 15 and 16 retrieve the right resource bundle and print the results. The output is as follows:

```
Hello
The zoo is open.

Bonjour
Le zoo est ouvert
```

Notice how much is happening behind the scenes here. Java uses the name of the bundle (Zoo) and looks for the relevant property file. You will see this again later in the chapter and learn how Java figures out which one to use.

Property File Format

The most common syntax is where a property file contains key/value pairs in the format:

```
animal=dolphin
```

There's more to it than that. There are actually two other formats that you can use to express these pairs. Even if you never use them in your job, you need to know them for the exam:

```
animal:dolphin
animal dolphin
```

You might wonder how to express some other ideas in a property file. The common ones are these:

- If a line begins with # or !, it is a comment.

- Spaces before or after the separator character are ignored.

- Spaces at the beginning of a line are ignored.

- Spaces at the end of a line are not ignored.

- End a line with a backslash if you want to break the line for readability.

- You can use normal Java escape characters like \t and \n.

Putting these together, we can write the following:

```
# one comment
! another comment
key =    value\tafter tab
long = abcdefghijklm\
 nopqrstuvwxyz
```

Printing out these two properties in a program gives us this:

```
value → after tab
abcdefghijklmnopqrstuvwxyz
```

Since a resource bundle contains key/value pairs, you can even loop through them to list all of the pairs. The ResourceBundle class provides a method to get a set of all keys:

```
Locale us = new Locale("en", "US");
ResourceBundle rb = ResourceBundle.getBundle("Zoo", us);

Set<String> keys = rb.keySet();
keys.stream().map(k -> k + " " + rb.getString(k))
             .forEach(System.out::println);
```

This example goes through all of the keys. It maps each key to a String with both the key and value before printing everything. This prints

```
name Vancouver Zoo
hello Hello
open The zoo is open
```

And yes, we could have used a traditional for loop. You need to know both loops and functional programming for the exam, so we use both approaches throughout the book.

In addition to ResourceBundle, Java supports a class named Properties. It is like a Map that you learned about in Chapter 3, "Generics and Collections." It was written before Map existed, so it doesn't use all of the same method names.

Properties has some additional features, including being able to pass a default. Converting from ResourceBundle to Properties is easy:

```
Properties props = new Properties();
rb.keySet().stream()
            .forEach(k -> props.put(k, rb.getString(k)));
```

Here we went through each key and used a Consumer to add it to the Properties object. Now that we have Properties available, we can get a default value:

```
System.out.println(props.getProperty("notReallyAProperty"));
System.out.println(props.getProperty("notReallyAProperty", "123"));
```

The first line prints null, since that property doesn't exist. The second prints 123, since the property wasn't found. If a key were passed that actually existed, both would have returned it.

Note that the method called is getProperty(). There is also a get() method as we'd expect with any collection. Only getProperty() allows for a default value.

Table 5.6 shows the different scenarios with getProperty(). As you can see, null is returned when we don't pass a default value and the key is not found. When we pass the default value, it is used instead.

TABLE 5.6 Return values for getProperty()

Key Found?	Yes	No
getProperty("key")	Value	null
getProperty("key", "default")	Value	"default"

Creating a Java Class Resource Bundle

Most of the time, a property file resource bundle is enough to meet the program's needs. It does have a limitation in that only String values are allowed. Java class resource bundles allow any Java type as the value. Keys are strings regardless.

To implement a resource bundle in Java, you create a class with the same name that you would use for a property file. Only the extension is different. Since we have a Java object, the file must be a .java file rather than a .properties file. For example, the following class is equivalent to the property file that you saw in the last section:

```
1:   import java.util.*;
2:   public class Zoo_en extends ListResourceBundle {
3:      protected Object[][] getContents() {
4:         return new Object[][] {
5:            { "hello", "Hello" },
6:            { "open", "The zoo is open" } };
7:      } }
```

Line 2 shows the superclass for Java class resource bundles. The ListResourceBundle abstract class leaves one method for subclasses to implement. The rest of the code creates a 2D array with the keys hello and open.

There are two main advantages of using a Java class instead of a property file for a resource bundle:

- You can use a value type that is not a String.
- You can create the values of the properties at runtime.

In our zoos, we realize that we need to collect taxes differently in each country. We decide to set up just the code for the United States first. This will give us the structure. Then we can give the work for the rest to another programmer. Pretend that we created UsTaxCode class. Then we can use a Java class resource bundle to retrieve it:

```
1:    package resourcebundles;
2:    import java.util.*;
3:    public class Tax_en_US extends ListResourceBundle {
4:        protected Object[][] getContents() {
5:            return new Object[][] { { "tax", new UsTaxCode() } };
6:        }
7:        public static void main(String[] args) {
8:            ResourceBundle rb = ResourceBundle.getBundle(
9:                "resourcebundles.Tax", Locale.US);
10:           System.out.println(rb.getObject("tax"));
11:    }}
```

Line 3 extends the ListResourceBundle so that we can define a resource bundle. This time, the class name specifies both the language code and country code. Lines 4–6 show the method to declare the key/value pairs. This time, the value is not a String. Lines 8–9 show that a resource bundle can be in a package. We just specify the name of the package before the name of the class. Line 10 shows how to retrieve a non-String resource bundle.

Determining Which Resource Bundle to Use

On the exam, there are two methods for getting a resource bundle:

```
ResourceBundle.getBundle("name");
ResourceBundle.getBundle("name", locale);
```

The first one uses the default locale. You are likely to use this one in programs that you write. The exam either tells you what to assume as the default locale or uses the second approach.

Java handles the logic of picking the best available resource bundle for a given key. It tries to find the most specific value. When there is a tie, Java class resource bundles are given preference. Table 5.7 shows what Java goes through when asked for resource bundle Zoo with the locale new Locale("fr", "FR") when the default locale is US English.

TABLE 5.7 Picking a resource bundle for French in France with default locale US English

Step	Looks for File	Reason
1	Zoo_fr_FR.java	The requested locale
2	Zoo_fr_FR.properties	The requested locale
3	Zoo_fr.java	The language we requested with no country
4	Zoo_fr.properties	The language we requested with no country
5	Zoo_en_US.java	The default locale
6	Zoo_en_US.properties	The default locale
7	Zoo_en.java	The default language with no country
8	Zoo_en.properties	The default language with no country
9	Zoo.java	No locale at all—the default bundle
10	Zoo.properties	No locale at all—the default bundle
11	If still not found, throw MissingResourceException.	

You do need to be able to create the 11-step list in Table 5.7. As another way of remembering it, learn these steps:

- Always look for the property file after the matching Java class.
- Drop one thing at a time if there are no matches. First drop the country and then the language.
- Look at the default locale and the default resource bundle last.

How many files do you think Java would need to look for to find the resource bundle with the code?

```
Locale.setDefault(new Locale("hi"));
ResourceBundle rb = ResourceBundle.getBundle("Zoo", new Locale("en"));
```

The answer is six. They are listed here:

1. `Zoo_hi.java`
2. `Zoo_hi.properties`
3. `Zoo_en.java`
4. `Zoo_en.properties`
5. `Zoo.java`
6. `Zoo.properties`

This time, we didn't specify any country codes so Java got to skip looking for those. If we ask for the default locale, Java will start searching the bundles starting with step 6 in Table 5.7 and going to the end (or until it finds a match.)

Got all that? Good—because there is a twist. The steps that we've discussed so far are for finding the matching resource bundle to use as a base. Java isn't required to get all of the keys from the same resource bundle. It can get them from any parent of the matching resource bundle. A parent resource bundle in the hierarchy just removes components of the name until it gets to the top. Table 5.8 shows how to do this.

TABLE 5.8   Listing the parent resource bundles

Matching Resource Bundle	Files Keys Can Come From
Zoo_fr_FR.java	Zoo_fr_FR.java Zoo_fr.java Zoo.java
Zoo_fr.properties	Zoo_fr.properties Zoo.properties

Let's put all of this together and print some information about our zoos. We have a number of property files this time:

Zoo.properties
```
name=Vancouver Zoo
```

Zoo_en.properties
```
hello=Hello
open=is open
```

Zoo_en_CA.properties
```
visitor=Canada visitor
```

Zoo_fr.properties
```
hello=Bonjour
open=est ouvert
```

Zoo_fr_CA.properties
```
visitor=Canada visiteur
```

Suppose that we have a visitor from Quebec (a default locale of French Canada) who has asked the program to provide information in English. What do you think this outputs?

```
2:    Locale locale = new Locale("en", "CA");
3:    ResourceBundle rb = ResourceBundle.getBundle("Zoo", locale);
4:    System.out.print(rb.getString("hello"));
5:    System.out.print(". ");
6:    System.out.print(rb.getString("name"));
7:    System.out.print(" ");
8:    System.out.print(rb.getString("open"));
9:    System.out.print(" ");
10:   System.out.print(rb.getString("visitor"));
```

The answer is Hello. Vancouver Zoo is open Canada visitor. First Java goes through the available resource bundles to find a match. It finds one right away with Zoo_en_CA.properties. This means the default locale is irrelevant.

Line 4 doesn't find a match for the key hello in Zoo_en_CA.properties, so it goes up the hierarchy to Zoo_en.properties. Line 6 has to go all the way to the top of the hierarchy to Zoo.properties to find the key name. Line 8 has the same experience as line 4. Finally, line 10 has an easier job of it and finds a matching key in Zoo_en_CA.properties.

 Real World Scenario

Handling Variables Inside Resource Bundles

In real programs, it is common to substitute variables in the middle of a resource bundle. string. The convention is to use a number inside brackets such as {0}. Although Java resource bundles don't support this directly, the MessageFormat class does.

For example, suppose that we had this property defined:

```
helloByName=Hello, {0}
```

In Java, we can read in the value normally. After that, we can run it through the MessageFormat class to substitute the parameters. As you might guess, the second parameter to format() is a varargs one. This means that you can pass many parameters.

```
String format = rb.getString("helloByName");
String formatted = MessageFormat.format(format, "Tammy");
System.out.print(formatted);
```

Formatting Numbers

Resource bundles are great for content that doesn't change. Text like a welcome greeting is pretty stable. When talking about dates and prices, the formatting varies and not just the text. Luckily, the java.text package has classes to save the day. The following sections cover how to format numbers, currency, and dates.

Format and Parse Numbers and Currency

Regardless of whether you want to format or parse, the first step is the same. You need to create a NumberFormat. The class provides factory methods to get the desired formatter. Table 5.9 shows the available methods.

TABLE 5.9   Factory methods to get a NumberFormat

Description	Using Default Locale and a Specified Locale
A general purpose formatter	NumberFormat.getInstance() NumberFormat.getInstance(locale)
Same as getInstance	NumberFormat.getNumberInstance() NumberFormat.getNumberInstance(locale)
For formatting monetary amounts	NumberFormat.getCurrencyInstance() NumberFormat.getCurrencyInstance(locale)
For formatting percentages	NumberFormat.getPercentInstance() NumberFormat.getPercentInstance(locale)
Rounds decimal values before displaying (not on the exam)	NumberFormat.getIntegerInstance() NumberFormat.getIntegerInstance(locale)

Once you have the NumberFormat instance, you can call format() to turn a number into a String and parse() to turn a String into a number.

> The format classes are not thread-safe. Do not store them in instance variables or static variables.

Formatting

The format method formats the given number based on the locale associated with the NumberFormat object. For marketing literature, we want to share the monthly number of visitors to the San Diego Zoo. The following shows printing out the same number in three different locales:

```
1:    import java.text.*;
2:    import java.util.*;
3:
4:    public class FormatNumbers {
5:       public static void main(String[] args) {
6:          int attendeesPerYear = 3_200_000;
7:          int attendeesPerMonth = attendeesPerYear / 12;
8:          NumberFormat us = NumberFormat.getInstance(Locale.US);
9:          System.out.println(us.format(attendeesPerMonth));
10:         NumberFormat g = NumberFormat.getInstance(Locale.GERMANY);
11:         System.out.println(g.format(attendeesPerMonth));
12:         NumberFormat ca = NumberFormat.getInstance(Locale.CANADA_FRENCH);
13:         System.out.println(ca.format(attendeesPerMonth));
14:    } }
```

The output looks like this:

```
266,666
266.666
266 666
```

Now our U.S., German, and French Canadian guests can all see the same information in the number format they are accustomed to using. In the United States, we use commas to separate parts of large numbers. Germans use a dot for this function. French Canadians use neither.

Formatting currency works the same way:

```
double price = 48;
NumberFormat us = NumberFormat.getCurrencyInstance();
System.out.println(us.format(price));
```

When run with the default locale of en_US, the output is $48.00. Java automatically formats with two decimals and adds the dollar sign. This is convenient even if you don't need to localize your program!

> In the real world, use int or BigDecimal for money and not double. Doing math on amounts with double is dangerous, and your boss won't appreciate it if you lose pennies during transactions.

Parsing

The NumberFormat class defines a parse method for parsing a String into a number using a specific locale. The result of parsing depends on the locale. For example, if the locale is the United States and the number contains commas, the commas are treated as formatting symbols. If the locale is a country or language that uses commas as a decimal separator, the comma is treated as a decimal point. In other words, the value of the resulting number depends on the locale.

The parse methods for the different types of formats throw the checked exception ParseException if they fail to parse. Often, you will see the code as a snippet and not in a method as in the next example. You can assume that exceptions are properly handled. If you see parsing logic inside a method, make sure that ParseException or Exception is handled or declared.

Let's look at an example. The following code parses a discounted ticket price with different locales:

```java
NumberFormat en = NumberFormat.getInstance(Locale.US);
NumberFormat fr = NumberFormat.getInstance(Locale.FRANCE);

String s = "40.45";
System.out.println(en.parse(s)); // 40.45
System.out.println(fr.parse(s)); // 40
```

In the United States, a dot is part of a number and the number is parsed how you might expect. France does not use a decimal point to separate numbers. Java parses it as a formatting character, and it stops looking at the rest of the number. The lesson is to make sure that you parse using the right locale!

What Does Java Do with Extra Characters When Parsing?

The parse method parses only the beginning of a string. After it reaches a character that cannot be parsed, the parsing stops and the value is returned. Do you see why each of these behaves as it does?

```java
NumberFormat nf = NumberFormat.getInstance();
String one = "456abc";
String two = "-2.5165x10";
String three = "x85.3";
System.out.println(nf.parse(one));  // 456
System.out.println(nf.parse(two));  // -2.5165
System.out.println(nf.parse(three));// throws ParseException
```

The first two lines parse correctly. There happen to be extra characters after the number, but that's OK. The third parsing fails because there are no numbers at the beginning of the String. Java instead throws a java.text.ParseException.

The parse method is also used for parsing currency. For example, we can read in the zoo's monthly income from ticket sales:

```
String amt = "$92,807.99";
NumberFormat cf = NumberFormat.getCurrencyInstance();
double value = (Double) cf.parse(amt);
System.out.println(value); // 92807.99
```

The currency string "$92,807.99" contains a dollar sign and a comma. The parse method strips out the characters and converts the value to a number. The return value of parse is a Number object. Number is the parent class of all the java.lang wrapper classes, so the return value can be cast to its appropriate data type. The Number is cast to a Double and then automatically unboxed into a double.

The NumberFormat classes have other features and capabilities, but the topics covered in this section address the content that you need to know for the OCP exam.

Formatting Dates and Times

The date and time classes support many methods to get data out of them:

```
LocalDate date = LocalDate.of(2020, Month.JANUARY, 20);
System.out.println(date.getDayOfWeek());     // MONDAY
System.out.println(date.getMonth());          // JANUARY
System.out.println(date.getYear());          // 2020
System.out.println(date.getDayOfYear());     // 20
```

We could use this information to display information about the date. However, it would be more work than necessary. Java provides a class called DateTimeFormatter to help us out. Unlike the LocalDateTime class, DateTimeFormatter can be used to format any type of date and/or time object. What changes is the format. DateTimeFormatter is in the package java.time.format.

```
LocalDate date = LocalDate.of(2020, Month.JANUARY, 20);
LocalTime time = LocalTime.of(11, 12, 34);
LocalDateTime dateTime = LocalDateTime.of(date, time);
System.out.println(date.format(DateTimeFormatter.ISO_LOCAL_DATE));
System.out.println(time.format(DateTimeFormatter.ISO_LOCAL_TIME));
System.out.println(dateTime.format(DateTimeFormatter.ISO_LOCAL_DATE_TIME));
```

ISO is a standard for dates. The output of the previous code looks like this:

```
2020-01-20
11:12:34
2020-01-20T11:12:34
```

This is a reasonable way for computers to communicate, but it is probably not how you want to output the date and time in your program. Luckily, there are some predefined formats that are more useful:

```
DateTimeFormatter shortDateTime =
   DateTimeFormatter.ofLocalizedDate(FormatStyle.SHORT);
System.out.println(shortDateTime.format(dateTime));    // 1/20/20
System.out.println(shortDateTime.format(date));        // 1/20/20
System.out.println(
   shortDateTime.format(time)); // UnsupportedTemporalTypeException
```

Here we say that we want a localized formatter in the predefined short format. The last line throws an exception because a time cannot be formatted as a date. The format() method is declared on both the formatter objects and the date/time objects, allowing you to reference the objects in either order. The following statements print exactly the same thing as the previous code:

```
DateTimeFormatter shortDateTime =
   DateTimeFormatter.ofLocalizedDate(FormatStyle.SHORT);
System.out.println(dateTime.format(shortDateTime));
System.out.println(date.format(shortDateTime));
System.out.println(time.format(shortDateTime));
```

In this book, we'll change around the orders to get you used to seeing it both ways. Table 5.10 shows the legal and illegal localized formatting methods.

TABLE 5.10   ofLocalized methods

DateTimeFormatter f = DateTimeFormatter. (FormatStyle.SHORT);	Calling f.format (localDate)	Calling f.format (localDateTime) or f.format (zonedDateTime)	Calling f.format (localTime)
ofLocalizedDate	Legal—shows whole object	Legal—shows just date part	Throws runtime exception
OfLocalizedDateTime	Throws runtime exception	Legal—shows whole object	Throws runtime exception
ofLocalizedTime	Throws runtime exception	Legal—shows just time part	Legal—shows whole object

There are two predefined formats that can show up on the exam: SHORT and MEDIUM. The other predefined formats involve time zones, which are not on the exam.

```
LocalDate date = LocalDate.of(2020, Month.JANUARY, 20);
LocalTime time = LocalTime.of(11, 12, 34);
LocalDateTime dateTime = LocalDateTime.of(date, time);
DateTimeFormatter shortF = DateTimeFormatter
    .ofLocalizedDateTime(FormatStyle.SHORT);
DateTimeFormatter mediumF = DateTimeFormatter
    .ofLocalizedDateTime(FormatStyle.MEDIUM);
System.out.println(shortF.format(dateTime));      // 1/20/20 11:12 AM
System.out.println(mediumF.format(dateTime));     // Jan 20, 2020 11:12:34 AM
```

If you don't want to use one of the predefined formats, you can create your own. For example, this code spells out the month:

```
DateTimeFormatter f = DateTimeFormatter.ofPattern("MMMM dd, yyyy, hh:mm");
System.out.println(dateTime.format(f));      // January 20, 2020, 11:12
```

Before we look at the syntax, know that you are not expected to memorize what the different numbers of each symbol mean. The most you will need to do is to recognize the date and time parts.

MMMM M represents the month. The more Ms you have, the more verbose the Java output. For example, M outputs 1, MM outputs 01, MMM outputs Jan, and MMMM outputs January.

dd d represents the day in the month. As with month, the more ds you have, the more verbose the Java output. dd means to include the leading zero for a single-digit day.

, Use , if you want to output a comma (this also appears after the year).

yyyy y represents the year. yy outputs a two-digit year and yyyy outputs a four-digit year.

hh h represents the hour. Use hh to include the leading zero if you're outputting a single-digit hour.

: Use : if you want to output a colon.

mm m represents the minute omitting the leading zero if present. mm is more common and represents the minutes using two digits.

 Real World Scenario

Formatting Dates in Java 7 and Earlier

Formatting is roughly equivalent to the old way, as shown in Table 5.11; it just uses a different class.

TABLE 5.11   Old vs. new way of formatting times

	Old Way	New Way (Java 8 and Later)
Formatting the times	`SimpleDateFormat sf = new SimpleDateFormat("hh:mm"); sf.format(jan3);`	`DateTimeFormatter f = DateTimeFormatter.ofPattern("hh:mm"); dt.format(f);`

Let's do a quick review. Can you figure out which of these lines will throw an exception?

```
4: DateTimeFormatter f = DateTimeFormatter.ofPattern("hh:mm");
5: f.format(dateTime);
6: f.format(date);
7: f.format(time);
```

If you get this question on the exam, think about what symbols represent. You have h for hour and m for minute. Remember M (uppercase) is month and m (lowercase) is minute. You can use this formatter only with objects containing times. Therefore, line 6 will throw an exception.

Now that you know how to convert a date or time to a formatted String, you'll find it easy to convert a String to a date or time. Just like the format() method, the parse() method takes a formatter as well. If you don't specify one, it uses the default for that type.

```
DateTimeFormatter f = DateTimeFormatter.ofPattern("MM dd yyyy");
LocalDate date = LocalDate.parse("01 02 2015", f);
LocalTime time = LocalTime.parse("11:22");
System.out.println(date);        // 2015-01-02
System.out.println(time);        // 11:22
```

Here we show using both a custom formatter and a default value. This isn't common, but you might have to read code that looks like this on the exam. Parsing is consistent in that if anything goes wrong, Java throws a runtime exception. It could be a format that doesn't match the String to be parsed or an invalid date.

Summary

A LocalDate contains just a date. A LocalTime contains just a time. A LocalDateTime contains both a date and time. A ZonedDateTime adds a time zone. All four have private constructors and are created using LocalDate.now() or LocalDate.of() (or the equivalents for that class). Instant represents a moment in time.

Dates and times can be manipulated using plus___ or minus___ methods. The Period class represents a number of days, months, or years to add to or subtract from a LocalDate, LocalDateTime, or ZonedDateTime. The Duration class represents hours, minutes, and seconds. It is used with LocalTime, LocalDateTime, or ZonedDateTime.

UTC represents the time zone offset from zero. Daylight savings time is observed in the United States and other countries by moving the clocks ahead an hour in the spring and an hour back in the fall. Java changes time and UTC offset to account for this.

You can create a Locale class with a desired language and optional country. The language is a two-letter lowercase code, and the country is a two-letter uppercase code. For example, en and en_US are locales for English and US English, respectively. ResourceBundle allows specifying key/value pairs in a property file or in a Java class. Java goes through candidate resource bundles from the most specific to the most general to find a match. If no matches are found for the requested locale, Java switches to the default locale and then finally the default resource bundle. Java looks at the equivalent Java class before the property file for each locale. Once a matching resource bundle is found, Java only looks in the hierarchy of that resource bundle to find keys.

NumberFormat uses static methods to retrieve the desired formatter, such as one for currency. DateTimeFormatter is used to output dates and times in the desired format. The date and time classes are all immutable, which means that the return value must be used or the operation will be ignored.

Exam Essentials

Recognize invalid uses of dates and times.   LocalDate does not contain time fields and LocalTime does not contain date fields. Watch for operations being performed on the wrong type. Also watch for adding or subtracting time and ignoring the result.

Differentiate between Period **and** Duration.   Period is for day, month, and year. It can only be used with LocalDate, LocalDateTime, and ZonedDateTime. Duration is for hours, minutes, and seconds. It can only be used with LocalTime, LocalDateTime, and ZonedDateTime.

Perform calculations with dates.   Be able to perform calculations between times using UTC. Whether the format is -05:00, GMT-5, or UTC-5, you calculate by subtracting the offset from the time and then seeing how far the resulting times are. Also be able to perform comparisons that include daylight savings time. In March, the United States springs ahead an hour, and in November, it falls back an hour.

Identify valid and invalid locale strings.   Know that the language code is lowercase and mandatory. The country code is uppercase if present and follows the language code and an underscore. Locale.Builder is an alternate way to create a Locale, and it allows calling the setters in either order.

Determine which resource bundle Java will use to look up a key. Know the order that Java uses to search for a matching resource bundle. Also recognize that the matching resource bundle hierarchy is searched once a matching resource bundle is found.

Understand which Property **value gets used as a default.** When calling get(), null is returned if the key is not found. When calling getProperty(), there are two options. The single-parameter version still returns null if the key is not found. The version that takes two parameters uses the second parameter as a return value if the key is not found.

Review Questions

1. Which of the following creates valid locales, assuming that the language and country codes follow standard conventions? (Choose all that apply.)

    A. `new Locale("hi");`

    B. `new Locale("hi", "IN");`

    C. `new Locale("IN");`

    D. `new Locale("IN", "hi");`

    E. `Locale.create("hi");`

    F. `Locale.create("IN");`

2. Which of the following are common types to localize? (Choose all that apply.)

    A. Booleans

    B. Class names

    C. Currency

    D. Dates

    E. Numbers

    F. Variable names

3. Which of the following are true? (Choose all that apply.)

    A. All keys must be in the same resource bundle file to be used.

    B. All resource bundles defined as Java classes can be expressed using the property file format instead.

    C. All resource bundles defined as property files can be expressed using the Java class list bundle format instead.

    D. Changing the default locale lasts for only a single run of the program.

    E. It is forbidden to have both `Props_en.java` and `Props_en.properties` in the classpath of an application.

4. Assume that all bundles mentioned in the answers exist and define the same keys. Which one will be used to find the key in line 8?

    ```
    6:   Locale.setDefault(new Locale("en", "US"));
    7:   ResourceBundle b = ResourceBundle.getBundle("Dolphins");
    8:   b.getString("name");
    ```

    A. `Dolphins.properties`

    B. `Dolphins_en.java`

    C. `Dolphins_en.properties`

    D. `Whales.properties`

E. `Whales_en_US.properties`

F. The code does not compile.

5. Suppose that we have the following property files and code. Which bundles are used on lines 8 and 9 respectively?

```
Dolphins.properties
name=The Dolphin
age=0
```

```
Dolphins_en.properties
name=Dolly
age=4
```

```
Dolphins_fr.properties
name=Dolly
```

```
5:    Locale fr = new Locale("fr");
6:    Locale.setDefault(new Locale("en", "US"));
7:    ResourceBundle b = ResourceBundle.getBundle("Dolphins", fr);
8:    b.getString("name");
9:    b.getString("age");
```

A. `Dolphins.properties` and `Dolphins.properties`

B. `Dolphins.properties` and `Dolphins_en.properties`

C. `Dolphins_en.properties` and `Dolphins_en.properties`

D. `Dolphins_fr.properties` and `Dolphins.properties`

E. `Dolphins_fr.properties` and `Dolphins_en.properties`

F. The code does not compile.

6. Which of the following can be inserted into the blank to create a date of June 21, 2014? (Choose all that apply.)

```
import java.time.*;

public class StartOfSummer {
   public static void main(String[] args) {
   LocalDate date = _____
} }
```

A. `new LocalDate(2014, 5, 21);`

B. `new LocalDate(2014, 6, 21);`

C. `LocalDate.of(2014, 5, 21);`

D. `LocalDate.of(2014, 6, 21);`

    E. `LocalDate.of(2014, Calendar.JUNE, 21);`

    F. `LocalDate.of(2014, Month.JUNE, 21);`

7. What is the output of the following code?

```
LocalDate date = LocalDate.parse(
"2018-04-30", DateTimeFormatter.ISO_LOCAL_DATE);
date.plusDays(2);
date.plusHours(3);
System.out.println(date.getYear() + " "
   + date.getMonth() + " "+ date.getDayOfMonth());
```

    A. `2018 APRIL 2`

    B. `2018 APRIL 30`

    C. `2018 MAY 2`

    D. The code does not compile.

    E. A runtime exception is thrown.

8. What is the output of the following code?

```
LocalDate date = LocalDate.of(2018, Month.APRIL, 40);
System.out.println(date.getYear() + " " + date.getMonth()
   + " "+ date.getDayOfMonth());
```

    A. `2018 APRIL 4`

    B. `2018 APRIL 30`

    C. `2018 MAY 10`

    D. Another date

    E. The code does not compile.

    F. A runtime exception is thrown.

9. What is the output of the following code?

```
LocalDate date = LocalDate.of(2018, Month.APRIL, 30);
date.plusDays(2);
date.plusYears(3);
System.out.println(date.getYear() + " "
   + date.getMonth() + " "+ date.getDayOfMonth());
```

    A. `2018 APRIL 2`

    B. `2018 APRIL 30`

    C. `2018 MAY 2`

    D. `2021 APRIL 2`

E. 2021 APRIL 30

F. 2021 MAY 2

G. A runtime exception is thrown.

10. What is the output of the following code?

```
LocalDateTime d = LocalDateTime.of(2015, 5, 10, 11, 22, 33);
Period p = Period.of(1, 2, 3);
d = d.minus(p);
DateTimeFormatter f = DateTimeFormatter.
    ofLocalizedTime(FormatStyle.SHORT);
System.out.println(d.format(f));
```

A. 3/7/14 11:22 AM

B. 5/10/15 11:22 AM

C. 3/7/14

D. 5/10/15

E. 11:22 AM

F. The code does not compile.

G. A runtime exception is thrown.

11. What is the output of the following code?

```
LocalDateTime d = LocalDateTime.of(2015, 5, 10, 11, 22, 33);
Period p = Period.ofDays(1).ofYears(2);
d = d.minus(p);
DateTimeFormatter f = DateTimeFormatter.
    ofLocalizedDateTime(FormatStyle.SHORT);
System.out.println(f.format(d));
```

A. 5/9/13 11:22 AM

B. 5/10/13 11:22 AM

C. 5/9/14

D. 5/10/14

E. The code does not compile.

G. A runtime exception is thrown.

12. Which of the answer choices is true given the following code? (Choose all that apply.)

```
2016-08-28T05:00 GMT-04:00
2016-08-28T09:00 GMT-06:00
```

A. The first date/time is earlier.

B. The second date/time is earlier.

C. Both date/times are the same.

D. The date/times are 2 hours apart.

E. The date/times are 6 hours apart.

F. The date/times are 10 hours apart.

13. Note that March 13, 2016, is the weekend that clocks spring ahead for daylight savings time. What is the output of the following?

```
LocalDate date = LocalDate.of(2016, Month.MARCH, 13);
LocalTime time = LocalTime.of(1, 30);
ZoneId zone = ZoneId.of("US/Eastern");
ZonedDateTime dateTime1 = ZonedDateTime.of(date, time, zone);
ZonedDateTime dateTime2 = dateTime1.plus(1, ChronoUnit.HOURS);

long hours = ChronoUnit.HOURS.between(dateTime1, dateTime2);
int clock1 = dateTime1.getHour();
int clock2 = dateTime2.getHour();
System.out.println(hours + "," + clock1 + "," + clock2);
```

A. 1,1,2

B. 1,1,3

C. 2,1,2

D. 2,1,3

E. The code does not compile.

F. A runtime exception is thrown.

14. Note that March 13, 2016, is the weekend that we spring forward, and November 6, 2016, is when we fall back for daylight savings time. Which of the following can fill in the blank without the code throwing an exception?

```
ZoneId zone = ZoneId.of("US/Eastern");
LocalDate date = _____;
LocalTime time1 = LocalTime.of(2, 15);
ZonedDateTime a = ZonedDateTime.of(date4, time1, zone);
```

A. LocalDate.of(2016, 3, 13)

B. LocalDate.of(2016, 3, 40)

C. LocalDate.of(2016, 11, 6)

D. LocalDate.of(2016, 11, 7)

E. LocalDate.of(2017, 2, 29)

15. Given the following code, which of the answer choices can fill in the blank to print true? (Choose all that apply.)

```
String m1 = Duration.of(1, ChronoUnit.MINUTES).toString();
String m2 = Duration.ofMinutes(1).toString();
String s = Duration.of(60, ChronoUnit.SECONDS).toString();

String d = Duration.ofDays(1).toString();
String p = Period.ofDays(1).toString();

System.out.println(_____);
```

A. m1 == m2

B. m1.equals(m2)

C. m1.equals(s)

D. d == p

E. d.equals(p)

16. Given the following, which answers can correctly fill in the blank? (Choose all that apply.)

```
LocalDate date = LocalDate.now();
LocalTime time = LocalTime.now();
LocalDateTime dateTime = LocalDateTime.now();
ZoneId zoneId = ZoneId.systemDefault();
ZonedDateTime zonedDateTime = ZonedDateTime.of(dateTime, zoneId);
long epochSeconds = 0;
Instant instant = _____;
```

A. Instant.now()

B. Instant.ofEpochSecond(epochSeconds)

C. date.toInstant()

D. dateTime.toInstant()

E. time.toInstant()

F. zonedDateTime.toInstant()

17. What is the output of the following method if props contains {veggies=brontosaurus, meat=velociraptor}?

```
private static void print(Properties props) {
    System.out.println(props.get("veggies", "none")
        + " " + props.get("omni", "none"));
}
```

    A. brontosaurus none

    B. brontosaurus null

    C. none none

    D. none null

    E. The code does not compile.

    F. A runtime exception is thrown.

18. Which of the following prints out all of the values in props?

    A. `props.keys().stream().map(k -> k .forEach(System.out::println);`

    B. `props.keys().stream().map(k -> props.get(k))`
        `.forEach(System.out::println);`

    C. `props.keySet().stream().map(k -> k) .forEach(System.out::println);`

    D. `props.keySet().stream().map(k -> props.get(k))`
        `.forEach(System.out::println);`

    E. `props.stream().map(k -> k) .forEach(System.out::println);`

    F. `props.stream().map(k -> props.get(k)) .forEach(System.out::println);`

19. Which of the following are stored in a `Period` object? (Choose all that apply.)

    A. Year

    B. Month

    C. Day

    D. Hour

    E. Minute

    F. Second

20. Which of the following objects could contain the information "eastern standard time"? (Choose all that apply.)

    A. `Instant`

    B. `LocalDate`

    C. `LocalDateTime`

    D. `LocalTime`

    E. `ZonedDateTime`

Chapter

6

Exceptions and Assertions

THE OCP EXAM TOPICS COVERED IN THIS CHAPTER INCLUDE THE FOLLOWING:

✓ **Exceptions and Assertions**

- Use try-catch and throw statements
- Use catch, multi-catch, and finally clauses
- Use Autoclose resources with a try-with-resources statement
- Create custom exceptions and Auto-closeable resources
- Test invariants by using assertions

You have already learned the basics of exceptions for the OCA. While reviewing these basics, we will point out the additional exception classes that you are expected to know for the OCP. We will also cover the more advanced features introduced in Java 7 for working with exceptions. We will end the chapter by introducing assertions.

Reviewing Exceptions

A program can fail for just about any reason. Here are just a few of the possibilities for program failure that are commonly covered on the OCP exam:

- Your program tries to read a file that doesn't exist.

- Your program tries to access a database, but the network connection to the database is unavailable.

- You made a coding mistake and wrote an invalid SQL statement in your JDBC code.

- You made a coding mistake and used the wrong format specifiers when using DateTimeFormatter.

As you can see, some of these are coding mistakes. Others are completely beyond your control. Your program can't help it if the network connection goes down. What it can do is deal with the situation.

Questions about exceptions can show up in any topic on the exam. This means that you might see a question that appears to be about threads, but it is really testing your knowledge about exception handling. We will show code using topics covered in later chapters in the book to get you used to this. We promise that the end-of-chapter questions will not assume that you know about these topics just yet.

Even if you mastered exceptions for the OCA, we recommend reading the following review sections in any event because they use classes that you didn't see on the OCA. We will cover the key terms used with exceptions, syntax, and rules for working with exceptions. We will also let you know which exception classes you should be familiar with.

Exceptions Terminology

An *exception* is Java's way of saying, "I give up. I don't know what to do right now. You deal with it." When you write a method, you can either deal with the exception or make it the calling code's problem.

The *happy path* is when nothing goes wrong. With bad code, there might not be a happy path. For example, your code might have a bug where it always throws a `NullPointerException`. In this case, you have an exception path but not a happy path, because execution can never complete normally.

Categories of Exceptions

For the OCA, you learned about the major categories of exception classes. Figure 6.1 reviews the hierarchy of these classes. Remember that a *runtime exception*, or unchecked exception, may be caught, but it is not required that it be caught. After all, if you had to check for `NullPointerException`, every piece of code that you wrote would need to deal with it. A *checked exception* is any class that extends `Exception` but is not a runtime exception. Checked exceptions must follow the *handle or declare rule* where they are either caught or thrown to the caller. An error is fatal and should not be caught by the program. While it is legal to catch an error, it is not a good practice.

FIGURE 6.1   Categories of exceptions

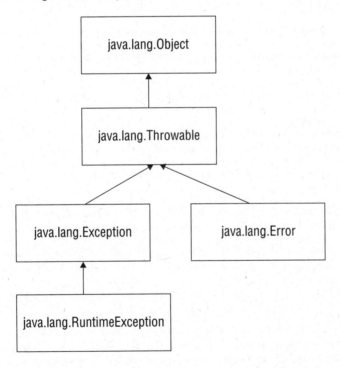

These rules are very important. Make sure that you can fill in Table 6.1 from memory. If you need more review on the differences, we recommend getting out your OCA study materials.

TABLE 6.1 Types of exceptions

Type	How to recognize	Recommended for program to catch?	Is program required to catch or declare?
Runtime exception	RuntimeException or its subclasses	Yes	No
Checked exception	Exception or its subclasses but not RuntimeException or its subclasses	Yes	Yes
Error	Error or its subclasses	No	No

Exceptions on the OCP

On the OCA, you had to know about only a handful of exceptions. As a review, these exceptions were as follows:

ArithmeticException   Thrown by the JVM when code attempts to divide by zero.

ArrayIndexOutOfBoundsException   Thrown by the JVM when code uses an illegal index to access an array.

ClassCastException   Thrown by the JVM when an attempt is made to cast an object to a subclass of which it is not an instance.

IllegalArgumentException   Thrown by the program to indicate that a method has been passed an illegal or inappropriate argument.

NullPointerException   Thrown by the JVM when there is a null reference where an object is required.

NumberFormatException   Thrown by the program when an attempt is made to convert a string to a numeric type, but the string doesn't have an appropriate format.

You also learned that java.io.IOException is an example of a checked exception. This made it easier, because the exam needed to tell you when an exception was a checked exception other than an IOException.

On the OCP, you need to know more exceptions. The objectives cover a number of APIs that throw a mix of checked and unchecked exceptions.

Table 6.2 and Table 6.3 provide a summary of the checked and runtime exceptions that you need to know for the exam. It's OK if you don't know what all of these do yet. Just remember that IO, parsing, and SQL exceptions are checked. Anything else is a runtime exception unless the exam states otherwise. You can come back to this later for review.

TABLE 6.2   OCP checked exceptions

Exception	Used when	Checked or unchecked?	Where to find more details
`java.text.ParseException`	Converting a `String` to a number.	Checked	Chapter 5
`java.io.IOException` `java.io.FileNotFound` `Exception` `java.io.NotSerializable` `Exception`	Dealing with IO and NIO.2 issues. `IOException` is the parent class. There are a number of subclasses. You can assume any `java.io` exception is checked.	Checked	Chapter 9
`java.sql.SQLException`	Dealing with database issues. `SQLException` is the parent class. Again, you can assume any `java.sql` exception is checked.	Checked	Chapter 10

TABLE 6.3   OCP runtime exceptions

Exception	Used when	Checked or unchecked?	Where to find more details
`java.lang.ArrayStoreException`	Trying to store the wrong data type in an array.	Unchecked	Chapter 3
`java.time.DateTimeException`	Receiving an invalid format string for a date.	Unchecked	Chapter 3
`java.util.MissingResourceException`	Trying to access a key or resource bundle that does not exist.	Unchecked	Chapter 5

TABLE 6.3   OCP runtime exceptions *(continued)*

Exception	Used when	Checked or unchecked?	Where to find more details
java.lang.IllegalStateException java.lang. UnsupportedOperationException	Attempting to run an invalid operation in collections and concurrency.	Unchecked	Chapters 3 and 7

Try Statement

On the OCA exam, you learned that the syntax of a try statement looks like Figure 6.2. The *try statement* consists of a mandatory try clause. It can include one or more *catch clause*s to handle the exceptions that are thrown. It can also include a *finally clause*, which runs regardless of whether an exception is thrown. This is all still true for both try statements and try-with-resources statements.

FIGURE 6.2   The syntax of a try statement

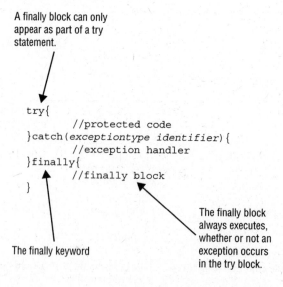

There is also a rule that says a try statement is required to have either or both of the catch and finally clauses. This is true for try statements, but is not true for try-with-resources statements, as you'll see later in the chapter.

There are two other rules that you need to remember from the OCA about the catch clauses:

- Java checks the catch blocks in the order in which they appear. It is illegal to declare a subclass exception in a catch block that is lower down in the list than a superclass exception because it will be unreachable code.

- Java will not allow you to declare a catch block for a checked exception type that cannot potentially be thrown by the try clause body. This is again to avoid unreachable code.

Throw vs. *Throws*

The exam might test whether you are paying attention to the difference between throw and throws. Remember that throw means an exception is actually being thrown and throws indicate that the method merely has the potential to throw that exception. The following example uses both:

```
10:    public String getDataFromDatabase() throws SQLException {
11:        throw new UnsupportedOperationException();
12:    }
```

Line 10 declares that the method might or might not throw a SQLException. Since this is a checked exception, the caller needs to handle or declare it. Line 11 actually does throw an UnsupportedOperationException. Since this is a runtime exception, it does not need to be declared on line 10.

This arrangement might seem strange but is actually a common pattern. The implementer of this method hasn't written the logic to go to the database yet. Maybe the database isn't available. The method still declares that it throws a SQLException, so any callers handle it right away and aren't surprised later by a change in method signature.

Remember to pay attention that throw and throws aren't reversed in the code that you see on the exam.

Creating Custom Exceptions

Java provides many exception classes out of the box. Sometimes, you want to write a method with a more specialized type of exception. You can create your own exception class to do this.

When creating your own exception, you need to decide whether it should be a checked or unchecked exception. While you can extend any exception class, it is most common to extend Exception (for checked) or RuntimeException (for unchecked.)

Creating your own exception class is really easy. Can you figure out whether the exceptions are checked or unchecked in this example?

```
1:    class CannotSwimException extends Exception {}
2:    class DangerInTheWater extends RuntimeException {}
3:    class SharkInTheWaterException extends DangerInTheWater {}
4:    class Dolphin {
5:      public void swim() throws CannotSwimException {
6:          // logic here
7:      }
8:    }
```

On line 1, we have a checked exception because it extends directly from Exception. Not being able to swim is pretty bad when we are trying to swim, so we want to force callers to deal with this situation. On line 2, we have an unchecked exception because it extends directly from RuntimeException. On line 3, we have another unchecked exception because it extends indirectly from RuntimeException. It is pretty unlikely that there will be a shark in the water. We might even be swimming in a pool where the odds of a shark are 0 percent! We don't want to force the caller to deal with everything that might remotely happen, so we leave this as an unchecked exception.

Lines 5–7 are a method that declares it might throw the checked CannotSwimException. The method implementation could be written to actually throw it or not. The method implementation could also be written to throw a SharkInTheWaterException, an ArrayIndexOutOfBoundsException, or any other runtime exception.

These one-liner exception declarations are pretty useful, especially on the exam where they need to communicate quickly whether an exception is checked or unchecked. Let's see how to pass more information in your exception.

The following example shows the three most common constructors defined by the Exception class:

```
public class CannotSwimException extends Exception {
    public CannotSwimException() {
        super();
    }
    public CannotSwimException(Exception e) {
        super(e);
    }
    public CannotSwimException(String message) {
        super(message);
    }
}
```

The first constructor is the default constructor with no parameters. The second constructor shows how to wrap another exception inside yours. The third constructor shows how to pass a custom error message.

Remember from the OCA that the default constructor is provided automatically if you don't write any constructors of your own.

Using a different constructor allows you to provide more information about what went wrong. We would get output like this if we wrote a main method with the line throw new CannotSwimException();:

```
Exception in thread "main" CannotSwimException
    at CannotSwimException.main(CannotSwimException.java:18)
```

This gives us just the exception and location. Now we change the main method to wrap an exception using the line throw new CannotSwimException(new RuntimeException());:

```
Exception in thread "main" CannotSwimException: java.lang.RuntimeException
    at CannotSwimException.main(CannotSwimException.java:19)
Caused by: java.lang.RuntimeException
    ... 1 more
```

This time, we find the underlying RuntimeException as well. Finally, we change the main method to pass a message using the line throw new CannotSwimException("broken fin");:

```
Exception in thread "main" CannotSwimException: broken fin
    at CannotSwimException.main(CannotSwimException.java:20)
```

This time we see the message text in the result. You might want to provide more information about the exception depending on the problem.

The error messages that we've been showing are called a *stack trace*. They show the exception along with the method calls it took to get there. Java automatically prints the stack trace when the program handles an exception.

You can also print the stack trace on your own:

```
try {
    throw new CannotSwimException();
} catch (CannotSwimException e) {
    e.printStackTrace();
}
```

Using Multi-catch

When something goes wrong in a program, it is common to log the error and convert it to a different exception type. In this example, we print the stack trace rather than write to a log. Next, we throw a runtime exception:

```
2:      public static void main(String[] args) {
3:          try {
```

```
 4:            Path path = Paths.get("dolphinsBorn.txt");
 5:            String text = new String(Files.readAllBytes(path));
 6:            LocalDate date = LocalDate.parse(text);
 7:            System.out.println(date);
 8:         } catch (DateTimeParseException e) {
 9:            e.printStackTrace();
10:            throw new RuntimeException(e);
11:         } catch (IOException e) {
12:            e.printStackTrace();
13:            throw new RuntimeException(e);
14:         } }
```

Lines 4 and 5 read a text file into a String. We cover this in Chapter 9, "NIO.2." For now, it does what it sounds like and throws an IOException if the operation fails. Line 6 converts that String to a LocalDate. You saw in Chapter 5, "Dates, Strings, and Localization," that this throws a DateTimeParseException on failure. The two catch blocks on lines 8–14 print a stack trace and then wrap the exception in a RuntimeException.

This works. However, duplicating code is bad. Think about what happens if we decide that we want to change the code to write to a log file instead of printing the stack trace. We have to be sure to change the code in two places. Before Java 7, there were two approaches to deal with this problem. One was to catch Exception instead of the specific types:

```
public static void main(String[] args) {
   try {
      Path path = Paths.get("dolphinsBorn.txt");
      String text = new String(Files.readAllBytes(path));
      LocalDate date = LocalDate.parse(text);
      System.out.println(date);
   } catch (Exception e) {     // BAD approach
      e.printStackTrace();
      throw new RuntimeException(e);
   } }
```

The duplicate code is gone. However, this isn't a good approach because it catches other exceptions too. For example, suppose that we had incorrect code that threw a NullPointerException. The catch block would catch it, which was never the intent.

The other approach is to extract the duplicate code into a helper method:

```
public static void main(String[] args) {
   try {
      Path path = Paths.get("dolphinsBorn.txt");
      String text = new String(Files.readAllBytes(path));
      LocalDate date = LocalDate.parse(text);
      System.out.println(date);
```

```
    } catch (DateTimeParseException e) {
        handleException(e);
    } catch (IOException e) {
        handleException(e);
    }
}
private static void handleException(Exception e) {
    e.printStackTrace();
    throw new RuntimeException(e);
}
```

The duplicate code is mostly gone now. We still have a little duplication in that the code calls handleException() in two places. The code also is longer and a bit harder to read.

The Java language designers recognized that this situation is an undesirable tradeoff. In Java 7, they introduced the ability to catch multiple exceptions in the same catch block, also known as *multi-catch*. Now we have an elegant solution to the problem:

```
public static void main(String[] args) {
    try {
        Path path = Paths.get("dolphinsBorn.txt");
        String text = new String(Files.readAllBytes(path));
        LocalDate date = LocalDate.parse(text);
        System.out.println(date);
    } catch (DateTimeParseException | IOException e) {
        e.printStackTrace();
        throw new RuntimeException(e);
    } }
```

This is much better. There's no duplicate code, the common logic is all in one place, and the logic is exactly where we would expect to find it.

Figure 6.3 shows the syntax of multi-catch. It's like a regular catch clause, except two or more exception types are specified separated by a pipe. The pipe is also used as the "or" operator, making it easy to remember that you can use either/or of the exception types. Notice how there is only one variable name in the catch clause. Java is saying that the variable named e can be of type Exception1 or Exception2.

FIGURE 6.3   The syntax of multi-catch

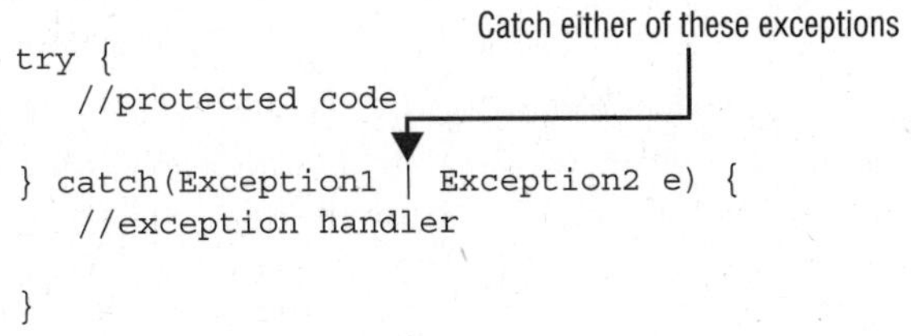

The exam might try to trick you with invalid syntax. Remember that the exceptions can be listed in any order within the catch clause. However, the variable name must appear only once and at the end. Do you see why these are valid or invalid?

```
catch(Exception1 e | Exception2 e | Exception3 e)     // DOES NOT COMPILE

catch(Exception1 e1 | Exception2 e2 | Exception3 e3) // DOES NOT COMPILE

catch(Exception1 | Exception2 | Exception3 e)
```

The first line is incorrect because the variable name appears three times. Just because it happens to be the same variable name doesn't make it OK. The second line is incorrect because the variable name again appears three times. Using different variable names doesn't make it any better. The third line does compile. It shows the correct syntax for specifying three exceptions.

Java intends multi-catch to be used for exceptions that aren't related, and it prevents you from specifying redundant types in a multi-catch. Do you see what is wrong here?

```
try {
    throw new IOException();
} catch (FileNotFoundException | IOException e) { } // DOES NOT COMPILE
```

FileNotFoundException is a subclass of IOException. Specifying it in the multi-catch is redundant, and the compiler gives a message such as this:

```
The exception FileNotFoundException is already caught by the alternative IOException
```

Since we can omit that exception type without changing the behavior of the program, Java does not allow declaring it. The correct code is as follows:

```
try {
    throw new IOException();
} catch (IOException e) { }
```

Multi-catch Is Effectively Final

This try statement is legal. It is a bad idea to reassign the variable in a catch block, but it is allowed:

```
try {
    // do some work
} catch(RuntimeException e) {
    e = new RuntimeException();
}
```

When adding multi-catch, this pattern is no longer allowed:

```
try {
   throw new IOException();
} catch(IOException | RuntimeException e) {
   e = new RuntimeException();          // DOES NOT COMPILE
}
```

With multi-catch, we no longer have a specific type of exception. Java uses the common Exception superclass for the variable internally. However, the intent isn't really to have any old random exception in there. It wouldn't make sense to shove an IllegalStateException in e. That would just make the code more complicated. Imagine that you wanted to rethrow the exception and it could be any old type. To avoid these problems and complexity, Java forbids reassigning the exception variable in a multi-catch situation.

This is scarcely a hardship given that it is bad practice to reassign the variable to begin with! Since Java is big on backward compatibility, this bad practice is still permitted when catching a single exception type.

To review multi-catch, see how many errors you can find in this try statement.

```
11:   public void doesNotCompile() {  // METHOD DOES NOT COMPILE
12:      try {
13:         mightThrow();
14:      } catch (FileNotFoundException | IllegalStateException e) {
15:      } catch (InputMismatchException e | MissingResourceException e) {
16:      } catch (SQLException | ArrayIndexOutOfBoundsException e) {
17:      } catch (FileNotFoundException | IllegalArgumentException e) {
18:      } catch (Exception e) {
19:      } catch (IOException e) {
20:      }
21:   }
22:   private void mightThrow() throws DateTimeParseException, IOException { }
```

This code is just swimming with errors. In fact, some errors hide others, so you might not see them all in the compiler. Once you start fixing some errors, you'll see the others. Here's what's wrong:

- Line 15 has an extra variable name. Remember that there can be only one exception variable per catch block.

- Line 18 and 19 are reversed. The more general superclasses must be caught after their subclasses. While this doesn't have anything to do with multi-catch, you'll see "regular" catch block problems mixed in with multi-catch.

- Line 17 cannot catch FileNotFoundException because that exception was already caught on line 15. You can't list the same exception type more than once in the same try statement, just like with "regular" catch blocks.

- Line 16 cannot catch SQLException because nothing in the try statement can potentially throw one. Again, just like "regular" catch blocks, any runtime exception may be caught. However, only checked exceptions that have the potential to be thrown are allowed to be caught.

Don't worry—you won't see this many problems in the same example on the exam!

Using Try-With-Resources

Multi-catch allows you to write code without duplication. Another problem arises with duplication in finally blocks. As you'll see in Chapters 8, 9, and 10, it is important to close resources when you are finished with them. For the exam, a resource is typically a file or database.

Imagine that you want to write a simple method to read the first line of one file and write it to another file. Prior to Java 7, your code would look like the following. Pay attention to the try-catch statements. You'll learn how to write the actual code by reading and writing code in Chapter 9.

```
10:    public void oldApproach(Path path1, Path path2) throws IOException {
11:        BufferedReader in = null;
12:        BufferedWriter out = null;
13:        try {
14:            in = Files.newBufferedReader(path1);
15:            out = Files.newBufferedWriter(path2);
16:            out.write(in.readLine());
17:        } finally {
18:            if (in != null) in.close();
19:            if (out != null) out.close();
20:        }
21:    }
```

That's twelve lines of code to do something quite simple, and we don't even deal with catching the exception. The sidebar, "Ensuring Resources Are Closed," explains why so much code is needed to do something so simple. Switching to the try-with-resources syntax introduced in Java 7, it can be rewritten as follows:

```
30:    public void newApproach(Path path1, Path path2) throws IOException {
31:        try (BufferedReader in = Files.newBufferedReader(path1);
32:            BufferedWriter out = Files.newBufferedWriter(path2)) {
```

```
33:            out.write(in.readLine());
34:      }
35:   }
```

The new version has half as many lines! There is no longer code just to close resources. The new *try-with-resources* statement automatically closes all resources opened in the try clause. This feature is also known as *automatic resource management*, because Java automatically takes care of the closing.

In the following sections, we will look at the try-with-resources syntax and how to indicate a resource can be automatically closed. We will introduce suppressed exceptions.

 Real World Scenario

Ensuring Resources Are Closed

Although it is beyond the scope of the exam, we sometimes come across code that appears to guarantee resource closure, but in fact it does not. Take a look at the following code snippet for closing resources:

```
} finally {
    if (in != null) in.close();
    if (out != null) out.close();
}
```

Can you spot any problem with this code snippet that could lead to a resource leak? If in.close() throws an exception, then out.close() will never be executed, leaving us with an unclosed resource! A better implementation follows:

```
} finally {
    try {
        in.close();
    } catch (IOException e) {}
    try {
        out.close();
    } catch (IOException e) {}
}
```

We swallow the exceptions to ensure both close methods are executed, although we could certainly note that the exceptions occurred in a local variable and rethrow them after both close requests have been made.

As you might imagine, writing this code correctly is error prone. You have to remember to close all of the resources that you open. You also have to make sure that they remain independent of each other. Luckily, try-with-resources avoids the need to keep writing code like this by hand!

Try-With-Resources Basics

You might have noticed that there is no `finally` block in the try-with-resources code. For the OCA exam, you learned that a `try` statement must have one or more catch blocks or a `finally` block. This is still true. The `finally` clause exists implicitly. You just don't have to type it.

> Remember that only a try-with-resources statement is permitted to omit both the `catch` and `finally` blocks. A traditional `try` statement must have either or both.

Figure 6.4 shows what a try-with-resources statement looks like. Notice that one or more resources can be opened in the try clause. Also, notice that parentheses are used to list those resources and semicolons are used to separate the declarations. This works just like declaring multiple indexes in a `for` loop.

FIGURE 6.4   The syntax of a basic try-with-resources

Any resources that should automatically be closed

```
try (BufferedReader r = Files.newBufferedReader(path1);
     BufferedWriter w = Files.newBufferedWriter(path2)) {
   // protected code

}
```

Resources are closed at this point

Figure 6.5 shows that a try-with-resources statement is still allowed to have catch and/or `finally` blocks. They are run in addition to the implicit one. The implicit `finally` block runs before any programmer-coded ones.

FIGURE 6.5   The syntax of try-with-resources including catch/finally

Any resources that should automatically be closed

```
try (BufferedReader r = Files.newBufferedReader(path1);
     BufferedWriter w = Files.newBufferedWriter(path2)) {
   //protected code

} catch (IOException e) {
   // exeption handler

} finally {
   // finally block

}
```

Optional clauses; resources still closed automatically

To make sure that you've wrapped your head around the differences, make sure you can fill in Table 6.4 and Table 6.5 with whichever combinations of catch and finally blocks are legal configurations.

TABLE 6.4   Legal vs. illegal configurations with a traditional try statement

	0 finally **blocks**	**1** finally **block**	**2 or more** finally **blocks**
0 catch **blocks**	Not legal	Legal	Not legal
1 or more catch **blocks**	Legal	Legal	Not legal

TABLE 6.5   Legal vs. illegal configurations with a try-with-resources statement

	0 finally **blocks**	**1** finally **block**	**2 or more** finally **blocks**
0 catch **blocks**	Legal	Legal	Not legal
1 or more catch **blocks**	Legal	Legal	Not legal

The resources created in the try clause are only in scope within the try block. This is another way to remember that the implicit finally runs before any catch/finally blocks that you code yourself. The implicit close has run already, and the resource is no longer available. Do you see why lines 6 and 8 don't compile in this example?

```
3:    try (Scanner s = new Scanner(System.in)) {
4:        s.nextLine();
5:    } catch(Exception e) {
6:        s.nextInt();  // DOES NOT COMPILE
7:    } finally{
8:        s.nextInt();  // DOES NOT COMPILE
9:    }
```

The problem is that Scanner has gone out of scope at the end of the try clause. Lines 6 and 8 do not have access to it. This is actually a nice feature. You can't accidentally use an object that has been closed. In a traditional try statement, the variable has to be declared before the try statement so that both the try and finally blocks can access it, which has the unpleasant side effect of making the variable in scope for the rest of the method, just inviting you to call it by accident.

AutoCloseable

You can't just put any random class in a try-with-resources statement. Java commits to closing automatically any resources opened in the try clause. Here we tell Java to try to close the Turkey class when we are finished with it:

```java
public class Turkey {
    public static void main(String[] args) {
        try (Turkey t = new Turkey()) {  // DOES NOT COMPILE
            System.out.println(t);
        }
    }
}
```

Java doesn't allow this. It has no idea how to close a Turkey. Java informs us of this fact with a compiler error:

```
The resource type Turkey does not implement java.lang.AutoCloseable
```

In order for a class to be created in the try clause, Java requires it to implement an interface called AutoCloseable. TurkeyCage does implement this interface:

```java
1:    public class TurkeyCage implements AutoCloseable {
2:        public void close() {
3:            System.out.println("Close gate");
4:        }
5:        public static void main(String[] args) {
6:            try (TurkeyCage t = new TurkeyCage()) {
7:                System.out.println("put turkeys in");
8:            }
9:        }
10:   }
```

That's much better. Line 1 declares that the class implements the AutoCloseable interface. This interface requires a close() method to be implemented, which is done on lines 2–4. Now, line 6 is allowed. Java does know how to close a TurkeyCage object. All Java has to do is to call the close() method.

The AutoCloseable interface has only one method to implement:

```java
public void close() throws Exception;
```

Wait—TurkeyCage didn't throw an Exception. That's OK because an overriding method is allowed to declare more specific exceptions than the parent or even none at all. By declaring Exception, the AutoCloseable interface is saying that implementers may throw any exceptions they choose.

The following shows what happens when an exception is thrown. Do you see any problems with it?

```java
public class StuckTurkeyCage implements AutoCloseable {
    public void close() throws Exception {
        throw new Exception("Cage door does not close");
    }
    public static void main(String[] args) {
        try (StuckTurkeyCage t = new StuckTurkeyCage()) { // DOES NOT COMPILE
            System.out.println("put turkeys in");
        }
    }
}
```

The try-with-resources statement throws a checked exception. And you know that checked exceptions need to be handled or declared. Tricky isn't it? This is something that you need to watch for on the exam. If the main() method declared an Exception, this code would compile.

Java strongly recommends that close() not actually throw Exception. It is better to throw a more specific exception. Java also recommends to make the close() method idempotent. *Idempotent* means that the method can called be multiple times without any side effects or undesirable behavior on subsequent runs. For example, it shouldn't throw an exception the second time or change state or the like. Both these negative practices are allowed. They are merely discouraged.

To better understand this, see which implementation you think is best:

```java
class ExampleOne implements AutoCloseable {
    public void close() throws IllegalStateException {
        throw new IllegalStateException("Cage door does not close");
    }
}
class ExampleTwo implements AutoCloseable {
    public void close() throws Exception {
        throw new Exception("Cage door does not close");
    }
}
class ExampleThree implements AutoCloseable {
    static int COUNT = 0;
    public void close()  {
        COUNT++;
    }
}
```

ExampleOne is the best implementation. ExampleTwo throws Exception rather than a more specific subclass, which is not recommended. ExampleThree has a side effect. It changes the state of a variable. Side effects are not recommended.

 Real World Scenario

AutoCloseable* vs. *Closeable

The AutoCloseable interface was introduced in Java 7. Before that, another interface existed called Closeable. It was similar to what the language designers wanted, with the following exceptions:

- Closeable restricts the type of exception thrown to IOException.

- Closeable requires implementations to be idempotent.

The language designers emphasize backward compatibility. Since changing the existing interface was undesirable, they made a new one called AutoCloseable. This new interface is less strict than Closeable. Since Closeable meets the requirements for AutoCloseable, it started implementing AutoCloseable when the latter was introduced.

Suppressed Exceptions

What happens if the close() method throws an exception? If the TurkeyCage doesn't close, the turkeys could all escape. Clearly we need to handle such a condition.

We already know that the resources are closed before any programmer-coded catch blocks are run. This means that we can catch the exception thrown by close() if we wish. Alternatively, we can allow the caller to deal with it. Just like a regular exception, checked exceptions must be handled or declared. Runtime exceptions do not need to be acknowledged.

The following shows how we can catch an exception thrown by close().

```java
public class JammedTurkeyCage implements AutoCloseable {
    public void close() throws IllegalStateException {
        throw new IllegalStateException("Cage door does not close");
    }
    public static void main(String[] args) {
        try (JammedTurkeyCage t = new JammedTurkeyCage()) {
            System.out.println("put turkeys in");
        } catch (IllegalStateException e) {
            System.out.println("caught: " + e.getMessage());
        }
    }
}
```

The close() method is automatically called by try-with-resources. The catch block catches it and prints caught: Cage door does not close.

Note that if JammedTurkeyCage's close() method threw a checked exception, the try statement in the main method would need to catch it, or the main method would need to throw it.

This seems reasonable enough. What happens if the try block also throws an exception? Java 7 added a way to accumulate exceptions. When multiple exceptions are thrown, all but the first are called *suppressed exceptions*. The idea is that Java treats the first exception as the primary one and tacks on any that come up while automatically closing, for example:

```
15:    try (JammedTurkeyCage t = new JammedTurkeyCage()) {
16:        throw new IllegalStateException("turkeys ran off");
17:    } catch (IllegalStateException e) {
18:        System.out.println("caught: " + e.getMessage());
19:        for (Throwable t: e.getSuppressed())
20:            System.out.println(t.getMessage());
21:    }
```

Line 16 throws the primary exception. At this point, the try clause ends and Java automatically calls the close() method. It throws an IllegalStateException, which is added as a suppressed exception. Then line 17 catches the primary exception. Line 18 prints the message for the primary exception. Line 19 loops through the one suppressed exception and line 20 prints it out. The output is

```
caught: turkeys ran off
Cage door does not close
```

Keep in mind that the catch block looks for matches on the primary exception. What do you think this code prints?

```
22:    try (JammedTurkeyCage t = new JammedTurkeyCage()) {
23:        throw new RuntimeException("turkeys ran off");
24:    } catch (IllegalStateException e) {
25:        System.out.println("caught: " + e.getMessage());
26:    }
```

Line 23 throws the primary exception. Java again calls the close() method and adds a suppressed exception. Line 24 would catch an IllegalStateException. However, we don't have one of those. The primary exception is a RuntimeException. Since this does not match the catch clause, the exception is thrown to the caller. Eventually the main method would output something like the following:

```
Exception in thread "main" java.lang.RuntimeException: turkeys ran off
    atJammedTurkeyCage.main(JammedTurkeyCage.java:20)
    Suppressed: java.lang.IllegalStateException: Cage door does not close
```

```
atJammedTurkeyCage.close(JammedTurkeyCage.java:5)
atJammedTurkeyCage.main(JammedTurkeyCage.java:21)
```

Java remembers the suppressed exceptions that go with a primary exception even if we don't handle them in the code. Now let's look at what happens if two exceptions are thrown while closing resources:

```
27:   try (JammedTurkeyCage t1 = new JammedTurkeyCage();
28:        JammedTurkeyCage t2 = new JammedTurkeyCage()) {
29:          System.out.println("turkeys entered cages");
30:   } catch (IllegalStateException e) {
31:      System.out.println("caught: " + e.getMessage());
32:      for (Throwable t: e.getSuppressed())
33:         System.out.println(t.getMessage());
34:   }
```

On line 29, the turkeys enter the cages without exception. Then Java tries to close both cages automatically. t2 is closed first, since Java closes resources in the reverse order from which it created them. This throws an exception. Since it is the first exception to occur, it becomes the primary exception. Then t1 is closed. Since an exception has already been thrown, this one becomes a suppressed exception. The output is

```
turkeys entered cages
caught: Cage door does not close
Cage door does not close
```

Finally, keep in mind that suppressed exceptions apply only to exceptions thrown in the try clause. The following example does not throw a suppressed exception:

```
35:   try (JammedTurkeyCage t = new JammedTurkeyCage()) {
36:      throw new IllegalStateException("turkeys ran off");
37:   } finally {
38:      throw new RuntimeException("and we couldn't find them");
39:   }
```

Line 36 throws an exception. Then Java tries to close the resource and adds a suppressed exception to it. Now we have a problem. The finally block runs after all this. Since line 38 throws an exception, the previous exception is lost. This has always been and continues to be bad programming practice. We don't want to lose exceptions.

Remember that Java needs to be backward compatible. try and finally were both allowed to throw an exception long before Java 7. When this happened, the finally block took precedence. This behavior needs to continue. Since automatic resource management was new with Java 7, the try-with-resources part was allowed to behave differently. Regular finally blocks could not change.

Putting It Together

You've learned two new rules for the order in which code runs in a try-with-resources statement:

- Resources are closed after the try clause ends and before any catch/finally clauses.
- Resources are closed in the reverse order from which they were created.

Based on these rules, can you figure out what this code prints?

```java
public class Auto implements AutoCloseable {
   int num;
   Auto(int num) { this.num = num; }
   public void close() {
      System.out.println("Close: " + num);
   }
   public static void main(String[] args) {
      try (Auto a1 = new Auto(1); Auto a2 = new Auto(2)) {
         throw new RuntimeException();
      } catch (Exception e) {
         System.out.println("ex");
      } finally {
         System.out.println("finally");
      }
   }
}
```

Since the resources are closed in the reverse order from which they were opened, we have Close: 2 and then Close: 1. After that, the catch block and finally block are run—just as they are in a regular try statement. The output is

```
Close: 2
Close: 1
ex
finally
```

Rethrowing Exceptions

It is a common pattern to log and then throw the same exception. Suppose that we have a method that declares two checked exceptions:

```java
public void parseData() throws SQLException,  DateTimeParseException {}
```

When calling this method, we need to handle or declare those two exception types. There are few valid ways of doing this. We could have two catch blocks and duplicate the logic. Or we could use multi-catch:

```
3:    public void multiCatch() throws SQLException, DateTimeParseException {
4:        try {
5:            parseData();
6:        } catch (SQLException | DateTimeParseException e) {
7:            System.err.println(e);
8:            throw e;
9:    } }
```

This doesn't seem bad. We only have one catch block on line 6, so we aren't duplicating code. Or are we? The list of exceptions in the catch block and the list of exceptions in the method signature of multiCatch() are the same. This is duplication.

Since there were a number of changes in Java 7, the language designers decided to solve this problem at the same time. They made it legal to write Exception in the catch block but really only a limited set of exceptions. The following code is similar to the preceding example:

```
3:    public void rethrowing() throws SQLException, DateTimeParseException {
4:        try {
5:            parseData();
6:        } catch (Exception e) {
7:            System.err.println(e);
8;            throw e;
9:    } }
```

We still have one catch block on line 6. This time, Java interprets Exception as the possible exceptions that can be thrown in the method. As long as all of these checked exceptions are handled or declared, Java is happy.

Notice how we said that the two examples are similar; that is, they are not the same. What happens if parseData() throws a NullPointerException? In the multi-catch version, the exception will not be caught in the catch block and will not be logged to System.err. In the rethrowing example, it will be caught, logged, and rethrown.

Now, suppose that parseData() changes implementation to use a file system instead of a database. The developers decided to change it slowly because they wanted to run both systems in parallel for a while. They added an exception to the method signature, giving us the following:

```
public void parseData() throws IOException, SQLException, DateTimeParseException
```

Let's think about how our methods need to change. In the multi-catch example, we need to make two changes:

```
public void multiCatch() throws IOException, SQLException, DateTimeParseException {
    try {
```

```
      parseData();
   } catch (IOException | SQLException | DateTimeParseException e) {
      System.err.println(e);
      throw e;
   } }
```

We had to add the new exception to both the multi-catch and the method signature. We also would likely have to update some of the callers of our method. Now we make the same change to our rethrowing example:

```
public void rethrowing() throws IOException, SQLException,
DateTimeParseException {
   try {
      parseData();
   } catch (Exception e) {
      System.err.println(e);
      throw e;
   } }
```

This time, we only had to update the method signature. Java is able to infer that Exception in the catch block now includes the additional type.

The developers finally finished their change and decided to remove SQLException from the method signature leaving us with

```
public void parseData() throws IOException, DateTimeParseException {
```

We get to change the multi-catch version yet again. This time, we have to remove an exception from the catch block, giving us the following:

```
public void multiCatch() throws IOException, SQLException,
DateTimeParseException {
   try {
      parseData();
   } catch (IOException | DateTimeParseException e) {
      System.err.println(e);
      throw e;
   } }
```

We decide to leave the method signature of our method alone, so that our callers don't need to change. After all, we are allowed to throw extra exceptions. The rethrowing example is better off. No code changes are required. Java merely interprets Exception to mean the remaining two exception types.

These changes are why many people prefer using unchecked exceptions. You don't have this trickle of changes when a method changes which exceptions it throws.

Working with Assertions

An *assertion* is a Boolean expression that you place at a point in your code where you expect something to be true. The English definition of the word *assert* is to state that something is true, which means that you assert that something is true. An *assert statement* contains this statement along with an optional String message.

An assertion allows for detecting defects in the code. You can turn on assertions for testing and debugging while leaving them off when your program is in production.

Why assert something when you know it is true? It is only true when everything is working properly. If the program has a defect, it might not actually be true. Detecting this earlier in the process lets you know something is wrong.

> When troubleshooting a problem at work, developers might tell people that they don't believe anything that they can't see. Often the process of verifying something they have verbally asserted to be true proves the assumption was false.

In the following sections, we cover the syntax for using an assertion, how to turn them on/off, and common uses of assertions.

The *assert* Statement

The syntax for an assert statement has two forms:

```
assert boolean_expression;
assert boolean_expression: error_message;
```

The boolean expression must evaluate to true or false. It can be inside optional parenthesis. The optional error message is a String used as the message for the AssertionError that is thrown.

That's right. An assertion throws an AssertionError if it is false. Since programs aren't supposed to catch an Error, this means that assertion failures are fatal and end the program.

The three possible outcomes of an assert statement are as follows:

- If assertions are disabled, Java skips the assertion and goes on in the code.

- If assertions are enabled and the boolean expression is true, then our assertion has been validated and nothing happens. The program continues to execute in its normal manner.

- If assertions are enabled and the boolean expression is false, then our assertion is invalid and a java.lang.AssertionError is thrown.

Presuming assertions are enabled, an assertion is a shorter/better way of writing the following:

```
if (!boolean_expression) throw new AssertionError();
```

The assert syntax is easier to read. But wait. Remember when we said a developer shouldn't be throwing an Error? With the assert syntax, you aren't. Java is throwing the Error.

Suppose that we enable assertions by running the following example with the command java -ea Assertions:

```
1:    public class Assertions {
2:        public static void main(String[] args) {
3:            int numGuests = -5;
4:            assert numGuests > 0;
5:            System.out.println(numGuests);
6:        }
7:    }
```

We made a typo in the code. We intended for there to be five guests and not negative five guests. The assertion on line 4 detects this problem. Java throws the AssertionError at this point. Line 5 never runs since an error was thrown.

The program ends with a stack trace similar to this:

```
Exception in thread "main" java.lang.AssertionError
    at asserts.Assertions.main(Assertions.java:7)
```

If we run the same program using the command line java Assertions, we get a different result. The program prints -5. Now, in this example, it is pretty obvious what the problem is since the program is only seven lines. In a more complicated program, knowing the state of affairs is more useful.

Enabling Assertions

By default, assert statements are ignored by the JVM at runtime. To enable assertions, use the -enableassertions flag on the command line:

```
java -enableassertions Rectangle
```

You can also use the shortcut -ea flag:

```
java -ea Rectangle
```

Using the -enableassertions or -ea flag without any arguments enables assertions in all classes except system classes. *System classes* are classes that are part of the Java runtime. You can think of them as the classes that come with Java. You can also enable assertions for a specific class or package. For example, the following command enables assertions only for classes in the com.wiley.demos package and any subpackages:

```
java -ea:com.wiley.demos... my.programs.Main
```

The three dots means any class in the specified package or subpackages. You can also enable assertions for a specific class:

```
java -ea:com.wiley.demos.TestColors my.programs.Main
```

You can disable assertions using the -disableassertions (or -da) flag for a specific class or package that was previously enabled. For example, the following command enables assertions for the com.wiley.demos package but disables assertions for the TestColors class:

```
java -ea:com.wiley.demos... -da:com.wiley.demos.TestColors my.programs.Main
```

Enabling assertions is an important aspect of using them, because if assertions are not enabled, assert statements are ignored at runtime. Assertions were added to the Java language in the Java 1.4 release, as was the new assert keyword. Keep an eye out for a question that contains an assert statement but that is not executed with assertions enabled; the assert statement is ignored in that situation.

Using Assertions

You can use assertions for many reasons, including the following. You won't be asked to identify the type of assertion on the exam. This is just to give you ideas of how they might be used.

Internal Invariants   You assert that a value is within a certain constraint. assert x < 0 is an example of an internal invariant.

Class Invariants   You assert the validity of an object's state. Class invariants are typically private methods within the class that return a boolean. The upcoming Rectangle class demonstrates a class invariant.

Control Flow Invariants   You assert that a line of code you assume is unreachable is never reached. The upcoming TestSeasons class demonstrates a control flow invariant.

Preconditions   You assert that certain conditions are met before a method is invoked.

Post Conditions   You assert that certain conditions are met after a method executes successfully.

The following example demonstrates a control flow invariant. Suppose that we have the following enum declaration. Notice how winter is missing from the list of seasons. This is intentional. Our zoo is closed in the winter because it is too cold for visitors.

```
public enum Seasons {
    SPRING, SUMMER, FALL
}
```

The following `TestSeasons` class contains a `switch` statement that switches on a Seasons object. Because there are only three possible outcomes, the `default` case statement on lines 11–12 should never execute:

```
1:    public class TestSeasons {
2:      public static void test(Seasons s) {
3:          switch (s) {
4:          case SPRING:
5:          case FALL:
6:              System.out.println("Shorter hours");
7:              break;
8:          case SUMMER:
9:              System.out.println("Longer hours");
10:             break;
11:         default:
12:             assert false: "Invalid season";
13:         }}}
```

Because the value of s on line 3 can only be SPRING, SUMMER, or FALL, and the switch statement has a case for all three of these outcomes, we can assert that line 12 is not reachable. This example is typical of when to use an assertion. We know that WINTER is not a choice because it is not in the enum. If this situation ever changes, the assertion will tell us about it. Notice that if it does, an AssertionError is thrown because the boolean is false.

Consider whether to throw a RuntimeException or use an assertion in these scenarios. In real programs, you might prefer the RuntimeException. If this were to fail in production, would you want the program to throw an exception or fail silently? The assertion would fail silently, since you'd have assertions off in production.

The only way this assertion will fail is if somehow the enum is modified. Suppose that you are working on a project that uses the Seasons enum, and the zoo decides to start opening in the winter. The assertion can help uncover the ripple effect of such a change. Suppose the new version of Seasons looks like this:

```
public enum Seasons {
    SPRING, SUMMER, FALL, WINTER
}
```

See if you can determine the output of the following main method added to the TestSeasons class:

```
public static void main(String [] args) {
    test (Seasons.WINTER);
}
```

Because WINTER is a new season and not one of the cases, the default block executes and the assert fails. (It has to fail because it uses false for the boolean expression.) Assuming assertions are enabled, an AssertionError is thrown and the following stack trace displays a message like this:

```
Exception in thread "main" java.lang.AssertionError: Invalid season
        at TestSeason.main(Test.java:12)
        at TestSeason.main(Test.java:18)
```

A control flow assertion is a common use of assert statements. You could place an assert statement at any location in your code that you assume will not be reached.

Assertions Should Not Alter Outcomes

Because assertions can, should, and probably will be turned off in a production environment, your assertions should not contain any business logic that affects the outcome of your code. For example, the following assertion is not a good design because it alters the value of a variable:

```
int x = 10;
assert ++x > 10;   // Not a good design!
```

When assertions are turned on, x is incremented to 11; but when assertions are turned off, the value of x is 10. This is not a good use of assertions because the outcome of the code will be different depending on whether assertions are turned on.

The following example demonstrates a class invariant. A Rectangle object is not considered valid if either its width or height is negative. Examine the following Rectangle class, and assuming that assertions are turned on, determine the output of running the main method:

```
1: public class Rectangle {
2:     private int width, height;
3:
4:     public Rectangle(int width, int height) {
5:         this.width = width;
6:         this.height = height;
7:     }
8:
9:     public int getArea() {
10:         assert isValid(): "Not a valid Rectangle";
11:         return width * height;
```

```
12:  }
13:
14:  private boolean isValid() {
15:      return (width >= 0 && height >= 0);
16:  }
17:
18:  public static void main(String [] args) {
19:      Rectangle one = new Rectangle(5,12);
20:      Rectangle two = new Rectangle(-4,10);
21:      System.out.println("Area one = " + one.getArea());
22:      System.out.println("Area two = " + two.getArea());
23:  }
24:}
```

The isValid method is an example of a class invariant. It is a private method that tests the state of the object. Line 10 invokes isValid in an assertion statement before computing the area. Within main, Rectangle one is valid and its area is output. Rectangle two has a negative width, so the assertion fails on line 10. The output is shown here:

```
Area one = 60
Exception in thread "main" java.lang.AssertionError: Not a valid Rectangle
        at Rectangle.getArea(Rectangle.java:10)
        at Rectangle.main(Rectangle.java:22)
```

Validating Method Parameters

Do not use assertions to check for valid arguments passed in to a method. Use an IllegalArgumentException instead. For example, the constructor of Rectangle should throw an IllegalArgumentException when either the width or height is negative:

```
public Rectangle(int width, int height) {
    if(width < 0 || height < 0) {
        throw new IllegalArgumentException();
    }
    this.width = width;
    this.height = height;
}
```

This constructor greatly improves the reliability of the Rectangle class, because there is no way to set the field's width and height except in the constructor. Remember, assertions are for situations where you are certain of something and you just want to verify it. You cannot be certain that someone instantiating a Rectangle will pass in positive values. However, with the Rectangle constructor defined here, you should be able to assert with a great deal of certainty that invoking isValid on any Rectangle object will return true.

Assertions are used for debugging purposes, allowing you to verify that something that you think is true during the coding phase is actually true at runtime.

Summary

An exception indicates that something unexpected happened. Subclasses of java.lang.Error are exceptions that a program should not attempt to handle. Subclasses of java.lang.RuntimeException are runtime (unchecked) exceptions. Subclasses of java.lang.Exception that do not subclass java.lang.RuntimeException are checked exceptions. Java requires checked exceptions to be handled or declared.

If a try statement has multiple catch blocks, at most one catch block can run. Java looks for an exception that can be caught by each catch block in the order in which they appear, and the first match is run. Then execution continues after the try statement to the finally block if present. If both catch and finally throw an exception, the one from finally gets thrown. Common checked exceptions include ParseException, IOException, and SQLException.

Multi-catch allows catching multiple exception types in the same catch block. The types are separated with a pipe (|). The multiple exception types are not allowed to have a subclass/superclass relationship. The variable in a multi-catch expression is effectively final.

Try-with-resources allows Java to take care of calling the close() method. This is called automatic resource management. Objects instantiated in the try clause must implement the AutoCloseable interface. This interface has a single method close() and can throw any type of Exception. Unlike traditional try statements, try-with-resources does not require a catch or finally block to be present. If the try clause and one or more of the close() methods throw an exception, Java uses suppressed exceptions to keep track of both. Similarly, if multiple close() methods throw an exception, the first one is the primary exception and the others are suppressed exceptions. getSuppressed() allows these exceptions to be retrieved.

An assertion is a boolean expression placed at a particular point in your code where you think something should always be true. A failed assertion throws an AssertionError. Assertions should not change the state of any variables. You saw how the –ea and –enable-assertion flags turn on assertions.

Exam Essentials

Determine if an exception is checked or unchecked.   Checked exceptions are in the Exception class hierarchy but not the RuntimeException hierarchy. DateTimeParseException, IOException, and SQLException are common checked exceptions.

Recognize when to use throw vs. throws.   The throw keyword is used when you actually want to throw an exception. For example, throw new RuntimeException(). The throws keyword is used in a method declaration.

Create code using multi-catch.   The multiple exception types are separated by a pipe (|). They are not allowed to have a subclass/superclass relationship.

Identify the similarities and differences between a traditional try statement and try-with-resources statement.   A traditional try statement is required to have at least one catch block or a finally block. A try-with-resources statement is allowed to omit both. A try-with-resources statement is allowed to create suppressed exceptions in the try clause or when closing resources. Neither is allowed to create suppressed exceptions by combining the try and finally (or catch) clauses.

Know how to enable assertions.   Assertions are disabled by default. Watch for a question that uses assertions but does not enable them or a question that tests your knowledge of how assertions are enabled from the command line.

Review Questions

1. Which of the following pairs fills in the blanks to make this code compile?

```
5:    public void read() _____ SQLException {
6:            _____ new SQLException();
7:    }
```

   A. throw on line 5 and throw on line 6
   B. throw on line 5 and throws on line 6
   C. throws on line 5 and throw on line 6
   D. throws on line 5 and throws on line 6
   E. None of the above. SQLException is a checked exception and cannot be thrown.
   F. None of the above. SQLException is a runtime exception and cannot be thrown.

2. Which of the following changes when made independently would make this code compile? (Choose all that apply.)

```
1:    public class StuckTurkeyCage implements AutoCloseable {
2:        public void close() throws Exception {
3:            throw new Exception("Cage door does not close");
4:        }
5:        public static void main(String[] args) {
6:            try (StuckTurkeyCage t = new StuckTurkeyCage()) {
7:                System.out.println("put turkeys in");
8:            }
9:        }
10:    }
```

   A. Remove throws Exception from the declaration on line 2.
   B. Add throws Exception to the declaration on line 5.
   C. Change line 8 to } catch (Exception e) {}.
   D. Change line 8 to } finally {}.
   E. None of the above will make the code compile.
   F. The code already compiles as is.

3. Which of the following fills in the blank to make the code compile? (Choose all that apply)

```
public static void main(String[] args)  {
    try {
        throw new IOException();
    } catch (_____) { }
}
```

A. `FileNotFoundException | IOException e`

B. `FileNotFoundException e | IOException e`

C. `FileNotFoundException | RuntimeException e`

D. `FileNotFoundException e | RuntimeException e`

E. `IOException | RuntimeException e`

F. `IOException e | RuntimeException e`

4. Which of the following are true statements? (Choose all that apply.)

A. A traditional `try` statement without a `catch` block requires a `finally` block.

B. A traditional `try` statement without a `finally` block requires a `catch` block.

C. A traditional `try` statement with only one statement can omit the `{}`.

D. A try-with-resources statement without a `catch` block requires a `finally` block.

E. A try-with-resources statement without a `finally` block requires a `catch` block.

F. A try-with-resources statement with only one statement can omit the `{}`.

5. What is the output of the following code?

```java
import java.io.*;
public class AutocloseableFlow {
    static class Door implements AutoCloseable {
        public void close() {
            System.out.print("D");
        } }
    static class Window implements Closeable {
        public void close() {
            System.out.print("W");
            throw new RuntimeException();
    } }
    public static void main(String[] args) {
        try (Door d = new Door(); Window w = new Window()) {
            System.out.print("T");
        } catch (Exception e) {
            System.out.print("E");
        } finally {
            System.out.print("F");
    } } }
```

A. TWF

B. TWDF

C. TWDEF

D. TWF followed by an exception

E.   TWDF followed by an exception

F.   TWEF followed by an exception

G.   The code does not compile.

6.   What is the output of the following code?

```java
import java.io.*;
public class AutocloseableFlow {
    static class Door implements AutoCloseable {
        public void close() {
            System.out.print("D");
            throw new RuntimeException();
        } }
    static class Window implements Closeable {
        public void close() {
            System.out.print("W");
            throw new RuntimeException();
    } }
    public static void main(String[] args) {
        try {
            Door d = new Door(); Window w = new Window()
        }
        {
            System.out.print("T");
        } catch (Exception e) {
            System.out.print("E");
        } finally {
            System.out.print("F");
        } } }
```

A.   TWF

B.   TWDF

C.   TWDEF

D.   TWF followed by an exception

E.   TWDF followed by an exception

F.   TWEF followed by an exception

G.   The code does not compile.

7.   What is the result of running `java EchoInput hi there` with the following code?

```java
public class EchoInput {
    public static void main(String [] args) {
```

```
        if(args.length <= 3) assert false;
        System.out.println(args[0] + args[1] + args[2]);
     }
  }
```

A. hithere

B. The assert statement throws an AssertionError.

C. The code throws an ArrayIndexOutOfBoundsException.

D. The code compiles and runs successfully, but there is no output.

E. The code does not compile.

8. Which of the following command lines cause this program to fail on the assertion? (Choose all that apply.)

```
public class On {
    public static void main(String[] args) {
        String s = null;
        assert s != null;
    }
}
```

A. java -da On

B. java -ea On

C. java -da -ea:On On

D. java -ea -da:On On

E. The code does not compile.

9. Which of the following prints OhNo with the assertion failure when the number is negative? (Choose all that apply.)

A. assert n < 0: "OhNo";

B. assert n < 0, "OhNo";

C. assert n < 0 ("OhNo");

D. assert(n < 0): "OhNo";

E. assert(n < 0, "OhNo");

10. Which of the following are true of the code? (Choose all that apply.)

```
4:     private int addPlusOne(int a, int b) {
5:         boolean assert = false;
6:         assert a++ > 0;
7:         assert b > 0;
8:         return a + b;
9:     }
```

A. Line 5 does not compile.

B. Lines 6 and 7 do not compile because they are missing the `String` message.

C. Lines 6 and 7 do not compile because they are missing parentheses.

D. Line 6 is an appropriate use of an assertion.

E. Line 7 is an appropriate use of an assertion.

11. Which of the following are runtime exceptions? (Choose all that apply.)

A. `IllegalFormatException`

B. `IllegalStateException`

C. `IOException`

D. `MissingResourceException`

E. `DateTimeParseException`

F. `SQLException`

12. Which of the following can legally fill in the blank? (Choose all that apply.)

```
public class AhChoo {
    static class SneezeException extends Exception { }
    static class SniffleException extends SneezeException { }
    public static void main(String[] args) throws SneezeException {
        try {
            throw new SneezeException();
        } catch (SneezeException e) {
            _____
            throw e;
        } } }
```

A. `// leave line blank`

B. `e = new Exception();`

C. `e = new RuntimeException();`

D. `e = new SneezeException();`

E. `e = new SniffleException();`

F. None of the above; the code does not compile.

13. Which of the following can legally fill in the blank? (Choose all that apply.)

```
public class AhChoo {
    static class SneezeException extends Exception { }
    static class SniffleException extends SneezeException { }
    public static void main(String[] args) throws SneezeException {
        try {
            throw new SneezeException();
        } catch (SneezeException | RuntimeException e) {
```

```
        _____
        throw e;
      } } }
```

A. // leave line blank

B. e = new Exception();

C. e = new RuntimeException();

D. e = new SneezeException();

E. e = new SniffleException();

F. None of the above; the code does not compile.

14. Which of the following can legally fill in the blank? (Choose all that apply.)

```
public class AhChoo {
    static class SneezeException extends Exception { }
    static class SniffleException extends SneezeException { }
    public static void main(String[] args) throws SneezeException {
        try {
            throw new SneezeException();
        } catch (SneezeException | SniffleException e) {

            _____
            throw e;
        } } }
```

A. // leave line blank

B. e = new Exception();

C. e = new RuntimeException();

D. e = new SneezeException();

E. e = new SniffleException();

F. None of the above; the code does not compile.

15. Which of the following are checked exceptions? (Choose all that apply.)

```
class One extends RuntimeException{}
class Two extends Exception{}
class Three extends Error{}
class Four extends One{}
class Five extends Two{}
class Six extends Three{}
```

A. One

B. Two

C. Three

D. Four

E. Five

F. Six

16. What is the output of the following?

```java
public class SnowStorm {
    static class Walk implements AutoCloseable {
    public void close() {
        throw new RuntimeException("snow");
    }
}
    public static void main(String[] args) {
        try (Walk walk1 = new Walk(); Walk walk2 = new Walk();) {
            throw new RuntimeException("rain");
        } catch(Exception e) {
            System.out.println(e.getMessage()
                + " " + e.getSuppressed().length);
    } } }
```

A. rain 0

B. rain 1

C. rain 2

D. show 0

E. snow 1

F. snow 2

G. The code does not compile.

17. Fill in the blank: A class that implements _____ may be in a try-with-resource statement. (Choose all that apply.)

A. AutoCloseable

B. Closeable

C. Exception

D. RuntimeException

E. Serializable

18. Which pairs fill in the blanks? The close() method is *not* allowed to throw a(n) _____ in a class that implements _____. (Choose all that apply.)

A. Exception, AutoCloseable

B. Exception, Closeable

C. IllegalStateException, AutoCloseable

D. IllegalStateException, Closeable

E. IOException, AutoCloseable

F. IOException, Closeable

19. Which of the following *cannot* fill in the blank? (Choose all that apply.)

```
public void read() throws SQLException {
    try {
        readFromDatabase();
    } catch (_____ e) {
        throw e;
    }
}

private void readFromDatabase() throws SQLException { }
```

A. Exception

B. RuntimeException

C. SQLException

D. SQLException | IOException

E. SQLException | RuntimeException

20. Which of the following is true when creating your own exception class?

A. One or more constructors must be coded.

B. Only checked exceptions may be created.

C. Only unchecked exceptions may be created.

D. The toString() method must be coded.

E. None of the above.

Chapter

7

Concurrency

THE OCP EXAM TOPICS COVERED IN THIS CHAPTER INCLUDE THE FOLLOWING:

✓ **Java Concurrency**

- Create worker threads using Runnable, Callable, and use an ExecutorService to concurrently execute tasks

- Identify potential threading problems among deadlock, starvation, livelock, and race conditions

- Use synchronized keyword and java.util.concurrent.atomic package to control the order of thread execution

- Use java.util.concurrent collections and classes including CyclicBarrier and CopyOnWriteArrayList

- Use parallel Fork/Join Framework

- Use parallel Streams including reduction, decomposition, merging processes, pipelines, and performance.

As you shall learn in Chapter 8, "IO," and Chapter 10, "JDBC," computers are capable of reading and writing data to external resources. Unfortunately, as compared to CPU operations, these disk/network operations tend to be extremely slow. So slow, in fact, that if your computer's operating system were to stop and wait for every disk or network operation to finish, your computer would appear to freeze or lock up constantly.

Luckily, all modern operating systems support what is known as multi-threaded processing. The idea behind multi-threaded processing is to allow an application or group of applications to execute multiple tasks at the same time. This allows tasks waiting for other resources to give way to other processing requests.

Since its early days, Java has supported multi-threading programming using the Thread class. In 2004, Java 5 was released and the Concurrency API was introduced in the java.util.concurrent package. It included numerous classes for performing complex thread-based tasks. The idea was simple: managing complex thread interactions is quite difficult for even the most skilled developers; therefore a set of reusable features was created. The Concurrency API has grown over the years to include numerous classes and frameworks to assist you in developing complex, multi-threaded applications. In this chapter, we will introduce you to the concept of threads and provide numerous ways to manage threads using the Concurrency API.

Threads and concurrency tend to be one of the more challenging topics for many programmers to grasp, as problems with threads can be frustrating even for veteran developers to understand. In practice, concurrency issues are among the most difficult problems to diagnose and resolve.

While previous versions of the exam expected you to know how to create your own thread classes and manage thread life cycles, the OCP 8 exam instead relies heavily on your knowledge of the Concurrency API. Since we believe that you need to walk before you can run, we provide a basic overview of threads in the first part of this chapter, as we believe it will help you better understand the Concurrency API used throughout the rest of the chapter.

Introducing Threads

We begin this chapter by reviewing common terminology associated with threads. A *thread* is the smallest unit of execution that can be scheduled by the operating system. A *process* is a group of associated threads that execute in the same, shared environment. It follows, then, that a *single-threaded process* is one that contains exactly one thread, whereas a *multi-threaded process* is one that contains one or more threads.

By *shared environment*, we mean that the threads in the same process share the same memory space and can communicate directly with one another. Yes, you will finally see how static variables can be useful for performing complex, multi-threaded tasks! Remember from your OCA studies that static methods and variables are defined on a single class object that all instances share. For example, if one thread updates the value of a static object, then this information is immediately available for other threads within the process to read.

In this chapter, we will talk a lot about tasks and their relationships to threads. A *task* is a single unit of work performed by a thread. Throughout this chapter, a task will commonly be implemented as a lambda expression. A thread can complete multiple independent tasks but only one task at a time.

Refer to Figure 7.1 for an overview of threads and their shared environment within a process.

FIGURE 7.1 Process model

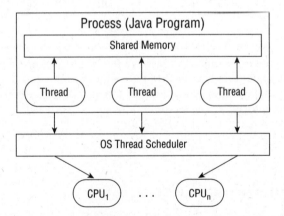

The process model shows a single process with three threads. It also shows how they are mapped to an arbitrary number of *n* CPUs available within the system. Keep this diagram in mind as we discuss task schedulers in the next section.

Distinguishing Thread Types

It might surprise you that all Java applications, including all of the ones that we have presented in this book, are all multi-threaded. Even a simple Java application that prints Hello World to the screen is multi-threaded. To help you understand this, we introduce the concepts of system threads and user-defined threads.

A *system thread* is created by the JVM and runs in the background of the application. For example, the garbage-collection thread is a system thread that is created by the JVM and runs in the background, helping to free memory that is no longer in use. For the most part, the execution of system-defined threads is invisible to the application developer. When a system-defined thread encounters a problem and cannot recover, such as running out of memory, it generates a Java Error, as opposed to an Exception.

As discussed in Chapter 6, "Exceptions and Assertions," even though it is possible to catch an Error, it is considered a very poor practice to do so, since it is rare that an application can recover from a system-level failure.

Alternatively, a *user-defined thread* is one created by the application developer to accomplish a specific task. All of the applications that we have created up to this point have been multi-threaded, but they contained only one user-defined thread, which calls the main() method. For simplicity, we commonly refer to threads that contain only a single user-defined thread as a single-threaded application, since we are often uninterested in the system threads.

Although not required knowledge for the exam, a *daemon thread* is one that will not prevent the JVM from exiting when the program finishes. A Java application terminates when the only threads that are running are daemon threads. For example, if the garbage-collection thread is the only thread left running, the JVM will automatically shut down. Both system and user-defined threads can be marked as daemon threads.

Understanding Thread Concurrency

At the start of the chapter, we mentioned that multi-threaded processing allows operating systems to execute threads at the same time. The property of executing multiple threads and processes at the same time is referred to as *concurrency*. Of course, with a single-core CPU system, only one task is actually executing at a given time. Even in multi-core or multi-CPU systems, there are often far more threads than CPU processors available. How does the system decide what to execute when there are multiple threads available?

Operating systems use a *thread scheduler* to determine which threads should be currently executing, as shown in Figure 7.1. For example, a thread scheduler may employ a *round-robin schedule* in which each available thread receives an equal number of CPU cycles with which to execute, with threads visited in a circular order. If there are 10 available threads, they might each get 100 milliseconds in which to execute, with the process returning to the first thread after the last thread has executed.

When a thread's allotted time is complete but the thread has not finished processing, a context switch occurs. A *context switch* is the process of storing a thread's current state and later restoring the state of the thread to continue execution. Be aware that there is often a cost associated with a context switch by way of lost time saving and reloading a thread's state.

Finally, a thread can interrupt or supersede another thread if it has a higher thread priority than the other thread. A *thread priority* is a numeric value associated with a thread that is taken into consideration by the thread scheduler when determining which threads should currently be executing. In Java, thread priorities are specified as integer values. The Thread class includes three important `static` constants, as shown in Table 7.1. By default, user-defined threads receive a thread priority value of `Thread.NORM_PRIORITY`. If you have a thread that must be executed right away, you can increase this value to 6 or higher or use the `Thread.MAX_PRIORITY` value. If two threads have the same priority, the thread scheduler will arbitrarily choose the one to process first in most situations.

TABLE 7.1   Java thread priority constants

Constant Variable	Value
Thread.MIN_PRIORITY	1
Thread.NORM_PRIORITY	5
Thread.MAX_PRIORITY	10

 Real World Scenario

The Importance of Thread Scheduling

Even though multi-core CPUs are quite common these days, single-core CPUs were the standard in personal computing for many decades. During this time, operating systems developed complex thread-scheduling and context-switching algorithms that allowed users to execute dozens or even hundreds of threads on a single-core CPU system. These scheduling algorithms allowed users to experience the illusion that multiple tasks were being performed at the exact same time within a single-CPU system. For example, a user could listen to music while writing a paper and receive notifications for new messages.

Since the number of threads often far outweighs the number of processors available even in multi-core systems, these thread-scheduling algorithms are still employed in operating systems today.

Introducing *Runnable*

As we mentioned in Chapter 4, "Functional Programming," java.lang.Runnable, or Runnable for short, is a functional interface that takes no arguments and returns no data. The following is the definition of the Runnable interface:

```
@FunctionalInterface public interface Runnable {
    void run();
}
```

The Runnable interface is commonly used to define the work a thread will execute, separate from the main application thread. We will be relying on the Runnable interface throughout this chapter, especially when we discuss applying parallel operations to streams.

The following lambda expressions each rely on the Runnable interface:

```
() -> System.out.println("Hello World")
() -> {int i=10; i++;}
() -> {return;}
() -> {}
```

Notice that all of these lambda expressions start with a set of empty parentheses, (). Also, note that none of them return a value. For these reasons, the following lambdas, while valid for other functional interfaces, are not compatible with Runnable:

```
() -> ""
() -> 5
() -> {return new Object();}
```

These examples are invalid Runnable expressions because they each return a value.

Creating *Runnable* Classes

Even though Runnable was made a functional interface in Java 8, the interface Runnable has existed since the very first version of Java. It was, and still is, commonly used to define a thread task by creating a class that implements the Runnable interface, as shown in the following code:

```
public class CalculateAverage implements Runnable {
    public void run() {
        // Define work here
    }
}
```

It is also useful if you need to pass information to your Runnable object to be used by the run() method, such as in the following class constructor:

```java
public class CalculateAverages implements Runnable {
   private double[] scores;
   public CalculateAverages(double[] scores) {
      this.scores = scores;
   }

   public void run() {
      // Define work here that uses the scores object
   }
}
```

In this chapter, we focus on creating lambda expressions that implicitly implement the Runnable interface. Just be aware that it is commonly used in class definitions.

Creating a Thread

The simplest way to execute a thread is by using the java.lang.Thread class, or Thread for short. Executing a task with Thread is a two-step process. First you define the Thread with the corresponding task to be done. Then you start the task by using the Thread.start() method.

As we shall discuss later in the chapter, Java does not provide any guarantees about the order in which a thread will be processed once it is started. It may be executed immediately or delayed for a significant amount of time.

Remember that order of thread execution is not often guaranteed. The exam commonly presents questions in which multiple tasks are started at the same time, and you must determine the result.

Defining the task, or work, that a Thread instance will execute can be done two ways in Java:

- Provide a Runnable object or lambda expression to the Thread constructor.
- Create a class that extends Thread and overrides the run() method.

The following are examples of these techniques:

```java
public class PrintData implements Runnable {
   public void run() {
      for(int i=0; i<3; i++)
         System.out.println("Printing record: "+i);
```

```
    }
    public static void main(String[] args) {
        (new Thread(new PrintData())).start();
    }
}

public class ReadInventoryThread extends Thread {
    public void run() {
        System.out.println("Printing zoo inventory");
    }
    public static void main(String[] args) {
        (new ReadInventoryThread()).start();
    }
}
```

The first example creates a Thread using a Runnable instance, while the second example uses the less common practice of extending the Thread class and overriding the run() method. Anytime you create a Thread instance, make sure that you remember to start the task with the Thread.start() method. This starts the task in a separate operating system thread. For example, what is the output of the following code snippet using these two classes?

```
public static void main(String[] args) {
    System.out.println("begin");
    (new ReadInventoryThread()).start();
    (new Thread(new PrintData())).start();
    (new ReadInventoryThread()).start();
    System.out.println("end");
}
```

The answer is that it is unknown until runtime. For example, the following is just one possible output:

```
begin
Printing zoo inventory
Printing record: 0
end
Printing zoo inventory
Printing record: 1
Printing record: 2
```

This sample uses a total of four threads—the main() user thread and three additional threads created by the main() method. While the order of thread execution once the threads have been started is indeterminate, the order within a single thread is still linear.

For example, the for() loop in PrintData is still ordered, as is the end appearing after the begin in the main() method.

On the exam, be careful about cases where a Thread or Runnable is created but no start() method is called. While the following code snippets will compile, none will actually execute a task on a separate processing thread. Instead, the thread that made the call will be used to execute the task, causing the thread to wait until each run() method is complete before moving on to the next line.

```
new PrintData().run();
(new Thread(new PrintData())).run();
(new ReadInventoryThread()).run();
```

In general, you should extend the Thread class only under very specific circumstances, such as when you are creating your own priority-based thread. In most situations, you should implement the Runnable interface rather than extend the Thread class.

We conclude our discussion of the Thread class here. While previous versions of the exam were quite focused on understanding the difference between extending Thread and implementing Runnable, the OCP 8 exam strongly encourages developers to use the Concurrency API to create and manage Thread objects for them.

 Real World Scenario

For Interviews, Be Familiar with Thread-Creation Options

Despite the fact that the exam no longer focuses on creating threads by extending the Thread class and implementing the Runnable interface, it is extremely common when interviewing for a Java development position to be asked to explain the difference between extending the Thread class and implementing Runnable. The following are some reasons to prefer one method over the other in Java:

- If you need to define your own Thread rules upon which multiple tasks will rely, such as a priority Thread, extending Thread may be preferable.

- Since Java doesn't support multiple inheritance, extending Thread does not allow you to extend any other class, whereas implementing Runnable lets you extend another class.

- Implementing Runnable is often a better object-oriented design practice since it separates the task being performed from the Thread object performing it.

- Implementing Runnable allows the class to be used by numerous Concurrency API classes.

If asked this question, you should answer it accurately. You should also mention that you can now use the ExecutorService, which we will discuss in the next section, to perform thread tasks without having to create Thread objects directly.

Polling with Sleep

Oftentimes, you need a thread to poll for a result to finish. *Polling* is the process of intermittently checking data at some fixed interval. For example, let's say that you have a thread that modifies a shared static counter value and your main() thread is waiting for the thread to increase the value above 100, as shown in the following class:

```
public class CheckResults {
   private static int counter = 0;
   public static void main(String[] args) {

      new Thread(() -> {
         for(int i=0; i<500; i++) CheckResults.counter++;
      }).start();

      while(CheckResults.counter<100) {
         System.out.println("Not reached yet");
      }
      System.out.println("Reached!");
   }
}
```

How many times will the while() loop in this code execute and output Not reached yet? The answer is, we don't know! It could output zero, ten, or a million times. If our thread scheduler is particularly poor, it could operate infinitely! Using a while() loop to check for data without some kind of delay is considered a very bad coding practice as it ties up CPU resources for no reason.

We can improve this result by using the Thread.sleep() method to implement polling. The Thread.sleep() method requests the current thread of execution rest for a specified number of milliseconds. When used inside the body of the main() method, the thread associated with the main() method will pause, while the separate thread will continue to run. Compare the previous implementation with the following one that uses Thread.sleep():

```
public class CheckResults {
   private static int counter = 0;
   public static void main(String[] args) throws InterruptedException {

      new Thread(() -> {
         for(int i=0; i<500; i++) CheckResults.counter++;
      }).start();

      while(CheckResults.counter<100) {
         System.out.println("Not reached yet");
         Thread.sleep(1000); // 1 SECOND
      }
      System.out.println("Reached!");
```

```
    }
}
```

In this example, we delay 1,000 milliseconds at the end of the loop, or 1 second. While this may seem like a small amount, we have now prevented a possibly infinite loop from executing and locking up our main program. Notice that we also changed the signature of the main method, since `Thread.sleep()` throws the checked `InterruptedException`. Alternatively, we could have wrapped each call to the `Thread.sleep()` method in a `try`/`catch` block.

How many times does the `while()` loop execute in this revised class? Still unknown! While polling does prevent the CPU from being overwhelmed with a potentially infinite loop, it does not guarantee when the loop will terminate. For example, the separate thread could be losing CPU time to a higher-priority process, resulting in multiple executions of the `while()` loop before it finishes.

Another issue to be concerned about is the shared counter variable. What if one thread is reading the counter variable while another thread is writing it? The thread reading the shared variable may end up with an invalid or incorrect value. We will discuss these issues in detail in the upcoming section on synchronization.

Creating Threads with the *ExecutorService*

With the announcement of the Concurrency API, Java introduced the `ExecutorService`, which creates and manages threads for you. You first obtain an instance of an `ExecutorService` interface, and then you send the service tasks to be processed. The framework includes numerous useful features, such as thread pooling and scheduling, which would be cumbersome for you to implement in every project. Therefore, it is recommended that you use this framework anytime you need to create and execute a separate task, even if you need only a single thread.

Introducing the Single-Thread Executor

Since `ExecutorService` is an interface, how do you obtain an instance of it? The Concurrency API includes the `Executors` factory class that can be used to create instances of the `ExecutorService` object. As you may remember from Chapter 2, "Design Patterns and Principles," the factory pattern is a creational pattern in which the underlying implementation details of the object creation are hidden from us. You will see the factory pattern used again throughout Chapter 9, "NIO.2."

Let's start with a simple example using the `newSingleThreadExecutor()` method to obtain an `ExecutorService` instance and the `execute()` method to perform asynchronous tasks:

```java
import java.util.concurrent.*;

public class ZooInfo {
    public static void main(String[] args) {
```

```
ExecutorService service = null;
try {
   service = Executors.newSingleThreadExecutor();

   System.out.println("begin");
   service.execute(() -> System.out.println("Printing zoo inventory"));
   service.execute(() -> {for(int i=0; i<3; i++)
      System.out.println("Printing record: "+i);}
   );
   service.execute(() -> System.out.println("Printing zoo inventory"));
   System.out.println("end");
} finally {
   if(service != null) service.shutdown();
}
   }
}
```

As you may notice, this is just a rewrite of our earlier PrintData and ReadInventoryThread classes to use Runnable-based lambda expressions and an ExecutorService instance.

In this example, we used the newSingleThreadExecutor() method, which is the simplest ExecutorService that we could create. Unlike our earlier example, in which we had three extra threads for newly created tasks, this example uses only one, which means that the threads will order their results. For example, the following is a possible output for this code snippet:

```
begin
Printing zoo inventory
Printing record: 0
Printing record: 1
end
Printing record: 2
Printing zoo inventory
```

With a single-thread executor, results are guaranteed to be executed in the order in which they are added to the executor service. Notice that the end text is output while our thread executor tasks are still running. This is because the main() method is still an independent thread from the ExecutorService, and it can perform tasks while the other thread is running.

Executing Multiple Tasks

In the previous example, it is possible that all three tasks were submitted for execution before the first task was even started. In this case, the single thread executor will queue the tasks and wait until the previous task completes before executing the next task.

Although tasks are guaranteed to be executed in the order in which they are submitted for a single-thread executor, you avoid relying on this behavior to order events. As you will see later in the chapter, when we increase the number of threads in the executor service, this guarantee disappears.

Shutting Down a Thread Executor

Once you have finished using a thread executor, it is important that you call the shutdown() method. A thread executor creates a non-daemon thread on the first task that is executed, so failing to call shutdown() will result in your application never terminating.

The shutdown process for a thread executor involves first rejecting any new tasks submitted to the thread executor while continuing to execute any previously submitted tasks. During this time, calling isShutdown() will return true, while isTerminated() will return false. If a new task is submitted to the thread executor while it is shutting down, a RejectedExecutionException will be thrown. Once all active tasks have been completed, isShutdown() and isTerminated() will both return true. Figure 7.2 shows the life cycle of an ExecutorService object.

FIGURE 7.2   ExecutorService life cycle

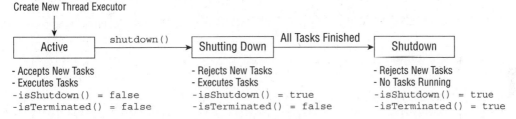

Create New Thread Executor

| Active | shutdown() → | Shutting Down | All Tasks Finished → | Shutdown |

- Accepts New Tasks
- Executes Tasks
- isShutdown() = false
- isTerminated() = false

- Rejects New Tasks
- Executes Tasks
- isShutdown() = true
- isTerminated() = false

- Rejects New Tasks
- No Tasks Running
- isShutdown() = true
- isTerminated() = true

For the exam, you should be aware that shutdown() does not actually stop any tasks that have already been submitted to the thread executor. What if you want to cancel all running and upcoming tasks? The ExecutorService provides a method called shutdownNow(), which attempts to stop all running tasks and discards any that have not been started yet. Note that shutdownNow() *attempts* to stop all running tasks. It is possible to create a thread that will never terminate, so any attempt to interrupt it may be ignored. Lastly, shutdownNow() returns a List<Runnable> of tasks that were submitted to the thread executor but that were never started.

Real World Scenario

Finally Shutting Down a Thread Executor

As you learned in Chapter 6, resources such as thread executors should be properly closed to prevent memory leaks. Unfortunately, the ExecutorService interface does not implement AutoCloseable, so you cannot use a try-with-resources statement. You can still use a finally block, as we do throughout this chapter. While not required, it is considered a good practice to do so.

```
ExecutorService service = null;
try {
    service = Executors.newSingleThreadExecutor();

    // Add tasks to thread executor
    …
} finally {
    if(service != null) service.shutdown();
}
```

Although this solution works for thread executors that are used once and thrown away, it does not work for thread executors that are persistent throughout the life of the application. For example, you can create a static instance of a thread executor and have all processes share it.

In such a scenario, you would need to define a static method that can be called anytime the user signals that they wish to exit the program. Remember that failure to shut down a thread executor after at least one thread has been created will result in the program hanging.

Submitting Tasks

You can submit tasks to an ExecutorService instance multiple ways. The first method we presented, execute(), is inherited from the Executor interface, which the ExecutorService interface extends. The execute() method takes a Runnable lambda expression or instance and completes the task asynchronously. Because the return type of the method is void, it does not tell us anything about the result of the task. It is considered a "fire-and-forget" method, as once it is submitted, the results are not directly available to the calling thread.

Fortunately, the writers of the Java added submit() methods to the ExecutorService interface, which, like execute(), can be used to complete tasks asynchronously. Unlike execute(), though, submit() returns a Future object that can be used to determine if the task is complete. It can also be used to return a generic result object after the task has been completed.

Table 7.2 shows the five methods, including execute() and two submit() methods, which you should know for the exam.

TABLE 7.2 ExecutorService methods

Method Name	Description
void execute(Runnable command)	Executes a Runnable task at some point in the future

Method Name	Description
`Future<?> submit(Runnable task)`	Executes a Runnable task at some point in the future and returns a Future representing the task
`<T> Future<T> submit(Callable<T> task)`	Executes a Callable task at some point in the future and returns a Future representing the pending results of the task

`<T> List<Future<T>> invokeAll(`
`Collection<? extends Callable<T>> tasks)`
`throws InterruptedException`
	Executes the given tasks, synchronously returning the results of all tasks as a Collection of Future objects, in the same order they were in the original collection

`<T> T invokeAny(`
`Collection<? extends Callable<T>> tasks)`
`throws InterruptedException,`
`ExecutionException`
	Executes the given tasks, synchronously returning the result of one of finished tasks, cancelling any unfinished tasks

In practice, using the submit() method is quite similar to using the execute() method, except that the submit() method return a Future object that can be used to determine whether or not the task has completed execution. Don't worry if you haven't seen Future or Callable before; we will discuss them in detail shortly.

Submitting Tasks: *execute()* vs *submit()*

As you might have noticed, the execute() and submit() methods are nearly identical when applied to Runnable expressions. The submit() method has the obvious advantage of doing the exact same thing execute() does, but with a return object that can be used to track the result. Because of this advantage and the fact that execute() does not support Callable expressions, we tend to prefer submit() over execute(), even if you don't store the Future reference. Therefore, we use submit() in the majority of the examples in this chapter.

For the exam, you need to be familiar with both execute() and submit(), but in your own code we recommend submit() over execute() whenever possible.

Submitting Task Collections

The last two methods listed in Table 7.2 that you should know for the exam are invokeAll() and invokeAny(). Both of these methods take a Collection object containing a list of tasks to execute. Both of these methods also execute synchronously. By synchronous, we mean that unlike the other methods used to submit tasks to a thread executor, these methods will wait until the results are available before returning control to the enclosing program.

The invokeAll() method executes all tasks in a provided collection and returns a List of ordered Future objects, with one Future object corresponding to each submitted task, in the order they were in the original collection. Even though Future.isDone() returns true for each element in the returned List, a task could have completed normally or thrown an exception.

The invokeAny() method executes a collection of tasks and returns the result of one of the tasks that successfully completes execution, cancelling all unfinished tasks. While the first task to finish is often returned, this behavior is not guaranteed, as any completed task can be returned by this method.

Finally, the invokeAll() method will wait indefinitely until all tasks are complete, while the invokeAny() method will wait indefinitely until at least one task completes. The ExecutorService interface also includes overloaded versions of invokeAll() and invokeAny() that take a timeout value and TimeUnit parameter. We will see how to use these types of parameters in the next section when discussing the Future class.

Waiting for Results

How do we know when a task submitted to an ExecutorService is complete? As mentioned in the last section, the submit() method returns a java.util.concurrent. Future<V> object, or Future<V> for short, that can be used to determine this result:

```
Future<?> future = service.submit(() -> System.out.println("Hello Zoo"));
```

The Future class includes methods that are useful in determining the state of a task, as shown in Table 7.3.

TABLE 7.3   Future methods

Method Name	Description
boolean isDone()	Returns true if the task was completed, threw an exception, or was cancelled.
boolean isCancelled()	Returns true if the task was cancelled before it completely normally.
boolean cancel()	Attempts to cancel execution of the task.
V get()	Retrieves the result of a task, waiting endlessly if it is not yet available.
V get(long timeout, TimeUnit unit)	Retrieves the result of a task, waiting the specified amount of time. If the result is not ready by the time the timeout is reached, a checked TimeoutException will be thrown.

The following is an updated version of our earlier polling example CheckResults class, which uses a Future instance to poll for the results:

```
import java.util.concurrent.*;
public class CheckResults {
   private static int counter = 0;
   public static void main(String[] args) throws InterruptedException,
                ExecutionException {
      ExecutorService service = null;
      try {
         service = Executors.newSingleThreadExecutor();
         Future<?> result = service.submit(() -> {
            for(int i=0; i<500; i++) CheckResults.counter++;
         });

         result.get(10, TimeUnit.SECONDS);
         System.out.println("Reached!");
      } catch (TimeoutException e) {
         System.out.println("Not reached in time");
      } finally {
         if(service != null) service.shutdown();
      }
   }
}
```

This example is similar to our earlier polling implementation, but it does not use the Thread class directly. In part, this is the essence of the Concurrency API: to do complex things with threads without using the Thread class directly. It also waits at most 10 seconds, throwing a TimeoutException if the task is not done.

What is the return value of this task? As Future<V> is a generic class, the type V is determined by the return type of the Runnable method. Since the return type of Runnable.run() is void, the get() method always returns null. In the next section, you will see that there is another task class compatible with ExecutorService that supports other return types.

As you saw in the previous example, the get() method can take an optional value and enum type java.util.concurrent.TimeUnit. We present the full list of TimeUnit values in Table 7.4 in increasing order of duration. Note that numerous methods in the Concurrency API use the TimeUnit enum.

TABLE 7.4   TimeUnit values

Enum Name	Description
TimeUnit.NANOSECONDS	Time in one-billionth of a second (1/1,000,000,000)
TimeUnit.MICROSECONDS	Time in one-millionth of a second (1/1,000,000)
TimeUnit.MILLISECONDS	Time in one-thousandth of a second (1/1,000)

TABLE 7.4 TimeUnit values *(continued)*

Enum Name	Description
TimeUnit.SECONDS	Time in seconds
TimeUnit.MINUTES	Time in minutes
TimeUnit.HOURS	Time in hours
TimeUnit.DAYS	Time in days

Introducing *Callable*

When the Concurrency API was released in Java 5, the new java.util.concurrent. Callable interface was added, or Callable for short, which is similar to Runnable except that its call() method returns a value and can throw a checked exception. As you may remember from the definition of Runnable, the run() method returns void and cannot throw any checked exceptions. Along with Runnable, Callable was also made a functional interface in Java 8. The following is the definition of the Callable interface:

```
@FunctionalInterface public interface Callable<V> {
   V call() throws Exception;
}
```

The Callable interface was introduced as an alternative to the Runnable interface, since it allows more details to be retrieved easily from the task after it is completed. The ExecutorService includes an overloaded version of the submit() method that takes a Callable object and returns a generic Future<T> object.

Ambiguous Lambda Expressions: *Callable* vs. *Supplier*

You may remember from Chapter 4 that the Callable functional interface strongly resembles the Supplier functional interface, in that they both take no arguments and return a generic type. One difference is that the method in Callable can throw a checked Exception. How do you tell lambda expressions for these two apart? The answer is sometimes you can't. Consider the following example, which uses the same lambda expression for three different method calls:

```
public class AmbiguousLambdaSample {
   public static void useCallable(Callable<Integer> expression) {}
```

```
    public static void useSupplier(Supplier<Integer> expression) {}

    public static void use(Supplier<Integer> expression) {}
    public static void use(Callable<Integer> expression) {}
    public static void main(String[] args) {
        useCallable(() -> {throw new IOException();});   // COMPILES
        useSupplier(() -> {throw new IOException();});   // DOES NOT COMPILE
        use(() -> {throw new IOException();});           // DOES NOT COMPILE
    }
}
```

The first line of the main() method compiles, as Callable is permitted to throw checked exceptions. The second line of the main() method does not compile, as Supplier does not support checked exceptions.

What about the last line? The use() method is overloaded to take both Callable and Supplier parameters. The compiler does not take into account the fact that the body of the lambda expression happens to throw an exception; therefore, it does not know how to tell them apart. As you might have already guessed, when the compiler doesn't know what to do, it reports an error and does not compile. When the compiler is unable to assign a functional interface to a lambda expression, it is referred to as an *ambiguous lambda expression*.

Note that the ambiguity can be resolved with an explicit cast. For example, the following corrected line of code does compile:

```
    use((Callable<Integer>)() -> {throw new IOException("");});  // COMPILES
```

With an explicit cast, the lambda expression is no longer ambiguous and the compiler can handle it without issue.

Unlike Runnable, in which the get() methods always return null, the get() methods on a Future object return the matching generic type or null.

Let's take a look at an example using Callable:

```
import java.util.concurrent.*;

public class AddData {
    public static void main(String[] args) throws InterruptedException,
            ExecutionException {
        ExecutorService service = null;
        try {
            service = Executors.newSingleThreadExecutor();
            Future<Integer> result = service.submit(() -> 30+11);
```

```
        System.out.println(result.get());
    } finally {
        if(service != null) service.shutdown();
    }
  }
}
```

We can now retrieve and print the output of the Callable results, 41 in this example. The results could have also been obtained using Runnable and some shared, possibly static, object, although this solution that relies on Callable is a lot simpler and easier to follow.

Since Callable supports a return type when used with ExecutorService, it is often preferred over Runnable when using the Concurrency API. That said, we use both interfaces throughout this chapter, as they are interchangeable in situations where the lambda does not throw an exception and there is no return type.

Checked Exceptions in *Callable* and *Runnable*

Besides having a return type, the Callable interface also supports checked exceptions, whereas the Runnable interface does not without an embedded try/catch block. Given an instance of ExecutorService called service, which of the following lines of code will or will not compile?

```
service.submit(() -> {Thread.sleep(1000); return null;});
service.submit(() -> {Thread.sleep(1000);});
```

The first line will compile, while the second line will not. Why? Recall that Thread. sleep() throws a checked InterruptedException. Since the first lambda expression has a return type, the compiler treats this as a Callable expression that supports checked exceptions. The second lambda expression does not return a value; therefore, the compiler treats this as a Runnable expression. Since Runnable methods do not support checked exceptions, the compiler will report an error trying to compile this code snippet.

Waiting for All Tasks to Finish

After submitting a set of tasks to a thread executor, it is common to wait for the results. As you saw in the previous sections, one solution is to call get() on each Future object returned by the submit() method. If we don't need the results of the tasks and are finished using our thread executor, there is a simpler approach.

First, we shut down the thread executor using the shutdown() method. Next, we use the awaitTermination(long timeout, TimeUnit unit) method available for all thread executors. The method waits the specified time to complete all tasks, returning sooner if all tasks finish or an InterruptedException is detected. You can see an example of this in the following code snippet:

```
ExecutorService service = null;
try {
   service = Executors.newSingleThreadExecutor();

   // Add tasks to the thread executor
   ...
} finally {
   if(service != null) service.shutdown();
}
if(service != null) {
   service.awaitTermination(1, TimeUnit.MINUTES);
   // Check whether all tasks are finished
   if(service.isTerminated())
      System.out.println("All tasks finished");
   else
      System.out.println("At least one task is still running");
}
```

In this example, we submit a number of tasks to the thread executor and then shut down the thread executor and wait up to one minute for the results. Notice that we can call isTerminated() after the awaitTermination() method finishes to confirm that all tasks are actually finished.

Scheduling Tasks

Oftentimes in Java, we need to schedule a task to happen at some future time. We might even need to schedule the task to happen repeatedly, at some set interval. For example, imagine that we want to check the supply of food for zoo animals once an hour and fill it as needed. The ScheduledExecutorService, which is a subinterface of ExecutorService, can be used for just such a task.

Like ExecutorService, we obtain an instance of ScheduledExecutorService using a factory method in the Executors class, as shown in the following snippet:

```
ScheduledExecutorService service = Executors.newSingleThreadScheduledExecutor();
```

Note that we could implicitly cast an instance of ScheduledExecutorService to ExecutorService, although doing so would remove access to the scheduled methods that we want to use.

Refer to Table 7.5 for our discussion of `ScheduledExecutorService` methods.

TABLE 7.5   ScheduledExecutorService methods

Method Name	Description
`schedule(Callable<V> callable, long delay, TimeUnit unit)`	Creates and executes a `Callable` task after the given delay
`schedule(Runnable command, long delay, TimeUnit unit)`	Creates and executes a `Runnable` task after the given delay
`scheduleAtFixedRate(Runnable command, long initialDelay, long period, TimeUnit unit)`	Creates and executes a `Runnable` task after the given initial delay, creating a new task every period value that passes.
`scheduleAtFixedDelay(Runnable command, long initialDelay, long delay, TimeUnit unit)`	Creates and executes a `Runnable` task after the given initial delay and subsequently with the given delay between the termination of one execution and the commencement of the next

In practice, these methods are among the most convenient in the Concurrency API, as they perform relatively complex tasks with a single line of code. The delay and period parameters rely on the `TimeUnit` argument to determine the format of the value, such as seconds or milliseconds.

The first two `schedule()` methods in Table 7.5 take a `Callable` or `Runnable`, respectively, perform the task after some delay, and return a `ScheduledFuture<V>` instance. `ScheduledFuture<V>` is identical to the `Future<V>` class, except that it includes a `getDelay()` method that returns the delay set when the process was created. The following uses the `schedule()` method with `Callable` and `Runnable` tasks:

```
ScheduledExecutorService service = Executors.newSingleThreadScheduledExecutor();

Runnable task1 = () -> System.out.println("Hello Zoo");
Callable<String> task2 = () -> "Monkey";

Future<?> result1 = service.schedule(task1, 10, TimeUnit.SECONDS);
Future<?> result2 = service.schedule(task2, 8, TimeUnit.MINUTES);
```

The first task is scheduled 10 seconds in the future, whereas the second task is scheduled 8 minutes in the future.

While these tasks are scheduled in the future, the actual execution may be delayed. For example, there may be no threads available to perform the task, at which point they will just wait in the queue. Also, if the `ScheduledExecutorService` is shut down by the time the scheduled task execution time is reached, they will be discarded.

The last two methods in Table 7.5 might be a little confusing if you have not seen them before. Conceptually, they are very similar as they both perform the same task repeatedly, after completing some initial delay. The difference is related to the timing of the process and when the next task starts.

The scheduleAtFixedRate() method creates a new task and submits it to the executor every period, regardless of whether or not the previous task finished. The following example executes a Runnable task every minute, following an initial five-minute delay:

```
service.scheduleAtFixedRate(command,5,1,TimeUnit.MINUTE);
```

One risk of using this method is the possibility a task could consistently take longer to run than the period between tasks. What would happen if the task consistently took five minutes to execute? Despite the fact that the task is still running, the ScheduledExecutorService would submit a new task to be started every minute. If a single-thread executor was used, over time this would result in endless set tasks being scheduled, which would run back to back assuming that no other tasks were submitted to the ScheduledExecutorService.

On the other hand, the scheduleAtFixedDelay() method creates a new task after the previous task has finished. For example, if the first task runs at 12:00 and takes five minutes to finish, with a period of 2 minutes, then the second task will start at 12:07.

```
service.scheduleAtFixedDelay(command,0,2,TimeUnit.MINUTE);
```

Notice that neither of the methods, scheduleAtFixedDelay() and scheduleAtFixedRate(), take a Callable object as an input parameter. Since these tasks are scheduled to run infinitely, as long as the ScheduledExecutorService is still alive, they would generate an endless series of Future objects.

Each of the ScheduledExecutorService methods is important and has real-world applications. For example, you can use the schedule() command to check on the state of processing a task and send out notifications if it is not finished or even call schedule() again to delay processing.

The scheduleAtFixedRate() is useful for tasks that need to be run at specific intervals, such as checking the health of the animals once a day. Even if it takes two hours to examine an animal on Monday, this doesn't mean that Tuesday's exam should start any later.

Finally, scheduleAtFixedDelay() is useful for processes that you want to happen repeatedly but whose specific time is unimportant. For example, imagine that we have a zoo cafeteria worker who periodically restocks the salad bar throughout the day. The process can take 20 minutes or more, since it requires the worker to haul a large number of items from the back room. Once the worker has filled the salad bar with fresh food, he doesn't need to check at some specific time, just after enough time has passed for it to become low on stock again.

If you are familiar with creating Cron jobs in Linux to schedule tasks, then you should know that scheduleAtFixedRate() is the closest built-in Java equivalent.

Increasing Concurrency with Pools

All of our examples up until now have been with single-thread executors, which, while interesting, weren't particularly useful. After all, the name of this chapter is "Concurrency," and you can't do a lot of that with a single-thread executor!

We now present three additional factory methods in the Executors class that act on a pool of threads, rather than on a single thread. A *thread pool* is a group of pre-instantiated reusable threads that are available to perform a set of arbitrary tasks. Table 7.6 includes our two previous single-thread executor methods, along with the new ones that you should know for the exam.

TABLE 7.6   Executors methods

Method Name	Return Type	Description
newSingleThreadExecutor()	ExecutorService	Creates a single-threaded executor that uses a single worker thread operating off an unbounded queue. Results are processed sequentially in the order in which they are submitted.
newSingleThreadScheduled Executor()	Scheduled ExecutorService	Creates a single-threaded executor that can schedule commands to run after a given delay or to execute periodically.
newCachedThreadPool()	ExecutorService	Creates a thread pool that creates new threads as needed, but will reuse previously constructed threads when they are available.
newFixedThreadPool(int nThreads)	ExecutorService	Creates a thread pool that reuses a fixed number of threads operating off a shared unbounded queue.
newScheduledThreadPool(int nThreads)	Scheduled ExecutorService	Creates a thread pool that can schedule commands to run after a given delay or to execute periodically.

As shown in Table 7.6, these methods return the exact same instance types, ExecutorService and ScheduledExecutorService, that we used earlier in this chapter. In other words, all of our previous examples are compatible with these new pooled-thread executors! There are also overloaded versions of each of the methods in Table 7.6 that create threads using a ThreadFactory input parameter. For the exam, you are only required to know the methods to create thread executors in Table 7.6.

The difference between a single-thread and a pooled-thread executor is what happens when a task is already running. While a single-thread executor will wait for an available thread to become available before running the next task, a pooled-thread executor can execute the next task concurrently. If the pool runs out of available threads, the task will be queued by the thread executor and wait to be completed.

The newCachedThreadPool() method will create a thread pool of unbounded size, allocating a new thread anytime one is required or all existing threads are busy. This is commonly used for pools that require executing many short-lived asynchronous tasks. For long-lived processes, usage of this executor is strongly discouraged, as it could grow to encompass a large number of threads over the application life cycle.

The newFixedThreadPool() takes a number of threads and allocates them all upon creation. As long as our number of tasks is less than our number of threads, all tasks will be executed concurrently. If at any point the number of tasks exceeds the number of threads in the pool, they will wait in similar manner as you saw with a single-thread executor. In fact, calling newFixedThreadPool() with a value of 1 is equivalent to calling newSingleThreadExecutor().

The newScheduledThreadPool() is identical to the newFixedThreadPool() method, except that it returns an instance of ScheduledExecutorService and is therefore compatible with scheduling tasks. This executor has subtle differences in the way that the scheduleAtFixedRate() performs. For example, recall our previous example in which tasks took five minutes to complete:

```
ScheduledExecutorService service = Executors.newScheduledThreadPool(10);
service.scheduleAtFixedRate(command,3,1,TimeUnit.MINUTE);
```

Whereas with a single-thread executor and a five-minute task execution time, an endless set of tasks would be scheduled over time. With a pooled executor, this can be avoided. If the pool size is sufficiently large, 10 for example, then as each thread finishes, it is returned to the pool and results in new threads available for the next tasks as they come up.

 Real World Scenario

Choosing a Pool Size

In practice, it can be quite difficult to choose an appropriate pool size. In general, you want at least a handful more threads than you think you will ever possibly need. On the other hand, you don't want to choose so many threads that your application uses up too many resources or too much CPU processing power. Oftentimes, the number of CPUs available is used to determine the thread size using this command:

```
Runtime.getRuntime().availableProcessors()
```

It is a common practice to allocate thread pools based on the number of CPUs, as well as how CPU intensive the task is. For example, if you are performing very CPU-intensive tasks, then creating a 16-thread pool in a 2-CPU computer will cause the computer to perform quite slowly, as your process is chewing up most of the CPU bandwidth available for other applications. Alternatively, if your tasks involve reading/writing data from disk or a network, a 16-thread pool may be appropriate, since most of the waiting involves external resources.

Fortunately, most tasks are dependent on some other resources, such as a database, file system, or network. In those situations, creating large thread pools is generally safe, as the tasks are not CPU intensive and may involve a lot of waiting for external resources to become available.

Synchronizing Data Access

Recall that thread safety is the property of an object that guarantees safe execution by multiple threads at the same time. Now that we have multiple threads capable of accessing the same objects in memory, we have to make sure to organize our access to this data such that we don't end up with invalid or unexpected results. Since threads run in a shared environment and memory space, how do we prevent two threads from interfering with each other?

Imagine that our zoo has a program to count sheep, preferably one that won't put the zoo workers to sleep! Each zoo worker runs out to a field, adds a new sheep to the flock, counts the total number of sheep, and runs back to us to report the results. We present the following code to represent this conceptually:

```java
import java.util.concurrent.*;

public class SheepManager {

   private int sheepCount = 0;
   private void incrementAndReport() {
      System.out.print((++sheepCount)+" ");
   }

   public static void main(String[] args) {
      ExecutorService service = null;
      try {
         service = Executors.newFixedThreadPool(20);

         SheepManager manager = new SheepManager();
         for(int i=0; i<10; i++)
            service.submit(() -> manager.incrementAndReport());
      } finally {
         if(service != null) service.shutdown();
      }
   }
}
```

Notice that we use the pre-increment ++ operator to update the sheepCount variable. Remember that the pre-increment operator is shorthand for the following expression in which the newly assigned value is returned:

```
sheepCount = sheepCount + 1;
```

A problem occurs when two threads both execute the right side of the expression, reading the "old" value before either thread writes the "new" value of the variable. The two assignments become redundant; they both assign the same new value, with one thread overwriting the results of the other. Figure 7.3 demonstrates this problem with two threads, assuming that sheepCount has a starting value of 1.

FIGURE 7.3   Lack of thread synchronization

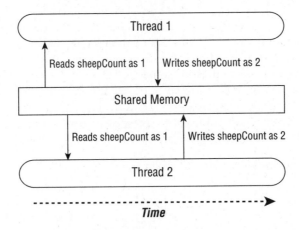

You can see in Figure 7.3 that both threads read and write the same values, causing one of the two ++sheepCount operations to be lost. Therefore, the increment operator ++ is not thread-safe. As you will see later in this chapter, the unexpected result of two tasks executing at the same time is referred to as a *race condition*.

Returning to our SheepManager application, we choose a large thread size of 20 so that all tasks can be run concurrently. Let's say that each lambda expression submitted to the thread executor corresponds to a zoo worker. Each time a zoo worker increments the sheep counter, they run back to report the results. What would you expect the output of this program to be? Although the output will vary, the following are some samples created by this program:

```
1 2 2 3 4 5 6 7 8 9

2 4 5 6 7 8 1 9 10 3

2 1 3 4 5 6 7 8 9 10
```

In this example, multiple workers are sharing the sheepCount variable. In the first sample, two zoo workers both call ++sheepCount at the same time, resulting in one of the increment operations actually being lost, with the last total being 9 instead of 10. In the other examples, results from earlier threads are output before ones that started later, such as 3 being output after 4 in the second example. We know that we had 10 workers, but the results are incomplete and out of order.

The idea here is that some zoo workers may run faster on their way to the field but more slowly on their way back and report late. Others may get to the field last but somehow be the first ones back to report the results.

Protecting Data with Atomic Classes

With the release of the Concurrency API, Java added a new java.util.concurrent.atomic package to help coordinate access to primitive values and object references. As with most classes in the Concurrency API, these classes are added solely for convenience.

In our first SheepManager sample output, the same value, 2, was printed twice, with the highest counter being 9 instead of 10. As we demonstrated in the previous section, the increment operator ++ is not thread-safe. Furthermore, the reason that it is not thread-safe is that the operation is not atomic, carrying out two tasks, read and write, that can be interrupted by other threads.

Atomic is the property of an operation to be carried out as a single unit of execution without any interference by another thread. A thread-safe atomic version of the increment operator would be one that performed the read and write of the variable as a single operation, not allowing any other threads to access the variable during the operation. Figure 7.4 shows the result of making the sheepCount variable atomic.

FIGURE 7.4   Thread synchronization using atomic operations

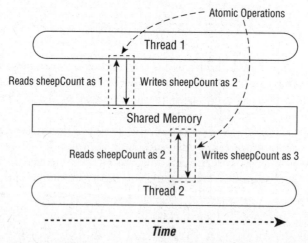

Figure 7.4 resembles our earlier Figure 7.3, except that reading and writing the data is atomic with regard to the sheepCount variable. Any thread trying to access the sheepCount variable while an atomic operation is in process will have to wait until the atomic operation on the variable is complete. Of course, this exclusivity applies only to the threads trying to access the sheepCount variable, with the rest of the memory space not affected by this operation.

Since accessing primitives and references in Java is common in shared environments, the Concurrency API includes numerous useful classes that are conceptually the same as our primitive classes but that support atomic operations. Table 7.7 lists the atomic classes with which you should be familiar for the exam.

TABLE 7.7   Atomic classes

Class Name	Description
AtomicBoolean	A boolean value that may be updated atomically
AtomicInteger	An int value that may be updated atomically
AtomicIntegerArray	An int array in which elements may be updated atomically
AtomicLong	A long value that may be updated atomically
AtomicLongArray	A long array in which elements may be updated atomically
AtomicReference	A generic object reference that may be updated atomically
AtomicReferenceArray	An array of generic object references in which elements may be updated atomically

How do we use an atomic class? Each class includes numerous methods that are equivalent to many of the primitive built-in operators that we use on primitives, such as the assignment operator = and the increment operators ++. We describe the common atomic methods that you should know for the exam in Table 7.8.

TABLE 7.8   Common atomic methods

Class Name	Description
get()	Retrieve the current value
set()	Set the given value, equivalent to the assignment = operator
getAndSet()	Atomically sets the new value and returns the old value
incrementAndGet()	For numeric classes, atomic pre-increment operation equivalent to ++value
getAndIncrement()	For numeric classes, atomic post-increment operation equivalent to value++
decrementAndGet()	For numeric classes, atomic pre-decrement operation equivalent to --value
getAndDecrement()	For numeric classes, atomic post-decrement operation equivalent to value--

In the following example, we update our SheepManager class with an AtomicInteger:

```java
private AtomicInteger sheepCount = new AtomicInteger(0);
    private void incrementAndReport() {
        System.out.print(sheepCount.incrementAndGet()+" ");
    }
```

How does this implementation differ from our previous examples? When we run this modification, we get varying output, such as the following:

```
2 3 1 4 5 6 7 8 9 10

1 4 3 2 5 6 7 8 9 10

1 4 3 5 6 2 7 8 10 9
```

Unlike our previous sample output, the numbers 1 through 10 will always be output. As you might notice, the results are still not ordered, although we'll get to that soon enough. The key here is that using the atomic classes ensures that the data is consistent between workers and that no values are lost due to concurrent modifications.

Improving Access with Synchronized Blocks

How do we improve the results so that each worker is able to increment and report the results in order? The most common technique is to use a monitor, also called a *lock*, to synchronize access. A *monitor* is a structure that supports mutual exclusion or the property that at most one thread is executing a particular segment of code at a given time.

In Java, any Object can be used as a monitor, along with the synchronized keyword, as shown in the following example:

```java
SheepManager manager = new SheepManager();
synchronized(manager) {
    // Work to be completed by one thread at a time
}
```

This example is referred to as a *synchronized block*. Each thread that arrives will first check if any threads are in the block. In this manner, a thread "acquires the lock" for the monitor. If the lock is available, a single thread will enter the block, acquiring the lock and preventing all other threads from entering. While the first thread is executing the block, all threads that arrive will attempt to acquire the same lock and wait for first thread to finish. Once a thread finishes executing the block, it will release the lock, allowing one of the waiting threads to proceed.

NOTE

In order to synchronize access across multiple threads, each thread must have access to the same Object. For example, synchronizing on different objects would not actually organize the results.

Let's revisit our SheepManager example and see if we can improve the results so that each worker increments and outputs the counter in order. Let's say that we replaced our for() loop with the following implementation:

```
for(int i=0; i<10; i++) {
    synchronized(manager) {
        service.submit(() -> manager.incrementAndReport());
    }
}
```

Does this solution fix the problem? No, it does not! Can you spot the problem? We've synchronized the *creation* of the threads but not the *execution* of the threads. In this example, each thread would be created one at a time, but they may all still execute and perform their work at the same time, resulting in the same type of output that you saw earlier. Diagnosing and resolving threading problems is often one of the most difficult tasks in any programming language.

We now present a corrected version of the SheepManager class, which does order the workers:

```
import java.util.concurrent.*;

public class SheepManager {

    private int sheepCount = 0;
    private void incrementAndReport() {
        synchronized(this) {
            System.out.print((++sheepCount)+" ");
        }
    }

    public static void main(String[] args) {
        ExecutorService service = null;
        try {
            service = Executors.newFixedThreadPool(20);

            SheepManager manager = new SheepManager();
            for(int i=0; i<10; i++)
                service.submit(() -> manager.incrementAndReport());
        } finally {
            if(service != null) service.shutdown();
        }
    }
}
```

When this code executes, it will consistently output the following:

```
1 2 3 4 5 6 7 8 9 10
```

Although all threads are still created and executed at the same time, they each wait at the synchronized block for the worker to increment and report the result before entering. In this manner, each zoo worker waits for the previous zoo worker to come back before running out on the field. While it's random which zoo worker will run out next, it is guaranteed that there will be at most one on the field.

We could have synchronized on any object, so long as it was the same object. For example, the following code snippet would have also worked:

```java
private final Object lock = new Object();
private void incrementAndReport() {
    synchronized(lock) {
        System.out.print((++sheepCount)+" ");
    }
}
```

Although we didn't need to make the lock variable final, doing so ensures that it is not reassigned after threads start using it.

We could have used an atomic count variable along with the synchronized block in this example, although it is unnecessary. Since synchronized blocks allow only one thread to enter, we're not gaining any improvement by using an atomic variable if the only time that we access the variable is within a synchronized block.

Synchronizing Methods

In the previous example, we established our monitor using synchronized(this) around the body of the method. Java actually provides a more convenient compiler enhancement for doing so. We can add the synchronized modifier to any instance method to synchronize automatically on the object itself. For example, the following two method definitions are equivalent:

```java
private void incrementAndReport() {
    synchronized(this) {
        System.out.print((++sheepCount)+" ");
    }
}

private synchronized void incrementAndReport() {
    System.out.print((++sheepCount)+" ");
}
```

The first uses a synchronized block, whereas the second uses the synchronized method modifier. Which you use is completely up to you.

We can also add the synchronized modifier to static methods. What object is used as the monitor when we synchronize on a static method? The class object, of course! For example, the following two methods are equivalent for static synchronization inside our SheepManager class:

```
public static void printDaysWork() {
    synchronized(SheepManager.class) {
        System.out.print("Finished work");
    }
}

public static synchronized void printDaysWork() {
    System.out.print("Finished work");
}
```

As before, the first uses a synchronized block, with the second example using the synchronized modifier. You can use static synchronization if you need to order thread access across all instances, rather than a single instance.

Understanding the Cost of Synchronization

We complete this section by noting that synchronization, while useful, may be costly in practice. While multi-threaded programming is about doing multiple things at the same time, synchronization is about taking multiple threads and making them perform in a more single-threaded manner.

For example, let's say that we have a highly concurrent class with numerous methods that synchronize on the same object. Let's say that 50 concurrent threads access it. Let's also say that, on average, each thread takes a modest 100 milliseconds to execute.

In this example, if all of the threads try to access the monitor at the same time, how long will it take for them to complete their work, assuming that 50 threads are available in the thread pool?

```
50 threads x 100 milliseconds
    = 5,000 milliseconds
    = 5 seconds
```

Even though five seconds may not seem like a lot, it's actually pretty long in computer time. What if 50 new tasks are created before the five seconds are up? This will pile onto the workload, resulting in most threads constantly entering a waiting or "stuck" state. In the application, this may cause tasks that would normally be quick to finish in a non-synchronized environment to take a significantly long amount of time to complete.

Synchronization is about protecting data integrity at the cost of performance. In many cases, performance costs are minimal, but in extreme scenarios the application could slow down significantly due to the inclusion of synchronization. Being able to identify synchronization problems, including finding ways to improve performance in synchronized multi-threaded environments, is a valuable skill in practice.

Using Concurrent Collections

Besides managing threads, the Concurrency API includes interfaces and classes that help you coordinate access to collections across multiple tasks. By collections, we are of course referring to the Java Collections Framework that we introduced in Chapter 3, "Generics and Collections." In this section, we will demonstrate many of the new concurrent classes available to you when using the Concurrency API.

Introducing Concurrent Collections

The first question you might be asking is "Do we really need new concurrent collection classes?" After all, in the previous section you saw that we can use the synchronized keyword on any method or block, so couldn't we do the same for our existing collection classes? The short answer is "We could." For example, take a look at the following code that accesses a Map using the synchronized keyword:

```
public class ZooManager {
    private Map<String,Object> foodData = new HashMap<String,Object>();
    public synchronized void put(String key, String value) {
        foodData.put(key, value);
    }
    public synchronized Object get(String key) {
        return foodData.get(key);
    }
}
```

So then, why use a concurrent collection class? Like using ExecutorService to manage threads for us, using the concurrent collections is extremely convenient in practice. It also prevents us from introducing mistakes in own custom implementation, such as if we forgot to synchronize one of the accessor methods. In fact, the concurrent collections often include performance enhancements that avoid unnecessary synchronization. Accessing collections from across multiple threads is so common that the writers of Java thought it would be a good idea to have alternate versions of many of the regular collections classes just for multi-threaded access.

The following is an alternate version of our implementation that does not use the synchronized keyword but instead uses a concurrent collection class:

```
public class ZooManager {
    private Map<String,Object> foodData = new ConcurrentHashMap<String,Object>();
```

```
    public void put(String key, String value) {
        foodData.put(key, value);
    }
    public Object get(String key) {
        return foodData.get(key);
    }
}
```

You might notice that this code is nearly identical to our previous implementation. In fact, even our reference type for the object, Map, remained unchanged. As you may remember from our discussion of polymorphism in Chapter 2, even though the reference type changes, the underlying object is still a ConcurrentHashMap. Also, notice that since ConcurrentHashMap implements Map, it uses the same get()/put() methods. Therefore, there is no need to use the ConcurrentHashMap reference type in this example.

Understanding Memory Consistency Errors

The purpose of the concurrent collection classes is to solve common memory consistency errors. A *memory consistency error* occurs when two threads have inconsistent views of what should be the same data. Conceptually, we want writes on one thread to be available to another thread if it accesses the concurrent collection after the write has occurred.

When two threads try to modify the same non-concurrent collection, the JVM may throw a ConcurrentModificationException at runtime. In fact, it can happen with a single thread. Take a look at the following code snippet:

```
Map<String, Object> foodData = new HashMap<String, Object>();
foodData.put("penguin", 1);
foodData.put("flamingo", 2);
for(String key: foodData.keySet())
    foodData.remove(key);
```

This snippet will throw a ConcurrentModificationException at runtime, since the iterator keyset() is not properly updated after the first element is removed. Changing the first line to use a ConcurrentHashMap will prevent the code from throwing an exception at runtime:

```
Map<String, Object> foodData = new ConcurrentHashMap<String, Object>();
foodData.put("penguin", 1);
foodData.put("flamingo", 2);
for(String key: foodData.keySet())
    foodData.remove(key);
```

Although we don't usually modify a loop variable, this example highlights the fact that the ConcurrentHashMap is ordering read/write access such that all access to the class is consistent. In this code snippet, the iterator created by keySet() is updated as soon as an object is removed from the Map.

The concurrent classes were created to help avoid common issues in which multiple threads are adding and removing objects from the same collections. At any given instance, all threads should have the same consistent view of the structure of the collection.

Working with Concurrent Classes

There are numerous collection classes with which you should be familiar for the exam. Luckily, you already know how to use most of them, as the methods available are a superset to the non-concurrent collection classes that you learned about in Chapter 3.

You should use a concurrent collection class anytime that you are going to have multiple threads modify a collections object outside a synchronized block or method, even if you don't expect a concurrency problem. On the other hand, if all of the threads are accessing an established immutable or read-only collection, a concurrent collection class is not required.

In the same way that we instantiate an ArrayList object but pass around a List reference, it is considered a good practice to instantiate a concurrent collection but pass it around using a non-concurrent interface whenever possible. This has some similarities with the factory pattern that you learned about in Chapter 2, as the users of these objects may not be aware of the underlying implementation. In some cases, the callers may need to know that it is a concurrent collection so that a concurrent interface or class is appropriate, but for the majority of circumstances, that distinction is not necessary.

Table 7.9 lists the common concurrent classes with which you should be familiar for the exam.

TABLE 7.9   Concurrent collection classes

Class Name	Java Collections Framework Interface	Elements Ordered?	Sorted?	Blocking?
ConcurrentHashMap	ConcurrentMap	No	No	No
ConcurrentLinkedDeque	Deque	Yes	No	No
ConcurrentLinkedQueue	Queue	Yes	No	No
ConcurrentSkipListMap	ConcurrentMap SortedMap NavigableMap	Yes	Yes	No
ConcurrentSkipListSet	SortedSet NavigableSet	Yes	Yes	No
CopyOnWriteArrayList	List	Yes	No	No
CopyOnWriteArraySet	Set	No	No	No
LinkedBlockingDeque	BlockingQueue BlockingDeque	Yes	No	Yes
LinkedBlockingQueue	BlockingQueue	Yes	No	Yes

Based on your knowledge of collections from Chapter 3, classes like `ConcurrentHashMap`, `ConcurrentLinkedQueue`, and `ConcurrentLinkedDeque` should be quite easy for you to learn. Take a look at the following code samples:

```
Map<String,Integer> map = new ConcurrentHashMap<>();
map.put("zebra", 52);
map.put("elephant", 10);
System.out.println(map.get("elephant"));

Queue<Integer> queue = new ConcurrentLinkedQueue<>();
queue.offer(31);
System.out.println(queue.peek());
System.out.println(queue.poll());

Deque<Integer> deque = new ConcurrentLinkedDeque<>();
deque.offer(10);
deque.push(4);
System.out.println(deque.peek());
System.out.println(deque.pop());
```

As you may have noticed, these samples strongly resemble the collections snippets that you saw earlier in this book, with the only difference being the object creation call. In each of the samples, we assign an interface reference to the newly created object and use it the same way as we would a non-concurrent object.

The `ConcurrentHashMap` implements the `ConcurrentMap` interface, also found in the Concurrency API. You can use either reference type, `Map` or `ConcurrentMap`, to access a `ConcurrentHashMap` object, depending on whether or not you want the caller to know anything about the underlying implementation. For example, a method signature may require a `ConcurrentMap` reference to ensure that object passed to it is properly supported in a multi-threaded environment.

Understanding Blocking Queues

As you may have noticed, Table 7.9 included two queue classes that implement blocking interfaces: `LinkedBlockingQueue` and `LinkedBlockingDeque`. The `BlockingQueue` is just like a regular `Queue`, except that it includes methods that will wait a specific amount of time to complete an operation.

Since `BlockingQueue` inherits all of the methods from `Queue`, we skip the inherited methods and present the new waiting methods in Table 7.10.

TABLE 7.10   BlockingQueue waiting methods

Method Name	Description
`offer(E e, long timeout, TimeUnit unit)`	Adds item to the queue waiting the specified time, returning `false` if time elapses before space is available

TABLE 7.10 BlockingQueue waiting methods *(continued)*

Method Name	Description
poll(long timeout, TimeUnit unit)	Retrieves and removes an item from the queue, waiting the specified time, returning null if the time elapses before the item is available

A LinkedBlockingQueue, as the name implies, maintains a linked list between elements. The following sample is using a LinkedBlockingQueue to wait for the results of some of the operations. The methods in Table 7.10 can each throw a checked InterruptedException, as they can be interrupted before they finish waiting for a result; therefore they must be properly caught.

```
try {
    BlockingQueue<Integer> blockingQueue = new LinkedBlockingQueue<>();

    blockingQueue.offer(39);
    blockingQueue.offer(3, 4, TimeUnit.SECONDS);

    System.out.println(blockingQueue.poll());
    System.out.println(blockingQueue.poll(10, TimeUnit.MILLISECONDS));
} catch (InterruptedException e) {
    // Handle interruption
}
```

As shown in this example, since LinkedBlockingQueue implements both Queue and BlockingQueue, we can use methods available to both, such as those that don't take any wait arguments.

Table 7.9 also includes the LinkedBlockingDeque class that maintains a doubly linked list between elements and implements a BlockingDeque interface. The BlockingDeque interface extends Deque much in the same way that BlockingQueue extends Queue, providing numerous waiting methods. Refer to Table 7.11 for the waiting methods defined in BlockingDeque.

TABLE 7.11 BlockingDeque waiting methods

Method Name	Description
offerFirst(E e, long timeout, TimeUnit unit)	Adds an item to the front of the queue, waiting a specified time, returning false if time elapses before space is available
offerLast(E e, long timeout, TimeUnit unit)	Adds an item to the tail of the queue, waiting a specified time, returning false if time elapses before space is available

Method Name	Description
pollFirst(long timeout, TimeUnit unit)	Retrieves and removes an item from the front of the queue, waiting the specified time, returning null if the time elapses before the item is available
pollLast(long timeout, TimeUnit unit)	Retrieves and removes an item from the tail of the queue, waiting the specified time, returning null if the time elapses before the item is available

The following is a sample of using a LinkedBlockingDeque. As before, since the methods in Table 7.11 each throw a checked InterruptedException, they must be properly caught in the code that uses them.

```
try {
    BlockingDeque<Integer> blockingDeque = new LinkedBlockingDeque<>();

    blockingDeque.offer(91);
    blockingDeque.offerFirst(5, 2, TimeUnit.MINUTES);
    blockingDeque.offerLast(47, 100, TimeUnit.MICROSECONDS);
    blockingDeque.offer(3, 4, TimeUnit.SECONDS);

    System.out.println(blockingDeque.poll());
    System.out.println(blockingDeque.poll(950, TimeUnit.MILLISECONDS));
    System.out.println(blockingDeque.pollFirst(200, TimeUnit.NANOSECONDS));
    System.out.println(blockingDeque.pollLast(1, TimeUnit.SECONDS));
} catch (InterruptedException e) {
    // Handle interruption
}
```

This example creates a LinkedBlockingDeque and assigns it to a BlockingDeque reference. Since BlockingDeque extends Queue, Deque, and BlockingQueue, all of the previously defined queue methods are available for use.

Understanding *SkipList* Collections

The SkipList classes, ConcurrentSkipListSet and ConcurrentSkipListMap, are concurrent versions of their sorted counterparts, TreeSet and TreeMap, respectively. They maintain their elements or keys in the natural ordering of their elements. When you see SkipList or SkipSet on the exam, just think "sorted" concurrent collections and the rest should follow naturally.

Like other queue examples, it is recommended that you assign these objects to interface references, such as SortedMap or NavigableSet. In this manner, using them is the same as the code that you worked with in Chapter 3.

Understanding *CopyOnWrite* Collections

Table 7.9 included two classes, CopyOnWriteArrayList and CopyOnWriteArraySet, that behave a little differently than the other concurrent examples that you have seen. These classes copy all of their elements to a new underlying structure anytime an element is added, modified, or removed from the collection. By a *modified* element, we mean that the reference in the collection is changed. Modifying the actual contents of the collection will not cause a new structure to be allocated.

Although the data is copied to a new underlying structure, our reference to the object does not change. This is particularly useful in multi-threaded environments that need to iterate the collection. Any iterator established prior to a modification will not see the changes, but instead it will iterate over the original elements prior to the modification.

Let's take a look at how this works with an example:

```
List<Integer> list = new CopyOnWriteArrayList<>(Arrays.asList(4,3,52));
for(Integer item: list) {
    System.out.print(item+" ");
    list.add(9);
}
System.out.println();
System.out.println("Size: "+list.size());
```

When executed as part of a program, this code snippet outputs the following:

```
4 3 52
Size: 6
```

Despite adding elements to the array while iterating over it, only those elements in the collection at the time the for() loop was created were accessed. Alternatively, if we had used a regular ArrayList object, a ConcurrentModificationException would have been thrown at runtime. With either class, though, we avoid entering an infinite loop in which elements are constantly added to the array as we iterate over them.

> The CopyOnWrite classes are similar to the immutable object pattern that you saw in Chapter 2, as a new underlying structure is created every time the collection is modified. Unlike the immutable object pattern, though, the reference to the object stays the same even while the underlying data is changed. Therefore, strictly speaking, this is not an immutable object pattern, although it shares many similarities.

The CopyOnWrite classes can use a lot of memory, since a new collection structure needs be allocated anytime the collection is modified. They are commonly used in multi-threaded environment situations where reads are far more common than writes.

Obtaining Synchronized Collections

Besides the concurrent collection classes that we have covered, the Concurrency API also includes methods for obtaining synchronized versions of existing non-concurrent collection objects. These methods, defined in the Collections class, contain synchronized methods that operate on the inputted collection and return a reference that is the same type as the underlying collection. We list these methods in Table 7.12.

TABLE 7.12   Synchronized collections methods

Method Name
synchronizedCollection(Collection<T> c)
synchronizedList(List<T> list)
synchronizedMap(Map<K,V> m)
synchronizedNavigableMap(NavigableMap<K,V> m)
synchronizedNavigableSet(NavigableSet<T> s)
synchronizedSet(Set<T> s)
synchronizedSortedMap(SortedMap<K,V> m)
synchronizedSortedSet(SortedSet<T> s)

When should you use these methods? If you know at the time of creation that your object requires synchronization, then you should use one of the concurrent collection classes listed in Table 7.9. On the other hand, if you are given an existing collection that is not a concurrent class and need to access it among multiple threads, you can wrap it using the methods in Table 7.12.

While the methods in Table 7.12 synchronize access to the data elements, such as the get() and set() methods, they do not synchronize access on any iterators that you may create from the synchronized collection. Therefore, it is imperative that you use a synchronization block if you need to iterate over any of the returned collections in Table 7.12, as shown in the following example:

```
List<Integer> list = Collections.synchronizedList(
   new ArrayList<>(Arrays.asList(4,3,52)));
synchronized(list) {
   for(int data: list)
      System.out.print(data+" ");
}
```

Unlike the concurrent collections, the synchronized collections also throw an exception if they are modified within an iterator by a single thread. For example, take a look at the following modification of our earlier example:

```
Map<String, Object> foodData = new HashMap<String, Object>();
foodData.put("penguin", 1);
foodData.put("flamingo", 2);
Map<String,Object> synchronizedFoodData = Collections.synchronizedMap(foodData);
for(String key: synchronizedFoodData.keySet())
    synchronizedFoodData.remove(key);
```

This code throws a ConcurrentModificationException at runtime, whereas our example that used ConcurrentHashMap did not. Other than iterating over the collection, the objects returned by the methods in Table 7.12 are inherently safe to use among multiple threads.

Working with Parallel Streams

In Chapter 4, you learned that the Streams API enabled functional programming in Java 8. One of the most powerful features of the Streams API is that it has built-in concurrency support. Up until now, all of the streams with which you have worked have been serial streams. A *serial stream* is a stream in which the results are ordered, with only one entry being processed at a time.

A *parallel stream* is a stream that is capable of processing results concurrently, using multiple threads. For example, you can use a parallel stream and the stream map() method to operate concurrently on the elements in the stream, vastly improving performance over processing a single element at a time.

Using a parallel stream can change not only the performance of your application but also the expected results. As you shall see, some operations also require special handling to be able to be processed in a parallel manner.

By default, the number of threads available in a parallel stream is related to the number of available CPUs in your environment. In order to increase the thread count, you would need to create your own custom class.

Creating Parallel Streams

The Streams API was designed to make creating parallel streams quite easy. For the exam, you should be familiar with the two ways of creating a parallel stream.

parallel()

The first way to create a parallel stream is from an existing stream. You just call parallel() on an existing stream to convert it to one that supports multi-threaded processing, as shown in the following code:

```
Stream<Integer> stream = Arrays.asList(1,2,3,4,5,6).stream();
Stream<Integer> parallelStream = stream.parallel();
```

Be aware that parallel() is an intermediate operation that operates on the original stream.

parallelStream()

The second way to create a parallel stream is from a Java collection class. The Collection interface includes a method parallelStream() that can be called on any collection and returns a parallel stream. The following is a revised code snippet that creates the parallel stream directly from the List object:

```
Stream<Integer> parallelStream2 = Arrays.asList(1,2,3,4,5,6).parallelStream();
```

We will use parallelStream() on Collection objects throughout this section.

The Stream interface includes a method isParallel() that can be used to test if the instance of a stream supports parallel processing. Some operations on streams preserve the parallel attribute, while others do not. For example, the Stream.concat(Stream s1, Stream s2) is parallel if either s1 or s2 is parallel. On the other hand, flatMap() creates a new stream that is not parallel by default, regardless of whether the underlying elements were parallel.

Processing Tasks in Parallel

As you may have noticed, creating the parallel stream is the easy part. The interesting part comes in using it. Let's take a look at a serial example:

```
Arrays.asList(1,2,3,4,5,6)
   .stream()
   .forEach(s -> System.out.print(s+" "));
```

What do you think this code will output when executed as part of a main() method? Let's take a look:

```
1 2 3 4 5 6
```

As you might expect, the results are ordered and predictable because we are using a serial stream. What happens if we use a parallel stream, though?

```
Arrays.asList(1,2,3,4,5,6)
   .parallelStream()
   .forEach(s -> System.out.print(s+" "));
```

With a parallel stream, the forEach() operation is applied across multiple elements of the stream concurrently. The following are each sample outputs of this code snippet:

```
4 1 6 5 2 3
```

```
5 2 1 3 6 4
```

```
1 2 6 4 5 3
```

As you can see, the results are no longer ordered or predictable. If you compare this to earlier parts of the chapter, the forEach() operation on a parallel stream is equivalent to submitting multiple Runnable lambda expressions to a pooled thread executor.

Ordering forEach Results

The Streams API includes an alternate version of the forEach() operation called forEachOrdered(), which forces a parallel stream to process the results in order at the cost of performance. For example, take a look at the following code snippet:

```
Arrays.asList(1,2,3,4,5,6)
   .parallelStream()
   .forEachOrdered(s -> System.out.print(s+" "));
```

Like our starting example, this outputs the results in order:

```
1 2 3 4 5 6
```

Since we have ordered the results, we have lost some of the performance gains of using a parallel stream, so why use this method? You might be calling this method in a section of your application that takes both serial and parallel streams, and you need to ensure that the results are processed in a particular order. Also, stream operations that occur before/after the forEachOrdered() can still gain performance improvements for using a parallel stream.

Understanding Performance Improvements

Let's look at another example to see how much using a parallel stream may improve performance in your applications. Let's say that you have a task that requires processing 4,000 records, with each record taking a modest 10 milliseconds to complete. The following is a sample implementation that uses Thread.sleep() to simulate processing the data:

```java
import java.util.*;

public class WhaleDataCalculator {

    public int processRecord(int input) {
        try {
            Thread.sleep(10);
        } catch (InterruptedException e) {
            // Handle interrupted exception
        }
        return input+1;
    }

    public void processAllData(List<Integer> data) {
        data.stream().map(a -> processRecord(a)).count();
    }

    public static void main(String[] args) {
        WhaleDataCalculator calculator = new WhaleDataCalculator();

        // Define the data
        List<Integer> data = new ArrayList<Integer>();
        for(int i=0; i<4000; i++) data.add(i);

        // Process the data
        long start = System.currentTimeMillis();
        calculator.processAllData(data);
        double time = (System.currentTimeMillis()-start)/1000.0;

        // Report results
        System.out.println("\nTasks completed in: "+time+" seconds");
    }
}
```

Given that there are 4,000 records, and each record takes 10 milliseconds to process, by using a serial stream(), the results will take approximately 40 seconds to complete this task. Each task is completed one at a time:

```
Tasks completed in: 40.044 seconds
```

If we use a parallel stream, though, the results can be processed concurrently:

```java
public void processAllData(List<Integer> data) {
    data.parallelStream().map(a -> processRecord(a)).count();
}
```

Depending on the number of CPUs available in your environment, the following is a possible output of the code using a parallel stream:

```
Tasks completed in: 10.542 seconds
```

You see that using a parallel stream can have a four-fold improvement in the results. Even better, the results scale with the number of processors. *Scaling* is the property that, as we add more resources such as CPUs, the results gradually improve.

Does that mean that all of your streams should be parallel? Not exactly. Parallel streams tend to achieve the most improvement when the number of elements in the stream is significantly large. For small streams, the improvement is often limited, as there are some overhead costs to allocating and setting up the parallel processing.

> As with earlier examples in this chapter, the performance of using parallel streams will vary with your local computing environment. There is never a guarantee that using a parallel stream will improve performance. In fact, using a parallel stream could slow the application due to the overhead of creating the parallel processing structures. That said, in a variety of circumstances, applying parallel streams could result in significant performance gains.

Understanding Independent Operations

Parallel streams can improve performance because they rely on the property that many stream operations can be executed independently. By independent operations, we mean that the results of an operation on one element of a stream do not require or impact the results of another element of the stream. For example, in the previous example, each call to processRecord() can be executed separately, without impacting any other invocation of the method.

As another example, consider the following lambda expression supplied to the map() method, which maps the stream contents to uppercase strings:

```
Arrays.asList("jackal","kangaroo","lemur")
    .parallelStream()
    .map(s -> s.toUpperCase())
    .forEach(System.out::println);
```

In this example, mapping jackal to JACKAL can be done independently of mapping kangaroo to KANGAROO. In other words, multiple elements of the stream can be processed at the same time and the results will not change.

Many common streams including map(), forEach(), and filter() can be processed independently, although order is never guaranteed. Consider the following modified version of our previous stream code:

```
Arrays.asList("jackal","kangaroo","lemur")
    .parallelStream()
```

```
.map(s -> {System.out.println(s); return s.toUpperCase();})
.forEach(System.out::println);
```

This example includes an embedded print statement in the lambda passed to the map() method. While the return values of the map() operation are the same, the order in which they are processed can result in very different output. We might even print terminal results before the intermediate operations have finished, as shown in the following generated output:

```
kangaroo
KANGAROO
lemur
jackal
JACKAL
LEMUR
```

When using streams, you should avoid any lambda expressions that can produce side effects.

 NOTE   For the exam, you should remember that parallel streams can process results independently, although the order of the results cannot be determined ahead of time.

Avoiding Stateful Operations

Side effects can also appear in parallel streams if your lambda expressions are stateful. A *stateful lambda expression* is one whose result depends on any state that might change during the execution of a pipeline. On the other hand, a stateless lambda expression is one whose result does not depend on any state that might change during the execution of a pipeline.

Let's take a look an example to see why stateful lambda expressions should be avoided in parallel streams:

```
List<Integer> data = Collections.synchronizedList(new ArrayList<>());
Arrays.asList(1,2,3,4,5,6).parallelStream()
   .map(i -> {data.add(i); return i;}) // AVOID STATEFUL LAMBDA EXPRESSIONS!
   .forEachOrdered(i -> System.out.print(i+" "));

System.out.println();
for(Integer e: data) {
   System.out.print(e+" ");
}
```

The following is a sample generation of this code snippet using a parallel stream:

```
1 2 3 4 5 6
2 4 3 5 6 1
```

The forEachOrdered() method displays the numbers in the stream sequentially, whereas the order of the elements in the data list is completely random. You can see that a stateful lambda expression, which modifies the data list in parallel, produces unpredictable results at runtime.

Note that this would not have been noticeable with a serial stream, where the results would have been the following:

```
1 2 3 4 5 6
1 2 3 4 5 6
```

It strongly recommended that you avoid stateful operations when using parallel streams, so as to remove any potential data side effects. In fact, they should generally be avoided in serial streams wherever possible, since they prevent your streams from taking advantage of parallelization.

 Real World Scenario

Using Concurrent Collections with Parallel Streams

We applied the parallel stream to a synchronized list in the previous example. Anytime you are working with a collection with a parallel stream, it is recommended that you use a concurrent collection. For example, if we had used a regular ArrayList rather than a synchronized one, we could have seen output such as the following:

```
1 2 3 4 5 6
null 2 4 5 6 1
```

For an ArrayList object, the JVM internally manages a primitive array of the same type. As the size of the dynamic ArrayList grows, a new, larger primitive array is periodically required. If two threads both trigger the array to be resized at the same time, a result can be lost, producing the unexpected value shown here. As briefly mentioned earlier, and also discussed later in this chapter, the unexpected result of two tasks executing at the same time is a race condition.

Processing Parallel Reductions

Besides possibly improving performance and modifying the order of operations, using parallel streams can impact how you write your application. Reduction operations on parallel streams are referred to as *parallel reductions*. The results for parallel reductions can be different from what you expect when working with serial streams.

Performing Order-Based Tasks

Since order is not guaranteed with parallel streams, methods such as findAny() on parallel streams may result in unexpected behavior. Let's take a look at the results of findAny() applied to a serial stream:

```
System.out.print(Arrays.asList(1,2,3,4,5,6).stream().findAny().get());
```

This code consistently outputs the first value in the serial stream, 1.

With a parallel stream, the JVM can create any number of threads to process the stream. When you call findAny() on a parallel stream, the JVM selects the first thread to finish the task and retrieves its data:

```
System.out.print(Arrays.asList(1,2,3,4,5,6).parallelStream().findAny().get());
```

The result is that the output could be 4, 1, or really any value in the stream. You can see that with parallel streams, the results of findAny() are no longer predictable.

Any stream operation that is based on order, including findFirst(), limit(), or skip(), may actually perform more slowly in a parallel environment. This is a result of a parallel processing task being forced to coordinate all of its threads in a synchronized-like fashion.

On the plus side, the results of ordered operations on a parallel stream will be consistent with a serial stream. For example, calling skip(5).limit(2).findFirst() will return the same result on ordered serial and parallel streams.

 Real World Scenario

Creating Unordered Streams

All of the streams with which you have been working are considered ordered by default. It is possible to create an unordered stream from an ordered stream, similar to how you create a parallel stream from a serial stream:

```
Arrays.asList(1,2,3,4,5,6).stream().unordered();
```

This method does not actually reorder the elements; it just tells the JVM that if an order-based stream operation is applied, the order can be ignored. For example, calling skip(5) on an unordered stream will skip any 5 elements, not the first 5 required on an ordered stream.

For serial streams, using an unordered version has no effect, but on parallel streams, the results can greatly improve performance:

```
Arrays.asList(1,2,3,4,5,6).stream().unordered().parallel();
```

Even though unordered streams will not be on the exam, if you are developing applications with parallel streams, you should know when to apply an unordered stream to improve performance.

Combining Results with *reduce()*

As you learned in Chapter 4, the stream operation reduce() combines a stream into a single object. Recall that first parameter to the reduce() method is called the *identity*, the second parameter is called the *accumulator*, and the third parameter is called the *combiner*.

We can concatenate a string using the reduce() method to produce wolf, as shown in the following example:

```
System.out.println(Arrays.asList('w', 'o', 'l', 'f')
    .stream()
    .reduce("",(c,s1) -> c + s1,
        (s2,s3) -> s2 + s3));
```

> The naming of the variables in this stream example is not accidental. The variable c is interpreted as a char, whereas s1, s2, and s3 are String values. Recall that in the three-argument version of reduce(), the accumulator is a BiFunction, while the combiner is BinaryOperator.

On parallel streams, the reduce() method works by applying the reduction to pairs of elements within the stream to create intermediate values and then combining those intermediate values to produce a final result. Whereas with a serial stream, wolf was built one character at a time, in a parallel stream, the intermediate strings wo and lf could have been created and then combined.

With parallel streams, though, we now have to be concerned about order. What if the elements of a string are combined in the wrong order to produce wlfo or flwo? The Streams API prevents this problem, while still allowing streams to be processed in parallel, as long as the arguments to the reduce() operation adhere to certain principles.

Requirements for reduce() Arguments

- The *identity* must be defined such that for all elements in the stream u, combiner.apply(identity, u) is equal to u.

- The *accumulator* operator op must be associative and stateless such that (a op b) op c is equal to a op (b op c).

- The *combiner* operator must also be associative and stateless and compatible with the identity, such that for all u and t combiner.apply(u,accumulator.apply(identity,t)) is equal to accumulator.apply(u,t).

If you follow these principles when building your reduce() arguments, then the operations can be performed using a parallel stream and the results will be ordered as they would be with a serial stream. Note that these principles still apply to the identity and accumulator when using the one- or two-argument version of reduce() on parallel streams.

> While the requirements for the input arguments to the reduce() method hold true for both serial and parallel streams, you may not have noticed any problems in serial streams because the result was always ordered. With parallel streams, though, order is no longer guaranteed, and an argument that violates one of these rules is much more likely to produce side effects and/or unpredictable results.

Let's take a look at an example using a non-associative accumulator. In particular, subtracting numbers is not an associative operation; therefore the following code can output different values depending on whether you use a serial or parallel stream:

```
System.out.println(Arrays.asList(1,2,3,4,5,6)
    .parallelStream()
    .reduce(0,(a,b) -> (a-b))); // NOT AN ASSOCIATIVE ACCUMULATOR
```

It may output -21, 3, or some other value, as the accumulator function violates the associativity property.

You can see other problems if we use an identity parameter that is not truly an identity value. For example, what do you expect the following code to output?

```
System.out.println(Arrays.asList("w","o","l","f")
    .parallelStream()
    .reduce("X",String::concat));
```

In fact, it can output XwXoXlXf. As part of the parallel process, the identity is applied to multiple elements in the stream, resulting in very unexpected data.

Using the Three-Argument *reduce()* Method

Although the one- and two-argument versions of reduce() do support parallel processing, it is recommended that you use the three-argument version of reduce() when working with parallel streams. Providing an explicit combiner method allows the JVM to partition the operations in the stream more efficiently.

Combing Results with *collect()*

Like reduce(), the Streams API includes a three-argument version of collect() that takes accumulator and combiner operators, along with a supplier operator instead of an identity. Also like reduce(), the accumulator and combiner operations must be associative and stateless, with the combiner operation compatible with the accumulator operator, as previously discussed. In this manner, the three-argument version of collect() can be performed as a parallel reduction, as shown in the following example:

```
Stream<String> stream = Stream.of("w", "o", "l", "f").parallel();
SortedSet<String> set = stream.collect(ConcurrentSkipListSet::new, Set::add,
    Set::addAll);
System.out.println(set); // [f, l, o, w]
```

Recall that elements in a ConcurrentSkipListSet are sorted according to their natural ordering.

You should use a concurrent collection to combine the results, ensuring that the results of concurrent threads do not cause a ConcurrentModificationException.

Using the One-Argument *collect()* Method

Recall that the one-argument version of collect()takes a collector argument, as shown in the following example:

```
Stream<String> stream = Stream.of("w", "o", "l", "f").parallel();
Set<String> set = stream.collect(Collectors.toSet());
System.out.println(set); // [f, w, l, o]
```

Performing parallel reductions with a collector requires additional considerations. For example, if the collection into which you are inserting is an ordered data set, such as a List, then the elements in the resulting collection must be in the same order, regardless of whether you use a serial or parallel stream. This may reduce performance, though, as some operations are unable to be completed in parallel.

The following rules ensure that a parallel reduction will be performed efficiently in Java using a collector.

Requirements for Parallel Reduction with collect()

- The stream is parallel.

- The parameter of the collect operation has the Collector.Characteristics.CONCURRENT characteristic.

- Either the stream is unordered, or the collector has the characteristic Collector.Characteristics.UNORDERED.

Any class that implements the Collector interface includes a characteristics() method that returns a set of available attributes for the collector. While Collectors.toSet() does have the UNORDERED characteristic, it does not have the CONCURRENT characteristic; therefore the previous collector example will not be performed as a concurrent reduction.

The Collectors class includes two sets of methods for retrieving collectors that are both UNORDERED and CONCURRENT, Collectors.toConcurrentMap() and Collectors.groupingByConcurrent(), and therefore it is capable of performing parallel reductions efficiently. Like their non-concurrent counterparts, there are overloaded versions that take additional arguments.

Here is a rewrite of an example from Chapter 4 to use a parallel stream and parallel reduction:

```
Stream<String> ohMy = Stream.of("lions", "tigers", "bears").parallel();
ConcurrentMap<Integer, String> map = ohMy
    .collect(Collectors.toConcurrentMap(String::length, k -> k,
        (s1, s2) -> s1 + "," + s2));
System.out.println(map); // {5=lions,bears, 6=tigers}
System.out.println(map.getClass()); // java.util.concurrent.ConcurrentHashMap
```

We use a ConcurrentMap reference, although the actual class returned is likely ConcurrentHashMap. The particular class is not guaranteed; it will just be a class that implements the interface ConcurrentMap.

Finally, we can rewrite our groupingBy() example from Chapter 4 to use a parallel stream and parallel reduction:

```
Stream<String> ohMy = Stream.of("lions", "tigers", "bears").parallel();
ConcurrentMap<Integer, List<String>> map = ohMy.collect(
    Collectors.groupingByConcurrent(String::length));
System.out.println(map); // {5=[lions, bears], 6=[tigers]}
```

As before, the returned object can be assigned a ConcurrentMap reference.

Encouraging Parallel Processing

Guaranteeing that a particular stream will perform reductions in a parallel, as opposed to single-threaded, is often difficult in practice. For example, the one-argument reduce() operation on a parallel stream may perform concurrently even when there is no explicit combiner argument. Alternatively, you may expect some collectors to perform well on a parallel stream, resorting to single-threaded processing at runtime.

The key to applying parallel reductions is to encourage the JVM to take advantage of the parallel structures, such as using a groupingByConcurrent() collector on a parallel stream rather than a groupingBy() collector. By encouraging the JVM to take advantage of the parallel processing, we get the best possible performance at runtime.

Managing Concurrent Processes

The Concurrency API includes classes that can be used to coordinate tasks among a group of related threads. These classes are designed for use in specific scenarios, similar to many of the design patterns that you saw in Chapter 2. In this section, we present two classes with which you should be familiar for the exam, CyclicBarrier and ForkJoinPool.

Creating a *CyclicBarrier*

Our zoo workers are back, and this time they are cleaning pens. Imagine that there is a lion pen that needs to emptied, cleaned, and then filled back up with the lions. To complete the task, we have assigned four zoo workers. Obviously, we don't want to start cleaning the cage while a lion is roaming in it, lest we end up losing a zoo worker! Furthermore, we don't want to let the lions back into the pen while it is still being cleaned.

We could have all of the work completed by a single worker, but this would be slow and ignore the fact that we have three zoo workers standing by to help. A better solution would be to have all four zoo employees work concurrently, pausing between the end of one set of tasks and the start of the next.

To coordinate these tasks, we can use the `CyclicBarrier` class. For now, let's start with a code sample without a `CyclicBarrier`:

```java
import java.util.concurrent.*;

public class LionPenManager {

    private void removeAnimals() { System.out.println("Removing animals"); }
    private void cleanPen() { System.out.println("Cleaning the pen"); }
    private void addAnimals() { System.out.println("Adding animals"); }

    public void performTask() {
        removeAnimals();
        cleanPen();
        addAnimals();
    }

    public static void main(String[] args) {
        ExecutorService service = null;
        try {
            service = Executors.newFixedThreadPool(4);
            LionPenManager manager = new LionPenManager();
            for(int i=0; i<4; i++)
                service.submit(() -> manager.performTask());
        } finally {
            if(service != null) service.shutdown();
        }
    }
}
```

The following is sample output based on this implementation:

```
Removing animals
Removing animals
Cleaning the pen
Adding animals
Removing animals
Cleaning the pen
Adding animals
Removing animals
```

```
Cleaning the pen
Adding animals
Cleaning the pen
Adding animals
```

Although within a single thread the results are ordered, among multiple workers the output is entirely random. We see that some animals are still being removed while the cage is being cleaned, and other animals are added before the cleaning process is finished. In our conceptual example, this would be quite chaotic and would not lead to a very clean cage.

We can improve these results by using the CyclicBarrier class. The CyclicBarrier takes in its constructors a limit value, indicating the number of threads to wait for. As each thread finishes, it calls the await() method on the cyclic barrier. Once the specified number of threads have each called await(), the barrier is released and all threads can continue.

The following is a reimplementation of our LionPenManager class that uses CyclicBarrier objects to coordinate access:

```java
import java.util.concurrent.*;

public class LionPenManager {

    private void removeAnimals() { System.out.println("Removing animals"); }
    private void cleanPen() { System.out.println("Cleaning the pen"); }
    private void addAnimals() { System.out.println("Adding animals"); }

    public void performTask(CyclicBarrier c1, CyclicBarrier c2) {
        try {
            removeAnimals();
            c1.await();
            cleanPen();
            c2.await();
            addAnimals();
        } catch (InterruptedException | BrokenBarrierException e) {
            // Handle checked exceptions here
        }
    }
    public static void main(String[] args) {
        ExecutorService service = null;
        try {
            service = Executors.newFixedThreadPool(4);

            LionPenManager manager = new LionPenManager();
            CyclicBarrier c1 = new CyclicBarrier(4);
            CyclicBarrier c2 = new CyclicBarrier(4,
                    () -> System.out.println("*** Pen Cleaned!"));
```

```
        for(int i=0; i<4; i++)
            service.submit(() -> manager.performTask(c1,c2));
    } finally {
        if(service != null) service.shutdown();
    }
  }
}
```

In this example, we have updated the performTask() to use CyclicBarrier objects. Like synchronizing on the same object, coordinating a task with a CyclicBarrier requires the object to be static or passed to the thread performing the task. We also add a try/catch block in the performTask() method, as the await() method throws multiple checked exceptions.

The following is sample output based on this revised implementation of our LionPenManager class:

```
Removing animals
Removing animals
Removing animals
Removing animals
Cleaning the pen
Cleaning the pen
Cleaning the pen
Cleaning the pen
*** Pen Cleaned!
Adding animals
Adding animals
Adding animals
Adding animals
```

As you can see, all of the results are now organized. Removing the animals all happens in one step, as does cleaning the pen and adding the animals back in. In this example, we used two different constructors for our CyclicBarrier objects, the latter of which called a Runnable method upon completion.

Thread Pool Size and Cyclic Barrier Limit

If you are using a thread pool, make sure that you set the number of available threads to be at least as large as your CyclicBarrier limit value. For example, what if we changed the code to allocate only two threads, such as in the following snippet?

```
ExecutorService service = Executors.newFixedThreadPool(2);
```

In this case, the code will hang indefinitely. The barrier would never be reached as the only threads available in the pool are stuck waiting for the barrier to be complete. As you shall see in the next section, this is a form of deadlock.

The CyclicBarrier class allows us to perform complex, multi-threaded tasks, while all threads stop and wait at logical barriers. This solution is superior to a single-threaded solution, as the individual tasks, such as removing the animals, can be completed in parallel by all four zoo workers.

There is a slight loss in performance to be expected from using a CyclicBarrier. For example, one worker may be incredibly slow at removing lions, resulting in the other three workers waiting for him to finish. Since we can't start cleaning the pen while it is full of lions, though, this solution is about as concurrent as we can make it.

Reusing *CyclicBarrier*

After a CyclicBarrier is broken, all threads are released and the number of threads waiting on the CyclicBarrier goes back to zero. At this point, the CyclicBarrier may be used again for a new set of waiting threads. For example, if our CyclicBarrier limit is 5 and we have 15 threads that call await(), then the CyclicBarrier will be activated a total of three times.

Applying the Fork/Join Framework

Suppose that we need to measure the weight of all of the animals in our zoo. Further suppose that we ask exactly one person to perform this task and complete it in an hour. What's the first thing that person is likely to do? Probably ask for help!

In most of the examples in this chapter, we knew at the start of the process exactly how many threads and tasks we needed to perform. Sometimes, we aren't so lucky. It may be that we have five threads, or five zoo workers in our example, but we have no idea how many tasks need to be performed. When a task gets too complicated, we can split the task into multiple other tasks using the fork/join framework.

Introducing Recursion

The fork/join framework relies on the concept of recursion to solve complex tasks. *Recursion* is the process by which a task calls itself to solve a problem. A recursive solution is constructed with a base case and a recursive case:

Base case: A non-recursive method that is used to terminate the recursive path

Recursive case: A recursive method that may call itself one or multiple times to solve a problem

For example, a method that computes the factorial of a number can be expressed as a recursive function. In mathematics, a *factorial* is what you get when you multiply a number by all of the integers below it. The factorial of 5 is equal to 5 * 4 * 3 * 2 * 1 = 120. The following is a recursive factorial function in Java:

```
public static int factorial(int n)  {
   if(n<=1) return 1;
   else return n * factorial(n-1);
}
```

In this example, you see that 1 is the base case, and any integer value greater than 1 triggers the recursive case.

One challenge in implementing a recursive solution is always to make sure that the recursive process arrives at a base case. For example, if the base case is never reached, the solution will continue infinitely and the program will hang. In Java, this will result in a StackOverflowError anytime the application recurses too deeply.

Let's use an array of Double values called weights. For simplicity, let's say that there are 10 animals in the zoo; thus our array is of size 10.

```
Double[] weights = new Double[10];
```

We are further constrained by the fact that the animals are spread out, and a single person can weigh at most three animals in an hour. If we want to complete this task in an hour, our zoo worker is going to need some help.

Conceptually, we start off with a single zoo worker who realizes that they cannot perform all 10 tasks in time. They perform a recursive step by dividing the set of 10 animals into two sets of 5 animals, one set for each zoo worker. The two zoo workers then further subdivide the set until each zoo worker has at most three animals to weigh, which is the base case in our example.

Applying the fork/join framework requires us to perform three steps:

1. Create a ForkJoinTask.
2. Create the ForkJoinPool.
3. Start the ForkJoinTask.

The first step is the most complex, as it requires defining the recursive process. Fortunately, the second and third steps are easy and can each be completed with a single line of code. For the exam, you should know how to implement the fork/join solution by extending one of two classes, RecursiveAction and RecursiveTask, both of which implement the ForkJoinTask interface.

The first class, RecursiveAction, is an abstract class that requires us to implement the compute() method, which returns void, to perform the bulk of the work. The second class, RecursiveTask, is an abstract generic class that requires us to implement the compute() method, which returns the generic type, to perform the bulk of the work. As you might have guessed, the difference between RecursiveAction and RecursiveTask is analogous to the difference between Runnable and Callable, respectively, which you saw at the start of the chapter.

Let's define a WeighAnimalAction that extends the fork/join class RecursiveAction:

```java
import java.util.*;
import java.util.concurrent.*;

public class WeighAnimalAction extends RecursiveAction {
    private int start;
    private int end;
    private Double[] weights;
    public WeighAnimalAction(Double[] weights, int start, int end) {
        this.start = start;
        this.end = end;
        this.weights = weights;
    }

    protected void compute() {
        if(end-start <= 3)
            for(int i=start; i<end; i++) {
                weights[i] = (double)new Random().nextInt(100);
                System.out.println("Animal Weighed: "+i);
            }
        else {
            int middle = start+((end-start)/2);
            System.out.println("[start="+start+",middle="+middle+",end="+end+"]");
            invokeAll(new WeighAnimalAction(weights,start,middle),
                    new WeighAnimalAction(weights,middle,end));
        }
    }
}
```

We start off by defining the task and the arguments on which the task will operate, such as start, end, and weights. We then override the abstract compute() method, defining our base and recursive processes. For the base case, we weigh the animal if there are at most three left in the set. For simplicity, this base case assigns a random number from 0 to 100 as the weight.

For the recursive case, we split the work from one WeighAnimalAction object into two WeighAnimalAction instances, dividing the available indices between the two tasks. Some subtasks may end up with little or no work to do, which is fine, as long as they terminate in a base case.

 Dividing tasks into recursive subtasks may not always result in evenly divided sets. In our zoo example, one zoo worker may end up with three animals to weigh, while others may have only one animal to weigh. The goal of the fork/join framework is to break up large tasks into smaller ones, not to guarantee every base case ends up being exactly the same size.

Once the task class is defined, creating the ForkJoinPool and starting the task is quite easy. The following main() method performs the task on 10 records and outputs the results:

```
public static void main(String[] args) {
    Double[] weights = new Double[10];

    ForkJoinTask<?> task = new WeighAnimalAction(weights,0,weights.length);
    ForkJoinPool pool pool = new ForkJoinPool();
    pool.invoke(task);

    // Print results
    System.out.println();
    System.out.print("Weights: ");
    Arrays.asList(weights).stream().forEach(
        d -> System.out.print(d.intValue()+" "));
}
```

By default, the ForkJoinPool class will use the number of processors to determine how many threads to create. The following is a sample output of this code:

```
[start=0,middle=5,end=10]
[start=0,middle=2,end=5]
Animal Weighed: 0
Animal Weighed: 2
[start=5,middle=7,end=10]
Animal Weighed: 1
Animal Weighed: 3
Animal Weighed: 5
Animal Weighed: 6
Animal Weighed: 7
Animal Weighed: 8
Animal Weighed: 9
Animal Weighed: 4

Weights: 94 73 8 92 75 63 76 60 73 3
```

The key concept to take away from this example is that the process was started as a single task, and it spawned additional concurrent tasks to split up the work after it had already started. As you may have noticed in the sample output, some tasks reached their base case while others were still performing recursive work. Likewise, the order of the output cannot be guaranteed, since some zoo workers may finish before others.

> Creating a ForkJoinTask and submitting it to a ForkJoinPool does not guarantee it will be executed immediately. For example, a recursive step may generate 10 tasks when there are only four threads available. Like a pooled thread executor, the tasks will wait for an available thread to start processing the data.

Working with a *RecursiveTask*

Let's say that we want to compute the sum of all weight values while processing the data. Instead of extending RecursiveAction, we could extend the generic RecursiveTask to calculate and return each sum in the compute() method. The following is an updated implementation that uses RecursiveTask<Double>:

```
public class WeighAnimalTask extends RecursiveTask<Double>  {
   private int start;
   private int end;
   private Double[] weights;
   public WeighAnimalTask(Double[] weights, int start, int end) {
      this.start = start;
      this.end = end;
      this.weights = weights;
   }

   protected Double compute() {
      if(end-start <= 3) {
         double sum = 0;
         for(int i=start; i<end; i++) {
            weights[i] = (double)new Random().nextInt(100);
            System.out.println("Animal Weighed: "+i);
            sum += weights[i];
         }
         return sum;
      } else {
         int middle = start+((end-start)/2);
         System.out.println("[start="+start+",middle="+middle+",end="+end+"]");
         RecursiveTask<Double> otherTask = new WeighAnimalTask(weights,start,middle);
         otherTask.fork();
```

```
        return new WeighAnimalTask(weights,middle,end).compute() + otherTask.join();
   }
  }
}
```

While our base case is mostly unchanged, except for returning a sum value, the recursive case is quite different. Since the invokeAll() method doesn't return a value, we instead issue a fork() and join() command to retrieve the recursive data. The fork() method instructs the fork/join framework to complete the task in a separate thread, while the join() method causes the current thread to wait for the results.

In this example, we compute the [middle, end] range using the current thread, since we already have one available, and the [start, middle] range using a separate thread. We then combine the results, waiting for the otherTask to complete. We can then update our main() method to include the results of the entire task:

```
ForkJoinTask<Double> task = new WeighAnimalTask(weights,0,weights.length);
ForkJoinPool pool pool = new ForkJoinPool();
Double sum = pool.invoke(task);
System.out.println("Sum: "+sum);
```

Given our previous sample run, the total sum would have been 617.

One thing to be careful about when using the fork() and join() methods is the order in which they are applied. For instance, while the previous example was multi-threaded, the following variation operates with single-threaded performance:

```
        RecursiveTask<Double> otherTask = new WeighAnimalTask(weights,start,middle);
        Double otherResult = otherTask.fork().join();
        return new WeighAnimalTask(weights,middle,end).compute() + otherResult;
```

In this example, the current thread calls join(), causing it to wait for the [start,middle] subtask to finish before starting on the [middle,end] subtask. In this manner, the results are actually performed in a single-threaded manner. For the exam, make sure that fork() is called before the current thread begins a subtask and that join() is called after it finishes retrieving the results, in order for them to be done in parallel.

Identifying Fork/Join Issues

Unlike many of our earlier Concurrency API classes and structures, the fork/join framework can be a bit overwhelming for developers who have not seen it before. With that in mind, we have created the following list of tips for identifying issues in a fork/join class on the exam.

Tips for Reviewing a Fork/Join Class

- The class should extend RecursiveAction or RecursiveTask.

- If the class extends RecursiveAction, then it should override a protected compute() method that takes no arguments and returns void.

- If the class extends RecursiveTask, then it should override a protected compute() method that takes no arguments and returns a generic type listed in the class definition.

- The invokeAll() method takes two instances of the fork/join class and does not return a result.

- The fork() method causes a new task to be submitted to the pool and is similar to the thread executor submit() method.

- The join() method is called after the fork() method and causes the current thread to wait for the results of a subtask.

- Unlike fork(), calling compute() within a compute() method causes the task to wait for the results of the subtask.

- The fork() method should be called before the current thread performs a compute() operation, with join() called to read the results afterward.

- Since compute() takes no arguments, the constructor of the class is often used to pass instructions to the task.

Obviously, this is a lot to look for when taking the exam, so we recommend that you practice with the framework by writing your own fork/join classes. You can also time the results with System.currentTimeMillis() to see how the fork/join can improve performance.

Identifying Threading Problems

A threading problem can occur in multi-threaded applications when two or more threads interact in an unexpected and undesirable way. For example, two threads may block each other from accessing a particular segment of code.

The Concurrency API was created to help eliminate potential threading issues common to all developers. As you have seen, the Concurrency API creates threads and manages complex thread interactions for you, often in just a few lines of code.

Although the Concurrency API reduces the potential for threading issues, it does not eliminate it. In practice, finding and identifying threading issues within an application is often one of the most difficult tasks a developer can undertake.

Understanding Liveness

As you have seen in this chapter, many thread operations can be performed independently, but some require coordination. For example, synchronizing on a method requires all threads that call the method to wait for other threads to finish before continuing. You also saw earlier in the chapter that threads in a CyclicBarrier will each wait for the barrier limit to be reached before continuing.

What happens to the application while all of these threads are waiting? In many cases, the waiting is ephemeral and the user has very little idea that any delay has occurred. In other cases, though, the waiting may be extremely long, perhaps infinite.

Liveness is the ability of an application to be able to execute in a timely manner. Liveness problems, then, are those in which the application becomes unresponsive or in some kind of "stuck" state. For the exam, there are three types of liveness issues with which you should be familiar: deadlock, starvation, and livelock.

Deadlock

Deadlock occurs when two or more threads are blocked forever, each waiting on the other. We can illustrate this principle with the following example. Imagine that our zoo has two foxes: Foxy and Tails. Foxy likes to eat first and then drink water, while Tails likes to drink water first and then eat. Furthermore, neither animal likes to share, and they will finish their meal only if they have exclusive access to both food and water.

The zookeeper places the food on one side of the environment and the water on the other side. Although our foxes are fast, it still takes them 100 milliseconds to run from one side of the environment to the other.

What happens if Foxy gets the food first and Tails gets the water first? The following application models this behavior:

```java
import java.util.concurrent.*;

public class Food {}
public class Water {}

public class Fox {

    public void eatAndDrink(Food food, Water water) {
        synchronized(food) {
            System.out.println("Got Food!");
            move();
            synchronized(water) {
                System.out.println("Got Water!");
            }
        }
    }

    public void drinkAndEat(Food food, Water water) {
        synchronized(water) {
            System.out.println("Got Water!");
            move();
            synchronized(food) {
```

```
            System.out.println("Got Food!");
        }
    }
}

public void move() {
    try {
        Thread.sleep(100);
    } catch (InterruptedException e) {
        // Handle exception
    }
}

public static void main(String[] args) {
    // Create participants and resources
    Fox foxy = new Fox();
    Fox tails = new Fox();
    Food food = new Food();
    Water water = new Water();

    // Process data
    ExecutorService service = null;
    try {
        service = Executors.newScheduledThreadPool(10);
        service.submit(() -> foxy.eatAndDrink(food,water));
        service.submit(() -> tails.drinkAndEat(food,water));
    } finally {
        if(service != null) service.shutdown();
    }
}
}
```

In this example, Foxy obtains the food and then moves to the other side of the environment to obtain the water. Unfortunately, Tails already drank the water and is waiting for the food to become available. The result is that our program outputs the following and it hangs indefinitely:

```
Got Food!
Got Water!
```

This example is considered a deadlock because both participants are permanently blocked, waiting on resources that will never become available.

Preventing Deadlocks

How do you fix a deadlock once it has occurred? The answer is that you can't in most situations. On the other hand, there are numerous strategies to help prevent deadlocks from ever happening in the first place. One common strategy to avoid deadlocks is for all threads to order their resource requests. For example, if both foxes have a rule that they need to obtain food before water, then the previous deadlock scenario will not happen again. Once one of the foxes obtained food, the second fox would wait, leaving the water resource available.

There are some advanced techniques that try to detect and resolve a deadlock in real time, but they are often quite difficult to implement and have limited success in practice. In fact, many operating systems ignore the problem altogether and pretend that *deadlocks never happen*.

Starvation

Starvation occurs when a single thread is perpetually denied access to a shared resource or lock. The thread is still active, but it is unable to complete its work as a result of other threads constantly taking the resource that they trying to access.

In our fox example, imagine that we have a pack of very hungry, very competitive foxes in our environment. Every time Foxy stands up to go get food, one of the other foxes sees her and rushes to eat before her. Foxy is free to roam around the enclosure, take a nap, and howl for a zookeeper but is never able to obtain access to the food. In this example, Foxy literally and figuratively experiences starvation. Good thing that this is just a theoretical example!

Livelock

Livelock occurs when two or more threads are conceptually blocked forever, although they are each still active and trying to complete their task. Livelock is a special case of resource starvation in which two or more threads actively try to acquire a set of locks, are unable to do so, and restart part of the process.

Livelock is often a result of two threads trying to resolve a deadlock. Returning to our fox example, imagine that Foxy and Tails are both holding their food and water resources, respectively. They each realize that they cannot finish their meal in this state, so they both let go of their food and water, run to opposite side of the environment, and pick up the other resource. Now Foxy has the water, Tails has the food, and neither is able to finish their meal!

If Foxy and Tails continue this process forever, it is referred to as livelock. Both Foxy and Tails are active, running back and forth across their area, but neither is able to finish their meal. Foxy and Tails are executing a form of failed deadlock recovery. Each fox notices that they are potentially entering a deadlock state and responds by releasing all of its locked resources. Unfortunately, the lock and unlock process is cyclical, and the two foxes are conceptually deadlocked.

In practice, livelock is often very difficult issue to detect. Threads in a livelock state appear active and able to respond to requests, even when they are in fact stuck in an endless cycle.

Managing Race Conditions

A *race condition* is an undesirable result that occurs when two tasks, which should be completed sequentially, are completed at the same time. We encountered two examples of race conditions earlier in the chapter when we introduced synchronization and parallel streams.

While Figure 7.3 shows a classical thread-based example of a race condition, we now provide a more illustrative example. Imagine two zoo patrons, Olivia and Sophia, are signing up for an account on the zoo's new visitor website. Both of them want to use the same username, ZooFan, and they each send requests to create the account at the same time, as shown in Figure 7.5.

FIGURE 7.5   Race condition on user creation

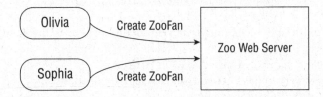

What result does the web server return when both users attempt to create an account with the same username in Figure 7.5?

Possible Outcomes for This Race Condition

- Both users are able to create accounts with username ZooFan.

- Both users are unable to create an account with username ZooFan, returning an error message to both users.

- One user is able to create the account with the username ZooFan, while the other user receives an error message.

Which of these results is most desirable when designing our web server? The first possibility, in which both users are able to create an account with the same username, could cause serious problems and break numerous invariants in the system. Assuming that the username is required to log into the website, how do they both log in with the same username and different passwords? In this case, the website cannot tell them apart. This is the worst possible outcome to this race condition, as it causes significant and potentially unrecoverable data problems.

What about the second scenario? If both users are unable to create the account, both will receive error messages and be told to try again. In this scenario, the data is protected since no two accounts with the same username exist in the system. The users are free to try again with the same username, ZooFan, since no one has been granted access to it. Although this might seem like a form of livelock, there is a subtle difference. When the users try to create their account again, the chances of them hitting a race condition tend to diminish. For example, if one user submits their request a few seconds before the other, they might avoid another race condition entirely by the system informing the second user that the account name is already in use.

The third scenario, in which one user obtains the account while the other does not, is often considered the best solution to this type of race condition. Like the second situation, we preserve data integrity, but unlike the second situation, at least one user is able to move forward on the first request, avoiding additional race condition scenarios. Also unlike the previous scenario, we can provide the user who didn't win the race with a clearer error message because we are now sure that the account username is no longer available in the system.

> For the third scenario, which of the two users should gain access to the account? For race conditions, it often doesn't matter as long as only one player "wins" the race. A common practice is to choose whichever thread made the request first, whenever possible.

For the exam, you should understand that race conditions lead to invalid data if they are not properly handled. Even the solution where both participants fail to proceed is preferable to one in which invalid data is permitted to enter the system.

Race conditions tend to appear in highly concurrent applications. As a software system grows and more users are added, they tend to appear more frequently. One solution is to use a monitor to synchronize on the relevant overlapping task. In the previous example, the relevant task is the method that determines whether an account username is in use and reserves it in the system if it is available. We could also use singletons, described in Chapter 2, to coordinate access to shared resources.

Summary

This chapter introduced you to threads and showed you how to process tasks in parallel using the Concurrency API. For the exam, you should know how to create threads indirectly using an ExecutorService and a fork/join recursive framework. The work that a thread performs can be defined in an instance of Runnable or Callable. As of Java 8, these tasks can now be expressed as lambda expressions.

We presented techniques for organizing tasks among multiple threads using atomic classes, synchronization blocks, synchronized methods, and the CyclicBarrier class. The Concurrency API includes numerous collections classes that support multi-threaded processing. For the exam, you should also be familiar with the CopyOnWriteArrayList class, which creates a new underlying structure anytime the list is modified.

We then introduced the notion of parallel streams and showed you how using them can improve performance in your application. Parallel streams can also cause unexpected results, since the results are no longer ordered. We also reviewed parallel reductions and showed how they differed from reductions on serial streams.

We concluded this chapter by discussing potential threading issues with which you should be familiar for the exam including deadlock, starvation, livelock, and race conditions. You need to know only the basic theory behind these concepts for the exam. In professional software development, however, finding and resolving such problems is often quite challenging.

Exam Essentials

Create concurrent tasks with a thread executor service using Runnable **and** Callable. An ExecutorService creates and manages a single thread or a pool of threads. Instances of Runnable and Callable can both be submitted to a thread executor and will be completed using the available threads in the service. Callable differs from Runnable in that Callable returns a generic data type and can throw a checked exception. A ScheduledExecutorService can be used to schedule tasks at a fixed rate or a fixed interval between executions.

Be able to synchronize blocks and methods. A monitor can be used to ensure that only one thread processes a particular section of code at a time. In Java, monitors are commonly implemented as synchronized blocks or using synchronized methods. In order to achieve synchronization, two threads must synchronize on the same shared object.

Be able to apply the atomic classes. An atomic operation is one that occurs without interference by another thread. The Concurrency API includes a set of atomic classes that are similar to the primitive classes, except that they ensure that operations on them are performed atomically.

Be able to use the concurrent collection classes. The Concurrency API includes numerous collections classes that include built-in support for multi-threaded processing, such as ConcurrentHashMap and ConcurrentDeque. It also includes a class CopyOnWriteArrayList that creates a copy of its underlying list structure every time it is modified and is useful in highly concurrent environments.

Understand the impact of using parallel streams. The Streams API allows for easy creation of parallel streams. Using a parallel stream can cause unexpected results, since the order of operations may no longer be predictable. Some operations, such as reduce() and collect(), require special consideration to achieve optimal performance when applied to a parallel stream.

Manage process with the CyclicBarrier **class and the fork/join framework.** The CyclicBarrier class can be used to force a set of threads to wait until they are at a certain stage of execution before continuing. The fork/join framework can be used to create a task that spawns additional tasks to solve problems recursively.

Identify potential threading problems. Deadlock, starvation, and livelock are three threading problems that can occur and result in threads never completing their task. Deadlock occurs when two or more threads are blocked forever. Starvation occurs when a single thread is perpetually denied access to a shared resource. Livelock is a form of starvation where two or more threads are active but conceptually blocked forever. Finally, race conditions occur when two threads execute at the same time, resulting in an unexpected outcome.

Review Questions

1. Given an instance of a `Stream`, s, and a `Collection`, c, which are valid ways of creating a parallel stream? (Choose all that apply.)

   A. `new ParallelStream(s)`

   B. `c.parallel()`

   C. `s.parallelStream()`

   D. `c.parallelStream()`

   E. `new ParallelStream(c)`

   F. `s.parallel()`

2. Which of the following statements about the `Callable call()` and `Runnable run()` methods are correct? (Choose all that apply.)

   A. Both can throw unchecked exceptions.

   B. `Callable` takes a generic method argument.

   C. `Callable` can throw a checked exception.

   D. Both can be implemented with lambda expressions.

   E. `Runnable` returns a generic type.

   F. `Callable` returns a generic type.

   G. Both methods return void.

3. Which lines need to be changed to make the code compile? (Choose all that apply.)

   ```
   ExecutorService service = Executors.newSingleThreadScheduledExecutor();
   service.scheduleWithFixedDelay(() -> { // w1
           System.out.println("Open Zoo");
           return null; // w2
       }, 0, 1, TimeUnit.MINUTES);
   Future<?> result = service.submit(() -> System.out.println("Wake Staff")); // w3
   System.out.println(result.get()); // w4
   ```

   A. It compiles and runs without issue.

   B. Line w1

   C. Line w2

   D. Line w3

   E. Line w4

   F. It compiles but throws an exception at runtime.

4. What statement about the following code is true?

   ```
   AtomicLong value1 = new AtomicLong(0);
   final long[] value2 = {0};
   ```

```
IntStream.iterate(1, i -> 1).limit(100).parallel()
   .forEach(i -> value1.incrementAndGet());
IntStream.iterate(1, i -> 1).limit(100).parallel()
   .forEach(i -> ++value2[0]);
System.out.println(value1+" "+value2[0]);
```

- **A.** It outputs 100 100.
- **B.** It outputs 100 99.
- **C.** The output cannot be determined ahead of time.
- **D.** The code does not compile.
- **E.** It compiles but throws an exception at runtime.
- **F.** It compiles but enters an infinite loop at runtime.

5. Fill in the blanks: _____ occur(s) when two or more threads are blocked forever but both appear active. _____occur(s) when two or more threads try to complete a related task at the same time.
- **A.** Livelock, Deadlock
- **B.** Deadlock, Starvation
- **C.** Race conditions, Deadlock
- **D.** Livelock, Race conditions
- **E.** Starvation, Race conditions
- **F.** Deadlock, Livelock

6. Which happens when more tasks are submitted to a thread executor than available threads?
- **A.** The thread executor will throw an exception when a task is submitted that is over its thread limit.
- **B.** The task will be added to an internal queue and completed when there is an available thread.
- **C.** The thread executor will discard any task over its thread limit.
- **D.** The call to submit the task to the thread executor will wait until there is a thread available before continuing.
- **E.** The thread executor creates new temporary threads to complete the additional tasks.

7. What is the result of executing the following code snippet?

```
List<Integer> l1 = Arrays.asList(1,2,3);
List<Integer> l2 = new CopyOnWriteArrayList<>(l1);
Set<Integer> s3 = new ConcurrentSkipListSet<>();
s3.addAll(l1);

for(Integer item: l2) l2.add(4); // x1
for(Integer item: s3) s3.add(5); // x2
System.out.println(l1.size()+" "+l2.size()+" "+s3.size());
```

A. It outputs 3 6 4.

B. It outputs 6 6 6.

C. It outputs 6 3 4.

D. The code does not compile.

E. It compiles but throws an exception at runtime on line x1.

F. It compiles but throws an exception at runtime on line x2.

G. It compiles but enters an infinite loop at runtime.

8. What statements about the following code are true? (Choose all that apply.)

```
Integer i1 = Arrays.asList(1,2,3,4,5).stream().findAny().get();
synchronized(i1) { // y1
    Integer i2 = Arrays.asList(6,7,8,9,10)
        .parallelStream()
        .sorted()  // y2
        .findAny().get(); // y3
    System.out.println(i1+" "+i2);
}
```

A. It outputs 1 6.

B. It outputs 1 10.

C. The code will not compile because of line y1.

D. The code will not compile because of line y2.

E. The code will not compile because of line y3.

F. It compiles but throws an exception at runtime.

G. The output cannot be determined ahead of time.

H. It compiles but waits forever at runtime.

9. Assuming MyTask is an abstract class that implements the ForkJoinTask interface, what statements about the following code are true? (Choose all that apply.)

```
import java.util.concurrent.*;
public class FindMin extends MyTask {
    private Integer[] elements;
    private int a;
    private int b;
    public FindMin(Integer[] elements, int a, int b) {
        this.elements = elements;
        this.a = a;
        this.b = b;
    }
```

```
public Integer compute() {
   if ((b-a) < 2)
      return Math.min(elements[a], elements[b]);
   else {
      int m = a + ((b-a) / 2);
      System.out.println(a + "," + m + "," + b);
      MyTask t1 = new FindMin(elements, a, m);
      int result = t1.fork().join();
      return Math.min(new FindMin(elements, m, b).compute(), result);
   }
}

public static void main(String[] args) throws InterruptedException,
                                              ExecutionException {
   Integer[] elements = new Integer[] { 8, -3, 2, -54 };
   MyTask task = new FindMin(elements, 0, elements.length-1);
   ForkJoinPool pool = new ForkJoinPool(1);
   Integer sum = pool.invoke(task);
   System.out.println("Min: " + sum);
}
}
```

A. The code correctly finds the minimum value in the array.

B. MyTask inherits RecursiveAction.

C. MyTask inherits RecursiveTask.

D. The code produces a ForkJoinPool at runtime.

E. The class produces single-threaded performance at runtime.

F. The code does not compile.

10. What statements about the following code are true? (Choose all that apply.)

```
System.out.println(Arrays.asList("duck","chicken","flamingo","pelican")
   .parallelStream().parallel() // q1
   .reduce(0,
      (c1, c2) -> c1.length() + c2.length(), // q2
      (s1, s2) -> s1 + s2)); // q3
```

A. It compiles and runs without issue, outputting the total length of all strings in the stream.

B. The code will not compile because of line q1.

C. The code will not compile because of line q2.

D. The code will not compile because of line q3.

E. It compiles but throws an exception at runtime.

11. What statements about the following code snippet are true? (Choose all that apply.)

```java
Object o1 = new Object();
Object o2 = new Object();
ExecutorService service = Executors.newFixedThreadPool(2);
Future<?> f1 = service.submit(() -> {
    synchronized (o1) {
        synchronized (o2) { System.out.println("Tortoise"); } // t1
    }
});
Future<?> f2 = service.submit(() -> {
    synchronized (o2) {
        synchronized (o1) { System.out.println("Hare"); } // t2
    }
});
f1.get();
f2.get();
```

A. If the code does output anything, the order cannot be determined.

B. The code will always output Tortoise followed by Hare.

C. The code will always output Hare followed by Tortoise.

D. The code does not compile because of line t1.

E. The code does not compile because of line t2.

F. The code may produce a deadlock at runtime.

G. The code may produce a livelock at runtime.

H. It compiles but throws an exception at runtime.

12. What is the result of executing the following application? (Choose all that apply.)

```java
import java.util.concurrent.*;
public class CountNumbers extends RecursiveAction {
    private int start;
    private int end;
    public CountNumbers(int start, int end) {
        this.start = start;
        this.end = end;
    }
    protected void compute() {
        if (start<0) return;
```

```
        else {
            int middle = start + ((end-start) / 2);
            invokeAll(new CountNumbers(start, middle),
                new CountNumbers(middle, end)); // m1
        }
    }
    public static void main(String[] args) {
        ForkJoinTask<?> task = new CountNumbers(0, 4); // m2
        ForkJoinPool pool = new ForkJoinPool();
        Object result = pool.invoke(task); // m3
    }
}
```

A. It compiles and runs without issue.

B. The code will not compile because of m1.

C. The code will not compile because of m2.

D. The code will not compile because of m3.

E. It compiles but throws an exception at runtime.

F. It compiles but hangs at runtime.

13. What statements about the following code snippet are true? (Choose all that apply.)

```
4: Stream<String> cats = Stream.of("leopard","lynx","ocelot","puma").parallel();
5: Stream<String> bears = Stream.of("panda","grizzly","polar").parallel();
6: ConcurrentMap<Boolean, List<String>> data = Stream.of(cats,bears)
7:    .flatMap(s -> s)
8:    .collect(Collectors.groupingByConcurrent(s -> !s.startsWith("p")));
9: System.out.println(data.get(false).size()+" "+data.get(true).size());
```

A. It outputs 3 4.

B. It outputs 4 3.

C. The code will not compile because of line 6.

D. The code will not compile because of line 7.

E. The code will not compile because of line 8.

F. It compiles but throws an exception at runtime.

G. The collect() operation is always executed in a single-threaded fashion.

14. What is the result of calling the following method?

```
3: public void addAndPrintItems(BlockingDeque<Integer> deque) {
4:     deque.offer(103);
5:     deque.offerFirst(20, 1, TimeUnit.SECONDS);
```

```
6:      deque.offerLast(85, 7, TimeUnit.HOURS);
7:      System.out.print(deque.pollFirst(200, TimeUnit.NANOSECONDS));
8:      System.out.print(" "+deque.pollLast(1, TimeUnit.MINUTES));
9: }
```

A. It outputs 20 85.

B. It outputs 103 85.

C. It outputs 20 103.

D. The code will not compile.

E. It compiles but throws an exception at runtime.

F. The output cannot be determined ahead of time.

15. Which of the following are valid `Callable` expressions? (Choose all that apply.)

    A. `a -> {return 10;}`

    B. `() -> {String s = "";}`

    C. `() -> 5`

    D. `() -> {return null}`

    E. `() -> "The" + "Zoo"`

    F. `(int count) -> count+1`

    G. `() -> {System.out.println("Giraffe"); return 10;}`

16. What is the result of executing the following application? (Choose all that apply.)

```
import java.util.concurrent.*;
import java.util.stream.*;
public class PrintConstants {
    public static void main(String[] args) {
        ExecutorService service = Executors.newScheduledThreadPool(10);
        DoubleStream.of(3.14159,2.71828) // b1
            .forEach(c -> service.submit( // b2
                () -> System.out.println(10*c))); // b3
        service.execute(() -> System.out.println("Printed")); // b4
    }
}
```

    A. It compiles and outputs the two numbers, followed by `Printed`.

    B. The code will not compile because of line b1.

    C. The code will not compile because of line b2.

    D. The code will not compile because of line b3.

    E. The code will not compile because of line b4.

    F. It compiles but the output cannot be determined ahead of time.

G. It compiles but throws an exception at runtime.

H. It compiles but waits forever at runtime.

17. Assuming 100 milliseconds is enough time for the tasks submitted to the thread executor to complete, what is the result of executing the following program? (Choose all that apply.)

```java
import java.util.concurrent.*;
public class SheepManager {
    private static AtomicInteger sheepCount1 = new AtomicInteger(0); // w1
    private static int sheepCount2 = 0;

    public static void main(String[] args) throws InterruptedException {
        ExecutorService service = null;
        try {
            service = Executors.newSingleThreadExecutor(); // w2

            for(int i=0; i<100; i++)
                service.execute(() ->
                    {sheepCount1.getAndIncrement(); sheepCount2++;}); // w3
            Thread.sleep(100);
            System.out.println(sheepCount1+" "+sheepCount2);
        } finally {
            if(service != null) service.shutdown();
        }
    }
}
```

A. It outputs `100 99`.

B. It outputs `100 100`.

C. The output cannot be determined ahead of time.

D. The code will not compile because of line w1.

E. The code will not compile because of line w2.

F. The code will not compile because of line w3.

G. It compiles but throws an exception at runtime.

18. What is the result of executing the following application? (Choose all that apply.)

```java
import java.util.concurrent.*;
import java.util.stream.*;
public class StockRoomTracker {
    public static void await(CyclicBarrier cb) { // j1
        try { cb.await(); } catch (InterruptedException |
BrokenBarrierException e) {
```

```
            // Handle exception
         }
      }
      public static void main(String[] args) {
         CyclicBarrier cb = new CyclicBarrier(10,
            () -> System.out.println("Stock Room Full!")); // j2
         IntStream.iterate(1, i -> 1).limit(9)
            .parallel().forEach(i -> await(cb)); // j3
      }
   }
```

   A.   It outputs Stock Room Full!

   B.   The code will not compile because of line j1.

   C.   The code will not compile because of line j2.

   D.   The code will not compile because of line j3.

   E.   It compiles but throws an exception at runtime.

   F.   It compiles but waits forever at runtime.

19. What statements about the following class definition are true? (Choose all that apply.)

```
public class TicketManager {
   private TicketManager() { super(); }
   private static TicketManager instance;
   public static synchronized TicketManager getInstance() { // k1
      if (instance == null) instance = new TicketManager(); // k2
      return instance;
   }

   private int tickets;
   public int getTicketCount() { return tickets; }
   public void makeTicketsAvailable(int value) { tickets += value; } // k3
   public void sellTickets(int value) {
      synchronized (this) { // k4
         tickets -= value;
      }
   }
}
```

   A.   It compiles without issue.

   B.   The code will not compile because of line k2.

   C.   The code will not compile because of line k3.

   D.   The lock locks acquired on k1 and k4 are on the same object.

E. The class correctly prevents concurrency issues for the value of `tickets` when accessed by multiple threads.

F. At most one instance of `TicketManager` will be created in the application.

20. Which of the following properties of concurrency are true? (Choose all that apply.)

A. By itself, concurrency does not guarantee which task will be completed first.

B. Concurrency always improves the performance of an application.

C. Computers with a single processor do not benefit from concurrency.

D. Applications with many resource-heavy tasks tend to benefit more from concurrency than ones with CPU-intensive tasks.

E. Concurrent tasks do not share the same memory.

21. Assuming an implementation of the `performCount()` method is provided prior to runtime, which of the following are possible results of executing the following application? (Choose all that apply.)

```java
import java.util.*;
import java.util.concurrent.*;
import java.util.stream.*;
public class CountZooAnimals {
    public static Integer performCount(int exhibitNumber) {
        // IMPLEMENTATION OMITTED
    }

    public static void printResults(Future<?> f) {
        try {
            System.out.println(f.get()); // o1
        } catch (Exception e) {
            System.out.println("Exception!");
        }
    }

    public static void main(String[] args) throws InterruptedException,
    ExecutionException {
        ExecutorService service = Executors.newSingleThreadExecutor();
        final List<Future<?>> results = new ArrayList<>();
        IntStream.range(0, 10)
            .forEach(i -> results.add(
                service.submit(() -> performCount(i)))); // o2
        results.stream().forEach(f -> printResults(f));
        service.shutdown();
    }
}
```

A. It outputs a number 10 times.

B. It outputs a `Boolean` value 10 times.

C. It outputs a `null` value 10 times.

D. It outputs `Exception!` 10 times.

E. It hangs indefinitely at runtime.

F. It throws an unhandled exception at runtime.

G. The code will not compile because of line o1.

H. The code will not compile because of line o2.

22. What is the result of executing the following program?

```
import java.util.*;
import java.util.concurrent.*;
import java.util.stream.*;

public class PrintCounter {
   static int counter = 0;
   public static void main(String[] args) throws InterruptedException,
   ExecutionException {
      ExecutorService service = Executors.newSingleThreadExecutor();
      List<Future<?>> results = new ArrayList<>();
      IntStream.iterate(0,i -> i+1).limit(5).forEach(
            i -> results.add(service.execute(() -> counter++)) // n1
      );
      for(Future<?> result : results) {
         System.out.print(result.get()+" "); // n2
      }
      service.shutdown();
   }
}
```

A. It prints `0 1 2 3 4`

B. It prints `1 2 3 4 5`

C. It prints `null null null null null`

D. It hangs indefinitely at runtime.

E. The output cannot be determined.

F. The code will not compile because of line n1.

G. The code will not compile because of line n2.

Chapter

8

IO

THE OCP EXAM TOPICS COVERED IN THIS CHAPTER INCLUDE THE FOLLOWING:

✓ **Java I/O Fundamentals**

- Read and write data from the console
- Use BufferedReader, BufferedWriter, File, FileReader, FileWriter, FileInputStream, FileOutputStream, ObjectOutputStream, ObjectInputStream, and PrintWriter in the java.io.package.

What can Java applications do outside the scope of managing objects and attributes in memory? How can they save data so that information is not lost every time the program is terminated? They use files, of course! You can design code that writes the current state of an application to a file every time the application is closed and then reloads the data when the application is executed the next time. In this manner, information is preserved between program executions.

This chapter focuses on using the java.io API to interact with files and streams. We start by describing how files and directories are organized within a file system and show how to access them with the java.io.File class. We then show how to read and write file data with the stream classes. Finally, we conclude this chapter by discussing ways of reading user input at runtime using the Console class.

In the next chapter, "NIO.2," we will revisit the discussion of files and show how Java now provides more powerful techniques for managing files.

Understanding Files and Directories

We begin this chapter by describing what a file is and what a directory is within a file system. We then present the java.io.File class and demonstrate how to use it to read and write file information.

Conceptualizing the File System

Before we start working with files and directories, we present the terminology that we will be using throughout this chapter.

A *file* is record within a file system that stores user and system data. Files are organized using directories. A *directory* is a record within a file system that contains files as well as other directories. For simplicity, we often refer to a directory reference as a file record throughout this chapter, since it is stored in the file system with a unique name and with attributes similar to a file. For example, a file and directory can both be renamed with the same operation. Finally, the *root directory* is the topmost directory in the file system, from which all files and directories inherit. In Windows, it is denoted with a drive name such as c:\, while on Linux it is denoted with a single forward slash /.

In order to interact with files, we need to connect to the file system. The *file system* is in charge of reading and writing data within a computer. Different operating systems use different file systems to manage their data. For example, Windows-based systems use a different file system than Unix-based ones. As you shall see, Java includes numerous methods, which automatically connect to the local file system for you, allowing you to perform the same operations across multiple file systems.

A *path* is a String representation of a file or directory within a file system. Each file system defines its own path separator character that is used between directory entries. In most file systems, the value to the left of a separator is the parent of the value to the right of the separator. For example, the path value /user/home/zoo.txt means that the file zoo.txt is inside the home directory, with the home directory inside the user directory. You will see that paths can be absolute or relative later in this chapter.

We show how a directory and file system is organized in a hierarchical manner in Figure 8.1. In this diagram, directories are represented as rectangles and files as ovals. Directories can be empty, as shown with the c:\zoo and c:\app\employees directories.

FIGURE 8.1   Directory and file hierarchy

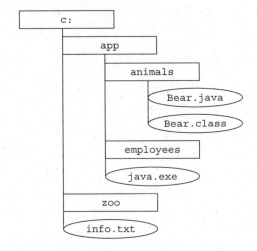

Introducing the File Class

The first class that we will discuss is one of the most commonly used in the java.io API, the java.io.File class, or File class for short. The File class is used to read information about existing files and directories, list the contents of a directory, and create/delete files and directories.

An instance of a File class represents the pathname of a particular file or directory on the file system. The File class cannot read or write data within a file, although it can be passed as a reference to many stream classes to read or write data, as you shall see in the next section.

One common mistake new Java developers make is forgetting that the File class can be used to represent directories as well as files.

Creating a File Object

A File object often is initialized with String containing either an absolute or relative path to the file or directory within the file system. The *absolute path* of a file or directory is the full path from the root directory to the file or directory, including all subdirectories that contain the file or directory. Alternatively, the *relative path* of a file or directory is the path from the current working directory to file or directory. For example, the following is an absolute path to the zoo.txt file:

/home/smith/data/zoo.txt

The following is a relative path to the same file, assuming the user's current directory was set to /home/smith.

data/zoo.txt

Different operating systems vary in their format of path names. For example, Unix-based systems use the forward slash / for paths, whereas Windows-based systems use the backslash \ character. That said, many programming languages and file systems support both types of slashes when writing path statements. For convenience, Java offers two options to retrieve the local separator character: a system property and a static variable defined in the File class. Both of the following examples will output the separator character:

System.out.println(System.getProperty("file.separator"));

System.out.println(java.io.File.separator);

The following code creates a File object and determines if the path it references exists within the file system:

```java
import java.io.File;

public class FileSample {
   public static void main(String[] args) {
      File file = new File("/home/smith/data/zoo.txt");
      System.out.println(file.exists());
   }
}
```

This example uses the absolute path to a file and outputs true or false, depending on whether the file exists. The most common File constructor we will use throughout this chapter takes a single String as an argument representing the relative or absolute path. There are other constructors, such as the one that joins an existing File path with a relative child path, as shown in the following example:

```java
File parent = new File("/home/smith");
File child = new File(parent,"data/zoo.txt");
```

In this example, we create a path that is equivalent to our previous example, using a combination of a child path and a parent path. If the parent object happened to be null, then it would be skipped and the method would revert to our single String constructor.

Working with a File Object

The File class contains numerous useful methods for interacting with files and directories within the file system. We present the most commonly used ones in Table 8.1. Although this table may seem like a lot of methods to learn, many of them are self-explanatory. For example, exists() returns true if the file or directory path exists and false otherwise.

TABLE 8.1   Commonly used java.io.File methods

Method Name	Description
exists()	Returns true if the file or directory exists.
getName()	Returns the name of the file or directory denoted by this path.
getAbsolutePath()	Returns the absolute pathname string of this path.
isDirectory()	Returns true if the file denoted by this path is a directory.
isFile()	Returns true if the file denoted by this path is a file.
length()	Returns the number of bytes in the file. For performance reasons, the file system may allocate more bytes on disk than the file actually uses.
lastModified()	Returns the number of milliseconds since the epoch when the file was last modified.
delete()	Deletes the file or directory. If this pathname denotes a directory, then the directory must be empty in order to be deleted.
renameTo(File)	Renames the file denoted by this path.
mkdir()	Creates the directory named by this path.
mkdirs()	Creates the directory named by this path including any nonexistent parent directories.
getParent()	Returns the abstract pathname of this abstract pathname's parent or null if this pathname does not name a parent directory.
listFiles()	Returns a File[] array denoting the files in the directory.

The following is a sample program that given a file path outputs information about the file or directory, such as whether it exists, what files are contained within it, and so forth:

```java
import java.io.File;

public class ReadFileInformation {
   public static void main(String[] args) {
      File file = new File("C:\\data\\zoo.txt");
      System.out.println("File Exists: "+file.exists());
      if(file.exists()) {
         System.out.println("Absolute Path: "+file.getAbsolutePath());
         System.out.println("Is Directory: "+file.isDirectory());
         System.out.println("Parent Path: "+file.getParent());
         if(file.isFile()) {
            System.out.println("File size: "+file.length());
            System.out.println("File LastModified: "+file.lastModified());
         } else {
            for(File subfile: file.listFiles()) {
               System.out.println("\t"+subfile.getName());
            }
         }
      }
   }
}
```

If the path provided did not point to a file, it would output the following:

```
File Exists: false
```

If the path provided pointed to a valid file, it would output something similar to the following:

```
File Exists: true
Absolute Path: C:\data\zoo.txt
Parent Path: C:\data
Is Directory: false
File size: 12382
File LastModified: 1420070400000
```

Finally, if the path provided pointed to a valid directory, such as C:\data, it would output something similar to the following:

```
File Exists: true
Absolute Path: C:\data
Parent Path: C:\
```

```
Is Directory: true
  employees.txt
  zoo.txt
  zoo-backup.txt
```

In these examples, you see that the output of an I/O-based program is completely dependent on the directories and files available at runtime in the underlying file system.

Note that we used a Windows-based path in the previous sample, which requires a double backslash in the String literal for the path separator. You may remember from Chapter 5, "Dates, Strings and Localization," that the backslash \ is a reserved character within a String literal and must be escaped with another backslash to be used within a String.

Introducing Streams

In this section, we present the concept of streams in Java and show how they are used for input/output (I/O) processing. I/O refers to the nature of how data is accessed, either by reading the data from a resource (input), or writing the data to a resource (output). This section will focus on the common ways that data is input and output using files accessed by streams.

Note that the I/O streams that we discuss in this chapter are data streams and completely unrelated to the new Stream API that you saw in Chapter 4, "Functional Programming." Even we agree that the naming of the new Stream API can be a little confusing when discussing I/O streams.

Stream Fundamentals

The contents of a file may be accessed or written via a *stream*, which is a list of data elements presented sequentially. Streams should be conceptually thought of as a long, nearly never-ending "stream of water" with data presented one "wave" at a time.

It may be helpful to visualize a stream as being so large that all of the data contained in it could not possibly fit into memory. For example, a 1 terabyte file could not be stored entirely in memory by most computer systems (at the time this book is being written). The file can still be read and written by a program with very little memory, since the stream allows the application to focus on only a small portion of the overall stream at any given time.

We demonstrate this principle in Figure 8.2. The stream is so large that once we start reading it, we have no idea where the beginning or the end is. We just have a pointer to our current position in the stream and read data one block at a time.

FIGURE 8.2   Visual representation of a stream

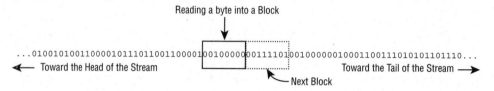

Reading a byte into a Block

...010010100110000101110110011000010010000000111101001000000100011001110101011101110...

← Toward the Head of the Stream   Toward the Tail of the Stream →

Next Block

Each type of stream segments data into a "wave" or "block" in a particular way. For example, some stream classes read or write data as individual byte values. Other stream classes read or write individual characters or strings of characters. On top of that, some stream classes read or write groups of bytes or characters at a time, specifically those with the word Buffered in their name.

 Real World Scenario

All Java Streams Use Bytes

Although the java.io API is full of streams that handle characters, strings, groups of bytes, and so on, nearly all are built on top of reading or writing an individual byte or an array of bytes at a time. The reasoning behind more high-order streams is for convenience as well as performance.

For example, writing a file one byte at a time is time consuming and slow in practice because the round-trip between the Java application and the file system is relatively expensive. By utilizing a BufferedOutputStream, the Java application can write a large chunk of bytes at a time, reducing the round-trips and drastically improving performance.

Although streams are commonly used with file I/O, they are more generally used to handle reading/writing of a sequential data source. For example, you might construct a Java application that submits data to a website using an input stream and reads the result via an output stream.

In fact, you have been using streams since your first "Hello World" program! Java provides three built-in streams, System.in, System.err, and System.out, the last of which we have been using to output data to the screen throughout this book. We will discuss these three streams in detail later in this chapter when we discuss user input.

Stream Nomenclature

The java.io API provides numerous classes for creating, accessing, and manipulating streams—so many that it tends to overwhelm most new Java developers. Stay calm! We will review the major differences between each stream class and show you how to distinguish between them. Even if you do come across a particular stream on the exam that you do not recognize, often the name of the stream gives you enough information to understand exactly what it does.

The goal of this section is to familiarize you with common terminology and naming conventions used with streams. Don't worry if you don't recognize the particular stream class names used in this section or their function; we'll be covering each in detail in the next part of the chapter.

Byte Streams vs. Character Streams

The `java.io` API defines two sets of classes for reading and writing streams: those with `Stream` in their name and those with `Reader/Writer` in their name. For example, the `java.io` API defines both a `FileInputStream` class as well as a `FileReader` class, both of which define a stream that reads a file. The difference between the two classes is based on how the stream is read or written.

Differences between Streams and Readers/Writers

1. The stream classes are used for inputting and outputting all types of binary or byte data.
2. The reader and writer classes are used for inputting and outputting only character and `String` data.

It is important to remember that even though readers/writers do not contain the word `Stream` in their class name, they are still in fact streams! The use of `Reader/Writer` in the name is just to distinguish them from byte streams. Throughout the chapter, we will often refer to `Reader/Writer` classes as streams, since conceptually they are streams.

Why Use Character Streams?

Since the byte stream classes can be used to input and output all types of binary data, including strings, it naturally follows that you can write all of your code to use the byte stream classes, never really needing the character stream classes.

There are advantages, though, to using the reader/writer classes, as they are specifically focused on managing character and string data. For example, you can use a `Writer` class to output a `String` value to a file without necessarily having to worry about the underlying byte encoding of the file.

For this reason, the character stream classes are sometimes referred to as convenience classes for working with text data.

The `java.io` API is structured such that all of the stream classes have the word `InputStream` or `OutputStream` in their name, while all `Reader/Writer` classes have either `Reader` or `Writer` in their name.

Pay close attention to the name of the java.io class on the exam, as decoding it often gives you context clues as to what the class does. For example, without needing to look it up, it should be clear that FileReader is a class that reads data from a file as characters or strings. Furthermore, ObjectOutputStream sounds like a class that writes object data to a byte stream.

Input and Output

Most Input stream classes have a corresponding Output class and vice versa. For example, the FileOutputStream class writes data that can be read by a FileInputStream. If you understand the features of a particular Input or Output stream class, you should naturally know what its complementary class does.

It follows, then, that most Reader classes have a corresponding Writer class. For example, the FileWriter class writes data that can be read by a FileReader.

There are exceptions to this rule. For the exam, you should know that PrintWriter has no accompanying PrintReader class. Likewise, the PrintStream class has no corresponding InputStream class. We will discuss these classes later this chapter.

Low-Level vs. High-Level Streams

Another way that you can familiarize yourself with the java.io API is by segmenting streams into low-level and high-level streams.

A *low-level stream* connects directly with the source of the data, such as a file, an array, or a String. Low-level streams process the raw data or resource and are accessed in a direct and unfiltered manner. For example, a FileInputStream is a class that reads file data one byte at a time.

Alternatively, a *high-level stream* is built on top of another stream using wrapping. *Wrapping* is the process by which an instance is passed to the constructor of another class and operations on the resulting instance are filtered and applied to the original instance. For example, take a look at the FileWriter and BufferedWriter objects in the following sample code:

```
try (
    BufferedReader bufferedReader = new BufferedReader(
                                new FileReader("zoo-data.txt"))) {
    System.out.println(bufferedReader.readLine());
}
```

In this example, FileReader is the low-level stream reader, whereas BufferedReader is the high-level stream that takes a FileReader as input. Many operations on the high-level stream pass through as operations to the underlying low-level stream, such as read() or close(). Other operations override or add new functionality to the low-level stream methods. The high-level stream adds new methods, such as readLine(), as well as performance enhancements for reading and filtering the low-level data.

High-level streams can take other high-level streams as input. For example, although the following code might seem a little odd at first, the style of wrapping a stream is quite common in practice:

```
try (ObjectInputStream objectStream = new ObjectInputStream(
                                new BufferedInputStream(
                                    new FileInputStream("zoo-data.txt")))) {
    System.out.println(objectStream.readObject());
}
```

In this example, `FileInputStream` is the low-level stream that interacts directly with the file, which is wrapped by a high-level `BufferedInputStream` to improve performance. Finally, the entire object is wrapped by a high-level `ObjectInputStream`, which allows us to filter the data as Java objects.

For the exam, the only low-level stream classes you need to be familiar with are the ones that operate on files. The rest of the non-abstract stream classes are all high-level streams.

 Real World Scenario

Use Buffered Streams When Working with Files

As briefly mentioned, `Buffered` classes read or write data in groups, rather than a single byte or character at a time. The performance gain from using a `Buffered` class to access a low-level file stream cannot be overstated. Unless you are doing something very specialized in your application, you should always wrap a file stream with a `Buffered` class in practice.

The reason that `Buffered` streams tend to perform so well in practice is that file systems are geared for sequential disk access. The more sequential bytes you read at a time, the fewer round-trips between the Java process and the file system, improving the access of your application. For example, accessing 16 sequential bytes is a lot faster than accessing 16 bytes spread across the hard drive.

Stream Base Classes

The `java.io` library defines four abstract classes that are the parents of all stream classes defined within the API: `InputStream`, `OutputStream`, `Reader`, and `Writer`. For convenience, the authors of the Java API include the name of the abstract parent class as the suffix of the child class. For example, `ObjectInputStream` ends with `InputStream`, meaning it has `InputStream` as an inherited parent class. Although most stream classes in `java.io` follow this pattern, `PrintStream`, which is an `OutputStream`, does not.

The constructors of high-level streams often take a reference to the abstract class. For example, `BufferedWriter` takes a `Writer` object as input, which allows it to take any subclass of `Writer`.

The advantage of using a reference to the abstract parent class in the class constructor should be apparent in the previous high-level stream example. With high level-streams, a class may be wrapped multiple times. Furthermore, developers may define their own stream subclass that performs custom filtering. By using the abstract parent class as input, the high-level stream classes can be used much more often without concern for the particular under-lying stream subclass.

One common area where the exam likes to play tricks on you is mixing and matching stream classes that are not compatible with each other. For example, take a look at each of the following examples and see if you can determine why they do not compile.

```
new BufferedInputStream(new FileReader("zoo-data.txt"));      // DOES NOT COMPILE

new BufferedWriter(new FileOutputStream("zoo-data.txt"));      // DOES NOT COMPILE

new ObjectInputStream(new FileOutputStream("zoo-data.txt")); // DOES NOT COMPILE

new BufferedInputStream(new InputStream());                   // DOES NOT COMPILE
```

The first two examples do not compile because they mix Reader/Writer classes with InputStream/OutputStream classes, respectively. The third example does not compile because we are mixing an OutputStream with an InputStream. Although it is possible to read data from an InputStream and write it to an OutputStream, wrapping the stream is not the way to do so. As you shall see later in this chapter, the data must be copied over, often iteratively. Finally, the last example does not compile because InputStream is an abstract class, and therefore you cannot instantiate an instance of it.

Decoding Java I/O Class Names

Given that there are so many different java.io stream classes, it is reasonable to think that you might encounter one on the exam whose name you may have forgotten. Luckily, the function of most stream classes can be understood by decoding the name of the class. We summarize these properties in the following list.

Review of java.io Class Properties

- A class with the word InputStream or OutputStream in its name is used for reading or writing binary data, respectively.
- A class with the word Reader or Writer in its name is used for reading or writing character or string data, respectively.
- Most, but not all, input classes have a corresponding output class.
- A low-level stream connects directly with the source of the data.
- A high-level stream is built on top of another stream using wrapping.
- A class with Buffered in its name reads or writes data in groups of bytes or characters and often improves performance in sequential file systems.

When wrapping a stream you can mix and match only types that inherit from the same abstract parent stream.

Table 8.2 describes those java.io streams you should be familiar with for the exam. Note that most of the information about each stream, such as whether it is an input or output stream or whether it accesses data using bytes or characters, can be decoded by the name alone.

TABLE 8.2   The `java.io` stream classes

Class Name	Low/High Level	Description
InputStream	N/A	The abstract class all `InputStream` classes inherit from
OutputStream	N/A	The abstract class all `OutputStream` classes inherit from
Reader	N/A	The abstract class all `Reader` classes inherit from
Writer	N/A	The abstract class all `Writer` classes inherit from
FileInputStream	Low	Reads file data as bytes
FileOutputStream	Low	Writes file data as bytes
FileReader	Low	Reads file data as characters
FileWriter	Low	Writes file data as characters
BufferedReader	High	Reads character data from an existing Reader in a buffered manner, which improves efficiency and performance
BufferedWriter	High	Writes character data to an existing `Writer` in a buffered manner, which improves efficiency and performance
ObjectInputStream	High	Deserializes primitive Java data types and graphs of Java objects from an existing `InputStream`
ObjectOutputStream	High	Serializes primitive Java data types and graphs of Java objects to an existing `OutputStream`
InputStreamReader	High	Reads character data from an existing `InputStream`
OutputStreamWriter	High	Writes character data to an existing `OutputStream`
PrintStream	High	Writes formatted representations of Java objects to a binary stream
PrintWriter	High	Writes formatted representations of Java objects to a text-based output stream

We will discuss these java.io classes in more detail including examples in upcoming sections.

Common Stream Operations

Before we delve into specific stream classes, let's review some common processes when working with streams.

Closing the Stream

Since streams are considered resources, it is imperative that they be closed after they are used lest they lead to resource leaks. As you saw in Chapter 6, "Exceptions and Assertions," you can accomplish this by calling the close() method in a finally block or using the try-with-resource syntax.

In a file system, failing to close a file properly could leave it locked by the operating system such that no other processes could read/write to it until the program is terminated. Throughout this chapter, we will close stream resources using the try-with-resource syntax, since this is the preferred way of closing resources in Java.

Flushing the Stream

When data is written to an OutputStream, the underlying operating system does not necessarily guarantee that the data will make it to the file immediately. In many operating systems, the data may be cached in memory, with a write occurring only after a temporary cache is filled or after some amount of time has passed.

If the data is cached in memory and the application terminates unexpectedly, the data would be lost, because it was never written to the file system. To address this, Java provides a flush() method, which requests that all accumulated data be written immediately to disk.

The flush() method helps reduce the amount of data lost if the application terminates unexpectedly. It is not without cost, though. Each time it is used, it may cause a noticeable delay in the application, especially for large files. Unless the data that you are writing is extremely critical, the flush() method should only be used intermittently. For example, it should not necessarily be called after every write but after every dozen writes or so, depending on your requirements. For reasonably small files, you may need to call flush() only once.

You do not need to call the flush() method explicitly when you have finished writing to a file, since the close() method will automatically do this. In some cases, calling the flush() method intermittently while writing a large file, rather than performing a single large flush when the file is closed, may appear to improve performance by stretching the disk access over the course of the write process.

Marking the Stream

The InputStream and Reader classes include mark(int) and reset() methods to move the stream back to an earlier position. Before calling either of these methods, you should call the markSupported() method, which returns true only if mark() is supported. Not all java.io input stream classes support this operation, and trying to call mark(int) or reset() on a class that does not support these operations will throw an exception at runtime.

Once you've verified that the stream can support these operations, you can call mark(int) with a read-ahead limit value. You can then read as many bytes as you want up to the limit value. If at any point you want to go back to the earlier position where you last called mark(), then you just call reset() and the stream will "revert" to an earlier state. In practice, it's not actually putting the data back into the stream but storing the data that was already read into memory for you to read again. Therefore, you should not call the mark() operation with too large a value as this could take up a lot of memory.

Assume that we have an InputStream instance whose next values are ABCD. Consider the following code snippet:

```
InputStream is = ...
System.out.print ((char)is.read());
if(is.markSupported()) {
    is.mark(100);
    System.out.print((char)is.read());
    System.out.print((char)is.read());
    is.reset();
}
System.out.print((char)is.read());
System.out.print((char)is.read());
System.out.print((char)is.read());
```

The code snippet will output the following if the mark() operation is supported:

ABCBCD

It first outputs A before the if/then statement. Since we are given that the stream supports the mark() operation, it will enter the if/then statement and read two characters, BC. It then calls the reset() operation, moving our stream back to the state that it was in after the A was read, therefore BC are read again, followed by D.

If the mark() operation is not supported, it will output this instead, skipping the if/then statement entirely:

ABCD

Notice that regardless of whether the mark() operation was supported, we took care to have the stream end at the same position.

Finally, if you call reset() after you have passed your mark() read limit, an exception may be thrown at runtime since the marked position may become invalidated. We say "an exception *may* be thrown" as some implementations may use a buffer to allow extra data to be read before the mark is invalidated.

Skipping over Data

The InputStream and Reader classes also include a skip(long) method, which as you might expect skips over a certain number of bytes. It returns a long value, which indicates the number of bytes that were actually skipped. If the return value is zero or negative, such as if the end of the stream was reached, no bytes were skipped.

Assume that we have an InputStream instance whose next values are TIGERS. Consider the following code snippet:

```
InputStream is = ...
System.out.print ((char)is.read());
is.skip(2)
is.read();
System.out.print((char)is.read());
System.out.print((char)is.read());
```

The code will read one character, T, skip two characters, IG, and then read three more characters, ERS, only the last two of which are printed to the user, which results in the following output.

```
TRS
```

You may notice in this example that calling the skip() operation is equivalent to calling read() and discarding the output. For skipping a handful of bytes, there is virtually no difference. On the other hand, for skipping a large number of bytes, skip() will often be faster, because it will use arrays to read the data.

Working with Streams

Now that we've reviewed the types of streams and their properties, it's time to jump in and work with some stream code! Some of the techniques for accessing streams may seem a bit new to you, but as you will see they are very similar among different stream classes.

The *FileInputStream* and *FileOutputStream* Classes

The first stream classes that we are going to discuss in detail are the most basic file stream classes, FileInputStream and FileOutputStream. They are used to read bytes from a file or write bytes to a file, respectively. These classes include constructors that take a File object or String, representing a path to the file.

The data in a FileInputStream object is commonly accessed by successive calls to the read() method until a value of -1 is returned, indicating that the end of the stream—in this case the end of the file—has been reached. Although less common, you can also choose to stop reading the stream early just by exiting the loop, such as if some search String is found.

When reading a single value of a `FileInputStream` instance, the `read()` method returns a primitive `int` value rather than a byte value. It does this so that it has an additional value available to be returned, specifically -1, when the end of the file is reached. If the class did return a byte instead of an `int`, there would be no way to know whether the end of the file had been reached based on the value returned from the `read()` method, since the file could contain all possible byte values as data. For compatibility, the `FileOutput-Stream` also uses `int` instead of byte for writing a single byte to a file.

The `FileInputStream` class also contains overloaded versions of the `read()` method, which take a pointer to a byte array where the data is written. The method returns an integer value indicating how many bytes can be read into the byte array. It is also used by Buffered classes to improve performance, as you shall see in the next section.

A `FileOutputStream` object is accessed by writing successive bytes using the `write(int)` method. Like the `FileInputStream` class, the `FileOutputStream` also contains overloaded versions of the `write()` method that allow a byte array to be passed and can be used by Buffered classes.

The following code uses `FileInputStream` and `FileOutputStream` to copy a file:

```java
import java.io.*;

public class CopyFileSample {
    public static void copy(File source, File destination) throws IOException {
        try (InputStream in = new FileInputStream(source);
            OutputStream out = new FileOutputStream(destination)) {
            int b;
            while((b = in.read()) != -1) {
                out.write(b);
            }
        }
    }

    public static void main(String[] args) throws IOException {
        File source = new File("Zoo.class");
        File destination = new File("ZooCopy.class");
        copy(source,destination);
    }
}
```

The `main()` method creates two `File` objects, one for the source file to copy from and one for the destination file to copy to. If the destination file already exists, it will be overridden by this code. Both `File` objects are created using relative paths, so the application would search for the `Zoo.class` in the current directory to read from, throwing a `FileNotFoundException` if the file is not found, which is a subclass of an `IOException`.

The copy() method creates instances of FileInputStream and FileOutputStream, and it proceeds to read the FileInputStream one byte at a time, copying the value to the FileOutputStream as it's read. As soon as the in.read() returns a -1 value, the loop ends. Finally, both streams are closed using the try-with-resource syntax presented in Chapter 6.

Note that the performance for this code, especially for large files, would not be particularly good because the sample does not use any byte arrays. As you shall see in the next section, we can improve the implementation using byte arrays and buffered streams.

The *BufferedInputStream* and *BufferedOutputStream* Classes

We can enhance our implementation with only a few minor code changes by wrapping the FileInputStream and FileOutputStream classes that you saw in the previous example with the BufferedInputStream and BufferedOutputStream classes, respectively.

Instead of reading the data one byte at a time, we use the underlying read(byte[]) method of BufferedInputStream, which returns the number of bytes read into the provided byte array. The number of bytes read is important for two reasons. First, if the value returned is 0, then we know that we have reached the end of the file and can stop reading from the BufferedInputStream. Second, the last read of the file will likely only partially fill the byte array, since it is unlikely for the file size to be an exact multiple of our buffer array size.

For example, if the buffer size is 1,024 bytes and the file size is 1,054 bytes, then the last read will be only 30 bytes. The length value tells us how many of the bytes in the array were actually read from the file. The remaining bytes of the array will be filled with leftover data from the previous read that should be discarded.

The data is written into the BufferedOutputStream using the write(byte[],int,int) method, which takes as input a byte array, an offset, and a length value, respectively. The offset value is the number of values to skip before writing characters, and it is often set to 0. The length value is the number of characters from the byte array to write.

Why Use the Buffered Classes?

Although we could have rewritten our earlier examples to use byte arrays without introducing the Buffered classes, we chose to present them together. In practice, it's quite common to use Buffered classes anytime you are reading or writing data with byte arrays. The Buffered classes contain numerous performance enhancements for managing stream data in memory.

For example, the BufferedInputStream class is capable of retrieving and storing in memory more data than you might request with a single read() call. For successive calls to the read() method with small byte arrays, this would be faster in a wide variety of situations, since the data can be returned directly from memory without going to the file system.

Here's a modified form of our copy() method, which uses byte arrays and the Buffered stream classes:

```java
import java.io.*;

public class CopyBufferFileSample {
    public static void copy(File source, File destination) throws IOException {
        try (
            InputStream in = new BufferedInputStream(new FileInputStream(source));
            OutputStream out = new BufferedOutputStream(
                                        new FileOutputStream(destination))) {
            byte[] buffer = new byte[1024];
            int lengthRead;
            while ((lengthRead = in.read(buffer)) > 0) {
                out.write(buffer,0,lengthRead);
                out.flush();
            }
        }
    }
}
```

You can see that this sample code that uses byte arrays is very similar to the nonbuffered sample code, although the performance improvement for using both the Buffered classes and byte arrays is an order of magnitude faster in practice. We also added a flush() command in the loop, as previously discussed, to ensure that the written data actually makes it to disk before the next buffer of data is read.

 Real World Scenario

Buffer Size Tuning

We chose a buffer size of 1024 in this example, as this is appropriate for a wide variety of circumstances, although in practice you may see better performance with a larger or smaller buffer size. This would depend on a number of factors including file system block size and CPU hardware.

It is also common to choose a power of 2 for the buffer size, since most underlying hardware is structured with file block and cache sizes that are a power of 2. The Buffered classes allow you to specify the buffer size in the constructor. If none is provided, they use a default value, which is a power of 2 in most JVMs.

Regardless of which buffer size you choose, the biggest performance increase you will see is moving from nonbuffered to buffered file access. Adjusting the buffer size may improve performance slightly, but unless you are using an extremely small or extremely large buffer size, it is unlikely to have a significant impact.

The *FileReader* and *FileWriter* classes

The FileReader and FileWriter classes, along with their associated buffer classes, are among the most convenient classes in the java.io API, in part because reading and writing text data are among the most common ways that developers interact with files.

Like the FileInputStream and FileOutputStream classes, the FileReader and FileWriter classes contain read() and write() methods, respectively. These methods read/write char values instead of byte values; although similar to what you saw with streams, the API actually uses an int value to hold the data so that -1 can be returned if the end of the file is detected. The FileReader and FileWriter classes contain other methods that you saw in the stream classes, including close() and flush(), the usage of which is the same.

The Writer class, which FileWriter inherits from, offers a write(String) method that allows a String object to be written directly to the stream. Using FileReader also allows you to pair it with BufferedReader in order to use the very convenient readLine() method, which you will see in the next example.

The *BufferedReader* and *BufferedWriter* Classes

Let's take a look at a sample program that makes use of both the BufferedReader and BufferedWriter classes using the associated readLine() and write(String) methods. It reads a text file, outputs each line to screen, and writes a copy of the file to disk. Since these classes are buffered, you can expect better performance than if you read/wrote each character one at a time.

```java
import java.io.*;
import java.util.*;

public class CopyTextFileSample {
    public static List<String> readFile(File source) throws IOException {
        List<String> data = new ArrayList<String>();
        try (BufferedReader reader = new BufferedReader(new FileReader(source))) {
            String s;
            while((s = reader.readLine()) != null) {
                data.add(s);
            }
        }
        return data;
    }

    public static void writeFile(List<String> data, File destination) throws
    IOException {
        try (BufferedWriter writer = new BufferedWriter(
                                        new FileWriter(destination))) {
            for(String s: data) {
                writer.write(s);
```

```
            writer.newLine();
        }
    }
}

public static void main(String[] args) throws IOException {
    File source = new File("Zoo.csv");
    File destination = new File("ZooCopy.csv");
    List<String> data = readFile(source);
    for(String record: data) {
        System.out.println(record);
    }
    writeFile(data,destination);
}
}
```

This example is similar to the file copy example that you saw previously, with some important differences. First, in the readFile() method, we use a temporary String reference s to hold the value of the data in loop as we read it. Unlike FileInputStream and FileReader, where we used -1 to check for file termination of an int value, with BufferedReader, we stop reading the file when readLine() returns null.

Next, instead of immediately copying the data we read from the file into the output file, we store it in a List of String objects in the readFile() method. This allows us to both display and modify the data, prior to writing it to disk later.

For example, let's say that we wanted to replace one person's name in a text file with another. We would just use the String.replaceAll() method on the data as we wrote it to disk, and the new file would have the replacement. By working entirely with String values instead of byte values, we have access to the all of the methods in the String API to manipulate data.

The last major difference between this code and the previous copy file example is in how data is written in the writeFile() method. Unlike the previous examples where we had to write the code one byte at a time or by using a byte array, we can write the entire String in a single call. The write(String) method is quite convenient in practice. We then use the writer.newLine() method to insert a line break into the copied file, as our reader.readLine() method split on line breaks.

Note that we used the .csv file extension in this example to represent comma-separated values files, as these are commonly text based. This example also assumes that the CSV file is small enough to fit entirely in memory.

Let's say that the file is so large that it cannot fit in memory. If you wanted to write it directly to disk, rather than storing it in a List object, you could take our earlier copy file stream example and replace it with Reader/Writer methods.

Comparing the Two Copy Applications

Although both this example and the previous InputStream/OutputStream solution can successfully copy the file, only the Reader/Writer solution gives us structured access to the text data. In order to accomplish the same feat with the InputStream/OutputStream classes, the application would have to detect the end of each line, which could be a lot of extra work. For example, if we are using a BufferedInputStream, multiple end-of-line characters could appear in the buffer array, meaning that we would have to go searching for them and then reconstruct the strings contained within the buffer array manually.

We would also have to write code to detect and process the character encoding. The *character encoding* determines how characters are encoded and stored in bytes and later read back or decoded as characters. Although this may sound simple, Java supports a wide variety of character encodings, ranging from ones that may use one byte for Latin characters, UTF-8 and ASCII for example, to using two or more bytes per character, such as UTF-16. For the exam, you don't need to memorize the character encodings, but you should be familiar with the names if you come across them on the exam.

Character Encoding in Java

In Java, the character encoding can be specified using the Charset class by passing a name value to the static Charset.forName() method, such as in the following examples:

```
Charset usAsciiCharset = Charset.forName("US-ASCII");
Charset utf8Charset = Charset.forName("UTF-8");
Charset utf16Charset = Charset.forName("UTF-16");
```

Java supports numerous character encodings, each specified by a different standard name value.

The key point here is that although you can use InputStream/OutputStream instead of Reader/Writer to read and write text files, it is inappropriate to do so. Recall that the character stream classes were created for convenience, and you should certainly take advantage of them when working with text data.

The *ObjectInputStream* and *ObjectOutputStream* Classes

Throughout this book, we have been managing our data model using classes, so it makes sense that we would want to write these objects to disk. The process of converting an in-memory object to a stored data format is referred to as *serialization*, with the reciprocal process of converting stored data into an object, which is known as *deserialization*. In this section, we will show you how Java provides built-in mechanisms for serializing and deserializing streams of objects directly to and from disk, respectively.

Although understanding serialization is important for using ObjectInputStream and ObjectOutputStream, we should mention that Oracle has a long history of adding and removing serialization from the list of exam objectives. Please check the latest list of objectives prior to taking the exam to determine if it is present.

The *Serializable* Interface

In order to serialize objects using the java.io API, the class they belong to must implement the java.io.Serializable interface. The Serializable interface is a tagging or marker interface, which means that it does not have any methods associated with it. Any class can implement the Serializable interface since there are no required methods to implement.

The purpose of implementing the Serializable interface is to inform any process attempting to serialize the object that you have taken the proper steps to make the object serializable, which involves making sure that the classes of all instance variables within the object are also marked Serializable. Many of the built-in Java classes that you have worked with throughout this book, including the String class, are marked Serializable. This means that many of the simple classes that we have built throughout this book can be marked Serializable without any additional work.

Note that the requirement for properly marking an object as Serializable may involve nested objects. For example, if a Cat class is marked as Serializable and contains a reference to a Tail object, then the class definition for the Tail object must also be marked as Serializable. Therefore, any object references contained within the Tail class must belong to classes that are also marked as Serializable, and so on.

A process attempting to serialize an object will throw a NotSerializableException if the class or one of its contained classes does not properly implement the Serializable interface. Let's say that you have a particular object within a larger object that is not serializable, such as one that stores temporary state or metadata information about the larger object. You can use the transient keyword on the reference to the object, which will instruct the process serializing the object to skip it and avoid throwing a NotSerializableException. The only limitation is that the data stored in the object will be lost during the serialization process.

Besides transient instance variables, static class members will also be ignored during the serialization and deserialization process. This should follow logically, as static class variables do not belong to one particular instance. If you need to store static class information, it will be need to be copied to an instance object and serialized separately.

Why Not Mark Every Class as *Serializable*?

You might be wondering why we don't just mark every class with the Serializable interface since there is no cost to doing so. The reason that we do not is that there are some classes that we want to instruct the JVM not to serialize. In particular, process-heavy classes such as the Thread class or any of the Stream classes would be difficult, often impossible, to save to persistent storage, since much of their work involves managing JVM processes or resources in real time.

By refraining from marking a class as `Serializable`, we are actively encouraging developers using it within their `Serializable` object either to make the reference to the class a local variable or, if they choose to include it in their class definition, to make sure that they mark it as `transient`, so that they realize the contents of the object will not be saved when the larger object is serialized.

The following program is an example of our `Animal` class that implements a `Serializable` properly:

```java
import java.io.Serializable;

public class Animal implements Serializable {
    private static final long serialVersionUID = 1L;
    private String name;
    private int age;
    private char type;

    public Animal(String name, int age, char type) {
        this.name = name;
        this.age = age;
        this.type = type;
    }

    public String getName() { return name; }
    public int getAge() { return age; }
    public char getType() { return type; }

    public String toString() {
        return "Animal [name=" + name + ", age=" + age + ", type=" + type + "]";
    }
}
```

All that was required to make our previous `Animal` class serializable in Java was to add `implements Serializable` to the class definition. Notice that we also added a variable called `serialVersionUID`. Although this is certainly not required as part of implementing the `Serializable` interface, it is considered a good practice to do so and update this `static` class variable anytime you modify the class.

This `serialVersionUID` is stored with the serialized object and assists during the deserialization process. The serialization process uses the `serialVersionUID` to identify uniquely a version of the class. That way, it knows whether the serialized data for an object will match the instance variable in the current version of the class. If an older version of the class is encountered during deserialization, an exception may be thrown. Alternatively, some deserialization tools support conversions automatically.

Real World Scenario

Maintaining a Serial UID

We recommend that you do not rely on the generated serialVersionUID provided by the Java compiler and that you explicitly declare one in each of your Serializable classes. Different Java compiler versions across different platforms may differ in their implementation of the generated serialVersionUID.

For example, you may end up with different serial ID values for the same class, if you are working with the Oracle implementation of Java 8 on a Windows platform versus a colleague using the OpenJDK Java 6 product on a Linux platform. This would lead to class incompatibility issues when deserializing the data, even though the data format is actually the same. Therefore, it is recommended that you provide and manage the serialVersionUID in all of your Serializable classes, updating it anytime the instance variables in the class are changed.

Serializing and Deserializing Objects

The java.io API provides two stream classes for object serialization and deserialization called ObjectInputStream and ObjectOutputStream.

The ObjectOutputStream class includes a method to serialize the object to the stream called void writeObject(Object). If the provided object is not Serializable, or it contains an embedded reference to a class that is not Serializable or not marked transient, a NotSerializableException will be thrown at runtime.

For the reciprocal process, the ObjectInputStream class includes a deserialization method that returns an object called readObject(). Notice that the return type of this method is the generic type java.lang.Object, indicating that the object will have to be cast explicitly at runtime to be used.

We now provide a sample program that reads and writes Animal data objects:

```java
import java.io.*;
import java.util.*;
public class ObjectStreamSample {
    public static List<Animal> getAnimals(File dataFile) throws IOException,
                                                ClassNotFoundException {
        List<Animal> animals = new ArrayList<Animal>();
        try (ObjectInputStream in = new ObjectInputStream(
                new BufferedInputStream(new FileInputStream(dataFile)))) {
            while(true) {
                Object object = in.readObject();
                if(object instanceof Animal)
                    animals.add((Animal)object);
            }
```

```
        } catch (EOFException e) {
            // File end reached
        }
        return animals;
    }

    public static void createAnimalsFile(List<Animal> animals, File dataFile)
                                                    throws IOException {
        try (ObjectOutputStream out = new ObjectOutputStream(
            new BufferedOutputStream(new FileOutputStream(dataFile)))) {
            for(Animal animal: animals)
                out.writeObject(animal);
        }
    }

    public static void main(String[] args) throws IOException,
                                            ClassNotFoundException {
        List<Animal> animals = new ArrayList<Animal>();
        animals.add(new Animal("Tommy Tiger",5,'T'));
        animals.add(new Animal("Peter Penguin",8,'P'));

        File dataFile = new File("animal.data");
        createAnimalsFile(animals,dataFile);
        System.out.println(getAnimals(dataFile));
    }
}
```

From a high-level, the program first creates a list of Animal objects in memory that includes two Animal instances. It then writes the list data into memory to an animal.data file saved in the current working directory. Finally, it reads the data from the file and outputs the following text:

```
[Animal [name=Tommy Tiger, age=5, type=T], Animal [name=Peter Penguin, age=8,
type=P]]
```

For performance reasons, we wrap each low-level file stream with a Buffered stream and then chain the result to an Object stream. The createAnimalsFile() method should be somewhat straightforward since we are just iterating over the List object and serializing each Animal object to disk using the writeObject() method.

The getAnimals() method is a little more complex, as we must take special care to deserialize the objects from disk. First, we need to check that the object we are reading is actually an instance of the Animal class before explicitly casting it, or else we might get a ClassCastException at runtime. In practice, we may want to throw an exception or log additional details if we encounter a class type that we did not expect.

Next, the readObject() throws the checked exception, ClassNotFoundException, since the class of the deserialized object may not be available to the JRE. Therefore, we need to catch the exception or rethrow in our method signatures; in this case, we chose the latter.

Finally, since we are reading objects, we can't use a -1 integer value to determine when we have finished reading a file. Instead, the proper technique is to catch an EOFException, which marks the program encountering the end of the file. Notice that we don't do anything with the exception other than finish the method. This is one of the few times when it is perfectly acceptable to swallow an exception.

 Real World Scenario

EOF Check Methods

You may come across code that reads from an InputStream and uses the snippet while(in.available()>0) to check for the end of the stream, rather than checking for an EOFException.

The problem with this technique, and the Javadoc does echo this, is that it only tells you the number of blocks that can be read without blocking the next caller. In other words, it can return 0 even if there are more bytes to be read. Therefore, the InputStream available() method should never be used to check for the end of the stream.

We conclude our discussion of the Object stream classes by noting that they do support reading and writing null objects. Therefore, it is important to check for null values when reading from a serialized data stream. In our sample application, we rely on the property of the instanceof operator always to return false for null values to skip explicitly needing to check for null values.

Understanding Object Creation

For the exam, you need be aware of how a deserialized object is created. When you deserialize an object, the constructor of the serialized class is not called. In fact, Java calls the first no-arg constructor for the first nonserializable parent class, skipping the constructors of any serialized class in between. Furthermore, any static variables or default initializations are ignored.

Let's take a look at a modified version the Animal class and see how the output of the ObjectStreamSample program would change with some modifications to our attributes and add a new constructor:

```
public class Animal implements Serializable {
    private static final long serialVersionUID = 2L;
    private transient String name;
    private transient int age = 10;
    private static char type = 'C';
```

```
   {this.age = 14;}
   public Animal() {
       this.name = "Unknown";
       this.age = 12;
       this.type = 'Q';
   }
   public Animal(String name, int age, char type) {
       this.name = name;
       this.age = age;
       this.type = type;
   }
   // Same methods as before
   ...
}
```

As we said earlier, transient means the value won't be included in the serialization process, so it's safe to assume name and age will be left out of the serialized file. More interestingly, the values of age being set to 10, 12, or 14 in the class are all ignored when the object is deserialized, as no class constructor or default initializations are used. The following is the output of the ObjectStreamSample program with the new Animal class definition:

```
[Animal [name=null, age=0, type=P], Animal [name=null, age=0, type=P]]
```

As expected, you can see that the values for name and age are lost on serialization and not set again during deserialization. The JVM initializes these variables with the default values based on the data types String and int, which are null and 0, respectively. Since the type variable is static, it is not serialized to disk. The sample program displays a value for type, as the variable is shared by all instances of the class and is the last value in our sample program.

For the exam, make sure that you understand that the constructor and any default initializations are ignored during the deserialization process.

The *PrintStream* and *PrintWriter* Classes

The PrintStream and PrintWriter classes are high-level stream classes that write formatted representation of Java objects to a text-based output stream. As you may have ascertained by the name, the PrintStream class operates on OutputStream instances and writes data as bytes, whereas the PrintWriter class operates on Writer instances and writes data as characters.

For convenience, both of these classes include constructors that can open and write to files directly. Furthermore, the PrintWriter class even has a constructor that takes an OutputStream as input, allowing you to wrap a PrintWriter class around an OutputStream.

These classes are primarily convenience classes in that you could write the low-level primitive or object directly to a stream without a PrintStream or PrintWriter class, although using one is helpful in a wide variety of situations.

In fact, the primary method class we have been using to output information to screen throughout this book uses a PrintStream object! For the exam, you should be aware that System.out and System.err are actually PrintStream objects.

Because PrintStream inherits OutputStream and PrintWriter inherits from Writer, both support the underlying write() method while providing a slew of print-based methods. For the exam, you should be familiar with the print(), println(), format(), and printf() methods. Unlike the underlying write() method, which throws a checked IOException that must be caught in your application, these print-based methods do not throw any checked exceptions. If they did, you would have been required to catch a checked exception anytime you called System.out.println() in your code! Both classes provide a method, checkError(), that can be used to detect the presence of a problem after attempting to write data to the stream.

For the rest of this section, we will use PrintWriter in our examples, as writing String data as characters instead of byte values is recommended. Keep in mind that the same examples could be easily rewritten with a PrintStream object.

> You might remember from Chapter 5 that String formatting is no longer a part of the OCP 8 exam. For the exam, you should be aware that the Console class includes two methods, format() and printf(), which take an optional vararg and format the output, although you're no longer required to know the various rules for formatting for the exam. For this chapter, we will provide the first String argument to these methods only.

print()

The most basic of the print-based methods is print(), which is overloaded with all Java primitives as well as String and Object. In general, these methods perform String.valueOf() on the argument and call the underlying stream's write() method, although they also handle character encoding automatically. For example, the following sets of print/write code are equivalent:

```
PrintWriter out = new PrintWriter("zoo.log");

out.print(5); // PrintWriter method
out.write(String.valueOf(5)); // Writer method

out.print(2.0); // PrintWriter method
out.write(String.valueOf(2.0)); // Writer method

Animal animal = new Animal();
out.print(animal); // PrintWriter method
out.write(animal==null ? "null": animal.toString()); // Writer method
```

You may remember from your OCA study material that valueOf() applied to an object calls the object's toString() method or returns null if the object is not set.

As these examples show, you could write to the same stream without the PrintWriter methods, but having the convenience of methods that convert everything to String values for you is extremely useful in practice.

println()

The next methods available in the PrintStream and PrintWriter classes are the println() methods, which are virtually identical to the print() methods, except that they insert a line break after the String value is written. The classes also include a version of println() that takes no arguments, which terminates the current line by writing a line separator.

These methods are especially helpful, as the line break or separator character is JVM dependent. For example, in some systems a line feed symbol, \n, signifies a line break, whereas other systems use a carriage return symbol followed by a line feed symbol, \r\n, to signify a line break. As you saw earlier in the chapter with file.separator, the line. separator value is available as a Java system property at any time:

```
System.getProperty("line.separator");
```

Although you can use print() instead of println() and insert all line break characters manually, it is not recommended in practice. As the line break character is OS dependent, it is recommended that you rely on println() for inserting line breaks since it makes your code more lightweight and portable.

format() and printf()

Like the String.format() methods discussed in Chapter 5, the format() method in PrintStream and PrintWriter takes a String, an optional locale, and a set of arguments, and it writes a formatted String to the stream based on the input. In other words, it is a convenience method for formatting directly to the stream. Refer to Chapter 5 for more details about how String values can be formatted in Java.

For convenience, as well as to make C developers feel more at home in Java, the PrintStream and PrintWriter APIs also include a set of printf() methods, which are straight pass-through methods to the format() methods. For example, although the names of the following two methods differ, their input values, output value, and behavior are identical in Java. They can be used interchangeably:

```
public PrintWriter format(String format, Object args...)
public PrintWriter printf(String format, Object args...)
```

Sample *PrintWriter* Application

We conclude this section with sample code of the PrintWriter class in action, as well as the accompanying output file:

```java
import java.io.*;

public class PrintWriterSample {
   public static void main(String[] args) throws IOException {
      File source = new File("zoo.log");
      try (PrintWriter out = new PrintWriter(
            new BufferedWriter(new FileWriter(source)))) {
         out.print("Today's weather is: ");
         out.println("Sunny");
         out.print("Today's temperature at the zoo is: ");
         out.print(1/3.0);
         out.println('C');
         out.format("It has rained 10.12 inches this year");
         out.println();
         out.printf("It may rain 21.2 more inches this year");
      }
   }
}
```

Note that we used a BufferedWriter along with FileWriter to access the file. We could have also used the PrintWriter(String filename) constructor in this example, as we did earlier in this section. The following are the contents of the file generated by the preceding code.

```
Today's weather is: Sunny
Today's temperature at the zoo is: 0.3333333333333333C
It has rained 10.12 inches this year
It may rain 21.2 more inches this year
```

You should pay close attention to the line breaks in the sample. For example, we called println() after our format(), since format() does not automatically insert a line break after the text. One of the most common bugs with printing data in practice is failing to account for line breaks properly.

Review of Stream Classes

We conclude this part of the chapter with Figure 8.3, which shows the various java.io stream classes that we have discussed and how they are related to one another via inheritance. The classes on the left side of the diagram are the abstract parent classes. The classes on the right side with dotted borders are low-level streams, and the ones with solid borders are high-level streams. Note that this diagram does not include all java.io stream classes, just the ones with which you should be familiar for the exam.

FIGURE 8.3   Diagram of `java.io` classes

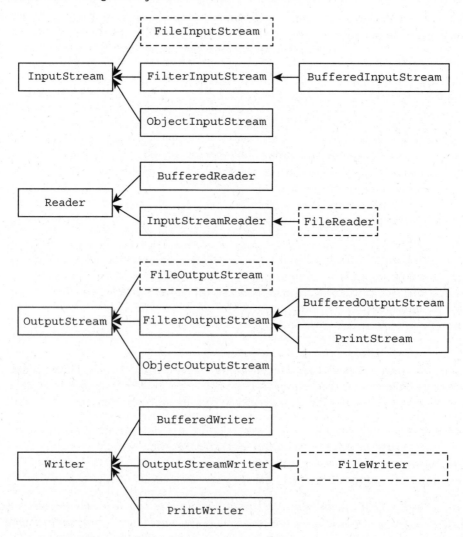

Other Stream Classes

The high-level `InputStreamReader` and `OutputStreamWriter` presented in Figure 8.3 are out of scope for the exam but useful in practice. The `InputStreamReader` class takes an `InputStream` instance and returns a `Reader` object. Likewise, the `OutputStreamWriter` class takes an `OutputStream` instance and returns a `Writer` object. In this manner, these classes convert data between character and byte streams. These classes are also unique in that they are the only `java.io` stream classes to have both `Stream` and `Reader/Writer` in their name.

Likewise, the DataInputStream and DataOutputStream are no longer required for the exam. They function quite similarly to the Object stream classes but are tailored to write only primitives and String values. In practice, they are rarely used as they require values and their associated types to be read in the precise order in which they were written. For example, if you wrote a String followed by an int and then a float, you would need to repeat this order exactly to read the data properly. In this manner, the files created by the DataOutputStream methods tend to be too rigid and too cumbersome to use in professional software development.

Finally, the parent classes FilterInputStream and FilterOutputStream were not discussed in this section, but they are also presented in the Figure 8.3, since we did discuss classes that inherit from them. The Filter classes are the superclass of all classes that filter or transform data. These classes will not be on the exam, though.

Interacting with Users

The java.io API includes numerous classes for interacting with the user. For example, you might want to write an application that asks a user to log in and reads their login details. In this section, we present the final java.io class that we will be covering in this book, the java.io.Console class, or Console class for short.

The Console class was introduced in Java 6 as a more evolved form of the System.in and System.out stream classes. It is now the recommended technique for interacting with and displaying information to the user in a text-based environment.

The Old Way

Before we delve into the Console class, let's review the old way of obtaining text input from the user. Similar to how System.out returns a PrintStream and is used to output text data to the user, System.in returns an InputStream and is used to retrieve text input from the user. It can be chained to a BufferedReader to allow input that terminates with the Enter key. Before we can apply the BufferedReader, though, we need to wrap the System.in object using the InputStreamReader class, which allows us to build a Reader object out of an existing InputStream instance. The result is shown in the following application:

```
import java.io.*;

public class SystemInSample {
    public static void main(String[] args) throws IOException {
        BufferedReader reader = new BufferedReader(
                                        new InputStreamReader(System.in));
        String userInput = reader.readLine();
        System.out.println("You entered the following: "+userInput);
    }
}
```

When run, this application fetches a single line of text from the user and then outputs it to the user before terminating. Notice that we did not close the stream, as closing System.in would prevent our application from accepting user input for the remainder of the application execution.

The New Way

The System.in and System.out objects have been available since the earliest versions of Java. In Java 6, the java.io.Console class was introduced with far more features and abilities than the original techniques. After all, System.in and System.out are just raw streams, whereas Console is a class with multiple convenience methods, one that is capable of containing additional methods in the future.

To begin, the Console class is a singleton, which as you may remember from Chapter 2 means that there is only one version of the object available in the JVM. It is created automatically for you by the JVM and accessed by calling the System.console() method. Be aware that this method will return null in environments where text interactions are not supported.

Next, let's look at our previous sample code rewritten using the Console class:

```
import java.io.Console;

public class ConsoleSample {
    public static void main(String[] args) {
        Console console = System.console();
        if(console != null) {
            String userInput = console.readLine();
            console.writer().println ("You entered the following: "+userInput);
        }
    }
}
```

The sample code first retrieves an instance of the Console singleton and determines if the Console is available by checking it for a null value. If the Console is available, it then retrieves a line of input from the user using the readLine() method, and it outputs the result using the Console's built-in PrintWriter object, accessed via the writer() method.

As you can see, the sample with System.in and System.out is very similar to the Console example by design. We will now review the various methods available in the Console class you should be familiar with for the exam, as well as note how the Console class has far more options than the System.in and System.out resources.

reader() and writer()

The Console class provides access to an instance of Reader and PrintWriter using the methods reader() and writer(), respectively. Access to these classes is analogous to calling System.in and System.out directly, although they use the Reader/Writer classes instead of the InputStream/OutputStream classes, which are more appropriate for working with character and String data. In this manner, they handle the underlying character encoding automatically.

These reader() and writer() methods are the most general ones in the Console class, and they are used by developers who need raw access to the user input and output stream or who may be in the process of migrating away from System.in.

format() and *printf()*

For outputting data to the user, you can use the PrintWriter writer() object or use the convenience format(String,Object...) method directly. The format() method takes a String format and list of arguments, and it behaves in the exact same manner as String. format() described in Chapter 5. For convenience to C developers, there is also a printf() method in the Console class, which is identical in every way but name to the format() method, and it can be used in any place format() is used.

Note that the Console class defines only one format() method, and it does not define a format() method that takes a locale variable. In this manner, it uses the default system locale to establish the formatter. Of course, you could always use a custom locale by retrieving the Writer object and passing your own locale instance, such as in the following example:

```
Console console = System.console();
console.writer().format(new Locale("fr", "CA"),"Hello World");
```

The following sample Console application prints information to the user:

```
import java.io.*;

public class ConsoleSamplePrint {
   public static void main(String[] args) throws NumberFormatException,
IOException {
      Console console = System.console();
      if(console == null) {
         throw new RuntimeException("Console not available");
      } else {
         console.writer().println("Welcome to Our Zoo!");
         console.format("Our zoo has 391 animals and employs 25 people.");
         console.writer().println();
         console.printf("The zoo spans 128.91 acres.");
      }
   }
}
```

You can see that a wide variety of methods are available to present text data to the user, including using the underlying console.writer() instance directly.

flush()

The flush() method forces any buffered output to be written immediately. It is recommended that you call the flush() method prior to calling any readLine() or readPassword() methods in order to ensure that no data is pending during the read. Failure to do so could result in a user prompt for input with no preceding text, as the text prior to the prompt may still be in a buffer.

readLine()

The basic readLine() method retrieves a single line of text from the user, and the user presses the Enter key to terminate it.

The Console class also supports an overloaded version of the readLine() method with the signature readLine(String format, Object... args), which displays a formatted prompt to the user prior to accepting text.

The following sample application reads information from the user and writes it back to the screen:

```java
import java.io.*;

public class ConsoleReadInputSample {
    public static void main(String[] args) throws NumberFormatException,
IOException {
        Console console = System.console();
        if(console == null) {
            throw new RuntimeException("Console not available");
        } else {
            console.writer().print("How excited are you about your trip today? ");
            console.flush();
            String excitementAnswer = console.readLine();
            String name = console.readLine("Please enter your name: ");

            Integer age = null;
            console.writer().print("What is your age? ");
            console.flush();
            BufferedReader reader = new BufferedReader(console.reader());
            String value = reader.readLine();
            age = Integer.valueOf(value);
            console.writer().println();

            console.format("Your name is "+name);
            console.writer().println();
            console.format("Your age is "+age);
            console.printf("Your excitement level is: "+excitementAnswer);
        }
    }
}
```

The example includes multiple ways to read input from the user including the `console.readLine()` method, as well as creating a `BufferedReader` out of the `console.read()` object. The information is printed back to the user via a variety of different writer methods available in the `Console` class.

readPassword()

The `readPassword()` method is similar to the `readLine()` method, except that echoing is disabled. By disabling echoing, the user does not see the text they are typing, meaning that their password is secure if someone happens to be looking at their screen.

Also like the `readLine()` method, the `Console` class offers an overloaded version of the `readPassword()` method with the signature `readPassword(String format, Object... args)` used for displaying a formatted prompt to the user prior to accepting text. Unlike the `readLine()` method, though, the `readPassword()` method returns an array of characters instead of a `String`.

Why Does *readPassword()* Return a Character Array?

As you may remember from your OCA study material, `String` values are added to a shared memory pool for performance reasons in Java. This means that if a password that a user typed in were to be returned to the process as a `String`, it might be available in the `String` pool long after the user entered it.

If the memory in the application is ever dumped to disk, it means that the password could be recovered by a malicious individual after the user has stopped using the application. The advantage of the `readPassword()` method using a character array should be clear. As soon as the data is read and used, the sensitive password data in the array can be "erased" by writing garbage data to the elements of the array. This would remove the password from memory long before it would be removed by garbage collection if a `String` value were used.

The last sample application that we will present retrieves two passwords from the user and verifies that they are correct:

```java
import java.io.*;
import java.util.Arrays;

public class PasswordCompareSample {
    public static void main(String[] args) throws NumberFormatException,
                                                                IOException {
        Console console = System.console();
        if(console == null) {
            throw new RuntimeException("Console not available");
        } else {
            char[] password = console.readPassword("Enter your password: ");
```

```
console.format("Enter your password again:   ");
console.flush();
char[] verify = console.readPassword();
boolean match = Arrays.equals(password,verify);

// Immediately clear passwords from memory
for(int i=0; i<password.length; i++) {
    password[i]='x';
}
for(int i=0; i<verify.length; i++) {
    verify[i]='x';
}

console.format("Your password was "+(match ? "correct": "incorrect"));
        }
    }
}
```

You can see that this sample application uses both overloaded versions of the console. readPassword() method. For security reasons, we immediately clear the character arrays that store the password as soon as they are no longer needed in the application. Note that you could also use Array.fill(password,'x') to wipe an array's data.

Summary

The bulk of this chapter focused on teaching you how to use Java to interact with files. We started off by introducing you to the concept of files and directories, and then we showed you how to reference them using path Strings. We presented the java.io.File class, and we showed you how to use it to read basic file information.

We then introduced java.io streams to read/write file contents, and we described their various attributes, including low-level vs. high-level, byte vs. character, input vs. output, and so on. The description of the stream is designed to help you remember the function of the stream by using its name as a context clue.

We visited many of the byte and character stream classes that you will need to know for the exam in increasing order of complexity. A common practice is to start with a low-level resource or file stream and wrap it in a buffered stream to improve performance. You can also apply a high-level stream to manipulate the data, such as a data stream. We described what it means to be serializable in Java, and we showed you how to use the object stream classes to persist objects directly to and from disk.

We concluded the chapter by showing you how to read input data from the user, using both the legacy System.in method and the newer Console class. The Console class has many advanced features, such as support for passwords and built-in support for String formatting.

Exam Essentials

Understand files, directories, and streams.   Files are records that store data to a persistent storage device that is available after the application has finished executing. Files are organized within a file system in directories, which in turn may contain other directories. Files can be accessed using streams, which present the data in sequential blocks.

Be able to use the `java.io.File` **class.**   Java `File` instances can be created by passing a path `String` to the new `File()` constructor. The `File` class includes a number of instance methods for retrieving information about both files and directories. It also includes methods to create/delete files and directories, as well as retrieve a list of files within the directory.

Distinguish between byte and character streams.   The `java.io` API supports both byte and character streams. Byte streams have the word `InputStream` or `OutputStream` in their name and are useful for interacting with binary data. Character streams have the word `Reader` or `Writer` in their name and are convenient for working with `String` or character data.

Distinguish between low-level and high-level streams.   A low-level stream is one that operates directly on the underlying resource, such as a stream that reads file data from the file system. A high-level stream is one that operates on a low-level or other high-level stream to filter or convert data or to improve read/write performance with the buffer.

Be able to recognize and know how to use the following classes: `BufferedReader`, `BufferedWriter`, `File`, `FileReader`, `FileWriter`, `FileInputStream`, `FileOutputStream`, `ObjectOutputStream`, `ObjectInputStream`, **and** `PrintWriter`.   The `java.io` API reuses terms in the stream class name, which are useful in decoding the function of the class, such as `InputStream`, `OutputStream`, `Reader`, `Writer`, `Buffered`, `File`, `Object`, and `Print`. You should know how to use the stream classes listed here, including how to chain the streams together.

Be able to perform common stream operations including `close()`, `flush()`, `mark()`, `markSupported()`, `reset()`, **and** `skip()`.   The `java.io` API includes numerous methods common to both input and output stream classes. The `close()` method is shared by all stream classes and can be used implicitly by using try-with-resource syntax. The `flush()` method is used in output stream classes to force the writing of the data to the underlying resource. The `markSupported()`, `mark()`, and `reset()` methods are used in conjunction with the input stream classes to mark a position in the stream and return to it later on. Not all `java.io` input stream classes support the `mark()` and `reset()` operations. Finally, the `skip()` method is used in input stream classes to skip past a number of bytes.

Understand how to use Java serialization.   Classes can implement the `java.io.Serializable` interface to indicate that they support serializing their data to disk. The interface requires that all instance members of the class are `Serializable` or marked transient. The String class and all Java primitives are Serializable. The ObjectInputStream and ObjectOutputStream classes can be used to read and write a Serializable object from and to a stream, respectively.

Be able to interact with the user via the Console **class.**   Java 6 introduced the Console class as a replacement to System.in and System.out for reading and writing data from the user, respectively. The Console class includes special methods for retrieving passwords that are more secure than the standard ways of retrieving String values.

Review Questions

1. Which classes will allow the following to compile? (Choose all that apply.)

   ```
   InputStream is = new BufferedInputStream(new FileInputStream("zoo.txt"));
   InputStream wrapper = new _____ (is);
   ```

   A. BufferedInputStream

   B. FileInputStream

   C. BufferedWriter

   D. ObjectInputStream

   E. ObjectOutputStream

   F. BufferedReader

2. Why does Console.readPassword() return a char[] array instead of a String object? (Choose all that apply.)

   A. It improves performance.

   B. It is more secure.

   C. To encrypt the password data.

   D. To support all character encodings.

   E. Because Java puts all String values in a reusable pool.

   F. So that the value can be removed from memory immediately after use.

3. Which of the following are true? (Choose all that apply.)

   A. A new Console object is created every time System.console() is called.

   B. Console can only be used for reading input and not writing output.

   C. Console is obtained using the singleton pattern.

   D. When getting a Console object, it might be null.

   E. When getting a Console object, it will never be null.

4. Which of the following can fill in the blank to make the code compile? (Choose all that apply.)

   ```
   Console c = System.console();
   String s = _____;
   ```

   A. c.input()

   B. c.read()

   C. c.readLine()

   D. c.readPassword()

    E. `c.readString()`

    F. None of the above

5. What is the result of executing the following code? (Choose all that apply.)

```
String line;
Console c = System.console();
Writer w = c.writer();
if ((line = c.readLine()) != null)
    w.append(line);
w.flush();
```

    A. The code runs without error but prints nothing.

    B. The code prints what was entered by the user.

    C. An `ArrayIndexOutOfBoundsException` might be thrown.

    D. A `NullPointerException` might be thrown.

    E. An `IOException` might be thrown.

    F. The code does not compile.

6. Which of the following are true statements about serialization in Java? (Choose all that apply.)

    A. The process of converting serialized data back into memory is called deserialization.

    B. All non-thread classes should be marked `Serializable`.

    C. The `Serializable` interface requires implementing `serialize()` and `deserialize()` methods.

    D. The `Serializable` interface is marked `final` and cannot be extended.

    E. The `readObject()` method of `ObjectInputStream` may throw a `ClassNotFoundException` even if the return object is not explicitly cast.

7. Fill in the blank: _____ is the topmost directory on a file system.

    A. Absolute

    B. Directory

    C. Parent

    D. Root

    E. Top

8. Assuming / is the root directory, which of the following are true statements? (Choose all that apply.)

    A. `/home/parrot` is an absolute path.

    B. `/home/parrot` is a directory.

    C. `/home/parrot` is a relative path.

    D. The path pointed to from a `File` object must exist.

    E. The parent of the path pointed to by a `File` object must exist.

9. What are the requirements for a class that you want to serialize with `ObjectOutputStream`? (Choose all that apply.)

    A. The class must implement the `Serializable` interface.

    B. The class must extend the `Serializable` class.

    C. The class must declare a `static serialVersionUID` variable.

    D. All instance members of the class must be `Serializable`.

    E. All instance members of the class must be marked `transient`.

    F. Any class can be serialized with `ObjectOutputStream`.

10. The following method is designed to delete a directory tree recursively. Which of the following properties reflect the method definition? (Choose all that apply.)

    ```
    1: public static void deleteTree(File file) {
    2:    if(!file.isFile())
    3:       for(File entry: file.listFiles())
    4:          deleteTree(entry);
    5:    else file.delete();
    6: }
    ```

    A. It can delete a directory that contains only files.

    B. It can delete a directory tree of arbitrary length.

    C. It can delete a single file.

    D. The code will not compile because of line 2.

    E. The code will not compile because of line 3.

    F. It compiles but may throw an exception at runtime.

11. Which of the following are methods available to instances of the `java.io.File` class? (Choose all that apply.)

    A. `mv()`

    B. `createDirectory()`

    C. `mkdirs()`

    D. `move()`

    E. `renameTo()`

    F. `copy()`

    G. `mkdir()`

12. Suppose that the file `c:\book\java` exists. Which of the following lines of code creates an object that represents the file? (Choose all that apply.)

    A. `new File("c:\book\java");`

    B. `new File("c:\\book\\java");`

    C. `new File("c:/book/java");`

    D. `new File("c://book//java");`

    E. None of the above

13. Which of the following are built-in streams in Java? (Choose all that apply.)

    A. `System.err`

    B. `System.error`

    C. `System.in`

    D. `System.input`

    E. `System.out`

    F. `System.output`

14. Which of the following are not `java.io` classes? (Choose all that apply.)

    A. `BufferedReader`

    B. `BufferedWriter`

    C. `FileReader`

    D. `FileWriter`

    E. `PrintReader`

    F. `PrintWriter`

15. Assuming `zoo-data.txt` is a multiline text file, what is true of the following method?

```
private void echo() throws IOException {
    try (FileReader fileReader = new FileReader("zoo-data.txt");
        BufferedReader bufferedReader = new BufferedReader(fileReader)) {
        System.out.println(bufferedReader.readLine());
    }
}
```

    A. It prints the first line of the file to the console.

    B. It prints the entire contents of the file.

    C. The code does not compile because the reader is not closed.

    D. The code does compile, but the reader is not closed.

    E. The code does not compile for another reason.

16. Why shouldn't every class be marked `Serializable`? (Choose all that apply.)

    A. The compiler will throw an exception if certain classes are marked `Serializable`.

    B. Only `final` classes can be marked `Serializable`.

    C. Classes can implement only one interface, so marking them `Serializable` would prevent them from using any other interface.

    D. The data of some classes cannot be easily serialized, such as those managing threads or processes.

    E. Only concrete classes can be marked `Serializable`.

    F. Classes that store most of their data in `static` fields would not be easily serialized.

17. Which of the following stream classes are high-level? (Choose all that apply.)

    A. `ObjectInputStream`

    B. `PrintStream`

    C. `FileWriter`

    D. `PrintWriter`

    E. `OutputStream`

    F. `FileInputStream`

    G. `ObjectOutputStream`

18. Which values when inserted into the blank would allow the code to compile? (Choose all that apply.)

```
1: Console console = System.console();
2: String color = console.readLine("What is your favorite color? ");
3: console._____("Your favorite color is "+color);
```

    A. `print`

    B. `printf`

    C. `println`

    D. `format`

    E. `writer().println`

    F. `out`

19. Suppose that you need to write data that consists of int, double, boolean, and String values to a file that maintains the format of the original data. For performance reasons, you also want to buffer the data. Which three java.io classes can be chained together to best achieve this result?

    A. `FileWriter`

    B. `FileOutputStream`

    C. `BufferedOutputStream`

    D. `ObjectOutputStream`

    E. `DirectoryStream`

    F. `PrintWriter`

    G. `PipedOutputStream`

20. What are some reasons to use a character stream, such as Reader/Writer, over a byte stream, such as InputStream/OutputStream? (Choose all that apply.)

    A. More convenient code syntax when working with String data

    B. Improved performance

    C. Automatic character encoding

    D. Built-in serialization and deserialization

    E. Character streams are high-level streams

    F. Multi-threading support

21. Assuming the following class has proper `public` getter/setter methods for all of its `private` fields, which of the following fields will always be `null` after an instance of the class is serialized and then deserialized? (Choose all that apply.)

```java
public class Zebra implements Serializable {
    private static final long serialUID = 1L;
    private transient String name = "George";
    private static String birthPlace = "Africa";
    private transient Integer age;
    private java.util.List<Zebra> friends = new java.util.ArrayList<>();
    private Object tail = null;
    { age = 10;}

    public Zebra() {
        this.name = "Sophia";
    }
}
```

    A. `name`

    B. `tail`

    C. `age`

    D. `friends`

    E. `birthPlace`

    F. The code does not compile.

    G. The code compiles but throws an exception at runtime.

22. What is the value of name after an instance of `Eagle` is serialized and then deserialized?

```java
public class Bird implements Serializable {
    protected transient String name = "Bridget";
    public void setName(String name) { this.name = name; }
    public String getName() { return name; }
    public Bird() {
        this.name = "Matt";
    }
}
```

```
public class Eagle extends Bird implements Serializable {
    { this.name = "Janette"; }
    public Eagle() {
        this.name = "Daniel";
    }
}
```

A. Bridget

B. Matt

C. Janette

D. Daniel

E. null

F. The code does not compile.

G. The code compiles but throws an exception at runtime.

H. The value may not be known until runtime.

23. Assume that you have an InputStream whose next bytes are XYZABC. What is the result of calling the following method on the stream, using a count value of 3?

```
public static String pullBytes(InputStream is, int count) throws IOException
{
    is.mark(count);
    final StringBuilder sb = new StringBuilder();
    for(int i=0; i<count; i++)
        sb.append((char)is.read());
    is.reset();
    is.skip(1);
    sb.append((char)is.read());
    return sb.toString();
}
```

A. It will return a String value of XYZ.

B. It will return a String value of XYZA.

C. It will return a String value of XYZX.

D. It will return a String value of XYZB.

E. It will return a String value of XYZY.

F. The code does not compile.

G. The code compiles but throws an exception at runtime.

H. The result cannot be determined with the information given.

Chapter

9

NIO.2

THE OCP EXAM TOPICS COVERED IN THIS CHAPTER INCLUDE THE FOLLOWING:

✓ **Java File I/O (NIO.2)**

- Use Path interface to operate on file and directory paths

- Use Files class to check, read, delete, copy, move, manage metadata of a file or directory

- Use Stream API with NIO.2

In Chapter 8, "IO," we presented the java.io API and discussed how to use it to interact with files. In this chapter, we focus on the java.nio version 2 API, or NIO.2 for short, to interact with files. NIO.2 is an acronym that stands for the second version of the Non-blocking Input/Output API, and it is sometimes referred to as the "New I/O."

In this chapter, we will show how the NIO.2 API allows us to do a lot more with files and directories than the original java.io API. We will also show you how to read and modify the attributes of a file. We will conclude the chapter by introducing new NIO.2 methods that were added in Java 8, which rely on streams to perform complex operations with only a single line of code.

Unless otherwise stated, when we refer to *streams* in this chapter we are referring to the new functional programing specification, as discussed in Chapter 4, "Functional Programming." These are not to be mistaken for java.io streams defined in Chapter 8, although we agree the naming choice can be a bit confusing.

Introducing NIO.2

In Java, file I/O has undergone a number of revisions over the years. The first version of file I/O available in Java was the java.io API. As we discussed in Chapter 8, the java.io API uses byte streams to interact with file data. Although the java.io API has grown over the years, the underlying byte stream concept has not changed significantly since it was introduced.

Java introduced a replacement for java.io streams in Java 1.4 called Non-blocking I/O, or NIO for short. The NIO API introduced the concepts of buffers and channels in place of java.io streams. The basic idea is that you load the data from a file channel into a temporary buffer that, unlike byte streams, can be read forward and backward without blocking on the underlying resource.

Unfortunately, the NIO API released in Java 1.4 was never particularly popular, so much so that nothing from the original version of NIO will be on the OCP exam. Most Java developers working with large data structures such as file and web pages still use java.io streams today. With that in mind, this book is geared toward teaching you NIO.2.

Java 7 introduced the NIO.2 API. While the NIO API was intended as a replacement for java.io streams, the NIO.2 API is actually a replacement for the java.io.File class and related interactions that we discussed in Chapter 8. Unlike the NIO API, the NIO.2 API is on the OCP exam, and this chapter will discuss the usage and features of this API. People sometimes refer to NIO.2 as just NIO, although for clarity and to distinguish it from the first version of NIO, we will refer to it as NIO.2 throughout the chapter.

The goal of the NIO.2 API implementation is to provide a more intuitive, more feature-rich API for working with files. As you shall see in this chapter, it also provides a number of notable performance improvements over the existing java.io.File class.

Introducing *Path*

The java.nio.file.Path interface, or Path interface for short, is the primary entry point for working with the NIO.2 API. A Path object represents a hierarchical path on the storage system to a file or directory. In this manner, Path is a direct replacement for the legacy java.io.File class, and conceptually it contains many of the same properties. For example, both File and Path objects may refer to a file or a directory. Both also may refer to an absolute path or relative path within the file system. As we did in Chapter 8 and continue to do in this chapter, for simplicity's sake, we often refer to a directory reference as a file record since it is stored in the file system with similar properties.

Unlike the File class, the Path interface contains support for symbolic links. A *symbolic link* is a special file within an operating system that serves as a reference or pointer to another file or directory. In general, symbolic links are transparent to the user, as the operating system takes care of resolving the reference to the actual file. The NIO.2 API includes full support for creating, detecting, and navigating symbolic links within the file system.

Creating Instances with Factory and Helper Classes

The NIO.2 API makes good use of the factory pattern as discussed in Chapter 2, "Design Patterns and Principles." Remember that a factory class can be implemented using static methods to create instances of another class. For example, you can create an instance of a Path interface using a static method available in the Paths factory class. Note the s at the end of the Paths class to distinguish it from the Path interface.

Why Is *Path* an Interface?

You might be wondering, "If Path is the primary NIO.2 entry point, why don't I call a Path constructor directly?" The reason why Path is an interface and not a class is that creating a file or directory is considered a file system–dependent task in NIO.2. When you obtain a Path object from the default file system in NIO.2, the JVM gives you back an object that unlike java.io.File transparently handles system-specific details for the current platform.

If you didn't use the factory pattern to create an instance, you would have to know what the underlying file system was and use this in every create method. This would make your code complex and difficult to port to other file systems. In fact, the only time you would ever implement or instantiate a Path object directly is if you were writing code to interact with your own type of file system.

The advantage of using the factory pattern here is that you can write the same code that will run on a variety of different platforms. As you shall see in this chapter, not all file systems are the same; therefore, the same code may have different results when run on various file systems. For example, Linux systems are case sensitive, while Windows-based systems are not, and this difference could change the expected results of a program. By providing a different Path implementation for each platform, Java can handle these differences effectively.

NIO.2 also includes helper classes such as java.nio.file.Files, whose primary purpose is to operate on instances of Path objects. Helper or utility classes are similar to factory classes in that they are often composed primarily of static methods that operate on a particular class. They differ in that helper classes are focused on manipulating or creating new objects from existing instances, whereas factory classes are focused primarily on object creation.

You should become comfortable with this paradigm, if you are not already, as most of your interactions with the NIO.2 API will require accessing at least two classes: an interface and a factory or helper class. As a guideline for this section, we present the NIO.2 class and interface relationships in Figure 9.1.

FIGURE 9.1   NIO.2 class and interface relationships

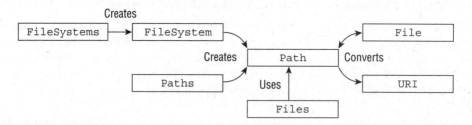

Creating Paths

Since Path is an interface, you need a factory class to create instances of one. The NIO.2 API provides a number of classes and methods that you can use to create Path objects, which we will review in this section.

Using the *Paths* Class

The simplest and most straightforward way to obtain a Path object is using the java.nio.files.Paths factory class, or Paths for short. To obtain a reference to a file or directory, you would call the static method Paths.getPath(String) method, as shown in the following examples:

```
Path path1 = Paths.get("pandas/cuddly.png");

Path path2 = Paths.get("c:\\zooinfo\\November\\employees.txt");

Path path3 = Paths.get("/home/zoodirector");
```

The first example creates a Path reference to a relative file in the current working directory. The second example creates a Path reference to an absolute file in a Windows-based system. The third example creates a Path reference to an absolute directory in a Linux or Mac-based system.

Absolute vs. Relative Is File System Dependent

In the explanation of the previous examples, we described the paths as absolute or relative within a specific file system. This is because some paths that are considered absolute in some file systems are considered relative in others. For example, the path c:\zooinfo\ November\employees.csv in the previous example set is considered relative in a Linux or Mac-based system, since it does not start with a forward slash, /. Likewise, the path /home/zoodirector is considered relative in a Windows-based system, since it does not start with a drive letter.

For the exam and throughout this text, you can use the following rules to determine whether a path is absolute or relative. Just be aware that this may differ depending on your actual file system.

- If a path starts with a forward slash, it is an absolute path, such as /bird/parrot.

- If a path starts with a drive letter, it is an absolute path, such as C:\bird\emu.

- Otherwise, it is a relative path, such as ..\eagle.

You can also create a Path using the Paths class using a vararg of type String, such as Paths.get(String,String...). This allows you to create a Path from a list of String values in which the operating system-dependent path.separator is automatically inserted between elements. As you may remember from Chapter 8, System.getProperty("path.separator") can be used to get the operating system-dependent file separator from the JVM. That said, most JVM implementations support both forward and backward slashes regardless of the file system, allowing the same code to run on multiple operating systems without having to rewrite the slashes.

```
Path path1 = Paths.get("pandas","cuddly.png");

Path path2 = Paths.get("c:","zooinfo","November","employees.txt");

Path path3 = Paths.get("/","home","zoodirector");
```

These examples are a rewrite of our previous set of Path examples, using the parameter list of String values instead of a single String value. The advantage of using this overloaded method is that it is more robust when manually constructing path values, as it inserts the proper path separator for you.

Be Wary of *Path* vs. *Paths* on the Exam

As you saw in Chapter 3, "Generics and Collections," with the Collection interface and Collections class, Java is fond of using one name for the data class and the plural form of that name for the factory or helper class. When you see questions with Path or Paths on the exam, be sure that the class reference and usage are correct. For example, the following usage is incorrect and will not compile:

```
Paths path1 = Paths.get("/alligator/swim.txt");   // DOES NOT COMPILE
```

```
Path path2 = Path.get("/crocodile/food.csv");   // DOES NOT COMPILE
```

In the first example, the Path object is being assigned to a Paths instance, which is incompatible. In the second example, there is attempt to access a method that does not exist, Path.get("String").

The key to remember is that the singular form Path represents the instance with which you want to work, whereas the plural form Paths is the factory class containing methods for creating Path instances.

Another way to construct a Path using the Paths class is with a URI value. A *uniform resource identifier* (URI) is a string of characters that identify a resource. It begins with a schema that indicates the resource type, followed by a path value. Examples of schema values include file://, http://, https://, and ftp://. The java.net.URI class is used to create and manage URI values.

```
Path path1 = Paths.get(new URI("file://pandas/cuddly.png")); // THROWS EXCEPTION
                                                             // AT RUNTIME
```

```
Path path2 = Paths.get(new URI("file:///c:/zoo-info/November/employees.txt"));
```

```
Path path3 = Paths.get(new URI("file:///home/zoodirectory"));
```

These examples show how the Paths.get(URI) method can be used to obtain a reference to a URI-based resource. Notice that these are actually rewrites of our earlier examples, as we can use URI values for both local and network paths. The first example actually throws an exception at runtime, as URIs must reference absolute paths at runtime. The URI class does have an isAbsolute() method, although this is related to whether or not the URI has a schema, not the file location.

We now present two additional methods that use other types of non-local file system schemas. For the exam, you do not need to know the syntax of these schemas, but you should be aware that they exist.

```
Path path4 = Paths.get(new URI("http://www.wiley.com"));

Path path5 = Paths.get(
   new URI("ftp://username:password@ftp.the-ftp-server.com"));
```

Note that the constructor new URI(String) does throw a checked URISyntaxException, which would have to be caught in any application where the previous code snippets are used.

Finally, the Path interface also contains a reciprocal method toUri() for converting a Path instance back to a URI instance, as shown in the following sample code:

```
Path path4 = Paths.get(new URI("http://www.wiley.com"));
URI uri4 = path4.toUri();
```

Accessing the Underlying *FileSystem* Object

The Path.getPath() method used throughout the previous examples is actually short-hand for the class java.nio.file.FileSystem method getPath(). The FileSystem class has a protected constructor, so we use the plural FileSystems factory class to obtain an instance of FileSystem, as shown in the following example code:

```
Path path1 = FileSystems.getDefault().getPath("pandas/cuddly.png");

Path path2 = FileSystems.getDefault().getPath("c:","zooinfo","November",
   "employees.txt");

Path path3 = FileSystems.getDefault().getPath("/home/zoodirector");
```

Again, we are able to rewrite our previous set of examples, with this code behaving in the exact same manner as before.

While most of the time we want access to a Path object that is within the local file system, the FileSystems factory class does give us the ability to connect to a remote file system, as shown in the following sample code:

```
FileSystem fileSystem = FileSystems.getFileSystem(
   new URI("http://www.selikoff.net"));

Path path = fileSystem.getPath("duck.txt");
```

This code is useful when we need to construct Path objects frequently for a remote file system. The power of the NIO.2 API here is that it lets us rely on the default file system for files and directories as before, while giving us the ability to build more-complex applications that reference external file systems.

Working with Legacy File Instances

When Path was added in Java 7, the legacy java.io.File class was updated with a new method, toPath(), that operates on an instance File variable:

```
File file = new File("pandas/cuddly.png");
Path path = file.toPath();
```

For backward compatibility, the Path interface also contains a method toFile() to return a File instance:

```
Path path = Paths.get("cuddly.png");
File file = path.toFile();
```

As you can see, the Java API is quite flexible, and it allows easy conversion between legacy code using the File class and newer code using Path. Although Java supports both methods for working with files, it is generally recommended that you rely on the Path API in your applications going forward as it is more feature rich and has built-in support for various file systems and symbolic links.

Interacting with Paths and Files

Now that we've covered how to obtain an instance of the Path object, you might ask, what can we do with it? The NIO.2 API provides a rich plethora of methods and classes that operate on Path objects—far more than were available in the java.io API. We will discuss the methods that you should know for the exam in this section.

Path Object vs. Actual File

One thing to keep in mind when reading this section is that a Path object is not a file but a representation of a location within the file system. In this manner, most operations available in the Path and Paths classes can be accomplished regardless of whether the underlying file that the Path object references actually exists. For example, retrieving the parent or root directory of a Path object does not require the file to exist, although the JVM may access the underlying file system to know how to process the path information.

As you shall see in this section, a handful of operations in the Path and Paths classes, such as Path.toRealPath(), do require the file to exist and will throw a checked exception if the file is not available.

Providing Optional Arguments

Throughout this section, we introduce numerous methods for interacting with files and directories in NIO.2. Many of the methods in the NIO.2 API that interact with real files and directories take additional options flags in the form of a vararg.

For the exam, you do not need to memorize which of the dozens of NIO.2 methods take which optional arguments, but you should be able to recognize what they do when you see them on the exam. Table 9.1 lists the values that you should know for the exam. Note that these descriptions apply to both files and directories. If you are not familiar with the operations to which these attributes apply, don't worry; we'll explain them later in this chapter.

TABLE 9.1   Common optional arguments in NIO.2

Enum Value	Usage	Description
NOFOLLOW_LINKS	Test file existing Read file data Copy file Move file	If provided, symbolic links when encountered will not be traversed. Useful for performing operations on symbolic links themselves rather than their target.
FOLLOW_LINKS	Traverse a directory tree	If provided, symbolic links when encountered will be traversed.
COPY_ATTRIBUTES	Copy file	If provided, all metadata about a file will be copied with it.
REPLACE_EXISTING	Copy file Move file	If provided and the target file exists, it will be replaced; otherwise, if it is not provided, an exception will be thrown if the file already exists.
ATOMIC_MOVE	Move file	The operation is performed in an atomic manner within the file system, ensuring that any process using the file sees only a complete record. Method using it may throw an exception if the feature is unsupported by the file system.

For simplicity as well as better readability, we purposely omit the enum class names to which the values belong throughout the text, although we do include them in any practice questions. For example, the copy methods take a list of CopyOption interface values, of which StandardCopyOption is an enum that implements the interface and includes StandardCopyOption.COPY_ATTRIBUTES as an option. As we said, for simplicity, we omit these details as the exam won't require you to understand this relationship.

While the name of many of these options gives a basic description of their function, the ATOMIC_MOVE option may be completely new to you. An *atomic operation* is any operation that is performed as a single indivisible unit of execution, which appears to the rest of the system as occurring instantaneously. Furthermore, an atomic *move* is one in which any process monitoring the file system never sees an incomplete or partially written file. If the file system does not support this feature, an AtomicMoveNotSupportedException will be thrown.

For the remainder of the chapter, we leave out these enum values in the method definitions so that you can focus on the core functionality. For the exam, you should understand their effect if you see them provided to a method.

 Real World Scenario

NIO.2 Varargs and Encapsulation

You might wonder why the authors of Java used a vararg to pass these values to NIO.2 methods, despite the fact that many methods take only one possible enum value. For example, they could have just added a boolean parameter or an overloaded method to accomplish the same goal.

The answer is that they were trying to future-proof the method. By using a vararg, the existing method calls are insulated from changes in future versions of Java in which additional values may be added. Per our discussion of design principles in Chapter 2, this would be a loosely coupled approach, as it allows changes in the options available for the method without changing the method signature.

Using *Path* Objects

The Path interface includes numerous methods for using Path objects. You have already seen two of them, toFile() and toUri(), used to convert Path objects to other types of resources.

Many of the methods in the Path interface transform the path value in some way and return a new Path object, allowing the methods to be chained. We demonstrate chaining in the following example, the details of which we'll discuss in this section of the chapter.

```
Paths.get("/zoo/../home").getParent().normalize().toAbsolutePath();
```

 If you start to feel overwhelmed by the number of methods available in the Path interface, just remember: the function of many of them can be inferred by their method name, such as getParent(), getNameCount(), toAbsolutePath(), and so on. In this section, we organize the methods by related functionality.

Viewing the *Path* with *toString()*, *getNameCount()*, and *getName()*

The Path interface contains three methods to retrieve basic information about the path representative. The first method, toString(), returns a String representation of the entire path. In fact, it is the only method in the Path interface to return a String. Most of the other methods that we will discuss in this section return a new Path object.

The second and third methods, getNameCount() and getName(int), are often used in conjunction to retrieve the number of elements in the path and a reference to each element, respectively. For greater compatibility with other NIO.2 methods, the getName(int) method returns the component of the Path as a new Path object rather than a String.

The following sample code uses these methods to retrieve path data:

```
Path path = Paths.get("/land/hippo/harry.happy");
System.out.println("The Path Name is: "+path);

for(int i=0; i<path.getNameCount(); i++) {
    System.out.println("   Element "+i+" is: "+path.getName(i));
}
```

As you might remember from our discussion of PrintStream/PrintWriter in Chapter 8, printing an object automatically invokes the object's toString() method. The output of this code snippet is the following:

```
The Path Name is: /land/hippo/harry.happy
   Element 0 is: land
   Element 1 is: hippo
   Element 2 is: harry.happy
```

Notice that the root element / is not included in the list of names. If the Path object represents the root element itself, then the number of names in the Path object returned by getNameCount() will be 0.

What if we ran the preceding code using the relative path land/hippo/harry.happy? The output would be as follows:

```
The Path Name is: land/hippo/harry.happy
   Element 0 is: land
   Element 1 is: hippo
   Element 2 is: harry.happy
```

Notice that the individual names are the same. For the exam, you should be aware that the getName(int) method is zero-indexed, with the file system root excluded from the path components.

Accessing *Path* Components with *getFileName()*, *getParent()*, and *getRoot()*

The Path interface contains numerous methods for retrieving specific subelements of a Path object, returned as Path objects themselves. The first method, getFileName(), returns a Path instance representing the filename, which is the farthest element from the root. Like most methods in the Path interface, getFileName() returns a new Path instance rather than a String.

The next method, getParent(), returns a Path instance representing the parent path or null if there is no such parent. If the instance of the Path object is relative, this method will stop at the top-level element defined in the Path object. In other words, it will not traverse outside the working directory to the file system root.

The last method, getRoot(), returns the root element for the Path object or null if the Path object is relative.

We present a sample application that traverses absolute and relative Path objects to show how each handles the root differently:

```java
import java.nio.file.*;

public class PathFilePathTest {
    public static void printPathInformation(Path path) {

        System.out.println("Filename is: "+path.getFileName());
        System.out.println("Root is: "+path.getRoot());

        Path currentParent = path;
        while((currentParent = currentParent.getParent()) != null) {
            System.out.println("   Current parent is: "+currentParent);
        }
    }

    public static void main(String[] args) {
        printPathInformation(Paths.get("/zoo/armadillo/shells.txt"));
        System.out.println();
        printPathInformation(Paths.get("armadillo/shells.txt"));
    }
}
```

The while loop in the printPathInformation() method continues until getParent() returns null. This sample application produces the following output:

```
Filename is: shells.txt
Root is: /
   Current parent is: /zoo/armadillo
   Current parent is: /zoo
   Current parent is: /
```

```
Filename is: shells.txt
Root is: null
   Current parent is: armadillo
```

Reviewing the sample output, you can see the difference in the behavior of getRoot() on absolute and relative paths. Also, notice that traversing the second path stopped at the top of the relative directory. As you can see in the example, it does not traverse relative directories outside the working directory.

Checking *Path* Type with *isAbsolute()* and *toAbsolutePath()*

The Path interface contains two methods for assisting with relative and absolute paths. The first method, isAbsolute(), returns true if the path the object references is absolute and false if the path the object references is relative. As discussed earlier in this chapter, whether a path is absolute or relative is often file system dependent, although we, like the exam writers, adopt common conventions for simplicity throughout the book.

The second method, toAbsolutePath(), converts a relative Path object to an absolute Path object by joining it to the current working directory. If the Path object is already absolute, then the method just returns an equivalent copy of it.

The following code snippet shows usage of both of these methods:

```
Path path1 = Paths.get("C:\\birds\\egret.txt");
System.out.println("Path1 is Absolute? "+path1.isAbsolute());
System.out.println("Absolute Path1: "+path1.toAbsolutePath());

Path path2 = Paths.get("birds/condor.txt");
System.out.println("Path2 is Absolute? "+path2.isAbsolute());
System.out.println("Absolute Path2 "+path2.toAbsolutePath());
```

The output for the code snippet is shown in the following sample code. Since the precise output is file system dependent, we'll treat the first example as being run on a Windows-based system, whereas the second example is run in a Linux or Mac-based system with the current working directory of /home.

```
Path1 is Absolute? true
Absolute Path1: C:\birds\egret.txt

Path2 is Absolute? false
Absolute Path2 /home/birds/condor.txt
```

Keep in mind that if the Path object already represents an absolute path, then the output is a new Path object with the same value.

As discussed earlier in this chapter, absolute and relative path types are actually file system dependent. In fact, you might be surprised by the output of the following lines of code on various operating systems:

```
System.out.println(Paths.get("/stripes/zebra.exe").isAbsolute());

System.out.println(Paths.get("c:/goats/Food.java").isAbsolute());
```

Although the first line outputs true on a Linux or Mac-based system, it outputs false on a Windows-based system since it is missing a drive letter prefix. In the same manner, the second path outputs true on Windows but false on a Linux or Mac-based system, as it is missing the root forward slash, /.

Creating a New Path with *subpath()*

The method subpath(int,int) returns a relative subpath of the Path object, referenced by an inclusive start index and an exclusive end index. It is useful for constructing a new relative path from a particular parent path element to another parent path element, as shown in the following example:

```
Path path = Paths.get("/mammal/carnivore/raccoon.image");
System.out.println("Path is: "+path);

System.out.println("Subpath from 0 to 3 is: "+path.subpath(0,3));
System.out.println("Subpath from 1 to 3 is: "+path.subpath(1,3));
System.out.println("Subpath from 1 to 2 is: "+path.subpath(1,2));
```

You might notice that the subpath() and getName(int) methods are similar in that they both return a Path object that represents a component of an existing Path. The difference is that the subpath() method may include multiple path components, whereas the getName(int) method only includes one.

The output of this code snippet is the following:

```
Path is: /mammal/carnivore/raccoon.image
Subpath from 0 to 3 is: mammal/carnivore/raccoon.image
Subpath from 1 to 3 is: carnivore/raccoon.image
Subpath from 1 to 2 is: carnivore
```

This code demonstrates that the subpath(int,int) method does not include the root of the file. Notice that the 0-indexed element is mammal in this example and not the root directory; therefore, the maximum index that can be used is 3.

The following two examples both throw java.lang.IllegalArgumentException at runtime:

```
System.out.println("Subpath from 0 to 4 is: "+path.subpath(0,4)); // THROWS
                                                    // EXCEPTION AT RUNTIME

System.out.println("Subpath from 1 to 1 is: "+path.subpath(1,1)); // THROWS
                                                    // EXCEPTION AT RUNTIME
```

The first example throws an exception at runtime, since the maximum index value allowed is 3. The second example throws an exception since the start and end indexes are the same, leading to an empty path value.

Using Path Symbols

Many file systems support paths that contain relative path information in the form of path symbols. For example, you might want a path that refers to the parent directory, regardless of what the current directory is. In this scenario, the double period value .. can be used to reference the parent directory. In addition, the single period value . can be used to reference the current directory within a path.

Table 9.2 lists symbols that are helpful to know while working with file paths.

TABLE 9.2   File system symbols

Symbol	Description
.	A reference to the current directory
..	A reference to the parent of the current directory

For example, the path value ../bear.txt refers to a file named bear.txt in the parent of the current directory. Likewise, the path value ./penguin.txt refers to a file named penguin.txt in the current directory. These symbols can also be combined for greater effect. For example, ../../lion.data refers to a file lion.data that is two directories up from the current working directory.

Deriving a Path with *relativize()*

The Path interface provides a method relativize(Path) for constructing the relative path from one Path object to another. Consider the following relative and absolute path examples using the relativize() method.

```
Path path1 = Paths.get("fish.txt");
Path path2 = Paths.get("birds.txt");
System.out.println(path1.relativize(path2));
System.out.println(path2.relativize(path1));
```

The code snippet produces the following output when executed:

```
..\birds.txt
..\fish.txt
```

If both path values are relative, then the relativize() method computes the paths as if they are in the same current working directory. Notice that ..\ is included at the start of the first set of examples. Since our path value points to a file, we need to move to the parent directory that contains the file.

Alternatively, if both path values are absolute, then the method computes the relative path from one absolute location to another, regardless of the current working directory. The following example demonstrates this property:

```
Path path3 = Paths.get("E:\\habitat");
Path path4 = Paths.get("E:\\sanctuary\\raven");
System.out.println(path3.relativize(path4));
System.out.println(path4.relativize(path3));
```

This code snippet produces the following output when executed:

```
..\sanctuary\raven
..\..\habitat
```

In this set of examples, the two path values are absolute, and the relativize() method constructs the relative path between the two absolute path values within the file system. Note that the file system is not accessed to perform this comparison. For example, the root path element E: may not exist in the file system, yet the code would execute without issue since Java is referencing the path elements and not the actual file values.

Compatible Path Types for _relativize()_

The relativize() method requires that both paths be absolute or both relative, and it will throw an IllegalArgumentException if a relative path value is mixed with an absolute path value. For example, the following would throw an exception at runtime:

```
Path path1 = Paths.get("/primate/chimpanzee");
Path path2 = Paths.get("bananas.txt");
Path1.relativize(path3); // THROWS EXCEPTION AT RUNTIME
```

On Windows-based systems, it also requires that if absolute paths are used, then both paths must have the same root directory or drive letter. For example, the following would also throw an IllegalArgumentException at runtime in a Windows-based system since they use different roots:

```
Path path3 = Paths.get("c:\\primate\\chimpanzee");
Path path4 = Paths.get("d:\\storage\\bananas.txt");
path3.relativize(path4); // THROWS EXCEPTION AT RUNTIME
```

Joining _Path_ Objects with _resolve()_

The Path interface includes a resolve(Path) method for creating a new Path by joining an existing path to the current path. To put it another way, the object on which the resolve() method is invoked becomes the basis of the new Path object, with the input argument being appended onto the Path. Let's see what happens if we apply resolve() to an absolute path and a relative path:

```
final Path path1 = Paths.get("/cats/../panther");
final Path path2 = Paths.get("food");
System.out.println(path1.resolve(path2));
```

The code snippet generates the following output:

```
/cats/../panther/food
```

For the exam, you should be aware that, like the relativize() method, the resolve() method does not clean up path symbols, such as the parent directory .. symbol. For that, you'll need to use the normalize() method, which we will cover next.

In this example, the input argument to the resolve() method was a relative path, but what if had been an absolute path?

```
final Path path1 = Paths.get("/turkey/food");
final Path path2 = Paths.get("/tiger/cage");
System.out.println(path1.resolve(path2));
```

Since the input parameter path2 is an absolute path, the output would be the following:

```
/tiger/cage
```

For the exam, you should be cognizant of mixing absolute and relative paths with the resolve() method. If an absolute path is provided as input to the method, such as path1.resolve(path2), then path1 would be ignored and a copy of path2 would be returned.

Cleaning Up a Path with *normalize()*

As you saw with the relativize() method, file systems can construct relative paths using .. and . values. There are times, however, when relative paths are combined such that there are redundancies in the path value. Luckily, Java provides us with the normalize(Path) method to eliminate the redundancies in the path.

For example, let's take the output of one of our previous examples that resulted in the path value ..\user\home and try to reconstitute the original absolute path using the resolve() method:

```
Path path3 = Paths.get("E:\\data");
Path path4 = Paths.get("E:\\user\\home");

Path relativePath = path3.relativize(path4);
System.out.println(path3.resolve(relativePath));
```

The result of this sample code would be the following output:

```
E:\data\..\user\home
```

You can see that this path value contains a redundancy. Worse yet, it does not match our original value, E:\user\home. We can resolve this redundancy by applying the normalize() method as shown here:

```
System.out.println(path3.resolve(relativePath).normalize());
```

This modified last line of code nicely produces our original path value:

```
E:\user\home
```

Like relativize(), the normalize() method does not check that the file actually exists. As you shall see with our final Path method, toRealPath(), Java provides a way to verify that the file does exactly exist.

Checking for File Existence with *toRealPath()*

The toRealPath(Path) method takes a Path object that may or may not point to an existing file within the file system, and it returns a reference to a real path within the file system. It is similar to the toAbsolutePath() method in that it can convert a relative path to an absolute path, except that it also verifies that the file referenced by the path actually exists, and thus it throws a checked IOException at runtime if the file cannot be located. It is also the only Path method to support the NOFOLLOW_LINKS option.

The toRealPath() method performs additional steps, such as removing redundant path elements. In other words, it implicitly calls normalize() on the resulting absolute path.

Let's say that we have a file system in which we have a symbolic link from food.source to food.txt, as described in the following relationship:

```
/zebra/food.source → /horse/food.txt
```

Assuming that our current working directory is /horse/schedule, then consider the following code:

```
try {
   System.out.println(Paths.get("/zebra/food.source").toRealPath());

   System.out.println(Paths.get("../././food.txt").toRealPath());
} catch (IOException e) {
   // Handle file I/O exception...
}
```

Notice that we have to catch IOException, since unlike the toAbsolutePath() method, the toRealPath() method interacts with the file system to check if the path is valid. Given the symbolic link and current working directory as described, then the output would be the following:

```
/horse/food.txt
/horse/food.txt
```

In these examples, the absolute and relative paths both resolve to the same absolute file, as the symbolic link points to a real file within the file system.

Finally, we can also use the toRealPath() method to gain access to the current working directory, such as shown here:

```
System.out.println(Paths.get(".").toRealPath());
```

Interacting with Files

Great! We now have access to a Path object, and we can find out a ton of information about it, but what can we do with the file it references? For starters, many of the same operations available in java.io.File are available to java.nio.file.Path via a helper class called java.nio.file.Files, or Files for short. Unlike the methods in the Path and Paths class, most of the options within the Files class will throw an exception if the file to which the Path refers does not exist.

Be Wary of *File* vs. *Files* on the Exam

As you saw with Collection vs. Collections in Chapter 3 and Path vs. Paths earlier in this chapter, Java is fond of singular names for container classes and plural names for factory and helper classes. In this situation, though, the NIO.2 Files helper class is in no way related to the File class, as the Files class operates on Path instances, not File instances. Keep in mind that File belongs to the legacy java.io API, while Files belongs to the NIO.2 API.

The Files class contains numerous static methods for interacting with files, with most taking one or two Path objects as arguments. Some of these methods are capable of throwing the checked IOException at runtime, often when the file being referenced does not exist within the file system, as you saw with the Path method toRealPath().

 You may notice that the names for the methods in the NIO.2 Files class are a lot more straightforward than what you saw in the java.io.File class. For example, the name of the method to move a file was renameTo() in the File class, and it is now move() in the Files class. In addition, the name of the method to create a directory was mkdir() in the File class, and it is now createDirectory() in the Files class. Many new Java programmers tend to find these method names a lot easier to learn and more developer friendly than the legacy method names, which were based on operating system commands.

Testing a Path with *exists()*

The Files.exists(Path) method takes a Path object and returns true if, and only if, it references a file that exists in the file system.

Let's take a look at some sample code:

```
Files.exists(Paths.get("/ostrich/feathers.png"));
```

```
Files.exists(Paths.get("/ostrich"));
```

The first example checks whether a file exists, while the second example checks whether a directory exists. You can see that this method does not throw an exception if the file does not exist, as doing so would prevent this method from ever returning `false` at runtime.

Testing Uniqueness with *isSameFile()*

The `Files.isSameFile(Path,Path)` method is useful for determining if two `Path` objects relate to the same file within the file system. It takes two `Path` objects as input and follows symbolic links. Despite the name, the method also determines if two `Path` objects refer to the same directory.

The `isSameFile()` method first checks if the `Path` objects are equal in terms of `equal()`, and if so, it automatically returns `true` without checking to see if either file exists. If the `Path` object `equals()` comparison returns `false`, then it locates each file to which the path refers in the file system and determines if they are the same, throwing a checked `IOException` if either file does not exist.

NOTE   This `isSameFile()` method does not compare the contents of the file. For example, two files may have identical content and attributes, but if they are in different locations, then this method will return `false`.

Let's assume that all of the files in the following examples exist within the file system and that cobra is a symbolic link to the snake file. What would be the output of the following code snippet?

```
try {
    System.out.println(Files.isSameFile(Paths.get("/user/home/cobra"),
        Paths.get("/user/home/snake")));

    System.out.println(Files.isSameFile(Paths.get("/user/tree/../monkey"),
        Paths.get("/user/monkey")));

    System.out.println(Files.isSameFile(Paths.get("/leaves/./giraffe.exe"),
        Paths.get("/leaves/giraffe.exe")));

    System.out.println(Files.isSameFile(Paths.get("/flamingo/tail.data"),
        Paths.get("/cardinal/tail.data")));
} catch (IOException e) {
    // Handle file I/O exception...
}
```

Since cobra is a symbolic link to the snake file, the first example outputs true. In the second example, the symbol .. cancels out the tree path of the path, resulting in the method also outputting true. In the third example, the symbol . leaves the path unmodified, so the result is true as well. The final example returns false, assuming that neither file is a symbolic link to the other. Even if the files have the same name and the same contents, if they are at different locations, they are considered different files within the file system.

Making Directories with *createDirectory()* and *createDirectories()*

To create directories in the legacy java.io API, we called mkdir() or mkdirs() on a File object. In the NIO.2 API, we can use the Files.createDirectory(Path) method to create a directory. There is also a plural form of the method called createDirectories(), which like mkdirs() creates the target directory along with any nonexistent parent directories leading up to the target directory in the path.

The directory-creation methods can throw the checked IOException, such as when the directory cannot be created or already exists. For example, the first method, createDirectory(), will throw an exception if the parent directory in which the new directory resides does not exist.

Both of these methods also accept an optional list of FileAttribute<?> values to set on the newly created directory or directories. We will discuss file attributes in the next section.

We now present a code snippet that shows how to create directories using NIO.2:

```
try {
    Files.createDirectory(Paths.get("/bison/field"));

    Files.createDirectories(Paths.get("/bison/field/pasture/green"));
} catch (IOException e) {
    // Handle file I/O exception...
}
```

The first example creates a new directory, field, in the directory /bison, assuming /bison exists; or else an exception is thrown. Contrast this with the second example that creates the directory green along with any of the following parent directories if they do not already exist, such as /bison, /bison/field, or /bison/pasture.

Duplicating File Contents with *copy()*

Unlike the legacy java.io.File class, the NIO.2 Files class provides a set of overloaded copy() methods for copying files and directories within the file system. The primary one that you should know about for the exam is Files.copy(Path,Path), which copies a file or directory from one location to another. The copy() method throws the checked IOException, such as when the file or directory does not exist or cannot be read.

Directory copies are shallow rather than deep, meaning that files and subdirectories within the directory are not copied. To copy the contents of a directory, you would need to create a function to traverse the directory and copy each file and subdirectory individually:

```
try {
   Files.copy(Paths.get("/panda"), Paths.get("/panda-save"));

   Files.copy(Paths.get("/panda/bamboo.txt"),
       Paths.get("/panda-save/bamboo.txt"));
} catch (IOException e) {
   // Handle file I/O exception...
}
```

The first example performs a shallow copy of the panda directory, creating a new panda-save directory, but it does not copy any of the contents of the original directory. The second example copies the bamboo.txt file from the directory panda to the directory panda-save.

By default, copying files and directories will traverse symbolic links, although it will not overwrite a file or directory if it already exists, nor will it copy file attributes. These behaviors can be altered by providing the additional options NOFOLLOW_LINKS, REPLACE_EXISTING, and COPY_ATTRIBUTES, respectively, as discussed earlier in the chapter.

Copying Files with *java.io* and NIO.2

The NIO.2 Files API class contains two overloaded copy() methods for copying files using java.io streams, as described in Chapter 8. The first copy() method takes a *source* java.io.InputStream along with a *target* Path object. It reads the contents from the stream and writes the output to a file represented by a Path object.

The second copy() method takes a *source* Path object and *target* java.io.OutputStream. It reads the contents of the file and writes the output to the stream.

The following are examples of each copy() method:

```
try (InputStream is = new FileInputStream("source-data.txt");
     OutputStream out = new FileOutputStream("output-data.txt")) {

   // Copy stream data to file
   Files.copy(is, Paths.get("c:\\mammals\\wolf.txt"));

   // Copy file data to stream
   Files.copy(Paths.get("c:\\fish\\clown.xsl"), out);

} catch (IOException e) {
   // Handle file I/O exception...
}
```

In this example, the InputStream and OutputStream parameters could refer to any valid stream, including website connections, in-memory stream resources, and so forth.

Like the first copy() method, the copy(InputStream,Path) method also supports optional vararg options, since the data is being written to a file represented by a Path object. The second method, copy(Path,OutputStream), does not support optional vararg values, though, since the data is being written to a stream that may not represent a file system resource.

Changing a File Location with *move()*

The Files.move(Path,Path) method moves or renames a file or directory within the file system. Like the copy() method, the move() method also throws the checked IOException in the event that the file or directory could not be found or moved.

The following is some sample code that uses the move() method:

```
try {
   Files.move(Paths.get("c:\\zoo"), Paths.get("c:\\zoo-new"));

   Files.move(Paths.get("c:\\user\\addresses.txt"),
      Paths.get("c:\\zoo-new\\addresses.txt"));
} catch (IOException e) {
   // Handle file I/O exception...
}
```

The first example renames the zoo directory to zoo-new directory, keeping all of the original contents from the source directory. The second example moves the addresses.txt file from the directory user to the directory zoo-new, and it renames it to addresses2.txt.

By default, the move() method will follow links, throw an exception if the file already exists, and not perform an atomic move. These behaviors can be changed by providing the optional values NOFOLLOW_LINKS, REPLACE_EXISTING, or ATOMIC_MOVE, respectively, to the method. If the file system does not support atomic moves, an AtomicMoveNotSupportedException will be thrown at runtime.

The Files.move() method can be applied to non-empty directories only if they are on the same underlying drive. While moving an empty directory across a drive is supported, moving a non-empty directory across a drive will throw an NIO.2 DirectoryNotEmptyException.

Removing a File with *delete()* and *deleteIfExists()*

The Files.delete(Path) method deletes a file or empty directory within the file system. The delete() method throws the checked IOException under a variety of circumstances. For example, if the path represents a non-empty directory, the operation will throw the runtime DirectoryNotEmptyException. If the target of the path is a symbol link, then the symbolic link will be deleted, not the target of the link.

The deleteIfExists(Path) method is identical to the delete(Path) method, except that it will not throw an exception if the file or directory does not exist, but instead it will return a boolean value of false. It will still throw an exception if the file or directory does exist but fails, such as in the case of the directory not being empty.

We now provide sample code that performs delete() operations:

```
try {
    Files.delete(Paths.get("/vulture/feathers.txt"));
    Files.deleteIfExists(Paths.get("/pigeon"));
} catch (IOException e) {
    // Handle file I/O exception...
}
```

The first example deletes the features.txt file in the vulture directory, and it throws a NoSuchFileException if the file or directory does not exist. The second example deletes the pigeon directory assuming it is empty. If the pigeon directory does not exist, then the second line will not throw an exception.

Reading and Writing File Data with *newBufferedReader()* and *newBufferedWriter()*

The NIO.2 API includes methods for reading and writing file contents using java.io streams. In this manner, the NIO.2 API bridges information about streams, which you learned about in Chapter 8; the Path and Files classes are covered in this chapter.

The first method, Files.newBufferedReader(Path,Charset), reads the file specified at the Path location using a java.io.BufferedReader object. It also requires a Charset value to determine what character encoding to use to read the file. You may remember that we briefly discussed character encoding and Charset in Chapter 8. For this chapter, you just need to know that characters can be encoded in bytes in a variety of ways. It may also be useful to know that Charset.defaultCharset() can be used to get the default Charset for the JVM.

We now present an example of this method:

```
Path path = Paths.get("/animals/gopher.txt");
try (BufferedReader reader = Files.newBufferedReader(path,
            Charset.forName("US-ASCII"))) {
    // Read from the stream
    String currentLine = null;
    while((currentLine = reader.readLine()) != null)
        System.out.println(currentLine);
} catch (IOException e) {
    // Handle file I/O exception...
}
```

This example reads the contents of the files using a BufferedReader and outputs the contents to the user. As you shall see in the next section, there is a much simpler way to accomplish this, which uses functional programming streams.

The second method, `Files.newBufferedWriter(Path,Charset)`, writes to a file specified at the `Path` location using a `BufferedWriter`. Like the reader method, it also takes a `Charset` value:

```
Path path = Paths.get("/animals/gorilla.txt");
List<String> data = new ArrayList();
try (BufferedWriter writer = Files.newBufferedWriter(path,
        Charset.forName("UTF-16"))) {
   writer.write("Hello World");
} catch (IOException e) {
   // Handle file I/O exception...
}
```

This code snippet creates a new file with the specified contents, overwriting the file if it already exists. The `newBufferedWriter()` method also supports taking additional enum values in an optional vararg, such as appending to an existing file instead of overwriting it, although you do not need to memorize this list for the exam.

Since both of these methods create resources, we use the try-with-resource syntax as described in Chapter 6, as we did when working with streams in Chapter 8. Also, note that both of these methods use buffered streams rather than low-level file streams. As we mentioned earlier in the chapter, the buffered stream classes are much more performant in practice, so much so that the NIO.2 API includes methods that specifically return these stream classes, in part to encourage you always to use buffered streams in your application.

Reading Files with *readAllLines()*

The `Files.readAllLines()` method reads all of the lines of a text file and returns the results as an ordered `List` of `String` values. The NIO.2 API includes an overloaded version that takes an optional `Charset` value. The following sample code reads the lines of the file and outputs them to the user:

```
Path path = Paths.get("/fish/sharks.log");
try {
   final List<String> lines = Files.readAllLines(path);
   for(String line: lines) {
       System.out.println(line);
   }
} catch (IOException e) {
   // Handle file I/O exception...
}
```

The code snippet reads all of the lines of the file and then iterates over them. As you might expect, the method may throw an `IOException` if the file cannot be read.

Be aware that the entire file is read when readAllLines() is called, with the resulting String array storing all of the contents of the file in memory at once. Therefore, if the file is significantly large, you may encounter an OutOfMemoryError trying to load all of it into memory. Later on in the chapter, we will revisit this method and present a new stream-based NIO.2 method that is far more performant on large files.

Understanding File Attributes

In the previous section, we reviewed methods that could create, modify, read, or delete a file or directory. The Files class also provides numerous methods accessing file and directory metadata, referred to as *file attributes*. Put simply, *metadata* is data that describes other data. In this context, file metadata is data about the file or directory record within the file system and not the contents of the file.

For example, a file or directory may be hidden within a file system or marked with a permission that prevents the current user from reading it. The Files class provides methods for determining this information from within your Java application.

The one thing to keep in mind while reading file metadata in Java is that some methods are operating system dependent. For example, some operating systems may not have a notion of user-level permissions, in which case users can read only files that they have permission to read.

Discovering Basic File Attributes

We begin the discussion of file attributes by presenting the basic methods, defined directly within the Files class, for reading file attributes. These methods are usable within any file system although they may have limited meaning in some file systems. In the next section, we will present a more generalized approach using attribute views and show that they not only improve performance but also allow us to access file system-dependent attributes.

Reading Common Attributes with *isDirectory()*, *isRegularFile()*, and *isSymbolicLink()*

The Files class includes three methods for determining if a path refers to a directory, a regular file, or a symbolic link. The methods to accomplish this are named Files.isDirectory(Path), Files.isRegularFile(Path), and Files.isSymbolicLink(Path), respectively.

Java defines a *regular file* as one that contains content, as opposed to a symbolic link, directory, resource, or other non-regular file that may be present in some operating systems. If the symbolic link points to a real file or directory, Java will perform the check on the target of the symbolic link. In other words, it is possible for isRegularFile() to return true for a symbolic link, as long as the link resolves to a regular file.

Let's take a look at some sample code:

```
Files.isDirectory(Paths.get("/canine/coyote/fur.jpg"));

Files.isRegularFile(Paths.get("/canine/types.txt"));

Files.isSymbolicLink(Paths.get("/canine/coyote"));
```

The first example returns true if fur.jpg is a directory or a symbolic link to a directory and false otherwise. Note that directories can have extensions in many file systems, so it is possible for fur.jpg to be the name of a directory. The second example returns true if types.txt points to a regular file or alternatively a symbolic link that points to a regular file. The third example returns true if /canine/coyote is a symbolic link, regardless of whether the file or directory it points to exists.

We illuminate these concepts in Table 9.3. For this table, assume that the file system with the directory /canine/coyote and file /canine/types.txt exists. Furthermore, assume that /coyotes is a symbolic link within the file system that points to another path within the file system.

TABLE 9.3   isDirectory(), isRegularFile(), isSymbolicLink() examples

	isDirectory()	isRegularFile()	isSymbolicLink()
/canine/coyote	true	false	false
/canine/types.txt	false	true	false
/coyotes	true if the target is a directory	true if the target is a regular file	true

You see that the value of isDirectory() and isRegular() in Table 9.3 cannot be determined on the symbolic link /coyotes without knowledge of what the symbolic link points to.

 Real World Scenario

Exception Handling

You may notice when browsing the Files API that isDirectory(), isRegularFile(), and isSymbolicLink() do not throw an exception if the path does not exist, so the following code is redundant:

```
if(Files.exists(path) && Files.isDirectory(path)) {
```

This code could be replaced with a single `Files.isDirectory()` method call since the `exists()` call is unnecessary:

```
if(Files.isDirectory(path)) {
```

Checking File Visibility with *isHidden()*

The `Files` class includes the `Files.isHidden(Path)` method to determine whether a file or directory is hidden within the file system. In Linux- or Mac-based systems, this is often denoted by file or directory entries that begin with a period character (.), while in Windows-based systems this requires the hidden attribute to be set. The `isHidden()` method throws the checked `IOException`, as there may be an I/O error reading the underlying file information. We present illustrative usage of this method in the following sample code:

```
try {
   System.out.println(Files.isHidden(Paths.get("/walrus.txt")));
} catch (IOException e) {
   // Handle file I/O exception...
}
```

If the `walrus.txt` file is available and hidden within the file system, this method will return `true`.

Testing File Accessibility with *isReadable()* and *isExecutable()*

The `Files` class includes two methods for reading file accessibility: `Files.isReadable(Path)` and `Files.isExecutable(Path)`. This is important in file systems where the filename can be viewed within a directory, but the user may not have permission to read the contents of the file or execute it. We now present sample usage of each method:

```
System.out.println(Files.isReadable(Paths.get("/seal/baby.png")));
```

```
System.out.println(Files.isExecutable(Paths.get("/seal/baby.png")));
```

The first example returns `true` if the `baby.png` file exists and its contents are readable, based on the permission rules of the underlying file system. The second example returns `true` if the `baby.png` file is marked executable within the file system. Note that the file extension does not necessary determine whether a file is executable. For example, an image file that ends in `.png` could be marked executable within a Linux-based system.

Like the `isDirectory()`, `isRegularFile()`, and `isSymbolicLink()` methods, the `isReadable()` and `isExecutable()` methods do not throw exceptions if the file does not exist but instead return `false`.

Reading File Length with *size()*

The Files.size(Path) method is used to determine the size of the file in bytes. The size returned by this method represents the conceptual size of the data, and this may differ from the actual size on the persistence storage device due to file system compression and organization. The size() method throws the checked IOException if the file does not exist or if the process is unable to read the file information.

The following is a sample call to the size() method:

```
try {
   System.out.println(Files.size(Paths.get("/zoo/c/animals.txt")));
} catch (IOException e) {
   // Handle file I/O exception...
}
```

The example outputs the number of bytes in the file, expressed as a long value. As you may have already realized, we're repeating a lot of the methods defined in java.io.File, as discussed in Chapter 8. Since the NIO.2 API was defined as a replacement for the java.io API, it includes many of the same methods in one form or another.

 The Files.size() method is defined only on files. Calling Files.size() on a directory is system dependent and undefined. If you need to determine the size of a directory and its contents, you'll need to walk the directory tree, as described later in this chapter.

Managing File Modifications with *getLastModifiedTime()* and *setLastModifiedTime()*

Most operating systems support tracking a last-modified date/time value with each file. Some applications use this to determine when the file should be read again. For example, there might be a program that performs an operation anytime the file data changes. In the majority of circumstances, it is a lot faster to check a single file metadata attribute than to reload the entire contents of the file, especially if the file is large.

The Files class provides the method Files.getLastModifiedTime(Path), which returns a FileTime object to accomplish this. The FileTime class is a simple container class that stores the date/time information about when a file was accessed, modified, or created. For convenience, it has a toMillis() method that returns the epoch time.

The Files class also provides a mechanism for updating the last-modified date/time of a file using the Files.setLastModifiedTime(Path,FileTime) method. The FileTime class also has a static fromMillis() method that converts from the epoch time to a FileTime object.

Both of these methods have the ability to throw a checked IOException when the file is accessed or modified.

NOTE   You don't actually have to modify the file to change the last-modified date/time value. That said, it is considered a good practice to modify this attribute only when the file data changes, since changing this value arbitrarily could impact applications that access the file regularly.

We now present examples of both methods:

```
try {
    final Path path = Paths.get("/rabbit/food.jpg");
    System.out.println(Files.getLastModifiedTime(path).toMillis());

    Files.setLastModifiedTime(path,
            FileTime.fromMillis(System.currentTimeMillis()));

    System.out.println(Files.getLastModifiedTime(path).toMillis());
} catch (IOException e) {
    // Handle file I/O exception...
}
```

The first part of the code reads and outputs the last-modified time value of the food.jpeg file. The next line sets a last-modified date/time using the current time value. Finally, we repeat our earlier line and output the newly set last-modified date/time value.

Managing Ownership with *getOwner()* and *setOwner()*

Many file systems also support the notion of user-owned files and directories. In this manner, the Files.getOwner(Path) method returns an instance of UserPrincipal that represents the owner of the file within the file system.

As you may have already guessed, there is also a method to set the owner, called Files .setOwner(Path,UserPrincipal). Note that the operating system may intervene when you try to modify the owner of a file and block the operation. For example, a process running under one user may not be allowed to take ownership of a file owned by another user. Both the getOwner() and setOwner() methods can throw the checked exception IOException in case of any issues accessing or modifying the file.

In order to set a file owner to an arbitrary user, the NIO.2 API provides a UserPrincipalLookupService helper class for finding a UserPrincipal record for a particular user within a file system. In order to use the helper class, you first need to obtain an instance of a FileSystem object, either by using the FileSystems.getDefault() method or by calling getFileSystem() on the Path object with which you are working, as shown in the following two examples:

```
UserPrincipal owner = FileSystems.getDefault().getUserPrincipalLookupService()
                    .lookupPrincipalByName("jane");

Path path = ...
```

```
UserPrincipal owner = path.getFileSystem().getUserPrincipalLookupService()
                    .lookupPrincipalByName("jane");
```

We now present examples of the getOwner() and setOwner() methods, including an example of how to use the UserPrincipalLookupService:

```
try {
    // Read owner of file
    Path path = Paths.get("/chicken/feathers.txt");
    System.out.println(Files.getOwner(path).getName());

    // Change owner of file
    UserPrincipal owner = path.getFileSystem()
            .getUserPrincipalLookupService().lookupPrincipalByName("jane");
    Files.setOwner(path, owner);

    // Output the updated owner information
    System.out.println(Files.getOwner(path).getName());
} catch (IOException e) {
    // Handle file I/O exception...
}
```

The first set of lines reads the owner of the file and outputs the name of the user. The second set of lines retrieves a user named jane within the related file system and uses it to set a new owner for the file. Finally, we read the file owner name again to verify that is has been updated.

Improving Access with Views

Up until now, we have been accessing individual file attributes with single method calls. While this is functionally correct, there are often costs associated with accessing the file that make it far more efficient to retrieve all file metadata attributes in a single call. Furthermore, some attributes are file system specific and cannot be easily generalized for all file systems.

The NIO.2 API addresses both of these concerns by allowing you to construct views for various file systems in a single method call. A *view* is a group of related attributes for a particular file system type. A file may support multiple views, allowing you to retrieve and update various sets of information about the file.

If you need to read multiple attributes of a file or directory at a time, the performance advantage of using a view may be substantial. Although more attributes are read than in a single method call, there are fewer round-trips between Java and the operating system, whereas reading the same attributes with the previously described single method calls would require many such trips. In practice, the number of trips between Java and the operating system is more important in determining performance than the number of attributes read.

That's not to say that the single method calls we just finished discussing do not have their applications. If you only need to read exactly one file attribute, then there is little or no performance difference. They also tend to be more convenient to use given their concise nature.

Understanding Views

To request a view, you need to provide both a path to the file or a directory whose information you want to read, as well as a class object, which tells the NIO.2 API method which type of view you would like returned.

The Files API includes two sets of methods of analogous classes for accessing view information. The first method, Files.readAttributes(), returns a read-only view of the file attributes. The second method, Files.getFileAttributeView(), returns the underlying attribute view, and it provides a direct resource for modifying file information.

Both of these methods can throw a checked IOException, such as when the view class type is unsupported. For example, trying to read Windows-based attributes within a Linux file system may throw an UnsupportedOperationException.

Table 9.4 lists the commonly used attributes and view classes; note that the first row is required knowledge for the exam. The DOS and POSIX classes are useful for reading and modifying operating system–specific properties. They also both inherit from their respective attribute and view classes. For example, PosixFileAttributes inherits from BasicFileAttributes, just as DosFileAttributeView inherits from BasicFileAttributeView, meaning that all of the operations available on the parent class are available in the respective subclasses.

TABLE 9.4   The attributes and view classes

Attributes Class	View Class	Description
BasicFileAttributes	BasicFileAttributeView	Basic set of attributes supported by all file systems
DosFileAttributes	DosFileAttributeView	Attributes supported by DOS/Windows-based systems
PosixFileAttributes	PosixFileAttributeView	Attributes supported by POSIX systems, such as UNIX, Linux, Mac, and so on

For the exam, you should be familiar with the BasicFileAttributes and BasicFileAttributeView classes and their common methods, such as creationTime(), lastModifiedTime(), and so forth. You do not need to memorize the methods available to the DosFile and PosixFile classes for the exam, although you should be aware that they exist in case you come across them.

Reading Attributes

The NIO.2 API provides a Files.readAttributes(Path,Class<A>) method, which returns read-only versions of a file view. The second parameter uses generics such that the return type of the method will be an instance of the provided class.

BasicFileAttributes

All attributes classes extend from BasicFileAttributes; therefore it contains attributes common to all supported file systems. It includes many of the file attributes that you previously saw as single-line method calls in the Files class, such as Files.isDirectory(), Files.getLastModifiedTime(), and so on.

We now present a sample application that retrieves BasicFileAttributes on a file and outputs various metadata about the file:

```java
import java.io.IOException;
import java.nio.file.*;
import java.nio.file.attribute.BasicFileAttributes;

public class BasicFileAttributesSample {
    public static void main(String[] args) throws IOException {
        Path path = Paths.get("/turtles/sea.txt");
        BasicFileAttributes data = Files.readAttributes(path,
            BasicFileAttributes.class);

        System.out.println("Is path a directory? "+data.isDirectory());
        System.out.println("Is path a regular file? "+data.isRegularFile());
        System.out.println("Is path a symbolic link? "+data.isSymbolicLink());
        System.out.println("Path not a file, directory, nor symbolic link? "+
            data.isOther());

        System.out.println("Size (in bytes): "+data.size());

        System.out.println("Creation date/time: "+data.creationTime());
        System.out.println("Last modified date/time: "+data.lastModifiedTime());
        System.out.println("Last accessed date/time: "+data.lastAccessTime());
        System.out.println("Unique file identifier (if available): "+
            data.fileKey());
    }
}
```

The majority of these attributes should be familiar to you, as they were covered in the previous section of this chapter. The only ones that are new are isOther(), lastAccessTime(), creationTime(), and fileKey(). The isOther() method is used to check for paths that are not files, directories, or symbolic links, such as paths that refer to resources or devices in some file systems. The lastAccessTime() and creationTime() methods return other date/time information about the file. The fileKey() method returns a file system value that represents a unique identifier for the file within the file system or null if it is not supported by the file system.

Modifying Attributes

While the Files.readAttributes() method is useful for reading file data, it does not provide a direct mechanism for modifying file attributes. The NIO.2 API provides the Files.getFileAttributeView(Path,Class<V>) method, which returns a view object that we can use to update the file system–dependent attributes. We can also use the view object to read the associated file system attributes by calling readAttributes() on the view object.

BasicFileAttributeView

BasicFileAttributeView is used to modify a file's set of date/time values. In general, we cannot modify the other basic attributes directly, since this would change the property of the file system object. For example, we cannot set a property to change a directory into a file, since this leaves the files in the future in an ambiguous state. Likewise, we cannot change the size of the object without modifying its contents.

We now present a sample application that reads a file's basic attributes and increments the file's last-modified date/time values by 10,000 milliseconds, or 10 seconds:

```java
import java.io.IOException;
import java.nio.file.*;
import java.nio.file.attribute.*;

public class BasicFileAttributeViewSample {
    public static void main(String[] args) throws IOException {
        Path path = Paths.get("/turtles/sea.txt");

        BasicFileAttributeView view =
            Files.getFileAttributeView(path,BasicFileAttributeView.class);
        BasicFileAttributes data = view.readAttributes();

        FileTime lastModifiedTime = FileTime.fromMillis(
            data.lastModifiedTime().toMillis()+10_000);

        view.setTimes(lastModifiedTime,null,null);
    }
}
```

Notice that although we called Files.getFileAttributeView(), we were still able to retrieve a BasicFileAttributes object by calling readAttributes() on the resulting view. Since there is only one update method, setTimes(FileTime lastModifiedTime, FileTime lastAccessTime, FileTime createTime) in the BasicFileAttributeView class, and it takes three arguments, we need to pass three values to the method.

The NIO.2 API allows us to pass null for any date/time value that we do not wish to modify. For example, the following line of code would change only the last-modified date/time, leaving the other file date/time values unaffected:

```java
view.setTimes(lastModifiedTime,null,null);
```

Presenting the New Stream Methods

Prior to Java 8, the techniques used to perform complex file operations in NIO.2, such as searching for a file within a directory tree, were a tad verbose and often required you to define an entire class to perform a simple task. When Java 8 was released, new methods that rely on streams were added to the NIO.2 specification that allow you to perform many of these complex operations with a single line of code.

Conceptualizing Directory Walking

Before delving into the new NIO.2 stream methods, let's review some basic concepts about file systems. When we originally described a directory in Chapter 8, we mentioned that it was organized in a hierarchical manner. For example, a directory can contain files and other directories, which can in turn contain other files and directories. Every record in a file system has exactly one parent, with the exception of the root directory, which sits atop everything.

This is commonly visualized as a tree with a single root node and many branches and leaves, as shown in Figure 9.2. Notice that this tree is conceptually equivalent to Figure 8.1.

FIGURE 9.2   File and directory as a tree structure

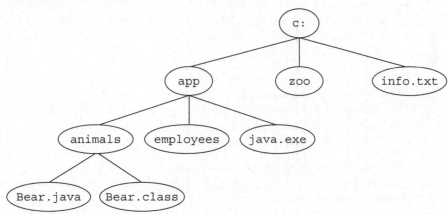

A common task in a file system is to iterate over the descendants of a particular file path, either recording information about them or, more commonly, filtering them for a specific set of files. For example, you may want to search a folder and print a list of all of the .java files. Furthermore, file systems store file records in a hierarchical manner. Generally speaking, if you want to search for a file, you have to start with a parent directory, read its child elements, then read their children, and so on.

Walking or traversing a directory is the process by which you start with a parent directory and iterate over all of its descendants until some condition is met or there are no more elements over which to iterate. The starting path is usually a relevant directory to the application; after all, it would be time consuming to search the entire file system if your application uses only a single directory!

Selecting a Search Strategy

There are two common strategies associated with walking a directory tree: a depth-first search and a breadth-first search. A *depth-first search* traverses the structure from the root to an arbitrary leaf and then navigates back up toward the root, traversing fully down any paths it skipped along the way. The *search depth* is the distance from the root to current node. For performance reasons, some processes have a maximum search depth that is used to limit how many levels deep the search goes before stopping.

Alternatively, a *breadth-first search* starts at the root and processes all elements of each particular depth, or distance from the root, before proceeding to the next depth level. The results are ordered by depth, with all nodes at depth 1 read before all nodes at depth 2, and so on.

For the exam, you don't have to understand the details of each search strategy that Java employs; you just need to be aware that the Streams API uses depth-first searching with a default maximum depth of Integer.MAX_VALUE.

 Real World Scenario

Depth-First Search vs. Breadth-First Search

In practice, each search strategy has its own advantages and disadvantages. For example, depth-first searches tend to require less memory, since breadth-first searches require maintaining all of the nodes on a particular level in memory in order to generate the next level.

On the other hand, breadth-first searches work better when the node for which you are searching is likely near the root, since depth-first searches can go many levels down a completely useless path before visiting all of the children of the root. For example, in Figure 9.2, we might traverse the entire c:\app tree before finding the file at c:\info.txt.

If you are interested in understanding search strategies in greater detail, there are numerous algorithm books and articles on the subject, including a detailed description of each search strategy on Wikipedia.

Walking a Directory

As presented in Chapter 4, Java 8 includes a new Streams API for performing complex operations in a single line of code using functional programming and lambda expressions. The first newly added NIO.2 stream-based method that we will cover is one used to traverse a directory. The Files.walk(path) method returns a Stream<Path> object that traverses the directory in a depth-first, lazy manner.

By *lazy*, we mean the set of elements is built and read while the directory is being traversed. For example, until a specific subdirectory is reached, its child elements are not loaded. This performance enhancement allows the process to be run on directories with a large number of descendants in a reasonable manner.

 Keep in mind that when you create a `Stream<Path>` object using `Files.walk()`, the contents of the directory have not yet been traversed.

The following is an example of using a stream to walk a directory structure:

```
Path path = Paths.get("/bigcats");

try {
   Files.walk(path)
      .filter(p -> p.toString().endsWith(".java"))
      .forEach(System.out::println);
} catch (IOException e) {
   // Handle file I/O exception...
}
```

This example iterates over a directory and outputs all of the files that end with a java extension. You can see that the method also throws a somewhat expected IOException, as there could be a problem reading the underlying file system. Sample output for this method would be similar to the following:

```
/bigcats/version1/backup/Lion.java
/bigcats/version1/Lion.java
/bigcats/version1/Tiger.java
/bigcats/Lion.java
```

If you are familiar with the FileVisitor interface pattern, which was required for version 7 of the OCP exam, you might have noticed that we did in one line what would normally require an entire class definition to do.

By default, the method iterates up to Integer.MAX_VALUE directories deep, although there is an overloaded version of walk(Path,int) that takes a maximum directory depth integer value as the second parameter. A value of 0 indicates the current path record itself. In the previous example, you would need to specify a value of at least 1 to print any child record. In practice, you may want to set a limit to prevent your application from searching too deeply on a large directory structure and taking too much time.

Why Is *Integer.MAX_VALUE* the Depth Limit?

Java used an integer value for its maximum depth because most file systems do not support path values deeper than what can be stopped in an int. In other words, using Integer.MAX_VALUE is effectively like using an infinite value, since you would be hard pressed to find a situation where this limit is exceeded.

You see that the Stream<Path> object returned by the walk() method visits every descendant path, with the filter being applied as each path is encountered. In the next section, you will see that there is a more useful method for filtering files available in the NIO.2 API.

 Real World Scenario

Disregarding *newDirectoryStream()*

While browsing the NIO.2 API, you may come across the method Files.newDirectoryStream() along with the generic object it returns, DirectoryStream<Path>. The method behaves quite similarly to Files.walk(), except the DirectoryStream<Path> object that it returns does not inherit from the java.util.stream.Stream class. In other words, despite its name, it is not actually a stream as described in Chapter 4, and therefore none of the useful stream operations can be applied.

Although this method was part of the OCP 7 objective, it had been removed at the time of the writing of this book. We bring it up now only to help guide you should you come across it in practice.

Avoiding Circular Paths

Unlike our earlier NIO.2 methods, the walk() method will not traverse symbolic links by default. Following symbolic links could result in a directory tree that includes other, seemingly unrelated directories in the search. For example, a symbolic link to the root directory in a subdirectory means that every file in the system may be traversed.

Worse yet, symbolic links could lead to a cycle. A *cycle* is an infinite circular dependency in which an entry in a directory is an ancestor of the directory. For example, imagine that we had a directory /birds/robin that contains a symbolic link called /birds/robin/allBirds that pointed to /birds. Trying to traverse the /birds/robin directory would result in an infinite loop since each time the allBirds subdirectory was reached, we would go back to the parent path.

If you have a situation where you need to change the default behavior and traverse symbolic links, NIO.2 offers the FOLLOW_LINKS option as a vararg to the walk() method. It is recommended to specify an appropriate depth limit when this option is used. Also, be aware that when this option is used, the walk() method will track the paths it has visited, throwing a FileSystemLoopException if a cycle is detected.

Searching a Directory

In the previous example, we applied a filter to the Stream<Path> object to filter the results, although the NIO.2 API provides a more direct method. The Files.find(Path,int,BiPredicate) method behaves in a similar manner as the Files.walk() method, except that it requires the depth value to be explicitly set along with a BiPredicate to filter the data. Like walk(), find() also supports the FOLLOW_LINK vararg option.

As you may remember from Chapter 4, a BiPredicate is an interface that takes two generic objects and returns a boolean value of the form (T, U) -> boolean. In this case, the two object types are Path and BasicFileAttributes, which you saw earlier in the chapter. In this manner, the NIO.2 automatically loads the BasicFileAttributes object for you, allowing you to write complex lambda expressions that have direct access to this object. We illustrate this with the following example:

```
Path path = Paths.get("/bigcats");
long dateFilter = 1420070400000l;

try {
    Stream<Path> stream = Files.find(path, 10,
        (p,a) -> p.toString().endsWith(".java")
            && a.lastModifiedTime().toMillis()>dateFilter);
    stream.forEach(System.out::println);
} catch (Exception e) {
    // Handle file I/O exception...
}
```

This example is similar to our previous Files.walk() example in that it will search a directory for files that end with the .java extension. It is more advanced, though, in that it applies a last-modified time filter using the BasicFileAttributes object. Finally, it sets the directory depth limit for search to 10, as opposed to relying on the default Integer.MAX_VALUE value that the Files.walk() method uses.

Listing Directory Contents

You may remember in Chapter 8 that we presented the method listFiles() that operated on a java.io.File instance and returned a list of File objects representing the contents of the directory that are direct children of the parent. Although you could use the Files. walk() method with a maximum depth limit of 1 to perform this same task, the NIO.2 API includes a new stream method, Files.list(Path), that does this for you.

Consider the following code snippet, assuming that the current working directory is /zoo:

```
try {
    Path path = Paths.get("ducks");
    Files.list(path)
        .filter(p -> !Files.isDirectory(p))
        .map(p -> p.toAbsolutePath())
        .forEach(System.out::println);
```

```
} catch (IOException e) {
   // Handle file I/O exception...
}
```

The code snippet iterates over a directory, outputting the full path of the files that it contains. Depending on the contents of the file system, the output might look something like the following:

```
/zoo/ducks/food.txt
/zoo/ducks/food-backup.txt
/zoo/ducks/weight.txt
```

Contrast this method with the `Files.walk()` method, which traverses all subdirectories. For the exam, you should be aware that `Files.list()` searches one level deep and is analogous to `java.io.File.listFiles()`, except that it relies on streams.

Printing File Contents

Earlier in the chapter, we presented `Files.readAllLines()` and commented that using it to read a very large file could result in an `OutOfMemoryError` problem. Luckily, the NIO.2 API in Java 8 now includes a `Files.lines(Path)` method that returns a `Stream<String>` object and does not suffer from this same issue. The contents of the file are read and processed lazily, which means that only a small portion of the file is stored in memory at any given time.

We now present `Files.lines()`, which is equivalent to the previous `Files.readAllLines()` sample code:

```
Path path = Paths.get("/fish/sharks.log");
try {
   Files.lines(path).forEach(System.out::println);
} catch (IOException e) {
   // Handle file I/O exception...
}
```

The first thing you may notice is that this example is a lot shorter, accomplishing in a single line what took multiple lines earlier. It is also more performant on large files, since it does not require the entire file to be read and stored in memory.

Taking things one step further, we can leverage other stream methods for a more powerful example:

```
Path path = Paths.get("/fish/sharks.log");
try {
   System.out.println(Files.lines(path)
      .filter(s -> s.startsWith("WARN "))
      .map(s -> s.substring(5))
```

```
      .collect(Collectors.toList()));
} catch (IOException e) {
   // Handle file I/O exception...
}
```

This sample code now searches for lines in the file that start with WARN, outputting everything after it to a single list that is printed to the user. You can see that lambda expressions coupled with NIO.2 allow us to perform very complex file operations concisely.

Assuming that the input file sharks.log is as follows,

```
INFO Server starting
DEBUG Processes available = 10
WARN No database could be detected
DEBUG Processes available reset to 0
WARN Performing manual recovery
INFO Server successfully started
```

then the sample output would be the following:

```
[No database could be detected, Performing manual recovery]
```

Files.readAllLines() vs. Files.lines()

For the exam, you should be familiar with both readAllLines() and lines() and with which one returns a List and which one returns a Stream. This is even more difficult since the forEach() method can be called on both Stream and Collection objects. For example, both of the following lines compile and run without issue:

```
Files.readAllLines(Paths.get("birds.txt")).forEach(System.out::println);
```

```
Files.lines(Paths.get("birds.txt")).forEach(System.out::println);
```

The first code snippet reads the entire file into memory and then performs a print operation on the resulting object. The second code snippet reads the lines lazily and prints them as they are being read. The advantage of the second code snippet is that it does not require the entire file to be stored in memory as it is being read.

You should also be aware of when they are mixing incompatible types on the exam. For example, can you determine which of the following two lines compiles?

```
Files.readAllLines(path).filter(s -> s.length()>2).forEach(System.out::println);
```

```
Files.lines(path).filter(s -> s.length()>2).forEach(System.out::println);
```

The first line does not compile because the filter() operation cannot be applied to a Collection without first converting it to a Stream using the stream() method.

Comparing Legacy *File* and NIO.2 Methods

We conclude this chapter with Table 9.5, which shows a comparison between some of the legacy java.io.File methods described in Chapter 8 and the new NIO.2 methods described in this chapter. In this table, file refers to an instance of the java.io.File class, while path refers to an instance of a NIO.2 Path interface.

TABLE 9.5   Comparison of legacy File and NIO.2 methods

Legacy Method	NIO.2 Method
file.exists()	Files.exists(path)
file.getName()	path.getFileName()
file.getAbsolutePath()	path.toAbsolutePath()
file.isDirectory()	Files.isDirectory(path)
file.isFile()	Files.isRegularFile(path)
file.isHidden()	Files.isHidden(path)
file.length()	Files.size(path)
file.lastModified()	Files.getLastModifiedTime(path)
file.setLastModified(time)	Files.setLastModifiedTime(path,fileTime)
file.delete()	Files.delete(path)
file.renameTo(otherFile)	Files.move(path,otherPath)
file.mkdir()	Files.createDirectory(path)
file.mkdirs()	Files.createDirectories(path)
file.listFiles()	Files.list(path)

Bear in mind that a number of methods and features are available in the NIO.2 API that are not available in the legacy API, such as support for symbolic links, setting a file owner, and so on. As expected, the NIO.2 API is a much more developed, much more powerful API than the legacy java.io.File class described in Chapter 8.

Summary

This chapter introduced the NIO.2 API for working with files and directories using the Path interface. For the exam, you need to know what the NIO.2 Path interface is and how it differs from the legacy java.io.File class. You should be familiar with how to create and use Path objects, including how to combine or resolve them with other Path objects.

We spent time reviewing various static methods available in the Files helper class. As discussed, the name of the function often tells you exactly what it does. We explained that most of these methods are capable of throwing an IOException and many take optional vararg enum values.

We also discussed how the NIO.2 API provides methods for reading and writing file metadata using views. Java uses views to retrieve all of the file system attributes for a file without numerous round-trips to the operating system. The NIO.2 API also includes support for operating system–specific file attributes, such as those found in Windows-, Mac-, and Linux-based file systems. For the exam, you should be familiar with the BasicFileAttributes and BasicFileAttributeView classes.

With the introduction of functional programming in Java 8, the NIO.2 Files class was updated with new methods that use the lambda expressions and streams to process files and directories. For the exam, you need to know how to apply the Streams API in NIO.2 to walk a directory tree, search for files, and list the contents of a directory or file.

Exam Essentials

Understand how to create and use Path objects.   Using the NIO.2 API, an instance of a Path object can be created from the Paths factory class by passing a path String to the static method Paths.getPath(). The Path interface includes numerous instance methods for reading and manipulating the abstract path value.

Understand how to interact with Path objects using the Files API.   The NIO.2 static Files helper class can be used to perform a variety of operations on a file or directory represented by a Path object, including creating directories, copying or moving a file/directory, deleting a file/directory, verifying that a file/directory exists, reading the contents of a file, and reading the metadata of a file or directory.

Be able to read and update file attributes using views.   The NIO.2 API supports file views that can be used to retrieve or update file system–specific attributes of a file or directory. While the NIO.2 API includes support for various file systems, only the BasicFileAttributes and BasicFileAttributeView classes are required knowledge for the exam. The views are accessed in one of two ways from the Files helper class: a read-only attribute set and an updateable view. Accessing all of the file properties in a single call is more performant in most file systems than accessing them one at a time.

Be able to read files using lambda expressions.   When Java 8 was updated with functional programming, the NIO.2 API gained four new methods for reading file data using lambda expressions and Stream instances in a lazy manner. The Files.walk() method traverses a directory tree in a depth-first manner. The Files.find() method traverses a directory finding those paths that match a specific set of search criteria. The Files.list() method retrieves the contents of a single directory level and makes them available as a stream. Finally, the Files.lines() method reads all of the lines in a file and processes them as they are read.

Review Questions

1. What is the output of the following code?

```
Path path = Path.get("/user/../../root","../kodiacbear.txt");
path.normalize().relativize("/lion");
System.out.println(path);
```

  A. /user/../../root/../kodiacbear.txt

  B. /user/./root/kodiacbear.txt/lion

  C. /kodiacbear.txt

  D. kodiacbear.txt

  E. ../lion

  F. The code does not compile.

2. For which values of path inserted on the blank line would it be possible for the following code to output Success? (Choose all that apply.)

```
Path path = _____;
if(Files.isDirectory(path))
    System.out.println(Files.deleteIfExists(path) ? "Success": "Try Again");
```

  A. path refers to a regular file in the file system.

  B. path refers to a symbolic link in the file system.

  C. path refers to an empty directory in the file system.

  D. path refers to a directory with content in the file system.

  E. path does not refer to a record that exists within the file system.

  F. The code does not compile.

3. What is the result of executing the following code? (Choose all that apply.)

```
1: Path path = Paths.get("sloth.schedule");
2: BasicFileAttributes attributes = Files.readAttributes(path, BasicFileAttributes.class);
3: if(attributes.size()>0 && attributes.creationTime().toMillis()>0) {
4:     attributes.setTimes(null,null,null);
5: }
```

  A. It compiles and runs without issue.

  B. The code will not compile because of line 2.

  C. The code will not compile because of line 3.

  D. The code will not compile because of line 4.

  E. The code compiles but throws an exception at runtime.

4. If the current working directory is /user/home, then what is the output of the following code?

```
Path path = Paths.get("/zoo/animals/bear/koala/food.txt");
System.out.println(path.subpath(1,3).getName(1).toAbsolutePath());
```

- **A.** animals/bear
- **B.** koala
- **C.** /user/home/bear
- **D.** /user/home/koala/koala
- **E.** /user/home/food.txt
- **F.** /user/home/koala/food.txt
- **G.** The code does not compile.

5. Assume /kang exists as a symbolic link to the directory /mammal/kangaroo within the file system. Which of the following statements are correct about this code snippet? (Choose all that apply.)

```
Path path = Paths.get("/kang");
if(Files.isDirectory(path) && Files.isSymbolicLink(path))
    Files.createDirectory(path.resolve("joey"));
```

- **A.** A new directory will always be created.
- **B.** A new directory will be created only if /mammal/kangaroo exists.
- **C.** If the code creates a directory, it will be reachable at /kang/joey.
- **D.** If the code creates a directory, it will be reachable at /mammal/kangaroo/joey.
- **E.** The code does not compile.
- **F.** The code will compile but always throws an exception at runtime.

6. Given that /animals is a directory that exists and it is empty, what is the result of the following code?

```
Path path = Paths.get("/animals");
boolean myBoolean = Files.walk(path)
    .filter((p,a) -> a.isDirectory() && !path.equals(p)) // w1
    .findFirst().isPresent();  // w2
System.out.println(myBoolean ? "No Sub-directory": "Has Sub-directory");
```

- **A.** It prints No Sub-directory.
- **B.** It prints Has Sub-directory.
- **C.** The code will not compile because of line w1.
- **D.** The code will not compile because of line w2.
- **E.** The output cannot be determined.
- **F.** It produces an infinite loop at runtime.

7. If the current working directory is /zoo, and the path /zoo/turkey does not exist, then what is the result of executing the following code? (Choose all that apply.)

```
Path path = Paths.get("turkey");
if(Files.isSameFile(path,Paths.get("/zoo/turkey")))   // x1
    Files.createDirectory(path.resolve("info"));  // x2
```

- **A.** The code compiles and runs without issue, but it does not create any directories.
- **B.** The directory /zoo/turkey is created.
- **C.** The directory /zoo/turkey/info is created.
- **D.** The code will not compile because of line x1.
- **E.** The code will not compile because of line x2.
- **F.** It compiles but throws an exception at runtime.

8. What is the output of the following code?

```
Path path1 = Paths.get("/pets/../cat.txt");
Path path2 = Paths.get("./dog.txt");
System.out.println(path1.resolve(path2));
System.out.println(path2.resolve(path1));
```

- **A.** /pets/../cat.txt/./dog.txt
     /pets/../cat.txt
- **B.** /pets/../cat.txt/./dog.txt
     ./dog.txt/pets/../cat.txt
- **C.** /cats.txt
     /dog.txt
- **D.** /cats.txt/dog.txt
     /cat.txt
- **E.** It compiles but throws an exception at runtime.

9. What are some advantages of using Files.lines() over Files.readAllLines()? (Choose all that apply.)
- **A.** It is often faster.
- **B.** It can be run on large files with very little memory available.
- **C.** It can be chained with stream methods directly.
- **D.** It does not modify the contents of the file.
- **E.** It ensures the file is not read-locked by the file system.
- **F.** There are no differences, because one method is a pointer to the other.

10. What is correct about the following code snippet? (Choose all that apply.)

```
Files.move(Paths.get("monkey.txt"), Paths.get("/animals"),
    StandardCopyOption.ATOMIC_MOVE,
    LinkOption.NOFOLLOW_LINKS);
```

A. If /animals exists, it will be overwritten at runtime.

B. If monkey.txt is a symbolic link, the file it points to will be moved at runtime.

C. If another process is monitoring the file system, it will not see an incomplete file at runtime.

D. The code will always throw an exception, since no filename is specified in the target folder path.

E. The metadata of the monkey.txt will be moved along with the file.

11. For the copy() method shown here, assume that the source exists as regular file and that the target does not. What is the result of the following code?

```
Path path1 = Paths.get("./goat.txt").normalize(); // k1
Path path2 = Paths.get("mule.png");
Files.copy(path1,path2,StandardCopyOption.COPY_ATTRIBUTES);   //k2
System.out.println(Files.isSameFile(path1, path2)); //k3
```

A. It will output false.

B. It will output true.

C. It does not compile because of line k1.

D. It does not compile because of line k2.

E. It does not compile because of line k3.

F. It compiles but throws an exception at runtime.

12. Which of the following methods *cannot* be used to obtain a Path instance? (Choose all that apply.)

A. new Path("jaguar.txt")

B. FileSystems.getDefault().getPath("puma.txt")

C. Paths.get(new URI("cheetah.txt"))

D. Paths.get("cats","lynx.txt")

E. new java.io.File("tiger.txt").toPath()

F. new FileSystem().getPath("leopard")

G. Paths.getPath("ocelot.txt")

13. Assume /monkeys exists as a regular directory containing multiple files, symbolic links, and subdirectories. What is true about the following code? (Choose all that apply.)

```
Path path = Paths.get("/monkeys");
Files.find(path, 0, (p,a) -> a.isSymbolicLink()).map(p -> p.toString())   // y1
    .collect(Collectors.toList())   // y2
    .stream() // y3
    .filter(x -> x.toString().endsWith(".txt")) // y4
    .forEach(System.out::println);
```

A. It will print all symbolic links in the directory tree ending in .txt.

B. It will print nothing.

C. It does not compile because of line y1.

D. It does not compile because of line y2.

E. It does not compile because of line y3.

F. It does not compile because of line y4.

G. It compiles but throws an exception at runtime.

14. Which NIO.2 method is most similar to the legacy java.io.File.listFiles() method?

A. `Path.listFiles()`

B. `Files.walk()`

C. `Files.find()`

D. `Files.files()`

E. `Files.list()`

F. `Files.lines()`

15. What are some advantages of using NIO.2 views to read metadata rather than individually from java.nio.Files methods? (Choose all that apply.)

A. It can be used on both files and directories.

B. For reading a single attribute, it is often more performant.

C. It allows you to read symbolic links.

D. It makes fewer round-trips to the file system.

E. It can be used to access file system–dependent attributes.

F. For reading multiple attributes, it is often more performant.

16. Assuming /squid/food-schedule.csv exists as a regular non-empty file that a program has access to read, what is correct about the following code snippet? (Choose all that apply.)

```
Path path = Paths.get("/squid/food-schedule.csv");
Files.lines(path) // r1
    .flatMap(p -> Stream.of(p.split(","))) // r2
    .map(s -> s.toUpperCase())  // r3
    .forEach(System.out::println);
```

A. It compiles but may throw an exception at runtime.

B. The code will not compile because of line r1.

C. The code will not compile because of line r2.

D. The code will not compile because of line r3.

E. It may not print anything at runtime.

F. If it prints anything, it will not include commas.

17. Assuming the current directory is /animals/cute, which are possible results of executing the following code? (Choose all that apply.)

```
Files.walk(Paths.get("..").toRealPath().getParent())  // u1
    .map(p -> p.toAbsolutePath().toString()) // u2
    .filter(s -> s.endsWith(".java")) // u3
    .collect(Collectors.toList())
    .forEach(System.out::println);
```

- **A.** It compiles but may throw an exception at runtime.
- **B.** The code will not compile because of line u1.
- **C.** The code will not compile because of line u2.
- **D.** The code will not compile because of line u3.
- **E.** It prints all .java files in the /animals directory tree.
- **F.** It prints all .java files in the /animals/cute directory tree.
- **G.** It prints all .java files in the root directory tree.

18. Assuming the directories and files referenced here all exist and are accessible within the file system, what is the result of the following code?

```
Path path1 = Paths.get("/lizard/./").resolve(Paths.get("walking.txt"));
Path path2 = new File("/lizard/././actions/../walking.txt").toPath();

System.out.print(Files.isSameFile(path1,path2));
System.out.print(" "+path1.equals(path2));
System.out.print(" "+path1.normalize().equals(path2.normalize()));
```

- **A.** true true true
- **B.** false false false
- **C.** false true false
- **D.** true false true
- **E.** true false false
- **F.** The code does not compile.

19. What are three advantages of the NIO.2 API over the legacy java.io.File class for working with files?

- **A.** NIO.2 supports file system–dependent attributes.
- **B.** NIO.2 can be used to list all the files within a single directory.
- **C.** NIO.2 allows you to traverse a directory tree directly.
- **D.** NIO.2 can be used to delete files and non-empty directories.
- **E.** NIO.2 supports symbolic links.
- **F.** NIO.2 can be used to read the last-modified time.

20. Assuming the current directory is /seals/harp/food, what is the result of executing the following code?

```
final Path path = Paths.get(".").normalize();  // h1
int count = 0;
for(int i=0; i<path.getNameCount(); ++i) {
    count++;
}
System.out.println(count);
```

A. 0

B. 1

C. 2

D. 3

E. 4

F. The code throws a runtime exception because of line h1.

Chapter

10

JDBC

THE OCP EXAM TOPICS COVERED IN THIS CHAPTER INCLUDE THE FOLLOWING:

✓ **Building Database Applications with JDBC**

- Describe the interfaces that make up the core of the JDBC API including the Driver, Connection, Statement, and ResultSet interfaces and their relationship to provider implementations

- Identify the components required to connect to a database using the DriverManager class including the JDBC URL

- Submit queries and read results from the database including creating statements, returning result sets, iterating through the results, and properly closing result sets, statements, and connections

JDBC stands for Java Database Connectivity. This chapter will introduce you to the basics of accessing databases from Java. We will cover the key interfaces for how to connect, perform queries, and process the results.

If you are new to JDBC, note that this chapter covers only the very basics of JDBC and working with databases. What we cover is enough for the exam. To be ready to use JDBC on the job, we recommend that you read books on SQL along with Java and databases. For example, you might try *SQL For Dummies* by Allen G. Taylor (Wiley, 2013) and *Practical Database Programming with Java* by Ying Bai (Wiley-IEEE Press, 2011).

For Experienced Developers

If you are an experienced developer and know JDBC well, you can skip the "Introducing Relational Databases and SQL" section. Read the rest of this chapter carefully, though. The authors have co-moderated the JDBC forum at CodeRanch for many years, and we found that the exam covers some topics that developers don't use in practice, while it omits some others that are critical, in particular these topics:

- You probably set up the URL once for a project for a specific database. Often, developers just copy and paste it from somewhere else. For the exam, you actually have to understand this rather than relying on looking it up.

- You are likely using a DataSource. For the exam, you have to remember or relearn how DriverManager works.

- You might know that you can skip Class.forName on a JDBC 3.0 driver that was ahead of its time in including the java.sql.Driver file in addition to the public driver class. For the exam, go with the simplified view of the world that says it is mandatory. Of course, you would probably be using a DataSource in the first place, making this a moot point.

- The exam talks about Statement. You should be using PreparedStatement in real code.

- Yes, we know that you use the default values for the ResultSet modes virtually all the time, and you probably don't know the alternatives by heart. For the exam, you have to memorize them.

- You'll probably never use Scrollable outside the exam, but you have to learn it in detail anyway. Sorry.

Introducing Relational Databases and SQL

Data is information. A piece of data is one fact, such as your first name. A *database* is an organized collection of data. In the real world, a file cabinet is a type of database. It has file folders, each of which contains pieces of paper. The file folders are organized in some way, often alphabetically. Each piece of paper is like a piece of data. Similarly, the folders on your computer are like a database. The folders provide organization, and each file is a piece of data.

A *relational database* is a database that is organized into *tables*, which consist of rows and columns. You can think of a table as a spreadsheet. There are two main ways to access a relational database from Java:

- *Java Database Connectivity Language (JDBC)*: Accesses data as rows and columns. JDBC is the API covered in this chapter.

- *Java Persistence API (JPA)*: Accesses data through Java objects using a concept called object-relational mapping (ORM). The idea is that you don't have to write as much code, and you get your data in Java objects. JPA is not on the exam, and therefore it is not covered in this chapter.

- A relational database is accessed through Structured Query Language (*SQL*).

- In addition to relational databases, there is another type of database called a *NoSQL database*. This is for databases that store their data in a format other than tables. NoSQL is out of scope for the exam as well.

- In the following sections, we introduce a small relational database that we will be using for the examples in this chapter and present the SQL to access it. We will also cover some vocabulary that you need to know.

Picking a Database

In all of the other chapters of this book, you need to write code and try lots of examples. This chapter is different. It's still nice to try out the examples, but you can probably get the JDBC questions correct on the exam from just reading this chapter and mastering the review questions.

Luckily, Java comes with an embedded database called JavaDB. JavaDB is a version of the open source Derby database that comes automatically with the JDK (http://db.apache.org/derby). To practice for the exam, Derby is sufficient.

There are also stand-alone databases that you can choose from if you want to install one. We like MySQL (https://www.mysql.com) or PostgreSQL (http://www.postgresql.org), both of which are open source and have been around for more than 20 years.

While the major databases all have many similarities, they do have important differences and advanced features. Choosing the correct database for use in your job is an important decision that you need to spend much time researching. For the exam, any database is fine for practice.

There are plenty of tutorials for installing and getting started with any of these. It's beyond the scope of the book and the exam to set up a database, but feel free to ask questions in the database/JDBC section of CodeRanch. You might even get an answer from the authors.

Identifying the Structure of a Relational Database

Our sample database has two tables. One has a row for each species that is in our zoo. The other has a row for each animal. These two relate to each other because an animal belongs to a species. These relationships are why this type of database is called a relational database. Figure 10.1 shows the structure of our database.

FIGURE 10.1   Tables in our relational database

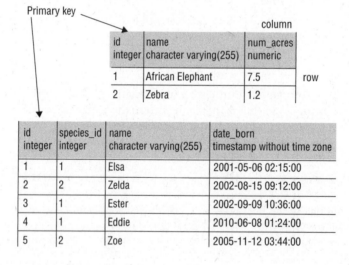

As you can see in Figure 10.1, we have two tables. One is named species and the other is named animal. Each table has a *primary key*, which gives us a unique way to reference each row. After all, two animals might have the same name, but they can't have the same ID. You don't need to know about keys for the exam. We mention it to give you a bit of context. In our example, it so happens that the primary key is only one column. In some situations, it is a combination of columns. For example, a student identifier and year might be a key.

There are two rows and three columns in the species table and five rows and four columns in the animal table. You do need to know about rows and columns for the exam.

The Code to Set Up the Database

We provide a program to set up JavaDB to run the examples in this chapter. You don't have to understand it for the exam. Parts of SQL called DDL (database definition language) and DML (database manipulation language) are used to do so. Don't worry–knowing how to read or write SQL is not on the exam! We include it only so that you can follow along if you'd like.

Before running the following code, you need to add a .jar file to your classpath. Add <JAVA_HOME>/db/lib/derby.jar to your classpath. Just make sure to replace <JAVA_HOME> with the actual path on your file system. On Linux or Mac, you run the program like this:

```
java -cp "/my/jdk/home/db/lib/derby.jar:." SetupDerbyDatabase
```

And on Windows, you run the program like this:

```
java -cp "c:\program files\jdk\db\lib\derby.jar;." SetupDerbyDatabase
```

The code is as follows. You can also find this code along with more details on setup at http://selikoff.net/ocp.

```java
import java.sql.*;

public class SetupDerbyDatabase {

    public static void main(String[] args) throws Exception {
        String url = "jdbc:derby:zoo;create=true";
        try (Connection conn = DriverManager.getConnection(url);
             Statement stmt = conn.createStatement()) {

stmt.executeUpdate("CREATE TABLE species ("
+ "id INTEGER PRIMARY KEY, "
+ "name VARCHAR(255), "
+ "num_acres DECIMAL)");
stmt.executeUpdate(
"CREATE TABLE animal ("
+ "id INTEGER PRIMARY KEY, "
+ "species_id integer, "
+ "name VARCHAR(255), "
+ "date_born TIMESTAMP)");

stmt.executeUpdate("INSERT INTO species VALUES (1, 'African Elephant', 7.5)");
stmt.executeUpdate("INSERT INTO species VALUES (2, 'Zebra', 1.2)");
```

```
        stmt.executeUpdate("INSERT INTO animal VALUES (1, 1, 'Elsa', '2001-05-06 02:15')");
        stmt.executeUpdate("INSERT INTO animal VALUES (2, 2, 'Zelda', '2002-08-15 09:12')");
        stmt.executeUpdate("INSERT INTO animal VALUES (3, 1, 'Ester', '2002-09-09 10:36')");
        stmt.executeUpdate("INSERT INTO animal VALUES (4, 1, 'Eddie', '2010-06-08 01:24')");
        stmt.executeUpdate("INSERT INTO animal VALUES (5, 2, 'Zoe', '2005-11-12 03:44')");
        }
    }
}
```

You don't need to understand this code. It is just to get you set up. In a nutshell, it connects to the database and creates two tables. Then it loads data into those tables.

Writing Basic SQL Statements

The only thing that you need to know about SQL for the exam is that there are four types of statements for working with the data in tables. Pay attention to the first word of each:

INSERT: Add a new row to the table

SELECT: Retrieve data from the table

UPDATE: Change zero or more rows in the table

DELETE: Remove zero or more rows from the table

That's it. You are not expected to determine if SQL statements are correct. You are not expected to spot syntax errors in SQL statements. You are not expected to write SQL statements. Notice a theme?

If you already know SQL, you can skip to the section on JDBC. We are covering the basics so that newer developers know what is going on, at least at a high level. We promise there is nothing else in this section on SQL that you need to know. In fact, you probably know a lot that isn't covered here. As far as the exam is concerned, joining two tables is a concept that doesn't exist!

Unlike Java, SQL keywords are case insensitive. This means select, SELECT, and Select are all equivalent. Most people use uppercase for the database keywords so that they stand out. It's also common practice to use underscores to separate "words" in column names. We follow these conventions. Now it's time to write some code.

SQL has a number of types. Most are self explanatory, like INTEGER and TIMESTAMP. There's also DECIMAL, which is like a double in Java. The strangest one is VARCHAR, standing for "variable character," which is like a String in Java. The *variable* part means that the database should use only as much space as it needs to store the value.

The INSERT statement is usually used to create one new row in a table, for example:

```
INSERT INTO species VALUES (3, 'Asian Elephant', 7.5);
```

If there are two rows in the table before this command is run, then there are three afterward. The INSERT statement lists the values that we want to insert. By default, it uses the same order in which the columns were defined. String data is enclosed in single quotes.

The SELECT statement reads data from the table:

```
SELECT * FROM SPECIES WHERE ID = 3;
```

The WHERE clause is optional. If you omit it, the contents of the entire table are returned. The * indicates to return all of the columns in the order in which they were defined. Alternatively, you can list out the columns that you want returned:

```
SELECT NAME, NUM_ACRES FROM SPECIES WHERE ID = 3;
```

It is preferable to list the column names for clarity. It also helps in case the table changes in the database.

You can also get information about the whole result without returning individual rows using special SQL functions:

```
SELECT COUNT(*), SUM(num_acres) FROM SPECIES;
```

This query tells us how many species we have and how much space we need for them. It returns only one row since it is combining information. Even if there are no rows in the table, the query returns one row that contains zero as the answer.

The UPDATE statement changes one or more rows in the database:

```
UPDATE SPECIES SET NUM_ACRES = NUM_ACRES + .5 WHERE NAME = 'Asian Elephant';
```

Again, the WHERE clause is optional. If it is omitted, all rows in the table will be updated. The UPDATE statement always specifies the table to update and the column to update.

The DELETE statement deletes one or more rows in the database:

```
DELETE FROM SPECIES WHERE NAME = 'Asian Elephant';
```

And yet again, the WHERE clause is optional. If it is omitted, the entire table will be emptied. So be careful!

All of the SQL shown in this section is common across databases. For more advanced SQL, there is variation across databases.

Introducing the Interfaces of JDBC

For the exam you need to know four key interfaces of JDBC. The interfaces are declared in the JDK. This is just like all of the other interfaces and classes that you've seen in this book. List is in the JDK, Path is in the JDK, and so forth.

As you know, interfaces need a concrete class to implement them in order to be useful. These concrete classes come from the JDBC driver. Each database has a different

JAR file with these classes. For example, PostgreSQL's JAR is called something like
`postgresql-9.4-1201.jdbc4.jar`. MySql's JAR is called something like `mysql-connector-java-5.1.36.jar`. The exact name depends on the version of the driver JAR.

This driver JAR contains an implementation of these key interfaces along with a number of others. The key is that the provided implementations know how to communicate with a database. There are different types of drivers; luckily, you don't need to know about this for the exam.

Figure 10.2 shows the four key interfaces that you need to know. It also shows that the implementation is provided by an imaginary Foo driver JAR. They cleverly stick the name Foo in all classes.

You've probably noticed that we didn't tell you what the implementing classes are called in any real database. The main point is that you shouldn't know. With JDBC, you use only the interfaces in your code and never the implementation classes directly. In fact, they might not even be `public` classes.

FIGURE 10.2   Key JDBC interfaces

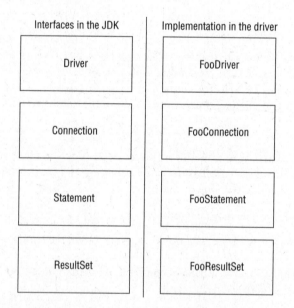

What do these four interfaces do? On a very high level, we have the following:

`Driver`: Knows how to get a connection to the database

`Connection`: Knows how to communicate with the database

`Statement`: Knows how to run the SQL

`ResultSet`: Knows what was returned by a `SELECT` query

All database classes are in the package `java.sql`, so we will omit the imports going forward.

In this next example, we show you what JDBC code looks like end to end. If you are new to JDBC, just notice that three of the four interfaces are in the code. If you are experienced, this is what JDBC looks like according to the OCP exam. Yes, we know—you wouldn't and shouldn't write code like this. We wouldn't either. It's OK. Grumble to yourself, and get it out of your system.

```java
package com.wiley.ocp.connection;

import java.sql.*;

public class MyFirstDatabaseConnection {

    public static void main(String[] args) throws SQLException {
        String url = "jdbc:derby:zoo";
        try (Connection conn = DriverManager.getConnection(url);
            Statement stmt = conn.createStatement();
            ResultSet rs = stmt.executeQuery("select name from animal")) {

            while (rs.next())
                System.out.println(rs.getString(1));

        }
    }
}
```

If the URL were using our imaginary Foo driver, DriverManager would return an instance of FooConnection. Calling createStatement() would then return an instance of FooStatement, and calling executeQuery() would return an instance of FooResultSet. Since the URL uses derby instead, it returns the implementations that derby has provided for these interfaces. You don't need to know their names. In the rest of the chapter, we will explain how to use all four of the interfaces and go into more detail about what they do. By the end of the chapter, you'll be writing code like this yourself.

Connecting to a Database

The first step in doing anything with a database is connecting to it. First we will show you how to build the JDBC URL. Then we will show you how the exam wants you to get a Connection to the database.

Building a JDBC URL

To access a website, you need to know the URL of the website. To access your email, you need to know your username and password. JDBC is no different. In order to access a database, you need to know this information about it.

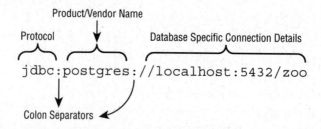

Unlike web URLs, a JDBC URL has a variety of formats. They have three parts in common, as shown in Figure 10.3. Well, there are three if you can count the third one as being in common. The first piece is always the same. It is the protocol jdbc. The second part is the name of the database such as derby, mysql, or postgres. The third part is "the rest of it," which is a database-specific format. Colons separate the three parts.

FIGURE 10.3 The JDBC URL format

The third part typically contains the location and the name of the database. The syntax varies. You need to know about the three main parts. You don't need to memorize the vendor-specific part. Phew! You've already seen one such URL:

jdbc:derby:zoo

Notice the three parts. It starts with jdbc, then comes derby, and it ends with the database name. Other examples are shown here:

jdbc:postgresql://**localhost**/**zoo**

jdbc:oracle:thin:@**123.123.123.123:1521:zoo**

jdbc:mysql://**localhost:3306/zoo**?profileSQL=true

You can see that each of these begins with jdbc, followed by a colon, and then followed by the vendor/product name. After that it varies. Notice how all of them include the location of the database, which are localhost, 123.123.123.123:1521, and localhost:3306, respectively. Also notice that the port is optional when using the default. Finally, notice that all of them include the name of the database, which is zoo.

To make sure you get this, do you see what is wrong with each of the following?

jdbc:postgresql://local/zoo

jdbc:mysql://123456/zoo

jdbc;oracle;thin;/localhost/zoo

The first one uses local instead of localhost. localhost is a specially defined name. You can't just make up a name. Granted, it is possible for our database server to be named *local*, but the exam won't have you assume names. If the database server has a special name, the question will let you know it. The second one says that the location of the database is 123456. This doesn't make sense. A location can be localhost or an IP address or a domain name. It can't be any random number. The third one is no good because it uses semicolons instead of colons.

In some databases, you use an alias rather than the database name. For the purposes of the exam, consider this alias to be a logical database name.

Getting a Database *Connection*

There are two main ways to get a Connection: DriverManager or DataSource. DriverManager is the one covered on the exam. Do not use a DriverManager in code someone is paying you to write. A DataSource is a factory, and it has more features than DriverManager. For example, it can pool connections or store the database connection info outside the application.

The DriverManager class is in the JDK, as it is an API that comes with Java. It uses the factory pattern, which means that you call a static method to get a Connection. As you learned in Chapter 2, "Design Patterns and Principles," the factory pattern means that you can get any implementation of the interface when calling the method. The good news is that the method has an easy-to-remember name—getConnection().

To get a Connection from the embedded database, you write the following:

```java
import java.sql.*;
public class TestConnect {

    public static void main(String[] args) throws SQLException {
        Connection conn = DriverManager.getConnection("jdbc:derby:zoo");
        System.out.println(conn);
    }
}
```

Running this example as java TestConnect will give you an error that begins with this:

```
Exception in thread "main" java.sql.SQLException: No suitable driver found for
jdbc:derby:zoo
        at java.sql.DriverManager.getConnection(DriverManager.java:689)
        at java.sql.DriverManager.getConnection(DriverManager.java:270)
```

The class SQLException means "something went wrong when connecting to or accessing the database." In this case, we didn't tell Java where to find the database driver JAR file. Remember that the implementation class for Connection is found inside a driver JAR.

We try this again by adding the classpath with java -cp "<*java_home*>/db/lib/ derby.jar:." TestConnect. Remember to substitute the location of where Java is installed on your computer for <*java_home*>. (If you are on Windows, replace the colon with a semicolon.) This time the program runs successfully and prints something like the following:

```
org.apache.derby.impl.jdbc.EmbedConnection40@1372082959
(XID = 156), (SESSIONID = 1), (DATABASE = zoo), (DRDAID = null)
```

The details of the output aren't important. Just notice that the class is not `Connection`. It is a vendor implementation of `Connection`.

There is also a signature that takes a username and password:

```java
import java.sql.*;
public class TestExternal {
    public static void main(String[] args) throws SQLException {
        Connection conn = DriverManager.getConnection(
            "jdbc:postgresql://localhost:5432/ocp-book",
            "username",
            "password");
        System.out.println(conn);
    }
}
```

Notice the three parameters that are passed to getConnection(). The first is the JDBC URL that you learned about in the previous section. The second is the username for accessing the database, and the third is the password for accessing the database. It should go without saying that our password is not "password." Also, don't put your password in real code. It's a horrible practice that Oracle should not be encouraging.

This time, now that we've included the driver file, the program runs successfully and prints something like this:

```
org.postgresql.jdbc4.Jdbc4Connection@eed1f14
```

Again, notice that it is a driver-specific implementation class. You can tell from the package name. Since the package is org.postgresql.jdbc4, it is part of the PostgreSQL driver. The command line tells Java where to find the driver JAR. It also includes the current directory so that Java can find TestConnect itself!

Unless the exam specifies a command line, you can assume that the correct JDBC driver JAR is in the classpath. The exam creators explicitly ask about the driver JAR if they want you to think about it.

The nice thing about a factory is that it takes care of the logic of creating a class for you. You don't need to know the name of the class that implements Connection, and you don't need to know how it is created. You are probably a bit curious, though.

The DriverManager class looks through the classpath for JARs that contain a Driver. DriverManager knows that a JAR is a driver because it contains a file called java.sql.Driver in the directory META-INF/services. In other words, a driver might contain this information:

```
META-INF
-service
-java.sql.Driver
```

```
com
-wiley
-MyDriver.class
```

Inside the java.sql.Driver file is one line. It is the fully qualified package name of the Driver implementation class. Remember those four key interfaces? Driver is the first one.

DriverManager then looks through any drivers it can find to see if they can handle the JDBC URL. If so, it creates a Connection using that Driver. If not, it gives up and throws a SQLException.

Real World Scenario

Using a *DataSource*

In real applications, you should use a DataSource rather than DriverManager to get a Connection. For one thing, there's no reason why you should have to know the database password. It's far better if the database team or another team can set up a data source that you can reference. Another reason is that a DataSource maintains a connection pool so that you can keep reusing the same connection rather than needing to get a new one each time. Even the JavaDoc says DataSource is preferred over DriverManager. But DriverManager is in the exam objectives, so you still have to know it.

You might see Class.forName() used in older code before getting a Connection. It looked like this:

```
public static void main(String[] args) throws SQLException,
ClassNotFoundException {
   Class.forName("org.postgresql.Driver");
   Connection conn = DriverManager.getConnection(
       "jdbc:postgresql://localhost:5432/ocp-book",
       "username",
       "password");
}
```

Class.forName() loads a class. This lets DriverManager use a Driver, even if the JAR doesn't have a META-INF/service/java.sql.Driver file. There's no harm in including Class.forName(), even if the newer driver does have this file.

When Class.forName() is used, the error about an invalid class occurs on that line and throws a ClassNotFoundException:

```
public static void main(String[] args) throws ClassNotFoundException {
   Class.forName("not.a.driver");
}
```

Obviously, this is not a valid driver name. The output begins with the following code:

```
Exception in thread "main" java.lang.ClassNotFoundException: not.a.driver
    at java.net.URLClassLoader.findClass(URLClassLoader.java:381)
    at java.lang.ClassLoader.loadClass(ClassLoader.java:424)
    at sun.misc.Launcher$AppClassLoader.loadClass(Launcher.java:331)
    at java.lang.ClassLoader.loadClass(ClassLoader.java:357)
    at java.lang.Class.forName0(Native Method)
    at java.lang.Class.forName(Class.java:264)
```

Having META-INF/service/java.sql.Driver inside the JAR became mandatory with JDBC 4.0 in Java 6. Before that, some drivers included it and some didn't. Table 10.1 sums up the current state of affairs.

TABLE 10.1   JDBC 3.0 vs. 4.0 drivers

	JDBC <= 3.0 Driver	JDBC >= 4.0 Driver
Required to contain java.sql.Driver	No	Yes
Java will use java.sql.Driver file if present	Yes	Yes
Required to use Class.forName	Yes	No
Allowed to use Class.forName	Yes	Yes

Obtaining a *Statement*

In order to run SQL, you need to tell a Statement about it. Getting a Statement from a Connection is easy:

```
Statement stmt = conn.createStatement();
```

As you will remember, Statement is one of the four core interfaces on the exam. It represents a SQL statement that you want to run using the Connection.

That's the simple signature. There's another one that you need to know for the exam:

```
Statement stmt = conn.createStatement(
  ResultSet.TYPE_FORWARD_ONLY, ResultSet.CONCUR_READ_ONLY);
```

This signature takes two parameters. The first is the ResultSet type, and the other is the ResultSet concurrency mode. You have to know all of the choices for these parameters and the order in which they are specified. Let's look at the choices for these parameters.

Choosing a *ResultSet* Type

By default, a ResultSet is in TYPE_FORWARD_ONLY mode. This is what you need most of the time. You can go through the data once in the order in which it was retrieved.

Two other modes that you can request when creating a Statement are TYPE_SCROLL_ INSENSITIVE and TYPE_SCROLL_SENSITIVE. Both allow you to go through the data in any order. You can go both forward and backward. You can even go to a specific spot in the data. Think of this like scrolling in a browser. You can scroll up and down. You can go to a specific spot in the result.

The difference between TYPE_SCROLL_INSENSITIVE and TYPE_SCROLL_SENSITIVE is what happens when data changes in the actual database while you are busy scrolling. With TYPE_ SCROLL_INSENSITIVE, you have a static view of what the ResultSet looked like when you did the query. If the data changed in the table, you will see it as it was when you did the query. With TYPE_SCROLL_SENSITIVE, you would see the latest data when scrolling through the ResultSet.

> You have to know forward only and scroll insensitive in detail for the exam. For scroll sensitive, you only have to know the name and that it isn't well supported. You don't need to read or write code with it.

We say "would" because most databases and database drivers don't actually support the TYPE_SCROLL_SENSITIVE mode. That's right. You have to learn something for the exam that you are almost guaranteed never to use in practice.

If the type you request isn't available, the driver can "helpfully" downgrade to one that is. This means that if you ask for TYPE_SCROLL_SENSITIVE, you will likely get a Statement that is TYPE_SCROLL_INSENSITIVE. Isn't that great? If you'd wanted insensitive, you'd have asked for that in the first place!

Table 10.2 sums up what you need to know about the ResultSet types.

TABLE 10.2 ResultSet type options

ResultSet **Type**	**Can Go Backward**	**See Latest Data from Database Table**	**Supported by Most Drivers**
ResultSet.TYPE_ FORWARD_ONLY	No	No	Yes
ResultSet.TYPE_ SCROLL_INSENSITIVE	Yes	No	Yes
ResultSet.TYPE_ SCROLL_SENSITIVE	Yes	Yes	No

Choosing a *ResultSet* Concurrency Mode

By default, a ResultSet is in CONCUR_READ_ONLY mode. This is what you need most of the time. It means that you can't update the result set. Most of the time, you will use INSERT, UPDATE, or DELETE SQL statements to change the database rather than a ResultSet.

There is one other mode that you can request when creating a Statement. Unsurprisingly, it lets you modify the database through the ResultSet. It is called CONCUR_UPDATABLE.

 You have to know read-only mode in detail for the exam. For updatable, you only have to know the name and that it is not universally supported.

Databases and JDBC drivers are not required to support CONCUR_UPDATABLE. Unlike TYPE_SCROLL_SENSITIVE, an updatable result set is at least used on rare occasions. Most of the time, it is the wrong choice for your program, though.

Again, if the mode you request isn't available, the driver can downgrade you. This means that if you ask for CONCUR_UPDATABLE, you will likely get a Statement that is CONCUR_READ_ONLY.

Table 10.3 sums up what you need to know about the ResultSet concurrency modes.

TABLE 10.3   ResultSet concurrency mode options

ResultSet **Type**	**Can Read Data**	**Can Update Data**	**Supported by All Drivers**
ResultSet.CONCUR_ READ_ONLY	Yes	Yes	No
ResultSet.CONCUR_ UPDATABLE	Yes	No	Yes

Executing a *Statement*

Now that we have a Statement, we can run a SQL statement. The way you run SQL varies depending on what kind of SQL statement it is. Remember that you aren't expected to be able to read SQL, but you do need to know what the first keyword means.

Let's start out with statements that change the data in a table. That would be SQL statements that begin with DELETE, INSERT, or UPDATE. They typically use a method called executeUpdate(). The name is a little tricky because the SQL UPDATE statement is not the only statement that uses this method.

The method takes the SQL statement to run as a parameter. It returns the number of rows that were inserted, deleted, or changed. Here's an example of all three update types:

```
11:   Statement stmt = conn.createStatement();
12:   int result = stmt.executeUpdate(
13:       "insert into species values(10, 'Deer', 3)");
14:   System.out.println(result);   // 1
15:   result = stmt.executeUpdate(
16:       "update species set name = '' where name = 'None'");
17:   System.out.println(result); // 0
18:   result = stmt.executeUpdate(
19:       "delete from species where id = 10");
20:   System.out.println(result);   // 1
```

For the exam, you don't need to read SQL. The question will tell you how many rows are affected if you need to know. Line 12 runs a statement to insert one row. Therefore, the result is 1 because one row was affected. Line 15 checks the whole table, but no records match, so the result is 0. Line 18 deletes the row created on line 12. Again one row is affected, so the result is 1.

Next, let's look at a SQL statement that begins with SELECT. This time, we use the executeQuery() method:

```
ResultSet rs =  stmt.executeQuery("select * from species");
```

Since we are running query to get a result, the return type is ResultSet. In the next section, we will show you how to process the ResultSet.

There's a third method called execute() that can run either a query or an update. It returns a boolean so that we know whether there is a ResultSet. That way, we can call the proper method to get more detail. The pattern looks like this:

```
boolean isResultSet = stmt.execute(sql);
if (isResultSet) {
   ResultSet rs = stmt.getResultSet();
   System.out.println("ran a query");
} else {
   int result = stmt.getUpdateCount();
   System.out.println("ran an update");
}
```

If sql is a SELECT, the boolean is true and we can get the ResultSet. If it is not a SELECT, we can get the number of rows updated.

Real World Scenario

The Importance of a *PreparedStatement*

On the exam, only Statement is covered. In real life, you should not use Statement directly. You should use a subclass called PreparedStatement. This subclass has three advantages: performance, security, and readability.

- Performance: In most programs you run similar queries multiple times. A Prepared-Statement figures out a plan to run the SQL well and remembers it.

- Security: Suppose you have this method:

```
private static void scaryDelete(Connection conn, String name) throws SQLException {
    Statement stmt = conn.createStatement();
    String sql = "delete from animal where name = '" + name + "'";
    System.out.println(sql);
    stmt.executeUpdate(sql);
}
```

This method appears to delete the row that matches the given name. Imagine that this program lets a user type in the name. If the user's String is "Asian Elephant", this works out well and one row gets deleted. What happens if the user's String is "any' or 1 = 1 or name='any"? The generated SQL is

```
delete from animal where name = 'any' or 1 = 1 or name='any'
```

This deletes every row in the table. That's not good. In fact, it is so bad that it has a name—SQL injection. Upon first glance, the solution is to prevent single quotes in the user's input. It turns out to be more complicated than that because the bad guys know many ways of doing bad things. Luckily, you can just write this:

```
PreparedStatement ps = conn.prepareStatement("delete from animal where name = ?");
ps.setString(1, name);
ps.execute();
```

The JDBC driver takes care of all the escaping for you. This is convenient.

- Readability: It's nice not to have to deal with string concatenation in building a query string with lots of variables.

What do you think happens if we use the wrong method for a SQL statement? Let's take a look:

```
Connection conn = DriverManager.getConnection("jdbc:derby:zoo");
Statement stmt = conn.createStatement();
```

```
int result = stmt.executeUpdate("select * from animal");
```

This throws a SQLException similar to the following:

```
A result was returned when none was expected.
```

We can't get a compiler error since the SQL is a String. We can get an exception, though, and we do. We also get a SQLException when using executeQuery() with SQL that changes the database:

```
No results were returned by the query.
```

Again, we get an exception because the driver can't translate the query into the expected return type.

To review, make sure that you know Table 10.4 and Table 10.5 well. Unlike many topics covered so far, this one is useful in the real world and not just on the exam. Table 10.4 shows which SQL statements can be run by each of the three key methods on Statement. Table 10.5 shows what is returned by each method.

TABLE 10.4   SQL runnable by execute method

Method	DELETE	INSERT	SELECT	UPDATE
stmt.execute()	Yes	Yes	Yes	Yes
stmt.executeQuery()	No	No	Yes	No
stmt.executeUpdate()	Yes	Yes	No	Yes

TABLE 10.5   Return types of executes

Method	Return Type	What Is Returned for SELECT	What Is Returned for DELETE/INSERT/UPDATE
stmt.execute()	boolean	true	false
stmt.executeQuery()	ResultSet	The rows and columns returned	n/a
stmt.executeUpdate()	int	n/a	Number of rows added/changed/removed

Getting Data from a *ResultSet*

By far, the most common type of ResultSet is of type forward-only. We will start by showing you how to get the data from one of these. Then after going through the different methods to get columns by type, we will show you how to work with a scrollable ResultSet.

Reading a *ResultSet*

When working with a forward-only ResultSet, most of the time you will write a loop to look at each row. The code looks like this:

```
20:   Map<Integer, String> idToNameMap = new HashMap<>();
21:   ResultSet rs = stmt.executeQuery("select id, name from species");
22:   while(rs.next()) {
23:       int id = rs.getInt("id");
24:       String name = rs.getString("name");
25:       idToNameMap.put(id, name);
26:   }
27:   System.out.println(idToNameMap); // {1=African Elephant, 2=Zebra}
```

There are a few things to notice here. First, we use the executeQuery() method on line 21, since we want to have a ResultSet returned. On line 22, we loop through the results. Each time through the loop represents one row in the ResultSet. Lines 23 and 24 show you the best way to get the columns for a given row.

A ResultSet has a *cursor*, which points to the current location in the data. Figure 10.4 shows the position as we loop through. At line 21, the cursor starts out pointing to the location before the ResultSet. On the first loop iteration, rs.next() returns true and the cursor moves to point to the first row of data. On the second loop iteration, rs.next() returns true again and the cursor moves to point to the second row of data. The next call to rs.next() returns false. The cursor advances past the end of the data. The false signifies that there is no data available to get.

FIGURE 10.4   The ResultSet cursor

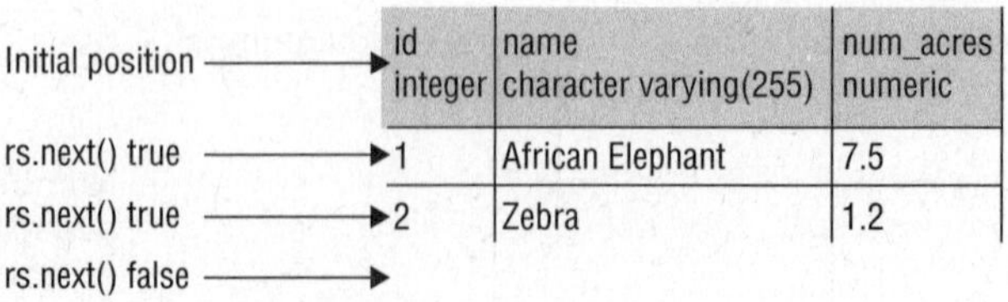

	id integer	name character varying(255)	num_acres numeric
Initial position →			
rs.next() true →	1	African Elephant	7.5
rs.next() true →	2	Zebra	1.2
rs.next() false →			

We did say the "best way." There is another way to access the columns. You can use an index instead of a column name. The column name is better because it is clearer what is going on when reading the code. It also allows you to change the SQL to reorder the columns. Rewriting this same example with column numbers looks like the following:

```
20:   Map<Integer, String> idToNameMap = new HashMap<>();
21:   ResultSet rs =  stmt.executeQuery("select id, name from species");
22:   while(rs.next()) {
23:       int id = rs.getInt(1);
24:       String name = rs.getString(2);
25:       idToNameMap.put(id, name);
26:   }
27:   System.out.println(idToNameMap); // {1=African Elephant, 2=Zebra}
```

This time, you can see the column positions on lines 23 and 24. Notice how the columns are counted starting with 1 rather than 0. This is really important, so we will repeat it.

NOTE   Remember that JDBC starts counting with one rather than zero.

Sometimes you want to get only one row from the table. Maybe you need only one piece of data. Or maybe the SQL is just returning the number of rows in the table. When you want only one row, you use an if statement rather than a while loop:

```
ResultSet rs =  stmt.executeQuery("select count(*) from animal");
if(rs.next())
   System.out.println(rs.getInt(1));
```

It is very important to check that rs.next() returns true before trying to call a getter on the ResultSet. That would throw a SQLException, so the if statement checks that it is safe to call. Alternatively, you can use the column name:

```
ResultSet rs =  stmt.executeQuery("select count(*) from animal");
if(rs.next())
   System.out.println(rs.getInt("count"));
```

The following code throws a SQLException:

```
int id = rs.getInt(0);  // BAD CODE
```

Attempting to access a column that does not exist throws a SQLException, as does getting data from a ResultSet when it isn't pointing at a valid row. You need to be able to recognize such code. Here a few examples to watch out for. Do you see what is wrong here when no rows match?

```
ResultSet rs =  stmt.executeQuery(
   "select * from animal where name= 'Not in table'");
rs.next();
rs.getInt(1); // throws SQLException
```

Calling rs.next() works. It returns false. However, calling a getter afterward does throw a SQLException because the result set cursor does not point to a valid position. If there actually were a match returned, this code would have worked. Do you see what is wrong with the following?

```
ResultSet rs =  stmt.executeQuery("select count(*) from animal");
rs.getInt(1); // throws SQLException
```

Not calling rs.next() at all is a problem. The result set cursor is still pointing to a location before the first row, so the getter has nothing to point to. How about this one?

```
ResultSet rs =  stmt.executeQuery("select count(*) from animal");
rs.next();
rs.getInt(0); // throws SQLException
```

Since column indexes begin with 1, there is no column 0 to point to and a SQLException is thrown. One more try. What is wrong with this one?

```
ResultSet rs =  stmt.executeQuery("select id from animal");
rs.next();
rs.getInt("badColumn"); // throws SQLException
```

Trying to get a column that isn't in the ResultSet is just as bad as an invalid column index, and it also throws a SQLException.

To sum up this section, it is very important to remember the following:

- Always use an if statement or while loop when calling rs.next().
- Column indexes begin with 1.

Getting Data for a Column

There are lots of get ____ methods on the ResultSet interface. The ones that you need to know for the exam are easy to remember since they are called get, followed by the name of the type you are getting. Table 10.6 shows the get methods that you need to know. The first column shows the method name, and the second column shows the type that Java returns. The third column shows the type name that could be in the database. There is some variation by databases, so check your specific database documentation. You need to know only the first two columns for the exam.

TABLE 10.6   ResultSet get methods

Method Name	Return Type	Example Database Type
getBoolean	boolean	BOOLEAN
getDate	java.sql.Date	DATE
getDouble	double	DOUBLE
getInt	int	INTEGER
getLong	long	BIGINT
getObject	Object	Any type
getString	String	CHAR, VARCHAR
getTime	java.sql.Time	TIME
getTimeStamp	java.sql.TimeStamp	TIMESTAMP

You might notice that not all of the primitive types are in Table 10.6. There are getByte and getFloat methods, but you don't need to know about them for the exam. There is no getChar method. Luckily, you don't need to remember this. The exam will not try to trick you by using a get method name that doesn't exist for JDBC. Isn't that nice of it?

That takes care of the primitives. Now what about the three date types? In the database, we have the date/time of birth of one of our animals as 2001-05-06 02:15. Let's look at the three ways to get pieces of this information. First, we want to know what date Elsa the elephant was born:

```
ResultSet rs = stmt.executeQuery("select date_born from animal where name = 'Elsa'");
if (rs.next()) {
   java.sql.Date sqlDate = rs.getDate(1);
   LocalDate localDate = sqlDate.toLocalDate();
   System.out.println(localDate);  // 2001-05-06
}
```

When calling getDate, JDBC returns just the date part of the value. This is the year, month, and date. It returns a java.sql.Date object. This is an older class, but Java 8 adds a method to convert it to the new LocalDate type.

Now we want to know what time of day Elsa was born:

```
ResultSet rs = stmt.executeQuery("select date_born from animal where name = 'Elsa'");
if (rs.next()) {
    java.sql.Time sqlTime = rs.getTime(1);
    LocalTime localTime = sqlTime.toLocalTime();
    System.out.println(localTime); // 02:15
}
```

When calling getTime, JDBC returns just the time part of the value. This is the hours and minutes. It also optionally includes more granular pieces like seconds. Finally, let's suppose that we want to know both the date and time when Elsa was born:

```
ResultSet rs = stmt.executeQuery("select date_born from animal where name = 'Elsa'");
if (rs.next()) {
    java.sql.Timestamp sqlTimeStamp = rs.getTimestamp(1);
    LocalDateTime localDateTime = sqlTimeStamp.toLocalDateTime();
    System.out.println(localDateTime); // 2001-05-06T02:15
}
```

All three of these values came from the same column in the database. Table 10.7 reviews this mapping.

TABLE 10.7   JDBC date and time types

JDBC Type	Java 8 Type	Contains
java.sql.Date	java.time.LocalDate	Date only
java.sql.Time	java.time.LocalTime	Time only
java.sql.TimeStamp	java.time.LocalDateTime	Both date and time

Finally, the getObject method can return any type. For a primitive, it uses the wrapper class. Let's look at an example:

```
16:   ResultSet rs = stmt.executeQuery("select id, name from species");
17:   while(rs.next()) {
18:       Object idField = rs.getObject("id");
19:       Object nameField = rs.getObject("name");
20:       if (idField instanceof Integer) {
21:           int id = (Integer) idField;
22:           System.out.println(id);
```

```
23:      }
24:      if (nameField instanceof String) {
25:          String name = (String) nameField;
26:          System.out.println(name);
27:      }
28:  }
```

Lines 18 and 19 get the column as whatever type of Object is most appropriate. Lines 20–23 show you how to confirm that the type is Integer before casting and unboxing it into an int. Lines 24–27 show you how to confirm that the type is String and cast it as well. You probably won't use getObject() when writing code for a job, but it is good to know about it for the exam.

Scrolling *ResultSet*

A scrollable ResultSet allows you to position the cursor at any row. In this section, we will show you the options for doing so.

You've already learned the next() method. There's also a previous() method, which does the opposite. It moves backward one row and returns true if pointing to a valid row of data.

There are also methods to start at the beginning and end of the ResultSet. The first() and last() methods return a boolean for whether they were successful at finding a row. The beforeFirst() and afterLast() methods have a return type of void, since it is always possible to get to a spot that doesn't have data. Figure 10.5 shows these methods. You can see that beforeFirst() and afterLast() don't point to rows in the ResultSet.

FIGURE 10.5   First and last

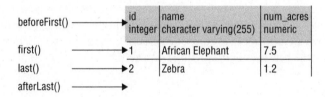

Ready to see these methods in action?

```
10:  Statement stmt = conn.createStatement(
11:      ResultSet.TYPE_SCROLL_INSENSITIVE,
12:      ResultSet.CONCUR_READ_ONLY);
13:  ResultSet rs = stmt.executeQuery("select id from species order by id");
14:  rs.afterLast();
15:  System.out.println(rs.previous());    // true
16:  System.out.println(rs.getInt(1));     // 2
```

```
17:    System.out.println(rs.previous());     // true
18:    System.out.println(rs.getInt(1));      // 1
19:    System.out.println(rs.last());         // true
20:    System.out.println(rs.getInt(1));      // 2
21:    System.out.println(rs.first());        // true
22:    System.out.println(rs.getInt(1));      // 1
23:    rs.beforeFirst();
24:    System.out.println(rs.getInt(1));      // throws SQLException
```

On lines 10–12, we create the statement. This time it is a scrollable result set type, so we can call these extra methods. Make sure that the type is scrollable whenever you see methods other than next(). Line 14 puts the cursor after the last row in the result. Line 15 moves it back one, and line 16 outputs id 2 since the cursor is on the last row. Line 17 moves one more back, which takes us to row number 1. Line 19 goes back to the last row, which is row 2. Line 21 goes to the first row, which is row 1. Line 23 goes to a point immediately before the first row. Line 24 throws an exception, since there is no data to read before the first row.

Now let's look at an example where the query doesn't return any rows:

```
Statement stmt = conn.createStatement(
   ResultSet.TYPE_SCROLL_INSENSITIVE,
   ResultSet.CONCUR_READ_ONLY);
ResultSet rs = stmt.executeQuery("select id from species where id  = -99");
System.out.println(rs.first());  // false
System.out.println(rs.last());   // false
```

When the cursor moves to the "first" or "last" row, the methods return false. There aren't any rows, which makes it impossible to point to a row of data.

Another method that you need to know is absolute(). It takes the row number to which you want to move the cursor as a parameter. A positive number moves the cursor to that numbered row. Zero moves the cursor to a location immediately before the first row. Figure 10.6 shows the row numbers starting from zero.

FIGURE 10.6   Absolute rows

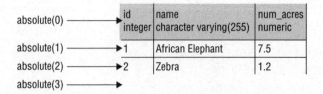

A negative number means to start counting from the end of the ResultSet rather than from the beginning. Figure 10.7 shows the negative row numbers.

FIGURE 10.7   Negative absolute rows

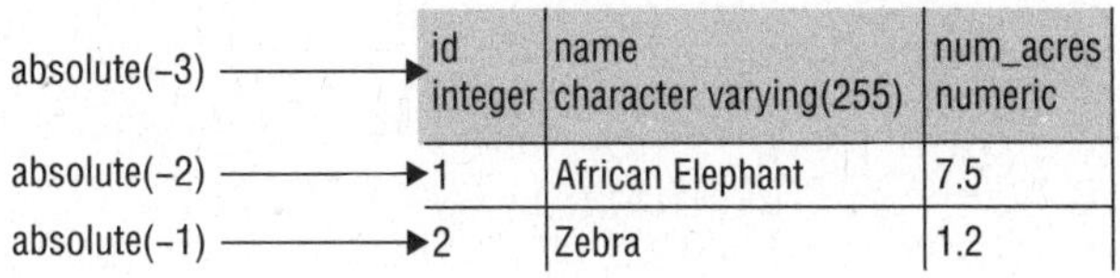

You can see that -1 is the last row. To better understand absolute(), we will use the data in Figure 10.8.

FIGURE 10.8   Animal table

id integer	species_id integer	name character varying(255)	date_born timestamp without time zone
1	1	Elsa	2001-05-06 02:15:00
2	2	Zelda	2002-08-15 09:12:00
3	1	Ester	2002-09-09 10:36:00
4	1	Eddie	2010-06-08 01:24:00
5	2	Zoe	2005-11-12 03:44:00

Try to follow along with this code example:

```
36:    Statement stmt = conn.createStatement(
37:       ResultSet.TYPE_SCROLL_INSENSITIVE,
38:       ResultSet.CONCUR_READ_ONLY);
39:    ResultSet rs = stmt.executeQuery("select id from animal order by id");
40:    System.out.println(rs.absolute(2));        // true
41:    System.out.println(rs.getString("id"));    // 2
42:    System.out.println(rs.absolute(0));        // false
43:    System.out.println(rs.absolute(5));        // true
44:    System.out.println(rs.getString("id"));    // 5
45:    System.out.println(rs.absolute(-2));       // true
46:    System.out.println(rs.getString("id"));    // 4
```

Line 40 positions the cursor at the second row of the ResultSet. The id column doesn't need to match the row number, of course. We did that to make it easier to follow. Line 42 puts the cursor before the result set, so absolute() returns false. Line 43 moves the cursor to the last row, showing that you can go to a valid row after going outside the table. Line 45 moves the cursor to the second-to-last row.

Finally, there is a relative() method that moves forward or backward the requested number of rows. It returns a boolean if the cursor is pointing to a row with data. Here's an example:

```
51:   Statement stmt = conn.createStatement(
52:      ResultSet.TYPE_SCROLL_INSENSITIVE,
53:      ResultSet.CONCUR_READ_ONLY);
54:   ResultSet rs = stmt.executeQuery("select id from animal order by id");
55:   System.out.println(rs.next());          // true
56:   System.out.println(rs.getString("id")); // 1
57:   System.out.println(rs.relative(2));     // true
58:   System.out.println(rs.getString("id")); // 3
59:   System.out.println(rs.relative(-1));    // true
60:   System.out.println(rs.getString("id")); // 2
61:   System.out.println(rs.relative(4));     // false
```

Line 55 moves the cursor to the first row of the result. Line 57 moves forward two rows to row 3. Line 59 moves backward one to row 2. Line 61 tries to move forward four rows, which would position the cursor by row 6. There is no row 6, so this is just after the last row. Since there is no row 6, the method returns `false`.

To review, the methods that you can use when traversing a `ResultSet` are listed in Table 10.8.

TABLE 10.8   Navigating a `ResultSet`

Method	Description	Requires Scrollable ResultSet
boolean absolute(int rowNum)	Move cursor to the specified row number	Yes
void afterLast()	Move cursor to a location immediately after the last row	Yes
void beforeFirst()	Move cursor to a location immediately before the first row	Yes
boolean first()	Move cursor to the first row	Yes
boolean last()	Move cursor to the last row	Yes
boolean next()	Move cursor one row forward	No
boolean previous()	Move cursor one row backward	Yes
boolean relative(int rowNum)	Move cursor forward or backward the specified number of rows	Yes

Closing Database Resources

As you saw in Chapter 8, "IO," and Chapter 9, "NIO.2," it is important to close resources when you are finished with them. This is true for JDBC as well. JDBC resources, such as a Connection, are expensive to create. Not closing them creates a *resource leak* that will eventually slow down your program.

Repeating the example from earlier in the chapter, we have the following:

```java
public static void main(String[] args) throws SQLException {
  String url = " jdbc:derby:zoo";
  try (Connection conn = DriverManager.getConnection(url);
      Statement stmt = conn.createStatement();
      ResultSet rs = stmt.executeQuery("select name from animal")) {

      while (rs.next())
          System.out.println(rs.getString(1));
  }
}
```

Notice how this code uses the try-with-resources syntax from Chapter 6, "Exceptions and Assertions." Remember that a try-with-resources statement closes the resources in the reverse order from which they were opened. This means that the ResultSet is closed first, followed by the Statement, and then the Connection. This is the standard order to close resources.

Closing Database Resources without Try-with-Resources Statements

Prior to Java 7, you had to write a lot of code to close JDBC resources properly. It looked like this:

```java
public static void main(String[] args) throws SQLException {
   String url = "jdbc:derby:zoo";
   Connection conn = null;
   Statement stmt = null;
   ResultSet rs = null;
   try {
      conn = DriverManager.getConnection(url);
      stmt = conn.createStatement();
      rs = stmt.executeQuery("select name from animal");
      while (rs.next())
         System.out.println(rs.getString(1));
```

```
      } finally {
         closeResultSet(rs);
         closeStatement(stmt);
         closeConnection(conn);
      }
   }
   private static void closeResultSet(ResultSet rs) {
      try {
         if (rs != null)
            rs.close();
      } catch (SQLException e) { }
   }
   private static void closeStatement(Statement stmt) {
      try {
         if (stmt != null)
            stmt.close();
      } catch (SQLException e) { }
   }
   private static void closeConnection(Connection conn) {
      try {
         if (conn != null)
            conn.close();
      } catch (SQLException e) { }
   }
```

This example closes the three resources in the same order as the Java 7 example. First comes the ResultSet, then the Statement, and last the Connection.

Each of the helper methods to close a resource has a try/catch block that ignores any SQLException thrown on closing. This is another reason why the Java 8 example is better. It doesn't lose such exceptions, instead treating them as suppressed exceptions. The helper methods also check if the resource is null in case the variable was never set.

While it is a good habit to close all three resources, it isn't strictly necessary. Closing a JDBC resource should close any resources that it created. In particular, the following are true:

- Closing a Connection also closes the Statement and ResultSet.
- Closing a Statement also closes the ResultSet.

There's another way to close a ResultSet. JDBC automatically closes a ResultSet when you run another SQL statement from the same Statement. How many resources are closed in this code?

```
14:    String url = jdbc:derby:zoo";
15:    try (Connection conn = DriverManager.getConnection(url);
16:         Statement stmt = conn.createStatement();
17:         ResultSet rs = stmt.executeQuery("select count(*) from animal")) {
18:
19:      if (rs.next()) System.out.println(rs.getInt(1));
20:
21:      ResultSet rs2 = stmt.executeQuery("select count(*) from animal");
22:      int num = stmt.executeUpdate(
23:          "update animal set name = 'clear' where name = 'other'");
24:    }
```

The correct answer is four. On line 21, rs is closed because the same Statement runs another query. On line 23, rs2 is closed because the same Statement runs another SQL statement. This shows you that both a query and an update cause the previous ResultSet to be closed. Then the try-with-resources statement runs and closes the Statement and Connection objects.

It is very important to close resources in the right order.

Dealing with Exceptions

Up until this point in the chapter, we've lived in a perfect world. Sure, we mentioned that a checked SQLException might be thrown by any JDBC method–but we never actually caught it. We just declared it and let the caller deal with it. Now let's catch the exception:

```
String url = " jdbc:derby:zoo";
try (Connection conn = DriverManager.getConnection(url ");
     Statement stmt = conn.createStatement();
     ResultSet rs = stmt.executeQuery("select not_a_column from animal")) {

     while (rs.next())
        System.out.println(rs.getString(1));

} catch (SQLException e) {
   System.out.println(e.getMessage());
   System.out.println(e.getSQLState());
   System.out.println(e.getErrorCode());
}
```

The output looks like this:

```
ERROR: column "not_a_column" does not exist
  Position: 8
42703
0
```

Each of these methods gives you a different piece of information. The getMessage() method returns a human-readable message as to what went wrong. The getSQLState() method returns a code as to what went wrong. You can Google the name of your database and the SQL state to get more information about the error. By comparison, getErrorCode() is a database-specific code. On this database, it doesn't do anything.

On the exam, either you will be told the names of the columns in a table or you can assume that they are correct. Similarly, you can assume that all SQL is correct.

Summary

There are four key SQL statements: SELECT reads data, INSERT creates a new row, UPDATE changes existing data, and DELETE removes existing data. On the exam, JDBC uses four key interfaces: Driver, Connection, Statement, and ResultSet. The interfaces are part of the Java API. A database-specific JAR file provides the implementations.

To connect to a database, you need the JDBC URL. A JDBC URL has three parts separated by colons. The first part is jdbc. The second part is the name of the vendor/product. The third part varies by database, but it includes the location and name of the database. The location is either localhost or an IP address followed by an optional port.

The DriverManager class provides a factory method called getConnection() to get a Connection implementation. Modern driver JARs contain a file in META-INF/service called java.sql.Driver. This is the name of the implementation class of Driver. Older JARs do not, and they require Class.forName() to load the driver.

There are three ResultSet types that you can request when creating a Statement. If the type you request isn't available, JDBC will downgrade your request to one that is available. The default, TYPE_FORWARD_ONLY, means that you can only go through the data in order. TYPE_SCROLL_INSENSITIVE means that you can go through the data in any order, but you won't see changes made in the database while you are scrolling. TYPE_SCROLL_SENSITIVE means that you can go through the data in any order, and you will see changes made in the database.

You can request either of two modes for ResultSet concurrency when creating a Statement. Again, JDBC will downgrade your request if needed. The default,

CONCUR_READ_ONLY, means that you can read the ResultSet but not write to it. CONCUR_ UPDATABLE means that you can both read and write to it.

When running a SELECT SQL statement, the executeQuery() method returns a ResultSet. When running a DELETE, INSERT, or UPDATE SQL statement, the executeUpdate() method returns the number of rows that were affected. There is also an execute() method that returns a boolean to indicate whether the statement was a query.

For a forward-only result set, call rs.next() from an if statement or while loop to set the cursor position. To get data from a column, call a method like getString(1) or getString("a"). Column indexes begin with 1, not 0. Aside from the primitive getters, there are getDate(), getTime(), and getTimeStamp(). They return just the date, just the time, or both, respectively. Also, getObject() can return any type.

For a scrollable result set, you can use methods to move to an absolute() position or relative() position. Scrolling to next() and previous() are also allowed. There are also methods to go to the first() and last() rows. All of these methods return true if the cursor is pointing to a row with data. Other methods allow you to go outside the ResultSet with beforeFirst() and afterLast().

It is important to close JDBC resources when finished with them to avoid leaking resources. Closing a Connection automatically closes the Statement and ResultSet objects. Closing a Statement automatically closes the ResultSet object. Also, running another SQL statement closes the previous ResultSet object from that Statement.

Exam Essentials

Name the core four JDBC interfaces that you need to know for the exam and where they are defined. The four key interfaces are Driver, Connection, Statement, and ResultSet. The interfaces are part of the core Java APIs. The implementations are part of a database JAR file.

Identify correct and incorrect JDBC URLs. A JDBC URL starts with jdbc:, and it is followed by the vendor/product name. Next comes another colon and then a database-specific connection string. This database-specific string includes the location, such as localhost or an IP address with an optional port. It also contains the name of the database.

Describe how to get a Connection using DriverManager. After including the driver JAR in the classpath, call DriverManager.getConnection(url) or DriverManager. getConnection(url, username, password) to get a driver-specific Connection implementation class.

Create a Statement using different options. When creating a Statement, you can use the defaults. Alternatively, you can specify the ResultSet type followed by the ResultSet concurrency mode. The options for ResultSet type are TYPE_FORWARD_ONLY, TYPE_SCROLL_ INSENSITIVE, and TYPE_SCROLL_SENSITIVE. The options for ResultSet concurrency mode are CONCUR_READ_ONLY and CONCUR_UPDATABLE.

Choose which method on Statement to run given a SQL statement.   For a SELECT SQL statement, use executeQuery() or execute(). For other SQL statements, use executeUpdate() or execute().

Loop through a forward only ResultSet.   Before trying to get data from a ResultSet, you call rs.next() inside an if statement or while loop. This ensures that the cursor is in a valid position. To get data from a column, call a method like getString(1) or getString("a"). Remember that column indexes begin with 1.

Navigate within a scrollable ResultSet.   The rows in a ResultSet are numbered starting with 1. Calling absolute(4) moves the cursor to the fourth row. Calling absolute(0) moves the cursor to a location immediately before the result. Calling absolute(-1) moves the cursor to the last row.

Identify when a resource should be closed.   If you're closing all three resources, the ResultSet must be closed first, followed by the Statement, and then followed by the Connection. Closing an object later in this list automatically closes those earlier in the list.

Review Questions

1. Which interfaces or classes are in a database-specific JAR file? (Choose all that apply.)

    A. Driver

    B. Driver's implementation

    C. DriverManager

    D. DriverManager's implementation

    E. Statement

    F. Statement's implementation

2. Which are required parts of a JDBC URL? (Choose all that apply.)

    A. Connection parameters

    B. Database name

    C. jdbc

    D. Location of database

    E. Port

    F. Password

3. Which of the following is a valid JDBC URL?

    A. jdbc:sybase:localhost:1234/db

    B. jdbc::sybase::localhost::/db

    C. jdbc::sybase:localhost::1234/db

    D. sybase:localhost:1234/db

    E. sybase::localhost::/db

    F. sybase::localhost::1234/db

4. What file is required inside a JDBC 4.0+ driver JAR?

    A. java.sql.Driver

    B. META-INF/java.sql.Driver

    C. META-INF/db/java.sql.Driver

    D. META-INF/database/java.sql.Driver

    E. META-INF/service/java.sql.Driver

5. Suppose that you have a table named animal with two rows. What is the result of the following code?

```
6:    Connection conn = new Connection(url, userName, password);
7:    Statement stmt = conn.createStatement();
8:    ResultSet rs = stmt.executeQuery("select count(*) from animal");
9:    if (rs.next()) System.out.println(rs.getInt(1));
```

A. 0

B. 2

C. There is a compiler error on line 6.

D. There is a compiler error on line 9.

E. There is a compiler error on another line.

F. A runtime exception is thrown.

6. Which of the following are true? (Choose all that apply.)

    A. Calling `Class.forName()` is mandatory in JDBC 4.0.

    B. `Class.forName()` throws a `ClassNotFoundException` if the driver class is not found.

    C. `Class.forName()` throws a `SQLException` if the driver class is not found.

    D. `DriverManager.getConnection()` throws a `ClassNotFoundException` if the driver class is not found.

    E. `DriverManager.getConnection()` throws a `SQLException` if the driver class is not found.

7. Which of the following can fill in the blank? (Choose all that apply.)

```
public void stmt(Connection conn, int b) throws SQLException {
    Statement stmt = conn.createStatement(_____, b);
}
```

    A. `ResultSet.CONCUR_READ_ONLY`

    B. `ResultSet.CONCUR_UPDATABLE`

    C. `ResultSet.TYPE_FORWARD_ONLY`

    D. `ResultSet.TYPE_REVERSE_ONLY`

    E. `ResultSet.TYPE_SCROLL_INSENSITIVE`

    F. `ResultSet.TYPE_SCROLL_SENSITIVE`

8. Given a valid conn object of type `Connection`, what will happen if you run this code when the requested mode is not supported?

```
conn.createStatement(ResultSet.TYPE_SCROLL_SENSITIVE, ResultSet.CONCUR_
UPDATABLE);
```

    A. A `ClassNotFoundException` is thrown.

    B. A `NoSuchTypeException` is thrown.

    C. A `SQLException` is thrown.

    D. A `TypeNotFoundException` is thrown.

    E. The code will run without throwing an exception.

    F. None of the above. The code will not compile.

9. Which of the options can fill in the blanks in order to make the code compile?

```
boolean bool = stmt._____(sql);
int num = stmt._____ (sql);
ResultSet rs = stmt._____ (sql);
```

A. execute, executeQuery, executeUpdate

B. execute, executeUpdate, executeQuery

C. executeQuery, execute, executeUpdate

D. executeQuery, executeUpdate, execute

E. executeUpdate, execute, executeQuery

F. executeUpdate, executeQuery, execute

10. Suppose that the table animal has five rows and this SQL statement updates all of them. What is the result of this code?

```
public static void main(String[] args) throws SQLException {
    Connection conn = DriverManager.getConnection("jdbc:derby:zoo");
    Statement stmt = conn.createStatement();
    int result = stmt.executeUpdate("update animal set name = name");
    System.out.println(result);
}
```

A. 0

B. 1

C. 5

D. The code does not compile.

E. A SQLException is thrown.

F. A different exception is thrown.

11. Suppose that the table food has five rows and this SQL statement updates all of them. What is the result of this code?

```
public static void main(String[] args) {
    Connection conn = DriverManager.getConnection("jdbc:derby:zoo");
    Statement stmt = conn.createStatement();
    int result = stmt.executeUpdate("update food set amount = amount + 1");
    System.out.println(result);
}
```

A. 0

B. 1

C. 5

D. The code does not compile.

E. A SQLException is thrown.

F. A different exception is thrown.

12. Which is the correct order in which to close database resources?

   A. `Connection, ResultSet, Statement`

   B. `Connection, Statement, ResultSet`

   C. `ResultSet, Connection, Statement`

   D. `ResultSet, Statement, Connection`

   E. `Statement, Connection, ResultSet`

   F. `Statement, ResultSet, Connection`

13. There are currently 100 rows in the table `species` before inserting a new row. What is the output of the following code?

```
try (Connection conn = DriverManager.getConnection("jdbc:derby:zoo");
    Statement stmt = conn.createStatement()) {

    ResultSet rs = stmt.executeQuery("select count(*) from species");
    int num = stmt.executeUpdate("INSERT INTO species VALUES (3, 'Ant', .05)");
    rs.next();
    System.out.println(rs.getInt(1));
}
```

   A. `100`

   B. `101`

   C. The code does not compile.

   D. A SQLException is thrown.

   E. A different exception is thrown.

14. Which of the following can fill in the blank correctly? (Choose all that apply.)

```
ResultSet rs = stmt.executeQuery(sql);
if (rs.next()) {

    _____

}
```

   A. `String s = rs.getString(0);`

   B. `String s = rs.getString(1);`

   C. `String s = rs.getObject(0);`

   D. `String s = rs.getObject(1);`

E. `Object s = rs.getObject(0);`

F. `Object s = rs.getObject(1);`

15. Which of the following can fill in the blank to print the month, date, year, hour, minute, and second?

   A. `rs.getDate("d");`

   B. `rs.getLocalDate("d");`

   C. `rs.getLocalDateTime("d");`

   D. `rs.getLocalTime("d");`

   E. `rs.getTime("d");`

   F. `rs.getTimeStamp("d");`

16. Suppose that you have a table with three rows. The names in those rows are Anna, Betty, and Cat. What does the following output?

```
String sql = "select name from animal";
try (Connection conn = DriverManager.getConnection("jdbc:derby:zoo");
    Statement stmt = conn.createStatement();

    ResultSet rs = stmt.executeQuery(sql)) {
    rs.next();
    rs.previous();
    rs.previous();
    rs.next();
    rs.next();
    rs.absolute(2);
    System.out.println(rs.getString(1));
}
```

   A. Anna

   B. Betty

   C. Cat

   D. The code does not compile.

   E. A `SQLException` is thrown.

17. Which of the following methods move the cursor without returning a `boolean`?

   A. `absolute()`

   B. `afterFirst()`

   C. `afterLast()`

   D. `beforeFirst()`

   E. `beforeLast()`

   F. `previous()`

18. Suppose that you have a table animal with three rows. The names in those rows are Anna, Betty, and Cat. What does the following output?

```
String sql = "select name from animal order by id";
try (Connection conn = DriverManager.getConnection("jdbc:derby:zoo");
    Statement stmt = conn.createStatement();

    ResultSet rs = stmt.executeQuery(sql)) {
    rs.absolute(0);
    rs.next();
    System.out.println(rs.getString(1));
}
```

A. Anna

B. Betty

C. Cat

D. The code does not compile.

E. A SQLException is thrown.

19. In a table animal with 10 rows, how many times does true get output by the following? (Choose all that apply.)

```
String sql = "select * from animal";
try (Connection conn = DriverManager.getConnection("jdbc:derby:zoo");
    Statement stmt = conn.createStatement(
        ResultSet.TYPE_SCROLL_INSENSITIVE, ResultSet.CONCUR_READ_ONLY);

    ResultSet rs = stmt.executeQuery(sql)) {
    System.out.println(rs.absolute(0));
    System.out.println(rs.absolute(5));
    System.out.println(rs.previous());
    System.out.println(rs.relative(-2));
    System.out.println(rs.relative(-100));
```

A. One

B. Two

C. Three

D. Four

E. Five

F. The code does not compile.

G. A SQLException is thrown.

20. In the table animal with 10 rows, how many times does true get output by the following? (Choose all that apply.)

```
String sql = "select * from animal";
try (Connection conn = DriverManager.getConnection("jdbc:derby:zoo");
        Statement stmt = conn.createStatement(
            ResultSet.TYPE_SCROLL_INSENSITIVE, ResultSet.CONCUR_READ_ONLY);

    ResultSet rs = stmt.executeQuery(sql));
    System.out.println(rs.beforeFirst());
    System.out.println(rs.absolute(5));
    System.out.println(rs.previous());
    System.out.println(rs.relative(-2));
    System.out.println(rs.afterLast());
```

- **A.** One
- **B.** Two
- **C.** Three
- **D.** Four
- **E.** Five
- **F.** The code does not compile.
- **G.** A SQLException is thrown.

Appendix A

Answers to Review Questions

Chapter 1: Advanced Class Design

1. A. Based on the equals() method in the code, objects are equal if they have the same employeeId. The hashCode() method correctly overrides the one from Object. The equals() method is an overload of the one from Object and not an override. It would be better to pass Object since an override would be better to use here. It is odd to override hashCode() and not equals().

2. A. hashCode() is correct and perfectly reasonable given that equals() also checks that field. ClassCastException is a runtime exception and therefore does not need to be handled or declared. The override in equals() is correct. It is common for equals() to refer to a private instance variable. This is legal because it is within the same class, even if it is referring to a different object of the same class.

3. C. s1 points to the string pool. s2 points to an object on the heap, since it is created at runtime. == checks for reference equality. These are different references, making B incorrect. String overrides equals() so the actual values are the same, making C correct. And yes, this question could have appeared on the OCA. Remember that the OCP is cumulative. A question may appear to be about one thing and actually be about a simpler concept.

4. C. The equals() method is correct. You are allowed to use any business logic that you want in determining equality. The hashCode() method is not correct. It violates the rule that two objects that return true for equals() must return the same hashCode(). It is also a bad idea for the hash code to contain values that could change.

5. A, D. The relevant rule is that two objects that return true for equals() objects must return the same hash code. Therefore A is correct and B is incorrect. Two objects with the same hash code may or may not be equal. This makes C incorrect and D correct. The fact that two objects are not equal does not guarantee or preclude them from sharing a hash code. Remember that hashCode() tells you which bucket to look in and equals() tells you whether you have found an exact match.

6. B. The ordinal() method of an enum returns its corresponding int value. Like arrays, enums are zero based. Remember that the index of an enum may change when you recompile the code and should not be used for comparison.

7. E. A case statement on an enum data type must be the unqualified name of an enumeration constant. For example, case VANILLA would be valid. You cannot use the ordinal equivalents. Therefore, the code does not compile.

8. C. Inner is a member inner class. Inner classes are not allowed to contain static methods or static variables. Only nested static classes are permitted to contain statics.

9. B. Outer.this.x is the correct way to refer to x in the Outer class. In Java 7, the answer would have been D because you used to have to declare variables as final to use them in a local inner class. In Java 8, this requirement was dropped and the variables only need to be effectively final, which means that the code would still compile if final were added.

10. C. The code compiles fine. A member inner class is allowed to be `private`, and it is allowed to refer to instance variables from the outer class. Two `.class` files are generated. `Book.class` matches the name of the outer class. The inner class does not compile to `BookReader.class`. That would introduce the possibility of a naming conflict. `Book$BookReader.class` is correct because it shows the scope of the class is limited to `Book`. You don't need to know that $ is the syntax, but you do need to know the number of classes and that `BookReader` is not a top-level class.

11. D. `FootballGame` is trying to refer to a `static` variable in another class. It needs a static import to do so. The correct syntax is `import static` and not static import. B is incorrect because * does not `import` classes in a package. C is incorrect because it does not refer to a `static` member.

12. E. The `main` method tries to cast a `Firefox` instance to IE. Since IE is not a subclass of `Firefox`, this throws a `ClassCastException`.

13. B. c is an instance of `Chipmunk`. It is an instance of any superclasses or interfaces it implements. In this case, those are `Furry`, `Mammal`, and `Object`. `null` is not an instance of any type. Therefore, the first two `if` statements execute and `result` is 3.

14. E. Code involving `instanceof` does not compile when there is no way for it to evaluate true. D not only compiles but it is always true. E does not compile because `ArrayList` is a concrete class that does not extend `Chipmunk`. F does compile because `Runnable` is an interface. In theory, someone could subclass `Chipmunk` and have the subclass implement `Runnable`.

15. B, E. `equals()` should `return false` when the object it passed in is not equal to the current object. This includes `null` and incorrect types. An `equals()` method should have a `null` check and an `instanceof` check.

16. E. This is a member inner class. It needs to be created using an instance of the outer class. The syntax looks weird, but it creates an object of the outer class and then an object of the inner class from it.

17. B, C. Enums are required to have a semicolon after the list of values if there is anything else in the enum. Don't worry; you won't be expected to track down missing semicolons on the whole exam—only on enum questions. Enums are not allowed to have a public constructor.

18. G. This question appears to be about enums but is really about `abstract` methods. Just as an `abstract` superclass requires concrete subclasses to have an implementation, `abstract` enum methods require each enum type to implement the method.

19. A, C. An override must have the same method signature. A and C both do. F is an overload because it has a different parameter list. E does not compile because it throws a checked exception not declared in the superclass. D compiles but is not an override because it is `static`. B has a different method name, so it is not even an overload.

20. C. Both objects are `BabyRhino` objects. Virtual method invocation says that the subclass method gets called at runtime rather than the type in the variable reference. However, we

are not calling methods here. We are referring to instance variables. With instance variables, the reference type does matter.

21. A, C, E. Remember that @Override means that we are implementing a method from a superclass or interface. The Object class declares methods with the signatures in Options A and C. Granted, it is a poor implementation of equals(), but it does compile. Option E is also correct because the method is declared in Otter. Option F is incorrect because methods from an interface are always public. Option B is incorrect because the parameter type does not match the one in Object. Option D is incorrect because the return type does not match the one in Object.

Chapter 2: Design Patterns and Principles

1. C, E. Option A is incorrect as a design pattern is focused on solving a specific commonly occurring problem. Option B is also incorrect, as design principles and design patterns are different, despite both promoting better code development. Option D is incorrect as design patterns may be applied to static or non-static classes alike. Options C and E are correct statements about design principles and design patterns.

2. E. The code does not compile because EasternChipmunk inherits the abstract method climb() but does not implement it, therefore the correct answer is E. B, C, and D are incorrect as they compile for various reasons. Line 2 compiles, as non-static and non-default interface methods are assumed to have the abstract modifier. Line 4 compiles without issue as an interface can extend another interface. Line 5 compiles without issue as an abstract class can implement an interface without implementing any of the abstract methods. F is incorrect, as Line 8 does not compile.

3. A, D. A is correct as Climb defines an interface with exactly one abstract method. B is incorrect, as abstract classes are not functional interfaces despite having a single abstract method. While functional interfaces may have any number of default methods, ArcticMountainClimb will not compile due to the default method getSpeed() missing an implementation body, so C is incorrect. D is correct, as the interface MountainClimb has exactly one abstract method defined in Climb. Finally, E is incorrect because A and D are correct.

4. A, D. The first lambda expression is valid, taking no arguments and returning the empty string, so A is correct. B is incorrect, as more than one parameter requires parentheses (). C is incorrect, as brackets {} are required when using return. D is correct, as the expression takes one Camel input and returns void. E is incorrect, as parentheses are required when using the data type Wolf. F is incorrect, as it has no right-side expression. Finally, G is incorrect, as specifying the data type for one parameter in a lambda expression requires you to specify the data type for all parameters in the expression. In this case, z has a data type and m does not, therefore the expression is invalid.

5. B, E, F. A is incorrect, as any method that changes the singleton breaks the singleton pattern. B is correct, as the constructor of the singleton class must be `private`, else other classes would be able to instantiate it, breaking the singleton pattern. C is incorrect, as the name of the object itself, as well as the method to retrieve the singleton, is not defined in the pattern. D is incorrect, as the object must be marked `private`. If it was marked `protected`, it would not be properly encapsulated and other classes would have access to it. E is correct, as the purpose of a singleton is to ensure that all threads share the same instance of the object in memory. F is correct, as a `public static` method is required for all threads to access the same singleton.

6. A. This code compiles and runs without issue so C, D, E, and F are incorrect. Line h1 creates a lambda expression that checks if the age is less than 5. Since there is only one parameter and it does not specify a type, the parentheses around the type parameter are optional. Line h2 uses the `Predicate` interface, which declares a `test()` method. Since `test()` returns `true` on the expression, match is output and A is correct.

7. C, E, G, H. A is incorrect, as there are definitely some problems with the immutable objects implementation. B is incorrect, as there is no such thing as the `Immutable` interface defined in the Java API. C is correct, as all instance variables should be `private` and `final` to prevent them from being changed by a caller. D is incorrect, as adding settings is the opposite of what you do with the immutable object pattern. E is correct, since `List<Seal>` is mutable, all direct access should be removed. F is incorrect, as this has nothing to do with immutability. G is correct, as we need to copy the mutable `List<Seal>` to prevent the caller of the constructor from maintaining access to a mutable structure within our class. H is also correct, as it prevents the methods of the class from being overridden.

8. C, F. A and B are both incorrect as interfaces can extend other interfaces, although not classes. C is correct since a class may implement multiple interfaces. D is incorrect as interfaces have `static` and `default` methods, as well as `static final` variables. E is incorrect as interfaces are assumed to be abstract, and abstract and final can never be used together. F is correct as interface methods and variables are each assumed `public`.

9. D, F. A is incorrect, as there are definitely some problems with the singleton implementation. B and C are incorrect, as naming of the instance variable and access method are not required as part of the pattern. The `public` modifier on the cheetahManager instance means that any class can access or even replace the instance, which breaks the singleton pattern; hence D is required to fix the implementation. E is incorrect, as marking the instance final would prevent lazy instantiation and as the code would not compile. F is also required, since without this step two threads could create two distinct instances of the singleton at the same time, which would violate the singleton pattern.

10. D. While Java supports multiple inheritance through interfaces, it does not support method overriding in interfaces, since it's not clear which parent method should be used. In this example, CanWalk and CanRun both implement a `default walk()` method. The definition of CanSprint extends these two interfaces and therefore won't compile as two `default` methods with the same signature from parent classes are detected, therefore the answer is D. None of the other lines of code cause problems, so the rest of the answers are not correct.

11. A, F. B is incorrect because it does not use the return keyword. C, D, and E are incorrect because the variable e is already in use from the lambda and cannot be redefined. Additionally, C is missing the return keyword and E is missing the semicolon. A and F are the only correct lambda expressions that match the functional interface.

12. C. The functional interface takes two int parameters. The code on line x1 attempts to use them as if one is an Object, resulting in a compiler error making C the correct answer. It also tries to return String even though the data type for the functional interface method is boolean. It is tricky to use types in a lambda when they are implicitly specified. Remember to check the interface for the real type.

13. B, C, E. Immutable objects may not be modified after creation. B, C, and E are correct statements that support this property. A is incorrect, as immutable objects may have getter methods, just not setter methods. D is incorrect, as static methods are not part of the immutable object pattern. F is also incorrect, as the getter methods are not required to be marked synchronized.

14. A, B, D, E. The blank can be filled with any class or interface that is a supertype of TurtleFrog. A is a superclass of TurtleFrog, and B is the same class, so both are correct. BrazilianHornedFrog is not a superclass of TurtleFrog, so C is incorrect. TurtleFrog inherits the CanHop interface, so D is correct. All classes inherit Object, so E is correct. Finally, Long is an unrelated class that is not a superclass of TurtleFrog, and it is therefore incorrect.

15. B, C. A reference to an object requires an explicit cast if referenced with a subclass, so A is incorrect. If the cast is to a superclass reference, then an explicit cast is not required, so C is correct. If a method takes the superclass of an object as a parameter, then any subclass references may be used without a cast, so B is correct. Some cast exceptions can be detected as errors at compile-time, but others can only be detected at runtime, so D is incorrect. Due to the nature of polymorphism, a public instance method can be overridden in a subclass and calls to it will be replaced even in the superclass in which it was defined, so E is incorrect.

16. F. The interface variable amount is correctly declared, with public, static, and final being assumed and automatically inserted by the compiler, so B is incorrect. The method declaration for eatGrass() on line 3 is incorrect because the method has been marked as static but no method body has been provided. The method declaration for chew() on line 4 is also incorrect, since an interface method that provides a body must be marked as default or static explicitly. Therefore, F is the correct answer since this code contains two compile-time errors.

17. B, C, F. Options B, C, and F are each correct statements about JavaBean encapsulation. A is incorrect, as that is a property of the immutable object pattern, not encapsulation. D is incorrect, as there is no such JavaBean interface defined in the Java API. Finally, E is incorrect, as handling instantiation is not part of encapsulation.

18. A, B, E. A is correct, and it is one of the reasons to prefer class inheritance over object composition. B is also correct, since object composition tends to lead to classes that are easier to reference, as they don't require knowledge of any parent classes. C is incorrect, as inheritance tends to use the is-a principle, whereas object composition relies on the has-a

principle. D is incorrect, as this is a statement about inheritance, not object composition. E is correct, as object composition has no notion of inheritance and variables must be exposed publically if they are to be used by other classes in different packages. F is incorrect, as neither are always the right answer. There are situations where inheritance is more appropriate, and situations where object composition is more appropriate.

19. B, D, E. A is incorrect, as that is a property of the immutable object pattern. B is correct, as caching data is one of the most common uses of the singleton pattern. While the singleton pattern may use lazy instantiation, it is not used to ensure that objects are lazily instantiated, so C is incorrect. D is correct, as we only want one class writing to a log file at once. E is also correct, as managing application-wide configuration data is another very common use of the singleton pattern. F is incorrect, as we only want one instance of a `static` object created when using the singleton pattern.

20. A. Although the definition of methods on lines 2 and 5 vary, both will be converted to `public abstract` by the compiler. Line 4 is fine, because an interface can have `public` or default access. Finally, the class `Falcon` doesn't need to implement the interface methods because it is marked as `abstract`. Therefore, the code will compile without issue.

Chapter 3: Generics and Collections

1. B. The answer needs to implement `List` because the scenario allows duplicates. Since you need a `List`, you can eliminate C, D, and E immediately. `HashMap` is a `Map` and `HashSet` is a `Set`. `LinkedList` is both a `List` and a `Queue`. You want a regular `List`. Option A, `Arrays`, is trying to distract you. It is a utility class rather than a `Collection`. An array is not a collection. By process of elimination, the answer is B.

2. D. The answer needs to implement `Map` because you are dealing with key/value pairs per the unique string text. You can eliminate A, C, E, and F immediately. `ArrayList` and `Vector` are `List`s. `HashSet` and `TreeSet` are `Set`s. Now it is between `HashMap` and `TreeMap`. Since the question talks about ordering, you need the `TreeMap`. Therefore, the answer is E.

3. E. The code does not compile. It attempts to mix generics and legacy code. Lines 3 through 7 create an `ArrayList` without generics. This means that we can put any objects in it. Line 7 should be looping through a list of `Objects` rather than `Strings` since we didn't use generics.

4. E. Since we call `push()` rather than `offer()`, we are treating the `ArrayDeque` as a LIFO (last-in, first-out) stack. On line 7, we remove the last element added, which is `"ola"`. On line 8, we look at the new last element (`"hi"`), but don't remove it. Lines 9 and 10, we remove each element in turn until none are left. Note that we don't use an `Iterator` to loop through the `ArrayDeque`. The order in which the elements are stored internally is not part of the API contract.

5. B, C, F. Option A does not compile because the generic types are not compatible. We could say HashSet<? extends Number> hs2 = new HashSet<Integer>();. Option B uses a lower bound, so it allows superclass generic types. Option C is a traditional use of generics where the generic type is the same and the List type uses the interface as the type. Option D does not compile because a Set is not a List. Option E does not compile because upper bounds are not allowed when instantiating the type. Finally, Option F does compile because the upper bound is on the correct side of =.

6. C. Line 7 gives a compiler warning for not using generics but not a compiler error. Line 4 compiles fine because toString() is defined on the Object class and is therefore always available to call. Line 6 creates the Hello class with the generic type String. Line 7 creates the Hello class with the generic type Object since no type is specified.

7. A, D. The code compiles fine. It uses the diamond operator, and it allows any implementation of Number to be added. HashSet does not guarantee any iteration order, making A and D correct.

8. C. TreeSet sorts the elements. Since uppercase letters sort before lowercase letters, the ordering is "ONE", "One", "one". The ceiling() method returns the smallest element greater than the specified one. "On" appears between "ONE" and "One". Therefore, the smallest element that is larger than the specified value is "One".

9. E. Trick question! The Map interface uses put() rather than add() to add elements to the map. If these examples used put(), the answer would be A and C. B is no good because a long cannot be shoved into a Double. D is no good because a char is not the same thing as a String.

10. A. The array is sorted using MyComparator, which sorts the elements in reverse alphabetical order in a case-insensitive fashion. Normally, numbers sort before letters. This code reverses that by calling the compareTo() method on b instead of a.

11. A. Line 3 uses the diamond operator to create the map. Lines 5 and 7 use autoboxing to convert between the int primitive and the Integer wrapper class. The keys map to their squared value. 1 maps to 1, 2 maps to 4, 3 maps to 9, 4 maps to 16, and so on.

12. A, B, D. The generic type must be Exception or a subclass of Exception since this is an upper bound. C and E are wrong because Throwable is a superclass of Exception. D uses an odd syntax by explicitly listing the type, but you should be able to recognize it as acceptable.

13. B, E. showSize() can take any type of List since it uses an unbounded wildcard. Option A is incorrect because it is a Queue and not a List. Option C is incorrect because the wildcard is not allowed to be on the right side of an assignment. Option D is incorrect because the generic types are not compatible. Option B is correct because a lower-bounded wildcard allows that same type to be the generic. Option E is correct because Integer is a subclass of Number. Vector is an old type of List. It isn't common in new code, but you still need to know it for the exam and in case you encounter old code.

14. C. This question is hard because it defines both Comparable and Comparator on the same object. t1 doesn't specify a Comparator so it uses the Comparable object's compareTo() method. This sorts by the text instance variable. t2 did specify a Comparator when calling the constructor, so it uses the compare() method, which sorts by the int.

15. D. The list is sorted in descending order. However, it is searched using the default order, which is sorted in ascending order. binarySearch() requires both to use the same sort order. Therefore, the precondition for binarySearch() is not met and the result is undefined.

16. B, D, F. The java.lang.Comparable interface is implemented on the object to compare. It specifies the compareTo() method, which takes one parameter. The java.util.Comparator interface specifies the compare() method, which takes two parameters.

17. B, D. Line 1 is a generic class that requires specifying a name for the type. Options A and C are incorrect because no type is specified. Line 3 tries to use the diamond operator to instantiate the class. Option E is incorrect because T is not a class and certainly not one compatible with String. Option F is incorrect because a wildcard cannot be specified on the right side when instantiating an object.

18. A, B. C is both a class and a type parameter. This means that within the class D, when we refer to C, it uses the type parameter. All of the choices that mention class C are incorrect because it no longer means the class C.

19. A, D. A LinkedList implements both List and Queue. The List interface has a method to remove by index. Since this method exists, Java does not autobox to call the other method. Queue has only the remove by object method, so Java does autobox there. Since the number 1 is not in the list, Java does not remove anything for the Queue.

20. E. This question looks like it is about generics, but it's not. It is trying to see if you noticed that Map does not have a contains() method. It has containsKey() and containsValue() instead. If containsKey() was called, the answer would be false because the 123 in the list is an Integer rather than a String.

21. A, F. You have to memorize this. hasNext() returns a boolean, and it is used in the loop. next() returns the next element.

22. B. When using generic types in a static method, the generic specification goes before the return type.

23. B, E. Both Comparator and Comparable are functional interfaces. However, Comparable is intended to be used on the object being compared, making choice B correct. removeIf was added in Java 8 to allow specifying the lambda to check when removing elements, making choice E correct.

24. F. Choice A is incorrect because forEach takes a Consumer parameter, which requires one parameter. Choices B and C are close. The syntax for a lambda is correct. However, s is already defined as a local variable and therefore the lambda can't redefine it. Choices D and E use incorrect syntax for a method reference. Choice F is correct.

25. F. The first call to merge() calls the mapping function and adds the two numbers to get 13. It then updates the map. The second call to merge() sees that the map currently has a null value for that key. It does not call the mapping function but instead replaces it with the new value of 3. Therefore choice F is correct.

Chapter 4: Functional Programming

1. D. No terminal operation is called, so the stream never executes. The methods chain to create a stream that would contain "2" and "12." The first line creates an infinite stream. The second line would get the first two elements from that infinite stream and map each element to add an extra character.

2. F. b1 is set to true since anyMatch() terminates. Even though the stream is infinite, Java finds a match on the first element and stops looking. However, when allMatch() runs, it needs to keep going until the end of the stream since it keeps finding matches. Since all elements continue to match, the program hangs.

3. E. An infinite stream is generated where each element is twice as long as the previous one. b1 is set to false because Java finds an element that doesn't match when it gets to the element of length 4. However, the next line tries to operate on the same stream. Since streams can be used only once, this throws an exception that the "stream has already been operated upon or closed." If two different streams were used, the result would be option A.

4. A, B. Terminal operations are the final step in a stream pipeline. Exactly one is required, because it triggers the execution of the entire stream pipeline. Therefore, options A and B are correct. Options C and F are true of intermediate operations rather than terminal operations. Option E is never true. Once a stream pipeline is run, the Stream is marked invalid.

5. A, B. Options D and E are incorrect because they are intermediate operations and not terminal operations. While option F is a reduction, it is incorrect because it is available only on primitive streams such as IntStream. Option C is incorrect because it is not a reduction—it does not look at each element in the stream.

6. A. Options C and D are incorrect because these methods do not take a Predicate parameter and do not return a boolean. Options B and E are incorrect because they cause the code to run infinitely. The stream has no way to know that a match won't show up later. Option A is correct because it is safe to return false as soon as one element passes through the stream that doesn't match.

7. F. The sorted() method is used in a stream pipeline to return a sorted Stream. A collector is needed to turn the stream back into a List. The collect() method takes the desired collector.

8. D, E. The sum() method returns an int rather than an OptionalInt because the sum of an empty list is zero. Therefore, option E is correct. The findAny() method returns an OptionalInt because there might not be any elements to find. Therefore, option D is correct. The average() method returns an OptionalDouble since averages of any type can result in a fraction. Therefore, options A and B are both incorrect.

9. B, D. Option A would work for a regular Stream. However, we have a LongStream and therefore need to call getAsLong(). Option C is missing the :: that would make it a method reference. Therefore, options B and D are correct.

10. F. The terminal operation must be right before the semicolon, which is line M. Remember that forEach() is a terminal operation while peek() is an intermediate operation. This eliminates all but choices C, E, and F. Choice E is incorrect because there is no limit() operation, which means that the code would run infinitely. Choice C is incorrect because filter() is called before limit(). No elements make it through the filter, so the code also runs infinitely. Choice F is correct.

11. B, C, E. As written, the code doesn't compile because the collector expects to get a String immediately before it in the chain. Option B fixes this, at which point nothing is output because the collector creates a String. Option E fixes this and causes the output to be 11111. Since the post-increment operator is used, the stream contains an infinite number of 1s. Option C fixes this and causes the stream to contain increasing numbers.

12. A, F, G. Line 6 doesn't take any parameters, and it returns a String, making it a Supplier. Another clue is that it uses a constructor reference, which should scream Supplier! This makes choice F correct. Line 7 takes two parameters, and it doesn't return anything making it a BiConsumer. The print statement should also be a clue that we are dealing with a Consumer or BiConsumer. This makes choice A correct. Choices C and D are there to mislead you; these interfaces don't actually exist. BinaryOperator spells out *binary*. The other functional interfaces use the prefix Bi. Finally, line 8 takes a single parameter, and it returns the same type, which is a UnaryOperator. Since the types are the same, only one generic is needed, making choice G correct.

13. F. If the map() and flatMap() calls were reversed, choice B would be correct. In this case, the Stream created from the source is of type Stream<List<Integer>>. The Function in map expects an Integer rather than a List<Integer>, so the code does not compile.

14. D. Line 4 should obviously look OK. It creates a Stream and uses autoboxing to put the Integer 1 inside. Line 5 converts to a primitive, again using autoboxing. Line 6 converts to a double primitive, which works since double d = 1; would work. Line 7 is where it all falls apart. Converting from a double to an int would require a cast inside the lambda.

15. D, E. Choices A and B do not compile, because they are invalid generic declarations. Primitives are not allowed as generics, and Map must have two generic types. Choice C is incorrect because partitioning only gives a Boolean key. Choices D and E are correct because the result Collection can be customized.

16. C. The partitioningBy() operation always returns a map with two Boolean keys, even if there are no corresponding values. By contrast, groupingBy() returns only keys that are actually needed.

17. E. A UnaryOperator is a special type of function where the parameter and return type are the same. Therefore, option E is correct. Notice that other options don't even compile because they have the wrong number of generic types for the functional interface provided.

18. D. The terminal operation is count(). Since there is a terminal operation, the intermediate operations run. The peek() operation comes before the filter, so both numbers are printed. The count happens to be 1 since the other number is filtered. However, the result of the stream pipeline isn't stored in a variable, and that result is ignored.

19. A, C, E. The three common types of double, int and, long have dedicated supplier classes. The only primitive functional interface that does not involve one of those three types is BooleanSupplier.

20. B. Both lists and streams have forEach() methods. There is no reason to collect into a list just to loop through it.

Chapter 5: Dates, Strings, and Localization

1. A, B. Choices E and F are incorrect because a Locale is created using a constructor. The convention is to use lowercase for a language code and uppercase for a country code. The language is mandatory when using a constructor, which makes choices A and B correct.

2. C, D, E. Localization refers to user-facing elements that a user sees. Currency, dates, and numbers are commonly used in different formats for different countries. Class and variable names are internal to the application, so there is no need to translate them for users. Booleans are true/false values with standard names.

3. C, D. Choice A is incorrect because Java will look at parent bundles. For example, Java will look at Props.properties if Props_en.properties does not contain the requested key. Java class resource bundles can have non-String values while property files are limited to strings. Therefore, choice B is incorrect and choice C is correct. Choice D is correct because the locale is only changed in memory. Choice E is incorrect because Java specifies that it will look for a Java class resource bundle before a property file of the same name.

4. B. Java will first look for the most specific matches it can find, starting with Dolphins_en_US.java and then Dolphins_en_US.properties. Since neither is found, it drops the country and looks for Dolphins_en.java. Since a match is found, there is no reason to go on to the next one, which is Dolphins_en.properties.

5. D. Java will use Dolphins_fr.properties as the matching resource bundle on line 7 because it is an exact match on the language of the requested locale. Line 8 finds a matching key in this file. Line 9 does not find a match in that file, and therefore it has to look higher up in the hierarchy. Once a bundle is chosen, only resources in that hierarchy are allowed.

6. D, F. Options A and B are incorrect because LocalDate does not have a public constructor. Option C is incorrect because months start counting with 1 rather than 0. Option E is incorrect because it uses the old Calendar constants for months, which begin with 0. Options D and F are both correct ways of specifying the desired date.

7. D. A LocalDate does not have a time element. Therefore, it has no method to add hours, and the code does not compile.

8. F. Java throws an exception if invalid date values are passed. There is no 40th day in April—or any other month for that matter.

9. B. The date starts out as April 30, 2018. Since dates are immutable and the plus methods have their return values ignored, the result is unchanged. Therefore, Option B is correct.

10. E. Even though d has both date and time, the formatter only outputs time.

11. B. Period does not allow chaining. Only the last Period method called counts, so only the two years are subtracted.

12. A, E. When dealing with time zones, it is best to convert to GMT first by subtracting the time zone. The first date/time is 9:00 GMT, and the second is 15:00 GMT. Therefore, the first one is earlier by 6 hours.

13. B. dateTime1 is 2016-03-13T01:30-05:00[US/Eastern] and dateTime2 is 2016-03-13T03:30-04:00[US/Eastern]. While the values are two hours apart, the time zone offset changes as well, making it only change from 6:30 GMT to 7:30 GMT.

14. A, C, D. Option B is incorrect because there is no March 40th. Option E is incorrect because 2017 isn't a leap year and therefore has no February 29th. Option D is correct because it is just a regular date and has nothing to do with daylight savings time. Options A and C are correct because Java is smart enough to adjust for daylight savings time.

15. B, C. Options A and D are incorrect because the String references do not point to the same object. Option E is incorrect because a Period format begins with a P and a Duration format begins with PT. They are different types and do not represent the same value even though they are both a day. Remember that Duration uses hours/minutes/seconds and Period uses years/months/days for measures. Options B and C are correct because m1, m2, and s all represent a duration of the same length.

16. A, B, F. Option A correctly creates the current instant. Option B correctly converts from seconds to an Instant. Option F is also a proper conversion. Options C, D, and E are incorrect because the source object does not represent a point in time. Without a time zone, Java doesn't know what moment in time to use for the Instant.

17. E. The Properties class defines a get() method that does not allow for a default value. It also has a getProperty() method, which returns the default value if the key is not provided.

18. D. Options E and F do not compile because you can't get a stream directly from a Properties object. Options A and B do not compile because the method is keySet(), not keys(). Option C outputs all of the keys, and Option D outputs all of the values.

19. A, B, C. Remember that Duration uses hours/minutes/seconds and Period uses years/months/days for measures.

20. E. Local_____ explicitly excludes time zones. Instant represents a point in time, but always uses GMT rather than the desired time zone.

Chapter 6: Exceptions and Assertions

1. C. The method should declare that it throws an exception and the body of the method actually would throw it. Options E and F are incorrect because both checked and unchecked (runtime) exceptions can be declared in a method signature. Also, option F is incorrect because SQLException is a checked exception.

2. B, C. Option A is incorrect because it will move the compilation error to the close() method since it does throw an exception that must be handled or declared. Option B is correct because the unhandled exception becomes declared. Option C is correct because the exception becomes handled. Option D is incorrect because the exception remains unhandled.

3. E. Options B, D, and F are incorrect because only one variable name is allowed in a multi-catch block. Option A is incorrect because FileNotFoundException is a subclass of IOException. A multi-catch statement does not allow redundancy, and just catching IOException would have been equivalent. Option C is incorrect because the IOException that is thrown is not handled.

4. A, B. A try-with-resources statement does not require a catch or finally block. A traditional try statement requires at least one of the two.

5. C. After opening both resources in the try-with-resources statement, T is printed. Then the try-with-resource completes and closes the resources in reverse order from which they were opened. After W is printed, an exception is thrown. However, the remaining resource is still closed and D is printed. The exception thrown is then caught and E is printed. Last, the finally block is run, printing F. Therefore the answer is TWDEF.

6. G. A try-with-resources statement uses parentheses rather than brackets for the try section. This is likely subtler than a question that you'll get on the exam, but it is still important to be on alert for details.

7. C. The code compiles fine, so option E is incorrect. The command line has only two arguments, so args.length is 2 and the if statement is true. However, because assertions are not enabled, it does not throw an AssertionError, so option B is incorrect. The println attempts to print args[2], which generates an ArrayIndexOutOfBoundsException, so the answer is option C.

8. B, C. Java uses the flags –ea or –enableassertions to turn on assertions. –da or –disableassertions turns off assertions. The colon indicates for a specific class. Choice B is correct because it turns on assertions for all code. Choice C is correct because it disables assertions but then turns them back on for this class.

9. A, D. An assertion consists of a boolean expression followed by an optional colon and message. The boolean expression is allowed to be in parenthesis, but this is not required. Therefore A and D are correct.

10. A, E. Line 5 does not compile because assert is a reserved word making Choice A correct. B and C are incorrect because the parenthesis and message are both optional. D is incorrect

because assertions should not have side effects. E is correct because checking an argument passed from elsewhere in the program is an appropriate use of an assertion.

11. A, B, D, E. You need to memorize the contents of Table 6.2 and Table 6.3 before the exam.

12. A, D, E. Since a single exception type is caught, only the same type of exception or a subclass is allowed to be assigned to the variable in the catch block. Therefore D and E are correct. Additionally A is correct because there are no changes to the variable.

13. A. Since a multi-catch is used, the variable in the catch block is effectively final and cannot be reassigned.

14. F. A multi-catch cannot catch both a superclass and subclass. Notice how similar questions can be while testing something that is entirely different.

15. B, E. A checked exception extends Exception but not RuntimeException. The entire hierarchy counts, so B and E are both correct.

16. C. The exception inside the try block becomes the primary exception since it is thrown first. Then two suppressed exceptions are added to it when trying to close the AutoCloseable resources.

17. A, B. Closeable was the original interface for IO classes. AutoCloseable was added in Java 7 along with try-with-resources. Closeable extends AutoCloseable for backward compatibility.

18. B. The main difference between AutoCloseable and Closeable is that AutoCloseable has Exception in the signature and Closeable has only IOException in the signature. Since IllegalStateException is a runtime exception, it can be thrown by any method.

19. D. Choice A is allowed because Java 7 and later "translates" Exception in a catch block to the correct one. Choices C and E are allowed because they actually catch a SQLException. Choice D is not allowed because there is no IOException declared. Choice B is allowed because a method does not have to handle an exception if it declares it.

20. E. You can create checked or unchecked exceptions. The default constructor is used if one is not supplied. There is no requirement to implement specific methods.

Chapter 7: Concurrency

1. D, F. There is no such class as ParallelStream, so A and E are incorrect. The method defined in the Stream class to create a parallel stream from an existing stream is parallel(); therefore F is correct and C is incorrect. The method defined in the Collection class to create a parallel stream from a collection is parallelStream(); therefore D is correct and B is incorrect.

2. A, C, D, F. Runnable and Callable statements both take no method arguments as input, so B is incorrect. Runnable returns void and Callable returns a generic type, so F is cor-

rect, and E and G are incorrect. All methods are capable of throwing unchecked exceptions, so A is correct. Only `Callable` is capable of throwing checked exceptions, so C is correct. Both `Runnable` and `Callable` can be implemented with lambda expressions, so D is correct.

3. B, C. The code does not compile, so A and F are incorrect. The first problem is that although a `ScheduledExecutorService` is created, it is assigned to an `ExecutorService`. Since `scheduleWithFixedDelay()` does not exist in `ExecutorService`, line w1 will not compile, and B is correct. The second problem is that `scheduleWithFixedDelay()` supports only `Runnable`, not `Callable`, and any attempt to return a value is invalid in a `Runnable` lambda expression; therefore line w2 will also not compile and C is correct. The rest of the lines compile without issue, so D and E are incorrect.

4. C. The code compiles and runs without throwing an exception or entering an infinite loop, so D, E, and F are incorrect. The key here is that the increment operator `++` is not atomic. While the first part of the output will always be 100, the second part is nondeterministic. It could output any value from 1 to 100, because the threads can overwrite each other's work. Therefore, C is the correct answer and A and B are incorrect.

5. D. Livelock occurs when two or more threads are conceptually blocked forever, although they are each still active and trying to complete their task. A race condition is an undesirable result that occurs when two tasks are completed at the same time, which should have been completed sequentially. For these reasons, D is the only correct answer.

6. B. If a task is submitted to a thread executor, and the thread executor does not have any available threads, the call to the task will return immediately with the task being queued internally by the thread executor. For this reason, B is the only correct answer.

7. A. The code compiles without issue, so D is incorrect. The `CopyOnWriteArrrayList` class is designed to preserve the original list on iteration, so the first loop will be executed exactly three times and E is incorrect. The `ConcurrentSkipListSet` class allows modifications while iterating, so it is possible that the second loop could generate an infinite loop. In this case, though, the second loop executes exactly four times, since elements in a set are unique and 5 can be added only once. For these reasons, F and G are also incorrect. Finally, despite using the elements of l1 to populate the collections, l2 and s3 are not backed by the original list, so the size of l1 is 3. Likewise, the size of l2 is 6 and the size of s3 is 4, so A is the correct answer.

8. G. The code compiles and runs without issue, so C, D, E, F, and H are incorrect. There are two important things to notice: first, synchronizing on the first output doesn't actually impact the results of the code. Second, sorting on a parallel stream does not mean that `findAny()` will return the first record. The `findAny()` method will return the value from the first thread that retrieves a record. Therefore, the output is not guaranteed for either serial or parallel stream. Since the results cannot be predicted ahead of time, G is the correct answer.

9. A, C, E. The code compiles without issue, so F is incorrect. Note that the `compute()` method is `protected` in the parent class, although you can override it with `public` without issue since this is a more accessible modifier. Since `compute()` returns a value,

RecursiveTask must be inherited instead of RecursiveAction, so C is correct and B is incorrect. The code does correctly find the minimum value on a non-empty array without entering an infinite loop, so A is correct and D is incorrect. Finally, since the code calls join() immediately after fork(), causing the process to wait, it does not perform any faster if there are 100 threads versus 1 thread, so E is also correct.

10. C. The code does not compile, so A and E are incorrect. The problem here is that c1 is a String but c2 is an int, so the code fails to combine on line q2, since calling length() on an int is not allowed, and C is correct. The rest of the lines compile without issue. Note that calling parallel() on an already parallel is allowed, and it may in fact return the same object.

11. A, F. The code compiles without issue, so D and E are incorrect. Since both tasks are submitted to the same thread executor pool, the order cannot be determined, so B and C are incorrect and A is correct. The key here is that the way the resources o1 and o2 are synchronized, a deadlock could appear if the first thread gets o1 and the second thread gets o2; therefore F is correct. The code cannot produce a livelock, since both threads are waiting, so G is incorrect. Finally, if a deadlock does occur, an exception will not be thrown, so H is incorrect.

12. E. The program compiles without issue, so B, C, and D are incorrect. Lines m2 and m3 throw a compiler warning about generics but still compile. Notice that RecursiveAction, unlike RecursiveTask, does not return a value. However, since we used a generic ForkJoinTask reference, the code still compiles. The issue here is that the base condition is not reached since the numbers start/end are consistently positive. This causes an infinite loop, although since memory is finite, Java detects this and throws a StackOverflowError, so E is correct. In practice, this could also generate a locking exception before the StackOverflowError when the program runs out of memory, but in either circumstance, the program will exit.

13. A, G. The code compiles and runs without issue, so C, D, E, and F are incorrect. The collect() operation groups the animals into those that do and do not start with the letter p. Note that there are four animals that do not start with the letter p and three animals that do. The negation operator ! before the startsWith() method means that results are reversed, so the output is 3 4 and A is correct, making B incorrect. Finally, the stream created by flatMap() is a new stream that is not parallel by default, even though its elements are parallel streams. Therefore, the performance will be single-threaded and G is correct.

14. D. The methods on line 5, 6, 7, and 8 each throw InterruptedException, which is a checked exception; therefore the method does not compile and C is the only correct answer. If the method signature was updated to include throws InterruptedException, then the answer would be F, because the deque may be blocked at runtime when the offerFirst(), offerLast(), pollFirst(), and pollLast() operations are called. Finally, if they were not blocked and there were no other operations on the deque, then the output would be 20 85, and the answer would be A.

15. C, E, G. A Callable lambda expression takes no values and returns a generic type; therefore C, E, and G are correct. A and F are incorrect because they both take an input parameter. B is a Runnable lambda expression, because it does not return a value, but it is not a

Callable one, so B is incorrect. D is not a valid lambda expression, because it is missing a semicolon at the end of the return statement, which is required when inside braces {}.

16. F, H. The application compiles and does not throw an exception, so B, C, D, E, and G are incorrect. Even though the stream is processed in sequential order, the tasks are submitted to a thread executor, which may complete the tasks in any order. Therefore, the output cannot be determined ahead of time and F is correct, making A incorrect. Finally, the thread executor is never shut down; therefore the code will run but it will never terminate, making H also correct.

17. B. The code compiles and runs without issue, so D, E, F, and G are incorrect. The key aspect to notice in the code is that a single-thread executor is used, meaning that no task will be executed concurrently. Therefore, the results are valid and predictable with 100 100 being the output, and B is the correct answer. If a pooled thread executor was used with at least two threads, then the sheepCount2++ operations could overwrite each other, making the second value indeterminate at the end of the program. In this case, C would be the correct answer.

18. F. The code compiles without issue, so B, C, and D are incorrect. The limit on the cyclic barrier is 10, but the stream can generate only up to 9 threads that reach the barrier; therefore the limit can never be reached, and F is the correct answer, making A and E incorrect. Note that even if the limit(9) statement was changed to limit(10), the program could still hang, since the JVM might not allocate 10 threads to the parallel stream.

19. A, F. The class compiles without issue so A is correct, and B and C are incorrect. The synchronized object on line k1 is TicketManager.class, while the synchronized object on line k4 is the instance of TicketManager. The class is not thread-safe because the makeTicketsAvailable() method is not synchronized, and E is incorrect. One thread could call sellTickets() while another thread has unblocked accessed to makeTicketsAvailable(), causing an invalid number of tickets to be reached as part of a race condition. Finally, F is correct because the class synchronizes using a static getInstance() method, preventing more than one instance from being created.

20. A, D. By itself, concurrency does not guarantee which task will be completed first, so A is correct. Furthermore, applications with numerous resource requests will often be stuck waiting for a resource, which allows other tasks to run. Therefore, they tend to benefit more from concurrency than CPU-intensive tasks, so D is also correct. B is incorrect because concurrency may in fact make an application slower if it is truly single-threaded in nature. Keep in mind that there is a cost associated with allocating additional memory and CPU time to manage the concurrent process. C is incorrect because single-processor CPUs have been benefiting from concurrency for decades. Finally, E is incorrect; there are numerous examples in this chapter of concurrent tasks sharing memory.

21. A, C, D, E. The code compiles and runs without issue, so G and H are incorrect. The return type of performCount() is Integer, so the submit() is interpreted as being applied to a Callable<Integer> value. In this manner, the Future<?> is really a Future<Integer> object. One possible implementation of performCount() is just to return the input parameter; therefore A is a correct answer. B is incorrect, because the return type is Integer, not Boolean. The performCount() method could just return null, so C is a correct choice.

The performCount() can also throw a runtime exception; therefore D is also a correct answer. It is also possible for our performCount() to hang indefinitely, such as in a deadlock. This would cause Future.get() to hang in printResults(), making E also a correct answer. Finally, any exception thrown in performCount() will appear as an exception in the get() operation. Since the get() operations are caught in a try/catch block in printResults(), none of them will be unhandled, and F is incorrect.

22. F. The key to solving this question is to remember that the execute() method returns void, not a Future object. Therefore, line n1 does not compile and F is the correct answer. If the submit() method had been used instead of execute(), then C would have been the correct answer, as the output of submit(Runnable) task is a Future<?> object which can only return null on its get() method.

Chapter 8: IO

1. A, D. The reference is for an InputStream object, so only a high-level input Stream class is permitted. B is incorrect because FileInputStream is a low-level stream that interacts directly with a file resource, not a stream resource. C and F are incorrect because you cannot use BufferedReader/BufferedWriter directly on a stream. E is incorrect because the reference is to an InputStream, not an OutputStream. A and D are the only correct options. Note that a BufferedInputStream can be wrapped twice, since high-level streams can take other high-level streams.

2. B, E, F. The method returns a char[] array so that the password value never enters the reusable String pool in memory, and the value can be immediately erased from memory after use. E and F support this principle. The result is that the value is more secure, so B is also correct. If the value did enter the reusable String pool, it might stay in memory long after the method using it completed, meaning that a memory dump of the application could retrieve it. A, C, and D are incorrect and not features of the readPassword() method.

3. C, D. A Console object is created by the JVM. Since only one exists, it is a singleton, making option C correct. If the program is run in an environment without a console, System.console() returns null, making D also correct. The other statements about Console are incorrect.

4. C. The readLine() method returns a String and reads a line of input from the console. readPassword() returns a char[]. The others do not exist.

5. B, D, E. This is correct code for reading a line from the console and writing it back out to the console, making option B correct. Options D and E are also correct. If no console is available, a NullPointerException is thrown. The append() method throws an IOException.

6. A, E. The first statement is the definition of deserialization, so A is correct. B is incorrect, because you may mark (or not mark) a class as serializable for a variety of reasons. C is incorrect because the Serializable interface has no method requirements, and any class

can implement the interface. D is also incorrect, because the `Serializable` interface may be extended by your own interface. Finally, E is correct, because the exception may be thrown within the `readObject()` even if the result is not cast.

7. D. The root directory is the top-level directory; therefore D is correct. The rest of the statements are invalid or incorrect.

8. A. Paths that begin with the root directory are absolute paths, so A is correct and C is incorrect. B is incorrect because the path could be a file or directory within the file system. A `File` object may refer to a path that does not exist within the file system, so D and E are incorrect.

9. A. First, the class must implement the `Serializable` interface, so A is correct. `Serializable` is not a class; therefore B is incorrect. Creating a `static serialVersionUID` variable is optional and recommended, but it is not required for use with the `ObjectOutputStream`, so C is incorrect. Every instance variable must either be `Serializable` or be marked `transient`, but all variables are not required to be either, so D and E are incorrect. F is incorrect, because the class must be `Serializable` and have instance members that are `Serializable` or marked `transient`.

10. C, F. The code compiles, so D and E are incorrect. There is a bug in the method in that `file.delete()` should be executed at the end of the method for both files and directories alike. As written, the method will delete all files within a directory but none of the directories themselves. Therefore, A and B are incorrect and C is correct. F is correct, because most methods in the `File` class that interact with the file system are capable of throwing an exception at runtime, such as when the directory does not exist.

11. C, E, G. To move a file using `java.io.File`, you should use the `renameTo()` method, since there are no `move()` or `mv()` methods. Therefore, E is correct, and A and D are incorrect. To create a directory or chain of directories using `java.io.File`, you should use `mkdir()` or `mkdirs()`, respectively, because there is no `createDirectory()` method. Therefore, C and G are correct, and B is incorrect. Finally, there is no `copy()` method in the `java.io.File` class, so F is incorrect. Copying a file with `java.io` would require reading the contents using a stream.

12. B, C. Option B is correct because Java requires a backslash to be escaped with another backslash. Option C is also correct because Java will convert the slashes to the right one when working with paths.

13. A, C, E. The `System` class has three streams: `in` is for input, `err` is for error, and `out` is for output. Therefore A, C, and E are correct. The others do not exist.

14. E. `PrintWriter` is the only `Writer` class that you need to know that doesn't have a complementary `Reader` class, so E is correct.

15. A. This code compiles and runs without issue, so C and E are incorrect. It uses a try-with-resource block to open the `FileReader` and `BufferedReader` objects. Therefore, both get closed automatically, and D is incorrect. The body of the `try` block reads in the first line of the file and outputs it to the user. Therefore, A is correct. Since the rest of the file is not read, B is incorrect.

16. D, F. Any class, abstract, concrete, or `final`, can be marked `Serializable`, so A, B, and E are incorrect. Classes can implement multiple interfaces, so C is also incorrect. D is correct, because process-heavy classes would be difficult to serialize since it may involve managing multiple threads. F is also correct because serialization of an object stores only the instance variable data, not the `static` class data. In other words, serializing an object throws away the `static` class data.

17. A, B, D, G. `ObjectOutputStream` and `ObjectInputStream` perform serialization and deserialization on a low-level stream, respectively, so A and G are correct. `PrintStream` and `PrintWriter` format text for a low-level `OutputStream` and `Writer`, respectively, so B and D are also correct. `FileWriter` and `FileInputStream` operate on a file directly and are low-level streams, so C and F are incorrect. Finally, `OutputStream` is an abstract parent class and is neither high-level nor low-level, so E is incorrect.

18. B, D, E. `Console` defines two output methods, `format()` and `printf()`, that are identical in function, so B and D are correct. A, C, and F are each incorrect, because there is no such method with that name defined in the `Console` class. You can also use the `writer()` method to gain access to the `Console`'s `PrintWriter` object, so E is correct.

19. B, C, D. Since you need to write primitives and `String` values, the `OutputStream` classes are appropriate. Therefore, you can eliminate A and F since they are not `OutputStream` classes. Next, `DirectoryStream` is not a `java.io` class, so E is incorrect. As you shall see in the next chapter, `DirectoryStream` is an NIO.2 class. The data should be written to the file directly using the `FileOutputStream` class, buffered with the `BufferedOutputStream` class and automatically serialized with the `ObjectOutputStream` class, so B, C, and D are correct. G is incorrect because it is not related to this task. We include it as an option to help you adapt to situations on the exam where you may come across a class with which you are not familiar. Just answer as best you can, based on what you know.

20. A, C. Character stream classes often include built-in convenience methods for working with `String` data, so A is correct. They also handle character encoding automatically, so C is also correct. The rest of the statements are irrelevant or incorrect and are not properties of all character streams.

21. A, C. The code compiles and runs without issue, so F and G are incorrect. Note that `serialUID` is not the same as `serialVersionUID`, although since `serialVersionUID` is recommended but not required, this does not pose any compilation issues. Just be aware that `serialUID` will not be used by the serialization process for version control. The `name` variable and `age` variable are both `transient`, which means that their values will not be saved upon serialization. Upon deserialization, the default initializations and constructor will be skipped, and they will both be `null`; therefore A and C are correct. B is incorrect because `tail` is not `transient` and could be set by a caller before being serialized. D is also incorrect because a serialized empty array is not the same as a `null` pointer. Even though these non-transient fields could be set to `null`, they are not guaranteed to be `null` after deserialization. E is incorrect because the `static` value will not be serialized; it will be available on the class after deserialization.

22. E. First off, even though the `Bird` class implements `Serializable`, it does not define a `static serialVersionUID` variable, which is recommended but not required; therefore

it compiles without issue and F is incorrect. The code also runs without issue, so G is incorrect. The key here is that Java will call the constructor for the first non-serializable no-argument parent class during deserialization, skipping any constructors and default initializations for serializable classes in between, including Eagle and Bird itself. Therefore, Object() is the first constructor called. All default initializations are skipped, so A, B, C, and D are all incorrect. Since the name is marked transient, the deserialized value is null and E is correct. H is also incorrect, because the caller cannot change the serialized value of name with setName(), since name is marked transient.

23. H. Not all java.io streams support the mark() operation; therefore, without calling mark-Supported() on the stream, the result is unknown until runtime. If the stream does support the mark() operation, then the result would be XYZY, because the reset() operation puts the stream back in the position before the mark() was called, and skip(1) will skip X, and E would be correct. If the stream does not support the mark() operation, a runtime exception would likely be thrown, and G would be correct. Since you don't know if the input stream supports the mark() operation, H is the only correct choice.

Chapter 9: NIO.2

1. F. The code snippet will not compile due to a bug on the first and second lines. The first line should use Paths.get(), because there is no method Path.get(). The second line passes a String to relativize() instead of a Path object. If both lines were corrected to use Paths.get(), then the correct answer would be A. Remember that the normalize() method, like most methods in the Path interface, does not modify the Path object, but instead it returns a new Path object. If it was corrected to reassign the new value to the existing path variable, then E would be correct.

2. B, C. The code snippet compiles without issue, so F is incorrect. If the value refers to a regular file, isDirectory() will return false and the statement will be skipped, so A is incorrect. Likewise, if the directory does not exist, the method also returns false, so E is also incorrect. A symbolic link can point to a real directory, and by default isDirectory() follows links, so B is possible. In this case, the symbolic link, not the directory, would be deleted. C is also possible and is the simple case of deleting an empty directory. D would allow the code to reach the execution block of the if/then statement, but the method deleteIfExists() would throw a DirectoryNotEmptyException if it had contents.

3. D. The setTimes() method is available only on BasicFileAttributeView, not the read-only BasicFileAttributes class, so line 4 will not compile and D is correct. You need to retrieve an instance of the view class to update the data. The rest of the lines compile without issue and only D is correct.

4. C. First off, the code compiles without issue, so G is incorrect. Let's take this one step at a time. First, the subpath() method is applied to the absolute path, which returns the relative path animals/bear. Next, the getName() method is applied to the relative path, and since this is indexed from zero, it returns the relative path bear. Finally, the toAbsolutePath()

method is applied to the relative path bear, resulting in the current directory being incorporated into the path. The final output is the absolute path /user/home/bear, so C is correct.

5. B, C, D. The first clause of the if/then statement will be true only if the target of the symbolic link, /mammal/kangaroo, exists, since by default isDirectory() follows symbolic links, so B is correct. Option A is incorrect because /mammal/kangaroo may not exist or /mammal/kangaroo/joey may already exist. If /mammal/kangaroo does exist, then the directory will be created at /mammal/kangaroo/joey, and because the symbolic link would be accessible as /kang/joey, C and D are both correct. E is incorrect, because the code compiles without issue. F is incorrect because the code may throw an exception at runtime, such as when the file system is unavailable or locked for usage; thus it is not guaranteed to throw an exception at runtime.

6. C. The code does not compile since the stream output by Files.walk() is Stream<Path>, therefore we need a Predictate, not a BiPredicate, on line w1, and the answer is C. If the Files.find() method had been used instead, and the lambda had been passed as an argument to the method instead of on filter(), the output would be B, Has Sub-directory, since the directory is given to be empty. For fun, we reversed the expected output of the ternary operation to make sure that you understood the process.

7. F. The code compiles without issue, so D and E are incorrect. The method Files.isSame-File() first checks to see if the Path values are the same in terms of equals(). Since the first path is relative and the second path is absolute, this comparison will return false, forcing isSameFile() to check for the existence of both paths in the file system. Since we know /zoo/turkey does not exist, a NoSuchFileException is thrown and F is the correct answer. A, B, and C are incorrect since an exception is thrown at runtime.

8. A. The code compiles and runs without issue, so E is incorrect. For this question, you have to remember two things. First, the resolve() method does not normalize any path symbols, so C and D are not correct. Second, calling resolve() with an absolute path as a parameter returns the absolute path, so A is correct and B is incorrect.

9. B, C. The methods are not the same, because Files.lines() returns a Stream<Path> and Files.readAllLines() returns a List<String>, so F is incorrect. A is incorrect, because performance is not often the reason to prefer one to the other. Files.lines() reads the file in a lazy manner, while Files.readAllLines() reads the entire file into memory all at once; therefore Files.lines() works better on large files with limited memory available, and B is correct. Although a List can be converted to a stream with the stream() method, this requires an extra step; therefore C is correct since the resulting object can be chained directly to a stream. Finally, D and E are incorrect because they are not relevant to these methods.

10. C, E. The REPLACE_EXISTING flag was not provided, so if the target exists, it will throw an exception at runtime and A is incorrect. Next, the NOFOLLOW_LINKS option means that if the source is a symbolic link, the link itself and not the target will be copied at runtime, so B is also incorrect. The option ATOMIC_MOVE means that any process monitoring the file system will not see an incomplete file during the move, so C is correct. D is incorrect, since you could rename a file not to have an extension. Note that in this example, if monkey.txt is a file, then the resulting /animals would be a file, not a directory. Likewise, if the source

is a directory, the result would also be a directory. E is correct, because moving always preserves the metadata even if the COPY_ATTRIBUTES flag is not set.

11. A. The code compiles and runs without issue, so C, D, E, and F are incorrect. Even though the file is copied with attributes preserved, the file is considered a separate file, so the output is false and A is correct and B is incorrect. Remember, isSameFile() returns true only if the files pointed to in the file system are the same, without regard to the file contents.

12. A, F. For this question, you need to rule out the answers that *can* be used to obtain a Path instance. D and G both use the Paths.get() method, one with optional vararg values. C uses an overloaded version of Paths.get() that takes a URI. B is a longer form for getting a Path using a specific file system, in this case the default file system. Finally, E uses a method added to java.io.File to make it easily compatible with Path. The remaining choices A and F are the correct ones, because they call constructors on Path and FileSystem, respectively, instead of using the underlying factory methods. The rest are invalid since they do not use the factory methods to gain access to instances.

13. B. The code compiles and runs without issue, so C, D, E, F, and G are incorrect. Note that the sample code creates a stream, collects it as a list, and then converts it back to a stream before outputting the filenames. The key here is that the depth parameter specified as the second argument to find() is 0, meaning the only record that will be searched is the top-level directory. Since we know that the top directory is regular and not a symbolic link, no other paths will be visited and nothing will be printed. For these reasons, B is the correct answer and A is incorrect.

14. E. First off, recall that the java.io.File.listFiles() method retrieves the members of the current directory without traversing any subdirectories. The methods Path.listFiles() and Files.files() do not exist, so A and D are incorrect. Files.walk() and Files.find() recursively traverse a directory tree rather than list the contents of the current directory; therefore, they are not a close match, and B and C are incorrect. Note that you could use these methods to perform the same operation if you set the depth limit to 1 and used a lambda with Files.find() that always returns true, but the question was about which method is most similar to java.io.File.listFiles(). In that regard, Files.list() is the closest match since it always reads only a single directory, and E is correct. Note that instead of an array, a stream of Path values is returned. Finally, F is incorrect because it reads the contents of a file, not a directory.

15. D, E, F. Whether a path is a symbolic link, file, or directory is not relevant, so A and C are incorrect. Using a view to read multiple attributes leads to fewer round-trips between the process and the file system and better performance, so D and F are correct. For reading single attributes, there is little or no expected gain, so B is incorrect. Finally, views can be used to access file system–specific attributes that are not available in java.nio.Files methods; therefore E is correct.

16. F. The code compiles without issue, so B, C, and D are incorrect. The code snippet breaks a file into lines and then further separates the lines by commas using the flatMap() method. The result is printed with one entry on a single line, but all original line breaks and commas from the file are removed; therefore F is correct. Since we are told that the file is non-empty and regular, and the program has access to read it, A and E are incorrect.

17. A, G. The code compiles without issue, so B, C, and D are incorrect. The first line actually resolves to the root path since `..` and `getParent()` are conceptually equivalent. Therefore, G is correct and E and F are incorrect. A is also correct since it may encounter a file that it does not have access to read, which is common when trying to read an entire file system.

18. D. The code compiles and runs without issue, so F is incorrect. The one thing to notice about these paths is that they represent the same path within the file system. Therefore, `isSameFile()` would return `true` and B and C are incorrect. The second output is `false`, because `Path.equals()` does not resolve the path within the file system, so A is incorrect. Finally, the normalized paths are `equals()`, since all extra symbols have been removed; therefore D is correct and E is incorrect.

19. A, C, E. While all of the answers are applicable to the NIO.2, only A, C, and E are options that are not supported by the legacy `java.io.File` class and therefore give NIO.2 an advantage over `java.io.File`.

20. B. The `normalize()` method does not convert a relative path into an absolute path; therefore, the path value after the first line is just the current directory symbol. The `for()` loop iterates the name values, but since there is only one entry, the loop terminates after a single iteration. Therefore, B is correct and the rest of the answers are incorrect.

Chapter 10: JDBC

1. B, F. The `Driver`, `Connection`, `Statement`, and `ResultSet` interfaces are part of the JDK, making choices A and E incorrect. The concrete `DriverManager` class is also part of the JDK, making choices C and D incorrect. Choices B and F are correct since the implementation of these interfaces is part of the database-specific driver JAR file.

2. B, C. A JDBC URL has three parts. The first part is the string `jdbc`, making choice C correct. The second part is the vendor/product name. The third part is database specific, but it includes a database name, making choice B correct as well. The location, such as IP address and port, is optional.

3. A. A JDBC URL has three main parts separated by single colons, making choices B, C, E, and F incorrect. The first part is always `jdbc`. Therefore, the correct answer is A. Notice that you can get this right even if you've never heard of the Sybase database before.

4. E. Starting with JDBC 4.0, driver implementations were required to provide the name of the class implementing `Driver` in a file named `java.sql.Driver` in the directory `META-INF/service`.

5. C. A `Connection` is created using a static method on `DriverManager`. It does not use a constructor. Therefore, choice C is correct. If the `Connection` was created properly, the answer would be choice B.

6. B, E. `Class.forName()` was used with old JDBC drivers to load the driver. It is not needed in JDBC 4.0, making choice A incorrect. If it is called, it throws a `ClassNotFoundException`. By contrast, `DriverManager.getConnection()` throws a `SQLException` when the driver cannot be found. Therefore, choices B and E are correct.

7. C, E, F. The first parameter is the `ResultSet` type. The second parameter is the `ResultSet` concurrency mode. Choices A and B are incorrect because they represent the second parameter. Choice D is incorrect because it is not a constant in JDBC. Choices C, E, and F are correct.

8. E. When a `Statement` is requested with an unsupported mode, the JDBC driver will downgrade the request to one that is supported. Therefore, choice E is correct. No exception is thrown. Furthermore, choices B and D are incorrect because exceptions with those names do not exist.

9. B. The first line has a return type of boolean because any type of SQL statement can be run, making it an `execute()` call. The second line returns the number of modified rows, making it an `executeUpdate()` call. The third line returns the results of a query, making it an `executeQuery()` call.

10. C. This code works as expected. It updates each of the five rows in the table and returns the number of rows updated. Therefore, choice C is correct.

11. D. JDBC code throws a `SQLException`, which is a checked exception. The code does not handle or declare this exception, and therefore it doesn't compile. If the exception were handled or declared, the answer would be choice C.

12. D. JDBC resources should be closed in the reverse order from that in which they were opened. The order for opening is `Connection`, `Statement`, and `ResultSet`. The order for closing is `ResultSet`, `Statement`, and `Connection`.

13. D. A `Statement` automatically closes the open `ResultSet` when another SQL statement is run. This means that rs is no longer open by the `println`, and a `SQLException` is thrown because the `ResultSet` is closed.

14. B, F. In a `ResultSet`, columns are indexed starting with 1, not 0. Therefore, choices A, C, and E are incorrect. There are methods to get the column as a `String` or `Object`. However, choice D is incorrect because an `Object` cannot be assigned to a `String` without a cast.

15. F. Choices B, C, and D are incorrect because they are not JDBC methods. Choice A is incorrect because it outputs just the month, date, and year. Choice E is incorrect because it outputs just the hours, minutes, and seconds.

16. E. By default, a `Statement` is not scrollable. The first call to `previous()` throws a `SQLException` because the `ResultSet` type is `TYPE_FORWARD_ONLY`.

17. C, D. Choices B and E are incorrect because those methods don't exist. Choices A and F are incorrect because these methods return a boolean. Choices C and D are correct.

18. A. The call to `absolute(0)` moves the cursor to a location immediately before the results, and then `next()` goes to the first row, so the answer is choice A.

19. C. The first `println` outputs `false` because the cursor is immediately before the result. The second `println` outputs `true` because the cursor is pointing to the fifth row. The third `println` outputs `true` because the cursor is pointing to the fourth row. The fourth `println` outputs `true` because the cursor is pointing to the second row. The fifth `println` outputs `false` because the cursor is located before the beginning of the result.

20. F. The first and last `println` statements do not compile. The `beforeFirst()` and `afterLast()` methods have a void return type. Therefore, the code does not compile and choice F is correct.

Appendix B

Study Tips

This appendix offers suggestions and recommendations for how to prepare for the certification exam. Since you need to hold a previous Java certification in order to take the OCP exam, we expect that if you are reading this book, this will not be your first Java certification exam. We recommend that you review this appendix, as it provides tips and strategies specific to the OCP exam, especially if you took your last Java certification exam a long time ago.

Studying for the Test

Before you even sign up to take the test, you need to study the material. Studying includes the following tasks:

- Creating a study plan
- Reading the Study Guide material
- Creating and running sample applications
- Solving the Review Questions at the end of each chapter
- Creating flashcards and/or using the ones we've provided
- Taking the three practice exams

The book is divided into chapters, each with corresponding exam objectives, to make it easier to assimilate. The early chapters define the building blocks of Java 8, while the later chapters present commonly used Java 8 frameworks. Unless we explicitly state something is out of scope for the exam, you will be required to have a strong understanding of all of the information in this book.

Creating a Study Plan

Rome wasn't built in a day, so you shouldn't attempt to study for the exam in only one day. Even if you have been certified with a previous version of Java, the new test includes features and components unique to Java 8 that are covered in this text.

Once you have decided to take the test (which we assume that you have already done since you're reading this book), you should construct a study plan that fits with your schedule. We recommend that you set aside some amount of time each day, even if it's just a few minutes during lunch, to read or practice for the exam. The idea is to keep your momentum going throughout the exam preparation process. The more consistent you are in how you study, the better prepared you will be for the exam. Try to avoid taking a few days or weeks off from studying, or you're likely to spend a lot of time relearning existing material instead of moving on to new material.

Let's say that you begin studying on January 1. Assuming that you allot two weeks per chapter, you could use the study plan that we constructed in Table B.1 as a schedule throughout the study process. Of course, if you've been programming in Java only a short time, two weeks per chapter may not be enough; if you're an experienced Java developer, you may need only a few days per chapter.

TABLE B.1   Sample study plan

Date	Task
January 1–January 11	Read Introduction, Appendix B, and Chapter 1
January 12–January 14	Answer Chapter 1 Review Questions
January 15–January 25	Read Chapter 2
January 26–January 28	Answer Chapter 2 Review Questions
January 29–February 8	Read Chapter 3
February 9–February 11	Answer Chapter 3 Review Questions
February 12–February 22	Read Chapter 4
February 23–February 25	Answer Chapter 4 Review Questions
February 26–March 8	Read Chapter 5
March 9–March 11	Answer Chapter 5 Review Questions
March 12–March 22	Read Chapter 6
March 23–March 25	Answer Chapter 6 Review Questions
March 26–April 5	Read Chapter 7
April 6–April 8	Answer Chapter 7 Review Questions
April 9–April 19	Read Chapter 8

TABLE B.1   Sample study plan *(continued)*

Date	Task
April 20–April 22	Answer Chapter 8 Review Questions
April 23–May 3	Read Chapter 9
May 4–May 6	Answer Chapter 9 Review Questions
May 7–May 17	Read Chapter 10
May 18–May 20	Answer Chapter 10 Review Questions
May 21–May 28	Take practice exams and practice with flashcards
May 29	Take exam

Your own study plan will vary based on your familiarity with Java, your personal and work schedules, and your learning abilities. It also may change if you are studying for an upgrade exam, which may emphasize some chapters more than others with a slightly different set of objectives. See Appendix C, "Upgrading from Java 6 or Earlier," for more information about the Java upgrade exams. The idea is to create a plan early on that has self-imposed deadlines, which you can follow throughout the studying process. When someone asks how you're doing preparing for the exam, you should have a strong sense of what you've learned so far, what you're currently studying, and how many weeks you need to be prepared to the take the exam.

Comparing Previous Exams

For those who already have a Java 6 or earlier certification, or for those who have only taken an OCA exam, be aware that the OCP exam is a lot more comprehensive than the previous exams that you have taken. Even if you are an experienced Java developer, the OCP exam may include numerous topics that you have never used before, such as NIO.2, the Concurrency API, and JDBC to name just a few. We recommend allocating a lot more time to study for this exam than for the OCA certification.

If you are OCP 7 certified already, then most of the new stuff that you need to study revolves around lambdas, streams, and the date/time changes in Java 8. Since lambda and streams methods have been added to nearly every Java framework covered by the exam, we recommend reading the book thoroughly to make sure that you don't miss any methods or frameworks new to Java 8.

Creating and Running Sample Applications

Although some people can learn Java just by reading a textbook, that's not how we recommend that you study for a certification exam. We want you to be writing your own Java sample applications throughout this book so that you don't just learn the material, but that you understand the material as well. For example, it may not be obvious why the following line of code does not compile, but if you try to compile it yourself, the Java compiler will tell you the problem.

```
float value = 102.0;    // DOES NOT COMPILE
```

In this section, we will discuss how to test Java code and the tools available to assist you in this process.

A lot of people post the question "Why does this code not compile?" on the CodeRanch.com forum. We encourage you to post the compiler error message any time you need help. We also recommend that you read the compiler message when posting, since it may provide meaningful information about why the code failed to compile.

In the previous example, the compiler failed to compile with the message Type mismatch: cannot convert from double to float. This message indicates that you are trying to convert a double value, 102.0, to a float variable reference using an implicit cast. If you add an explicit cast to (float) or change the value to 102.0f, the code will compile without issue.

Sample Test Class

Throughout this book, we present numerous code snippets and ask you whether they'll compile or not and what their output will be. You will place these snippets inside a simple Java application that starts, executes the code, and terminates. You can accomplish this by compiling and running a public class containing a public static void main(String[] args) method and adding the necessary import statements, such as the following:

```
// Add any necessary import statements here

public class TestClass {
    public static void main(String[] args) {
        // Add test code here

        // Add any print statements here
```

```
    System.out.println("Hello World!");
  }
}
```

This application isn't particularly interesting—it just outputs "Hello World!" and exits. That said, you could insert many of the code snippets presented in this book in the main() method to determine if the code compiles, as well as what the code outputs when it does compile. We strongly recommend that you become familiar with this sample application, so much so that you could write it from memory without the comments.

We recommend that while reading this book you make note of any sections that you do not fully understand and revisit them when in front of a computer screen with a Java compiler and Java runtime. You should start by copying the code snippet into your test class and then try experimenting with the code as much as possible. For example, we indicated that the previous sample line of code would not compile, but would any of the following compile?

```
float value1 = 102;
float value2 = (int)102.0;
float value3 = 1f * 0.0;
float value4 = 1f * (short)0.0;
float value5 = 1f * (boolean)0;
```

Try out these samples on your computer, and see if the result matches your expectation. Here's a hint: Two of these fives lines will not compile.

 Real World Scenario

IDE Software

While studying for the exam, you should develop code using a text editor and command-line Java compiler. Some of you may have prior experience with Integrated Development Environments (IDEs) such as Eclipse or IntelliJ. An IDE is a software application that facilitates software development for computer programmers.

Although such tools are extremely valuable in developing software, they can interfere with your ability to spot problems readily on the exam. For example, when a line of code does not compile, the IDE will often underline it in red, whereas on the exam, you'll have to find the line that does not compile, if there is one, on your own.

If you do choose to study with an IDE, make sure that you understand everything it is doing in the background for you. For the exam, you'll need to know how to compile code manually from the command line, and this experience is rarely learned using an IDE. You'll also need to understand why the code does not compile without relying on the tips and suggestions provided by the IDE.

Identifying Your Weakest Link

The best advice that we can give you to do well on the exam is to practice writing sample applications that push the limits of what you already know, as much and as often as possible. For example, if the previous samples with float values were too difficult for you, then you should spend even more time studying numeric promotion and casting expressions.

Prior to taking the OCP exam, you may already be an experienced Java developer, but there is a difference between being able to write Java code and being an Oracle Certified Java Programmer. For example, you may have never used JDBC, but since it is on the exam, you need to understand the basics. You may also be unaware of some of the more complex features that exist within the Java language. On top of that, there are new features of Java 8, such as lambda expressions and default interface methods, which experienced developers are just beginning to embrace.

The Review Questions in each chapter are designed to help you hone in on those features of the Java language where you may be weak and that are required knowledge for the exam. For each chapter, you should note which questions you got wrong, understand why you got them wrong, and study those areas even more.

Often, the reason you got a question wrong on the exam is that you did not fully understand the concept. Many topics in Java have subtle rules that you often need to see for yourself to truly understand. For example, you cannot write a class that implements two interfaces that define the same default method unless you override the default method in the class. Writing and attempting to compile your own sample interfaces and classes that reference the default method may illuminate this concept far better than it could ever be explained.

Finally, we find that developers who practice writing code while studying for the Java certification tend to write better Java code in their professional careers. Anyone can write a Java class that can compile, but just because a class compiles does not mean it is well designed. For example, imagine a class where all class methods and variables were declared public simply because the developer did not understand the other access modifiers, such as protected and private. Studying for the certification helps you learn those features that may not only be applicable in your daily coding experience but also that you never knew existed within the Java language.

"Overstudying" Practice Exams

Although we recommend reading this book and writing your own sample applications multiple times, redoing practice exams over and over can have a negative impact in the long run. For example, some individuals study the practice exam questions so much that they end up memorizing them. In this scenario, they can easily become overconfident; that is, they can achieve perfect scores on the practice exams but may fail the actual exam.

If you get a practice exam question correct, you should move on, and if you get it incorrect, you should review the part of the chapter that covers it until you can answer it correctly. For legal reasons we cannot publish real exam questions, so it is important that you learn the material on which questions are based.

On the other hand, we recommend that you repeat Review Questions as often as you like to master a chapter. Review Questions are designed to teach you important concepts in the chapter, and you should understand them completely before leaving a section. Furthermore, they help improve your ability to recognize certain types of problems present in many code snippets.

Taking the Test

Studying how to take a test can be just as important as the studying the material itself. For example, you could answer every question correctly but only make it halfway through the exam, resulting in a failing score! This section contains notes that are relevant to many software certification exams.

Understanding the Question

The majority of questions on the exam will contain code snippets and ask you to answer questions about them. For those items containing code snippets, the number-one question we recommend that you answer before attempting to solve the question is this:

Does the Code Compile?

It sounds simple, but many people dive into answering the question without checking whether or not the code actually compiles. If you can determine whether or not a particular set of code compiles, and what line or lines cause it to not compile, answering the question often becomes easy.

Although we recommend first checking for compilation problems, be aware that, unlike the OCA exam, the OCP does not focus as much on syntactical issues. The OCP exam tends to emphasize conceptual topics that require detailed knowledge of a framework or API. For example, you need to understand the difference between intermediate and terminal stream operations and why you can apply only one terminal operation on a stream. In this manner, the OCP exam tends to have more answers that throw an exception at runtime or cannot be predicted ahead of time.

That's not to say that there won't be any questions that rely solely on basic syntax and determining whether or not the code compiles. The exam expects you to be able to do both in a short amount of time. You should get into the habit of quickly scanning a code block to look for compiler issues, as you did on previous exams, before trying to understand what the code actually does.

Checking the Answers

To determine whether the code will compile, you should briefly review the answer choices to see what options are available. If there are no choices of the form "The code does not compile," then you can be reasonably assured that all of the lines of the code will compile and you do not need to spend time checking syntax. These questions are often, but not always, among the easiest questions because you can skip determining whether the code compiles and instead focus on what it does.

If the answer choices do include some answers of the form "Does not compile due to line w1," you should immediately focus on those lines and determine whether they compile. For example, take a look at the answer choices for the following question:

18. What is the output of the following code?
   - *Code Omitted -*

   A. Monday

   B. Tuesday

   C. Friday

   D. The code does not compile due to line w1.

   E. The code does not compile due to line w2.

The answer choices act as a guide instructing you to focus on line w1 or line w2 for compilation errors. If the question indicates only one answer choice is allowed, it also tells you that at most only one line of code contains a compilation problem and the other line is correct. Although the reason line w1 or line w2 may not compile could be related to other lines of code, the key is that those other lines do not throw compiler errors themselves. By quickly browsing the list of answers, you can save time by focusing only on those lines of code that are possible candidates for not compiling.

If you are able to identify a line of code that does not compile, you will be able to finish the question a lot quicker. Often, the most difficult questions are the ones where the code does in fact compile, but one of the answer choices is "Does not compile" without indicating any line numbers. In these situations, you will have to spend extra time verifying that each and every line compiles. If these questions are taking too much time, we recommend marking these for review and coming back to them later.

Eliminating Answers without Reading the Entire Question

Many times you can eliminate answer choices quickly without reading the entire question. In some cases, you may even be able to solve the question based solely on the answer choices. If you come across such questions on the exam, consider it a gift. Can you correctly answer the following question in which the application code has been left out?

5.   Which two lines, when inserted independently at line m1, allow the code to compile?
- *Code Omitted -*

A.   `public abstract final int swim();`

B.   `public abstract void swim();`

C.   `public abstract swim();`

D.   `public abstract void swim() {}`

E.   `public void swim();`

F.   `public void swim() {}`

If you remember your rules for modifiers and method declarations, this question should be easy. For example, option A declares the method both `abstract` and `final`, while option C is missing a return type; therefore, neither will compile. Options D and E also do not compile, as option D provides an implementation for an `abstract` method, while option E does not provide an implementation for a non-`abstract` method.

As the question is asking for exactly two choices, options B and F must be the correct answers since they are the only ones capable of compiling in any environment. In this manner, you can answer the question without ever reading the code.

Of course, after answering a question like this, you should still verify that your answer matches the question details. For example, some questions could ask you to choose which lines of code *do not* compile. In the previous example, options A, C, D, and E would be correct as they do not compile, instead of options B and F.

Determining What the Question Is Asking

A lot of times, a question may appear to be asking one thing but will actually be asking another. For example, the following question may appear to be asking about method overloading and abstract classes:

12.   What is the output of the following code?

```
1: abstract class Mammal {
2:     protected boolean hasFur() { return false; }
3: }
4: class Capybara implements Mammal {
5:     public boolean hasFur() { return true; }
6:     public static void main(String[] args) {
7:         System.out.println(new Capybara().hasFur());
8:     }
9: }
```

It turns out this question is a lot simpler than it looks. A class cannot implement another class—it can only extend another class—so line 4 will cause the code to fail to compile. If you notice this compiler problem early on, you'll likely be able to answer this question quickly and easily.

Taking Advantage of Context Clues

Let's face it—there will be things that you're likely to forget on the day of the exam. Between being nervous about taking the test and being a bit overtired when you read a particular chapter, you're likely to encounter at least one question where you do not have a high degree of confidence. Luckily, you do not need to score a perfect 100 percent to pass.

One advanced test-taking skill that can come in handy is to use information from one question to help you to answer another. For example, we mentioned in an earlier section that you could assume that a question's code block will compile and run if "Does not compile" and "Throws an exception at runtime" are not available in the list of answers. If you have a piece of code that you know compiles and a related piece of code that you're not so sure about, you can use information from the former question to help solve the latter question.

Use a similar strategy when a question asks which single line will not compile. If you're able to determine the line that does not compile with some degree of confidence, you can use the remaining code that you know does compile as a guide to help answer other questions.

By using context clues of other questions on the exam, you may be able to solve questions that you are unsure about more easily.

Being Suspicious of Strong Words

Many questions on the exam include answer choices with descriptive sentences rather than lines of code. When you see such questions, be wary of any answer choice that includes strong words such as "must," "all," or "cannot." If you think about the complexities of programming languages, it is rare for a rule to have no exceptions or special cases. Therefore, if you are stuck between two answers, and one of them uses "must" while the other uses "can" or "may," you are better off picking the one with the weaker word since it is a more ambiguous statement.

Take a look at the answer choices in the following sample question:

9. Which of the three following statements about interfaces are true?

  A. Interfaces *may* be marked `abstract`.

  B. Interfaces *must* be explicitly marked `abstract`.

  C. An interface *can* extend another interface.

  D. *All* interface declarations *must* include at least one method.

  E. A `default` interface method *must* have a body.

Notice the use of the words "must," "may," "can," and "all" in the answer choices. You can see that options A and B differ on degree, with option A being a much weaker statement than option B. Option C is also a somewhat general statement, as an interface can extend another interface but does not have to do so. Option D is also a very strong statement that, if true, would dictate how you define interfaces. For example, can you think of one example where you've created an interface without a method defined? If you can, it is clear that option D is incorrect.

In this example, option E, which includes "must," is actually a correct statement; that is, you cannot define a `default` method without a body. We include it as a choice to remind you that while strong words tend to indicate a false statement, they are not guaranteed to be incorrect. You should be suspicious of such answer choices but not automatically rule them out. In case you are wondering, the correct answers to this question are options A, C, and E.

Working Backwards from Answer Choices

After you have determined that the code does in fact compile, or you notice that all of the answer choices assume that the code does compile, it is time to review the flow of the program itself. It may be helpful to work backwards from the answer choices and available print statements. Trying to understand the flow of the entire program can be time consuming. By reviewing the code from the answer choices and working backwards, you might be able to disregard entire sections of the code or methods that are irrelevant to solving the problem.

Reading Code Quickly

Although you can't know ahead of time what classes will be on the exam, there are some common structures that you'll encounter on the exam that you should be familiar with. As you learned in Chapter 2, "Design Patterns and Principles," encapsulation is a common software design principle in which the attributes of a class are wrapped in getter/setter methods, as shown in the following class declaration:

```java
public class Deer {
   private int age;
   private String name;

   public Deer(int age, String name) {
      super();
      this.age = age;
      this.name = name;
   }

   public int getAge() { return age; }
   public void setAge(int age) { this.age = age; }
   public String getName() { return name; }
   public void setName(String name) { this.name = name; }
}
```

Although this might look like lot of code, what it is defining is really quite simple. It's just saying that a Deer object has two attributes, age and name, and it defines some getters/setters and a constructor for it.

You should get into the habit of reading common structures like this quickly on the exam, as it will help make especially long code segments much shorter to review. In general, the exam does not often insert compiler errors in simple getter/setter methods. Therefore, you should look for compilation problems in other parts of the code and review getters/setters only if you have ruled out everything else.

Taking Advantage of the Exam Software

The exam software includes numerous tools to assist you in taking the exam, which we will now discuss. While present in the current version of the exam, we cannot guarantee them to be available when you take the exam. With that in mind, make sure that you know how to accomplish similar tasks with the writing material provided at the testing center.

Applying the Process of Elimination

Although you might not immediately know the correct answer to a question, if you can reduce the question from five answers to three, your odds of guessing the correct answer will be markedly improved. Moreover, if you can reduce a question from four answers to two, you'll double your chances of guessing the correct answer!

The exam software allows you to eliminate answer choices by right-clicking an answer choice, which causes the text to be struck through, as shown in the following example:

A. 123

~~**B.** Elephant~~

C. Vulture

~~**D.** The code does not compile due to line n1.~~

Even better, the exam software remembers which answer choices you have eliminated anytime you go back to the question. You can undo the crossed-out answer simply by right-clicking the choice again.

Marking Answers

The exam software also includes an option to "mark" a question and review all marked questions at the end of the exam. If you are pressed for time, answer a question as best you can and then mark it to come back to later. If you finish the exam early, you have the option of reviewing the marked questions, as well as all of the questions on the exam if you so choose.

Using the Provided Writing Material

Depending on your particular testing center, you may be provided with a sheet of blank paper or a whiteboard to use to help you answer questions. In our experience, a whiteboard with marker and eraser is more commonly handed out. If you sit down and you are not provided with anything, make sure to ask for such materials.

After you have determined that the program does compile, it is time to understand what the program does! One of the most useful applications of writing material is tracking the state of primitive and reference variables. For example, let's say that you encountered the following code snippet on the exam:

```
Object o = new Turtle();
Mammal m = new Monkey();
Animal a = new Rabbit();
o = m;
```

In a situation like this, it can be helpful to draw a diagram of the current state of the variable references, as shown in Figure B.1.

FIGURE B.1   Tracking objects and references

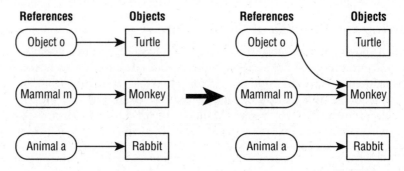

As each reference variable changes which object it points to, you would erase or cross out the arrow between them and draw a new one to a different object. Based on Figure B.1, you can see that the Turtle object is no longer reachable and is now eligible for garbage collection. You can also use the diagram to determine which casts are required and which are implicit. For example, trying to assign an Animal object to the m reference could require an explicit cast. In this manner, the diagram can help you find compilation errors that you may have missed the first time through.

Using the writing material to track state is also useful for complex questions that involve a loop, especially an embedded loop. Can you determine what the following code snippet outputs?

```
int x = 0;
int y = 10;
while (x < y) {
    System.out.println("<><>");
    for(int i=2; i<5; i++, x++) {
        x++;
        System.out.println("-");
    }
}
System.out.println(x+","+y);
```

The writing material can be essential in tracking variable changes as the loop progresses. In this case, the outer loop executes twice, with each inner loop executing three times, resulting in an output of 12,10, because x is incremented twice per inner loop.

The writing material can also be useful in questions involving String or array indices. For example, what is the output of the following code snippet?

```
String mammal = "DOLPHIN";
String modified = mammal.substring(2,mammal.indexOf('I'));
modified += "x" + mammal.substring(4);
System.out.println(modified);
```

For this problem, it may be helpful to draw a diagram of the String, complete with indices, as shown in Figure B.2.

FIGURE B.2   Marking indices

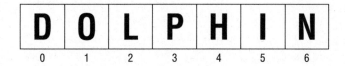

This diagram shows that the index of I used on the second line of the code snippet is 5. For the two substring() calls, remember that the first index is inclusive, while the second index is exclusive. You can then use Figure B.2 to see that the substring from 2 to 5 is LPH, while the substring from 4 to the end of the String is HIN. The resulting output is LPHxHIN. In addition to String values, similar diagrams can be constructed for primitive arrays and collections.

Finally, we should mention that if you do use the writing material and decide to come back to the question later, you might have to redo some of the work. This is especially true with whiteboards, since they tend to have limited space.

Although you aren't allowed to bring any written notes with you into the exam, you're allowed to write things down that you remember at the start of the exam on the writing material provided. If there's a particular facet of the Java language that you have difficulty remembering, try memorizing it before the exam and write it down as soon as the exam starts. You can then use this as a guide for the rest of the exam. Of course, this strategy works for only a handful of topics, since there's a limit to what you're likely to remember in a short time.

For example, you may have trouble remembering the format of a JDBC connection String. If so, we recommend that you memorize that information before the exam and write it down as soon as the exam starts for use in various questions.

Choosing the Best Answer

Sometimes, you read a question and immediately spot a compiler error that tells you exactly what the question is asking. Other times, though, you may stare at a method declaration for a couple of minutes and have no idea what the question is asking. While you might not know for sure which answer is correct in these situations, there are some test-taking tips that can improve the probability that you will pick the correct answer.

Understanding Relationships between Answers

The exam writers, as well as the writers of this book, are fond of answers that are related to each other. You can apply the process of elimination to remove entire sets of answers from selection, not just a single answer. For example, take a look at the following question:

22. What is the output of the following application?

```
3: int x = 0;
4: while(++x < 5) { x+=1; }
5: String message = x > 5 ? "Greater than": "Less Than";
6: System.out.println(message+","+x);
```

- **A.** Greater than,5
- **B.** Greater than,6
- **C.** Greater than,7
- **D.** Less than,5
- **E.** Less than,6
- **F.** Less than,7

In this question, notice that half of the answers output Greater than, whereas the other half output Less than. Based on the code, as well as the answers available, the question cannot output both values. This means that if you can determine to what the ternary expression on line 5 evaluates, you can eliminate half the answers!

You might also notice that this particular question does not include any "Does not compile" or "Code throws an exception at runtime" answers, meaning that you can be assured that this snippet of code does compile and run without issue. If you have a question similar to this, you can compare the syntax and use this as a guide for solving other related questions.

Guessing the Correct Answer

Unlike some other standardized tests, there's no penalty for answering a question incorrectly versus leaving it blank. If you're nearly out of time, or you just can't decide on an answer, select a random answer and move on. If you've been able to eliminate even one answer, then your guess will be better than blind luck.

Answer All Questions!

You should set a hard stop at five minutes of time remaining on the exam to ensure that you've answered each and every question. Remember, if you fail to answer a question, you'll definitely get it wrong and lose points, but if you guess, there's at least a chance that you'll be correct. There's no harm in guessing!

When in doubt, we generally recommend picking a random answer that includes "Does not compile" if available, although which choice you select is not nearly as important as making sure that you do not leave any questions unanswered on the exam!

Optimizing Your Time

One of the most difficult test-taking skills to master is balancing your time on the exam. Although Oracle often varies the precise number of questions on the exam and the amount of time that you have to answer them, the general rule of thumb is that you have about one-and-a-half minutes per question.

Of course, it can be stressful to look frequently at the time remaining while taking the exam, so the key is pacing yourself. Some questions will take you longer than two minutes to solve, but hopefully others will take less than a minute. The more time you save on the easier questions, the more time you'll have for the harder questions.

Checking the Time Remaining

The exam software includes a clock that tells you the amount of time that you have left on the exam. We don't recommend checking the clock after each and every question to determine your pace. After all, doing such a calculation will waste time and probably make you nervous and stressed out. We do recommend that you check the time remaining at certain points while taking the exam to determine whether you should try to increase your pace.

For example, if the exam lasts two-and-a-half hours, and it is 90 questions long, the following would be a good pace to try to maintain:

- 150 minutes remaining: Start the exam.
- 110 minutes remaining: One-third of the exam is finished.
- 70 minutes remaining: Two-thirds of the exam is finished.
- 30 minutes remaining: First pass of all questions is complete.
- 5 minutes remaining: Finished reviewing all questions marked for review. Select answers to all questions left blank.

As you're taking the exam, you may realize that you're falling behind. In this scenario, you need to start allotting less time per question, which may involve more guessing, or you'll end up with some questions that you never answer. As discussed in the previous section, guessing an answer to a question is better than not answering the question at all.

Skipping Hard Questions

If you do find that you are having difficulty with a particular question, just pick your best guess, mark the question, and come back to it later if there is enough time. Remember that all questions on the exam, easy or difficult, are weighted the same. It is a far better use of your time to spend five minutes answering ten easy questions than spend the same amount of time answering one difficult question.

You might come to a question that looks difficult and immediately realize that it is going to take a lot of time. In this case, skip it before even starting on it. You can save the most difficult problems for the end so that you can get all of the easy ones solved early on. Of course, you shouldn't mark every question for review, so use that sparingly. For example, if you need only 30 more seconds to solve a specific question, it is better to finish it so that you do not have to come back to it later. One important test-taking skill is not getting stuck on a difficult question for a long period of time.

Being Prepared for Nested Questions

The exam includes questions that may ask you to solve multiple problems at once. For example, consider the following code snippet:

```
4: List<Integer> list1 = new CopyOnWriteArrayList<>(Arrays.asList(1,2,3,4,5,6));
5: List<Integer> list2 = Collections.synchronizedList(Arrays.asList(1,2,3,4,5,6));
6: for(Integer item: list1) list1.add(5);
7: for(Integer item: list2) list2.remove(0);
8: System.out.println(list1.size()+" "+list2.size());
```

Even though list1 and list2 are independent objects, the question will likely require you to understand how each of these separate lists is processed. Furthermore, a runtime exception on one list impacts the results of another list. For example, if the operation on list1 on line 6 were to throw an exception at runtime, then line 7 would never be executed, and no modification of list2 would be attempted.

Improving Your Test-Taking Speed with Practice

Answering certification exam questions quickly does not come naturally to most people. It takes a bit of practice and skill to look at a question, a code sample, plus four to six answer choices and be able to answer the question within a minute or two. The best way to practice is to keep solving the review questions at the end of each chapter until you can read, understand, and answer them in under a minute.

Once you've completed all of the material and practiced with the review questions enough that you can answer them quickly and correctly, you should try one of the three 60-question practice exams that come with this Study Guide. You should treat it like the real exam, setting aside two hours and finishing it in one sitting.

Although we recommend that you try to avoid taking the practice exams so much so that you memorize the questions and answers, we do recommend that you keep taking them until you can finish each practice exam in under two hours. Remember not to move on to the next one until you can pass the previous exam in the allotted time. If not, study more and go back to drilling on the Review Questions. The idea is that you want to be good at quickly reading through the question, honing in on the key concept the question is asking, and being able to select the answer that best represents it.

Getting a Good Night's Rest

Although a lot of people are inclined to cram as much material as they can in the hours leading up to the exam, most studies have shown that this is a poor test-taking strategy. The best thing we can recommend that you do before the exam is to get a good night's rest!

Given the length of the exam and number of questions, the exam can be quite draining, especially if this is your first time taking a certification exam. You might come in expecting to be done 30 minutes early, only to discover that you are only a quarter of the way through the exam with half time remaining. At some point, you may begin to panic, and it is in these moments that these test-taking skills are most important. Just remember to take a deep breath, stay calm, eliminate as many wrong answers as you can, and make sure to answer each and every question. It is for stressful moments like these that being well rested with a good night's sleep will be most beneficial!

Appendix C

Upgrading from Java 6 or Earlier

THE UPGRADE TO JAVA SE 8 OCP (JAVA SE 6 AND ALL PRIOR VERSIONS) EXAM (1Z0-813) TOPICS COVERED IN THIS APPENDIX INCLUDE THE FOLLOWING:

✓ **Java Collections**

- Develop code that uses diamond with generic declarations

✓ **Language Enhancements**

- Develop code that uses String objects in the switch statement, binary literals, and numeric literals, including underscores in literals

✓ **Localization**

- Format dates, numbers, and currency values for localization with the NumberFormat and DateFormat classes, including number and date format patterns

✓ **Concurrency**

- Use Lock, ReadWriteLock, and ReentrantLock classes in the java.util.concurrent.locks and java.util.concurrent.atomic packages to support lock-free thread-safe programming on single variables

✓ **Java File I/O (NIO.2)**

- Recursively access a directory tree by using the DirectoryStream and FileVisitor interfaces

- Observe the changes in a directory by using the WatchService interface

Oracle offers developers who hold a Java 6 or earlier professional certification a direct path to become OCP 8 certified in the form of a dedicated upgrade exam (1Z0-813). If you are studying for this particular exam, then you should pay close attention to this appendix, as it includes objectives that are not part of the other OCP exams. For example, those individuals with an OCJP 1.6 certification who skipped a Java 7 certification might not be aware that you can now use String values in switch statements.

If you are taking the full OCP exam (1Z0-809) or the upgrade from version Java 7 (1Z0-810), then you should already know many of the topics in this appendix from your time taking the OCA 8 or OCP 7 exam, respectively. In this case, you can skip the sections on localization, concurrency, and NIO.2 in this appendix, since these will not be on your exam. We recommend that everyone review the first section on language enhancements, though, as these topics can be included on any OCP question.

Since Oracle has been known to add or update objectives over time, we encourage you review the latest information on Oracle's exam page before taking any exam. We also maintain a comprehensive list of updates for this book, including changes to the exam objectives, on our blog at http://www.selikoff.net/ocp.

This appendix assumes that you have finished reading the main text. The topics in this appendix build on concepts and examples discussed throughout the book.

Enhancing the Java Language

With the release of Java 7, new features were added to the Java language. You might not be aware of these features if your last certification was in Java 6 or earlier. We cover three of them here: the diamond operator <>, new formats for literals, and switch statements.

Using the Diamond Operator

Since Java 5, you have been allowed to tell the compiler about the type of a class that uses generics by specifying it between < and >. Starting with Java 7, you can even omit that type from the right side. The < and > are still required, though. This is called the diamond operator because <> looks like a diamond. For example, these two statements are equivalent:

```
List<String> list1 = new ArrayList<String>();
List<String> list2 = new ArrayList<>();
```

The first line creates an ArrayList using the generic type String. It compiles on Java 5 or higher. The second line uses the diamond operator to shorten the code on the right. It compiles in Java 7 or higher.

One of the most powerful features of the diamond operator <> is that it can be used for embedded collection types. For example, consider the following two statements:

```
Map<Map<String,Integer>,List<Double>> map1
  = new HashMap<Map<String,Integer>, List<Double>>();

Map<Map<String,Integer>,List<Double>> map2 = new HashMap<>();
```

The two lines are equivalent, with the second line using the diamond operator <> to significantly reduce the text that needs to be typed. The idea is that the compiler can "fill in the blank" with the declaration on the right side of the assignment. Do you see what is wrong with this code?

```
Map<Map<String,Integer>,List<Double>> map3
  = new HashMap<<>,<>>(); // DOES NOT COMPILE
```

The diamond operator asks you to infer everything about the generics. Nesting diamond operators is not allowed.

There is one limitation to using the diamond operator <>, in that it is allowed only on the right side of an assignment operation. For example, the following will not compile:

```
List<> list1 = new ArrayList<String>(); // DOES NOT COMPILE
```

Java uses the declared type to infer the diamond operator type. This does not work when the declaration tries to use the diamond operator <>. Thus it is not allowed.

Creating Literals

When a number is present in the code, it is a type of *literal*. By default, Java assumes that you are defining an int value with a literal. In this example, the number listed is bigger than what fits in an int. Remember that you aren't expected to memorize the maximum value for an int. The exam will include it in the question if it comes up.

```
long max = 3123456789;  // DOES NOT COMPILE
```

Java complains that the number is out of range. And it is—for an int. However, we don't have an int. The solution is to add the character L to the number:

```
long max = 3123456789L;  // now Java knows it is a long
```

Alternatively, you could add a lowercase l to the number. But please use the uppercase L. The lowercase l looks like the number 1. Another way to specify numbers is to change the base. When you learned how to count, you studied the digits 0–9. This numbering system is called base 10 since there are 10 numbers. It is also known as the decimal number system. Java allows you to specify digits in several other formats:

Octal (Digits 0-7)   This format uses the number 0 as a prefix, for example, 017.

Hexadecimal (Digits 0-9 and Letters A-F)   This format uses the number 0 followed by x or X as a prefix, for example, 0xFF.

Binary (Digits 0-1)   This format uses the number 0 followed by b or B as a prefix, for example, 0b10.

You won't need to convert between number systems on the exam. You'll have to recognize valid literal values that can be assigned to numbers.

Literals with Underscore Characters

The other thing you that need to know about numeric literals is a feature added in Java 7. You can have underscores in numbers to make them easier to read:

```
int million1 = 1000000;
int million2 = 1_000_000;
```

We'd rather be reading the latter example because the zeroes don't run together. You can add underscores anywhere except at the beginning of a literal, the end of a literal, right before a decimal point, or right after a decimal point. Let's look at a few examples:

```
double notAtStart = _1000.00;      // DOES NOT COMPILE
double notAtEnd = 1000.00_;        // DOES NOT COMPILE
double notByDecimal = 1000_.00;    // DOES NOT COMPILE
double annoyingButLegal = 1_00_0.0_0;  // this one compiles
```

Making Decisions with *Switch*

If you're taking an OCP upgrade exam, then you're sure to have encountered switch statements on a previous exam. Those new to Java 7 or Java 8, though, might not be aware that Oracle made some changes to switch statements that we will discuss in this section.

To review, a *switch statement*, as shown in Figure C.1, is a complex decision-making structure in which a single value is evaluated and flow is redirected to the first matching branch, known as a *case statement*. If no such case statement is found that matches the value, an optional *default statement* will be called. If no such default option is available, then the entire switch statement will be skipped. For the OCP exam, you are expected to know the basic rules about switch statements that you encountered on previous exams, such as the rule that case values must be unique.

FIGURE C.1   The structure of a switch statement

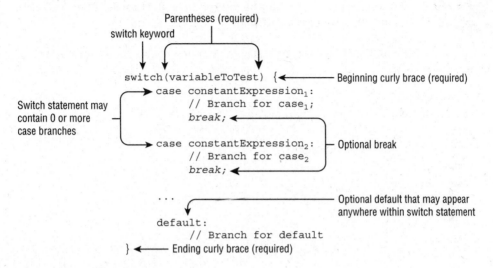

Supported Data Types

As shown in Figure C.1, a switch statement has a target variable that is not evaluated until runtime. Prior to Java 5.0, this variable could only be int values or those values that could be promoted to int, specifically byte, short, or char. When enum was added in Java 5.0, support was added to switch statements for enum values. In Java 7, switch statements were updated further to allow matching on String values. Finally, the switch statement also supports the equivalent primitive numeric wrapper classes, such as Byte, Short, Character, or Integer.

Data types supported by switch statements include the following:

- int and Integer
- byte and Byte
- short and Short
- char and Character
- String
- enum values

For the exam, we recommend that you memorize this list. Note that boolean and long and their associated wrapper classes are not supported by switch statements.

Compile-Time Constant Values

The values in each case statement must be compile-time constant values of the same data type as the switch value. This means that you can use only literals, enum constants, or final constant variables of the same data type. By final constant, we mean that the variable must be marked with the final modifier and initialized with a literal value in the same expression in which it is declared.

The variable must actually be marked as final. The new "effectively final" concept in Java 8 is insufficient.

Let's look at a simple example using the day of the week, with 0 for Sunday, 1 for Monday, and so on:

```java
int dayOfWeek = 5;
switch(dayOfWeek) {
   default:
      System.out.println("Weekday");
      break;
   case 0_0:
      System.out.println("Sunday");
      break;
   case 6:
      System.out.println("Saturday");
      break;
}
```

With a dayOfWeek value of 5, this code will output

```
Weekday
```

In this example, we use the numeric literal 0_0, which the compiler interprets as 0. You can see that there is a break statement at the end of each case and default section used to terminate the switch statement and return flow control to the closing statement. If you leave out the break statement, flow will continue to the next case or default block automatically.

Next, we see that the default block is not at the end of the switch statement. There is no requirement that the case or default statements be in a particular order, unless you are going to have pathways that reach multiple sections of the switch block in a single execution. In fact, there's no requirement that a switch statement have a case or default entry, since the following is a valid, albeit useless, statement:

```java
switch(dayOfWeek) {}
```

Consider the following variation:

```java
int dayOfWeek = 5;
switch(dayOfWeek) {
   case 0_0:
      System.out.println("Sunday");
```

```
default:
   System.out.println("Weekday");
case 6:
   System.out.println("Saturday");
}
```

This code looks a lot like the previous example, except that the break statements have been removed and the order has been changed. This means that if dayOfWeek is 5, then the code will jump to the default block and then execute all of the proceeding case statements in order until it finds a break statement or finishes the structure:

```
Weekday
Saturday
```

The order of the case and default statements is now important since placing the default statement at the end of the switch statement would cause only one word to be output.

What if the value of dayOfWeek was 6 in this example? Would the default block still be executed? The output of this example with dayOfWeek set to 6 would be as follows:

```
Saturday
```

Even though the default block came before the case block, only the case block was executed. If you recall the definition of the default block, it is branched to only if there is no matching case value for the switch statement, regardless of its position within the switch statement.

Finally, if the value of dayOfWeek was 0, all three statements would be output:

```
Sunday
Weekday
Saturday
```

In this last example, the default section is executed since there was no break statement at the end of the preceding case block. While the code will not branch to the default statement if there is a matching case value within the switch statement, it will execute the default statement if it encounters it after a case statement for which there is no terminating break statement.

The exam creators are fond of switch examples that are missing break statements! When evaluating switch statements on the exam, always consider that multiple branches may be visited in a single execution.

We conclude our discussion on switch statements by acknowledging that the data type for case statements must match the data type of the switch variable. As already discussed, the case statement value must also be a literal, enum constant, or final constant variable. For example, given the following switch statement, which case statements will compile?

```
private int getSortOrder(String firstName, final String lastName) {
    String middleName = "Patricia";
    final String suffix = "JR";
    int id = 0;
    switch(firstName) {
        case "Test":
            return 52;
        case middleName:    // DOES NOT COMPILE
            id = 5;
            break;
        case suffix:
            id = 0;
            break;
        case lastName:      // DOES NOT COMPILE
            id = 8;
            break;
        case 5:             // DOES NOT COMPILE
            id = 7;
            break;
        case 'J':           // DOES NOT COMPILE
            id = 10;
            break;
        case Month.JANUARY: // DOES NOT COMPILE
            id=15;
            break;
    }
    return id;
}
```

The first case statement, "Test", compiles without issue using a String literal, and it is a good example of how a return statement, like a break statement, can be used to exit the switch statement early. The second case statement, middleName, does not compile because middleName is not a final variable, despite having a known value at this particular line of execution. The third case statement, suffix, compiles without issue because suffix is a final constant variable.

The fourth case statement, lastName, does not compile, as the final variable is a method argument that can change at runtime. Finally, the last three case statements don't compile because none of them have a matching type of String, with the last one being an enum value.

Formatting and Parsing

Chapter 5, "Dates, Strings, and Localization," covers most of what you need to know on the exam about formatting and parsing. In particular, you learned how to format numbers and currency for a specific locale. You also learned how to format Java 8 dates. The following sections cover two more things that you need to know for the upgrade exam: special format flags for numbers and how to format/parse the pre-Java 8 date format.

Using *DecimalFormat* Flags

There is a special subclass of NumberFormat called DecimalFormat, which is typically used when you want specific formatting. When creating a DecimalFormat object, you use a constructor rather than a factory method. You pass the pattern that you would like to use. The patterns can get complex, but you only need to know about two formatting characters:

DecimalFormat Formatting Characters

means to omit the position if no digit exists for it.

0 means to put a 0 in the position if no digit exists for it.

An example helps to understand what is going on here:

```
12:    double d = 1234567.437;
13:    DecimalFormat one = new DecimalFormat("###,###,###.###");
14:    System.out.println(one.format(d)); // 1,234,567.437
15:
16:    DecimalFormat two = new DecimalFormat("000,000,000.00000");
17:    System.out.println(two.format(d)); // 001,234,567.43700
18:
19:    DecimalFormat three = new DecimalFormat("$#,###,###.##");
20:    System.out.println(three.format(d)); // $1,234,567.44
```

Line 14 displays just the digits in the number. The extra positions are omitted because we used #. Line 17 adds leading and trailing zeros to make the output the desired length. Line 20 shows prefixing a non-formatting character ($ sign) along with rounding because fewer digits are printed than available.

Using *DateFormat*

As with NumberFormat, you need to create a DateFormat before formatting or parsing. In fact, both classes extend a common Format superclass. The DateFormat class provides factory methods to get the desired formatter. Table C.1 shows the available methods.

TABLE C.1 Factory methods to get a DateFormat

Description	Using Default Locale and a Specified Locale

For formatting dates	`DateFormat.getDateInstance()`
	`DateFormat.getDateInstance(style)`
	`DateFormat.getDateInstance(style, locale)`

For formatting times	`DateFormat.getTimeInstance()`
	`DateFormat.getTimeInstance(style)`
	`DateFormat.getTimeInstance(style, locale)`

For formatting dates and times	`DateFormat.getDateTimeInstance()`
	`DateFormat.getDateTimeInstance(`
	    `dateStyle, timeStyle)`
	`DateFormat.getDateTimeInstance(`
	    `dateStyle, timeStyle, locale)`

Many of the factory methods take a style parameter. You can pass FULL, LONG, MEDIUM, and SHORT to specify the amount of detail that you want in the format. Once you have the DateFormat instance, you can call format() to turn a number into a String and parse() to turn a String into a number.

Formatting

The DateFormat class defines three format methods, but you need to know only one of these for the exam: `public final String format(Date date)`.

The date parameter is of type java.util.Date, a useful class that represents a specific instant in time as milliseconds. A Date object is instantiated by passing in a long that represents the time in milliseconds from January 1, 1970, at 00:00:00 GMT. (The no-argument constructor of Date returns the current time on the underlying platform.) The format method returns the String representation of the given Date based on the specified locale of the DateFormat object.

Let's look at an example. The following code creates a Date object for January 31, 1984, and it formats the date in all four styles:

```
DateFormat s = DateFormat.getDateInstance(DateFormat.SHORT);
DateFormat m = DateFormat.getDateInstance(DateFormat.MEDIUM);
DateFormat l = DateFormat.getDateInstance(DateFormat.LONG);
DateFormat f = DateFormat.getDateInstance(DateFormat.FULL);

Date d = new GregorianCalendar(2015, Calendar.JULY, 4).getTime();
System.out.println(s.format(d)); // 7/4/15
```

```
System.out.println(m.format(d)); // Jul 4, 2015
System.out.println(l.format(d)); // July 4, 2015
System.out.println(f.format(d)); // Saturday, July 4, 2015
```

Don't worry—you don't need to memorize the differences in output formatting. You just need to know that there are four styles.

To include the time in the format of a date, use a DateFormat object from the getDateTimeInstance method. The following statement formats the same Date object from the previous code using a MEDIUM date style and a FULL time style:

```
DateFormat dtf = DateFormat.getDateTimeInstance(
  DateFormat.MEDIUM, DateFormat.FULL);
System.out.println(dtf.format(d));
```

The output of the previous statements depends on the time zone and locale, but it will look something like this:

```
Jul 4, 2015 12:00:00 AM EDT
```

Notice that the two formats are independent of each other. Also note that the time defaults to midnight since we never specified a time. Let's try a similar format with the same date but a different locale. The following statements use a DateFormat object for the country Germany:

```
DateFormat de = DateFormat.getDateTimeInstance(
   DateFormat.MEDIUM, DateFormat.FULL, Locale.GERMANY);
System.out.println(de.format(d));
```

The output of the statements looks something like this:

```
31.01.1984 17.47 Uhr MST
```

Between the various date styles, time styles, and locales, you have a lot of options for formatting dates and times using the DateFormat class. The class is also used for parsing dates, as the next section shows.

Parsing

The DateFormat class contains the following parse method for parsing strings into dates: public Date parse(String source) throws ParseException.

The return value is of type java.util.Date, and the ParseException is thrown when the beginning of the string cannot be parsed into a date successfully.

The format of the String object depends on both the style and the locale of the DateFormat object. The following statements parse a date string in the SHORT style of the U.S. locale and then format the resulting Date object in the FULL style of the France locale:

```
DateFormat shortFormat = DateFormat.getDateInstance(
   DateFormat.SHORT, Locale.US);
String s = "01/31/1984";

Date date = shortFormat.parse(s);
DateFormat fullFormat = DateFormat.getDateInstance(
   DateFormat.FULL, Locale.FRANCE);
System.out.println(fullFormat.format(date));
```

The shortFormat object has the SHORT date style and U.S. locale and parses on it the string 01/31/1984. The resulting Date object is printed using a FULL style with the France locale. The output is as follows:

```
mardi 31 janvier 1984
```

The parse method throws a ParseException if the beginning of the string cannot be parsed. As with the parse method in NumberFormat, the parse method in DateFormat successfully parses a string if the beginning of the string is in the proper format.

Custom Date Formats

When you want to specify a custom format pattern, you use the SimpleDateFormat subclass. As with DecimalFormat, you use a constructor and pass in the desired format pattern.

There are many symbols for date formats. The most that you will need to do is to recognize the date and time parts.

MMMM M represents the month. The more Ms that you have, the more verbose the Java output is. For example, M outputs 1, MM outputs 01, MMM outputs Jan, and MMMM outputs January.

dd d represents the day in the month. As with month, the more ds that you have, the more verbose the Java output is. dd means to include the leading zero for a single-digit day.

yyyy y represents the year. yy outputs a two-digit year, and yyyy outputs a four-digit year.

hh h represents the hour. Use hh to include the leading zero if you're outputting a single-digit hour.

mm m represents the minute. As with month and day, mm means to include the leading zero for a single-digit minute.

ss represents the second. As with minute, ss means to include the leading zero for a single-digit second.

Let's look at an example:

```
14:   SimpleDateFormat f1 = new SimpleDateFormat("MM dd yyyy hh:mm:ss");
15:   SimpleDateFormat f2 = new SimpleDateFormat("MMMM yyyy");
16:   SimpleDateFormat f3 = new SimpleDateFormat("hh");
```

```
17:    Date date = f1.parse("01 26 2016 01:22:33");
18:    System.out.println(f2.format(date));  // January 2016
19:    System.out.println(f3.format(date));  // 01
```

First notice that the format string is passed into the constructor. Line 14 shows a common format for dates. Lines 15 and 16 show you how to use formats that are not common at all. You just assemble them from existing specifiers. Line 17 parses a String and stores it in a Date object. Lines 18 and 19 show how to format a Date object to turn it into a String.

Applying Locks

In Chapter 7, "Concurrency," you learned how to use the synchronized keyword on a block of code or method to create a monitor that allows only one thread to access a particular segment of code. Unfortunately, a synchronized block or method supports only a limited set of functionality. For example, what if we want to check if a lock is available and, if it is not, perform some other task? Furthermore, if the lock is never available and we synchronize on it, we enter a deadlock condition in which the thread hangs forever.

The Concurrency API includes the Lock framework that is conceptually similar to using the synchronized keyword, but with a lot more features and options available than the standard monitor that you saw in Chapter 7. For the upgrade exam, you should be familiar with the Lock interface and the classes that implement this interface.

Understanding the *Lock* Framework

The Lock framework works in a similar manner to the synchronized code that you saw in Chapter 7, except that the methods to acquire and release the lock are explicitly called. Also, instead of being able to synchronize on any Object, we can only synchronize on an object that implements the Lock interface.

Consider our synchronized example from Chapter 7 along with a variation that is conceptually equivalent to using a Lock object. Since Lock is an interface, we need an implementation class to use it. For now, we'll use the ReentrantLock class, since it most closely resembles the behavior of the synchronized keyword. As you will see later in this section, there are other lock classes that we can use.

```
// Implementation #1 with synchronization
Object object = new Object();
synchronized(object) {
    System.out.print(" "+(++birdCount));
}

// Implementation #2 with a Lock
Lock lock = new ReentrantLock();
try {
```

```
   lock.lock();
   System.out.print(" "+(++birdCount));
} finally {
   lock.unlock();
}
```

The first example uses the synchronized keyword on an Object, while the second example uses a Lock object as a monitor to ensure that only one thread has access to the work of the method. Once the Lock is established, the code explicitly calls lock() before modifying the birdCount variable, and then it ensures that the lock is released by calling unlock() in a finally block.

> While the two snippets of code are conceptually equivalent, they are not compatible with each other. For example, if one thread calls lock() on a Lock object while another thread uses the synchronized keyword on the same Lock object, the code will not be thread-safe. In other words, you can't mix and match the Lock framework and the synchronized keyword, as the Lock framework is an alternative to synchronization.

The Lock framework ensures that once a thread has called the lock() method, all other threads that call lock() will wait until the thread that acquired the lock calls the unlock() method. As far as which thread gets the lock next, that depends on the lock implementation class and parameters used.

Releasing the Lock

The most important part about obtaining a lock is to guarantee that it is released after the thread no longer needs it. After all, if the unlock() method is never called after obtaining a lock, other threads that try to obtain the lock will wait indefinitely.

For this reason, it is considered a good code practice to put the unlock() method in a finally block, as you saw in the previous example. This is similar to avoiding memory or database leaks by closing resources, as you saw in Chapter 8, "IO," and Chapter 10, "JDBC," respectively.

Variations in Lock Syntax

Oracle documentation and the exam can vary on whether or not the lock() call is inside the try/finally block. For example, you may see either of the following formats used on the exam:

```
Lock lock = new ReentrantLock();

// Syntax #1: lock() inside try/finally
try {
```

```
   lock.lock();
   // Implementation details
} finally {
   lock.unlock();
}

// Syntax #2: lock() outside try/finally
lock.lock();
try {
   // Implementation details
} finally {
   lock.unlock();
}
```

Although either implementation is technically correct, we tend to use the first syntax in this book, as it more closely resembles how file and database resources are requested and released.

Besides always making sure to release a lock, you also need to make sure that you only release a lock that you actually have. If you attempt to release a lock that you do not have, you will get an exception at runtime in the form of an IllegalMonitorStateException. We demonstrate this in the following code snippet:

```
Lock lock = new ReentrantLock();
lock.unlock();   // Throws IllegalMonitorStateException at runtime
```

This code skips the lock-acquisition step and attempts to release a lock that it does not have, which results in an IllegalMonitorStateException at runtime.

Attempting to Acquire a Lock

While the lock() method allows you to wait for a lock, it suffers from the same problem as the synchronized keyword. A thread could end up waiting a significantly long amount of time, perhaps forever, to obtain a lock. Luckily, the Lock interface includes two methods that allow the thread to test for a lock.

tryLock()

The tryLock() method will attempt to acquire a lock and immediately return a boolean result indicating whether or not the lock was obtained. Unlike the lock() method, it does not wait if another thread already holds the lock, although like lock(), it should be used with a try/finally block to ensure that the lock is released. The following is a sample implementation using the tryLock() method:

```
Lock lock = new ReentrantLock();
if(lock.tryLock()) {
```

```
      try {
         System.out.print(" "+(++birdCount));
      } finally {
         lock.unlock();
      }
   } else {
      System.out.println("Unable to acquire lock, doing something else");
   }
```

Besides ensuring that the lock is released in a try/finally block, you can see that we only need to release the lock with unlock() if it was successfully acquired. Remember that calling unlock() on a lock that you do not actually have will lead to a IllegalMonitorStateException at runtime.

tryLock(long time, TimeUnit unit)

The Lock interface includes an overloaded version of tryLock() and waits up to a specified amount of time trying to acquire a lock. It returns true as soon as the lock is acquired within the time specified, and it returns false after the time elapses. The following code snippet waits up to 10 seconds when trying to acquire the lock:

```
Lock lock = new ReentrantLock();
if(lock.tryLock(10,TimeUnit.SECONDS)) {
   try {
      System.out.print(" "+(++birdCount));
   } finally {
      lock.unlock();
   }
} else {
   System.out.println("Unable to acquire lock, doing something else");
}
```

Recall that the TimeUnit class is an enum that supports various units of time. Refer to Table 7.3 in Chapter 7 for a full list of values.

Using a *ReentrantLock*

The ReentrantLock, which we have been using in all of our lock examples up until now, is simple monitor lock that implements the Lock interface and supports mutual exclusion. In other words, at most one thread is allowed to hold the lock at any given time. As we described earlier, the ReentrantLock behaves most like the locks created by the synchronized keyword but with the enhancements defined in the Lock framework, such as supporting the tryLock() method.

Recall our sheep-counting program from Chapter 7. Each zoo worker runs out to a field, adds a new sheep to the flock, counts the total number sheep, and runs back to us to report the results. We present a modified version of our SheepManager class from that program, which uses a ReentrantLock:

```java
import java.util.concurrent.*;
import java.util.concurrent.locks.*;

public class SheepManager {

   private int sheepCount = 0;
   private Lock lock = new ReentrantLock();

   private void incrementAndReport() {
      try {
         lock.lock();
         System.out.print(" " + (++sheepCount));
      } finally {
         lock.unlock();
      }
   }

   public static void main(String[] args) {
      ExecutorService service = null;
      try {
         service = Executors.newFixedThreadPool(20);

         SheepManager manager = new SheepManager();
         for (int i = 0; i < 10; i++)
            service.submit(() -> manager.incrementAndReport());
      } finally {
         if (service != null) service.shutdown();
      }
   }
}
```

This code prints out the numbers in order, using a Lock instead of a synchronized block to order the results:

```
1 2 3 4 5 6 7 8 9 10
```

You see that the code is quite similar to using a synchronized block. One advantage to using the Lock framework is that we can use tryLock() to avoid deadlocking on the call to acquire the lock.

Duplicating Lock Requests

Another difference between using the synchronized keyword and the ReentrantLock class is what happens on duplicate lock requests. For example, what would you expect the following code snippet to output?

```java
Lock lock = new ReentrantLock();
try {
   lock.lock();
   lock.lock();
   ++birdCount;
} finally {
   lock.unlock();
}

new Thread(() -> {
   if(lock.tryLock()) {
      try {
         System.out.println("Acquired");
      } finally {
         lock.unlock();
      }
   } else {
      System.out.println("Unavailable");
   }
}).start();
```

In this example, we attempt to lock the object twice in one thread using the lock() method and once in a separate thread using the tryLock() method. Like using synchronization, if a thread requests a lock that it already has, it is trivially granted. Unlike synchronization, though, the ReentrantLock class maintains a counter on the number of times the lock has been given out. The result is that the unlock() method *must be called the same number of times* as the lock() method in order to release the lock. Therefore, this code outputs Unavailable, since the lock is still maintained by the original thread.

> **NOTE** The previous example uses a separate thread to show that the first thread still holds the lock, making the lock unavailable to the second thread. Note that if all lock requests are made by the same thread, then the program would instead output Acquired, as locks are automatically granted if the thread already has the lock.

We can address this problem by calling unlock() once for each lock() request, as shown in the following modified example:

```
Lock lock = new ReentrantLock();
try {
   lock.lock();
   try {
      lock.lock();
      ++birdCount;
   } finally {
      lock.unlock();
   }
} finally {
   lock.unlock();
}

new Thread(() -> {
   if(lock.tryLock()) {
      try {
         System.out.println("Acquired");
      } finally {
         lock.unlock();
      }
   } else {
      System.out.println("Unavailable");
   }
}).start();
```

The separate thread is now able to obtain the lock, printing Acquired. Note that we used two try/finally blocks to ensure that each request for a lock is properly unlocked.

Anytime you see a Lock object on the exam, make sure that it calls unlock() the same number of times that it calls lock().

Fair Lock Management

By default, when a ReentrantLock releases a lock, it then assigns it to a waiting thread at random if there are any, in the same manner as synchronized. This could potentially lead to thread starvation, as a thread that has been waiting a long time may continually lose the lock to another thread.

The ReentrantLock class has the optional feature that the thread that has been waiting the longest can be guaranteed the lock the next time it is released. This property is often referred to as *fairness*, and it corresponds to a FIFO ordering, as discussed in Chapter 3, "Generics and Collections."

Consider the following example that uses the `ReentrantLock` constructor that takes a `boolean` fairness value:

```
Lock lock = new ReentrantLock(true);
```

When the `boolean` value is set to `true`, fairness is enabled and the longest waiting thread is guaranteed to obtain the lock the next time it is released. When the `boolean` value is set to `false`, the lock defaults to its normal, no-argument constructor behavior, and it assigns the lock randomly upon its release.

 As even Oracle's documentation for the `ReentrantLock` class points out, enabling fairness may not have the desired outcome and could significantly slow down your program under certain circumstances. Therefore, you should use it only in situations where you really need your requests ordered in a particular manner.

Understanding Read/Write Locks

While a single lock guarantees mutually exclusivity of an object, it is also costly, as all threads need to wait each time an object is accessed. In a variety of systems, reading data from an object is far more common than writing to an object.

For example, imagine that our zoo uses a data-driven system to keep track of zoo employee names. The list of names might be read by hundreds of processes throughout the day, from assigning schedules, to printing paychecks, to mailing letters. By comparison, an employee might only join or leave the zoo staff at an average rate of two a week.

In this common situation, reads are far more common than writes; therefore, it would be helpful to have a lock that introduces a delay only when a write needs to happen. Unlike a monitor lock, reads would happen quickly as threads would not block and wait for each other on read operations.

The `ReadWriteLock` interface solves this problem and theoretically improves concurrency over a single-lock monitor by declaring two `ReadWriteLock` interface methods that each return a `Lock` instance:

`Lock readLock()` Returns a lock that may be held simultaneously by multiple threads and is therefore not mutually exclusive.

`Lock writeLock()` Returns a lock that is exclusive to all other locks, read and write, and may only be held by a single thread.

Note that the `ReadWriteLock` interface does not actually implement the `Lock` interface, but it contains two methods that return `Lock` objects.

The idea is that many threads can be granted a lock to read the object, but a write object is special and can be granted only if no threads are holding any locks on the object. Once a write lock is granted, all requests for locks are held until the write lock is released. In this manner, threads performing read operations can continue reading the data concurrently, stopping to wait only when a single thread has been granted a write access.

Using a *ReentrantReadWriteLock*

The ReentrantReadWriteLock class provided by the Concurrency API implements the ReadWriteLock interface. Like the ReentrantLock class, it also accepts an optional fairness boolean parameter in its constructor.

   The following sample application submits numerous read requests and two write requests that use a shared ReentrantReadWriteLock. Note that we could have used a concurrent collection class in this application, but for the purpose of this example, assume that we are modeling something more complex, such as access to a file or database:

```java
import java.util.*;
import java.util.concurrent.*;
import java.util.concurrent.locks.*;

public class ZooEmployeeNameManager {
    private ReadWriteLock readWriteLock = new ReentrantReadWriteLock();
    private List<String> names = new ArrayList<>();

    public ZooEmployeeNameManager() {
        names.add("John Smith");
        names.add("Sarah Smith");
        names.add("James Johnson");
    }

    private String readNames(int i) {
        Lock lock = readWriteLock.readLock();
        try {
            lock.lock();
            System.out.println("Read Lock Obtained!");
            return names.get(i % names.size());
        } finally {
            System.out.println("Read Lock Released!");
            lock.unlock();
        }
    }

    private void addName(String name) {
        Lock lock = readWriteLock.writeLock();
        try {
            lock.lock();
            System.out.println("Write Lock Obtained!");
            Thread.sleep(1000);
```

```
        names.add(name);
      } catch (InterruptedException e) {
        // Handle thread interrupted exception
      } finally {
        System.out.println("Write Lock Released!");
        lock.unlock();
      }
    }

  public static void main(String[] args) {
    ZooEmployeeNameManager manager = new ZooEmployeeNameManager();
    ExecutorService service = null;
    try {
      service = Executors.newFixedThreadPool(20);
      for(int i=0; i<100; i++) {
        final int employeeNumber = i;
        service.submit(() -> manager.readNames(employeeNumber));
      }
      service.submit(() -> manager.addName("Grace Hopper"));
      service.submit(() -> manager.addName("Josephine Davis"));
    } finally {
      if(service != null) service.shutdown();
    }
  }
}
```

When this code is executed, the output should be similar to the following:

```
...
Read Lock Obtained!
Read Lock Released!
Write Lock Obtained!
Write Lock Released!
Write Lock Obtained!
Write Lock Released!
Read Lock Obtained!
Read Lock Released!
...
```

We artificially inserted a delay in the write process to show that when one thread held a write lock, no other thread was active. In other words, no other thread was granted or held a read or write lock, while the single thread had the write lock. In this manner, the write lock is shown to be mutually exclusive.

We can further understand the difference between read and write locks by changing the writeLock() call in the addName() method to request a readLine() instead. The following is an updated implementation of the addName() method:

```java
private void addName(String name) {
    Lock lock = readWriteLock.readLock();
    try {
        lock.lock();
        System.out.println("Write Lock Obtained!");
        Thread.sleep(1000);
        names.add(name);
    } catch (InterruptedException e) {
        // Handle thread interrupted exception
    } finally {
        System.out.println("Write Lock Released!");
        lock.unlock();
    }
}
```

This change causes a noticeable change in the expected output:

```
Write Lock Obtained!
Read Lock Obtained!
Write Lock Obtained!
Read Lock Released!
...
Read Lock Released!
Write Lock Released!
Write Lock Released!
```

You can see that with this modification, the addName() method is no longer mutually exclusive, as other threads were able to act on the data while the addName() method was sleeping.

Working with Directories

In Chapter 9, "NIO.2," we presented a variety of classes and methods for interacting with files and directories in Java. In this section, we cover two additional NIO.2 topics that are not part of the full OCP exam but that are on the exam for those upgrading from Java 6 or earlier.

Traversing Directories

As you may recall from Chapter 9, we showed you how to traverse a directory by using the `Files.walk(Path)` method and search a directory using the `Files.find(Path,int,BiPredicate)` method. Both of these methods were added to Java 8 as part of the `Streams` API and returned a `Stream<Path>` object, which we then processed in a lazy manner.

Prior to Java 8, though, there was another set of techniques for walking and searching a directory that you need to know, part of the Java 7 release. We consider these techniques to be far less concise and convenient than the `Streams` API approach that you learned about in Chapter 9.

Reading a Directory with *DirectoryStream*

The NIO.2 API includes an interface called `DirectoryStream`, which can be used to read a single directory. Although this might sound confusing, the `DirectoryStream` interface does *not* implement or extend the generic `java.util.stream.Stream` inter-face, and it is therefore unrelated to the `Streams` API that you learned about in Chapter 4, "Functional Programming." It is also not related to `java.io` streams that you learned about in Chapter 8. Blame the authors of Java for this quite ambiguous naming choice!

Getting back to the topic at hand, the `DirectoryStream` interface can be used to iterate over a directory, similar to the `java.io.File.listFiles()` method. Consider the following example:

```
DirectoryStream<Path> stream = Files.newDirectoryStream(path);
```

You can see that we call the `newDirectoryStream()` method on a `Path` object and it returns a generic `DirectoryStream<Path>` object. The `DirectoryStream` object is similar to an instance of the `Collection` or `java.util.stream.Stream` interface in that it can be iter-ated over, but strictly speaking it does not implement either of these interfaces. Also, unlike a collection, a `DirectoryStream` instance represents a resource to a process that operates on a file system that, like an I/O stream, can access only one element at a time, and it must be closed when no longer used.

The following example uses a `DirectoryStream` to iterate over the single level of a directory:

```
Path path = Paths.get("/user/home");
try (DirectoryStream<Path> stream = Files.newDirectoryStream(path)) {
   for(Path element: stream) {
      System.out.println(element.getFileName()+"\t"+Files.isDirectory(element));
   }
}
```

This example code iterates over the /user/home directory and outputs the name of the path along with whether or not it represents a directory. Notice that we use the try-with-resource syntax as described in Chapter 6, "Exceptions and Assertions," since we need to ensure that the `DirectoryStream` object is closed when we are finished with it.

Remember for the exam that the DirectoryStream process traverses only a single directory and does not visit any subdirectories that it encounters. This distinguishes it from the FileVisitor process that you will see in the next section.

Since DirectoryStream does not inherit java.util.stream.Stream, we cannot apply any stream-based methods. For example, the following does not compile:

```
Path path = Paths.get("/user/home");
DirectoryStream<Path> stream = Files.newDirectoryStream(path)
    .filter(p -> p.getFileName().startsWith("zoo"))          // DOES NOT COMPILE
    .forEach(System.out::println);
```

This example does not compile because it tries to apply stream-based methods to a DirectoryStream instance. As we mentioned earlier, the naming of these classes is a tad ambiguous and confusing. Just know that when you see a DirectoryStream on the exam, it is not a stream in the context of Streams API that you learned about in Chapter 4.

Walking a Directory Tree with *FileVisitor*

While the DirectoryStream interface is used to visit the contents of a single directory, the FileVisitor<T> interface is used to visit an entire directory tree. This is useful for recursive tasks, such as deleting all of the files contained with a directory tree or searching a directory tree for a particular type of file. Although FileVisitor<T> is a generic interface that can be constructed using any class, we use Path as the type throughout this section.

The idea is simple. You create a class that implements the FileVisitor<Path> interface and then pass it to a Files.walkFileTree() method. The walkFileTree() method handles the complex process of loading the next directory and file for you, and it recursively calls the methods in your FileVisitor implementation as it encounters each entry.

Understanding the *FileVisitor* Structure

Before we start walking a directory tree, we need to define the structure of the FileVisitor<T> interface that you will need to implement. Using Path as the generic type, the FileVisitor<Path> interface requires four methods:

visitFile(Path,BasicFileAttributes) throws IOException   This method is called when a file is visited, and it automatically includes the file's attributes in a BasicFileAttributes object.

visitFileFailed(Path,IOException) throws IOException   This method is called when a file cannot be visited along with exception information about the reason for the failure.

preVisitDirectory(Path,BasicFileAttributes) throws IOException   This method is called before a directory's contents are visited, and it automatically includes the directory's attributes in a BasicFileAttributes object.

postVisitDirectory(Path,IOException) throws IOException   This method is called after a directory's contents are visited, and it includes exception information when applicable. The directory-based exception sent to this method, if provided, is analogous to the file-based exception sent to the `visitFileFailed()` method.

The following is a simple implementation of `FileVisitor` that searches for the file `zoo.txt` in a directory tree. Once it finds the file, it copies it within the directory and terminates the walk process. It also stops the process if it encounters an entry it failed to process.

```java
import java.io.*;
import java.nio.file.*;
import java.nio.file.attribute.BasicFileAttributes;

public class FindAndCopyFile implements FileVisitor<Path> {
    public FileVisitResult preVisitDirectory(Path dir,
            BasicFileAttributes attrs) throws IOException {
        return FileVisitResult.CONTINUE;
    }

    public FileVisitResult visitFile(Path file,
            BasicFileAttributes attrs) throws IOException {
        if (file.getFileName().equals("Zoo.txt")) {
            Files.copy(file, Paths.get("Zoo2.txt"));
            return FileVisitResult.TERMINATE;
        } else {
            return FileVisitResult.CONTINUE;
        }
    }

    public FileVisitResult visitFileFailed(Path file,
            IOException exc) throws IOException {
        return FileVisitResult.TERMINATE;
    }

    public FileVisitResult postVisitDirectory(Path dir,
            IOException exc) throws IOException {
        return FileVisitResult.CONTINUE;
    }
}
```

Each method in `FileVisitor` returns a `FileVisitResult` enum that instructs the process on what the next step in the walk should be by using the `FileVisitor`. The full list of values is shown in Table C.2.

TABLE C.2   The `FileVisitResult` options

Enum Value	Description
CONTINUE	Continue to the next item in the file walk.
TERMINATE	Immediately terminate the file walk.
SKIP_SUBTREE	Used by the `preVisitDirectory()` method to indicate that the current directory and its descendants should be skipped.
SKIP_SIBLINGS	Used by the `preVisitDirectory()` and `postVisitDirectory()` methods to indicate that all remaining unvisited siblings should be skipped. If used in `preVisitDirectory()`, then the directory entries are also skipped.

The process using the `FileVisitor` continues until one of the following three conditions is reached: the contents of the directory have been exhausted, a TERMINATE value is returned by one of the `FileVisitor` methods, or an uncaught `IOException` is thrown within one of the `FileVisitor` methods.

The SKIP_SUBTREE and SKIP_SIBLINGS options, when returned from the `preVisitDirectory()` method, allow the `FileVisitor` class to direct the flow of the process using the `FileVisitor` class. For example, we can use the SKIP_SUBTREE value to skip directories whose name begins with `init.d`.

The SKIP_SIBLINGS value is useful for skipping unneeded directories during a search process. For example, imagine we have a process that is checking for the existence of a particular file within each top-level directory on the hard drive. As soon as we find the file in the current directory path, we want to skip searching the rest of current path and go on to the next top-level directory on the hard drive. We can use the SKIP_SIBLINGS options, along with some instance variables to track where the file was found, to direct the process using the `FileVisitor` to skip the rest of the current directory tree.

Using the *SimpleFileVisitor* class

As you saw in the previous example, oftentimes we only want to "do something interesting" in a single `FileVisitor` method. The authors of Java foresaw this scenario and added a convenience class called `SimpleFileVisitor` that implements `FileVisitor` to the NIO.2 API. While most of the methods in the `SimpleFileVisitor` class just return CONTINUE, `visitFileFailed()` and `postVisitDirectory()` rethrow any `IOException` that they encounter.

To use the `SimpleFileVisitor` class, you simply extend it and overwrite the methods that you want to implement, relying on the default implementation for any methods that you do not overwrite.

The following DeletePath class is used to walk the file tree, deleting all files and directories that it encounters. The last entry processed in the tree will delete the original file or directory path to which the class was applied.

```java
import java.io.IOException;
import java.nio.file.*;
import java.nio.file.attribute.BasicFileAttributes;

public class DeletePath extends SimpleFileVisitor<Path> {
    public FileVisitResult visitFile(Path file,
            BasicFileAttributes attrs) throws IOException {
        System.out.println("Deleting file: "+file.toAbsolutePath());
        Files.delete(file);
        return FileVisitResult.CONTINUE;
    }

    public FileVisitResult postVisitDirectory(Path dir, IOException exc) throws
                                                            IOException {
        if(exc != null) {
            System.out.println("Exception encountered "+exc.toString());
            throw exc;
        }
        System.out.println("Deleting directory: "+dir.toAbsolutePath());
        Files.delete(dir);
        return FileVisitResult.CONTINUE;
    }
}
```

By extending the SimpleFileVisitor class, we can conveniently skip declaring the visitFileFailed() and preVisitDirectory() methods, instead relying on the default implementations. Notice that we delete the directory in the postVisitDirectory() method, since this is executed after the contents of the directory have been deleted. If we tried instead to delete the directory in the preVisitDirectory() method, an exception would be thrown if the directory was not empty. Finally, we check for the presence of exception in the postVisitDirectory() method, such as if the directory itself was unable to be read.

Applying *walkFileTree(Path, FileVisitor<? super Path>)*

By itself, a FileVisitor instance does not actually do anything. It must be paired with one of two Files.walkFileTree() methods. The simplest version of the walkFileTree()

method takes a path and FileVisitor object, and it walks the tree. The following application uses our DeletePath class to walk and delete files in a directory:

```java
import java.io.IOException;
import java.nio.file.*;

public class DeletePathSample {
    public static void main(String[] args) throws IOException {
        Files.walkFileTree(Paths.get("/user/home/test"), new DeletePath());
    }
}
```

Like the Files.walk() method that you saw in Chapter 9, the order in which a tree is searched is in depth-first manner. The result is that anytime the postVisitDirectory() method is called, we know that all of the available descendants of the directory have already been processed.

Applying *walkFileTree(Path, Set<FileVisitOption>, int, FileVisitor<? super Path>)*

The NIO.2 API provides an overloaded version of Files.walkFileTree() that takes the path and FileVisitor instance, along with two additional parameters: a Set of FileVisitOption parameters and maximum depth value.

The walkFileTree() method will not follow symbolic links by default. To force the method to traverse symbolic links, you can pass a Set that contains the FileVisitOption.FOLLOW_LINKS option. There is some risk following symbolic links while traversing a directory in that the symbolic link could contain a cycle. Recall from Chapter 9 that a cycle is an infinite circular reference in which an entry in a directory is an ancestor of the directory.

If a symbolic link does contain a circular reference, the process could traverse the directory infinitely, as each time it encounters the symbolic link it would return to a parent and traverse the tree again. The NIO.2 API detects and stops this behavior by blocking the read of a file in which an infinite loop is detected and instead calls visitFileFailed() with a FileSystemLoopException. It is important when enabling the FOLLOW_LINKS option in your application to account for this exception, since the default behavior of SimpleFileVisitor is to throw an exception and stop walking the tree on calling visitFileFailed().

The other parameter, int maxDepth, is used to limit the depth from the root to a node that the walkFileTree() method will visit. It is often used to improve performance in situations where the files or directories on which you are operating are expected to be close to the root. Bear in mind, using this parameter breaks the depth-first assumption that all descendants of a directory have been processed prior to calling postVisitDirectory() on the directory. The default value of maxDepth is Integer.MAX_VALUE in the previous walkFileTree() method, indicating that all directories should be visited.

The following sample `FileVisitor` class and test application searches for all files whose name ends in txt using the overloaded version of `walkFileTree()` discussed in this section:

```java
import java.io.IOException;
import java.nio.file.*;
import java.nio.file.attribute.BasicFileAttributes;
import java.util.EnumSet;

public class FindTextFiles extends SimpleFileVisitor<Path> {
    public FileVisitResult visitFile(Path file,
            BasicFileAttributes attrs) throws IOException {
        if(file.getFileName().endsWith("txt")) {
            System.out.println("Found file: "+file.toAbsolutePath());
        }
        return FileVisitResult.CONTINUE;
    }


    public FileVisitResult visitFileFailed(Path file, IOException exc) throws
                                                        IOException {
        if (exc instanceof FileSystemLoopException) {
            System.err.println("Circular reference detected: "+file.toString());
        } else if(exc != null) {
            throw exc;
        }
        return FileVisitResult.CONTINUE;
    }
}

public class FindTextFilesSample {
    public static void main(String[] args) throws IOException {
        Files.walkFileTree(Paths.get("/user/home"),
            EnumSet.of(FileVisitOption.FOLLOW_LINKS),
            5,
            new FindTextFiles());
    }
}
```

The sample application searches for all of the text files at most five levels deep from the /user/home root, following all symbolic links it finds. If a circular reference is detected, it outputs a message and continues processing the request. Remember that the NIO.2 API method will skip the processing of a file it has already read if a circular link is detected, and it will instead call the `visitFileFailed()` method.

Real World Scenario

Use the Stream-Based File Search Methods Whenever Possible

Although you need to know both the DirectoryStream and FileVisitor interfaces for the upgrade exam, we recommend that you use the newer Java 8 stream-based methods described in Chapter 9 whenever possible, as they produce significantly shorter and easier-to-read code. For example, other than the circular error handling, the previous FindTextFiles class can be rewritten into a single stream-based statement:

```
Files.walk(Paths.get("/user/home"), 5, FileVisitOption.FOLLOW_LINKS)
   .filter(p -> p.getFileName().endsWith("txt"))
   .forEach(p -> System.out.println("Found file: "+p.toAbsolutePath()));
```

It is clear that this approach is a lot simpler to read and maintain. There are some situations where the longer form is acceptable, such as if you need to reuse the FileVisitor implementation in multiple processes. You may also prefer the FileVisitor approach if you are hiding the implementation details from a caller using a compiled version of your class.

Monitoring a Directory for Changes

The Java NIO.2 API includes the WatchService framework for monitoring changes to directories in real time. In modern operating systems, it is common for two processes to access the same files in the same directory during their execution. If we expect a directory or its contents to be changed over time by another process, we can use the WatchService API to monitor the directory for changes and react to those changes as soon as they occur.

Applying the WatchService API to monitor a directory requires a number of steps. The following is a high-level overview of the WatchService process:

Overview of WatchService API

1. Create an instance of WatchService from the file system.
2. Register each directory and event type.
3. Create a loop that repeatedly queries the WatchService for changes.
4. Retrieve a WatchKey.
5. Retrieve all pending events for the WatchKey and do something with them.

6.   Reset the WatchKey.

7.   Once you no longer need the WatchService, close the resource.

If it seems like a lot of steps, don't worry! In this section, we start with the first step and build out from there—one step at a time.

Creating and Shutting Down the *WatchService*

The first step is the easiest. We use the FileSystems helper class to obtain a reference to the default FileSystem. We then use the FileSystem object to obtain a new WatchService instance, as shown in the following code snippet:

```
WatchService service = FileSystems.getDefault().newWatchService();
```

If the WatchService is being created and closed within a single method, we can apply the try-with-resource syntax, as WatchService extends Closeable in order to complete the first and last steps in an abridged fashion:

```
import java.io.IOException;
import java.nio.file.*;

public class WatchServiceSample {
    public static void main(String[] args) throws IOException {
        try (WatchService service = FileSystems.getDefault().newWatchService()) {
            ...
        }
    }
}
```

Alternatively, if we are not creating and closing the WatchService instance within a single method, we need to explicitly call the close() method on the WatchService instance after we have finished using it. Failure to close the WatchService after we have finished with it could lead to resource-contention issues within the file system.

Registering for Events

The next step is one of the most interesting, that is, determining what events we want to monitor. The WatchService can be used on any class that implements the Watchable interface, which requires the class to implement register() methods. In the NIO.2 API, the Path interface extends the Watchable interface; therefore we can use our WatchService instance to monitor any number of Path objects by calling a register() method.

Along with the WatchService instance, the register() method takes a vararg of StandardWatchEventKinds enum values, which indicates the events for which we want to listen. The WatchService API supports the four event types listed in Table C.3.

TABLE C.3   Available WatchService events

Enum Value	Description
StandardWatchEventKinds.ENTRY_CREATE	An element is added to the directory.
StandardWatchEventKinds.ENTRY_DELETE	An element is removed from the directory.
StandardWatchEventKinds.ENTRY_MODIFY	An existing element is modified in the directory.
StandardWatchEventKinds.OVERFLOW	An event may have been lost. It is possible to receive this event even if it is not registered for.

We expand our original implementation with a new version that registers for events:

```
import java.io.IOException;
import java.nio.file.*;

public class WatchServiceSample {
    public static void main(String[] args) throws IOException {
        try (WatchService service = FileSystems.getDefault().newWatchService()) {

            // Register for events
            Path zooData = Paths.get("/user/home/zoo/data");
            Path zooLog = Paths.get("/user/home/zoo/log");
            zooData.register(service,StandardWatchEventKinds.ENTRY_CREATE,
                    StandardWatchEventKinds.ENTRY_DELETE,
                    StandardWatchEventKinds.ENTRY_MODIFY);
            zooLog.register(service,StandardWatchEventKinds.ENTRY_MODIFY);
        }
    }
}
```

In this sample code, we register for events on two different directories. The first path is registered for the create/delete/modify events, while the second path is registered for only modify events. Note that overflow events can be received, even if no path registered for them. Finally, while any class can register for events, the only one that you need to be familiar with for the exam is Path.

Looping Over the *WatchService*

In order to use the WatchService, we need to set up a process that repeatedly polls the WatchService for changes in the data. The simplest way to do this is with an infinite loop, although we could also iterate a finite amount of times. Note that the WatchService API is one of the few places where we ever suggest creating an infinite loop on purpose.

The following updated sample creates such an infinite loop:

```java
import java.io.IOException;
import java.nio.file.*;

public class WatchServiceSample {
    public static void main(String[] args) throws IOException {
        try (WatchService service = FileSystems.getDefault().newWatchService()) {

            // Register for events
            Path zooData = Paths.get("/user/home/zoo/data");
            Path zooLog = Paths.get("/user/home/zoo/log");
            zooData.register(service,StandardWatchEventKinds.ENTRY_CREATE,
                    StandardWatchEventKinds.ENTRY_DELETE,
                    StandardWatchEventKinds.ENTRY_MODIFY);
            zooLog.register(service,StandardWatchEventKinds.ENTRY_MODIFY);

            // Poll for events
            for(;;) {
                // Handling of events
            }
        }
    }
}
```

Regardless of whether we use an infinite or finite loop, we can always use the break command from within the loop to exit under certain conditions. Note that for(;;) and while(true) are equivalent statements and either could be used here.

Spawning a *WatchService* Thread

Creating a process that loops infinitely on a WatchService instance is great if the entire purpose of your application is to detect changes in a directory. More likely, though, detecting changes in a directory is an ancillary process in your application.

For example, the primary function of your application might be to present a set of data to the user, and you need to monitor the data file for changes. Obviously, you would not want the application to be frozen constantly while polling for changes in the data file. As you may recall from Chapter 7, you can improve processes such as these by spawning a separate thread to monitor for changes to the file system.

Retrieving a *WatchKey*

The next step is to poll the WatchService to determine if an event has occurred. The WatchService API has three methods that check for and return an event key, which differ only in how they handle a lack of available events:

poll()   This method retrieves and removes the next WatchKey, returning null if none are present.

poll(long,TimeUnit)   This method retrieves and removes the next WatchKey, waiting a specified amount of time if none are present. If the time limit is reached without any events, the method returns null.

take()   This method retrieves and removes the next WatchKey, waiting indefinitely if none are present.

The second and third methods can throw an InterruptedException if the process is interrupted by another thread before the task could be completed. You saw numerous methods that threw this type of exception in Chapter 7.

The following is our updated sample application with the take() method:

```java
import java.io.IOException;
import java.nio.file.*;

public class WatchServiceSample {
    public static void main(String[] args) throws Exception {
        try (WatchService service = FileSystems.getDefault().newWatchService()) {

            // Register for events
            Path zooData = Paths.get("/user/home/zoo/data");
            Path zooLog = Paths.get("/user/home/zoo/log");
            zooData.register(service,StandardWatchEventKinds.ENTRY_CREATE,
                    StandardWatchEventKinds.ENTRY_DELETE,
                    StandardWatchEventKinds.ENTRY_MODIFY);
            zooLog.register(service,StandardWatchEventKinds.ENTRY_MODIFY);

            // Poll for events
            for(;;) {
```

```
        WatchKey key;
        try {
            key = service.take();
        } catch (InterruptedException x) {
            break;
        }
      }
    }
  }
}
```

In this sample application, if the WatchService process is interrupted while requesting a key, we break out of the infinite loop.

We prefer the take() method to the no-argument poll() method in this sample application, as it is used inside an infinite loop. Since the no-argument poll() method returns immediately, using it inside an infinite loop would cause the process to iterate constantly, wasting precious CPU cycles in performing the iterations. We could also use the poll() method that takes a wait time value, as this at least bounds the process from cycling over the loop instantly.

Processing and Resetting the *WatchKey*

Now that we have WatchKey, we can use that to retrieve a list of available events and process them. This is the core of our WatchService functionality, as it is where we decide what to do when something has changed. For example, we might reload a window that the user is viewing if we notice that the file data on which it is based has changed. We might also take a more complex action, such as sending an email or text message to an individual letting them know about the change in data.

To keep things simple in our sample application, we are just going to output the information about the directory change to the System.out stream. First, we request all available events by calling pollEvents() on our WatchKey instance. For each event found, we read and process the event details. The event details include the type of the event, which is retrieved by calling the kind() method. It also includes a reference to the Path associated with the event, which is retrieved by using the context() method.

Once we have processed all of the events available to the WatchKey, we must call the reset() method on the current WatchKey instance before the next call to retrieve a new WatchKey.

Failure to call the reset() method on the current WatchKey would result in not being able to retrieve any further WatchKey events. When using the WatchService API, it is critical not to skip the reset() method call.

We present the completed version of our sample application:

```
import java.io.IOException;
import java.nio.file.*;
```

```java
public class WatchServiceSample {
   public static void main(String[] args) throws IOException {
      try (WatchService service = FileSystems.getDefault().newWatchService()) {

         // Register for events
         Path zooData = Paths.get("/user/home/zoo/data");
         Path zooLog = Paths.get("/user/home/zoo/log");
         zooData.register(service,StandardWatchEventKinds.ENTRY_CREATE,
               StandardWatchEventKinds.ENTRY_DELETE,
               StandardWatchEventKinds.ENTRY_MODIFY);
         zooLog.register(service,StandardWatchEventKinds.ENTRY_MODIFY);

         // Poll for events
         for(;;) {
            WatchKey key;
            try {
               key = service.take();
            } catch (InterruptedException x) {
               break;
            }

            // Retrieve events for key
            for (WatchEvent<?> event: key.pollEvents()) {
               WatchEvent.Kind<?> kind = event.kind();
               if (kind == StandardWatchEventKinds.OVERFLOW) {
                  continue;
               }

               // Process event
               WatchEvent<Path> watchEvent = (WatchEvent<Path>)event;
               Path path = watchEvent.context();
               System.out.println("[eventType="+kind
                  +", path="+path.getFileName()+"]");
            }

            // Remember to always reset event key
            if(!key.reset()) {
               break;
            }
         }
      }
   }
}
```

In this application we first check the event type and discard OVERFLOW events, since they do not provide details about what data was lost. We then explicitly cast the event to a WatchEvent<Path> reference, allowing us to access the Path object associated with the WatchEvent using the context() method. As we mentioned earlier, any class can register for an event, so WatchService<T> is generic. For the exam, though, you only need to know how to use it with Path objects. Finally, we print the information about the event to System.out.

Once we have finished reading all of the events, we call reset() on the WatchKey instance. If the method reset() returns false, it means that the key is no longer valid, and we use this error condition as an indication that we should stop the WatchService loop.

The following is sample output from this application on a file system:

```
[eventType=ENTRY_CREATE, path=/user/home/zoo/data/NewFile.txt]
[eventType=ENTRY_DELETE, path=/user/home/zoo/data/NewFile.txt]
[eventType=ENTRY_CREATE, path=/user/home/zoo/data/ZooData.txt]
[eventType=ENTRY_MODIFY, path=/user/home/zoo/log/out.log]
[eventType=ENTRY_MODIFY, path=/user/home/zoo/data/ZooData.txt]
[eventType=ENTRY_MODIFY, path=/user/home/zoo/log/out.log]
[eventType=ENTRY_DELETE, path=/user/home/zoo/data/ZooData.txt]
```

In this sample execution, a file NewFile.txt was created and then immediately renamed to ZooData.txt. The content of the ZooData.txt was modified and the file itself was eventually deleted. While this was going on, the out.log file was modified by a separate process in the /log directory.

 Real World Scenario

Limitations of the WatchService API

Even though the WatchService API allows us to monitor a directory for changes, it does so with a number of known drawbacks. First off, it is possible to miss directory change events, hence the need for the OVERFLOW event to tell the application that a set of changes was discarded.

Second, when events are lost, we do not get any information about the lost events, other than we know that something was lost. Receiving no information about precisely which events were lost might make some people refrain from using the WatchService API altogether.

Finally, some JVMs implementations of the WatchService API are inefficient, with significant delays between the time that the directory is modified and the moment that the application is notified about the change. Some developers have even reported delays of up to five seconds. This may not seem like a significant amount of time to you, but for someone writing an application that continuously monitors a directory for changes, this may have a drastic impact on their application.

Summary

This appendix covers additional topics that you need to know if you are studying for the Java 6 or earlier OCP upgrade exam (1Z0-813). If you already took the OCA 8 or OCP 7 exam, then you should already know some of the topics in this appendix.

In this appendix, we presented some of the language changes made in Java 7, for those whose last certification was Java 6 or earlier. These included the diamond operator <>, numeric literals with underscore characters, as well as the new data types allowed in switch statements.

NumberFormat and DateFormat use factories to format and parse using common pattern formats. The subclasses DecimalFormat and SimpleDateFormat use pattern strings to work with custom formats.

The Concurrency API includes a Lock framework for managing locks beyond the standard monitor implemented with the synchronized keyword. Besides supporting a number of features beyond using the synchronized keyword, the Lock framework also includes the ReadWriteLock interface, which can improve performance in environments where reads are more common than writes.

We presented the DirectoryStream class and showed you how to use it to read a single level of a directory. We then expanded our discussion to the recursive FileVisitor class for walking a directory tree. Finally, we presented the NIO.2 WatchService API and showed you how to use it to monitor a directory.

Exam Essentials

Identify correct and incorrect uses of the diamond operator. The diamond operator is <>. It is used on the right side of an expression, and it means to use the same generic type as in the declaration, for example: Map<String,List<Integer>> m = new HashMap<>().

Create numeric and binary literals using the underscore character. Numeric literals may contain underscores between two digits and begin with 1-9, 0, 0x, 0X, 0b, and 0b. Underscores are allowed to occur anywhere in the literal except the first position, last position, immediately before a decimal point, or immediately after a decimal point.

Evaluate acceptable data types for a switch statement. The switch statement accepts the primitive types int, byte, short, and char, as well as their associated wrapper classes, Integer, Byte, Short, and Character. It also accepts String and enum values.

Know the common format patterns for DecimalFormat and SimpleDateFormat. For DecimalFormat, # means to omit the position and 0 means to put 0 in the position if no digit exists for it. For SimpleDateFormat, M is month, d is date, y is year, h is hour, m is minute, and s is second. Repeating these characters changes the format.

Understand how to use and apply the Lock **and** ReadWriteLock **interfaces.** The Lock interface with implementation class ReentrantLock is used as a mutually exclusive lock, similar to using the synchronized keyword. Unlike using the synchronized keyword, though, a Lock supports methods for obtaining locks and returning instantly or after a specified amount of time has elapsed if the lock cannot be obtained. The ReadWriteLock interface with implementation class ReentrantReadWriteLock holds two locks, one for reading that can be given to multiple threads and one for writing that is mutually exclusive. It is commonly used in data-driven environments where reads are more common than writes.

Understand how to traverse directories with DirectoryStream **and** FileVisitor. The NIO.2 DirectoryStream interface is used to retrieve the single-level contents of a directory. The NIO.2 FileVisitor interface is used to define a class with a set of methods that supports walking a directory tree in a recursive, depth-first manner. Both interfaces are used in conjunction with methods in the Files helper class to interact with the file system.

Be able to write code that can monitor a directory for changes using WatchService **API.** The WatchService API defines a set of NIO.2 interfaces and classes that can be applied to a directory to monitor it for changes. First, a set of Path values is registered for various event types with the WatchService object. Then the WatchService process repeatedly polls for events that represent changes in the file system. The WatchService process may poll infinitely, or it may exit under a developer-defined condition.

Review Questions

1. What is the result of the following code snippet?

```
final char a = 'A', d = 'D'; // p1
char grade = 'B';
switch(grade) {
    case a:  // p2
    case 'B': System.out.print("great");
    case 'C': System.out.print("good"); break;
    case d:  // p3
    case 'F': System.out.print("not good");
}
```

A. great

B. greatgood

C. The code will not compile because of line p1.

D. The code will not compile because of line p2.

E. The code will not compile because of lines p2 and p3.

2. What is the output of the following code?

```
DecimalFormat df = new DecimalFormat("#,000.0#");
double pi = 3.141592653;
System.out.println(df.format(pi));
```

A. 3.141592653

B. 0,003.14

C. ,003.1

D. 003.14

E. 00.04

F. The code does not compile.

G. None of the above

3. Assuming that we have access to a WatchService object, which has been properly initialized and registered with at least one Path, what two problems make the code unusable?

```
1: for(;;) {
2:     WatchKey key = watchService.poll();
3:     for (WatchEvent<?> event: key.pollEvents())
4:     System.out.println(event.kind()+","+event.context());
5: }
```

A. It does not check if the WatchKey is null.

B. It does not use the factory pattern.

C. The event type is not checked for OVERFLOW.

D. It does not cast WatchEvent<?> to WatchEvent<Path>.

E. It does not reset the WatchKey after use.

F. It uses an infinite loop that never ends.

4. What is the result of the following code snippet?

```
3: int x = 10 % 2 + 1;
4: switch(x) {
5:    case: 0 System.out.print("Too High"); break;
6:    case: 1 System.out.print("Just Right"); break;
7:    default: System.out.print("Too Low");
8: }
```

A. Too High

B. Just Right

C. Too Low

D. JustRightTooLow

E. The code will not compile because of line 3.

F. The code will not compile because of lines 5 and 6.

5. What is the result of applying the Files.walkFileTree() method to the current directory and an instance of the following FileVisitor class?

```
1: public class FilePrinter implements FileVisitor<Path> {
2:    public FileVisitResult visitFile(Path file, BasicFileAttributes attrs)
3:                                            throws IOException {
4:       System.out.println("Found file: "+file.getFileName());
5:       return FileVisitResult.CONTINUE;
6:    }
7: }
```

A. It prints out all of the filenames in the current directory.

B. It recursively prints out all of the filenames in the directory tree.

C. It recursively prints out all file and directory names in the directory tree.

D. The code will not compile because of line 1.

E. The code will not compile because of line 5.

F. The code compiles but it throws an exception at runtime.

6. What is the result of the following code snippet? (Choose all that apply.)

```
3:  final int movieRating = 4;
4:  int badMovie = 9;
5:  switch(badMovie) {
6:      case 0:
7:      case badMovie: System.out.println("Awful"); break;
8:      case movieRating:  System.out.println("Great"); break;
9:      case 4:
10:     default:
11:     case (int)'a':
12:     case 1*1: System.out.println("Too be determined"); break;
13: }
```

A. The code will not compile because of line 6.

B. The code will not compile because of line 7.

C. The code will not compile because of line 9.

D. The code will not compile because of line 11.

E. The code will not compile because of line 12.

7. Which of the following are possible results of running the following application? (Choose all that apply.)

```
import java.util.concurrent.locks.*;
import java.util.stream.IntStream;

public class AcquireLocks {
    public static void main(String[] args) {
        Lock lock = new ReentrantLock();
        IntStream.iterate(1, i -> 1).limit(10).parallel().forEach(x -> { // w1
            lock.tryLock(); // w2
            System.out.println("Got Lock!");
            lock.unlock(); // w3
        });
        System.out.print("Finished");
    }
}
```

A. It prints Got Lock! *at least* one time.

B. It prints Got Lock! ten times.

C. It prints Finished.

D. It hangs indefinitely at runtime.

E. The code will not compile because of line w1.

F. The code will not compile because of line w2.

G. The code will not compile because of line w3.

H. It throws an exception at runtime.

8. Which of the following compile? (Choose all that apply.)

    A. `List<Integer> l1 = new ArrayList();`

    B. `List<Integer> l2 = new ArrayList<>();`

    C. `List<Integer> l3 = new ArrayList<Integer>();`

    D. `List<> l4 = new ArrayList<Integer>();`

    F. `List<Integer> l5 = new List<Integer>();`

    G. `ArrayList<int> l6 = new List<int>();`

9. Which of these lines compile? (Choose all that apply.)

```
1: public class Rich {
2: public void money() {
3:     int _million = 1_000_000;
4:     double aThousand = 1_000_.00;
5:     double 100 = 100;
6:     int hundred = 100.00;
7:     float ten = 10d;
8:     short one = 1;
9: } }
```

    A. 3

    B. 4

    C. 5

    D. 6

    E. 7

    F. 8

10. What is the difference between the `WatchService` method `take()` and the no-argument version of `poll()`? (Choose all that apply.)

    A. Only `take()` can throw an `InterruptedException`.

    B. Only `poll()` can throw an `InterruptedException`.

    C. `take()` returns immediately; `poll()` waits indefinitely.

    D. Unlike `take()`, `poll()` returns `null` if no keys are present.

E. By default, take() waits up to one minute for a key.

F. None. The methods behave identically.

11. What is the result of the following program when run in the United States?

```
import java.util.Locale;
import java.text.NumberFormat;

public class MyParser {
    public static void main(String [] args) {
        NumberFormat nf = NumberFormat.getInstance(Locale.FRANCE);
        String value = "444,33";
        System.out.println(nf.parse(value));
    }
}
```

A. 444.33

B. 444,33

C. There is one compiler error.

D. There is more than one compiler error.

E. An exception is thrown at runtime.

12. Given that Germany uses a comma and the United States uses a period for the decimal point, what is the output of the following code?

```
Locale.setDefault(Locale.GERMANY);
DecimalFormat df = new DecimalFormat("#00.00##");
double pi = 3.141592653;
System.out.println(df.format(pi));
```

A. 3,1415

B. 3,1416

C. 03,1415

D. 03,1416

E. 003,1415

F. 003,1416

G. The code does not compile.

13. What are the possible results of executing the following code? (Choose all that apply.)

```
1: Path path = Paths.get("turtle.txt");
2: try (DirectoryStream<Path> directoryStream = Files.newDirectoryStream(path)) {
```

```
3:     for (Path entry: directoryStream)
4:         System.out.println(entry.getFileName());
5: }
```

A. It compiles and runs without issue.

B. The code will not compile because of line 2.

C. The code will not compile because of line 3.

D. It compiles but throws an InterruptedException at runtime.

E. It compiles but throws an IOException at runtime.

14. Given the following class, which of the following lines of code can replace INSERT CODE HERE to make the code compile? (Choose all that apply.)

```
public class Price {
    public void admission() {
        // INSERT CODE HERE
        System.out.println(amount);
} }
```

A. int amount = 9L;

B. int amount = 0b101;

C. int amount = 0xE;

D. double amount = 0xE;

E. double amount = 1_2_.0_0;

F. int amount = 1_2_;

G. None of the above

15. What is the result of the following code snippet?

```
3: int x = 10;
4: switch(x % 4.) {
5:     default: System.out.print("Not divisible by 4");
6:     case 0: System.out.print("Divisible by 4");
7: }
```

A. Not divisible by 4

B. Divisible by 4

C. Not divisible by 4Divisible by 4

D. The code does not output any text.

E. The code will not compile because of line 4.

16. What is the result of executing the following code? (Choose all that apply.)

```
1:   import java.io.IOException;
2:   import java.nio.file.*;
3:   import java.nio.file.attribute.*;
4:   public class DeleteFilesWithExtension extends SimpleFileVisitor<Path> {
5:       private String extension;
6:       public DeleteFilesWithExtension(String extension) {
7:          this.extension = extension;
8:       }
9:
10:      public FileVisitResult visitFile(Path file, BasicFileAttributes attrs)
11:                                              throws IOException {
12:        if(file.getFileName().endsWith(extension) && !attrs.isSymbolicLink())
13:           Files.delete(file);
14:              return FileVisitResult.CONTINUE;
15:       }
16:
17:      public static void main(String[] args) throws IOException {
18:          Files.walkFileTree(Paths.get("/zoo/data"),
19:            new DeleteFilesWithExtension("txt"));
20:      }
21: }
```

A. It compiles and is capable of deleting all matching files in the /zoo/data directory only.

B. It compiles and is capable of recursively deleting all matching files in the /zoo/data directory tree.

C. The code will not compile because of lines 10-11.

D. The code will not compile because of line 13.

E. The code will not compile because of lines 19–20.

F. It compiles but may throw an exception at runtime.

17. Which of the following is *not* accomplished using a static method? (Choose all that apply.)

A. Getting a DateFormat

B. Getting a DecimalFormat

C. Getting a NumberFormat

D. Getting a ResourceBundle

E. Getting a SimpleDateFormat

18. Which of the following are possible results of running the following application? (Choose all that apply.)

```java
import java.util.concurrent.*;
import java.util.concurrent.locks.*;

public class ManageData {
    public static void main(String[] args) throws Exception {

        ExecutorService service = null;
        try {
            ReadWriteLock readWriteLock = new ReentrantReadWriteLock(); // m1
            service = Executors.newFixedThreadPool(20);
            service.submit(() -> {
                readWriteLock.writeLock().lock(); // m2
                System.out.println("Got Write Lock!");
            });
            for (int i = 0; i < 10; i++) {
                service.submit(() -> {
                    readWriteLock.readLock().lock(); // m3
                    System.out.println("Got Read Lock!");
                });
            }
        } finally {
            if (service != null) service.shutdown();
        }
        System.out.print("Finished");
    }
}
```

A. It prints `Got Read Lock!`

B. It prints `Got Write Lock!`

C. It prints `Finished`.

D. It hangs indefinitely at runtime.

E. The code will not compile because of line m1.

F. The code will not compile because of line m2.

G. The code will not compile because of line m3.

H. It throws an exception at runtime.

19. Which of the following lines of code compile? (Choose all that apply.)

A. `int i1 = 1_234;`

B. `double d1 = 1_234_.0;`

C. `double d2 = 1_234._0;`

D. `double d3 = 1_234.0_;`

E. `double d4 = 1_234.0;`

F. None of the above

20. Which of the following steps are required to use the `WatchService` correctly? (Choose all that apply.)

A. Iterate over the `WatchService` with an infinite loop.

B. Stop using the `WatchService` if an `OVERFLOW` event is reported.

C. Read the object returned by the `WatchEvent` `context()` method that is associated with the event.

D. Reset a `WatchKey` when you are finished with it.

E. Register `WatchService` with at least one object and event.

F. Close the `WatchService` when you are finished with it.

21. What is the result of the following program? (Choose all that apply.)

```
import java.util.concurrent.*;
import java.util.concurrent.locks.*;

public class BeachManager {
   public static void goSwimming(Lock lock) {
      try {
         lock.lock(); // y1
         if(lock.tryLock()) { // y2
            System.out.println("Swim!");
         }
      } finally {
         lock.unlock();
      }
   }
   public static void main(String[] args) {
      Lock lock = new ReentrantLock();
      ExecutorService service = null;
      try {
```

```
        service = Executors.newFixedThreadPool(2);
        for(int i=0; i<2; i++)
            service.submit(() -> goSwimming(lock));
    } finally {
        if (service != null) service.shutdown();
    }
    System.out.print("Tasks Complete");
    }
}
```

A. It prints Swim!*at least* one time.
B. It prints Swim! exactly twice.
C. It prints Tasks Complete.
D. It hangs indefinitely at runtime.
E. The code will not compile because of line y1.
F. The code will not compile because of line y2.
G. It throws an exception at runtime.

Answers to Review Questions

1. B. The code compiles and runs without issue, so options C, D, and E are not correct. The value of grade is 'B', and there is a matching case statement that will cause "great" to be printed. There is no break statement after the case, though, so the next case statement will be reached and "good" will be printed. There is a break after this case statement, though, so the switch statement will end. The correct answer is thus option B.

2. D. DecimalFormat uses a constructor rather than a factory. The 0 means a mandatory position and the # means an optional position. The format says that there must be either three or four digits before the decimal. Since we only have one, Java uses the smaller number. The format also says that there must be either one or two digits after the decimal. Since we have many digits, Java uses the larger number.

3. A,E. First off, the WatchService.poll() method returns immediately with a value of null if there are no events available. Unless the file system is constantly busy, this code is likely to produce a NullPointerException on line 3 almost immediately after it starts, rendering the code unusable; therefore A is correct. The other major problem with this code is that the WatchKey method reset() is not called after the WatchKey is processed, meaning that this code can receive at most one event, at which point it loops infinitely; therefore E is correct. B is irrelevant information and therefore incorrect. For event type, it is recommended that you check for OVERFLOW events but it is not required, so C is incorrect. The event details can be outputted without casting to WatchEvent<Path>, so D is incorrect. Infinite loops are common with the WatchService API, so F is incorrect.

4. F. This question is designed to test your ability to spot syntax errors with switch statements. In particular, the colon (:) goes after the value in the case statement, not before. Therefore neither line 5 nor line 6 will compile, and option F is the correct answer. If the colon were moved after the values, the output would be Just Right, and the answer would be option B.

5. D. The code does not compile because in order to implement the FileVisitor interface, all four visitor methods must be provided, so D is correct. If instead of implementing the FileVisitor interface, it extended the SimpleFileVisitor class, which does not require any methods to be overridden, then the code would compile and produce the list of file-names in the directory tree, making B the correct answer.

6. B,C. The code will not compile due to problems with the case values. First, badMovie is not a constant value; therefore line 6 will not compile. If it was marked final, it would compile, so B is correct. Next, Line 9 has the same case value of 4 as Line 8. Since there's no option to remove Line 8 available in the choices, Line 9 should be removed and C is correct. The other answers are incorrect, because the rest of the lines of the code compile.

7. A,B,C,H. The application compiles without issue, so E, F, and G are incorrect. The tryLock() method attempts to obtain a lock but returns immediately with a value of false if the lock cannot be acquired. The application does not check whether or not the lock was actually acquired;

therefore the call to `unlock()` on w3 would produce an `IllegalMonitorStateException` at runtime if a thread that did not get a lock attempted to release it, and H is correct. The answer A is also correct, because the first thread to run will obtain the lock without issue. This behavior is indeterminate, though. If the threads are processed in order, with all of the threads able to obtain the lock, then the code will complete without throwing an exception, making B and C also correct. Finally, D is incorrect since `tryLock()` returns immediately if it cannot obtain the lock. Note that this code does not use a `try/finally` block to ensure that the `unlock()` method is called whenever a lock is obtained. Although using `try/finally` is strongly recommended, it is not required for the code to compile and run.

8. A,B,C. Option A compiles since it is allowed to use generics on just one side in a declaration. Option B compiles using the diamond operator. Option C is a longer form of option B; it spells out the generics type. Option D does not compile because the diamond operator is allowed only on the right side. Option E does not compile because `List` is allowed only on the left side, since it's an interface rather than a concrete type. Option F does not compile because primitives are not allowed to be `ArrayList` types. Autoboxing works only when working with the `ArrayList`, not when declaring it.

9. A,F. Option A is correct. Identifiers are allowed to begin with underscores. Numeric values are allowed to have underscores between two digits. Option B is incorrect because underscores are not allowed adjacent to a decimal point. Option C is incorrect because identifiers are not allowed to start with digits. Option D is incorrect because decimal values are not allowed in `int` variables—they can only go in `float` or `double` types. Option E is incorrect because 10d declares a `double`, and a `double` is bigger than a `float`. Option F is correct because it is a straightforward variable assignment.

10. A,D. Remember that `take()` waits indefinitely for a key, whereas the no-argument `poll()` returns immediately with `null` if there are no keys; therefore D is correct. Since `take()` waits indefinitely, it can throw an `InterruptedException`, so A is correct. B is incorrect, because the method does not wait. C has the descriptions of the methods reversed, and it is thus incorrect. E and F are completely false statements.

11. C. The parse methods throw a checked `ParseException`. Checked exceptions must be caught.

12. D. The 0 means a mandatory position and the # means an optional position. The format says that there must be either two or three digits before the decimal. Since we only have one, Java uses the smaller number. The format also says that there must be two, three, or four digits after the decimal. Since we have many digits, Java uses the larger number and rounds.

13. A,E. First off, the code compiles without issue, so B and C are incorrect. Next, it is possible for a directory to have an extension in the name, so A is correct, albeit uncommon. D is an incorrect answer, and it relates to threading, not a `DirectoryStream` walk process. E is correct, at least tangentially, because `NotDirectoryException` and `NoSuchFileException` extend `IOException`.

14. B,C,D. 0b is the prefix for a binary value, making option B correct. 0X is the prefix for a hexadecimal value. This value can be assigned to many primitive types, including `int` and double, making options C and D correct. Option A is incorrect because 9L is a long value. long amount = 9L would be allowed. Option E is incorrect because the underscore is immediately before the decimal. Option F is incorrect because the underscore is the very last character.

15. E. For this problem you need to remember your rules about numeric promotion as well as what data types are allowed in a switch statement. The expression x % 4. automatically promotes the x to a double; since 4. is a double, the result is a double. Because a switch statement does not accept the type double, the code fails to compile due to line 4, so option E is the correct answer.

16. B,F. The code compiles without issue, so C, D, and E are each incorrect. Because a subclass of FileVisitor was used and not the DirectoryStream class, the code will recursively delete all matching files in the /zoo/data directory, so B is correct and A is incorrect. Finally, if the directory path does not exist or is not accessible in the file system, an exception will be thrown at runtime, so F is also correct.

17. B,E. DecimalFormat and SimpleDateFormat use a constructor and take a pattern format string as a parameter. Options A and C are incorrect because they use a variety of factory methods to get an instance. Choice D is incorrect because ResourceBundle.getBundle is used.

18. A,B,C,D. The application compiles without issue so E, F, and G are incorrect. The problem with this code is that none of the locks that are acquired are ever released. Since the executor service is pooled, the requests could come in any order, so A and B are both possible outputs and therefore are correct answers. C is also possible, because Finished could be outputted before any of the threads have requested their first lock. Since the tasks could be processed in any order and none of the locks are released, the write lock request will hang indefinitely if any read lock requests have been granted and vice versa, making D a correct answer. H is incorrect, since there is nothing in the code that will produce a runtime exception.

19. A,E. Underscores are allowed as long as they are directly between two other digits. This means that options A and E are correct. Options B and C are incorrect because the underscore is adjacent to the decimal point. Option D is incorrect because the underscore is the last character.

20. D,E,F. Infinite loops are optional but not required when using the WatchService API, so A is incorrect. Ignoring OVERFLOW events is left to your discretion, so B is incorrect. There are no guidelines for how to process or respond to events when they happen, so C is incorrect. D is correct, because failure to reset a WatchKey will prevent you from receiving all future event notifications, rendering the WatchService useless. E is also correct in that if you do not register any objects, the WatchService does not do anything. Finally, F is correct, because the WatchService should be closed after use, preferably with a try-with-resource block if opened and closed in the same method.

21. A,C,D. The application compiles without issue, so E and F are incorrect. The most important thing to notice is that the goSwimming() method performs two lock requests, via lock() and tryLock(), but it has only one call to unlock(). Recall that for Reentrant

locks, a thread must call `unlock()` the same number of times it locks the object, or else the lock will not be released. Therefore, only one thread is able to acquire the lock and print `Swim`! For these reasons, A is correct and B is incorrect. C is also correct, since the lock requests are performed on separate threads from the main execution thread. Since the lock is never released by the first thread, the second thread will hang indefinitely, making D a correct answer. Finally, H is incorrect, because this code does not throw any exceptions at runtime.

Index

Y

Z

Comprehensive Online Learning Environment

Register on Sybex.com to gain access to the comprehensive online interactive learning environment and test bank to help you study for your OCA Java SE 8 Programmer II certification.

The online test bank includes:

- **Assessment Test** to help you focus your study to specific objectives
- **Chapter Tests** to reinforce what you learned
- **Practice Exams** to test your knowledge of the material
- **Digital Flashcards** to reinforce your learning and provide last-minute test prep before the exam
- **Searchable Glossary** gives you instant access to the key terms you'll need to know for the exam

Go to `http://sybextestbanks.wiley.com` **to register and gain access to this comprehensive study tool package.**